FREE AND FAITHFUL IN CHRIST

"You shall know the truth, and the truth will set you free"

(Jn 8:32)

BERNARD HÄRING

Free and Faithful in Christ

Moral Theology for Priests and Laity

VOLUME 2
The Truth will set you free

TH
08
HA-FR
V2

A CROSSROAD BOOK
The Seabury Press • New York

1979
THE SEABURY PRESS
815 Second Avenue
New York, N.Y. 10017

Printed in the United States of America

LIBRARY OF CONGRESS CATALOGING IN PUBLICATION DATA
Häring, Bernard, 1912–
Free and faithful in Christ.
"A Crossroad book."
Includes bibliographical references and index.
CONTENTS: v. 1. General moral theology.—v. 2.
The truth will set you free.
1. Christian ethics—Catholic authors. I. Title.
BX1758.2.H27   1978   241'.04'2   78-12253
ISBN 0-8164-0398-8 (v. 1)   ISBN 0-8164-0205-1 (v. 2)

ACKNOWLEDGMENTS

The fact that the second volume is to be published less than a year after the publication date of the first volume is the merit of the excellent cooperation of my publisher and his staff and many other people.

My heartfelt thanks, again, to Mrs. Josephine Ryan for her competent and indefatigable assistance in the care of the English expression and style, and for her numerous good suggestions regarding the content.

A word of special appreciation to Sr. Mary Gallagher of the College of our Lady of the Elms, Chicopee, for her generous and careful work on the Index.

I received, again, generous help in the transcription of the more than forty tapes of my text from Sr. Gabrielle L. Jean, Sr. Joyce Gadoua, Mrs. Virginia Malachaowski, Miss Marion McCracken, Mrs. John B. Mayotte, Miss Maria E. Motzko, and Mrs. Alice Paroby. Miss Marion also patiently helped checking all the Bible quotes.

B.H.

CONTENTS

Chapter Four
SALVATION, LIBERATION THROUGH FAITH

Chapter Five
FAITH-EDUCATION AND EVANGELIZATION
IN A CRITICAL AGE

Chapter Six
FAITH AND ECUMENISM

Chapter Seven
FAITH IN AN AGE OF UNBELIEF

ix

Chapter Eight
HOPE ASSURED BY FAITH

Chapter Nine
ACTUALIZING THE TRUTH IN LOVE

Introduction

The truth will set you free (Jn 8:32)

The first volume of this work tried to give a comprehensive view and understanding of the freedom for which Christ has freed us. In it we saw Christ as the Covenant of the People, who has chosen us as his associates to carry on the work of redemption and liberation in fidelity to him who is freedom and fidelity incarnate.

In this second volume the unifying theme is the truth by which Christ sets us free. Here our task is to see how truth and liberty are related. "Wherever freedom divorced itself from truth, it lost its substance and degenerated into anarchy and chaos. But it is equally true that the truth can unfold itself only in a climate of internal and external freedom".[1] Just as God's gift of freedom is not something man simply owns, so truth is at the same time a gift of God offered to us and an ongoing and difficult task. Christian morality can be understood as speaking and doing the truth in love, and thus growing fully into Christ (cf. Eph 4:15).

Our leitmotif, "free and faithful in Christ", leads with inner logic to a passionate interest in truth. Our very fidelity to Christ, the Liberator, means that we shall never stop searching for a better understanding of what true liberty is. To explore constantly all the implications of the freedom for which Christ calls us is an essential dimension of that fidelity. We can be free and faithful in Christ only to the extent that we are grounded in him who is the Way, the Truth, and the Life, and who has promised to send us the Spirit of Truth to guide us into all the truth (Jn 14:6).

1

The hunger and thirst to know Christ ever more intimately, and to know all his truth that makes us free (cf. Jn 8:31), is an act of grateful love for Christ and for our neighbour. Christ shares with us his liberating truth in order that, in him and with him, we may become the light of the world and salt for the earth. (This will be the theme of the third and last volume.)

However, it would not be accurate to describe this second volume as individual moral theology while the third is dedicated to social ethics. Here in this second volume, too, we explore truth always in a dimension of sharing, of solidarity in Christ, the Saving Truth. Hence the social dimension is equally present in all parts of this moral theology, and especially in this second volume.

TURNING OUR EYES TO CHRIST, we explore the conditions of knowing the truth. Being taught by the Word of God that we are known by God, we ask how we come to know him in and through his words and works. We are particularly interested in all the ways of searching and sharing truth that give us a share in Christ's liberating fidelity. We note especially the diversity of the individual situations and the cultural circumstances in which we search and express truth, and how this very diversity can enrich our purpose to be truthful in all our thinking, our desiring, our speaking and doing. We shall see that fidelity to Christ and in him coincides with our relationship to truth (Chapter One).

Those familiar with traditional manuals of Catholic moral theology may be surprised to note the special attention we give to the value of beauty, but I hope to convince the reader that this is not at all a luxury in the understanding of a specifically Christian ethic. Wherever God reveals himself and his design for his people, there is a wondrous beauty, his glory, the splendour of his goodness and truth. It is through this beauty that he draws us to himself and sharpens our hunger to know him in his truth and goodness. And by thus revealing himself in all his works, and especially in the human person made to his image and likeness, he calls us to be co-artists with him by developing our creativity in freedom and fidelity (Chapter Two).

The beatitude and glory of the Holy Trinity is in the sharing of truth, love, and life among the Divine Persons. All of creation and redemption is a sharing, a communication of blissful and attractive truth and love. Christian moral theology, therefore, has to give particular attention to the manifold ways of discerning truth and communicating it, sharing it. This leads us to see the modern means of communication in this light. There we all have a common vocation to learn together and to share together the liberating and consoling truth (Chapter Three).

In all this we are fully aware that salvation and liberation come by faith. The phenomenology of truth, of searching and sharing truth and the splendour of truth, leads us to the summit, to the most liberating relationship to truth, which is faith. Here we remember what we have learned about the reciprocity of consciences. Relationships determined by faith are marked by the truthfulness and reverence that are an essential part of the beauty and splendour of truth and goodness. Yet we cannot neglect a problem that was treated again and again in tradition, namely, how we can be faithful and truthful in the complexities of life and in a sinful world (Chapter Four).

The pluralistic character of modern society, the constant encounter with other cultures and religions, the birth pangs of the ecumenical movement, as well as the impact of modern atheism and paganism force today's Christians, as individuals and groups, to become more discerning, more critical about themselves and about current ideologies. The future of Christianity will be characterized not by those who are Christians simply by birth but by those who have freely chosen their faith in courageous honesty. All this means that moral theology has to approach many problems in a new way, in full awareness that we live and profess our faith in a critical era (Chapter Five).

Christ, the liberating truth, has come to tear down all the man-made barriers that divided Jews and Samaritans, Jews and Gentiles, in a world torn by hostile ideologies and the lust for power. We Christians can never deplore enough our own divisions, for it has not been truth but rather lack of honesty and courage to search for truth together that has divided the one Church into separate churches and sects. God in his goodness has awakened, in our time, a liberating longing for unity, and in this historical moment, moral theology would be absolutely unfaithful to its task if, in its whole content, it did not give particular attention to ecumenism. Here we present a special chapter on ecumenism, but surely not in order to dispense our-

selves from ecumenical alertness in all that we are writing
and saying (Chapter Six).

Nothing challenges us Christians to be thoroughly converted
to the liberating truth more than does modern atheism in all its
various forms and shades. This atheism cannot be faced by any
form of indifferentism or any kind of apologetics; it can only
be faced with absolute truthfulness. We can hope to enter into
a fruitful dialogue with at least some modern atheists, however,
if first we have the courage and honesty to search out the
hidden atheism in ourselves, in some of our traditions and practices, and in our partial unreadiness to search for truth in order
to put it into practice. We have also to examine ourselves about
our own share of accountability for the rise and oppressive
power of atheism. Dialogue with atheism is possible only for
Christians who are sharply aware of their own identity and are
radically committed to the truth revealed in Jesus Christ
(Chapter Seven).

God who has so wonderfully revealed himself in Jesus
Christ, the saving Truth, remains for us, nevertheless, the hidden
God. While we adore God's unconcealment of his truth, we
adore even more God in his truth, who is always infinitely
greater than our understanding. Since we live our faith in the
"already" and the "not yet", we have to give particular attention
to the hope dimensions of Christian faith. "Faith gives substance to our hopes and makes us certain of realities we do not
see" (Heb 11:1). In its profound relationship with liberating
truth, faith implies ongoing conversion and growth in the
Faithful One. Hope tells us that, through faith, we are always
on the road (Chapter Eight).

"God is Love". This is the heart of the liberating truth
revealed in Jesus Christ. In the phenomenology of truth and
knowledge, we come always to the same conclusion that the
unconcealment of truth is an event of freedom and love. Truth
reveals itself only to those who love and are ready to learn
to love more truthfully. We are far from a sentimental understanding of the phrase, "Love and do what you will", but with
Augustine we would emphasize "Have true love and do what
love wills".[2] The saving truth discloses the true countenance
of love and therefore the way "to do truth in love" (Eph 4:15)
(Chapter Nine).

Repeatedly our reflections on the saving truth lead us to the insight that it is not so much by abstract concepts but rather by images and symbols that the unconcealment of truth becomes liberating. Christ is the supreme and all-embracing symbol, the visible sign of the truth that saves. And it is the vocation of each and all of us to become, by our words, our deeds, and even by our silences, eloquent signs of God's attractive truth and goodness. Some readers, looking first at the table of contents, might be surprised to find no special chapter on the sacraments. But after a careful reading of the whole book they will, hopefully, realize that the sacramental vision is all pervasive: the christocentric dimension of Christian life, the presence of the Church as universal sacrament of salvation and unity, the seven sacraments energizing and illumining faith, hope and love, and resulting in "adoration of God in spirit and truth". For this reason it seems logical to treat immediately after the chapter on love of God and neighbour human sexuality that is sanctified by a special sacrament, the marital covenant of love. And, once we have chosen this approach, it becomes also clearer that celibacy for the kingdom of God is best understood in the light of that sacramentality which shines forth in all those who are totally dedicated to witness to the love of God in their whole state of life.

While a certain school tried to derive ethical norms mainly from the biological finality of sexuality, newer efforts attempt to decipher its meaning and norms as language whose main message is love. Like language, it communicates. All languages have their specificity, but all human languages have enough in common to allow translation and meaningful dialogue on their truths. Similarly, we can consider sexuality as a language common to humankind, and yet, in its "dialects", deeply affected by the concrete cultural and historical circumstances. Our emphasis is on the truthfulness of "sexual language", whereby people can "know" each other truthfully and share faithful love. Then, the transmission of life would never be severed from sharing the liberating truth of love (Chapter Ten).

---

[1] A. Dondeyne, "Liberté et verité, Etude philosophique", in H. v. Waegenbergh, Univ. Louvain (ed.), *Liberté et verité*, Louvain, 1954, 41.

[2] Augustine, "Dilige et quod vis fac". The emphasis is on "dilige", that means "authentic love".

Chapter One

What Is The Liberating Truth?

I. CHRIST HIMSELF, THE SAVING TRUTH

Pilate asks Jesus a political question: "You are a king?" Jesus responds on a totally different level, " 'King' is your word. My task is to bear witness to the truth. For this was I born; for this I came into the world, and all who are not deaf to truth listen to my voice". Pilate then asks, "What is truth?" (Jn 18:36-38). His questions are all ambiguous, distorted by false concerns, yet Christ's response and even his very silence impel Pilate to try to liberate him from his enemies. The disciples' questions are less direct but Jesus gives the full response. "I am the way; I am the truth and I am life; no one comes to the Father except by me" (Jn 14:6).

Jesus comes from the Father and, as the Saving Truth, he leads his disciples to the Father. Faced with Jesus Christ, we realize the imperfection of our own question, "What is the liberating truth?" for when we come into personal contact with Jesus Christ, we know that the real question is, "Who is he who embodies the liberating truth?"

1. Christ, Truth incarnate

Throughout the history of salvation, God reveals himself as the One who *is*. He is the liberating, the saving truth, but at the summit of God's self-revelation we learn that one of us, the Son of Man, Jesus of Nazareth, can call himself "the

7

Truth". The words he speaks with all his being and by all his witness are not his but the Father's. "I have taught them all that I learned from thee, and they have received it; they know with certainty that I came from thee" (Jn 17:8).

Christ is sent as the messenger and the message. He is the one who fulfils the word of the Father, and the one in whom truthfulness and faithfulness to the mission are embodied. Or differently expressed, he is a sacramental word, the visible Word of the Father, in whom divinity is transparent in all his human reality. "Anyone who has seen me has seen the Father" (Jn 14:9).

By his very fidelity to the mission the Father has given him, and by all that he is and does and speaks, Jesus of Nazareth is the truth and, at the same time, the faithful one. Truth, gladdening and attractive, shines through in all his being and life. It never imposes itself like alien law. "Grace and truth came through Jesus Christ" (Jn 1:17). Christ, sharing himself with his disciples, is liberating grace and truth. Against gnostic tendencies, the first letter of John insists that "It was there from the beginning; we have heard it; we have seen it with our own eyes; we looked upon it and felt it with our own hands . . . and we write this in order that the joy of us all may be complete" (1 Jn 1:1-4).

Jesus comes as the manifestation that God is light, and since he shares with us his life and his light, we can walk in the truth (1 Jn 1:5-7). In him we Christians adore the eternal Word of God by whom all things were made. He, the incarnate Word, the Lord, is the goal of human history, the focal point of the longings of history and of civilization, the centre of the human race, the joy of every heart and the answer to all its yearnings.[1]

The objectivist approach to all this sees revelation as primarily conceptual, and the Christian religion as a system of well-defined truths, sometimes even as a system of control over truths. The symbolic approach is different. As Gregory Baum writes, it "understands revelation in symbolic terms and the Christian religion as a set of symbols which people assimilate and celebrate, and out of which they define their lives and create their world".[2]

What gives meaning and unity to all these symbols is the Christ symbol. Christ, the visible image of God, is a real and historically effective symbol, for in him truth has taken the flesh of history. He is also the unifying symbol. What the created universe and history teach us receives its finality and meaning in him, who is the summit of history. Each of us finds his final truth in him.

In the light of Christ, the incarnate Truth, we come also to a better understanding of God's knowledge about the world. "His knowledge is causative and his causality is cognitive. He knows things into being".[3] Christ knows us as God knows us and, at the same time, with a human heart and mind. Sharing his truth with us is a new way of knowing us into being; he makes us a "new creation". And, responding to this way of being known, we realize also that the truth we receive has to take flesh in our own life and in the world around us.

The presence of Christ, the saving Truth, is felt everywhere and throughout the whole of history. But only through faith responding to the unique revelation can we come to know the God of history who, in absolute freedom, has revealed himself. Dietrich Bonhoeffer insists on the specifically Christian way of responding: "Since God is accessible in his self-revelation, men can find God only in Jesus Christ".[4] In Jesus Christ, God enters history, and no human attempt can grasp him beyond that history of which Christ is the point Omega.

2. *Christ, the truth that breathes love*

Truth in creation and redemption is the primordial mystery of the divine Truth. "In the beginning was the Word, and the Word was with God; and the Word was God" (Jn 1:1). The eternal Father utters the mystery of his heart in his Word, his consubstantial Son. St Augustine has this reflection: "As though uttering himself, the Father begot the Word equal to himself in all things; for he would not have uttered himself wholly and perfectly if there were in his Word anything more or less than in himself. And this Word can never have anything false because it is unchangeable, as he is from whom it is".[5] And since, in this Word of truth, the Father utters the mystery of his heart, the Word is response in the same love, as St Thomas Aquinas says beautifully: "The Son, however, is the Word, but not simply any kind of word, but the Word breathing forth love".[6]

Thus the mystery of the Holy Trinity, revealed in Jesus Christ and by the effusion of the Holy Spirit tells us the most important truth about our own way of being "in the Truth" as image and likeness of God. The fruitfulness of divine truth is absolute. It is the language of love flowing from the Father's heart. And since its goal is the exultation of love, it rests on love and shines forth resplendently in the Word breathing love, breathing the Holy Spirit.

The divine truth is communicative, which means it is sharing love, love and truth sharing themselves, love bounteously bestowing and returning. It is the truth and bliss of love. All truth in the created world is suffused with the holiness of this truth of the intimate divine life, for "all things were made through him and without him was made nothing that has been made" (Jn 1:3).

Hence the most momentous reality in history is not confrontation of knowledge and error as such, but rather confrontation between the truth that comes forth from love and breathes love and, on the other hand, darkness and artificial systems of knowledge and of practice that arise from lack of love, falsify the truth about love, and breathe hatred.

In Jesus of Nazareth, the Messiah, the Word of the Father that breathes love has found its full embodiment, its incarnation. In the graciousness and gentleness of the attractive way Christ shares truth, there is the unique presence of the divine Word. "Out of his full store we have all received grace upon grace; while the law was given to Moses, the gracious truth came through Jesus Christ. No one has ever seen God; but God's only Son, who is nearest to the Father's heart, he has made him known" (Jn 1:16-18). Christ's graciousness and co-humanity, his truth-sharing love and his love-sharing truth, point to the Father's heart.

When we say that Christ himself is the law or the norm of Christian life, we leave behind the narrow concepts of normative ethics, but we find a true criterion or ultimate norm for searching and sharing truth. Is all our knowledge grounded in the basic freedom of love, and does it strengthen the bond of love, in the image and likeness of him who is the truth and breathes love? All who have made their fundamental option for true love will love the truth and thus experience its liberating power. This is Christ's great promise to us: "You shall know the truth, and the truth will set you free" (Jn 8:32). In the same context Jesus says later: "If then the Son sets you free you will indeed be free" (Jn 8:36). Only the Father's beloved Son, who breathes love and has taken flesh in Jesus of Nazareth, who is anointed by the Holy Spirit, can set us free. There can be no freedom where truths are divorced from love and where love does not seek the fullness of truth.

The evil one is a murderer; he is filled with hatred. "He is not rooted in the truth; there is no truth in him" (Jn 8:44). Ideologies may contain a lot of half-truths and can assemble volumes of statistics, but if they breathe enmity, hatred, division, they do not share in the truth of the One who breathes love. Their "truths" will never free anyone.

3. *The Spirit of Truth*

Jesus is the anointed one, the Messiah (Christ). He is anointed by the Spirit to proclaim the liberating truth of the Gospel. "The Spirit of the Lord is upon me because he has anointed me; he has sent me to announce good news to the poor, to proclaim release for prisoners and recovery of sight for the blind; to let the broken victims go free" (Lk 4:18).

At his baptism in the Jordan, the Spirit gives witness to Jesus that he is the messenger of saving truth. The Spirit empowers him to give the final witness in the true baptism, baptism in his blood. John testified, "I saw the Spirit coming down from heaven like a dove and resting upon him. I did not know him but he who sent me to baptize in water had told me, 'when you see the Spirit coming down upon someone and resting upon him, you will know that this is he who is to baptize in the Holy Spirit' " (Jn 1:32-33; cf. Mt 3:16-17).

The Spirit drives Jesus into the wilderness (Mt 4:1) to live and to bring to completion the exodus, the liberating poverty that allows Jesus to live in a unique way by the Word that comes from the mouth of the Father. Jesus is "armed with the power of the Spirit" (Lk 4:14) when he begins to preach the saving truth and to share himself with the people.

Before giving the final witness to truth in self-giving love, Jesus promises his disciples to send the "Spirit of truth". "If you love me you will heed my commands; and I will ask the Father, and he will give you another to be your advocate, who will be with you forever, the Spirit of truth" (Jn 14:15-16). Those who open themselves to this Spirit will learn how to love and thus will know the truth. "He who loves me will be loved by my Father, and I will love him and disclose myself to him" (Jn 14:21). Whoever loves Jesus and the Father is taught by the Spirit and will come to an ever fuller knowledge of who Christ is, the truth he is and the truth he has lived and taught.

"Your advocate, the Holy Spirit, whom the Father will send in my name, will teach you everything, and will call to mind all that I have told you" (Jn 14:26). The teaching imparted by the "Spirit of truth" means bearing witness to Christ. Those who are taught by the Spirit will join Christ in his witness. "And you also are my witnesses, because you have been with me from the first" (Jn 15:26-27). The Spirit of truth is inseparable from Christ and his witness. He will give his disciples the joy and the strength to live the truth and thus to know it ever better. "When he comes who is the Spirit of truth, he will guide you into all the truth, for he will not speak on his own authority, but will tell you only what he hears" (Jn 16:13).

The Spirit is the sharing between the Father and the Son. Through the hypostatic union and through the anointing by the Spirit, Jesus is fully participating in that sharing between the Father and his Word. Therefore, the words he speaks are the Father's. "All that the Father has is mine, and that is why I said, 'Everything that he (the Spirit of truth) makes known to you, he will draw from what is mine'" (Jn 16:15).

Those who have a loving knowledge of God can "distinguish the Spirit of truth from the spirit of error" (1 Jn 4:6). The first letter of John speaks not only about the "Spirit of truth" but also says "the Spirit is truth" (5:6). And Paul insists that he can proclaim the saving truth only by a spiritual power, taught by the Spirit. "Things beyond our seeing, things beyond our hearing, things beyond our imagining, all prepared by God for those who love him, these it is that God has revealed through the Spirit. For the Spirit explores everything, even the depths of God's own nature . . . only the Spirit of God knows what God is. It is the Spirit that we have received from God, and not the spirit of the world, so that we may know all that God of his own grace has given us; and because we are interpreting spiritual truths to those who have the Spirit, we speak of these gifts of God in words found for us not by our human wisdom, but by the Spirit" (1 Cor 2:9-13).

The Holy Spirit who proceeds from the Father and the Son (or from the Father through the Son) is the gift, personified, of truth in love and love in truth. Believers receive the Holy Spirit and his gifts from the riches of the triune life of God. They can be received only in gratitude. "Christian life, a life of grace, of faith and love is a life arising from the fullness and therefore a life in gratitude . . . Eucharist".[7]

The Spirit of truth promised by Christ, who is Truth incarnate, is never a "loveless pneumatic enthusiasm". It does not dispense us from good reasoning, from sharing experience and reflection, but is an openness to the Spirit that protects us from arrogance and from cold reasoning. The believer knows that "all activity of the reason is bound to the Spirit (cf. 1 Cor 12:8, Col 1:9), if it wants to be truly good and helpful reasoning".[8] Docility to the Spirit of truth makes us able to learn together to share truth in love.

4. *Sanctification in, by, and for the truth*

After having promised the Spirit of truth Jesus prays for his disciples: "Consecrate them by the truth; thy word is truth. As thou hast sent me into the world, I have sent them into the world, and for their sake I now consecrate myself, that they, too, may be consecrated by the truth" (Jn 17:17-19). Consecrated by the Spirit to bear witness for the truth, Jesus' word is truth and has a purifying and sanctifying power. Accepting the word of Christ implies accepting him who is life-giving truth, and dedicating ourselves to the witness of truth.

Christ has consecrated himself to be the all-embracing sacrament of solidarity. He is the saving truth, and his truth sanctifies and unites believers. They give themselves for the sake of unity in truth and love. The Spirit of truth who makes us holy makes us also one in Christ.

To be possessed by the divine Truth and to bear witness to

it in the whole realm of life unto the glory of God is a prerequisite for the right disposition for the worship of God:
"Oh Lord, who shall sojourn in your tent? Who shall dwell
on your holy mountain? He who walks blamelessly and does
justice; he who thinks the truth in his heart and slanders none
with his tongue" (Ps 15:1ff).

The words of Jesus are "spirit and life" (Jn 6:63). In all his
words and deeds he gives himself for humankind to the glory
of the Father. The Spirit, in whom Christ baptizes believers, is
life-giving (Jn 6:63). If we live by the Spirit of truth we can be,
with Christ, adorers of the Father "in spirit and truth" (Jn 4:23),
honouring him not only with our lips but by giving ourselves
to him in the service of our brothers and sisters as Christ did,
always guided by the Spirit of truth. The Spirit gives and
requests the total and self-giving truthfulness of our life, and
this creates holy people. We find this motivation already in the
Shepherd of Hermas, although in other words: "again he said
to me, 'Love the truth, and let nothing but truth proceed from
your mouth, that the Spirit which the Lord has placed in your
flesh may be found truthful before all people; and the Lord,
who dwells in you will be glorified, because the Lord is truthful
in every word, and in him is no falsehood' ".[9]

5.   Christ, the Revealer of the truth about man

Christology and anthropology cannot be separated. Only in
Christ do we come to the full truth about humanity. The truth
revealed in Jesus Christ is greater than man's, for he *is* Truth
and what he reveals about man and his total calling is more
than any man could have thought out.[10]

In Jesus Christ the truth of each individual receives its place
and fullness. The Second Vatican Council speaks eloquently about
how all things find their truth and purpose in Christ. "The
Church believes that Christ, who died and was raised for all,
can through his Spirit offer man the light and the strength to
measure up to his supreme destiny. Nor has any other name
under heaven been given to man by which it is fitting for him
to be saved. She likewise holds that in her most benign Lord
and Master can be found the key, the focal point, and the goal
of all human history ... hence in the light of Christ, the image

of the unseen God, the first-born of every creature, the Council wishes to speak to all men in order to illuminate the mystery of man".[11]

Christ not only unmasks all the falsehood of man and about men; he shows us what the human person and the community of people can truly be. "The truth is that only in the mystery of the incarnate Word does the mystery of man take on light. For Adam, the first man, was a figure of him who was to come, namely, Christ the Lord. Christ, the final Adam, by the revelation of the mystery of the Father and his love, fully reveals man to man himself and makes his supreme calling clear... He worked with human hands, he thought with a human mind, acted by human choice, and loved with a human heart. Born of the Virgin Mary, he has truly been made one of us, like us in all things except sin".[12]

The Council gives particular attention to Christ as the Covenant, the model and summit of human solidarity. "God did not create man for life in isolation, but for the formation of social unity. So also it has pleased God to make men holy and save them not merely as individuals, without any mutual bonds, but by making them into a single people, a people which acknowledges him in truth and serves him in holiness... This communitarian character is developed and consummated in the work of Jesus Christ. For the very Word made flesh willed to share in the human fellowship".[13]

Men learn from each other and with each other about their nature and vocation, for we are all created in the image and likeness of God; we are made in Christ and in view of him. "Yet there is no human being who can be more than a pointer in his knowledge and particularly in his being to the final encounter with truth".[14]

Knowing Christ from Scripture, from tradition, and from the living community of faith does not resolve all the riddles about man. Moreover, our initial knowledge of Christ is frequently very imperfect. However, as long as we have the fundamental trust in Christ, we do not lose orientation even if many doubts remain about human nature. Even in the moments of darkness we stay on the road of truth as long as we can say truthfully, "I believe in you, Jesus of Nazareth. I trust that in you has

become manifest that meaning which allows me to take up the
purpose of my life patiently and courageously".[15]

As Christians we do not start with speculations about "the
order of being", although we face this kind of philosophical
search. Rather, we find our programme of life, above all, through
faith in Jesus Christ, true God and true man. We say yes to
Christ by sincerity, by fidelity to our conscience, by a profound
trust that we are accepted and loved, and by hope and trust
that the whole of life has a profound meaning and purpose.[16]

II.   MAN, SEARCHER FOR TRUTH

Modern man has invented the art of invention. Modern science
is an on-going process of learning, working out new models and
theories and testing them again and again empirically. But it is
not only in the field of empirical science and historical research
that man is a searcher; it is also true in the field of philosophy
and even in the search for religious truth.

In the study of the Old Testament we find a clear indication
of a gradual unfolding of salvation truth which comes from
God but which is also the harvest of man's steadfast search for
better knowledge about God and man. The fact that in Christ
the fullness of revelation has been given does not dispense his
disciples and the Church throughout the ages from uniting all
energies in the search for a better and more vital understanding
of salvation truth and its application to new cultures, new
languages, and new situations of life.

1.   *The right and duty to learn and to share in the common search for truth*

Man is known by God in a causative knowledge. Humankind
remains faithful to this origin by its constant effort to grasp the
meaning of life. The search for meaning of life is the first and
most important task. Whenever man stops searching for more
light and truth, identifying his partial knowledge with *the* truth,
he becomes intolerant and intolerable and is locking the doors
to the divine truth. To consider one's own knowledge as perfect
or absolute is nothing less than idolatry. All our knowledge is

fragmented. "Now we see only puzzling reflections in a mirror, but then we shall see face-to-face. My knowledge now is partial" (1 Cor 13:12). If anyone "assumes his truth is absolute and uninfluenced by his personal interests rather than simply his most honest approximation to truth, he may become a dangerous dogmatist".[17]

Human life is either growth or decay. This is also true of our grasp of truth, especially of the basic truths of meaning, purpose, salvation. "We undergo and undertake change in and through knowledge, and our knowledge changes with the other changes of human existence. Therefore, in one and the same man, the grasp of truth is different in the different cycles of life. Similarly there is a change in the course of the generations, but certain characteristics of the grasp of truth return in each generation again".[18] Since the search for truth depends on communication, the modality, the depth and the breadth of the process of knowledge of each person is to be seen in interdependence with cultural changes and with the whole collective destiny of humankind. We depend to a great extent on the wealth of fidelity to tradition.

A lively conscience becomes ever more conscious that its own integrity depends on how sincerely the person is searching for truth and to what kind of truth he gives preference.[19] The Synod of Bishops gathered in Rome in 1977 declared that "Nobody in the world has the right to hinder the human person from freely searching and accepting truth and striving towards the full knowledge and the free communication of truth". This freedom to search for ever better knowledge of truth includes the right to honest doubt about one's own opinions and about doctrines that others have tried to impose. Doubt has a great relevance if lived in openness to better knowledge and in readiness to revise one's own way of thinking and acting.

In its origin and final goal the truth is one. It is truth for man. But the great question for human existence is how each person shares in truth and makes it his own. This is a perennial task. The zealous search, the sincere longing for the knowledge of truth is fundamentally already a yearning for *the* truth. Through his eager search for truth man is already on the road, and he who is the Truth is with him. And the more the human person is experiencing the goodness and beauty of truth, the

more eagerly will he yearn for the final truth. The inborn hunger
for greater and even final knowledge manifests man's dignity and
rests on God's intention and promise to give man a blissful
sharing in his own truth.

2. The team

All of humankind, people of all cultures and generations,
should understand themselves as a great team in the search for
truth and in its practice. Since the knowledge of truth is a
solidaric task, the greater the solidarity is among people, the
closer we come to truth. Both the secular world and the Church
need model teams of persons who are eager to learn together
the art of dialogue and sharing.[20]

Each person has a distinctive see-level determined by his
or her kind of education, environment, culture and sub-culture,
and level of personal growth. No doubt there are difficulties in
communicating one's own truth, but there is a real possibility
if one is eager to do so. The better we know the limitedness,
the finiteness of our own see-level, and the more gratefully we
accept others in their diversity, the greater will be the chance
to grow in the knowledge and practice of truth. Teamwork is
a realization of the reciprocity of consciences. Each person
translates his own personal experience, and we can understand
the meaning and the wealth of this experience if we look not
only at the words but always at the person in the basic appreciation that says, "You who are different from me are necessary
for my truth".[21]

3. Dialogue

In authentic dialogue everyone is as eager to receive as to
give, and all try to be detached from the desire to impose their
own opinion or viewpoint. We shall never listen just to words
but to people, for people give the meaning to words. The same
word can have opposite meanings for different people or in
different circumstances. As believers we know that we cannot
be docile to the Spirit unless we are attentive to others and try
to understand not only what they say but what they are.

As long as we are eager to learn together and to search

earnestly for truth and unity, a pluriformity of convictions and doctrines will not be destructive. We will refrain from emphasizing theories or doctrines that, here and now, cannot help anyone, for what does language serve if I communicate nothing that helps others or furthers the solidaric task of knowing and doing the truth?

If we understand that all good things — and especially such a sublime thing as knowledge of truth — need time, then we will also appreciate that there is a time to speak and a time to be silent. As true believers who know that the supreme truth is love, we shall also understand that our commitment to truth implies a total commitment to love. "At all times both truth and love must be observed. As much as truth can be lived only in love, so true love can only be fulfilled in dedication to truth".[22] Like love, so the common search for truth is "patient, never boastful, nor conceited nor rude, never selfish, not quick to take offence" (1 Cor 13:4-5).

4. *Knowledge of truth from below*

Truth comes from above, from God, through his creation and revelation. But it has to be grasped from below. Nobody has a monopoly on truth that would allow him to dictate to others what they have to think or to believe. We can only share our experience, our reflections and our insights.

The first encyclical of Pope Paul VI, *Ecclesiam Suam*, emphasizes the importance of dialogue as the basic relationship in both the Church and the secular world. We cannot speak truly of dialogue if one person or group claims possession of the truth and the right to dictate to others. Dialogue presupposes the readiness on both sides to acknowledge their limitedness and to search for more light.

Before the Council there was sometimes a tendency to distinguish, and even to separate unduly, the teaching and learning functions in the Church. Today there is a clearer insight that those who are teachers must be the outstanding learners.[23] Today's moral theology realizes how important it is to learn from people in ordinary circumstances of life. Shared experience becomes a main source of better understanding about the access to truth and the various ways to learn together.[24] The Lord himself gives us a clear direction by his prayer, "I praise you, Father, Lord of heaven and earth, for hiding these things from the learned and wise and revealing them to the simple. Yes, Father, such was thy choice" (Lk 10:21).

Harvey Cox offers a hermeneutic for learning from people's religion.[25] We not only give attention to the historical and cultural context but also consider each detail, not with aloofness but rather with a willingness to respond and to confront our own life story with that of others. This confrontation is sincere if we are willing to modify our own opinions and lifestyles. "We cannot see that our culture and, in many places, our religion continue to be imposed on the poor, and that since ours is not a culture that they have participated in creating, both our culture and our religion become means of control".[26] It is no wonder that people, especially those of the Third World, sometimes react as a great part of the working class reacted in the nineteenth and early twentieth centuries. They rejected both the imposed culture and the religion as they were presented to them. Only in a genuine learning process can we share the deepest of our insights in moral meaning and religious values.

The Second Vatican Council, especially in the constitution on the Church in the Modern World, offers clear orientations for this sharing. "May the faithful, therefore, live in very close union with the people of their times. Let them strive to understand perfectly their way of thinking and feeling, as expressed in their culture. Let them blend modern science and its theories, and the understanding of the most recent discoveries, with Christian morality and doctrine. Thus their religious practice and morality can keep pace with their scientific knowledge and with an ever advancing technology. Thus, too, they will be able to test and interpret all things in a truly Christian spirit".[27]

III. PHENOMENOLOGY AND SOCIOLOGY OF TRUTH

The Synod of Bishops, Rome, 1977, sent out this message: "All educational effort has to take as its point of departure the aspirations of young people for creativity, for justice, for freedom and truth, as well as their desire for co-responsibility in the life of the church and society".[28] These are desires that are inborn, an essential part of human nature. At the centre is the desire to realize creatively, in freedom and truth, one's own vocation.

As an authentic Christian moral theologian, John Michael Sailer views human dedication to truth as the way of sharing in God's life and as discipleship of Christ. Therefore he looks first to the primordial pattern in God: "For every true adorer, God is ultimate truth AS BEING: he is *true*. He is ultimate truth as seeing: he knows himself and everything. He is ultimate truth as revealed: he manifests himself as the One who is and who knows".[29]

From this divine reality there flows, for man, the image and likeness of God, the capacity and the calling: "First, to *be* true, for such is the law governing his will; second, to *think* truth, for such is the law governing all thinking; third, to *act* in truth, for such is the law of all external life; fourth, to *speak* the truth, for such is the law of all discourse".[30]

1. Creative liberty and fidelity in truth and for truth

a) To be true

Just as we receive our being through God's creative sharing, so is our relation to truth (our being and becoming truthful) possible only as sharing in God's initiative. God acts truthfully and faithfully in creating and freeing us for truth. We can know him and his design only because he has first known us. His knowledge is causative, and all his words and works are truths. It is not possible to be true without honouring God's initiative that gives content and force to Christian life.[31]

God *is* love. In the most intimate love the Father speaks out his own Being in his Word who is the Truth that breathes love. Knowing us into being, God gives us a share in his life and his truth. We can adore him in truth, know and acknowledge him, for he has first known and acknowledged us (cf. Gal 4:9). "Anyone who loves God is known by him" (1 Cor 8:3). Although our knowledge now is only partial, we hope for that knowledge that corresponds to God's knowledge of us. "Then it will be whole, like God's knowledge of me" (1 Cor 13:12).

If our morality is based on God's initiative and accords

with what he does and reveals about freedom and truth, then our life is authentic and we dwell in his truth. Then we shall never stop yearning for greater truthfulness and a more Christ-like freedom. We are "in the truth" and growing in truth when we open ourselves to "that sincere longing that is an echo of the calling".[32] We are truly free and freely true when we respond to the revelation of God's love in Jesus Christ, when we allow his word to dwell in us and to guide us. Then we shall know what the Lord means when he tells us, "You shall know the truth and the truth will set you free" (Jn 8:32).

Our being "in the truth" is an ongoing process of purification and conversion which, again, is to be understood as our response to how the divine truth in Jesus Christ shines in the countenance he turns to us. Paul, having experienced how Christ knows him, exults, "All I care for is to know Christ" (Phil 3:10). But measuring his own knowledge and response in the light of Christ's initiative, he realizes how earnestly he must strive. "I have not yet reached perfection, but I press on hoping to take hold of that for which Christ once took hold of me" (Phil 3:12).

To the extent that we allow the truth to take hold of us, we come closer to truth and to truthfulness, and thus discover the hidden truth of our own being and our highest possibili-ties. Our truth is fidelity to the divine truth, to the way God reveals himself as the true and faithful One. Fidelity to his truth and to the truth of our being gives us the inner freedom to open ourselves to God's active presence and to all the ways he guides us into his truth.[33]

Our trust in God's active and faithful presence in history, and our gratitude for his having called us to freedom and truth, give us the courage and clear-sightedness to create space for freedom and mutual trust in the search for truth.[34] Our grasp on the meaning and on the truth of our being is never pure light. It is light and at the same time darkness, unconcealment and concealment. The unconcealment of meaning happens when we allow truth to reveal itself and to make its request.[35] Those who truly adore God, acknowledging him as the Source in all their thinking and doing, and allowing others to be and to reveal themselves, are gradually drawn into a full share of truth by the truth itself.

b) Thinking truth and doing the truth

Our being "in the truth" unfolds through our fidelity in thinking truth and acting according to it. God reveals his thoughts, his designs of love, by his deeds. His deeds are words and his words are deeds. In the sacraments we venerate God's acting word. The word and the sign are one; they effect what they signify. As the believer opens himself to this powerful word, he comes closer to truth.

Even our most hidden thoughts depend on communication which occurs not through isolated words but through a language that is thoroughly rooted in the culture, in all the ways people share with each other truth, half-truth and, unfortunately, sometimes untruth. In all our thinking and searching for truth, we have as a starting point that previous understanding that is *given* to us by language and other experiences of the common understanding.[36]

The more openly and creatively we meet the others, the better we come to an existential grasp. And if we use language creatively in our thinking, we are already on the wave-length of communication by words and deeds. Our thinking is leading us into truth whenever we sincerely want to do the truth and to share it with others by words and actions, by words that invite truthful action and by actions that communicate the truth of love and justice.

The very complexity and richness of our languages require a creative use. The educated adult uses two thousand words a day, of which the five hundred most frequently used have fourteen thousand dictionary definitions![37] This applies as much to thinking as to speaking.

Thinking cannot be severed from the thinking person who gives consistence and existential meaning to thoughts and words. Our thinking is true in the deepest sense if it is filled with love for the others and for oneself, and if its main purpose is to understand better the true nature of love. "For love consists, above all, in the communication of the truth".[38]

The truthfulness of thinking depends on that respect for others and that kind of culture and society that allow truthful communication and thus truthful thinking. But the freedom for truthful thinking is, above all, an inner reality: truthfulness

towards oneself, the courage to unmask prejudices, and that freedom from selfishness that allows us to hear those voices and
truths that ask from us an ongoing conversion.[39]

To be true in one's thinking, a person must allow the fullness
of reality to be the norm. The knowledge of truth begins with
perception, with receiving and accepting the reality and its
language. For the human person, truth is fidelity to Being as it
manifests itself in its mysterious and appealing presence. However, this receptivity has nothing to do with laziness or passivity.[40]

One can sin against truth in thinking by arbitrarily limiting
oneself to a partial truth as, for instance, to the world of empirical
science while neglecting the search for ultimate meaning and
truth. Thinking is also partial and untrue whenever a person
so absolutizes his own truth that he does not equally honour
the truth of the other. Integrity in thinking requires the courage
to be critical of oneself and one's opinions, and to accept doubts
as constructive elements for a more courageous and patient
search for truth and for greater openness to others. To risk
doubt and error is a necessary part of that freedom without
which we never can reach a greater fullness of truth.[41]

Man receives millions of pieces of information and has
treasured even more in his cerebral cortex; but for both perception and memory he has a selective power. The kind of
memory one has and how it functions for truth depends on
one's own truth. A person who has a profound disposition to
remember all that is good, all that is right, beautiful and honest,
is true in thinking and will be true in word and action.

Truth has to be acquired by each person individually. And
since it is the highest social good, we cannot be true in our
thinking unless we are committed to spreading the truth. But
this is not only an individual responsibility. All the institutions,
and especially the Church, have to do everything possible to
cultivate the best matrix and the best climate for the search for
truth and for its communication.[42]

2. Conscience and truth

It is an essential part of our humanity that we are born
for truth. The inborn longing for ever greater fullness of truth
and for people's unity in truth is a part of our conscience and

the reciprocity of consciences. The individual person who yearns for wholeness and integrity in openness to truth can be helped or hindered by the high or low level of the zest for truth in the environment.

Christ's discourses about hypocrisy seem to indicate that there was a trend in the whole social class to repress the inborn desire for truthfulness. Friedrich Nietzsche opposes the man of probity (*Redlichkeit*) to the inertia and falsehood of the crowd driven by herd instinct. He insists that talk about truth and criteria about the good make sense only in a radical turn to probity.[43]

For Karl Jasper, sincerity is the healthy conscience for truth. Honesty and sincerity towards oneself is "the foundation of veracity".[44] The conscience of truth impels a person, above all, to ask the truth about himself: what he is and what he is meant to be. "In all that he does, man is accompanied by the conscience of being bound to the objectivity of his own being; and this conscience, this companion, is he himself".[45]

Viktor Frankl sees logos and love as the two aspects of one and the same reality, of Being itself.[46] Man cannot find wholeness and inner unity unless he follows faithfully the conscience of truth, unless he is searching for the ultimate meaning of his life. We find ourselves and our integration if we find the truth of our life in self-transcending love. The genuine encounter of persons is not only oriented towards the logos; it also helps partners to transcend themselves towards the logos. "The self-transcendence of the human person happens either in the service of a purpose or in the love of a person. That is, it is directed either towards the logos in itself or the logos that is incarnate".[47]

The whole research and writing of Abraham Maslow similarly explores the human need to know the truth about oneself and to transcend oneself in the search for truth and in the service of others.[48] The higher needs that impel people to search for ultimate meaning are sustained by wonderment, admiration, astonishment and awe, whenever the beauty of truth and goodness reveals itself. "The unauthentic man is possessed by things, and he is not able to interpret himself as something else than a thing among things".[49] But man is marked by the capacity and the need to reflect on his own being, on "being a person", and by fulfilling this inner need he becomes ever more able to ask this wonderwork what it means to *be*.[50] Our capacity to admire, to be filled with awe and astonishment, and even more, our conscience about our own truthfulness, depend on our unceasing search for existential truth. In that search we experience our finiteness. We discover our errors, but also our capacity to overcome them.

Our truth-conscience is threatened in many ways, as Heidegger shows time and again. Man can become the slave of the flux of events and of impersonal thinking that make him a thing among things. He can be driven by the flux of events and by the lower needs and superficiality of the crowd. He can compromise truth and his own capacity for truth by his own inertia that so frequently celebrates the triumph of the status quo and of stereotyped doctrines and opinions.[51] He can be so much a part of a group, a party, or a religious sect that he sacrifices his good faith to a so-called "faith". But there cannot be this dilemma of either "faith" or good faith; there can only be the sacrifice of good faith to a wrong kind of faith. Such a sacrifice can be required only by a dead or sectarian faith. Bereft of sincerity, "faith" becomes naked obedience or madness.[52] Faith, in the religious sense, or dedication to a great cause, can go beyond reasons but can never go against reason.

Base selfishness, reinforced by an environment or institutions where the twin masters Pain and Pleasure, Promise and Threat, are almost the only teachers, can lead to a heretical structure of conscience. Such a deformed conscience looks first to possible reward or punishment, and only from there to truth. In a selective type of thinking, it will see only what the pain-and-pleasure masters allow. The Church and all parts of society should come to realize what great damage is done to human relations and to the truth of people's consciences when the reinforcers predominate.[53]

Jaspers insists that one of the constant sources of fallacy, error and untruth is human finiteness. But this very experience of finiteness can become the strongest incentive to search the depth of truth, the truth that holds all things together.[54] This search is not a blind jump but a courageous response to the deepest need of truth-conscience. It will not, however, become a way to truth by mere speculation or theory. Only if we allow truth to set us on fire, to purify us and to claim our total dedication does this encounter happen. An excellent criterion for the authenticity of our encounter with truth is an ever-increasing longing for greater truth, a yearning for that truth which bears fruit in our life.

Fruitfulness is not the same as utility. Where utility is the chief motive and criterion, the person has closed his mind to the region of higher truths and made himself unable to search authentically for the ultimate meaning of life. As criterion, fruitfulness functions differently within each region of existence, but it is unthinkable that something that bears no fruit at any level deserves to be called "truth".[55]

The Gospel of John, Chapter 15, uses the symbol of fruitfulness repeatedly. Whoever allows the word of Christ to dwell in him and to transform him will bear fruit in joy, the fruit of love and justice. The apostles are appointed to "go on and bear fruit, fruit that shall last". The Father cleans "every fruiting branch to make it more fruitful still". Similarly, the Apostle of the Gentiles speaks of the "fruit", the harvest of the Spirit. Those who renounce their selfish self and are guided by the Spirit will reap the harvest of "love, joy, peace, patience, kindness, goodness, fidelity, gentleness and self-control" (Gal 5:22-23).

3. *The various levels of truth*

Faith in creation by the word of God, and faith in the Word incarnate, impel the believer to honour all the dimensions and levels of truth. God has not only spoken in manifold ways to the prophets; he speaks also in various ways through the created reality and the history of the world.

Our culture today is marked by the diversification of the kinds and areas of knowledge, each of which has its own laws and exigencies that must be recognized in the pursuit of truth. Theology no longer considers herself as queen of all the sciences, but she does reflect on how all the different realities, and the many ways of approaching them, lead to better knowledge of God and better service to man.

Recognition of the autonomy of the different spheres of knowledge did not come without conflicts. Vatican II declares, "We cannot but deplore certain habits of mind sometimes found too, among Christians, which do not sufficiently attend to the rightful independence of science. The arguments and controversies which they spark led many minds to conclude that faith and science are mutually opposed".[56]

But while theologians, in a time of transition, could not see how different the approach of empirical science is, today the difficulty is the refusal of many scientists to acknowledge any other approach to truth than their own.

This method of positive science is impressive. It is empirical in a double sense. Not only are its theories based on perception of facts and processes; they are also constantly verified by further empirical research. Philosophical and religious knowledge is also grounded on perception and experience but it cannot be verified by empirical experiments. There, a totally different kind of thinking is necessary.

The word "scientism" expresses the various forms of reductionism. Since Descartes and Locke, some schools of philosophy have indulged in the conviction that experience is the reflection of truth and that therefore *the* system of reflection can be found only in the natural sciences. "Scientism is a philosophy of experience that has forgotten its own origin".[57]

After August Comtes, a certain trend at one time expected that the combination of all the perfected empirical sciences would be the complete reflection of reality. There was incredible optimism that if all the various branches of sciences were conducted empirically, they would fit together and make visible the total reality, the "truth". Even in psychology and psychiatry we still find this kind of reductionism. Adopting as completely as possible the methods and perspectives of the natural empirical sciences, many psychologists and psychiatrists act practically on the implicit "metaphysical" conviction that man has to be studied as a thing among other things.[58]

A science is this particular science and no other by the kind of questions it asks. The technical man is interested in how to control the world. If he has capitulated to the worldview of scientism, then man is, for him, no longer a subject but an object to be controlled. The subjective character, the person as a person, cannot be expressed in the categories of quantity. For this kind of scientist, people are functions in a system of tools, and as such, they can be calculated and measured. He does not know man in his dignity.

Scientism is not only an error in the mind; it can become a whole mentality that shapes one's relations with reality. People so thoroughly concerned and occupied with dominating the world lose the capacity to admire it. The more they own the world by technology, the less they are able to perceive and receive it in gratitude.[59]

The truth concerning ultimate meaning can only be received in gratitude. But for the person thoroughly shaped by the technological mentality, the world is something not to be received but to be conquered. All this is not the fault of empirical science and technology as such; it is rather the consequence of absolutizing what is relative, and taking this approach as the whole.

Even if this does not happen as theory, it can happen as praxis, as practical incapacity to approach higher knowledge. The higher the rank or level of a truth, the more intensive is its demand on man, not only on his intelligence but on all his being. Truth that is higher than the level of technical man can only be received in gratitude and in readiness to act on it for itself and not only for utility's sake.[60]

An outstanding economist, E.F. Schumacher, holds that a healthy revision of economy is possible only by a conversion to a total truth that radically understands technology as *means* for humanity, and that freedom can be restored even within the economy only by this broader vision of humanity. "Mankind has indeed a certain freedom of choice; it is not bound by trends, by the 'logic of production' or by any other fragmentary logic. But it is bound by truth. Only in the service of truth is perfect freedom, and even those who today ask us 'to free our imagination from bondage to the existent system' fail to point the way to the recognition of truth".[61]

Empirical sciences and mathematics, important as they are for people's life, are not asking questions of ultimate meaning and of holistic vision of life. But historical experiences show that they can fulfil their role only if they leave space in people's minds, imaginations and purposes for searching the truths that can give direction in all our life.

Schumacher has seen clearly that reductionism of all kinds

makes for unfreedom, while openness to truth in all its dimensions and on all its levels is liberating for each sphere and level of truth and life. Wholeness of vision and the wholeness of man are interrelated.

4. *Tension between a more static and a more dynamic vision of truth*

The Second Vatican Council's emphatic acknowledgment that the various levels of knowledge and spheres of reality enjoy a certain autonomy was the result of a more explicit vision of faith, dogma, and the whole created reality. "To a certain extent, the human intellect is also broadening its dominion over time; over the past by means of historical knowledge; over the future by the art of projecting and by planning ... History itself speeds along on so rapid a course that an individual person can scarcely keep abreast of it. The destiny of the human community has become all of a piece, where once the various groups of man had a kind of private history of their own. Thus the human race has passed from a rather static concept of reality to a more dynamic, evolutionary one. In consequence, there has arisen a new series of problems, a series as important as can be, calling for new efforts of analysis and synthesis".[62]

A morality that emphasizes creative liberty and fidelity cannot ignore these problems and the task they impose.

a) The biblical and the Greek concept of truth

In the Hellenistic worldview, history is a cycle of eternal repetition. Platonic truth dwells with eternal ideas. Only when the Greek culture came into intimate contact with other high cultures was the staticity of Greek knowledge somehow shaken.

The biblical vision is totally different. The theology of the Old Testament is narrative. Israel's religion is her history with God, with his faithful presence. The Hebrew word *'emet* can be translated as both "truth" and "fidelity". In the history of revelation, the unconcealment of truth is the experience of God's creative fidelity calling for a similar response from his people.

Dynamic truth is historical. It carries into the present the riches of past experience and reflections; the present shares in the gradual unfolding of knowledge. Truth itself is eternally in

God but the truth that gives direction to man is an event that happens now and bears in itself a sense of continuity. "Future has an open dimension for us, not only noetically — that is, for our grasp — but also ontologically in the unfolding of reality".[63]

In the historical act of unconcealment of truth, man takes part as actor and decision-maker. Future events and further discovery of truth contain our effort of knowledge and our decisions and actions.[64]

The greatest wealth of tradition can be known existentially only in God's active presence by people who are willing to be co-actors in creative liberty and fidelity.

The historical dimension of knowledge as unconcealment of truth is manifold. It happens time and again, yet is never completed. Each event of unconcealment of important truths presupposes a certain phase of the knowing subject's personal history which is interrelated with the collective history of a culture or of humanity in its search for ever better truths. "There is not one single truth that does not have a future, for each truth opens new breaches".[65]

Whoever considers his own truth as absolute in the sense of idealism, has in reality stopped having a history of knowledge. He has concealed himself from the further unconcealment of truth. The same is true of everyone who, following the system of realism, believes that he possesses truth in itself.

"Historicity of truth, however, does not mean that the truth of today is the untruth of tomorrow".[66] Of course, tomorrow I may recognize that what I saw yesterday was only an appearance and not really truth. But if I see truth today I can hope to see more of it tomorrow. Thus today's truth does not renounce yesterday's, but it becomes ever more integrated and complete. Only in this sense is truth, for me, immutable, unchangeable.

Just as technical inventions have their opportune time, so do important ethical truths have their *kairos*. When a great genius anticipates the time of discovery in a culture not yet prepared for it, there can arise dangerous conflicts. Sometimes it can be better to be temporarily silent and to prepare one's contemporaries to become receptive.[67]

An adequate grasp of existentially relevant truths presupposes emotional, affective and intellectual maturity and the readiness to respond to them with one's life. This explains why the grasp of truth is bound to the life history of both the individual person and the group and society.[68] All this proves how important for our approach to truth, and for our whole life, is the readiness to grow, to learn and to unlearn in an ongoing process of conversion.

b) The relevance of sociology of knowledge

Modern sociology of knowledge studies, empirically and systematically, the interrelation between the total shape of a past or present society, a certain culture, and economic and social processes on the one hand and, on the other, the type of knowledge, its growth and decay, the emphasis on certain truths and values, and blindness to others, and so on.[69]

Some of Max Scheler's discoveries that are fundamental for the sociology of knowledge cannot be ignored in theology. There is a functional interrelation and interdependence between the multiple forms of knowledge and its excentration in the total social reality. Each type of society, each group, and each era of civilization allows one sector of knowledge to develop particularly, bringing to the foreground some particular perspective and scale of values. Based on this insight is Scheler's appeal to intensify dialogue, cooperation and comparison between the different cultures and their ways of approaching the search for truth. Karl Mannheim follows him but gives more emphasis to how certain forms of knowledge can change and do change society and the course of history.[70]

George Gurvitch, synthesizing the results of a half-century's research, classifies the forms of knowledge thus:

1st, the perception and exploration of the external world;
2nd, knowledge of the "other" and the "we", the group and the societies;
3rd, knowledge of common sense;
4th, technological knowledge;
5th, political knowledge;
6th, scientific knowledge;
7th, philosophical knowledge.

Each of these basic forms, in turn, can have a different balance or tension:

1st, a more mystical or more rational knowledge;
2nd, a more empirical or more conceptual knowledge;
3rd, a positive or speculative knowledge;
4th, intuitive or reflective knowledge;
5th, symbolical or well-defined expression;
6th, collective or individual knowledge.

Gurvitch understands the interrelatedness not as causality in the sense of determinism but as functional, thus leaving open all the questions of epistemology. He explicitly rejects the Marxist sociology insofar as it considers knowledge and its forms as superstructure caused by the economic infra-structure. He holds that the empirical sociology of knowledge does not favour that theory.

Of particular interest to Gurvitch is the hierarchical roles the different forms of knowledge tend to take in the various types of society and culture. He considers the shape of each form of knowledge and its hierarchic rank as a functional part of the total expression and regulation of a society.[71] From the rich material available, I choose here only these examples that are of interest to our purpose, which is the understanding of the liberating truth.

Gurvitch notes that the knowledge of the others, the we, the group, had a relatively high rank in the city culture of antiquity. However, its dimension was greatly restricted by the kind of society. The foreigner, the slave, and to some extent women, were not at all included, or only in an accidental way. In the total structure of traditional India, the concept of the "other" and of the "we" was severely restricted and shaped by the caste society and the type of religion. Religion itself was highly marked and practically determined by this kind of knowledge of the others and by the whole societal structure. Modern democratic society and international cooperation since the time of the French Revolution, have given high priority to knowledge of the all-inclusive "we".

In most of the traditional patriarchal societies, the knowledge of common sense ranked very highly while, according to Gurvitch, it takes last place in a planned capitalistic society. In freely competitive capitalism it ranks only a little higher but has more places of refuge.

Systematic philosophy won its high place and developed in antiquity's city culture, in the late Middle Ages, and in modern times where it took its course in the effort to dethrone or replace theology. It does not rank highly in a capitalistic society.

In a freely competitive capitalistic society, the empirical sciences are given a place equal to or higher than technology, while in a planned capitalistic society technology and political science take first place and receive a somehow mythologized shape.

Sociology of knowledge does not intend to take the place of epistemology (the study or a theory of the nature and grounds of knowledge, especially with reference to its limits and validity). It does, however, pose pertinent questions to epistemology and can help it to come down to earth. It presses epistemology to give more attention to collective knowledge and not only to individual knowledge, to challenge the subject-object dichotomy, and to distinguish more clearly the different types of knowledge when it seeks to determine the question of validity. Of course it is epistemology's task to discern whether all the different perspectives of knowledge are equally valid, and how the contrasting hierarchies given to the various forms of knowledge affect the question of validity. It also has to deal more tentatively with the question of what does prevail, continuity or diversity or even contrast, among the different forms of knowledge, their hierarchy and perspectives.[72]

c) Some conclusions for practical and speculative theology

Sociology of knowledge makes us more sharply aware that our assent of faith is not given so much to a formulation as to the mystery to which it points, as Thomas Aquinas knew so well.[73]

Today's theological reflection can by no means ignore the sociology of knowledge and of morals. Our faith in the unity of truth must never lose sight of the plurality of approaches and cultural communications. The Second Vatican Council repeats the emphatic monition delivered by Pope John XXIII in a speech on October 22, 1962, at the beginning of the Council: "Recent studies and findings of science, history and philosophy raise new questions which influence life and demand new theological investigations. Furthermore, while adhering to the methods and requirements proper to theology, theologians are invited to seek continually for more suitable ways for communicating doctrine to the men of their times. For the deposit of faith or revealed truths are one thing; the manner in which they are formulated, without violence to their meaning and significance, is another. In pastoral care, appropriate use must be made not only of theological principles but also of the findings of the secular sciences, especially of psychology and sociology".[74]

Whoever has studied the sociology of knowledge in a historical dimension realizes in a new way that nobody, not even the Roman Catholic Church, has a monopoly of truth.[75] As Pope John insisted — after having experienced with great sympathy the different faith expressions and mentality of the Orthodox, the oriental Christians — it "needs painstaking labour to help people ... place the past on their shoulders, to change mentalities, tendencies and prejudices, and it is necessary to examine what time, tradition and customs have possibly superimposed on reality and truth".[76]

Sociology of knowledge helps us to understand better the relevance of what Vatican II says in its decree on Ecumenism about a complementarity of views and doctrines in different parts of Christianity, and about the hierarchy of truths.[77] This does not at all mean indulgence in a false conciliatory approach, but it can greatly help to remove misunderstandings that arose from historical contexts.

Sociology of knowledge can also alert theologians to the danger of uncritically following trends in their own environment and culture. It gives them a better understanding, too, of the legitimate diversity of theological schools like those of Alexandria and Antioch in antiquity, and of the extreme danger for their function whenever schools indulge in antagonisms.

For all large institutions, including the Church, sociology of knowledge can sound a warning about allowing knowledge of dominion and control too high a place in the hierarchy of knowledge, thus weakening their ability to adapt to new needs.[78] Karl Rahner draws particular attention to poor argumentation in moral theology, due to the inertia of theologians and the immobility of the institutions. "It is a part of the tragic history of the Church that, in practice and theory, she has defended moral rules with bad arguments because of problematic and historically conditioned convictions, 'prejudices', instead of overcoming them by her own initiative. Only when other historical circumstances eliminated them, the Church finally took up new convictions and acted as if the new vision were self-evident and the Church had never doubted".[79]

5. Objectivity and subjectivity: Questions of epistemology

It is not our purpose to enter into discussions with all the various schools of epistemology but, for a better understanding of what a liberating relationship to truth is, we do have to deal with some of the questions.

The school of existential phenomenology to which I am greatly indebted is equally distant from subjectivism and objectivism. It emphasizes subjectivity but always with the greatest attention to *inter*subjectivity. Existentially, enrichment comes from both the individual and the community, for whenever a person opens himself to truth, he participates in a dialogue. His existential involvement is by his own judgment, but his creative openness to truth happens within the realm of reciprocity of perspectives.[80]

The event of unconcealment of truth takes place in and through a subject. The subject, the thinking person, has an active role in it. Although, as believers, we do not forget God, the Truth, who is always the origin of truth itself and its revelation, we know that his presence is transcendental and we cannot ignore the human intersubjectivities. When searching for the truth and receiving it, the subject is indebted to all who share in the searching and discernment of truth.

Any effort to dissociate oneself from other subjects in order to entrust oneself to the objectivity of truth is self-deception. Each person must find his or her truth, the intimate meaning of life; but the road is marked by intentionality shared with the others who are equally searching for truth. To be ungrateful to those others who share their truth, or to be unconcerned for their searching, is to expel oneself from the paradise of truth.

That is why we consider an objectivistic metaphysics as contradiction.[81] The unconcealment of existential truth concerns a person in his wholeness, in his conscience and in his reciprocity with the consciences of others. This means that one can never proceed arbitrarily or with cold aloofness.

Whoever considers a human being's truth as an accurate mirror-image of reality in itself, or truth in itself, ignores the subject's creative involvement and his debt to others without whom he would never find truth. It is through creativity in receptivity, in openness to others, that one can realize one's openness to the Other, the Absolute Truth. When a person is creatively and receptively involved in the unconcealment of truth, he realizes that he is not the Lord of being but only the shepherd of being, and that this act of discovery is an act of response in co-responsibility (intersubjectivity). "All truth is subjective in the sense that truth is objective for a subject. Subjectivity for a subject is, of course, much more objective than in the interpretation of objectivism".[82]

The objectivist philosophy, more than any other epistemology, emphasizes that man is bound by truth itself. This aspect can be so exaggerated that human truths seem to be the absolute initiative of the objective reality. "The subject withdraws 'humbly' as unbiased observer, in the sense that it considers itself able to isolate itself from the event of truth. Then the objective truth becomes the objective subject for nobody ... and yet, the objectivist makes himself loudly heard. The 'humble' subject will presume to speak out pure objectivity. And thus humility turns into absolutism, for whatever the subject says is attributed to the initiative of objectivity itself".[83]

The objectivist believes in eliminating all the risk that a creative unconcealment of truth implies. But there is no greater risk to truth than to identify one's own thinking with absolute objectivity, completely ignoring all of one's sociological and psychological conditioning. Man is not a photographer of truth, and truth does not impress itself in the mind and will of a person who is not dedicated to it and not committed to discovering it.

The objectivist easily forgets existential conditions for discovering truth. Viktor Frankl writes, "Being is manifested and unconcealed only when I turn to it and dedicate myself to it;

and this dedication has to do with love. It is not accidental that in Hebrew the same word is used for knowledge and for conjugal union. According to Max Scheler, 'the act of knowledge is preceded by an act of love. I would like to say: in things there is a brighter longing for the spiritual being whose spirituality consists in being with' ".[84]

Karl Jaspers sees in all human knowledge a split between subject and object until one opens oneself to the truth that is all-embracing. This is the Absolute Truth, the transcendence with which human knowledge comes in contact only by a "leap" whereby the person leaves behind superficiality and finds himself in the truth.

Truth, transcendent and all-embracing, is demanding. "The truth opens itself to love; she comes to the fore in the decision that is gained in love".[85] This truth, this transcendence that gives meaning to all truth and helps man to overcome the object-subject split, is never a mere object. Man must know his limitedness. Only then can he experience unity as something that is given to him and enables him to give himself. In this kind of knowledge there is a profound existential truth: "only love can unconceal being and truth. Truth in its wholeness is accessible only to total love. Truth gives its final response through love".[86]

IV. TRUTHFULNESS AND DISCRETION IN COMMUNICATION

We have already seen that truthfulness in being and in searching for truth is essentially connected with sharing truth, and therefore with communication. Now we have to study the communication of truth, inasmuch as there can arise a tension between veracity and discretion. One's interior attachment to truth and love expresses itself in straightforwardness, uprightness, simplicity; but in an evil world it also demands great prudence and discretion, as Jesus' own words imply: "Look, I send you out like sheep among wolves; be wary as serpents, innocent as doves" (Mt 10: 16). Whatever may be the external difficulties and complexities of life, frankness and simple genuineness of character reveal themselves in one's language and one's whole deportment. Its opposite is duplicity, discord and perfidy.

1. *To the image and likeness of God*

True speech must be patterned on the divine Word, for that is what it reflects and imitates. From both its origin within us (the mental word, our knowledge) and its purpose (the revelation and exchange of love), it has to be viewed in this light.

No other Church Father's teaching has so enriched theology on this point as has St Augustine's. As the eternal Word is with the Father and reveals him, so our external truthfulness reveals the inner truthfulness. "The word that sounds outwardly is the sign of the word that gives light inwardly: the latter has the greater claim to be called a word".[87] As the eternal Word assumes human flesh to manifest itself, so the audible word must be in some measure an incarnation of the mental word: "When, therefore, that is in the word which is in the knowledge, then there is a true word and truth such as is looked for from man; thus that which is in the knowledge is also in the word, and what is not in the knowledge is also not in the word. Here may be recognized, 'Yes, yes; no, no' (Mt 5:37); and so this likeness of the image that is made approaches as nearly as possible that likeness of the image that is born, by which God the Son is declared to be 'in all things substantially like the Father' ".[88]

It is true that by our external word we cannot exhaustively and precisely express our inner word, our knowledge, just as our inner knowledge can never comprehensively grasp the fullness of reality. Nevertheless, the divine likeness must be so faithfully preserved within us that nothing in our external word may ever be found to contradict our inner word of knowledge or the purity of our intentions. "God the Father, the Begetter, has spoken out in his own co-eternal Word all that he is, and God the Son, his Word himself, has nothing either more or less in substance than is in him who, not lying but truthfully, has begotten the Word".[89]

God the Father expresses himself fully only in his Word. In creation and revelation he grants us participation in his truth only partially and gradually. This graduality does not contradict his truth. The Word of God, the Son of the Father, cannot lie. "This Word can never have anything false, because it is unchangeable, for He is from What It Is, for 'the Son can do nothing of himself but what he sees the Father do' (Jn 5:19)".[90]

Jesus Christ, the Word incarnate, remains absolutely faithful even when he does not reveal himself to those who are not searching for truth sincerely; he does not "cast pearls before swine" (Mt 7:6). The all-truthful and faithful One praises the Father, the source of all truth, for having hidden from the wise and arrogant what he revealed to the little and humble ones (Mt 11:25). As the first source and pattern of every true communication lays down the law of truthfulness for us, nothing in our utterance by words or deeds may contradict the loving truthfulness and intention of our mind. But we are not obliged and sometimes not even permitted, to express all that is in our mind.

For an adequate moral norm of true communication we go beyond the mere psychological concept of true speech (conformity of word with mind) to the divine source and pattern, and try to understand the end and purpose of human communication in the light of divine revelation. The goal is always to build up the human community in truth and love. Intellectual, moral and spiritual fellowship can exist only in the harmony of word and love. Whatever words and actions do not arise from true love for the good and for one's neighbour become contradictory, for they appear to be communication but are contradicting communion and fellowship.

As ultimate norm and guide for truth, the divine pattern teaches us not only the primacy of inner truthfulness but also the inseparable unity of inner truthfulness and loving communication. A loveless use of facts and half-truths destroys our inner truthfulness and damages community. The authentically truthful person cannot deal with truth in a heartless and calculating way, for he is taken up heart and soul with truth.

Discretion must guide all communication by words, gestures and deeds, for only thus can we truly share knowledge and search for the truth that bridges all differences, closes gaps, unmasks hypocrisy, heals wounds, binds the members of the Mystical Body together and testifies to our mission to be one in truth and love, in the image and likeness of God. Discretion is the sensibility of true love in the person dedicated to truth and truthful communication.

A realistic moral theology is grounded in our creation and re-creation in the image and likeness of God, but it also keeps in mind our unlikeness, our constant need of further purification, and our life in the midst of a disturbed and sometimes evil world.

Sincerity and candour indicate an openness of heart that has nothing to conceal. But the more a person progresses on the blessed road to purity of heart, the more he discovers the need for further purification in his thinking and longing, and the more he realizes that he cannot simply reveal himself to everyone at all times. While he humbly confesses his sins before God and in the sacrament of confession, he takes great care that, in his daily communications, his words and actions communicate only the best in himself. Further, even the sincere and upright person, for all his openheartedness, must conceal many things because of loving consideration for his neighbour. Therefore openness must be tempered by a reticence that spares the sensitivity of others and offers no occasion for thoughtless, cunning or malicious people to mar good works or damage good reputations so necessary for cooperation in a life of justice and peace.

The art of silence is a deep and clear fountain of truthful communication. One who does not know how to keep silent in order to allow the great truths and problems of life to mature within him cannot come to a closer likeness to God in sharing truth with others. Silence is a mysterious communication with the Source of all truths and of loving openness to others. In silence, truth and love and one's powers of communication flourish, while loquacity robs words of their gravity and depth, and often leads to superficiality, indifference to truth, and consequent distorted relationships.

2. Alas to the liar

In holy Scripture, truthfulness ranks among the highest values. History is seen as a battle between divine Truth and the Liar (Satan, the embodiment of untruthfulness and unfaithfulness) and all who follow him. The commandment, "You shall not bear false witness against your neighbour" (Ex 20:16; Lev 19:12) protects God's people from malicious and damaging untruths and infidelities. "The Old Testament condemns the lie insofar as it contradicts and destroys community based on fidelity which man owes to Yahweh and his fellowmen".[91] Untruthfulness aggressively contradicts the covenant that unites the people of God and calls for fidelity and reliability.[92] The grateful response to the gift of the covenant is fidelity and truthfulness before God and towards each other.

The New Testament reveals Jesus Christ, the Covenant and the Faithful Witness. The believer shares in his saving truth and in his mission to give faithful witness; the liar can have no share in this covenant.

The forceful passages about the exclusion of liars from the kingdom of God (cf. 1 Tim 1:10; Rev 21:8; 21:27; 22:15) do not deal with problems like the "white lie" but with the offences of those who open themselves to the delusions of the devil, the deceiver, or who by their whole conduct contradict the truth which they affirm by faith. It is a matter of self-deception from which all kinds of untruthfulness flows.[93]

As a basic normative ideal, the New Testament stresses the striving for exemplary truthfulness and trustworthiness (cf. Mt 5:37). All kinds of lying that damage community and credibility must be cast aside as the old self, the sinner (Eph 4:25; Col 3:9). Ananias and Sapphira, who purposely deceived their community and introduced an attitude of hypocrisy, were severely punished (Acts 5:1-11).

In both the Old and New Testaments, the problems of truthfulness and lying are seen in the light of God's own faithfulness and the believer's response to it in fidelity to the covenant. Truth and fidelity are so much a part of God's chosen ones that "lie" (*pseûdos*) is another name for sin and sinfulness (cf. Jn 8:44; Rom 1:25; 1 Jn 2:21; 2:27). Similarly, the word *apáte* can mean deception, illusion, fallacy, seduction (Mt 13:22; Eph 4:22; Col 2:8; 2 Thess 2:10; Heb 3:13). And the words *skótos* and *skotía*, meaning darkness, also infer that untruthfulness leads into the slavery of sin (cf. Jn 1:5; 3:19; 6:17; 8:12; 12:25; 12:46; Acts 26:18; Rom 13:12; 2 Cor 6:14; Eph 5:8; 5:11; 6:12; Col 1:13; 1 Pet 2:9; 1 Jn 1:16). These three biblical words mean the servitude to falsehood and, by inclusion, the individual act of lying or deceiving oneself and others, which flows from that servitude and worsens it.

3. *The gravity of sins of untruthfulness*

The untruthfulness which the Bible calls *pseûdos, apáte* or *skótos* is nothing other than a fundamental option for untruth in being, in thinking and acting. Individual acts that sin against truth in being, in the search for truth and its communication, can be expressions of that fundamental option and so participate in its servitude and malice. However, if there is a fundamental option for goodness and truth, the gravity of sins against truth depends on the behavioural direction. When they are incidents in a process of decay, of growing untruthfulness, they are grave venial sins that may prepare the fundamental option for darkness if there is not a decisive change. But if the overall direction is one of continuous conversion towards greater light, greater truthfulness, then sins against the search and communication of truth have to be judged differently.

In view of human weakness there is a presumption that an average person's lies, committed in weakness and with no intention to do damage to others, are "only" venial faults.[94] But it is dangerous to say, with Kern, that the lie is generally not against the order of love and therefore only venial sin.[95] This is particularly misleading in an ethics of acts which neglects attitudes. We can say, however, that people who care for truth and truthfulness can always hope not to have committed mortal sin by untruth if they continue to strive in the right direction. This corresponds with the great tradition represented, for instance, by Augustine and Thomas Aquinas. Yet tradition has also paid attention to the open caution of St Augustine who asked whether a perfect man might not commit a mortal sin when, in full freedom and consciousness, he speaks an ordinary lie.[96]

The tendency of some moralists to take sincerity in communication less seriously than protection of another's property goes directly against the quote, "Lying is by its nature a grave sin, as much as theft, calumny and similar faults".[97] Untruthfulness is diametrically opposed to the will of God who is Truth itself, and to our sanctification in truth. However, insincerity and falsehood are something quite different from an occasional lapse when, under sudden duress or out of excessive sympathy for another's feelings, one tells a lie. Such failings are not signs of fundamental falsehood.[98]

Some moralists have classified the "jocose lie" as venial sin. To my mind, it is not a lie at all, for a discourse must be taken as a whole and in its own context. A joking way of speaking can exhilirate others, can bring forth wisdom, wholesome laughter, and a greater willingness to accept human weaknesses. Besides, the initial deception is removed by what follows it, making the whole a kind of short comedy. Its value depends on graciousness and sensitivity for the other. Our neighbour must never be humiliated or disgraced.

The fanciful stories of quite young children should not ordinarily be censured as lies, since children do not yet adequately distinguish the lively play of fantasy from objective experience. At the proper time the educator will kindly help the child to make the necessary distinctions. Even when children consciously tell untruths, their lies are usually due to anxiety, fear, a previous experience of distrust, lack of confidence, or they simply imitate the lying practices of adults with whom the children are in contact. Education in truth can be effective only when it is built on the educator's exemplary pattern of truthfulness, and in an atmosphere of trust and kindly restraint in correction and punishment. Punishment, even if deserved, should usually be omitted when a child, out of uprightness and sincerity admits a fault.

A condemnatory attitude is also out of place in the case of pathological lying. It would not be correct, of course, to say that psychopaths bear no moral responsibility for whatever lies they tell, but a certain kind of psychopathic person suffers under a compulsory propensity for lying. Frequently in such cases the boundaries of truth, imagination and lie are blurred. Moral responsibility is diminished in proportion to the extent or degree of the mental illness. These people must be given the same kindly understanding as that given to children. But they should be led, step by step, to learn and to appreciate truthfulness.

4. Is the prohibition of lying a moral absolute?

The attitude of truthfulness, and consequently the verdict of untruthfulness, are moral absolutes. The question, however, is whether a truthful person might be allowed, in some situations of great complexity, to say something that in his own conviction is not true or not accurate, and if so, whether this should be considered a lie in the moral sense. For it is agreed that in a disordered world it can sometimes be a duty to conceal a truth or a true fact from those who want to abuse it in the pursuit of injustice. The question is then about what kind of language and conduct the truthful person may adopt to effect the necessary concealment.

a) Scripture and Tradition

The Old Testament frequently condemns lying, especially if it is destructive for the community; but it also tells about the lies of the venerated patriarchs: of Abraham (Gen 12:11-13; 21:15), of Isaac (Gen 26:7-11), of Jacob (Gen 27:8-27), of David and his friend Jonathan (1 Sam chs. 26-29).

It seems that at least some of these lies are not at all disapproved in the Bible. And the midwives who saved the Hebrew children by lies are praised as "God-fearing women". "God made the midwives prosper. He gave them homes and families of their own because they feared him" (Ex 1:15-21). Similarly, the Scriptures praise Judith who most ably deceived Holofernes and his soldiers in order to save her people (Jdt ch. 10).

In the New Testament there is no place where lying is praised or approved. On the other hand, neither do the strong and numerous texts that emphasize truthfulness and condemn liars suggest that the lying behaviour of the midwives in Egypt would now be wrong. But we can say that in the full light of the revelation of Christ, most of the patriarchs' lies would no longer receive implicit approval. There has been a growth of consciousness about the high value of sincerity.

There is no uniformity about this problem in the Christian tradition.[99] The most ancient tradition about the absolute or non-absolute prohibition of lying derives from Greek philosophy and from such passages of the Old Testament as we have just mentioned. Apart from Aristotle and Sophocles there is hardly any notable representative of Greek thought who condemns the lie as absolutely unlawful.

Because of this cultural background, and all the more because the lies of the patriarchs are not disapproved, great Church Fathers like Origen, Chrysostom, Hilary and Cassian sought to justify at least the use of the "officious lie" in certain circumstances, if it is absolutely unselfish and to the advantage of one's neighbour.

No Church Father has paid more attention to this problem or has more effectively influenced further tradition than St Augustine. Already in his work *Soliloquia*,[100] he clearly indicates that the intent to deceive belongs essentially to the definition of lying. In 395 he wrote his book, *On Lying*. He evidently rules out the "jocose lie" as a fault against truthfulness[101] or as lie in the moral sense. In this work Augustine, on principle, allows no exception to the prohibition against lying; it is absolute. However, in treating concrete questions, he is less coherent. A lie "that does not offend religion, the upright and benevolent sentiment, if it is said in the interest of the chastity of the body, is admissible".[102]

In his book, *Retractions*,[103] Augustine blames himself for lack of clarity in the earlier book. Twenty-five years after *On Lying*, he wrote the book, *Against Lying*. Here is his clearest expression on the absoluteness of the commandment to tell the truth and never to lie, even if the purpose is the protection of orthodoxy. The believer considers unbelievers and heretics as his neighbours and therefore would never lie against them. Augustine acknowledges that intention and purpose must be given close attention for the moral evaluation, but he holds that even the best purpose can never justify any lie, since it is objectively sinful.[104] No good that might be hoped from a morally wrong action can compensate for the evil.[105]

St Jerome who, in his commentary on *Galatians*, has justified the officious lie in serious situations, seems to have been won over to Augustine's point of view in the famous controversy between these two great doctors.[106] Subsequent theology follows Augustine's teaching throughout, declaring irrevocably that any consciously false utterance is unlawful.

In spite of his sincere veneration for Augustine, Luther departed from this tradition. "A good hearty lie for the sake of the good and for the Christian Church, a lie in case of necessity, a useful lie, a serviceable lie, would not be against God".[107] Despite this bold statement, H. Grisar overstates the case when he accuses Luther of constructing "nothing less than a theology of lying".[108] Most Lutherans hold to their leader's position while stressing, with great pathos, the inner truthfulness and laying down strict conditions for the exceptional cases. Calvin and his followers kept to the Augustinian tradition, condemning every lie as evil.

b) Newer efforts of reflection

Since the time of Hugh Grotius and Samuel Puffendorf, there has been wide acceptance in Protestant circles of the distinctions between lies which unjustly deceive the neighbour by withholding truth to which he is entitled, and *falsiloquium* (false speech) which is consciously false utterance where the other party has no right whatsoever to the truth at stake. The latter has been considered morally indifferent. Practically speaking, the purely mental reservation defended by a number of Catholic theologians in the seventeenth century did not differ from *falsiloquium*. It was condemned by the Holy Office in 1679.[109] The condemnation was deserved by the laxity that justified this purely mental restriction. Protestant authors accused it of having elements of hypocrisy that are not generally found in the theory of *falsiloquium*.

In recent times, a number of reputable Catholic theologians have distinguished a morally justifiable false utterance from lying.[110] Almost all hold as chief reason and as clear condition that the other party has no right to receive the accurate information and there is no other way to conceal truth although concealment is dutiful. Laros writes, "The patent violation of the right to truth by the inquiring party must enter the definition of lying".[111]

Karlheinz Peschke, in an excellent study of "the problem of the absolute sinfulness of lying", concentrates on "the affinity of veracity and faithfulness"[112] while also giving special attention to newer studies on the psychology of language.[113] He concludes that, in some complex situations, the most sincere person will not feel bound by the generally valid expectation of truthful information when this would do only unnecessary harm. Just as a person can become unworthy of the promise given to himself, so can there be situations where this general promise of truthfulness, inherent in human language and relationships, cannot or must not be fulfilled.

It seems to me that special attention must be given to the psychology and philosophy of language and of communication in general. An example may illustrate this point. During the time of Nazism, subservient followers of Hitler, employees of the state, came to Catholic hospitals and orphanages asking the nurses how many children they had with various hereditary diseases. Wherever a list of these children was supplied, the children were taken off to the gas chambers. In many cases, however, the nuns hid the children and responded that they had none. Did they lie? To my mind, they did not lie at all, although an analysis of the words alone could bring a verdict of "lie" or "false utterance". But in the concrete situation, what Hitler's men were really asking went beyond the words they uttered. Their actual question was, "How many children do you have for the gas chambers?" And the only response to that question could be "None". This was truthful communication or legitimate refusal of communication. Words have their meaning only within the context, and what, in abstraction, could be called "lie" or "false utterance" can be, in the actual situation, the proper response.

Axel Denecke, in a valuable book on truthfulness, presents criteria about lying to a sick person who is in a most serious condition and unable at the moment to bear the truthful information.[114] To me, it seems neither artificial nor evasive to judge as *not* a lie the temporary concealment which the doctor considers necessary, if it is part of a gradual process of truthful communication. If the doctor now conceals some of the facts, with a delicate intention to help the patient to prepare for further communication, his words must be seen in this dynamic context where the whole discourse is gradual and loving communication of truth.[115] If, however, a doctor simply gives false information with no further effort to communicate truth, I would consider it an unacceptable false utterance, indeed, objectively an unacceptable lie. The choice of words, the gestures, tone of voice, all will be different in the case of the doctor who simply decides to deceive the patient than in the case of one who temporarily withholds truth in order to reveal it gradually, lovingly, and at the proper time.

5. *The secret*

a) Basis and justification of the secret

The type of theology and its response to intricate and complex questions depend greatly on how aware the moral theologian is about the reality of sin in the world.

In a sinless humanity, people would be able to share their knowledge, their thoughts and desires in great simplicity. They would pay attention only to the law of growth. But God's own revelation finds barriers in the immaturity and sinfulness of receivers of his truth. There is not always a continual growth of knowledge of truth and love in humankind or even in the Church. Jesus reveals many things to his disciples which the others cannot yet grasp. And even at the end, he tells his privileged friends, "There is still much that I could say to you, but the burden would be too great for you" (Jn 16:12). And the messengers of the Good News are warned, "Do not give dogs what is holy; do not throw your pearls to swine; they will only trample on them and turn and tear you into pieces" (Mt 7:6).

Reverence for the divine Source of truth cautions us against revealing truth where there is no disposition to receive it sincerely or where we cannot actually bear meaningful witness to it. The communication of truth has its very purpose in acceptance and response. Many delicate problems and even grievances can be discussed with mature people, to everyone's profit, whereas public discussion of the same matter in open forum might result in disaster.

Respect for the intimate realm of one's own and other's life is a further and important reason for keeping certain things secret. Many times our best thoughts, desires and deeds need to be kept "in a secret place" (Mt 6:6), visible only to the Father who sees what is secret. Surely our good deeds should lead people to praise God, but this is possible only if, for the sake of the purity of our hearts, we are using discretion.

It is equally important to guard against making a show of one's intimate impulses that are not yet tested and approved. "Man has a right to the mask of exterior calm and self-mastery. The person who unmasks his inner self to the gaze of all, and indulges in free conversation about his innermost thoughts, cannot find his true self".[116] Secrecy and discretion are necessary not only for one's own peace but also to avoid scandal, distrust and the obstruction of good initiatives.

Everyone has to reckon with his own frailty as well as with the susceptibility of his neighbour. Human relations are never perfect, but if we are to have the best possible relations, we must allow our neighbours to decide how much they want to reveal of their inner life and their intimate concerns such as family life. As long as they do not infringe on anyone's right, respect for their secret must be absolute. We may never, through our indiscretion, deliver weapons of combat to enemies of the good. But it is even worse if one is spying on other people's secrets in order to turn the hidden knowledge against them as weapons.

Even in earthly enterprises, a lack of discretion can cause great damage to all involved, to entire families and communities. Our moral rules about the secret are, in great part, "ordinances of exigence in a disturbed world". On the other hand, it would be a grave fault to base our relationships more on distrust than on trust. The concern for our own and other people's secrets must always be animated by loving understanding and a common effort to create a climate of mutual trust. We all have need of others in whom we can confide when occasion demands. However, we have to discern whom we can trust in the various concerns of our life. In the most intimate and serious matters we can confide only in persons who are discreetly silent.

From all this it is evident that a proper sense of discretion and silence, and of sacred vigilance over committed secrets will always be open and sympathetic to basic confidence and will never deteriorate into a closed and forbidding reserve.

b) The various kinds of secret

(1) The *natural* secret includes all hidden truths or facts whose revelation, by the very nature of the case, would violate justice or charity.

(2) The *promised* secret embraces all hidden truths or facts which one has lawfully promised not to disclose even though, apart from the promise, there may be no other obligation to secrecy. But if the secrecy turns out to be absolutely mean-

less or even to conflict with a higher good and/or rights of others, the obligation of the promise ceases automatically.

(3) The *committed* secret embraces all the knowledge that one has obtained under conditions and activities which, by their nature, require secrecy. The most important in this class is the professional secret of physicians, midwives, lawyers, notaries, etc. The strictest and most sacred of professional secrets is protected under the seal of the confessional.

Priests or lay persons whom others have chosen as their spiritual guides, although they do not act as confessors, should consider secrecy as strictly as a confessor. It is not only a matter of grieving or damaging the individual person but also of undermining the general trust in those who are spiritual guides or who exercise professions that, by their nature, require secrecy.

c) Principal obligations regarding secrecy

Reverence and love forbid us to pry into the intimate life of our neighbour or to divulge secrets entrusted to us. The gravity of this sin is in proportion to the misuse of truth, the malice of purpose and the violation of justice and charity involved in the use of the information. If the motivation is only curiosity and there is no desire to exploit the knowledge sought, it is still a serious lack of respect for others — unless it is a pathological case.

Unauthorized eaves-dropping or spying on others is a gross impropriety. It is a serious offence to tape or record confidential remarks in an unguarded conversation without the knowledge and full consent of the speaker. If, however, it is not done to trip up or expose the other but only to protect oneself or others from grave and unjust damage, the moral evaluation is quite different. One must have just and proportionate reasons for probing into the secrets of others, for instance, to avert grave injustice threatening oneself, one's neighbour or the common good. Yet even in this case, the means must be honourable. If a confidential relationship is disturbed or destroyed by such action, one must be sure that the evil resulting will not be greater than the good one hopes to accomplish. This will seldom be the case.

To read the letters of others without authorization is a violation of justice in a very sensitive area. The state does have the right to restrict this privileged and secret form of communication but only to avert menace of great danger, as in times of war. However, in cases of censorship of private correspondence, the authorities must guarantee that no use of the information contained therein is made unless it is strictly demanded for the common welfare. It goes without saying that the officials concerned are bound by the professional secret regarding the contents of letters subjected to their censorship.

Parents and educators have the right to exercise control over the correspondence of immature persons if they have good reason to fear that privacy is gravely abused and may cause serious damage. However, in normal situations the atmosphere of trust is much more helpful than control.

No general norm can decide whether husbands and wives should dispense entirely with secrecy in private correspondence. Many things have to be taken into consideration. Neither spouse is allowed to read the other's correspondence against his or her will. Only in a case of very well grounded suspicion of danger, for instance, of an adulterous liaison by the other spouse, might it be permissible to read the letter which might contain the evidence or dissipate the suspicion. In most cases the interception of a spouse's letter will only increase the trouble.

The fact that, after Vatican II, most religious communities abolished censorship of mail by superiors is a sign of greater mutual trust and a shift from a system of controls to a greater emphasis on co-responsibility.

Legitimately obtained knowledge about secret matters may be used, especially for the benefit of the person whom the secret concerns or to protect oneself or others from grave injustice. Unjustly acquired information about such matters may not be used if the circumstances are such that its use would be practically a continuation or exploitation of the sin by which the secret was first obtained.

To divulge a natural secret or even a professional secret is a serious sin against justice, peace and love. It directly contradicts the liberating use of truth. The damage done by the violation of the professional secret must always be repaired in justice.

Obligation to secrecy ceases (a) if the one concerned reasonably permits or is obliged to permit disclosure; (b) if the matter has ceased to be a secret because of disclosure by others; (c) if disclosure effects a greater good for all concerned. In this case, secrecy itself stops.

The mere promise of secrecy when no higher good is involved cannot oblige one to expose oneself to disproportionate damage. If, in particular circumstances, safeguarding a secret would cause great damage to the community or to an innocent party, the matter must be disclosed as far as necessary, even though the promise of secrecy was given under oath. We must always bear in mind, however, that professional secrecy, above all, is an important factor in the common welfare and therefore outweighs many advantages of a lesser order.

To discuss a secret matter with an absolutely reliable person in order to be advised on a weighty matter or to be relieved of great mental strain is ordinarily permissible, but in any case the secret itself may not be endangered.

Physicians are faced with a knotty problem of professional secrecy when dealing with some criminal matters, for instance, criminal abortion. They are surely not bound to secrecy if, through their personal service and not through the confiding of the patient, they learn of a criminal action performed by an unscrupulous person from whom further damaging action can be anticipated. The difficulty is compounded if the doctor learns of the crime only through the confidential physician-patient relationship. To me, it seems certain that it is not permissible to betray the confidence by reporting the patient. But if the doctor can offer the greatest possible protection for the patient, then he may pursue a criminal who constitutes a menace to the common welfare, by having him reported and properly arraigned. In my opinion, the physician may sometimes even exert a moderate and respectful pressure on the patient to permit a judicial arraignment if this is necessary to prevent a great evil.

In no instance, however, may the physician consider himself an agent of criminal investigation or of police power. A doctor's service and professional secrecy belong, first of all, to the service of life and health: to the sick. Yet we may not justly expect him to reward by his silence a "confidence" which, in the first place, violates his sense of duty.

d) The concealing speech or action

Ordinarily, one protects the secret by silence in language and deportment. An indiscreet inquirer should not be answered at all or should be diverted by a counter-inquiry if that is possible. However, in some instances where silence or rebuff may not be enough to protect the secret, the only other way open may be a manner of speech which, though not untrue, serves the purpose of concealment more effectively. It cannot be said that this is against the purpose of speech, although it is not the normal purpose. Some people have been able, even in situations of exposure to brain-washing, to maintain their mental health and to protect the secret by a clever garrulity that mixed sense and nonsense.

Veiled speech or concealing action can be a response that has a deeper, almost hidden meaning. In the traditional moral theology this is called "perceptible mental reservation". While ambiguity of mind and intention must be excluded, one can use this ambiguous talk and deportment when secrecy is necessary to protect oneself or others against grave injustice and/or against the ambiguous inquirer. Language and deportment receive their final meaning from both the text and the context. The purpose of ambiguous discourse is not deception as such, but the concealment of truth from one who wants to abuse it. Misleading an indiscreet inquirer may be accepted as a consequence of his own improper approach to truth.

The "multiverse discourse" as concealing speech must always be an exception to be reluctantly tolerated only as dire necessity in an evil world. A disciple of Christ never has recourse to it for petty reasons or for selfish motives. Judiciously used, veiled speech is a manifestation of love for truth. Inopportunely used, however, it leads to mendacity.

In critical situations when the secret must be kept inviolate, the Christian can become as perplexed and confused as anyone else, and to such an extent that in groping for veiled speech he will hit upon words, signs and actions that are concretely and in fact like pure mental reservation. Objectively, that is equivalent to false utterance. But the perplexed conscience which, in the case of necessity, can see no other escape from the dilemma of violating secrecy on the one hand or false utterance on the other, should not be judged guilty of lie in the moral sense. This mild evaluation, however, applicable to cases of the perplexed conscience, may not be taken from a concrete context and distorted into a kind of flexible principle to justify deviations from truthfulness. Christian prudence, although not discarding criteria and quiet reflection, will never turn to lies but rather will trust in the guidance of the Holy Spirit to reveal truth or to conceal it as justice and love require (cf. Mt 10:20).

There are some situations in which recourse to veiled speech would be a betrayal of the Christian's mission to be a messenger of courageous and liberating truth. His speech will be straightforward when it is a matter of confessing the true faith, when it is necessary to fulfil justice and charity towards those in need, to defend the innocent against oppressors, or when one is lawfully questioned in court or is drawing up a bilateral contract.

The history of moral theology has seen unending disputes about whether, for proportionately great reasons, one is ever permitted to confirm a mental reservation (an equivocal response) under oath. Very many moralists have replied in the affirmative, with the provision that the mental reservation is a truly "perceptible" one and no danger of scandal is involved. A caution applies here, however. This opinion is advanced in view of extreme, almost inhuman, stress under oppressive law in certain epochs and certain countries where the accused is interrogated even under torture to extort information of every conceivable kind. In civilized states in which the accused has the right to decline to answer in all just and reasonable matters, the problem cannot arise at all.

V. TRUTH AND COVENANT FIDELITY

We have already seen that truth becomes a liberating force and event only for those who commit themselves to truth and to God who is the source of all truth. God is faithful in revealing himself as liberating truth to those who respond faithfully. A moral theology that chooses creative liberty and fidelity as leitmotif must surely give more attention to fidelity than is usually the case in our era.[117]

1. *The God of Faithfulness*

Throughout the history of salvation, the God of Israel, the Father of our Lord, Jesus Christ, reveals himself as the Faithful One. Creation and redemption are revelation of his faithfulness. He who, in absolute freedom for love has created the world, remains faithful to his work. He will bring it to completion.

We remember here that *berith* — covenant — is a key concept, if not the main concept, of the old Testament. All the Israelite liturgy is a great hymn to the faithful God who has committed himself in a covenant. Israel is free from other people's fear of a capricious, wayward God. Adam and Eve are sure that God is faithful; he will not abandon sinful humankind. Again and again, God offers a covenant to humankind until he finally chooses Abraham and his descendants as the people of the covenant. Israel is meant to be a sign for all nations that God is the faithful one. "God's superabundant grace, his faithfulness and fidelity, are central in Israel's spirituality, to the point that the praise of God's 'grace and fidelity' are predominant in her liturgy".[118] God's *chesed* is his faithful and loving concern for his handiwork. The people respond with praise and gratitude. They are becoming God's family.

God is faithful in his revelation. The Hebrew word *'emet* frequently means truth as God reveals it in fidelity to his original design. But his constancy has nothing to do with constant repetition of the same things and words. He is truthful throughout history; there is constancy in his revelation and in his loving action towards mankind.[119] "The programme of the God of the Bible is not so much that he continues being as that he commits himself. God is faithful, granting an oath of his faithful love to man although man is not the one on whom God can rely. God commits himself to Israel as the representative of humankind. He manifests his force through the weakness of the chosen ones. The message that God is faithful does not speak on his immobility but on his irrevocable choice".[120]

When Moses, seeing the people's unfaithfulness, had broken the tablets of the covenant, God appeared before him "and called aloud, 'Yahweh, the Lord, a God compassionate and gracious, long-suffering, ever constant and true, maintaining fidelity to thousands, forgiving iniquity, rebellion and sin, and not sweeping the guilty clean away' " (Ex 34:5-7).

The gravity of Israel's sins becomes clear to those who meditate on God's faithfulness (cf. Dt 32:3-7). Whatever may occur with humankind, "the word of our God endures for ever" (Is 40:8). The people trustfully implore God's mercy, for he keeps his promises and is a saviour to those who turn to him (Tob 14:4; Nb 23:19). Israel, who suffers distress and misery through her unfaithfulness, perceives the wonderful message, "I will betroth you to myself forever, betroth you in lawful wedlock with unfailing devotion and love. I will betroth you to myself to have and to hold, and you shall know the Lord" (Hos 2:19).

In response, the true Israelites will ever and ever remember God's fidelity shown by all the signs of his fatherly love and saving truth (cf. Ps 36:6; 89; 119:25-40). The praise of his fidelity is followed by a prayer that Israel, too, may respond faithfully (1 Kg 8:56ff). The Israelites reveal great trust that God's faithfulness will finally be met by the people's loving fidelity. "Love and fidelity have come together; justice and peace join hands. Fidelity springs up from earth and justice looks down from heaven" (Ps 85:10-11). God's promises culminate in the assurance that he will send a faithful servant and witness (Is 42:1ff; 49:3; 54:7-13).

Mary, the faithful daughter of Israel, recognizes in Jesus the fulfilment of the promises given to the forefathers (Lk 1:54-55.) In Jesus Christ, God's truth and fidelity receive their final proof. They become full reality in the incarnation, life, death and resurrection of Jesus Christ. His death on the cross is the seal of Christ's fidelity: "He said, 'It is accomplished'. He bowed his head and gave up his spirit" (Jn 19:30). Knowing his Father's fidelity, he entrusts his spirit into the Father's hands.

The spirituality of the New Testament is even more marked by the memorial of God's faithful presence and by praise of his fidelity. In salvation and judgment the believers experience God's faithfulness: "If we died with him, we shall live with him. If we endure we shall reign with him. If we deny him, he will deny us. If we are faithless, he keeps faith, for he cannot deny himself" (2 Tim 2:11-13).

The true disciples of Christ are called simply "the faithful" (*fidelis*). They are not only filled with faith but are also graced so that they can be faithful. Through his Spirit, Christ awakens faith and fidelity. "He will keep you firm to the end, without reproach on the day of our Lord Jesus Christ" (1 Cor 1: 8). If they allow Christ's word to abide in them, their life will bear fruit in faithful love (Jn 15:7-16). To live by and for the truth is to be faithful in Christ (2 Jn 4-6).

Christ's followers praise God's fidelity by their confidence and by their prayer for each other: "May the Lord direct your hearts towards God's love, the steadfastness of Christ (2 Thess 3:2-6). Trustful faith gives endurance (Rev 13:10; Heb 6:12; 1 Pet 1:7). The highest praise of Christ, the faithful One, is offered by those who seal their faith by martyrdom (Rev 20:4-7).

God shows his kindness and his fidelity to those in need, the poor, the oppressed, even the sinners. Therefore our response in fidelity to God implies fraternal relationships, kindness, compassion and forgiveness.[121] We are faithful to God, the creator and redeemer, insofar as we are faithful to his mercy and saving justice. This is an essential part of the covenant reality.

2.   Man's instability and the divine call to fidelity

a) Unstable man in an era of profound change

Fidelity and stability are not the same thing. In a static society, stability could be all too easily confused with fidelity. There is a stability that is unfaithful to the Lord of history and to one's own innate dynamism for growth. And there is also in man, as creature, a certain instability that must not be accused of lack of fidelity. We need only that degree of stability that befits the creature. There is, however, a dimension in humankind that is rightly called infidelity, and that is sinfulness. The sinner, as sinner, lacks fidelity towards God and towards his own vocation.

When we speak of man as sinner, we do not consider him simply and solely as sinner, We all are in need of redemption but not all are actually unfaithful in the same way. The converted person and community are on the road to ever greater faithfulness. Only if a person knows no fidelity, he is simply a sinner. "Unfaithfulness is not only a defect in one's character; it is rather the loss of character, and this is infinitely more serious than a defective character. Unfaithfulness is the loss of human substance and, altogether, dissolution".[122]

A most disturbing phenomenon of our time is the breakdown of so many marriages and the high percentage of priests and religious leaving their original vocation. As a consequence, young people have become unwilling to make a clear life-commitment. They want to experience marriage without the bond of marriage vows or any kind of public commitment. It seems that many of them need more time to grow to commitment on the level of a fundamental option. And even many of those who believe that they had acquired the degree of identity necessary for commitment to marriage or religious life now ask themselves whether the object of their commitment has become unrecognizable as their original commitment. All this points to profound cultural changes, to new views on marriage and celibacy, and even to the change in the self-understanding of the Church.[123]

Thirty years ago, theology called for a return to the sources. It rediscovered the importance of the memory of all our history, especially of the beginnings. Now we are passing from a society marked by memory to one characterized by imagination and one-sided attention to the future. Our certitudes have become more fragile. We are living, as it were, under the reign of the provisional.[124]

Under the impact of the rapid cultural changes and the influence of today's existentialist philosophy, people wonder how they can commit themselves for a whole future which is hidden from them. There are the great uncertainties about how the world around us will evolve, as well as anxieties and uncertainties about our own identity and steadfastness.[125] Yet all this may be a precious challenge that forces us to discover the deeper dimensions and riches of fidelity.

b) The risk to fidelity in view of one's own self

Today's ethics is deeply marked by the experience of the historicity of humankind and the psychology of development. Not only the world around us changes but we, too, are submitted to change and called to grow and to change. How, then, does a life commitment and the traditional concept of fidelity fit into this new life experience?

In today's language, a commitment is "above all, a self-commitment. I bind myself for the future".[126] A philosophy and psychology of self-fulfilment can lead to a one-sided and sometimes narcissistic attention to oneself. The dialogical character of fidelity — that is, fidelity to the other — is somehow ignored or underevaluated. The consequence is that a person can all too easily justify the revocation of his commitment in the name of fidelity to oneself.[127] Here we are faced with a real problem that cannot be resolved unless we come to the deeper insight that fidelity, unlike stability, is always commitment before the Other and the others.[128] "There can be no genuine fidelity towards oneself to the detriment of fidelity towards one's neighbour, and vice versa".[129]

c) The counterfeits of fidelity

Many people are afraid of fidelity and commitment because they know only the counterfeits of fidelity. Hence, to understand better what creative fidelity is, we have to take a look at its counterfeits.

The first that must be unmasked is the inertia that so frequently considers itself fidelity and stability. It is a clinging to stereotyped formulas, to the hang-ups of the past that hinder us from discovering the present opportunities, a laziness that keeps one from learning and unlearning. All this directly contradicts the biblical call to conversion. One cannot be faithful to the Lord without being willing to grow and to be more fully converted. This type of inertia can also be sacralized by institutions that have become immobile. Whatever hinders people from outgrowing infantilism, from freeing themselves from the conditionings of heredity, is never to be called fidelity. It is its enemy, a sham fidelity that leads to a loss of our freedom.[130]

A similar enemy of faithfulness is a total submissiveness in blind obedience or a mindless following of external laws without any fidelity to the scale of values or to those realities that cannot be defined by a static law.

Where the individual's self-interest prevails over the interests of the group, there is no real fidelity. On the contrary, there is the highest degree of vulnerability to manipulation and to the desire to manipulate others.[131]

Parents can cling to their children with such possessive affection that they prevent them from finding their own identity and autonomy. These people are faithful neither to their parental vocation nor to the person of the child.

One can hold to a cause or a principle because of mere fear of change, a lack of courage to face the unknown or the risk of responsibility. One can, for instance, keep to the promise of celibacy not so much for fidelity's sake as out of fear to face the difficulties of marriage or a new life situation.

A person can be so totally overpowered by his superego that his fidelities are inspired only by concern for the impression he makes on others. His loyalties and respectability are poisoned by hypocrisy. A spouse, for instance, who has inwardly broken his fidelity to the partner can try to save the marriage and the appearance of fidelity, not out of concern for the partner or for fidelity but only for the sake of respectability.

One who, through mere ambition, is clinging to a career or to a purpose, even though a noble one, should not use the word "fidelity".

A false understanding of social honour prevents many people from preserving their fidelity towards their children born out of wedlock.

An extreme form of sham fidelity is enslavement to another person to the point of running with him or her into final catastrophe as, for instance, shared suicide.[132]

d) A remnant of fidelity to truth

Each sin has a blinding power. One who breaks fidelity is easily tempted to denigrate the one whom he has abandoned. But there can be a remnant of fidelity that may lead back to the former fidelity, or at least to reparation. A spouse who has caused a marriage breakdown but still recognizes the goodness of his partner, to the point of confessing his own guilt, has preserved an important remnant of fidelity. The prodigal son can be saved because, in all the misery caused by his disloyalty towards his father, his healthy memory still recognizes that his father was good.

e) The call to true fidelity

The present explosion of restlessness that unmasks so many sham fidelities and the enormous suffering caused by broken fidelities is a challenge for all to be more concerned about the quality of their choices, the depth of their commitment and the constant need to renew and deepen their original option.[133] To be faithful, we need to accept the truth about our dignity and capacities, and equally the truth about ourselves that humbles us and alerts us. Then a renewed fidelity will further increase our capacity to open ourselves to truth in all its dimensions.[134]

Our commitments must be truthful also in observing the hierarchy of truths and values. "A person reaches his full maturity only by commitment to fidelities that are worth more than life".[135] No one can truthfully commit himself to fidelity unless he is sure about the justice of the cause and never forgets that persons are worth more than things. Fidelity is always grounded in a self-commitment that includes commitment to another. It is a matter of dedication to persons, and to causes only in view of persons. Our steadfastness becomes true fidelity only through a genuine discernment that eliminates the false fidelities and deepens the true ones.

Fidelity implies a commitment for all of the future. It has the character of unconditioned dedication, although we remain always aware of the continuing need to discern how this unconditioned commitment can be carried out under changing conditions of life. This is especially difficult if the other to whom we are committed changes his or her attitude completely. There might sometimes be a conflict between inner truthfulness and the external fulfilment of a commitment when the situations of life have changed or when we have come to a deeper understanding of truth and our commitment to it.[136]

3. *The partners of fidelity*

a) Faith and trust in God as the basis of fidelity

As we have seen, there are many cultural causes of the present crisis of fidelity, but the main crisis is that of faith. Where there is no faith in ultimate reality to give man trust and assurance, there is no ground for firm commitment and fidelity among people. But we can also say that as long as there is fidelity among us, there is a road to faith; there is already an implicit faith.

This theme of a mysterious reciprocity between faith and fidelity recurs in most of the writings of Gabriel Marcel. He says that faith appeared to him in a new light whenever he thought about fidelity, and that fidelity revealed itself to him in the sight of the Other from the experience of Presence.[137] In a more philosophical language he says, "Being is the locus of fidelity".[138] In other words, outside of transcendence, of the experience of Being that gives ground and meaning to all being, human fidelity cannot be imagined. Fidelity implies the sense of the sacred. "From there, fidelity reveals its true nature as testimony, as recognition. From that it follows also that an ethics which takes fidelity as its centre will irresistibly be led to ground it in what is more than human, in an unconditioned will that is, for us, the very mark of the Absolute".[139]

We pursue the question of "how, from this absolute fidelity which we can simply call faith, the other forms of fidelity are made possible; how, in it and in it alone, there can be found something that gives them firmness and guarantee?"[140]

Marcel speaks on faith in the most existential and, at the same time, ontological way. For him, faith is not something we "have"; it belongs to true existence. "It is my being, the ground of what I am". But immediately he poses the question, "Is there a total agreement between both? Am I the faith I manifest? Is my life this faith that has become evident?"[141]

The shaking reality is that all too much and too frequently the "I believe" is intermingled with the "I do not believe". But as long as we are truly human and able to be faithful, the "I believe" cannot be annulled by an ingredient of unbelief. The truthfulness of my faith depends on the truthfulness of my fidelity, as my fidelity is grounded in faith.

Neither faith nor fidelity can be understood in their truest and deepest sense without presence, without being-with. Fidelity to abstract ideas and principles can never fully commit a person, for a person is more than a principle. A deep experience of fidelity to truth already implies the experience of faith in the One who is Truth.

We would not be able to commit ourselves irrevocably to our fellowmen without a basic belief that, at the heart of being, there is Absolute Fidelity.[142] And nothing strengthens our faith in the One who is absolute fidelity more than fidelity as the mark of intersubjectivity. Through faith in Jesus Christ who is Fidelity incarnate, it becomes possible for us to identify ourselves with the love of God, for ultimate concern is faithfulness towards God. And we shall commit ourselves only to those fidelities that are valid in the sight of God. In his presence, our various commitments and fidelities are becoming a kind of polyphony; they strengthen and complete each other.[143] The believer makes each commitment in view of the divine fidelity assured to us. "It is in God himself who called you to share in the life of his Son, Jesus Christ, our Lord, and God keeps faith" (1 Cor 1: 9; cf. 10: 13).

Growth in the coherence of a faith decision follows the general rules of personal maturation. The depth of our faith commitment is always correlated with the truthfulness of our fidelity to our fellowmen. Whoever uses fully his freedom in his commitment and in his fidelity, prepares the possibility for greater depth and coherence.[144]

By creating man for freedom and entrusting to him the earth and the building up of a human community, God takes the initiative in giving trust and enabling us to be faithful.[145] God has first committed himself to us and shows his fidelity so abundantly that we, in gratitude, experience trust and are able to respond faithfully and to live on the covenant level. The Christian commitment has its very meaning as free response to God who freely commits himself to us. "Fidelity inspires confidence and trust and, on the other hand, trust calls for fidelity".[146]

b) Fidelity in the Thou-We-I relationships

The prophets and the pious people of Israel understood God's abiding and renewing fidelity as a call to fidelity among themselves. One cannot praise God's faithfulness except in the covenant community. The praise of God is always a recommitment to fidelity within his people. Yahweh's fidelity has its perfect sacrament — that is, its visible and effective sign —

in Jesus Christ who is faithful to the Father in and by his all-embracing solidarity. Christ is one with his brothers and sisters, as he is one with the Father. And he prays that his disciples, too, may live out their union with him and the Father by their mutual unity and fidelity (Jn 17:11-12). Thus the reciprocal fidelity of true disciples of Christ, and their fidelity to the poor in imitation of God's faithfulness, is a kind of sacrament in Jesus Christ, to lead the world to faith in God and in his messenger, Jesus Christ.

Our loyalty and fidelity to the Church has as its object not primarily the institution but rather the people of the covenant and all that serve their unity, thus indirectly including the institutional aspects. Those who are tempted to leave the Church because of institutional imperfections have to ask themselves if their commitment was ever personalized enough.

To speak of fidelity towards God without visible testimony of fidelity towards persons, the sons and daughters of God, conveys a false concept of transcendence. No one can honour the invisible God by fidelity without honouring him in one's brothers and sisters.

Although the fidelity we show to our fellowmen is the test and manifestation of our fidelity to God, the two fidelities do not simply coincide. Whatever may be the level of our mutual fidelity with others, our very faith in the Absolute Fidelity leads us to question the quality of our own faithfulness.[147] We are never allowed self-complacence. Our own and our partners' partial infidelities save us from idolatry. They force us, in our yearning for total experience of fidelity, to turn to him who is absolute fidelity, and to ground in him our efforts for greater faithfulness.

If our faith in the One who is absolute fidelity has not yet transformed our whole being, the painful experience of infidelity on the part of a beloved can shake it to the deepest ground. But this experience can also lead to a more radical faith and a more thoroughgoing dedication to him.

The fidelity of the believer towards his fellowmen will copy that of God who is faithful even when his people are greatly lacking in their response. He will continue, as artist and pedagogue, to awaken in the people the desire to live again according to the covenant and to discover the grace that allows a renewed fidelity. Therefore Christians are forgiving. And this is not so much an act of undeserved generosity towards the offender as an act of gratitude towards God who does not abandon us in our failures.

While a marriage cannot be a sacrament of the divine covenant when, from the very beginning, love and fidelity are excluded, the believer, when he has failed in his fidelity, will not abandon his partner with whom he has lived a sacrament of love and fidelity. Rather, he will do all in his power to heal the wounds and restore the faithful covenant. The greater the love and the stronger the self-commitment to the other was, the deeper will be the pain and suffering caused by the other's infidelity. This pain can be a sharing in Christ's redeeming suffering and lead to a deeper understanding of God's fidelity to us. But if one is unwilling to forgive and to heal, then the pain can be self-destructive and lead to disaster. Healing fidelity in the midst of an unfaithful world is, in a special sense, a sacrament, a sign of God's faithful presence.

In the most faithful and blissful human relationship, death is the experience of the limit. Through faith and trust in God's absolute fidelity, we know that our human fidelities have come at last not to their end but to their fulfilment.

4. *The dimensions of historicity*

a) A faithful memory

Fidelity implies not only the reciprocity of consciences but also the reciprocity of memories. God, who never forgets us, calls us to celebrate his wonderful deeds and all the signs of his fidelity, thus to develop a grateful and faithful memory.

The dynamism of our conscience, especially in view of fidelity, depends greatly on a healthy memory which treasures all the good we have received. From this arises a continuum and a disposition towards that faithfulness which continues to enrich human relationships and to give glory to God.

The peak experiences of our past that pointed the right direction for our lives will be effective only through a grateful memory. If we forget them, we are unfaithful to those splendid moments in which we experienced God's fidelity. The past obliges my memory the more it allows me to experience the depth of my true self in the reciprocity of relations.[148] An old proverb rightly says, "A grateful memory is the condition for a faithful heart".[149]

To the extent that we realize thankfully how much we are indebted to the whole history of truth and fidelity — to tradition in the best sense — we live truthfully the dimension of historicity. This memory allows us and urges us to enrich the stream of tradition by using every available opportunity to strengthen that history of faithfulness. Our commitment will be the best possible if we identify ourselves with the best of past history and with those of our past decisions which were made in truthfulness and fidelity. The memory of our past failures and partial untruthfulness can be an additional motive to build upon what was right, good and faithful.[150]

The best of what we have received in the past, including the tasks we were able to master, are made present and productive by a healthy memory. Through it we regain a clearer orientation and greater courage for the future.[151]

b) Presence

In its Latin root, the English word "presence" means to be for each other. The German word for presence, *Gegenwart*, means to wait for each other. Fidelity includes both of these. Presence, in the temporal dimension, has its full human wealth only through people's presence to each other in the presence of the Divine. Through faith-awareness of these dimensions of presence, we overcome the oppression of staleness and make our faithfulness to each other and to the past an expression of creative liberty.[152]

A grateful memory makes us appreciative and clearsighted about the present opportunities. We are creatively faithful to the here-and-now when we discover and act upon what can be done *now*. Thankful people have an eagle-eye for such things, while those who are forgetful, unrooted, thankless for the past, will find nothing worthwhile in the present hour. Gratitude united with vigilance sets us free from enslavements of the past and present, and gives us courage and wisdom to act out our fidelity with new initiatives. The small beginnings, too, have their own relevance for the history of fidelity.[153]

c) Commitment to the future

The courageous use of present opportunities growing out of the past gives us power over the future. While the future is never in our hands, yet we can make a great contribution to it, a contribution not only to our own future but also to that of all humankind.

Awareness of our insertion into the history of salvation strengthens our hope and awakens our sense of responsibility for all of the future, in view of the great moment of fulfilment of history. "Those of my decisions that have the power to inscribe themselves into the totality of history, according to the trustful expectation of others, will be in the best sense my own and my most free decisions".[154] These decisions will make visible the truth that commitment to the past is something altogether different from its mere repetition.

5. How creative is fidelity?

Since we have spoken all along on creative fidelity, it seems useful to give special attention to those dimensions and qualities that bring it forth.

Fidelity implies a concrete commitment. "The decision of a man faced with a multitude of possibilities implies always also the courage to leave behind and to renounce all those possibilities that lie outside the horizon of that concrete decision".[155]

In his absolute freedom, God has chosen this one world from an infinite number of possibilities. He has chosen a history of humankind. He always blends together the old and the new. Hence it is essential that our fundamental option is clear-cut and yet leaves enough space to unfold in that creative freedom that responds faithfully to new opportunities by keeping a clear direction.

By binding ourselves to God's design, to the covenant God offers us, we are set on the road to freedom. There is no creative freedom without fidelity, as there is no fidelity without freedom. The autonomy of a healthy conscience is both the result of freedom and the condition for it. Through fidelity we find our union with God and participate in his creative freedom.[156]

Since the gift of the covenant is a call to unity and solidarity, there is no way of entering into the paradise of true freedom without entering into the bonds of fidelity with the others. Only in faithfulness to the covenant and love for its people can our freedom grow strong. The enemy of faithfulness is not a surplus of freedom but a lack of it. It must be understood, however, that we are speaking of freedom for fidelity and of freedom that opens ever new horizons through fidelity.

For those firmly committed to covenant morality, the prohibitive laws are no longer a burden. Illumined and revitalized by the goal commandments, they are more than fulfilled by fidelity to the covenant.[157]

Creative fidelity can be lived only under the liberating law of grace by which one knows that God never asks for more than he gives. The believer knows himself to be faithful if he does what he can do now. He never dreams that he is already perfected in fidelity. The Apostle of the Gentiles, who counts everything as loss "because all is far outweighed by the gain of knowing Christ Jesus", does not think that he has "already achieved all this", but he presses on, "hoping to take hold of that for which Christ once took hold of me" (Phil 3:8-12).

This concept of fidelity is quite different from mere constancy. One can be coherent and perfectly observant of promises and laws, and yet become self-complacent. If we are faithful to God's covenant as pilgrim people, we will never think about being already perfected in faithfulness. Rather, trusting in him who calls us and guides us in his fidelity, we will always be open to new prophetic realizations.[158] Each step closer to the faithful God, in fidelity to the people of the covenant and to our commitment, will bring us a deeper appreciation of the scale and urgencies of values. By our faithful response to God's grace and call, we come to understand better both his gifts and his call.[159]

Fidelity of the heart looks in ever-increasing gratitude for the approximately best external expressions. When fidelity is wedded to freedom and freedom to fidelity, there is no clinging to the letter of the law; one is guided by the Spirit. Commitment is for love and active in love, and therefore creates ever new realities, stronger bonds of unity, and leads to greater light of truth.

Creative liberty and fidelity lead to inner integrity and to unity among people and groups. They are a being with and for

God, creator of all good and giver of the covenant.[160] Our commitment is for love and freedom, which is never an island but an espousal of my freedom for the freedom of all, an ongoing act of thanksgiving for those who faithfully have promoted true freedom and solidarity: gratitude especially for those who have shown us abiding fidelity.[161]

6. *Structures of fidelity*

a) Social manifestation of commitment

God has made his fidelity visible through all his works and through the visible signs and words by which he assured his covenant of fidelity. His promises and oaths are revelation of who God is. Man, too, by committing himself visibly and publicly, manifests his commitment and his determination to be faithful. The social nature of man, who is an embodied spirit, calls for visibility, "for the sign that manifests and celebrates fidelity".[162] His truth and fidelity are embodied in concrete acts and in the social reality. Whoever refuses this visibility refuses an essential part of human truth.

Solemn promises, vows, oaths, and various forms of consecration confirm, strengthen and publicly acknowledge the inner disposition. They are, in a way, points of arrival and departure. The inner disposition must have arrived at a certain degree of clarity before being manifested, and the manifestation is the beginning of a life in which each act can deepen the understanding and fulfilment of the commitment. As social beings, the persons who commit themselves are willing to give account and testimony of their fidelity. Religious vows such as baptismal vows, marriage vows and so on, are a covenant reality. It is not only commitment of the individual to the community or to the partner but reciprocity of commitment in mutual trust.

A solemn commitment needs a time of preparation and probing. The sacraments of initiation for adults are preceded by a catechumenate, a time of prayer and reflection on the gift and commitment. Religious vows, as commitment between a community and a person, need a time of knowing each other and experiencing what the mutual commitment means. Temporary vows and, similarly, the betrothal preceding marriage vows, are not provisional in the strict sense if the persons are faithful and serious in their promises but they provide a time of transition for facing new social and psychological conditions. The conditions must somehow be known. The candidates firmly intend a commitment for life unless grave obstacles arise that do not depend on their own freedom. If these promises are broken arbitrarily, fidelity is betrayed. If commitments are social in nature, a change of mind also needs social justification.

This can be exemplified by the qualitative difference between the African traditional concept of marriage as a developing reality, and the modern western "trial marriage". It was a great injustice when uninformed Westerners called the African marriage a "trial marriage", for in Africa it is not an arbitrary trial as understood by young people of Europe and North America. In Africa there are clearly defined stages oriented from the beginning towards final and irrevocable marriage commitment. Everyone knows the social conditions, and everything is arranged under the public eye and with social accountability. The commitment is clearly defined. What Gabriel Marcel says about the "infantilism" of those who want to experiment with marriage without being married, and the almost necessary failure of such a contradictory situation, cannot univocally be applied to the African and the western situations.[163] The difference is also in the mentality. In the traditional African arrangement, the purpose is communal and social, while the young western people who refuse the marriage commitment are usually looking chiefly for selfish self-fulfilment.[164]

It is important to see the essential difference between a commitment to a kind of covenant and, on the other hand, a contract. The covenant is on the level of being, of being-with, while the contract remains on the lower level of having and/or doing. The contracts about well-defined duties, things and works can gradually become socially controlled and enforced. A covenant is more than a contract of social relevance; however, by its very nature, it cannot be equally enforced or controlled by others. It can, however, be strengthened by the collective conscience and by favourable conditions in the community.

b) Sacramental quality of commitment and fidelity

A sacrament is a visible and effective sign of God's graciousness, his call and gift, and of man's response. At the heart of all the sacramental reality is God's covenant, made visible in creation and salvation. All genuine fidelity among people participates in the sacramental dignity of this covenant, whose embodiment is Christ.

The seven sacraments do not exhaust the sacramental reality but are privileged sacramental signs. They evidence and confirm a bond of fidelity between Christ and the Christian in the community of faith. They are God's creative works and a pledge of his fidelity, enabling us to give a response in adoring and faithful love in Christ and in the Church. The sacramental pledge is not a transient word uttered and straightaway forgotten, but a pledge to which the believer is bound by the new inner creation that boldly proclaims his bond with Christ and the people of the covenant.

For Christians, the prototype of all commitment is the solemn vow of the adult in *Baptism*. This is an eloquent expression of the covenant of fidelity between Christ and the baptized person. Christ wants to show his fidelity through a committed community. Hence it is natural that the baptismal vows should receive, as response from the community, a pledge to create a divine milieu that practises and fosters mutual fidelity.

The adult baptism is followed by *Confirmation*, which centres on an important dimension of our commitment to fidelity; that is, trust in the promptings of the Holy Spirit and grateful acceptance of the law of the Spirit who gives us life in Christ Jesus and helps us on the road of fidelity. In the case of infant baptism, there stands from the beginning Christ's commitment and the response-commitment of the community to guide the young person in a gradual awareness until he or she can respond with a commitment on the level of an established identity that allows a mature fundamental option.

The *Eucharist* not only renews and strengthens our grateful memory; it also teaches us how to celebrate the covenant fidelity in all our life.[165] Through the gift of self, Christ is "pledge of future glory" for the believer.[166] Faithful participation in the Eucharistic celebration, and a life nourished by it, are essential for preserving and deepening the covenant fidelity.

In the *Sacrament of Healing Forgiveness*, God gives us a tangible experience of his ever-renewing fidelity. The penitent opens himself to the gift and call of the sacrament by a renewed promise of fidelity in the ongoing conversion. As the conversion unfolds, the moral life assumes ever more clearly the covenant dimensions which include particularly fidelity to the "law", "Be merciful as your heavenly Father" (Lk 6:36).

The Sacrament of the *Anointing of the Sick* proclaims and celebrates God's fidelity as manifested in Christ's suffering and death, a fidelity that gives meaning and purpose to the Christian's suffering and sickness, and sustains him in his weakness. All the sacraments have their source and summit in Christ's sacrificial death, in the fidelity of the Father, sealed by Christ's resurrection and pointing to the final fulfilment in the new heaven and the new earth. Thus they are the very basis and effective signs of loyalty unto death. Receiving them gratefully and faithfully, we pray with the whole Church for the grace of final perseverance in the service of the Lord.

It is understandable that Protestants had difficulty in accepting Catholic teaching about the *Sacrament of Marriage* when the sacramentality was equated with "contract"about some acts. The Second Vatican Council views marriage as a covenant. "Thus a man and a woman who, by the marriage covenant of conjugal love, 'are no longer two but one flesh' (Mt 19:6) render mutual help and service to each other through an intimate union of their persons and of their actions. Through this union they experience the meaning of their oneness and attain to it with growing perfection day by day. As a mutual gift of two persons, this intimate union as well as the good of the children requires urgently the fidelity of the spouses and their unbreakable oneness".[167] A marriage is sacramental to the extent that, not only by celebration but by their whole life, the spouses manifest to each other and to the world around them a fidelity that is grounded in Christ's fidelity and is leading to him. Marital infidelity is not merely injustice but also wanton violation of loyalty to Christ who faithfully entwines this union into his own loving union with his bride, the Church (cf. Eph 5:21ff).

The *Ministerial Priesthood* implies a special covenant between Christ and the one he has chosen. This covenant becomes sacramentally visible through the commitment between the minister and the Church. The minister promises to serve and not to be served, thus to make Christ the Servant and prophetic High Priest visible to the others. The community, in turn, promises to sustain the priest by faithful cooperation, by prayer, good example and, if needed, by fraternal correction.

Celibacy is not necessarily connected with the ministerial priesthood. However, as long as it is made a condition for receiving ordination to the priesthood in the Latin Church, it must not be thought of as mere fulfilment of a legal requirement. In fact, celibacy for the kingdom of God is a charism that does not at all fit into categories of legal imposition. Hence nobody should promise celibacy unless he feels called to it and can embrace it as a part of his dedication to Christ and to his Church. This commitment can be fulfilled only as a part of total dedication in a climate where covenant morality and praise to God's fidelity reign.

Religious vows, although highly honoured in the Church, are not counted among the "seven sacraments of the Church". However, where religious communities and individual religious are outstanding signs of covenant morality, of fidelity and solidarity, there is surely a sacramental dimension. They are signs of the presence of God who calls all to fidelity.

Wherever Christians open themselves to the grace and call of the sacraments, they will discover in the midst of their secular reality the many signs of fidelity and the opportunities to build up and strengthen faithful relationships with their fellowmen. They become salt for the earth and light for the world by creating a divine milieu of justice, mercy and fidelity not only within the Church structures but within all the realms of life.

c) Fidelity and discipline

Creative fidelity is not purely spontaneous until our whole being is transformed by it. As long as we are at the same time saints and sinners, and live in a partially disordered world, we need the courage to renounce whatever holds us back on our road to God. While discipline is never a purpose in itself and should never diminish adaptability to new needs, a certain ordering of our daily life fosters the mutual reliability and confidence that insure faithful relationships. A reasonable discipline, by freeing us from many small decisions, releases our energies for creative decisions when new opportunities or problems arise. It also frees us from those subtle everyday temptations that can gradually erode our fidelities. An example could be our choices of entertainment. Television can bring to us an enormous diversity of impressions and appeals, as can the books we read and the places we visit for recreation. One who wants to live faithfully the marriage covenant will not deaden his sense of the beauty of truthful and faithful sexual love with pictures, impressions and themes that contradict the world of fidelity. Those who have committed themselves to celibate life will choose their programmes even more carefully and will never waste hour after hour on entertainment that leads to superficiality.

d) Fidelity and tolerance

Legalism tried to guarantee fidelity by rigid controls and sanctions. It is true that failure to keep one's commitments, especially if they are solemn ones, does hurt institutions, including the Church. The state, society and the Church have a legitimate interest in guaranteeing, as far as possible, the fulfilment of contracts and qualified promises.

Not just as an institution but as a sacrament of covenant-fidelity, the Church has a particular reason to strengthen fidelity. Control and sanctions are, however, only a very small and secondary part of this mission of the Church. Her whole life — evangelization, the celebration of the sacraments, the shape of Church communities — all can foster fidelity. And if these dimensions are given proper attention, then the canonical discipline, too, has its beneficial role. We agree, for instance, that marriage tribunals should be well staffed, and that requests about annulments should receive a prompt response, but if more attention and manpower are spent on the marriage tribunal (acting after the damage is done) than on the marriage catechumenate and for helping troubled marriages, then the cause of fidelity is not well served.[168]

In past centuries, the severe pressures of public opinion and the harsh treatment of those who failed in marriage or who left the priesthood or religious life seemingly were stabilizing factors. But it must be asked whether they truly strengthened fidelity as a covenant relationship with Christ. Furthermore, those who exercised such pressures and treated others like lepers were not faithful to Christ's mercy and to his commandment, "Do not judge".

In recent times, the sudden change in the cultural environment and in the self-understanding of the Church led to an increase in divorces and in departures from religious life and the priesthood. This only proves that too much trust had been placed earlier in the rigid structures of public opinion and sanction, while deeper motives for a more genuine fidelity were not sufficiently communicated. We have now to mobilize these deeper energies and motives. The transition is not easy. We have to harmonize absolute fidelity to the Lord's command not to judge others lovelessly, with an even firmer commitment to fidelity and to all the evangelical efforts to strengthen it within Church and world. As long as we can be "faithful" only by judging others harshly, our fidelity is not genuine.

There can be no doubt that some persons have good reasons for asking for dispensation from religious vows or from the exercise of the priestly ministry. We all have to become more discerning. Discernment is especially needed in relation to divorced and remarried people. Surely there are some who have sinned gravely against the fidelity due to their partner and to the whole Church. But there are others who have tried heroically to save their marriage and have made a decision only after a long period of struggle and prayer. Some have divorced their partner because they wanted to marry a more sexy or more wealthy person, but there are others who were abandoned in spite of good will, and made the decision to remarry mainly in order to guarantee for their children an orderly home. And finally, there are those who realize how gravely they sinned by breaking their conjugal vows or other commitments, and are trying to make reparation insofar as they can, and to live as faithful penitents. Each one and the whole Church will honour the Spirit and be more faithful to his grace by thinking, talking, and acting according to discernment.

VI.   HUMAN HONOUR

Throughout history, honour has been considered as one of the highest social goods. It is not directly a moral quality but it is of high moral relevance for the individual, the group, and for society.[169]

By "honour" we mean one's good name or public esteem. Its outward recognition is respect; its distinctive degree is praise based on one's particular worth or fame, superior standing, achievement and/or social rank. "Honour" connotes respect and self-respect, reverence that implies profound regard mingled with love, devotion, awe, homage, deference. We speak of honourableness (*honestas*), the high worth or quality of an honourable man who, because of his integrity, deserves honour. With Aristotle Thomas Aquinas defines honour as "manifestation of reverence in testimony of virtue".[170] For Thomas, glory (*gloria*) comes from the honour given to a person, insofar as social recognition and praise make his worth manifest to many.[171]

1. Honour in the light of truth and fidelity

We can search, find and practise truth only in the reciprocity of consciences in profound solidarity. This relationship requires mutual respect in which we accept and give honour. It has to be based on truthfulness. Honour, praise, reverence, truthfully offered and accepted, are visible signs of healthy human relationships which strengthen the social bonds of fidelity.[172] Where there is a right understanding and practice of honour, people abide in truth and unite in the search and practice of truth. Honour among those who together honour and praise God reveals the beauty of truthfulness and fidelity, and strengthens them.

2. The theological and moral significance of human honour

a) All true honour comes from God and leads to him

For people who have not yet found their full identity and integrity, and therefore are controlled from without, the common concern for good name can remain on the level of the superego. But wherever it is related to honourableness and reverence, it is rooted in and leads to high moral and religious dimensions.

For Max Scheler, the reverence that leads to the right way of receiving and manifesting honour is a profound spiritual sensitivity for the deep mystery of reality.[173] Without this reverence, social honour does not reach a high level and cannot guarantee more than a mediocre level of moral behaviour.

The fact that the honour and praise of God is so central in the Judeo-Christian tradition cannot be explained without the high evaluation of honour and praise in human relations. But it is equally true that the high quality of social honour, self-respect and reverence for others has its roots in the religious dimension of the human person and community and finally in the honour they render to God.

The God of Israel, who has revealed himself in Jesus Christ, accepts and requests honour and praise. "Blessed art thou, Lord God of our Father Israel, from of old and forever. Thine, O Lord, is the greatness, the power, the glory, the splendour and the majesty; for everything in heaven and on earth are thine" (1 Chr 29:10-11).

While praising God, the religious man knows also that all his honour and worth come from him. "Wealth and honour come from thee" (1 Chr 29:12). And this again is an urgent reason to praise God: " ... and now we give thee thanks, our God, and praise thy glorious name" (1 Chr 29:13). "All thy creatures praise thee, Lord, and thy servants bless thee. They talk of the glory of thy kingdom and tell of thy might" (Ps 145:10-11). The last book of holy Scripture re-echoes the tradition and religious consciousness that the worth of all people is honour and praise that come from God and can be upheld only if, by all their life, they praise him. "Praise and honour, glory and might to him who sits on the throne and to the lamb, forever and ever" (Rev 5:13).

The saints, as true adorers of God, know that the sole crown of honour is the glory of God. "As they lay their crowns before the throne, they cry, 'Thou art worthy, O Lord our God, to receive glory and honour and power, because thou didst create all things; by thy will they were created, and have their being' " (Rev 4:10-11). Paul indicates that those who refuse to honour God have lost their whole worth, their self-respect and their reverence for the other (cf. Rom 1:21ff). The consequence is the total breakdown of morality. "Thus, because they have not seen fit to acknowledge God, he has given them up to their own depraved reason. This leads them to break all rules of conduct" (Rom 1:28).

There is evidently a two-way relationship. Persons and groups must honour each other and mutually acknowledge their worth in order to be touched by God's glory and to adore him in truth. And reciprocally, to the extent that people stand in awe and bliss before God's glory and give him praise and thanks, they come to authentic self-respect and to social honour. Then they judge their worth and honour first before God and only then before the human community.[174]

True human honour is an important symbol of God's honour and glory, of the splendour of his self-transcending love. The biblical texts that warn against self-importance and vainglory are based on the truth that we have our honour only before God (cf. Gal 6:3). Only when the Christian stands before God in grateful humility can he properly receive and give honour. But whether honoured or dishonoured among men, we can boast only in the Lord (cf. Rom 5:1-11). Veneration of the saints is unrestricted honour, for it comes from God and leads to him.

b) Human honour in the light of the Paschal Mystery

Honour among people who have refused to honour God has degenerated into ambition, pride and arrogance. All too often it has caused enmities and wars. To redeem us, and to bring us home to the divine honour, the Word incarnate humbled himself to the point of dying on a cross (Phil 2:7ff). But the Paschal Mystery, the supreme sign of humility, is at the same time the supreme act of glorification of the Father and the source of honour and glory for the human person. We never sing about Christ dishonoured on the cross, without praising the Father and him for the divine love that shines forth in the glory of the Resurrection. The self-denial, even to the point of patiently accepting calumnies, which Christ asks of his disciples, is a way of liberation that prepares us for our share in the glory of the risen Lord.

A disciple of Christ cannot rejoice in any esteem that is not based on worth. We must be concerned, not with the reception of honour as such, but with the value of the good that honours God and is therefore worthy of esteem. "The worth of honour that thrives on honour itself is no better than for light to depend on its own reflection".[175]

Christ honours the Father not so much by suffering humiliation and calumny as by the love that motivates him. Therefore, the honour of his disciples needs this sacrificial spirit of love. It gives us the strength, at times, to renounce honour and to protect and defend the honour of others. For the sake of the kingdom of God, those who are disciples of Christ will be ready to suffer insult and disgrace from evil men, and even to endure the sometimes inevitable misunderstanding by well-meaning people. More than any flattering human deference, they will treasure the honour of being imitators of the crucified Christ, the stumbling block of contradiction which the unbelieving builders rejected. This is the honour of those who truly believe (cf. 1 Pet 2:7). "Let him who boasts, boast of the Lord" (1 Cor 1:31).

Christian honour can never be severed from the honour of Christ, the Servant (cf. Jn 12:26; Lk 22:27; Mt 23:8ff). The world's contempt of the true servant of Christ is an infinitely greater honour than all the world's acclaim. "If Christ's name is flung in your teeth as an insult, count yourselves happy, because then that glorious Spirit which is the Spirit of God is resting upon you ... If anyone suffers for being a Christian he should feel it no disgrace, but confess that name to the honour of God" (1 Pet 4:14-16).

The ineffable honour flowing from God to the disciples of Christ should create in their hearts an inner freedom about all human respect or deference. At the same time, they will strive always to render service with honour, because the gifts God bestows upon his people are proven, above all, in the service of his kingdom. It follows that a generous measure of personal honour is indispensable.

c) "Let your light shine before men"

All of creation and all the history of salvation are a reflection of God's glory; hence, the glorification of God's wonderful love and power is the supreme goal of humankind.

Christ tells his disciples how honoured they are. "You are salt to the world ... You are light for all the world" (Mt 5:13-14). He urges them, "Let your light shine among your fellows, so that when they see the good you do, they may give praise to your Father in heaven" (Mt 5:16). The indicative,

"You are light" is a title of honour from which follows the (imperative) vocation of the disciples to let their light shine in such a way that it returns to its source as praise and thanksgiving.

To make a show of religion before men (Mt 6:1) contradicts the very nature of the divine gift. The true disciple of Christ will watch over his motives, over his "purity of heart" and with equal fidelity he will do good "in the secret place" (Mt 6:6).

Human acclaim can never be the central basic motivation of a true disciple of Christ. But the human honour maintained in the shadow of the cross and in the light of Christ's resurrection — the honour directed to God's glory — should be judiciously upheld as an intrinsically worthy motive. It will be added to and illumined by the central motive of love and zeal for the kingdom of God. Then it will not only strengthen our leitmotif in hours of weakness but will also give it greater fullness and beauty.

Perhaps no other moral theologian has given so much attention as John Baptist Hirscher to the value of honour in the upbuilding of the kingdom of God. "The mature person, who respects himself, does so in view of God. Thus all recognition received and given to others lays the crowns before the throne of God, since they are the property of God. A countless multitude of dignities, honoured persons bowing before God, are eternally free from selfishness. And renouncing themselves forever, they are nothing other than servants of God. They all are to be revered, and none of them is alienated from God or introverted in the selfish self. They are all reverend, but nobody is that kind of 'nobleman' who is looking down on the crowd. They are all excellencies, because they belong to God, but they are servants because they are God's. ... Self-respect and mutual honour are brought home to the Creator, Redeemer and Sanctifier just as the work of creation, redemption and sanctification is to his honour. This is the kingdom".[176]

d) Christian self-esteem and respect for fellowmen

Presupposition for the truthful giving and receiving of honour is esteem for oneself and for one's neighbour. Without mutual respect there can be no healthy relationships and therefore no authentic honour.

Christian self-esteem is not self-admiration or complacency but humble and grateful response to the giver of all good things. It is not monological but rather a sharing in God's own freedom to honour his creatures. As participants in his covenant we have an unheard-of dignity, and whoever does not exult in this truth robs God of his honour; he fails to return to God the honour he has bestowed on those whom he calls to be his sons and daughters.

Just as Christian humility is totally alien to self-disparagement, so Christian self-esteem is far removed from pride. The exchange of honour in mutual reverence helps us to discover in ourselves and in others the highest potentialities, and to join hands in the service of the common good.

The genuineness of Christian self-respect manifests and proves itself in esteem for one's neighbour. If this is lacking, one has not yet truly recognized his dignity as a person before God. Indeed, since we have not the same need to see our neighbour's faults as to acknowledge our own, our esteem for him can be even more unquestioned than for ourselves. "There must be no room for rivalry and personal vanity among you, but you must humbly reckon others better than yourselves" (Phil 2:3). In a culture where sexism led so frequently to disregard of women, Peter admonished the Christian men, "You husbands must conduct your married life with understanding; pay honour to the woman's body, not only because it is weaker but mainly because you share together in the grace of God which gives you life" (1 Pet 3:7).

Misconception of one's own true worth before God, depreciation of the gifts God has granted us, self-disparagement in thought, word and deed: these are serious sins against Christian self-esteem. Vanity, stupid pride and arrogance that seek to base one's self-esteem on externals — charm, power, wealth, or even the sad courage to ignore and to dishonour God — are not only opposed to humility but are destructive of true self-esteem and of one's own humanity. Similarly, disdain for others because of external defects, or even for poverty and lack of success, contradicts the divine foundation of esteem and reverence.

Although moral defects may diminish respect for one's neighbour or for one's own person, these faults must never destroy respect, since the human person, made in the image and likeness of God, is still called by God's mercy to conversion and to the glory of eternal love.

False suspicion and rash judgment about moral integrity, which lower esteem for others or destroy it altogether, are serious sins. Rash judgment makes one unworthy of honour before God. "Do not judge and you shall not be judged" (Lk 6:37). The fault is graver if the suspicion or rash judgment is communicated to others, or if persons, who are otherwise highly esteemed and respected are suspected of outrageous offences. If, however, suspicion does not go beyond the reasons that gave rise to it, and does not burgeon out into actual rash judgment, and is not communicated to others, no sin is committed.[177]

A suspicious attitude is a great evil if it goes so far that distrust becomes greater than trust. This is a serious psychological deviation, and if it takes hold of a whole group, no healthy relationships are possible. Joy and enthusiasm for the good are stifled and courageous initiatives are discouraged.

3. *Social relevance of honour and aspiration*

a) Honour and social responsibility

Reconciling the sinner, God gives honour to him or her as a member of the communion of saints, as his son or daughter. The grateful awareness of this undeserved honour can be an effective motive to make oneself worthy of it by giving honour to one's fellowmen, our brothers and sisters in Christ.

To care for one's own and others' good name is an attitude that acknowledges the moral judgment of the community. It is a matter of responsibility for that common level of morality that is protected and enforced by the collective conscience. Although this might not be the highest form of morality, it would be irresponsible to ignore it or to destroy it through carelessness and disregard of the good name.[178]

One who looks for special honour beyond the simple level of good name can do so honourably only through achievements that are beyond the ordinary. The truly magnanimous person does not beg for honours but neither does he despise them. He rejoices to see his worth and his dedication acknowledged by the community which he is serving faithfully.[179]

St Augustine has clearly expressed the social dimension of both the simple "good name" and of "honour". "One who leads an unblemished life, free from misdeed and crime, does good for himself. But he who goes further by keeping his honour is considerate for others, for as our good life is necessary for ourselves, so is our good name for others".[180]

Special social groups — physicians, officers of the military, lawyers and such — who maintain high ethos of honour, render a precious social service under the condition, however, that they are truly élites serving the common good and not a privileged class concerned only for their collective interests.

Genuine Christians, and especially those dedicated to the service of the Gospel, will not only care for the good name of each individual and of the whole community, but will try to live up to their vocation to be light to the world. This motive is a part of their missionary zeal. And the more thoroughly the motive of esteem is subordinated to the good in itself (its own inner value), the more it will draw people to faith. The apostolic community of Jerusalem, which shared everything and lived brotherhood with unaffected joy, "enjoyed the favour of the whole people. And day by day the Lord added to their number those whom he was saving" (Acts 2:42-47). "They were all held in high esteem, for they had never a needy person among them" (Acts 4:34).

The Apostle of the Gentiles does not think that the motive of honourableness contradicts humility. "Care as much about each other as about yourselves. Do not be haughty, but go about with humble folk. Do not keep thinking how wise you are. ... Let your aims be such as all men count honourable" (Rom 12:16-17; cf. Phil 4:5; 1 Thess 4:12; 1 Pet 2:23; 3:16). The veneration of the saints is in the realm of honourableness and can be a strong appeal to live one's life according to the dignity of the sons and daughters of God in the service of the Gospel and of all people.

b) Today's role of ambition and pretension

In shaping the kind of good name, honour and aspiration that people are concerned with, the economic, social and cultural context plays an important role. Hans Joseph Buchkremer has made an interesting study of this connection.[181] Profound changes that mark our epoch have made it more difficult to find one's own identity, ego-strength and character. The young generation is no longer rooted in a family that includes several generations; the industrial and bureaucratic world tends to treat people as statistical numbers, counting only function and achievement; schools of the technocratic society are job-oriented, mirror-images of the "efficient society"; the environment in which many people live is depleted and constantly changing; and finally, the mass media destroy the earlier common conviction that unites people in one tradition and one kind of morals.[182] "In an epoch of confrontation of moral spheres and forms of ethos, it seems indicated to use the plural and to speak of morals and moralities".[183]

People who have become unable to judge their own moral value are like addicts in their craving for acknowledgment by others. And the kind of acknowledgment that is given in a society of efficiency is based on success and achievement. The danger then arises that instead of seeking honour by living honourably in a moral sense, people are driven by ambitions and pretensions that have nothing to do with their character and integrity. "All pretension is, in the final analysis, ambition for achievement, a craving for exaltation of one's individual self through recognition of achievement".[184] The ambition is frequently not for achievement as a value in itself but as a means of gaining recognition by the group or by the greatest possible admiring multitude. This can promote construction and production; it can check destruction and apathy; but it can scarcely promote human dignity. In such an environment the successful actor or businessman no longer feels the need to care for that kind of good name and honour that is based on an honourable life and character.

We no longer live in a society that offers firm and clear traditions able not only to guide people externally but also to help them to internalize the rules. Today, only persons who have internalized basic principles beyond detailed rules of conduct, and thus have come to a clear vision of life, can withstand the temptation of the new kind of ambition. Enslavement to it can be aggravated by an atmosphere of distrust. "The habitually ambitious individual thinks that he can become acceptable and respectable only through honour based on his achievement. Indeed, his ambitious dedication to efficiency is the result of mistrust of his own worth to be loved and to live his own life unbiased by the world around him".[185]

In old Israel and in the old Germanic world, the emphasis on honour was partially conditioned by the exodus situation. The German tribes who had no home felt that they had lost everything if they lost their honour, which was grounded on the basic ethos of loyalty to the leaders and thus to the group. The loyalty would be proven by their fortitude. For the Israelites who had left everything behind in order to gain their freedom and their homeland, honour was based on solidarity, on a life according to the covenant with God and in gratitude for the divine promises.

Things are quite different in a society where business efficiency and success tend to replace self-identification, integrity and character. "Without an ideal that strengthens the personal character, we all too quickly become slaves to social trends, to what other people are thinking about us, to our own pretensions, our social vanity and other herd instincts".[186]

c) Taming and integrating ambition

Ambition is good if exercised at the right time and place and for the right purpose. But where ambition and social honour are separated from the scale of values, we can easily understand that, time and again, youth rebels against the style of life produced by these base motives. The youth movements after the first world war, and even more the anti-culture movement of the 60s, were a loud protest against the emptiness of ambition and naked efficiency. But the protest itself can become an empty expression of insolence when it offers no higher and firm ideals, and especially if it gives little evidence of social responsibility.

Ambition can be channelled and ennobled by playfulness. The genuine competition in sports honours the competitor and keeps strict rules of honour. Where the sphere of play is rightly developed, aggression is transformed. The opponent is considered not as an enemy but as a companion. The happy comradeship of play should then also ennoble competition in school and professional activity.[187]

The healthy channelling of ambition depends greatly on the wisdom and attitude of parents. They can often stimulate ambition if the children are sure that the parents love and esteem them, and that this love does not depend on the children's achievements. Thus ambition is a secondary motive and does not lead to an "ambitious" character.[188] But if ambition becomes the prevailing and determining motive in a child's education, then objectivity and the direct interest in higher values like culture, good human relationships and dedication to the common good are seldom discovered.[189]

Ambition is an enormous source of energy. If it is simply ignored or denigrated, precious energies will be misguided. The goal should be to channel it into higher motives of social responsibility, fidelity and creativity. The main purpose of education and self-education is dedication to the highest values in healthy human relationships.

Except for a small minority of people who reach the ideal of serenity and dedication to the good, we all need at times to be spurred by ambition, and some need it at all times. But it is decisive to recognize that ambition has only relative value and should be subordinated to the higher values. Especially in the moral and religious fields, special care must be taken that it never becomes a determining force; otherwise it would lead to a pharisaical self-righteousness.[190]

4. Upholding one's own honour

Morally, stubborn indifference to one's own honour is no less questionable than inordinate ambition. This is particularly true if it is rooted in scorn for the opinions and sensitivities of others and a lack of social responsibility.

A disciple of Christ will not accept honours that are thrust upon him without his seeking if he knows that he does not deserve them. He will clearly reject them unless rejection would prove a disservice to the common good. In such a case he will try all the more to make himself worthy. For a mature person, unmerited esteem is more a cause of embarrassment than of joy.

But one's good name — if no more is involved — must be preserved even though one may not be, objectively, deserving of good repute. This is demanded insofar as one's sociability requires it. However, in order that the preservation of the good name may not degenerate into hypocrisy, the breach between repute and reality must be repaired by a deep sense of unworthiness before God and man, a zealous effort to regain the values that deserve honour, and an effort to give greater honour to others.

One who has an authentic sense of honour will, of course, refrain from blatant or officious self-praise. But for the sake of a higher cause, one is permitted to point prudently and modestly, to some good one has done with the help of God's grace, as St Paul did (cf. 1 Cor 9: 1-23; 2 Cor 3: 1-16; Gal 1: 10, 2: 2-6).

The obligation to preserve one's honour is especially grave for those whose social service depends greatly on good repute. Of course, this does not at all imply that one might become anxious about petty distinctions. Incidental matters, which do not really affect honour or good name, should ordinarily be ignored by the Christian in a spirit of love and out of concern for more important things.

The disciple of Christ will often even bear in silence harsh abuse and insult hurled in his face, so long as his social honour and activity are not jeopardized. In any case, it is contrary to the spirit of Christ to counter insult with insult (cf. Lk 6: 28; 1 Cor 4: 12; 1 Pet 2: 23). However, Christ's injunction to turn the other cheek when one is struck (Mt 5: 39) demands only a readiness to act with serenity, and not a literal compliance. This is clear from the Lord's own forthright rejection of the Pharisees' insults (cf. Jn 8: 48ff) and his calm and dignified reproof of the high priest's servant who struck him in the face (Jn 18: 22ff).

In extreme cases one may protect against unjust attack the high social good of one's reputation even by seeking legal redress in the courts of law. Of course this procedure, like every action in defence of personal rights, must be qualified:

1) Flowing from an awareness of the supremacy of God's honour and judgment, there must be a background of ultimate serenity about the insignificance of human judgment; 2) the action must be directed to the social service of honour itself, excluding all desire for revenge; 3) there must be at all times a willingness to come to full reconciliation; 4) one must be solicitous for the good name of others, even of the one who is guilty of the offence against us. Obviously, the bounds of truth and of justice in self-defence may never be transgressed.

The very concept of Christian honour excludes duels and similar measures of defence. Even less can they be a means of restoring true honour.

5. Sins against the honour of one's neighbour

Nobody can honour himself or be truly honourable unless he honours others on the true ground of reverence. This is easily seen in the case of racism and sexism. Whoever dishonours the other because of his colour can claim honour only for his own paleness but not for his personhood. And whoever dishonours the other person because she is a woman can claim honour only for his naked maleness but not for his personhood. So it is with all the other ways of insulting others or withholding honour on account of secondary attributes.

The following text takes up the main sins against the honour of others. But it always should be kept in mind that the one who dishonours his fellowmen dishonours himself even more.

a) Insult and refusal to honour

No one can give a complete catalogue of sins against other people's honour, because they are so manifold. Frequently, too, they are undetected by the sinner himself. All the sins committed by words and actions come from the heart; they make evident the disregard or contempt harboured in one's thoughts and desires. And we should not think only about the sins committed by words or actions but of all those committed by omission, by refusal to give to one's neighbour the honour that encourages and strengthens the bonds of community.

We can never honour others too much, but we can honour

them on false grounds and in false ways. For instance, praise may never degenerate into flattery. We should honour our neighbour for his own sake and not to obtain favours from him.

The Lord has told us how gravely sinful it can be to insult one's neighbour. "If anyone abuses his brother, he must answer for it to the court; if he sneers at him, he will have to answer for it in the fires of hell" (Mt 5:22).

A word of caution: the concrete meaning and consequent gravity of insult depends not only on words but on the total cultural context. In the sixteenth century, both reformers and Catholics indulged in language so rude that today it would be absolutely shocking. In some sub-cultures even now, gravely abusive terms seem to be acceptable as reproof and correction, or at least not judged as a serious insult. Of course, earnest effort should be made to replace with Christian reverence and courtesy such vulgar language.[191]

Serious violations of honour are not confined to the use of insulting language; gestures can be equally offensive. The deliberate and contemptuous neglect to greet another, or otherwise to show a lack of respect to which he is entitled under the circumstances, can be a serious offence.

Restitution must be made for the damage done by insult or refusal to show proper marks of deference. In most cases the best way is by positive manifestation of due respect. But an insult that is especially serious must be atoned for by explicit apology, at least if this is the custom among honourable people. Public insult demands public reparation. However, it is often advisable to delay one's apology until bitterness has at least partially subsided. A clumsy attempt to make good at an inopportune moment might merely exacerbate nervous tempers and lead to further rancour.

If two parties match insults, we cannot say that one offence cancels out the other. Although in such a situation there is no strict obligation in justice to repair the offence there is a serious obligation in charity encumbent on both parties to seek reconciliation as soon as possible and in the best possible way.

b) Calumny and detraction

Calumny is a false or exaggerated assertion about one's neighbour which is calculated to defame him.

Detraction is any unjustified assertion that infringes on the good name of another, even though it may not be formally untrue.

Both calumny and detraction are serious sins against justice and charity. In a society or environment in which honour and good name are appraised more highly than property, one can easily realize that it is even a greater sin than theft. "A good name is more desirable than great wealth" (Prov 22:1).

Detraction is sinful not only when it springs from malicious intent but also when it is due to conscious neglect. The gravity of this sin is to be judged by the foreseeable damage to honour, the anguish or vexation suffered, the disturbance of community bonds, the detriment to one's professional efficiency and the possible material loss. The degree of damage does not depend merely on the disturbing assertion but also, and substantially, on the circumstances involving the victim of the defamation, the detractor, and those who listen to the detractor.

Calumny or slander is a much graver sin than detraction. While detraction makes sinful use of "truth", slander violates not merely a conditional but an absolute right to one's good name in accordance with truth.

To me it seems erroneous to condone the divulgence of serious sins committed by a person who is already in ill-repute. It still hurts him and actually hinders the restitution of his good name.

Innuendos such as, "I don't want to hurt his/her reputation but ... " or, "If I were to divulge a mere fraction of what I know ... " are often more devastating than flat statements of facts. Wise people will not listen to these ambiguities or at least will not take them seriously.

It is particularly evil to deprive entire families, communities or ethnic groups of the honour due to them.

The dead retain the right to their good name, even though no loss of honour can hurt them personally anymore. But detraction or calumny does hurt their families and friends. The dead who sleep in the Lord must be held in esteem. Our judgment of the dead should always be reserved, for they have already faced the judgment of the all-holy God which we, too, shall have to face.

A person who has acted dishonourably has at the moment only a conditional right to his good name. He enjoys this right only insofar as, viewed as a whole, the preservation of his honour (inwardly undeserved) is for his own good and the good of the community. Therefore, disclosure of others' secret faults can be lawful and even obligatory under certain circumstances: when, for instance, this is necessary to preserve the community, oneself or others from unjust damage, or to restrain the evildoer from further evil.

But one who feels that he has the duty to reveal another's secret fault must carefully weigh both his motives and the foreseeable consequences. To divulge truthfully things which infringe on the honour of other people might be permitted to protect one's own honour and/or material goods from grave and unjust damage, if there is a certain proportion between the threatened evil and the loss of the other person's honour, and if no less harmful way is open. Nothing justifies one's divulging another's sins and faults which are not damaging to others, merely to make capital out of another's loss of honour as, for example, to eliminate their competition in business or politics, and so on.

One is allowed to expose swindlers in order to keep them from harming others. In the case of an engaged couple, it is permissible to reveal serious hidden faults of one party to the other if there is no other means of preventing a hapless marriage. Grave danger of seduction is almost always a compelling reason for revealing a secret to those who are endangered or to the parents or educators.

We are permitted to caution an employer or head of a house that an employee or domestic servant has "long fingers", in order to protect the establishment or the home from substantial loss and vexation through theft. However, if the servant or employee is threatened with much greater loss, material and social, or when a fraternal correction can be effective, the denunciation should be omitted.

Voters have a right to pertinent information about the qualifications of candidates for public office, but only those faults and defects can be divulged which make a candidate unfit or unworthy of the office he is seeking. Secret faults and past sins which have no bearing at all on the candidacy or fitness for public trust may not be revealed. This area of private honour is as inviolable for the office-seeker as for any private individual. A person who serves the common good or wants to serve it in an important position needs, even more than some others, a good personal reputation.

If a defamatory matter has been publicized in a grotesquely distorted manner, it can be an act of charity to lessen the damage of the offence by a truthful presentation of all the facts in the case. This is especially true if the reputation of a person in a position of public trust is at stake.

For any good reason, we may discuss publicly known matters despite their defaming character. Frivolous or meaningless gossip, however, is quite out of place.

Discreditable acts of other members of a family, institution, convent, monastery or other closed community, if known only in the community, may not be divulged outside this closed circle. Every member of the community is responsible for the honour of the community and of each of its members.

Where the circumstances are such that the discussion of publicly known facts prejudices neither another's good name nor love of neighbour, any proper motive is sufficient to justify serene conversation about these faults. It is not necessarily "idle talk", for at times it is better to speak with kind and loving mercy than to be morosely silent. However, as long as the sad situation is not known publicly, even though a number of people may know it, we cannot ignore the fact that our talking will make it known more widely. The argument that others will tell about it anyhow is specious. True disciples of Christ do not act on such superficial excuses.

There should be special merciful concern about those who have been condemned in a court of law. It is true that by public punishment the honour of the wrongdoer has been forfeited insofar as the crime under judgment is concerned, but it is against piety to publicize the names and mistakes of all those who have been involved even in a minor way.

Those who are actually caught and are detained for some time in jail are frequently not any worse than people of good reputation who avoid punishment because they are more influential or more callous. One who has been condemned has a right to merciful love, and needs a chance to restore his good reputation. It follows that if his crime is forgotten, or if he attempts to make a new start for a better life in a place where his past is not known or is already established in such a place, then it could be a grave sin to reopen the record of a remote, forgotten, or unknown affair. Only as long as a criminal continues to be a menace to the community has he no claim to a forfeited honour.

c) Talebearing

An especially venomous form of detraction is talebearing which tries to destroy the bond of love and peace between people. The motive eventually to supplant the injured party in the affection of his friend makes things no better. Even more than other forms of detraction, talebearing is a serious sin against charity and justice. "A curse on the scandalmonger and the deceitful, he has ruined many who lived in concord. The talk of a third party has wrecked the lives of many … Whoever pays heed to it will never find rest or live in peace of mind" (Sir 28:13-16).

Especially contemptible are anonymous talebearers and detractors. They should never be given any consideration or credence. Those in authority who would like to believe them should know that this destroys their own credibility and reliability.

One who is the object of talebearing has the right and sometimes the duty to unmask and/or confront the aggressor.

The breaking up of a dangerous sinful friendship, even though this involves disclosure of secret faults insofar as this is necessary for the purpose, is not to be characterized as talebearing. It can be, rather, an act of love.

d) Irresponsible cooperation in detraction

Whoever by his attitude, even though this be mere silence, effectively induces another to commit a sin of detraction is guilty of the same sin as the detractor. Nobody should listen to a detractor; one should either stop him openly, go away or introduce an indifferent topic of conversation. However, there is no general obligation to prevent or stop detraction when one fears that the attempt would merely harden the detractor in his determination to harm the other. At times, a stoic silence that allows the detractor to continue until he has run out of conversation can be better than an attempt to interrupt him, if it can be anticipated that the full story will be less damaging than the introductory hints or suggestions.

In any community or organization, those in authority have a special obligation in charity and justice to prevent detraction, to protect those entrusted to them from defamation by others; and therefore, they have to insist that reparation be made. Otherwise they participate somehow in the sin against the honour so necessary for the community and its members.

There should be no need to say that those who take pleasure in listening to detraction are no better than those who commit it. The damage done by calumny, detraction and talebearing can frequently not be repaired. However, a sincere conversion implies an effort to do whatever is in one's power to repair all the consequences of one's irresponsible talk and actions. The fact that a person may have acted thoughtlessly does not excuse him from the duty to prevent further damage as soon as he becomes aware of the consequences of his words and actions.

NOTES

[1] *Gaudium et Spes*, 45.
[2] G. Baum, *Religion and Alienation*, New York, Paramus, Toronto, 1975, 251ff; cf. A. Greeley, *The New Agenda*, New York, 1973. G. Baum rightly insists that the "symbolist" does not reject or minimize the historical dimension; cf. R. Bellah, *Beyond Belief*, New York, 1970, 220.
[3] J.H. Wright, S.J., "Divine Knowledge and Human Freedom", *Theol. St.* 38 (1977), 450-477, quote, p. 453.
[4] D. Bonhoeffer, *Gesammelte Schriften*, V, 219.
[5] Augustine, *De Trinitate* 15, cap. 14 PL 42, 1076ff.
[6] S.Th., I, q 43, a 3 ad 2.
[7] H.U.v. Balthasar, *Verbum Caro. Skizzen zur Theologie*, Einsiedeln, 1960, I, 179.
[8] A. Denecke, *Wahrheit. Eine evangelische Kasuistik*, Göttingen, 1972, 60ff.
[9] Pastor Hermae, *Mandatum* 3, 1ff.
[10] Cf. Ph. Dessauer, *Wahrheit als Weg*, München, 1946, 60ff.
[11] *Gaudium et Spes*, 10.
[12] *Gaudium et Spes*, 22.
[13] *Gaudium et Spes*, 32, cf. 45.
[14] E. McDonagh, "Morality and Spirituality", *Studia Moralia* 15 (1977), 121-137.

[15] J. Ratzinger, *Glaube und Zukunft*, München, 1970.

[16] Cf. H. Küng, *Christsein*, München, 1974, 35ff; A. Schmied, "Wahrhaftigkeit und Glaube", *Studia Moralia* 15 (1977), 545ff.

[17] R. May, *Man's Quest for Himself*, New York, 7th printing, 252.

[18] H. Schär, *Was ist Wahrheit? Eine theologisch-psychologische Untersuchung*. Zürich, 1970, 38ff.

[19] Cf. A. Schmied, l.c., 535.

[20] Cf. D. Donnelly, c.s.j., *Team, Theory and Practice*, New York, 1977. This is one of the most helpful books on how to share the search and practice of truth.

[21] R. Picker, *Pluriformes Christentum*, Wien, 1970, 62ff; cf. M. de Courteau, "Gibt es eine Sprache der Einheit?", *Concilium*, 1970, Heft 1, 40.

[22] A. Hartmann, S.J., *Toleranz und Christlicher Glaube*, Frankfurt, 1955, 115ff.

[23] R.A. McCormick, "Conscience, Theologians and the Magisterium", *The New Catholic World* 220 (1977), 269.

[24] Cf. R. Egenter, *Erfahrung ist Leben. Die Rolle der Erfahrung für das sittliche Leben*, München, 1974; P. Toinet, "Experience morale chrétienne et morales philosophiques", *Studia Moralia* 12 (1974), 9-46; J. Etienne, "Le rôle de l'experience en morale chrétienne", l.c., 47-54

[25] H. Cox, *The Seduction of the Spirit. The Use and Misuse of Peoples' Religion*, New York, 1973, 144-168.

[26] l.c., 170ff.

[27] *Gaudium et Spes*, 62. Cf. Commentary by R. Tucci, S.J., in *Lexikon Th.K.*, *Das Zweite Vatikanische Konzil*, vol. III, 476-485, esp. on the conflict between two opposite approaches. A traditionalist approach considers truth as the Church's static possession, with no attention to the psychological, social and historical condition of those who "possess" and teach the truth. On the other hand, modern culture looks at truth as something constantly to be sought for and discovered. The council debates have clearly manifested the passionate search for a better understanding of the revealed truth, and opening for new insights about the existential conditions for the better grasp of truth.

[28] Cf. Roman Synod 1977.

[29] J.M. Sailer, *Handbuch der christlichen Moral*, München, 1817, II, 52.

[30] l.c., II, 48.

[31] Y. Congar, "Réflexion et propos sur l'originalité d'une éthique chrétienne", *Studia Moralia* 15 (1977), 35.

[32] F.X. Durrwell, "Vous avez été appelés", *Studia Moralia* 15 (1977), 354.

[33] Cf. A. Dondaeyne, l.c., 55, 57.

[34] *Gaudium et Spes*, 62.

[35] Cf. W.A.M. Luijpen, *Existentielle Phänomenologie*, München, 1971, 102.

[36] Cf. A. Auer, "Das Vorverständnis des Sittlichen und seine Bedeutung für eine theologische Ethik", *Studia Moralia* 15 (1977), 219-244.

[37] D. Donnelly, l.c., 76.

[38] J. Nuttin, "Liberté et Verité psychologique", in *Liberté et Verité*, Louvain, 1954, 103.

[39] H. Schär, *Was ist Wahrheit?*, Zürich, 1970, 322.

[40] A. Dondeyne, l.c., 53-55.

[41] Cf. J. Messner, *Kulturethik*, Innsbruck, 1959[2], 568ff; H. Schär, l.c., 355ff.

[42] Cf. Ph. Dessauer, l.c., 81.

[43] Cf. A. Denecke, l.c., 16ff.

[44] K. Jaspers, *Von der Wahrheit, Philosophische Logik*, München, 1947, 381ff.

[45] Luijpen, l.c., 149.

[46] V. Frankl, *Der Wille zum Sinn*, Bern-Stuttgart, 1972, 85.

[47] l.c., 219.

[48] Cf. A. Maslow, "The Need to Know and the Fear of Knowing", *Journal of General Psychology* 68 (1963), 111-122.

[49] M. Heidegger, *Sein und Zeit*, Tübingen, 1949[6], 130.

[50] Cf. Luijpen, l.c., 126, 175; L. Landgrebe, *Der Weg der Phänomenologie*, Gütersloh, 1963, 77ff.

51 Cf. J.V. Morley, *On Compromise*, London, 1933, 22ff.
52 Cf. M. Merleau-Ponty, *Sense et non-sense*, Paris, 1966⁶, 318.
53 Cf. B. Häring, *Ethics of Manipulation*, Slough and New York, 1975, 13-43, 109-136.
54 K. Jaspers, *Der philosophiische Glaube angesichts der Offenbarung*, München, 1962, 530ff; *Von der Wahrheit*, 460.
55 Luijpen, l.c., 115.
56 *Gaudium et Spes*, 36; cf. Dondeyne, l.c., 52.
57 Luijpen, l.c., 84; cf. 82, 123.
58 l.c., 126.
59 G. Marcel, *Homo Viator*, Paris, 1944, 157.
60 Ph. Dessauer, l.c., 27.
61 E.F. Schuhmacher, *Small is Beautiful. Economics as if People Mattered*, New York, San Francisco, London, 1975, 296.
62 *Gaudium et Spes*, 5.
63 A. Denecke, l.c., 47.
64 Cf. Luijpen, l.c., 101; A. Dondeyne, *Foi chrétienne et pensée contemporaine*, Paris, 1952, 35-42.
65 Luijpen, l.c., 106ff.
66 l.c., 110.
67 l.c., 68.
68 V. Eid, "Sakramentales und christliches Ethos", *Studia Moralia* 15 (1977), 143; cf. Schär, l.c. 328.
69 Cf. M. Scheler, *Die Wissensformen und die Gesellschaft*, Leipzig, 1966; K. Mannheim, *Essays on the Sociology of Knowledge*, London, 1952; J. Schaaf, *Grundprinzipien der Wissenssoziologie*, Hamburg, 1956; W. Stark, *Sociology of Knowledge*, London, 1958; G. Gurvitch, *Les cadres sociaux de la connaissance*, Paris, 1966; Id., *Traité de sociologie*, II, Paris, 1968³, esp. 103-136.
70 G. Gurvitch, *Traité de sociologie*, 112-116.
71 l.c., 122, 126.
72 Problems of sociology of knowledge as well as of sociology of morals will be treated again, in volume III, in the chapters on culture, society and politics.
73 S.Th., I II, q 2, a 2: "Actus credentis non terminatur ad enuntiabile sed ad rem"; cf. Dondeyne, *Verité et liberté*, 64.
74 *Gaudium et Spes*, 62, and AAS 54 (1962), 792.
75 Cf. B. Häring, "Die Kirche darf nicht einer Monopolgesellschaft gleichen", in *Die gegenwärtige Heilsstunde*, Freiburg, 1964, 98-112. (This essay took as point of departure the "sociology of monopolies", concerning the sociology of knowledge.)
76 *Discorsi, messaggi, colloqui del Santo Padre Giovanhi XXIII*, III, 575.
77 *Decree on Ecumenism*, 11.
78 Cf. J. Neumann, *Menschenrechte auch in der Kirche?*, Zürich, 1976, 134ff.
79 K. Rahner, "Uber schlechte Argumentation in der Moraltheologie", *Studia Moralia* 15 (1977), 250.
80 G. Gurvitch, l.c., 133ff.
81 Cf. Luijpen, 130.
82 l.c., 99ff.
83 l.c., 104.
84 V. Frankl, *Der Wille zum Sinn*, Bern, Stuttgart, 1972, 85.
85 K. Jaspers, *Von der Wahrheit*, München, 1947, 987; cf. 597, 744.
86 l.c., 1004ff; cf. A. Gamoczy, "Wahrheitsfindung durch die Liebe", in H. Fischer (ed.), *Prinzip Liebe, Perspektiven der Theologie*, Freiburg i. B., 1975, 59-75.
87 Augustine, *De Trinitate* 15, 11 PL 42, 1071.
88 l.c., 15, 11 PL 42, 1072.
89 l.c., 15, 21 PL 42, 1088.
90 l.c., 15, 11 PL 42, 1073.
91 M.A. Klapfenstein, *Die Lüge im Alten Testament. Ihr Begriff, ihre Bedeutung und ihre Beurteilung*, Zürich-Frankfurt, 1964, 321ff.
92 l.c., 353.

98 WHAT IS THE LIBERATING TRUTH?

[93] Cf. R. Bultmann, *Theologie des Neuen Testaments*, Berlin, 1959³, 370.
[94] Cf. Augustine, *Enarrationes in Ps. 5*, PL 36, 86; Thomas, S.Th., II II, q 110, a 4.
[95] A. Kern, *Die Lüge*, Graz, 1930, 117.
[96] Cf. A. Landgraf, Sündhaftigkeit der Lüge nach der Lehre der Frühscholastik, *Zeitschr. für kath. Theol.* 63 (1939), 157-180.
[97] J. Mausbach, *Katholische Moraltheologie*, 5th ed., III, 244, and the latest, 10th ed., reworked by G. Ermecke, III, 596; cf. H. Küng, *Wahrhaftigkeit*, Freiburg, 1970¹⁰.
[98] Cf. Augustine, *De Mendacio* 17, PL 40, 510.
[99] The most complete study of the history of the problem is to be found in G. Müller, O.S.B., *Die Wahrhaftigkeitspflicht und die Problematik der Lüge*, Freiburg, 1962, 27-229 (bibliography pp. XVII-XXIV).
[100] *Soliloquia*, lib. II, 9, 16 PL 32, 892.
[101] *De Mendacio* II, 2 PL 40, 487.
[102] l.c., XX, 41 PL 40, 515.
[103] *Retractationes* I, 27 PL 32, 630.
[104] *Contra mendacium* VII, 17 PL 40, 527.
[105] l.c., IX, 20 PL 40, 530.
[106] Jerome, *Epist.* 85, cap. III, 11 PL 33, 257.
[107] Quoted in Kern, *Die Lüge*, 57 (Briefwechsel I, 269ff).
[108] H. Grisar, *Luther*, Freiburg, 1911, 460.
[109] Denz. Sch., 2126ff.
[110] A. Tanquerey, *Synopsis theologiae moralis*, 9th ed., III nn. 381-383; A. Vermeesch, "De mendacio", *Gregorianum* 1 (1920), 11-40; 425-474; J. Lindworski, S.J., "Das Problem der Lüge bei katholischen Ethikern und Moralisten", in O. Lipman (ed.), *Die Lüge*, Leipzig, 1927, 69ff; M. Ledrus, S.J., "De mendacio", *Periodica de re morali* 32 (1943), 5-58; 123-1 1; 33 (1944), 5-60; M. Laros, "Seid klug wie die Schlangen und einfältig wie die Tauben", Frankfurt, 1951; other authors, see G. Müller, l.c., 199-225.
[111] Laros, l.c., 82.
[112] K.-H. Peschke, "Das Problem der absoluten Sündhaftigkeit der Lüge", *Studia Moralia* 15 (1977), 697-711.
[113] Cf. F. Hainz, *Psychologie der Sprache*, Stuttgart, 1954; W.P. Robinson, *Language and Social Behaviour*, Harmondsworth, 1972.
[114] A. Dedecke, l.c.; E. Ansohn, *Die Wahrheit am Krankenbett. Grundfragen einer ärztlichen Sterbehilfe*, München, 1965, 115.
[115] Cf. B. Häring, *Medical Ethics*, Slough and Notre Dame, 1973, 203ff.
[116] R. Egenter, *Das Edle und der Christ*, München, 1935, 61.
[117] Cf. G. Marcel, "Fidelité créatrice", in *Du refus à l'invocation*, Paris, 1940, 199-217 (German title of the whole work: *Schöpferische Treue*, München-Zürich, 1963); M. Nédoncelle, *De la fidelité*, Paris, 1953; H. Bethge (ed.), *Eid, Gewissen, Treupflicht*, Frankfurt, 1965; A. Dumas and others, *Engagement et fidelité*, Paris, 1970; H. Kramer, *Sittliche Vorentscheidung*, Würzburg, 1970; Id., *Unwiderrufliche Entscheidungen im Leben des Christen*, München-Paderborn, 1974; R. Pesch, *Freie Treue. Die Christen und die Ehescheidung*, Freiburg, 1971; M. Joulin, *Vivre fidèle*, Paris, 1972; P. Kemp, *Théorie de l'engagement*, I, Paris, 1973; J.Cl. Sagne, *Conflict, changement, conversion. Vers une éthique de la conversion*, Paris, 1974; K. Demmer, *Die Lebensentscheidung. Ihre moraltheologische Grundlage*, München-Paderborn-Wien, 1974; V. Ayel, *Inventer la fidelité au temps des certitudes provisoires*, Lyon, 1976.
[118] E. Schillebeeckx, *Christus und die Christen*, Freiburg, 1977 (after having read the rich pages of the author on *chesed* and *'emet* in the Old Testament (l.c., 84-92) one is surprised that this book on Christ and Christians does not elaborate this dimension of fidelité in the New Testament. The reason seems to be that there is not much literature on fidelité in the New Testament, although nobody can deny the centrality of it).
[119] A. Denecke, l.c., 49.
[120] A. Dumas, "Théologie biblique de la fidelité", in *Engagement et fidelité*, Paris, 1970, 14.

[121] Cf. J. Guillet, *Thèmes bibliques*, Paris, 1950, 55ff.
[122] O.F. Bollnow, *Wesen und Wandel der Tugenden*, Frankfurt, 1972, 171.
[123] P. de Locht, *Les risques de la fidelité*, Paris, 1972, 48-52.
[124] V. Ayel, l.c., 39-44.
[125] Cf. M. Nédoncelle, l.c.
[126] P. Kemp, l.c., I, 17.
[127] This tendency is very strong in the otherwise excellent study of H. Kramer, l.c., 222ff.
[128] Cf. Bollnow, l.c., 174.
[129] K. Demmer, l.c., 88.
[130] Cf. Nédoncelle, l.c., 137ff.
[131] Cf. B. Häring, *Ethics of Manipulation*, Slough and New York, 1976, 109-129.
[132] Cf. Nédoncelle, l.c., 143ff.
[133] De Locht, l.c., 63.
[134] K. Demmer, l.c., 88ff.
[135] E. Mounier, *Le personalisme*, Paris, 1949, 68.
[136] Cf. Bollnow, l.c., 160ff.
[137] G. Marcel, *Schöpferische Treue*, München, 1961, 143.
[138] G. Marcel, *Etre et avoir*, Paris, 1935, 183.
[139] G. Marcel, *Homo viator*, Paris, 1944, 185.
[140] G. Marcel, *Schöpferische Treue*, 160.
[141] l.c., 164.
[142] Nédoncelle, l.c., 156.
[143] l.c., 113, cf. 104ff.
[144] K. Demmer, l.c., 100.
[145] V. Ayel, l.c., 149.
[146] V. Jankelevitch, "Le courage et la fidelité", in *Traité des vertus* II, 1970, 359-449, quote, p. 415.
[147] G. Marcel, *Schöpferische Treue*, 232.
[148] Nédoncelle, l.c., 52ff, 62ff; M. Joulin, l.c., 29ff.
[149] Jankelevitch, l.c., 411.
[150] Cf. K. Demmer, l.c., 83-87.
[151] H. Kramer, l.c., 231.
[152] Marcel, l.c., 148.
[153] Jankelevitch, l.c., 359.
[154] V. Ayel, l.c., 92.
[155] J.B. Metz, "Entscheidung", in H. Fries (ed.), *Handbuch theologischer Grundbegriffe*, München, 1962, I, 284.
[156] Nédoncelle, l.c., 111.
[157] Cf. K. Demmer, l.c., 100.
[158] Cf. V. Ayel, l.c., 107.
[159] l.c., 136.
[160] Cf. G. Marcel, *Positions et approches*, Paris, 1933, 287-292.
[161] Cf. V. Ayel, l.c., 79.
[162] l.c., 87, 133.
[163] G. Marcel, l.c., 156.
[164] Kramer not only emphasizes onesidedly "Selbsttreue" (fidelity towards the self) but also considers self-fulfilment as the main purpose of the marital vows, cf. l.c., 257. This, surely, is a strong trend in our culture.
[165] Cf. B. Häring, *The Eucharist and Our Everyday Life*, Slough, 1978.
[166] Denz. Sch., 1638, 1649.
[167] *Gaudium et Spes*, 48.
[168] Cf. B. Häring, "Theological Appraisal of Marriage Tribunals", in L.G. Wrenn (ed.), *Divorce and Remarriage in the Catholic Church*, New York, 1973, 16-28.
[169] Cf. M. Wundt, *Die Ehre als Quelle des sittlichen Lebens in Volk und Staat*, Langensalza, 1927; O.H. Nebe, *Die Ehre als theologisches Problem*, Berlin, 1936; F. Weidauer, *Die Wahrung der Ehre und die sittliche Tat*, Leipzig, 1936; H.E. Hengstenberg, *Von der Ehre, sofern sie den Christen angeht*, München, 1937; R. Egenter, *Von christlicher Ehrenhaftigkeit*, München, 1937;

Th. Steinbüchel, *Ehrfurcht*, Stuttgart, 1947; H. Reiner, *Die Ehre. Kritische Sicht einer abendländischen Lebensform*, Darmstadt, 1956; D.C. MacClelland, *The Achieving Society*, Princeton, N.J., 1961 (German tr., *Die Leistungsgesellschaft*, Stuttgart, 1966); W. Korff, *Ehre, Prestige, Gewissen*, Köln, 1966; O.F. Bollnow, "Ehre und guter Ruf", in *Einfache Sittlichkeit*, Göttingen, 1968⁴, 47-60; H. Buchkremer, *Ehrgeiz*, Stuttgart, 1972; F. Haider, *Die Ehre als menschliches Problem. Versuch einer pädagogischen Orientierung*, Padeborn, 1973; E. Schillebeeckx, "Ehre Gottes und das wahre, gute und glückliche Menschsein", in *Christus und die Christen*, Freiburg, 1977, 627-818.

170 *Quaestiones quodl.* 10, 6, 12, ob. 3.

171 S.Th., II II, 103, 1.

172 Bollnow, *Einfache Sittlichkeit*, 49.

173 M. Scheler, *Gesammelte Werke* 10, 628; cf. 10, 65ff.

174 R. Egenter, l.c., 101, 122ff.

175 M. Gierens, *Ehe, Mensur und Duell*, Paderborn, 1928, 46.

176 J.B. Hirscher, *Die christliche Moral als Lehre von der Verwirklichung des Gottesreiches in der Menschheit*, Sulzbach, 1851⁵, III, 144ff.

177 Cf. S.Th., II II, 60, 3.

178 Cf. Bollnow, l.c., 57.

179 Cf. R. Egenter, l.c., 73.

180 Augustine, *De bono viduitatis* XII, PL 40, 448.

181 H. Buchkremer, l.c.

182 l.c., 52-68.

183 A. Mitscherlich, *Die Unfähigkeit zu trauern*, München, 1962, 164.

184 Ph. Lersch, *Aufbau der Person*, München, 1962⁸, 192.

185 H. Buchkremer, l.c., 94; cf. D. Riesmann, *Die einsame Masse*, Berlin, 1956, 59.

186 F.W. Foerster, *Die Aufgaben der Erziehung*, Freiburg, 1959, 3.

187 Buchkremer, l.c., 110; A. Gehlen, *Urmensch und Spätkultur*, Frankfurt, 1964², 67.

188 Buchkremer, l.c., 84.

189 Cf. O. Willmann, *Didaktik*, Freiburg-Wien, 1957⁶, 309; Buchkremer, l.c., 114.

190 Buchkremer, l.c., 126: The author has very critical and pertinent remarks about ambition in priestly career and in certain traditions of religious orders (l.c., 70ff, 95ff).

191 Cf. St. Alphonsus, *Theologia moralis*, Lib. III, n. 966.

Chapter Two

A Morality of Beauty and Glory

In the previous chapter we have seen the indissoluble unity of truth and fidelity. The hunger and thirst for truth paves the way to fidelity; and fidelity, where it is at its best, opens ever new horizons of truth. We saw, too, that self-respect and the honour we offer to others and receive from others have their stability and beauty from truth and fidelity.

In this chapter we turn our attention to the dimension of beauty reflecting God's glory. We consider beauty in its broadest sense as the splendour of truth and goodness. Apart from it, truth and goodness cannot be known in all their bliss and majesty.

The dimensions we explore here have no place in a moral theology written only for confessors and controllers. But in a moral theology based on the Bible and understood in a perspective of creative liberty and fidelity, we cannot ignore the dimensions of beauty. We shall see that a morality under the law of grace is by its very nature a morality of beauty and creativity. We consider beauty first as divine revelation, as an ever-present quality of being (I). Then we try to understand the Christian's relation to art and to the artist, the significance of artistic creativity for a morality of creative freedom and fidelity (II). A morality of the beatitudes under the law of grace has to give attention also to feast and celebration (III), to play and dance (IV), and finally to the role of the sense of humour (V).

I. BEAUTY AS A DIMENSION OF GOD'S REVELATION

1. *The mystery that binds and liberates*

To dismiss the beautiful as something superfluous is to make life miserable, mean, barren. For a Christian who knows and adores God's glory and majesty, disparagement of the beautiful is betrayal of the Spirit, for beauty is a splendour of the true and the good.[1] In it man senses the attractive power of all that is good and true. One who, in all his being, knows truth and knows goodness is already caught by the love of the beautiful.

Beauty does not unfold itself to cold reasoning or to calculations of utility; it communicates its reality only through loving contemplation. Its radiance fills us with delight and lifts our spirits. The believer regards it as reflection of the Spirit in whom the human mind and heart repose, a blessed repose in truth and goodness beyond every purposiveness.

We do not know how angels might grasp the beautiful, but we do know that the human person experiences it most vitally and vividly in the totality of his or her being. Visible, audible, embodied beauty is in perfect harmony with the nature of the human person. The divine Artist expresses his message in sound, colour, figure. He shares the knowledge of the true and the good in such a way that their splendour speaks to the human heart and spirit, filling them with rapture.

We do not experience beauty as an addition to truth and goodness. The beautiful is as extensive as being. "The true and the good — being — is beautiful, that is, joy and bliss of spirit".[2] As the true and the good, so also the beautiful is a basis for fellowship and community of heart and mind. The new heaven and the new earth which we are expecting is the community in truth, in goodness, in love and joy, basking in God's beauty. The human community, insofar as it is on the way to the blessed community of love, cannot dispense with the beautiful and its gentle power to unite people in true and loving fellowship.

To the community of believers, "the beautiful" means far more than to those who lack knowledge of divine revelation.

Indeed, the Christian knows the name of the highest beauty. "Beauty", says Thomas Aquinas, "is one of the divine names".[3] God is the fullness and source of all beauty, beatifying light, undimmed splendour. "God is light, and in him is no darkness" (1 Jn 1:5). He is "the Father of glory" (Eph 1:17).

Created things are beautiful, for he who reveals himself in his works is all-beautiful. And beyond all external manifestation in creation and redemption, there is the divine glory, the splendour, the reflection of the triune life and love of God. From all eternity the Father communicates his glory with his Son who, as "the brightness of his glory and the image of his substance" (Heb 1:3) is called Beauty. The name is appropriate for the incarnate Son, the visible image of the Creator of all beauty. Acquiescing to St Augustine's thought, Thomas Aquinas again speaks of the eternal Word, the image of the Father: "Beauty has a likeness to that which is light and splendour of intellect. Augustine stresses this when he says, 'as the perfect Word who lacks nothing, being as it were the masterpiece of art of the omnipotent God ...' ".[4]

In the Creed we praise the only begotten Son of the Father as "light from light". We praise his glory, his beauty, as coming from the Father. In the Paschal Mystery this glory shines forth in the Word incarnate. "And now, Father, glorify me in thine own presence with the glory which I had with thee before the world began" (Jn 17:5).

All the created beauty and the glory of salvation history come from the mystery of the triune God and turn our eyes and our hearts to it. The primordial source of all beauty and all honour in heaven and on earth is the glory which God possesses in his own intimate life. In his eternal Word the Father communicates all his love, his truth, his glory to the Son. In his Son he sees reflected his own infinite beauty and majesty. And the Son, with equal love, communicates himself entirely to the Father in the love-glow of the Holy Spirit. The Holy Spirit, self-giving love, is the Spirit of glory. From all eternity, before the seraphim chanted their "Holy, holy, holy", God in his intimate triune life and love celebrates the holy Word and response of glory. The Father honours the Son, reflection of his splendour; the Son honours the Father in the Holy Spirit. Father and Son glorify the Spirit of love.

Since the triune love of God is fullness of being and beauty itself, where there is life in mutual love there is mutual honour, beauty, the splendour of truth and love. The contemplation of the eternal beauty of God stirred Augustine to exclaim in ecstasy, "How beautiful is everything, since you have made it, but how ineffably more beautiful are you, the Creator of all this".[5]

Uncreated beauty becomes fully visible in human form in the Word incarnate. "We saw his glory, such glory as befits the Father's only Son, full of grace and truth" (Jn 1:14). This goes far beyond the cloud of light which the people of the Old Testament saw over the Ark of the Covenant in the temple. The greatest beauty is that which shines forth in the countenance of Jesus Christ. Eternal beauty has become man. "It was there from the beginning; we have heard it; we have seen it with our own eyes; we looked upon it and felt it with our own hands; and it is of this we tell" (1 Jn 1:1).

Here again we are faced with the contrast harmony of concealment and unconcealment. The life of Jesus, and especially the Paschal Mystery, speaks also of the hiddenness of the divine glory. Only those who follow the lowliness, the *kenosis* of the Son of God will see his glory and share in it. "Let your bearing towards one another arise out of your life in Christ Jesus. For the divine nature was his from the first; yet he did not prize his equality with God, but made himself nothing, assuming the nature of a slave. Bearing the human likeness, revealed in human shape, he humbled himself and, in obedience, accepted death — death on a cross. Therefore God raised him to the heights" (Phil 2:5-10).

A morality of beauty and glory does not overlook the fulfilment of the prophecy: "He had no beauty, no majesty to draw our eyes, no grace to make us delight in him; his form disfigured, lost all the likeness of a man, his beauty changed beyond human semblance" (Is 53:2). He whose name is Beauty took upon himself our misery. For such was the consequence of sin that man no longer possessed the glory, the beauty and the right to honour which God had originally designed for him. Hence he who is the brightness of the Father's glory humbled himself to the ignominy of the cross in order to restore grace to all, and to grant a share in the Father's glory to all those who confess him as the Lord, "to the glory of God the Father" (Phil 2:11).

We cannot separate beauty and honour from its source, the divine glory. Only by joining Christ in the glorification of the Father can we live in the truth and rejoice in its glory. This work of glorification, so significant in salvation history, is effective in and through the Holy Spirit who is self-giving love. Jesus Christ, receiving everything from the Father and returning it to him in unlimited love, becomes for us the source of the living water, of the Spirit. The Spirit of truth whom he sends to those who follow him on the road of humility is "the Spirit of glory" (1 Pet 4:14).

The divine refulgence, radiating from the humanity of the risen Lord in his full glory, is the prerequisite and source of the transfiguration that gives the saints, the "just", a share in God's splendour in a glorious resurrection. The Christian expects not merely bliss of soul. He looks forward hopefully to the resurrection of his body in glory, in participation with the reflective splendour of Christ's own beauty. Therefore he not only reveres his own bodily reality as "a shrine of the indwelling Holy Spirit" but also understands the command "... then glorify God in your body" (1 Cor 6:20).

We honour Christ as "the light of the world" (Jn 8:12), as "the image of the invisible God" (Col 1:15), as "the bright morning star" (Rev 22:16). Giving to him, and with him to the Father, all glory in the Holy Spirit, we come to understand the good news that we, too, are light, "a light for the world". Those who serve the Lord in purity of heart understand their great vocation and mission, "And you, like the lamp, must shed light among your fellows, so that when they see the good you do, they may give praise to your Father in heaven" (Mt 5:16).

Our mission in the world and our final hope are presented in terms of beauty and glory. Until his glorious coming, Christ bestows the Spirit of truth, the Spirit of love, upon his disciples to make them sharers of his beauty and glory. He does the same for his Church, "so that he might present her to himself all-glorious, with no stain or wrinkle or anything of the sort, but holy and without blemish" (Eph 5:27).

The community of those who are totally consecrated to the glory of the Father will be glorious at the coming of the Lord, more so than any "bride adorned for her husband" (Rev 21:2). The Seer of Patmos rejoiced when the Lord showed him the holy city of Jerusalem "coming down out of heaven from God. It had the radiance of some priceless jewel, like jasper, clear as crystal" (Rev 21:11). "And the city had no need of sun or moon to shine upon it; for the glory of God gave it light, and its lamp was the Lamb... By its light shall the nations walk, and the kings of the earth shall bring into it all their splendour" (Rev 21:23-24). All the good done during history will enter into the full beauty of God's glory.

"The righteous will shine as brightly as the sun in the kingdom of their Father" (Mt 13:43), for they have renounced idolatry of created beauty and human honour, all falsity and self-exaltation, through union with Christ in his suffering and joy in his glory. "Alleluia! The Lord our God, sovereign over all, has entered on his reign! Exult and shout for joy and do him homage, for the wedding-day of the Lamb has come! His bride has made herself ready, and for her dress she has been given fine linen, clean and shining" (Rev 19:6-8).

One of the basic symbols of Christian faith and life is the woman "robed with the sun, beneath her feet the moon, and on her head a crown of twelve stars" (Rev 12:1). It is Mary, the mother of the Lord, the most beautiful of women, and the Church insofar as she joins Mary in the discipleship of Christ the Servant.

Some ask, "May the Christian love beauty?" But how is it possible not to love it, since beauty is surely the Christian's home, his hope! The whole life of the believers is turned to "the glory of God revealed in the face of Jesus Christ" (2 Cor 4:6), "until they will be taken up into his eternal glory".

For those who have contemplated God in the Word incarnate, and made the glorification of the Father their life's main purpose, Christ's high priestly prayer will be fulfilled: "The glory which thou gavest me I have given to them, that they may be one as we are one..., so that they may look upon my glory which thou hast given me because thou didst love me before the world began" (Jn 17:22-24).

God's own beauty is itself the primordial source of our joy, our strength, our love and our fellowship with all of his children.[6]

It will be our eternal bliss in the praise of God, the reflection of his truth and love in our final absorption in the very glory of his truth and love.

2. *Moral-psychological relevance of the beautiful*

Gratitude for beauty and openness to its message are of utmost importance in a sacramental vision of Christian life. Ralph Waldo Emerson warns, "Never lose an opportunity of seeing anything that is beautiful. For beauty is God's handwriting — a quasi-sacrament". The New Testament writers have chosen the word *charis*, which means the charm of beauty, to blend the message of God's grace and graciousness.[7]

For each person, the experience of the beautiful opens the way, in a singular and inescapable manner, to value-experience, to the good as a gracious gift, the good and the truth in their own attractive splendour. In the right encounter with the beautiful, we transcend the realm of profit or utility. We also leave behind a morality that speaks with an unattractive "must". Those who know beauty will never choose a morals of "must", detached from value. Rather, in wonderment, gratitude and joy, they sense the beautiful in all its delicacy and refinement, and soon discover that the beauty in nature and art opens new vistas to the stream of beauty that waters the earth through the moral sensibilities of its people.[8]

The graced nature of moral value will never be captured by anyone who cannot repose and rejoice before all the beauty that God has communicated to us. One might object that the experience of the beautiful has nothing to do with morality, since the value response to beauty re-echoes spontaneously, and as soon as one approaches it too purposefully and with imperatives, he is not on the right wave-length. Besides, it could be said that while morality cannot be severed from the majestic call to commitment, the beautiful grants and requests nothing else than delight.

To this objection we say that the focus is too much on naked duty and does not take seriously enough the sphere of the beautiful. It also tends to deprive the good of its attractive power and of its giftedness which generate gratitude, the very energy-source of a morality under the law of grace. While we can admire a person who does the good even though it might cost him great pain, we cannot at all appreciate a morality based on emotional starvation. Christ proclaims Gospel morality of graciousness and blessedness, and he promises his disciples his peace and the art of rejoicing even in the midst of difficulties.

The morality of beauty is something much deeper than that of "must" and "ought". Its experience is inescapably personal, a loving and grateful approach to life itself. The fullness of being is experienced as a beautifying gift, an attractive appeal that solicits a loving response. Anyone who allows the beautiful, in all its dimensions, to bring its message home, knows that life is meaningful, a wonderful gift and opportunity. Who, for instance, can be moved by the majestic beauty of the works of Mozart, Beethoven and Bach, and not experience wholeness, and not trust that life is worthwhile? The fragrance and beauty of a single flower, absorbed in gratitude, brings us closer to the giver of all good gifts.

A morality totally imprisoned in the question, "What have I to do?" ignores the moral implications of our response to the beautiful. But as soon as our basic moral question is, "What kind of person am I meant to be?" a new vista opens. Then we know the relevance of the beautiful for all of our lives. It will be a dimension in all our responsibilities, in our care for a healthy environment and for beautiful relationships with others.

Because beauty is simply and wholly a gift, our relation to it is unrestrained. But the very gratitude that makes us able to rejoice in it will motivate us to cultivate the beautiful in our lives. It needs space and time in the ordering of our life, not merely alongside other dimensions but as a formative force of all the facets of existence.

The genuine experience of the beautiful is holistic; it brings our whole being into contact with the all-embracing reality. The transcendental qualities of being — the good, the true and the beautiful — are inseparable; therefore, to neglect one of them has disastrous consequences for the others.[9] Take their splendour away from the good and the true, and you have condemned them to concealment. Make aesthetics a thoroughly separate sphere, and you destroy art itself. Block the access through the beautiful and you impoverish the good and the true.[10] Take beauty away, for example, from the life and spirituality of St

Francis of Assisi, and you can no longer understand him or rejoice with him.

Once we have understood that beauty is as much a tran-scendental dimension as oneness, truth and goodness, then we will see it clearly in God and all his works, in creation, in history, in the incarnation of the divine Word. Then it will be easier to overcome the split between the sphere of love and that of knowledge, "through the contemplation of the Divine Beauty where the Spirit of Truth is the shining splendour of the Divine Beauty".[11]

If, in education and theology, the value of the beautiful is neglected, nothing is left finally but the moral of despots or of hucksters, a purposive reckoning of man-the-maker who, like a beast of burden, no longer knows how to be an artist and to rejoice while he is producing and consuming things. Alienation from the beautiful among moralists and educators has made of biblical morality, with its gratitude, joy and wholeness, a fretful groaning under incomprehensive imperatives, laws and controls, a chilling encounter with duties, or a petty computation of merits for the other world. A morality that has no concern for the beautiful knows nothing of the blessedness that dwells within the good, which is the voice of the all-holy God.

3. Admiration and adoration

a) Freedom in adoration

For St Augustine, beauty is the voice by which all of creation praises God.[12] Only through praise and thanksgiving, he says, does man see "with the eye of the heart" the beauty that radiates from God's glory.[13]

Having lost the synthesis of patristic and medieval theology, Christians today turn their attention to what is most central, the glory of God (*doxa*) as presented in holy Scripture.[14] This entails the readiness "to become responsible guardians of the glory of God in his creation".[15] God is glorious in his beauty, in his word and work, in his gladdening news, in his grace and in his law. Therefore, his chosen ones know that they are destined "to be accepted as God's sons through Jesus Christ, in order that the glory of his gracious gift, so graciously bestowed on us in his beloved, might redound to his praise" (Eph 1:6). This is also the main purpose and message of the first draft of St Francis' rule. With all creation, Francis praises the love of God, his goodness and his beauty.[16] For him "Sister Poverty" becomes beautiful because she allows the redeemed to experience the gift character and beauty of all reality.

b) Beauty and praise of God in creation

Since creation is essentially an undeserved gift, a sign of God's graciousness, its beauty can be experienced only by those who applaud God in his works. Beauty is an essential predication of creation and redemption, since everything arises from God's superabundant love and might.[17] All that God creates and does re-echoes his own beatitude; and his people can share and rejoice in his glory by praise and thanksgiving. Knowing that we are created by God's infinite love and freedom, our gratitude and unceasing admiration allow us to discover and receive beauty everywhere.[18]

A person who is alienated from God is terrified by the forces of nature. He feels lost in the vastness of the universe or oppressed by its might. Or he may be overwhelmed by an impersonal pantheistic feeling of oneness in the midst of an ambiguous reality. He may offer an idolatrous cult to the majesty and beauty of things despite threatening experiences, or he may be turned, with hostile manichean distrust, against the splendour of material creation, seeing in it only a demoniac power that draws men away from the contemplation of pure ideas.

How different the view of the Christian who stands in reverential awe of creation! For him it is the handiwork of the Father, God's own enlightening word, the word of his bounty addressed lovingly to those whom he has made in his own image and likeness. The very first pages of sacred Scripture teach us that all that God has created is very good and very beautiful. Certainly the world was created for mankind in order that, harkening to its message, all might be filled with admiration and make use of it in a spirit of adoration.

But through man's guilt, and contrary to its abiding inner meaning, creation "was made the victim of frustration, not by its own choice but because of him who made it so, yet always with the hope that the universe itself is to be freed from the shackles of corruption and enter upon the liberty and splendour of the children of God. Up to the present, we know, the whole created universe groans in all its parts as if in the pangs of childbirth" (Rom 8:19-23).

God's most splendid and beautiful creation is humanity; men and women made to his image and likeness. And although sin has distorted and diminished this beauty, it has never been destroyed. Indeed, God has more wonderfully restored it in redemption. Those who praise God for this gift rejoice again in the splendour of the children of God and in a blessed freedom that should have its blissful consequences on man's milieu. Whereas the unbeliever is oppressed by the silence of creation,[19] the believer exults as, in faith and love, he understands the words of the psalms: "The heavens tell out the glory of God, the vault of heaven reveals his handiwork. One day speaks to another, night with night shares its knowledge, and this without speech or language. Their music goes out through all the earth, their words reach to the end of the world" (Ps 19:1-4).

The book of nature, in its tremendous beauty and its unfathomable majesty, is a mighty directive to the praise of God's wisdom. Only the fool does not understand this voice (cf. Job 38-42). The Christian knows how Jesus Christ rejoiced about the wonderful message of creation. To him, all its beauty speaks of the Father's goodness and care. It is the beauty of gift, the sign of God's love. All this enters into the message of the Sermon on the Mount. "Look at the birds of the air; they do not sow or reap or store in barns, yet your heavenly Father feeds them. Consider how the lilies grow in the fields; they do not work, they do not spin; and yet I tell you, even Solomon in all his splendour was not attired like one of these" (Mt 6:26-29).

The beauty of creation also occupies a place in the liturgy. It cannot be otherwise, since all this is a message and a gift brought to us through the Word of the Father. All points to Christ: "In him everything in heaven and on earth was created, things visible and invisible... The whole universe has been created through him and for him... Through him God chose to reconcile the whole universe to himself" (Col 1:16-20).

Hence it is necessary that all things be caught up in the worship which the Son renders to the heavenly Father in and through the Church. The psalms, which are adoration of the Creator, filled with loving wonderment, have formed the basis of Lauds, the Church's morning prayer, from the earliest times. They continue to resound in the Eucharistic celebration through whose transmuting power the precious gifts of the earth, bread and wine, water and oil, are taken up into the divine worship.

Anyone who does not sense the majesty of the Spirit's hovering over creation, who does not joyfully praise God when he beholds it in all its grandeur, lacks something of the basic preparation needed for the celebration of the Eucharist, and will not learn from it how to glorify God in his relation to all created things.

It is God's will that we should bring everything into explicit worship so that, from there, we have the criteria for worshipping God in our daily life, in our relationships with each other, and in the way we are shaping the world around us.

Biblical piety, poetry, feasts and celebrations praised, above all, the majesty and splendour made visible in salvation history, reflecting the power, the wisdom, love and patience of God. Many psalms, especially the great "Hallel" psalms, extolled in awe and wonder the splendid deeds of Yahweh before the fore-fathers and the chosen people of God. Since the most ancient times, these psalms have formed the basis of Vespers, the Church's evensong.

Salvation history centres on Jesus Christ, the Redeemer. His epiphany, the refulgence of his splendour in the work of salvation, imparts to Christian piety the perfect synthesis of all of life in the praise of God who reveals his majesty in all his deeds.

The glory of the risen Lord, the blissful rapture of the angels and saints in the celestial liturgy, is open here on earth only to the eyes of faith. The symbols and beauty of the liturgy should give to believers a foretaste of the heavenly liturgy. The liturgical celebrations open the eyes and hearts of all the faithful to the attractive signs that point to the highest mysteries. This is what Leo the Great expressed when he said that "the radiant visibility of Christ has been given over to the sacraments".[20]

The beauty of the liturgy, especially in the sacramental actions and signs, should speak not only to our reason but also to our hearts and minds of the Lord's joyous assurance that God continues in his faithful history with humankind. In the sacramental signs, God remains the hidden God but at the same time also the revealer of his bounties. The humble ones, those who know how to admire and adore, and who know intuitively the sign-values of all things and events, will frequently be touched by the sacramental experience. Carried away by holy ecstasy, the hearts of humble, loving people sing with Jesus, "I thank thee, Father, Lord of heaven and earth, for hiding these things from the learned and wise, and revealing them to the simple. Yes, Father, I thank thee that such was thy choice" (Lk 10:21).

The liturgy is designed to open us to the experience of God's wonderful way of acting with us. Salvation history, including our hope for the things to come, is present to our senses and to our intuition in an impressive unity of words and signs that call to mind the cooperation of man with the Divine Artist. This is further symbolized through the gifts from the bounty of the earth and of man, present in our celebration. Beauty is entrusted to us as co-workers, as co-artists.

4.   *A morality of beauty and glory*

I have already referred repeatedly to Hans Urs von Balthasar's five-volume theology in the perspective of glory. Etienne Souriau offers a similar contribution to moral theology in a perspective of ethics.[21] He shows convincingly how a creative ethics or moral theology might follow, as leitmotif, beauty in its fully human meaning. A point of departure is the fact that moral maturity, gentleness, generosity, magnanimity cannot be ignored if we want to understand the whole realm and full dimensions of beauty.

Surely morality is not just beauty, for it is more than that, and it cannot be confined to the narrow borders of an aesthetics. But if we see beauty in the theological dimension of the glory of God (*doxa*), then it is clear that morality expresses it in the highest degree. It is then a morality to the glory of God, the morality of a beauty that reflects God's own glory and looks forward to the glorification of man's total being in the light of the risen Lord.

A morality of beauty honours God as the Supreme Artist and praises him for calling us, his people, to be co-artists. God's design is to create us in his image and likeness and to complete man's vocation by making him his masterpiece. But he will not do this without the human person in a wonderful interplay, an inter-subjectivity with Christ, the Divine Master. His disciples are allowed to develop their own creativity not only in shaping the world but even more in working, together with Christ, so that they themselves and their brothers and sisters may recognize ever more clearly the divine design and their own capacities to be co-artists.

As Christians, we believe that we are called to holiness and that, from the life of Christ and his disciples, from the gifts God has bestowed on us, and from the needs of others, we can intuit the ideal image which lays before us as a normative value. It is the beauty of this ideal and its relation to God's glory that can raise us to the highest form of creative liberty and fidelity.

Jürgen Moltmann presents a vision of morality and religion in the light of play and feast. Whoever can celebrate the feast and play realizes that our relationship with God is not on the level of needs and consumption, and that a morality of "merits" has not the beauty that reflects his glories. If one looks first for usefulness and reward, he is still in an alien land where he cannot play and sing the songs of Zion. Neither can a Christian live his life as play and dance untouched by compassion for those who are suffering, or by being unmoved by their needs.

Yet to be strong in our liberating commitment, we must first be freed from that kind of religion that sees God as a gap-filler, useful only for discipline and order. We must free ourselves radically from all use of religion for alien goals and from all guilt complexes that arise from a morality of naked duty. Moltmann tells us that once a student asked him, "Is there, in your theology of hope, no place for joy?" And after a time of reflection, he found it most meaningful. "The more I laboured for the perspective of the political practice of Christian hope, the more I had the impression of discovering, as the other pole, the dimensions of rejoicing without purposive duties, abandoning oneself to play and joy in view of the beatitude of grace".[22]

There is a time for rejoicing and a time for action. But if there is no place for rejoicing and no everpresent dimension of joy and beauty, there will be an energy crisis in the outflow of proper action. The Protestant author, Gerhard Nebel, in his strong book, *The Event of the Beautiful*, writes, "Whoever is in love with the beautiful will, like Winkelmann, freeze in the barn of the reformation".[23] And, of course, we Catholics can say the same about the cold barn of a legalistic morality which we are trying to overcome. It is not sufficient to give attention to the beauty of liturgy while neglecting the beauty of the moral message and moral life. When beauty is a symbol of Christian morality, considered in the light of the divine glory, then we can easily integrate the insights of Aristotle for whom the *mesotes* — the good pace and measurement — is an essential moral quality.[24]

The dimension of praise and thanksgiving which has been emphasized throughout this work will not be fully human and vital without adoration inspired by the love of the beautiful, just as the beautiful alone remains ambiguous until it enters into the dimensions of God's glory and our response by praise and thanksgiving.

The beautiful is, however, not only a vital dimension of morality; it also has to play a special role in some areas where we would least expect it. E.F. Schumacher, in a ground-breaking work on economics, entitled, *Small is Beautiful,*[25] gives us an impressive vision of how economics and politics are destined to catastrophe unless they reconsider simplicity as a way to discover beauty. He tells of the beautiful in an economics that is totally geared to people's dignity and full humanity. We are reminded of the great lover of Sister Poverty, St Francis, who in his time was a counterforce against the early rise of capitalism.

Today, too, to sharpen our sense of responsibility and increase our capacities in ecology, we need people who can sing and rejoice in the beautiful. The depletion of the human environment by capitalistic and socialistic economists can be explained only by the general neglect of beauty in our age.

Schumacher speaks of our being "bound by truth". "Only in the service of truth is there perfect freedom, and even those who today ask us to free our imagination from bondage to the existing system fail to point the way to the recognition of truth".[26] And it is he, as a great economist and humanist, who points to the important dimension of beauty, the splendour of truth.

II. ART AND THE ARTIST

God did not create us to be mere observers of his works, prying into their secrets and marvelling at their grandeur. He has created us in his own image and likeness, and that means among other things that he created us to be co-creators and co-artists. There is already a sign of this in the very fact that we can discover the beauty and the meaning of God's design. But God has also entrusted to us nature and the world around us, to humanize it ever more, to transform it creatively so that truth and goodness can speak more to our hearts and the hearts of our fellowmen. In all that each of us does, we are to perfect ourselves as God's image and imprint in all that we touch something of his beauty.

Jesus himself chose to exercise a craft and thereby sanctify human labour for all times. Though the craft was modest indeed, we cannot but imagine that Jesus' work was beautiful. If we try to narrow the definition of art, we set it apart and impoverish other activities. "The division between fine arts and handicraft, despite its relevance in other respects, is not what logicians would call an 'essential division'. It is based on the purpose that art, in its other sense as fine art and useful art, can combine the double role, that of beauty and that of service. Such is the case especially in architecture".[27]

The sacred pages offer us striking examples about architecture in the Tabernacle of Yahweh and the temple in Jerusalem. In these centres of divine cult, there was a great display of all types of crafts and fine arts. The Lord himself endowed both the artists and artisans with the wisdom to further his glory and praise, and the joy of his people. The Lord spoke to Moses and said, "Mark this, I have especially chosen Bezalel, son of Uri, son of Hur, of the tribe of Judah. I have filled him with divine spirit, making him skilful and ingenious, expert in every craft and master of design, whether in gold, silver, copper or cutting stones to be set, or carving wood, for workmanship of every kind" (Ex 31:1-5; cf. Ex 35:10ff).

But how can we explain that not only geniuses like Plato and Rousseau but also outstanding religious men like Martin Luther and even such an ardent saint as Bernard of Clairvaux who felt that he had learned more from the beauty of nature than from books were vehement in their criticism of art and artists? And would not some strict moralists have agreed with André Gide, who maintains that "Every work of art presupposes cooperation with the devil?"[28]

To understand the conflicting, or apparently conflicting, statements of important men in this area, we first must inquire into the essential relation between art and morality (1). Next we look to the situation in which the artist is involved and which affects his relationship to his message, his mental attitudes and his public (2). Religious art in the service of the Church makes additional demands, and merits special treatment (3). Consideration must also be given to the lofty art of communicating the salvation message by appropriate symbols and our openness to them (4). And finally, we ask ourselves about the relevance of art for creative liberty and fidelity (5).

1. Art and morals

We agree emphatically with Maritain's denunciation of Gide's view: "It is manichaean blasphemy to maintain with André Gide that the devil has his imprints in every work of art. To think this is utterly absurd, for the evil one is not creative".[29]

The Christian point of view is well expressed by Pius XII: "One of the essential characteristics of art consists in a certain intrinsic affinity of art with religion, which in certain ways renders artists interpreters of the infinite perfections of God, and particularly of the beauty and harmony of God's creation. The function of all art lies, in fact, in breaking the narrow and tortuous enclosure of the finite in which man is immersed while living here below, and in providing a window on the infinite for his thirsting soul. Persons ennobled, elevated and prepared by art are thus better disposed to religious truths and the grace of Jesus Christ".[30]

Jacques Maritain has a beautiful evaluation, appreciated by many others: "We may say that art plays the same role in natural life which the 'sensible graces' play in the spiritual life. And in some way, even though it be very remotely and not consciously, it prepares the human race for contemplation".[31]

Great theologians compare the charism of the artist with that of the prophet. Karl Barth is convinced that great artists like Mozart knew more about the beauty and goodness of creation in its totality than many great Church Fathers and reformers, and much more than orthodox and liberal theologians with all their natural theology and their armour of word from the Scriptures. He gratefully extols Mozart for sharing his deep knowledge and magnificent vision with so many people.[32]

The artist's creativity arises from the longing for that perfect existence that cannot be found here below but which man, in spite of all illusions, is convinced must be.[33]

Emmanuel Kant has said many beautiful things about art, including the art of gardening.[34] But his interest seems too directly geared to moral teaching, and therefore he gives preference to beauty in nature as compared with art. He argues that "beauty in nature has an affinity with morality". One may not be convinced, but nevertheless he gives the illumining argument that beauty serves no other purpose than itself, and so brings home to man that the person is a goal in himself and may never be used as a means for purposes.[35]

Regarding the beauty of art, Kant is one-sidedly interested in the artist as a kind of moral preacher and communicator of clear ideas. Against Kant, Moltmann reasserts "the value of aesthetic joy against the absolute claims of ethics".[36]

We may now ask ourselves, "Do we accept the well-known slogan, 'art for art's sake' "? Regarding artistic production, our first query can not and may not be, "what profit do I derive from it?" Art has a value in itself, the value of the beautiful, which is loftier than the value of utility. Art wants to be loved for itself, and whoever views it merely as a means to another end has a narrow and false concept not only of the beautiful and of art but also of life itself. To subscribe to such a view is to risk losing oneself even in the religious sphere which would degenerate ultimately into a refined form of pragmatism.[37]

There can be a right understanding of the slogan, "art for art's sake", if it is art in the full sense, the beautiful communication of the splendour of truth and the good. But if the principle is understood as absolute separation of the spheres of values and the spheres of life, then it is a sad indication of "abandonment of means".[38]

All our basic reflections have this in mind: to show that the beautiful has majesty, dignity, loveableness in itself, insofar as and because it is an essential expression of being, of truth, of goodness, in the fullness of unity.

A true artist has a profound knowledge of wholeness, and he would betray his own vocation and his knowledge of the beautiful if he were to try to cultivate it through depreciation of the values of wholeness, goodness and truth. To violate or even to neglect the moral order and truth for the sake of exalting the autonomy of art is not only arrogant pride but the very alienation of art. Moral perversion cannot claim aesthetic originality, but by the same token, a pious or moral motive, the desire to edify or to serve the moral order, is no substitute for artistic inspiration or true dedication to the beautiful. "A work becomes beautiful neither by being edifying nor by being shameless ... There is laboured mediocrity of style both in edifying literature and in pornography".[39]

The artist produces a true work of art only if he is at home with the beautiful, as such. And it is precisely in the beautiful that he encounters the true and the good, the vision of wholeness, and unity in diversity. The artistic approach to the good and to truth is a genuinely human and even privileged one. True believers and true artists have a capacity to look beyond themselves and to reach out for the all-embracing reality.[40]

If we think of a moralist as one who inculcates his prohibitions and warnings, then we simply must say that a true artist can never be a moralist. But if we think of a moral teacher who is enchanted by the good and can enchant others, then he too is an artist. The artist, as artist, is a person of deep intuition. Often he sees the signs of the times before the theologian, and he can present truth in a more adaptive way than the abstract philosopher. Art can be a more original approach to holiness and goodness than a reflexive treatise on ethics, good as it may be. Above all, it is more enriching than an analytic treatise presented in difficult language. When reading Thomas Aquinas, I am grateful for his wonderful insights but sometimes I tire and my energies are drained. But if I hear the masterworks of Bach or Mozart, I am refreshed and feel closer to the world of truth and goodness because beauty opens the horizons.[41]

To enrich us and make us more open to the good, the

Christian artist who is both genius and true believer does not need a moralistic intention or a purposefully religious vein. He always acts as a whole person and as one who is at home in the world of salvation truth. He reaches it through the beautiful, bringing a message of wholeness and fascinating truth. The human message of beauty in art is liberating because it is the splendour of the good and the true. Thus, precisely because it is encompassed within the good, the world of art has its own autonomy.

2. The human conditions

The message of the prophets of Israel frequently reaches awe-inspiring beauty. But it was not of beauty they were speaking. They were seized by the mystery of God and of man. Art is a by-product of these religious geniuses. The artist's intention is immediately directed towards the beautiful; but unless he is seized by the mystery of good, by the mystery of God and of man, his art will be shallow. Philosophers explain that the beautiful is a transcendental, together with the good, truth, and unity and is the splendour of all the other transcendentals in their unity.[42]

This does not exclude, of course, that in the always imperfect realization of human beings, there can be a certain conflict between the perception of the beautiful and the knowledge of good and truth. "Only in God are all these perfections one in their formal sense. He alone *is* Truth, Beauty, Goodness and Unity. In things here below, on the contrary, truth, beauty, goodness are aspects of being which are distinct according to their formal reasons. They command distinct spheres of human activity. Therefore, all efforts to exclude, *a priori*, the possibility of conflicts on the pretext that the transcendentals are indissolubly bound up with one another is doomed to failure".[43] An artist may be a genius in his own field, yet his relation to the good and to truth can be disturbed by passions and/or social conditionings.

On the road to self-actualization as person and artist, the artist must be ready to sacrifice, at least temporarily, secondary values, subordinating them to the supreme and ultimate good. He reaches his freedom to perceive beauty as the splendour of the good and the truth, and the yearning of all things for unity, when he is dedicated to the power of love flowing from God.

The artist and the admirer of art must always respect the hierarchy of values. A clear insight into the more urgent and higher values will always be a challenge for them. The artist does not feel that his freedom as artist is threatened by the need to respect the laws governing the material he uses and their potentialities as medium of artistic communication. Wood carving, for instance, demands different procedures than work with metal. Similarly, the artist working in marble follows a totally different procedure than the stonecutter. His attention focuses entirely on the artistic expression, although he never forgets that he is dealing with marble. Likewise, an artist does not approach his art as a "moralist", yet he is fully conscious of moral values. Just as the sculptor handles the marble with infinitely greater care than the stonecutter, so every true artist has a privileged moral awareness simply as artist.

To the true artist and art lover, a work of art, "to the degree that it is immoral, is unaesthetic".[44] The genuine artist of noble character will sense the violation of moral value more keenly than one who is not an artist. To use immoral means in the production or sale of art would be, to him, nothing less than polluting his work.[45] And any effort to manipulate art in the service of untruth and immorality will outrage his sense of the beautiful as the splendour of goodness and truth. An artist who, in his own inner harmony with the good and true is dedicated to the harmony of all values, is God's masterpiece.

"A work of art that offends God also offends the Christian. And since it can no longer please and delight, it immediately loses for him all claim to beauty".[46] But a true artist will also disdain any form of naked moralism. He cannot imagine good without the radiance of beauty.

Similarly, a Christianity presented with cold legalistic morals is like a frost on our crop; it drives out the true artist. A biblical morality of grace, of the inner riches of spiritual life, a morality of the beatitudes, on the other hand, creates the soil in which Christian art can develop. Of course the genius is always, in a special way, a gift of God. But an authentic Christian artist has as his prelude a true joy in faith, "the power of the spirit of faith" as well as "a comparatively sound and healthy natural endowment, the openness to.being".[47]

The artist communicates a message of wholeness that always has an affinity with salvation. He is, in his own way, a teacher who teaches people's hearts and minds, and he should be aware of it.[48] He has to be aware of those to whom his art speaks. He will ask himself how they interpret his work and therefore will try to know their grammar of assent. He lives in a deep solidarity with people, for only thus can he communicate his knowledge of the mystery of man. Not only does he scrutinize human life but he also knows that he is constantly interrogated.[49] Art can communicate the yearning of creation for the original innocence, but the artist is also sharply aware of the conflicts, the tensions and the temptations of our fallen nature.[50]

Moral theology has to give special attention to motivation and theme in relation to both the artist and the public.

a) Motivation

Art has its own way of enforcing the beatitude, "How blest are those whose hearts are pure; they shall see God" (Mt 5:8). If the heart is not pure, if the basic intention and motives are not proper, disorder will constantly manifest itself in both the artist and his admirers. The pure heart will always see broader horizons and deeper dimensions; therefore it is not only a question of the immediate motive but of the basic intentions that guide all our life.

The artist who has chosen to glorify himself at whatever price, or to give himself to the service of evil, can still be a genius and have a great power of seduction. But his works will be palpably marked as filthy and spurious. "In the last analysis, 'immoral art' is a combination of two words in open contradiction to each other".[51]

No less than the artist, the public can be misguided by evil intentions. In fact, some who visit art galleries on the pretext of love of art or culture are more or less consciously impelled by a vile form of curiosity. The artist, of course, can do little to prevent this, for perverted motivations can profane even the reading of the sacred Scriptures. The public, too, has need of a stern moral caution: purge your hearts in order to approach art worthily.

The guile and bad taste of the public can constitute a great temptation for many artists, especially for those who must provide for their own livelihood day by day. What Pius XII stated thirty years ago is still true: "Unfortunately it is an undeniable fact that certain groups are drawn to indecent presentations and constantly demand still more shameless exhibitions". However, he was fundamentally optimistic: "True and wholesome works of art are accepted today, probably more than in the past, not only by professionals but also by ordinary, unsophisticated people".[52] H.U. von Balthasar is much less optimistic. He thinks that the negative attitude of a great number of Protestant theologians regarding art can be explained by the deep crisis of modern art.[53]

A clear realization of all this points to the need of a dual apostolate in the field of art: one directed towards the artist, including promotion of the authentic artistic vocation among the faithful, and the other to the public, to help everyone realize his chance and obligation in this area.

b) Problems in the choice of theme

No competent artist will dispute the necessity of right intention but it may be more difficult to convince him that a choice of theme must be subordinated to moral criteria. The artist cannot avoid presenting sometimes the problem of evil; he cannot be unrealistic. As holy Scripture does, he can deal with the story of evil by strengthening hope in the final triumph of good. But confronted with the problem of executing the design in his mind, the artist will ask himself whether his powers of achievement are equal to his good intention. The moral disenchantment of evil requires a high art which not all artists can claim. "In fact, even great artists are not always altogether equal to it."[54] The awareness of one's own moral and artistic limitations, humility of spirit, and a sense of responsibility in view of an immature public will impose limitations. The story is told that Michelangelo shattered a statue he had carved in a mythological motif, because despite all his genius, the work failed to measure up to the idea he sought to express.

However, since moralistic narrowness has done great harm in the past, a word of caution is warranted here against hasty judgment in these delicate matters. Only one who is fully conversant with the psychological and sociological data involved is competent to render a judgment and to offer a concrete contribution to the formation of the artist's conscience. What may be acceptable in one culture may not be at all admissible without qualification elsewhere. The more the criteria become concrete, the more we have to take into account the cultural context.

3. Religious art

Today we are more keenly aware of how difficult it is to speak on God. The difficulty can become even greater if our language is expressed by art; yet the artist is especially qualified to convey a religious message. Of itself, the beautiful is open to the experience of God's glory. It comes from him and leads to him. However, it can also enchant the self-centred human being and lead him to an idolatrous cult with beauty separated from its source.[55]

Christian faith is dedication to the personal God who has made his glory visible in Jesus Christ. It is a wonderful achievement if the artist can combine his inner experience of wholeness, of beauty, with a live faith in the personal God.

We understand the prohibition against making an image of God as a warning against all temptations to make an arbitrary image other than that revealed by God. Everyone, and especially the artist, will therefore give first attention to how God has made himself visible and has spoken to man.

It is generally agreed that, historically, art is greatly indebted to religion. It is inspired by the religious sense that has flourished wherever religious experience has been deep and strong. Especially the Christian Churches have been centres of art that have inspired the greatest artists. The Second Vatican Council says, "Very rightly the fine arts are considered to rank among the noblest expressions of human genius. This judgment applies especially to religious art and to its highest achievement, which is sacred art. By their very nature both are related to God's boundless beauty, for this is the reality which these human efforts are trying to express in some way. To the extent that these works aim exclusively at turning man's thoughts to God persuasively, devoutly, they are dedicated to God and to the cause of his greater honour and glory. Therefore, the Church has always been the friend of the fine arts".[56]

The liturgy of the Church has frequently been witness and source of inspired creativity. But since sacred art is an encounter with the Church, it greatly depends on creative liberty in theology and in the whole of the Church's life. Theology and religious art can inspire each other. Sacred art, particularly in the liturgy, is a significant medium in the proclamation of the Good News of salvation. Hence it has to be faithful to the same requirements as *kerygma* and liturgy, but in its own fashion, in the pattern of the beautiful. It is called, above all, to be faithful to the exalted mysteries which it intends to proclaim and glorify. Sacred art, at its noblest, will mirror the condescension of the Word of God as a lowly and humble servant. On the one hand, it will always shun the unauthentic, the superficial and tawdry, for here the contrast of any bad or muddled taste is especially marked.[57] On the other hand, as far as true artistic integrity permits, it must accommodate the tastes and feelings of the people. Of course this implies that very much is demanded of the artists. In every age, religious art tends to make a new encounter with all that is vital and life-giving in the spirit of the times; but in all ages, most of all in our own most dynamic culture, this encounter gives rise, on many levels, to critical problems for sacred art.

There is considerable danger of a rift between artists who are extremely sensitive to the transcendental and attuned to the new potentialities, and a vast number of priests and lay people who have grown used to an art form which at times has been quite pedestrian if not tasteless. Church authorities should be aware of their limited competence in these matters, so that outstanding artists will be given a certain freedom, the right of bold venture that will not betray itself into brashness. Without this measure of artistic freedom, no true progress and no sound conformity with the requirements of the various cultures and of our dynamic age is even conceivable.

The artist has to make every effort to avoid unnecessary scandal of the weak; but because of its affinity with prophecy, art should be a truly bold salvific scandal to all that is stuffy and pharisaical. Sacred art should never settle for mediocrity and thus alienate the efforts of noble minds and great visions.

The Second Vatican Council warns, "Let bishops carefully exclude from the house of God and from other sacred places those works of artists which are repugnant to faith, morals and Christian piety, and which offend true religious sense either by distortion of forms or lack of artistic worth, by mediocrity or pretence".[58]

While the Church objects to the overly far-fetched and unfamiliar, she has good reasons to oppose also what is unfortunately the too common stereotyped mediocrity in Church art, the trashy and sentimental. Pius XI said on this point, "With masters of art and with holy pontiffs, we have already many times expressed the thought that our hope, our ardent desire, our will can only be that such art not be admitted into our churches, while we open wide the portals and tender a sincere welcome to every good and progressive development of the approved and venerable traditions which, in so many centuries of Christian life, in such diversity of circumstances and of social and ethnic conditions, have given stupendous proof of their inexhaustible capacity to inspire new and beautiful forms, as often as they were investigated or studied and cultivated under the twofold light of genius and faith."[59]

The necessary stricture on what is beyond the grasp or tolerance of the faithful does not dispense artists from discharging their role as guides. They will succeed all the more in gradually educating the people to refinement in artistic taste and a genuine religious approach the more they "meet the faithful part way".[60] The ideal is mutual enrichment, a give-and-take between artists and the Christian community.

In sacral art, all is directed to prayer, to the praise of God in all our life. Thus, crowned in splendour by their queen, sacred art, the fine arts attain the height of their perfection.

Sacred art constantly teaches us that the beauty, the goodness and truth of God shine forth in man himself, who is God's own image, far more splendidly than in human works of art. This beauty of God manifests itself in man progressively if, in all his efforts to be really himself, he fixes his attention on God, the source of all beauty, goodness and truth. "Neither pictures nor statues", said Michelangelo in his old age, "can enchant people who are turned to the love of God whose arms are stretched out on the cross to embrace them".[61] But the Christian artist rejoices in bringing home the message of this love also through the works of his art.

4. *Importance of symbols*

Symbol means "something that stands for or suggests something else by reason of relationship, association, convention or accidental resemblance, especially: a visible sign of something invisible".[62]

The great sociologist, George Gurvitch, is convinced that a morality that presents the moral ideal by attractive symbols is a sign of a vital and genuine culture. And after reviewing the various types of morality, he makes the important observation that in the epoch of a morality of ideals in which we are living, symbolic images occupy a privileged place in the moral life.[63]

The Protestant theologian, Langdon Gilkey, being of the same opinion, suggests that for a lively celebration of the sacramental symbols, a fundamental task is to help us to understand the signs of the times and to bring to explicit expression at appropriate times the divine presence in all of life.[64] This is a task in itself, but it should be seen in relation to the liturgical celebration. Therefore we have to ask ourselves about the meaning and role of symbols.

Catholic theology presents Christ, the Word incarnate, as the primordial and most real symbol. He not only makes the Father visible; he is also a sign of the Father's real presence. Christ loved symbolic actions as the prophets of the Old Testament did. All his actions, accompanied by his words, and especially his death and resurrection, participate in his being the primal symbol.

Throughout all centuries, the Church has given the greatest attention to symbols; and we live in an age when psychologists alert us anew about their irreplaceable value for our moral and religious life.[65] Philosophers, liturgists and theologians have done no less in emphasizing the paramount importance of symbolism.[66] And it is especially important in view of the religious mystery and of effective motivation.

The mystery of God and the mystery of man are always infinitely deeper than what abstract concepts can express. We need symbols, symbolic images and symbolic language to point in the direction of the mystery, making us aware of its presence. Of course we also need the help of analytic and conceptual thinking; but where it is a matter of wholeness of vision, this must always be preceded and followed, grounded and crowned by symbols. Symbols address the whole person, spirit and heart, mind and imagination.

We have seen repeatedly how decisive for the formation of the moral person are the all-embracing leitmotif and inspiring attractive motives. Hence, moral discourse can never renounce the use of imaginative and symbolic language.[67]

Human beings communicate not only by words; they are a communication by what they are. This communication becomes a beautiful moral appeal if persons understand themselves as symbols, as image and likeness of God and co-artists with the Divine Artist. If this fundamental symbol is vitally grasped, all our gestures, our conduct, our clothing, our houses, architecture — all will become truthful symbols and more enriching communication.[68]

Von Balthasar said, "I am convinced that in education it is very helpful and even necessary to help people to grasp and understand symbols and to give them a proper place in their whole life".[69] This will also help to understand better and to deepen the experience of faith as the inner freedom to discover God's liberating action in us and in the world around us.

Bishop Klaus Hemmerle gives us an excellent example of how theology can use creatively one basic symbol.[70] He chooses play, and gives the phenomenology of play in all its symbolic richness, thus to help us to see the main truths of our faith insofar as the symbol of play is present and aids our understanding of them.

Each person should be an artist in the use and understanding of symbols. Education should therefore not only use symbols but also encourage and foster imagination, fantasy, creative painting, poetry and so on. However, humanity needs the genius of the great artists who have a special grasp of the symbol, of the archetypes and cultural symbols, and can bring them home to our senses, our imagination and our minds in a holistic experience. The work of art, in its perfection, is a symbolic representation of the fullness of life to which we are all on the way.[71]

The superficial artist who has no grasp of symbols can so load them with details and seductive splendour that they become practically unrecognizable. Just as rationalism and moralism can be the death of religion, so a false aestheticism can extinguish the light of religious and ethical symbols.[72] But it seems to me that philosophers and moralists frequently have done more damage to man's capacity for grasping symbols than artists have done. One can hardly imagine an authentic artist without a profound sense of symbols and symbolism.

5. *"The beautiful" and liberty*

The Divine Artist, in all his creation of beauty, intended that the human artist, in the image of God, would manifest that superabundance of freedom beyond pragmatic purposes.

I hope the reader has given special attention to the gratuitousness of the gift of beauty. In a world where so many, like B.F. Skinner and his followers, reduce man's life to automatic response to the twin masters of pain and pleasure, and as a consequence enforce manipulation by controllers, we can realize that creative freedom — or any freedom — can survive only if we rejoice in the beauty of God's creation and are creative ourselves beyond all utilitarian purposes.

We cannot extol God's grace and live according to its law if we do not appreciate all the gifts of God, particularly beauty and man's eros for beauty as Plato and other great thinkers have sung of it. Eros is the ascent to the heights through the attractive power of the beauty of the true and the good.[73]

I cannot but disagree with Rudolph Bultmann when he writes that "the idea of the beautiful has no vital significance for Christian faith". He sees in the beautiful the "temptation of a false transfiguration of the world that distracts attention from transcendence". For him, art does not disclose Christian faith in the depth of its reality, for this "cannot be grasped in a disinterested appraisal of it, but only in suffering".[74] Of course, we may not ignore the school of suffering in the service of neighbour and the pangs of childbirth in the hope of a better world.

I quote Bultmann because I know how concerned he is about

freedom and fidelity, and I feel that a negative attitude towards art and towards beauty itself, because of a danger in misinterpretation, is no better than if we were to ignore the concept and symbols of love because they, too, can be misinterpreted. Rather, for the sake of creative fidelity, the only way is to see beauty and the lofty vocation and mission of artists in the light of God's glory. Just as we cannot separate the love of God from the love which we experience among people, so we cannot separate our high purpose of glorifying God from all the beauty that praises him.

III. FEAST AND CELEBRATION

What would art in its various forms be without feast and celebration, and what would feast mean without art, without music, poetry, dancing? We speak of "feast" and not just of leisure pastimes that today are so frequently a part of the commercial world.[75]

1. *Phenomenology of feast and celebration*

Feast and celebration have given and still give people an opportunity to rediscover and develop play, fantasy, creativity, and thus make an essential contribution to the formation of persons and communities marked by creative liberty and fidelity.[76] The feasts not only allow the development of imagination and fantasy; they also encourage thoughts about utopias for the future and ask the right questions about our ideals and hopes for the future and our commitment to them.[77]

Christian hope looks forward to the everlasting feast in the new heaven and on the new earth. Feasts create new relationships through which, as Plato says, people experience that they are given to each other as fellow celebrants of the feast.[78]

A presupposition and reason for celebrating feasts is the basic conviction that it is good to live and that we have reason to rejoice together. The special reason for celebrating is that we have received what we are loving. By the feast we affirm, through common celebration, the goodness of being. And thus we discover a new dimension of the true and the good.[79]

It is not irrelevant how one views the relation between everyday work and feasts. One may be so taken up by the workday that he considers the feast only as a necessary relaxation for further work. Others consider the feast and celebration as meaningful only if they have first discovered the meaning of work. The feast bears meaning and message in itself, and thus opens new horizons. The feasts help us to find a deeper meaning in our everyday life, and to master it with greater freedom. This does not exclude that, coming down from the height of celebration, we may feel even more keenly the conflicts of life. But this, too, can be good, a challenge not only to celebrate feasts together but also to join hands to make our life more human and dignified.

The feast and dedication to culture assure a privileged space of freedom given by God to man who is burdened by sin and labour.[80]

Not without a certain degree of contemplation does the feast reach the human depth that gives a profound insight into the reasons for celebration. Like art, it addresses the whole person, body and spirit. The humanness of the feast allows laughter, wit, sense of humour, even exuberant manifestations of joy. As Harvey Cox notes, we can even break out in laughter about human foolishness.[81] One may have doubts about the genuine character of a feast like the annual Oktoberfest of Munich, when beer is at its very centre; but whoever knows the biblical language and human tradition cannot object to rejoicing in a festive meal with a good drink, as at the wedding party in Cana.[82]

A serious question, however, is how we can celebrate feasts in full awareness of the suffering and evil in the world.[83] The tradition of Israel and of the Church proves that the feast in no way denies or forgets the evil, but it shows confidence that the good will finally celebrate its victory. The celebrations in which we anticipate the final victory are not flights from the stress of life, but they can well be a source of trust and strength for facing life's troubles and withstanding evil. "The true witness to God, and the true expression of real possibilities both of joy and glory, will be found among those who can sing in exile, rejoice in struggle, and glimpse glory in hope as yet frustrated, because they have discovered, usually through one another, that the infinite distance of God is the measure of the power of his presence, and that the suffering of God is the measure of the power of his untroubled and invincible love".[84]

Only the ones who suffer with those in misery can rejoice together. As Christians, we celebrate the Easter feast with joy and thanksgiving for our liberation, and in deep solidarity with those still in the bondage of pain and sickness. If we can truly celebrate this event, then we can work with trust and confidence for the freedom of all.

Of course the celebration of feasts has its snares. One of them is superficiality in human relationships — thoughtlessness and distraction followed by escapism. Another is that feasts can be noisy and noisome. Loud laughter in drinking bouts is not celebration of the final victory of peace and love but more of a flight and effort to hide the inner despair. The political feasts of the French revolution, the big shows by Hitler, the new rituals and pseudofeasts for the powerful men of the Communist Party, these and similar events are degradations of the genuine sense of feast, comparable with bad art.[85]

2. *The cultic dimension of the feast*

The Book of Genesis sees the Sabbath as God's gift to man, wherein man reposes before his Creator and rejoices in him, and thus becomes and remains his image and likeness in ordering all that God has entrusted to him.

God has not only wrought wonderful signs for the liberation of Israel; he also has given Israel the liberating word to celebrate these events in feasts, thus to remain grateful and free. In Israel and in the Christian era, the feast is experienced as an invitation from God to rejoice with him and to find courage and strength through praise of God.

It seems that in all historically known cultures, the chief meaning of the feast is worship and rejoicing before God. But it belongs to the Good News for Christians that their feasts need not be fabricated, for they are offered by God himself who, in this way, keeps their memory alive, healthy and grateful, and assures them of the ongoing history of salvation.[86]

As we have seen earlier, the feast presupposes, psychologically, a basic trust in the goodness of life and in the final victory of the good. Paul Tillich sees in this fundamental trust of believers "the courage to be" that God himself assures.[87] The believer not only rejoices for having received wonderful gifts, but he celebrates feasts because he is assured of God's covenant, of his love, of his fidelity, and thus he keeps his response of gratitude and fidelity alive.

3. Feast and human existence as Eucharist

The source and summit of all Christian celebration is, of course, the Eucharist. The Christian knows, by faith assured by God himself, that he has always and everywhere reasons to render thanks and praise to God. We celebrate the Eucharist as memorial of the passion, death and resurrection of Christ, and we do so in union with the risen Lord. Therefore it is impossible to celebrate feasts with the Eucharist as centre if we are neglecting our suffering and downtrodden brothers and sisters. We can give thanks to the Lord and celebrate feasts only if we are using our God-given energies to cooperate for justice and peace. But we also are enabled to celebrate in view of our own suffering and the cost of discipleship, for we are assured of the victory. Full of hope, we look forward with joy and trust to the new creation. Although frustration and suffering are never in themselves a reason to celebrate, we know that because they are redeemed in Christ and we can join him, the victor, they can even give us new reasons to celebrate feasts and to play before the Lord.[88]

If we accept the Eucharist as the focal point, source and rule of our life, then all our feasts and celebrations, and indeed all of our life are signs of gratitude that open us to the wealth of the past history of salvation and to all the present opportunities.[89] Thus there will be no split between our worship and our life, between our everyday life and our feasts.

Legalistic manuals of moral theology treated the Eucharist only in a perspective of duties: the duty to celebrate the Mass and the duty to assist, with innumerable occasions for mortal sins by priests who might not observe scrupulously every detail of the rituals and rubrics. It was an obsessive question for confessors to know how many mortal sins a penitent had committed by not assisting at Mass. For me, the main moral question is, how could it ever happen that moralists, priests and lay people would consider the Eucharist primarily in a perspective of duty? If it is a question about sin, then it is directed above all to the theologians and priests who have not effectively helped the faithful to see and to experience the meaning of the celebration of feasts, especially of the Eucharist, and to respond with gratitude and joy to the Eucharistic invitation.

Of course there is an obligation to participate regularly in the Eucharist, but it is never a naked duty. It can be understood only by those who are evangelized, who understand and experience the joy of the Gospel, and therefore hear the beautiful and urgent invitation of the Lord to repose before him, to be with him, to receive his total love and to join him in his covenant love.

For a Christian who is evangelized and knows the Lord's wonderful invitation to join with him and his people in the praise of the Father, it should be a shaking experience if, by mere negligence and laziness, he begins to stay away from the regular Eucharistic celebrations.[90] And, of course, for a Christian, it can never be just a matter of being there. He will participate actively with heart, mind and will. The final fecundity of the Eucharist and the other sacraments is the Christian's transformation whereby his whole life becomes praise and thanksgiving in union with Christ, and total commitment to him and to his work of salvation.

4. The Christian's Sunday

The prophets and lawkeepers gave to the rhythm between work and repose — which is found also in other cultures — a theological meaning. The Israelites celebrated the seventh day, the Sabbath, as the day of completion of God's work, his transcendence beyond creation, his nearness to it, and especially his rejoicing in his creation. "And God saw all that he had made, and it was very good ... God blessed the seventh day and made it holy, because on that day he ceased from all the work he had set himself to do" (Gen 1: 31-2: 3). This is the cultic meaning of the Sabbath: man's repose before God.

Later the Sabbath was more and more used for the gathering of the people around the holy books. In Deuteronomy 5: 1ff., we find the prophetic ethical meaning of the Sabbath: it is the celebration of God's liberating action, a day of thanksgiving that imposes on the Israelites the duty not to overburden the servant. "The alien within your gates, your slaves and slave-girls may rest as you do. Remember that you were slaves in Egypt and the Lord your God brought you out with a strong hand and an outstretched arm, and for that reason the Lord your God commanded you to keep the Sabbath day". Thus the Sabbath participates in the significance of the great feasts of Israel.

While the regular celebration in mythological religions calls to mind the cycle of repetition in the course of nature and of history, in Israel it is the ongoing feast of the ongoing history of salvation.[91] Feast and Sabbath remind Israel of the messianic time. They give the people assurance that God will bring to completion the history of salvation, as he completed the work of creation.

The first generation of Christians continued to observe the Sabbath as a day of repose, of contemplation and especially of listening to the word of God in preparation for their celebration of the Eucharist which took place regularly on Sundays (cf. Acts 20:7; 1 Cor 16-2). Christ has freed his disciples from a ritualistic scrupulous observance of the Sabbath. For him, healing and other ways of doing good for others could sometimes be more urgent than the observance of Sabbath repose. "The Sabbath was made for the sake of man and not man for the Sabbath" (Mk 2:27).

In the early Christian generations, the Sunday was not conceived as a day of obligatory repose but as one of regular celebration of the memorial of the Lord's death and resurrection. It was to bring home to the redeemed that all of life is a feast.[92] St Augustine says, "In the house of God, there is ongoing festivity".[93] For those early Christians, Sunday was distinguished because the Lord had risen on the first day of the week and had sent the Holy Spirit (Pentecost) again on the first day.

Until the time of Constantine, the Roman Empire had as its day of repose the day of Saturn (Saturday) which, then, was the first day of the week, while the day of the Sun (Sunday) was the second. By Constantinian decree, the latter became the first day of the week, the day of repose and the day of celebration for Christians. So Sunday now became "the Lord's day" (cf. Rev 1:10). Until then, the Church had not even thought about imposing total repose on Sunday; it was only requested that time be kept free for the celebration of the Eucharist. Since the early times, the Lord's day was also considered as "the eighth day" (cf. Jn 20:26), a day of anticipation of the final day of fulfilment. Thus, prophetically, it commits the faithful to participate in the history of salvation "until the Lord comes".

A history of the theology of Sunday could somehow be an image of the whole history of the Church and of theology.[94] A flourishing Christianity knows Sunday as a day of joy and recommitment, as participation in the history of salvation. The emphasis is on partaking in the death and resurrection of Christ. In a time of decay, however, theology and practice fall back into rabbinic casuistry about how much work one can do on Sunday, what is or is not servile work, and so on. Time and again we can observe the tension between the prophetic history and ritualistic alienation.

What is most important for giving meaning to repose is to take time and give time for meditation and celebration, time to cultivate the community spirit, to rejoice together, to visit the sick and console those who are in sorrow. That the Sunday repose is also protected by law and by custom is good. It helps to make socially visible the fact that we are not slaves of work but are invited to leisure, to rejoicing together and to celebration.

5. The feast and freedom in fidelity

The messianic vision of Sunday and feast day implies that our everyday life should become ever more a feast day, a living out of the Sunday, and that the freedom and joy of the feast should gradually permeate all of our days. The freedom experienced on the feast days and Sundays should be the yeast for every day's joy, and give new meaning to suffering and to labour.[95]

Technocracy has robbed man of his selfhood. It tends to reduce the person to a tool. And if the human being, on one important level of existence, accepts the role of being not much more than a tool, then he cannot manifest himself on another level as person. We see this, for instance, in the fact that man shaped by technocracy does not know how to use his free time. He takes it almost for granted that commercial interests will provide it. And when he has lost his integral selfhood in the realm of work and organization, he is easily manipulated, too, by any form of advertisement or propaganda. Göbbels and other brain-washers have known this well.[96]

People bewitched by technocracy and by a craving for economic success are no longer their own masters while they try to subdue the earth.[97] Hence we cannot celebrate our feasts without being concerned for and committed to liberating action on all levels, especially in the realm of everyday activities and the organization of the whole world of work. To do this we need the experience of joy and freedom. "Joyful fulfilment in the *present* is an essential element of subjective freedom, even though human life is intrinsically future oriented. Just because, according to Christian faith, the future is assured by God's promise, we are set free to celebrate and enjoy the present".[98]

The idea of freedom and the purpose of liberation will inspire us to celebrate feasts if we experience freedom as a gift already given to us, and as a promise. It is the gratuitous character of freedom that allows us to celebrate and to rejoice together. But since, as Christians, we experience freedom as the gift of the one Father offered for all, our celebrations recommit us, time and again, to the cause of everyone's freedom.[99] As Christians we celebrate the love of God made visible in Jesus Christ and his followers. This celebration is authentic only if we accept our share in the all-embracing love of God. Thus our feasts fill us with joy and mutual love, and set us free for each other. It is precisely this profound experience that enables us to live in creative liberty and fidelity.

The messianic meaning of Sunday, feast and celebration, implies a healthy relation with the past which they memorialize. If we celebrate them with a grateful memory, we know that we can prove our gratitude for all that we have inherited from the past by shaping the future in creative fidelity. Feasts and celebrations play an important role in forming our personality. They give us strength, but they also provide occasion for self-examination and for developing a purposeful new way of thinking and acting.[100]

IV. PLAY

1. *Importance of play in people's life*

Having treated the beautiful in general and art in particular, the feast and celebration as a way of reaching out for truth and for living in liberating truth and fidelity, we turn our attention now to play.[101]

A chapter on play in a tract on moral theology dedicated to the formation of the responsible person may surprise some people. In manuals written for confessors, play was treated only in the context of occasion of sin. And of course, if it is presented only in that context, one is tempted more by sinful play. But we consider play as an essential part of human life. For us, "the playing man is not only a man who plays, but even more is one who conceives his whole being as a playing being".[102]

Before we try to understand man as a being who plays, we ask what kind of play people choose today. Many are more spectators of play than players who play before God, play with each other, play with their children.

The number of those who go to Mass is diminishing. First place is taken by television, movies, the great spectator sports of football, boxing, baseball, horseracing and car racing. All this somehow mirrors the quality of life in our times.[103] Car races, attracting thousands of spectators, are a kind of symbol of a general addiction to speed as a drug; speed that leaves no time or inclination for prayer, for contemplation, for profound feelings or thought, and which costs more lives every year than any of the most atrocious battles of World War I or II. If people would learn the rhythm of friendly play and joyous feast, they would be immunized against this kind of ruinous play. Those who rejoice and celebrate life together, and who learn the fair language of play, will not be disarmed when faced with the audiovisual aggressiveness of so many movies and television programmes.[104]

Historically, play and dance belong to the religious sphere almost as much as the feast. "The true cheerfulness and serenity of the playing man, for whom seriousness and wit are joined together, is a religious phenomenon; it is a matter of an earthly and heavenly man".[105] A Protestant author, who is well aware of the fallenness of humankind, writes, "Authentic humanness appears only when man begins to play in a self-forgetting and liberated way, and when he dares the greatest play to bring life itself, with its seemingly contradictory pieces and lacerating contradictions, to a unity. If he succeeds in this great play, then we can speak of culture".[106]

Whoever knows how to play and to dance can take things seriously. He is interested in what he is doing, yet his seriousness is serenity, joy, overflowing liberty. In play we learn the kind of seriousness that is completely human and so far away from the sad seriousness of those who see life only as a burden and not as a gift. The person who plays knows that his play is only play and that he has to fulfil his purposive task in the world seriously; but he knows this in a way that gives to his seriousness in all his tasks a spirit of freedom.[107]

H. Kutzner has noted the intimate relationship between play and the love of gardening.[108] Gardening for beauty and enjoyment symbolizes the entrustment of nature to man, to love it and take care of it. It is a part of nature set free simply for the sake of beauty, a kind of reconciliation between nature and history, a kind of tithing of nature for the sake of enjoyment and art.

Play is frequently as ambivalent as the whole human culture. But just as perverted love does not allow us to shy away from love, so perverted play is an appeal to us, as believers, to play to the honour of God, letting the whole realm of play experience redemption.

Romano Guardini compares the liturgy with a wonderful play before God in a magnificent mixture of profound earnestness and divine serenity.[109] And van Leeuw finds the paradigm of play useful for a deeper understanding of history and a better way of taking our part in it. "The oldest drama, that which covers the world, is the encounter between God and man. The great actor is God. We are his partners".[110] But the author adds that man can play *against* God and that is the most dangerous play, sharing its honour with the devil. Unless liturgy brings us to adoration and to true sacrifice, the beautiful drama disintegrates and becomes, instead, a tragedy or a miserable comedy.

Klaus Hemmerle sees in the realm of play a kind of preludium of theology, a true symbol in which theology is always present if the play is true art. It can be a kind of interpretative play that resembles creation and man's share in creativity.[111] Playing, we interpret ourselves and can come to a better self-understanding. We have won much if we learn to experience our life and the world around us as a great drama in which, from the very beginning, nothing is determined except the rules of play. As long as we observe them we can respond creatively to new happenings.[112]

Jürgen Moltmann questions himself about understanding Jesus as "the first liberated man in creation" in a perspective of play: "The life of Jesus in the gospels stands under the signs of manger and cross, homelessness and murder. In the face of such suffering, aesthetic categories fail rather abruptly. It is difficult to consider the sufferings of the forsaken Christ and his pain of death in a serious, loving game of God for man's benefit, as the mystics occasionally have done. At this point the categories of play seem misplaced ... I think we should literally and sincerely leave the cross out of the game. In spite of Bach, the dying agony of Jesus does not fit the categories of song ... After all, Golgotha was not Oberammergau". But with Moltmann, we know quite well that we can celebrate the one undivided mystery of cross and resurrection. "Easter is an altogether different matter; here indeed begins the laughing of the redeemed, the dancing of the liberated, and the created game of new, concrete concomitants of the liberty which has been opened for us, even if we still live under conditions with little cause for rejoicing".[113]

The redeemed can laugh, sing, dance even in the face of death. "Death is swallowed up in victory. Oh death, where is thy victory?" (1 Cor 15:55).

2. Unconcealment of truth in play

Holy Scripture itself uses play as a paradigm to unconceal the most sublime truths. Not only does divine wisdom prepare a great feast (cf. Prv 9:1-6), she also presents a wonderful play. "When he assigned the sea its boundaries, when he laid down

the foundations of the earth, I was by his side, a master crafts-
man, delighting him day after day, ever at play in his presence,
at play everywhere in his world, delighting to be with the sons
of man" (Prv 8:29-31).

There is a special exhilaration in play as interplay, as an
expression of partnership and shared joy. This is a paradigm
of all of God's works. Creation and incarnation, and the whole
history of salvation are expression and revelation of God's free
creative and redemptive love. Our whole existence is "at home"
if we know that we are in the hands of God and that his play
with us is holy and liberating, the highest manifestation of his
love. This is the deeper truth of the person who plays, the
source of his cheerfulness, serenity and his seriousness.[114] "It
cannot be denied that the origin and fulfilment of the play
directs us to a sacred mystery that is not at our disposal".[115]
And this mystery is a part of our life, for God himself invites
us. If we are a part of the play and observe its rules, playing
our role nobly, attentively and generously, then it reveals a
dimension of the transcendent truth. Our play becomes a symbol
in which God's own play is already present. "The whole great
play is God's play with us and for the world, with and for
humankind, a play that he himself has initiated and for which he
has laid down nothing other than the rules of play. The world
sustained by God shall play its own play, however, without allowing itself a game with God. And man is not a plaything of God
but invited to be his free partner".[116]

Hans Küng adds to this beautiful reflection a warning that
things should not be overly simplified. Although play is an
aesthetic category, the reality presented under this paradigm
must not be taken lightly. For all too often man is not honoured
by his fellowmen as a playmate but treated as an object of
gambling in a game with him against him.

God's way of playing with man and for man is always a
wonderful surprise. The greatest surprise is the coming of his
only begotten Son as our redeemer, and the Easter event after
Good Friday. Whenever we honour God's surprising initiatives,
we discover new insights, new opportunities, and experience
the honour of being free partners. And we shall play together
with the Lord for the freedom and joy of our fellowmen. Then
we too shall have, time and again, beautiful surprises in store.

The art of play and dance often reveals truth by unmasking dangerous errors. Whoever has seen beautiful and respectful dances, and especially sacred dances like David's before the ark of the Lord, is especially well armed against the manichean tendency to a dualism which despises the body.[117] Dance and play are poetry manifested by the bodily realities. They assure us of the biblical vision that the body is the human person who manifests his joy at being the work of the great Artist. In its gracious movements, the body speaks the language of an artist. Sacred play and dance can mediate religious experience. Historians have frequently pointed out the connection between religion and play. As play finds its meaning in itself so, and infinitely more, religion has its significance and value in itself and thus enriches all of life.[118]

Human language is itself a beautiful play or, rather, interplay. Speaking to each other with fantasy and imagination, discovering the great possibilities of our language, we are playmates helping each other to discover essential dimensions of truth.[119] The fact that one can make an empty play with words does not refute this truth; indeed, it only unmasks the one who does not observe the rules of the game. Genuine play with words is a source of joy. It is the experience that my truth is beautiful only if it becomes also your truth, and that I have not found my truth unless I am open to yours.

The paradigm of play helps us to understand better what it means that our life is to glorify God. "The joy is the meaning of human life, joy in thanksgiving and thanksgiving in joy ... Then we ask for what purpose do I exist? The answer does not lie in demonstrable purposes establishing my usefulness, but in the acceptance of my existence as such, and in what the Dutch biologist and philosopher Buytendijk has called 'demonstrative value of being' ".[120]

Moltmann rightly insists that "the notion that enjoying God implies enjoying our own existence has been obscured by our puritan training in self control".[121] Surely nature is full of purpose-free rejoicing, inviting us to rejoice, to sing and to play. Man's self-representation in art, in the play and in dancing is the human echo of God's pleasure in his creation. "The glorification of God lies in the demonstrative joy of existence ... Man, in his uninhibited fondness for this finite life, and by his affirmation of mortal beauty, shares the infinite pleasure of the Creator".[122]

3. *The art and morality of play*

Play can be literally re-creation; it has a healing power. The art of play and celebration teaches us also the art of living beautifully and nobly. To see this we need only compare the beautiful play with the shabby one. Dr Eric Berne has written an interesting book, *Games People Play*.[123] He presents the various human relationships under the paradigm of play, revealing the difference between the beautiful play and interplay in healthy relationships, and the disturbing plays that stem from repressions and all the disorders stored in the subconscious. These insights open an avenue for a therapy of play.

The Church Fathers, especially those of the Latin Church, were very harsh in their judgment of theatres, spectacles, and games of competition in their times. This judgment was historically conditioned[124] and probably necessary for a certain time because of dangerous situations; but in the long run, theology did a great disservice to human culture and human health when its approach remained negative, bedeviling all that is play, theatre. We cannot redeem the world by rigorism. Only through a positive appreciation and clear understanding of the significance of good play can we contribute to the promotion of culture. We need to praise the arduous vocations that bring this realm of life home into the great dimensions of redemption. Then we can also say a clear word against abuses as, for instance, the cruelty of boxing until the total knockout, against a senseless, hysterical starcult, against unworthty dances, obscene plays, and so on.

4. *Play and liberty*

In the joy of play and the cultivation and admiration of beauty, there is both a loving nearness and the freedom of distance. The person in whom the dimension of play, feast and beauty is fully developed can keep that distance from the world and from things which is necessary for joyous dedication to the truth beyond all pragmatism. He is free to transcend the "knowledge of dominion" for the knowledge of meaning, the knowledge of limited purpose for the sake of salvation knowledge. He keeps the practical knowledge — the "knowledge of dominion", serenely within the proper dimension.

F.G. Jünger tries to imagine the kind of man and the kind of human community where the dimension of playfulness is totally lacking. Where every movement has to serve a concrete purpose and everything is a means to something else, there will be a total dependence that allows no space for creative liberty.[125] Garaudy, on the other hand, invites us to imagine a political world shaped by people whose experience and spirit is formed by playfulness, by the creativity of artistic expression. Here there would be less temptation to violence, less unfair competition and more readiness for fair cooperation.[126]

The play age of children is of highest importance, and irreparable damage is done to them if it is unduly restricted and shortened. If parents know how to play with their children, it is as much to their own benefit as to that of the children. The pattern formed by the beautiful, by the feast and by play, gives greater openness to the future, fosters fantasy and creativity, forms people who can approach many problems with the ease of the playing person, and can discover the beauty and the joy of the good.

The purest phenomenon of play is the play of love. It is an irreplaceable dimension of conjugal love and, it seems to me, of all love.[127] One of the greatest perversions would be a conjugal intercourse for the sole purpose of procreation with no love and no play of love. God's works are the play of love. They arise from the superabundance of his freedom and love, and have as their final purpose man's free, creative and faithful response of love mutually given and received.

Christian morality is best expressed in the beatitudes. It is the celebration of love, a morality of freedom that is not only achieved but also is to be celebrated, for it cannot be achieved if it is not rejoiced in and celebrated.

Buytendijk sees play as a way to existential self-experience, a way to vital knowledge.[128] It opens an essential horizon of knowledge attuned to nearness, nobility and attractiveness. The moral appeal is grounded in the message of salvation, in the festive liberty that God's graciousness, the grace of the Holy Spirit, enables.

True, the moral appeal is also majestic; the good makes absolute demands. But these demands come to us in the joy of faith which leads us to see things in their proper dimensions. In the adoration of the all-holy and all-merciful God, we are liberated for that seriousness that is always accompanied by cheerfulness. If we understand our life as response to God's wonderful play, we shall never resist the challenge of the game of life, nor shall we ever be fascinated by a merely techno-cratic worldview that wants to monopolize seriousness and considers play as mere frivolity. We shall respond to God's wonderful initiative in joyous faith and that happy seriousness which is play and, of course, always more than play.[129] For Harvey Cox, genuine prayer is the play of free children before God, and such prayer is setting free all our energies to live the life of the redeemed.[130]

V. SENSE OF HUMOUR

1. *The meaning of sense of humour*

Humour is the noblest form of wit and fun. Here we are interested in what the sense of humour means for the liberating truth.

Since the nineteenth century, a sense of humour can be counted among the cardinal virtues of English-speaking people. It marks the best of the English and American style of life. These cultures have produced great geniuses of humour as, for instance, Dickens and Chesterton.

Edmund Bergier counts about eighty different theories on the nature and origin of the sense of humour.[131] Philip Dessauer says that "humour is the criterion of inner freedom, of the broadmindedness of a healthy, affirmative relationship with truth".[132] Cardinal Ratzinger thinks that it belongs to the basic criteria for the discernment of the spirits. "Where the sense of humour dies, there is surely not the spirit of Christ, and conversely, joy is a sign of grace".[133] Theodor Haecker, who wrote one of the finest essays on humour, calls it the "broadest and noblest milieu of humanness".[134]

Humour's laughter is cordial and sensitive, always a sign of human culture. It does not arise from a primitive instinct but is on the level of a proper evaluation of existence. The sense of humour allows itself some foolishness but it is always the foolishness of wisdom, a beautiful mixture of self-affirmation and sympathetic participation.[135]

A classical manifestation of sense of humour is Erasmus' book, *Enkomium Morias* (Praise of Foolishness). He dedicated it to his friend Thomas More, in whom he finds no foolishness but on whose name (More) he plays with the similitude "Moria". A superficial reading might consider this book as satire, for Erasmus sharply unmasks the foolishness and faults of his time and especially of the Roman Curia. But what distinguishes it from satire is that he makes it quite clear that he feels he is in the same boat, in the same Noah's ark with all the other animals, one of them. Combining a maximum of participation with a minimum of self-affirmation, his wit is never destructive but is an ultimate expression of his trust that we are not hopeless fools. The wise man knows the remnants of his foolishness and therefore can laugh kindly and cheerfully about the foolishness of others with whom he always includes himself. As a short definition of sense of humour we can offer, "the capacity to laugh in spite of all".[136]

2. The art and ethos of sense of humour

An outgoing sense of humour is a charism and is also a sign of maturity. Only an integrated person can, at the same time, sympathetically participate and graciously affirm his self-hood. Only those who are sure of their own selfhood can allow themselves the "wisdom of the fool". While wit can be a natural gift, sense of humour presupposes the synthesis of life. It can be cultivated only by cultivating humanness and co-humanity.

The true sense of humour cannot go to extremes. The person who is gifted with humour knows when to weep and when to laugh. This gift is never condescendent, never degenerates into irony or satire, is never immoral or vulgar. A person who has a sense of humour allows us to feel at home with him or her. It is a true virtue but a declared enemy of moralism.[137]

A sense of humour is the smile of love. It can never replace love but neither can it exist truly without a loving heart. "Where there is a sense of humour you always find love too. But this does not mean that love is lacking where there is not a special sense of humour".[138] Yet when the finesse of a sense of humour is added to genuine love, then we can play a powerful role as peacemakers in many difficult situations, and can protect the love of God and of neighbour in moments of temptation.

3. Being reconciled with an imperfect world

Heaven is plain joy. It does not need the help of humorous participation. But here in our imperfect world, we who are sharply aware of our participation in the world's imperfections, urgently need a sense of humour. It is a sign of redemption. "The Christians' sense of humour arises from the redeeming certainty of their being accepted; it should be every day's art to radiate the joy of the gospel in a humourless, hard, technocratic world".[139]

The ethos of the sense of humour is the art of the possible. The humourist is a master of this art through a synthesis of glad acceptance and renunciation, of wisdom and foolishness, of the simplicity of the child and the maturity of the adult. It is a beautiful manifestation of Christian ethics in its tension between the "already" and the "not yet".[140]

Philip Lersch considers humour as a kind of love of a world in spite of imperfection and malice, "a profound gratitude to God who allows us to live in this imperfect world".[141] Numerous authors think that the whole religious vision — the faith in the final victory of the good and the acceptance of the world — is an essential presupposition for a genuine sense of humour. Even though the truly humourous person might think of himself as an unbeliever, he has a profound faith in the ultimate meaning of life and in the victory of the good. "If life were considered only as a tragedy, there would be no sense of humour. Neither would there be a place for it if it were a shallow comedy".[142]

The humourist's faith may be tempted in many ways, yet

in his deepest heart he knows that hope is the response, hope is the remedy. He is not simply an optimist; he has a sharp eye for falsehood and all kinds of evil, but he has an even sharper eye for the good and he trusts that it will finally triumph. His humour and his laughter will never approve obscenity and other evil things, even if they present themselves under the guise of wit.

4. Humour and liberating truth

A sense of humour presupposes a good deal of experience of liberty. The humourous person graciously puts aside many obstacles to freedom and joy; he does not get lost in troublesome situations. Humour may induce us to some compromise but only to an open-ended compromise insofar as it leads into the wide open milieu of Christian joy and hope. Those who have a sense of humour take the next step in the right direction almost without thinking about it. They can do it creatively because they have accepted the foolishness of wisdom. Through this charism the "art of the possible" becomes a partial experience of the truth that "the truth will set you free" (Jn 8:32).

NOTES

[1] Cf. H. Charlier, "L'art dans la communauté", in Problèmes de l'art sacré, Paris, 1951, 138; H. Hermann, Glanz des Wahren. Von Wesen, Wirken und Lebensbedeutung der bildenden Kunst, Freiburg, 1952³.
[2] A. Marc, Dialectic de l'affermation, Paris, 1952, 238.
[3] Thomas Aquinas, De divinis nominibus, cap. 4, lectiones 5 et 6; cf. K. Barth, Kirchliche Dogmatik II/1, Zürich, 1946, 733ff.
[4] S.Th., I, q 39, a 8.
[5] Augustine, Confessiones XIII, cap. XX, 28 PL 32, 856.
[6] Augustine, De civitate Dei, XXI, 29-33 PL 41, 796-804.
[7] Cf. H.U. von Balthasar, Herrlichkeit. Eine Theologie der Aesthetik, tome I: Schau und Gestalt, Einsiedeln, 1961, 31.
[8] H.G. Gadamer, Wahrheit und Methode. Grundzüge einer philosophischen Hermeneutik, Tübingen, 1960, 36.
[9] Balthasar, l.c., 9.
[10] Cf. H.E. Bahr, Theologische Untersuchung der Kunst. Poiesis, München-Hamburg, 1965, 26ff.
[11] P. Evdokimov, La conoscenza di Dio secondo la tradizione Orientale, Roma, 1969, 16.
[12] Augustine, Enarrationes in Ps. 14, PL 37, 1964.
[13] Augustine, Enarrationes in Ps. 96, 19 PL 37, 1252.

[14] Balthasar, *Herrlichkeit* III/1, Einsiedeln, 1965, 27.
[15] l.c., 28.
[16] Cf. l.c., 341-344.
[17] Cf. G. Nebel, *Das Ereignis des Schönen*, Stuttgart, 1953, 48, 155ff.
[18] Cf. R.M. Rilke, *Briefe aus den Jahren 1904-1907*, Berlin, 1939, 210.
[19] B. Pascal, *Pensées*, N. 206.
[20] Leo the Great, *Sermo 72*, 4 PL 54, 398.
[21] E. Souriau, *La couronne d'herbes*, Paris, 1975.
[22] J. Moltmann, Introduction to G.M. Martin, "Wir wollen alle auf Erden schon...". *Das Recht auf Glück*, Stuttgart, 1970, 11.
[23] G. Nebel, l.c., 188.
[24] Cf. H.-G. Gadamer, l.c., 37.
[25] E.F. Schuhmacher, *Small is Beautiful*, New York-London, 1975.
[26] l.c., 296.
[27] J. Maritain, *Art et scholastique*, Paris, 1927, 245.
[28] Quoted by G. Jaquemet, "art et morale", in *Catholicisme*, 969; cf. Maritain, l.c., 122, 129.
[29] Maritain, l.c., 315.
[30] Pius XII, Address to Italian Artists, April 8, 1952, English translation in *Catholic Mind* 50 (1952), 697ff.
[31] Maritain, l.c., 130ff.
[32] K. Barth, *Wolfgang Amadeus Mozart 1756/1956*, Zollikon, 1957, 44; cf. H.E. Bahr, l.c., 87.
[33] Cf. R. Guardini, *Ueber das Wesen des Kunstwerkes*, Tübingen, 1954⁴, 50.
[34] *Kritik der Urteilskraft*, §49.
[35] l.c., §42; cf. Gadamer, l.c., 47ff.
[36] J. Moltmann, Preface to *Theology of Joy*, London, 1976².
[37] Y. de Montcheuil, *Problèmes de vie spirituelle*, Paris, 1947⁴, 131ff.
[38] Cf. H. Sedlmayr, *Verlust der Mitte*, Salzburg, 1956⁷; Id., *Der Tod des Lichtes, übergangene Perspektiven moderner Kunst*, Salzburg, 1965.
[39] G. Jaquemet, l.c., 872.
[40] Cf. D. Bonhoeffer, *Gesammelte Schriften* V, 357; A. Altenähr, "Dietrich Bonhoeffers Gedicht 'Stationen auf dem Weg zur Freiheit'?", *Studia Moralia* 15 (1977), 283.
[41] Cf. H.E. Bahr, l.c., 98ff.
[42] M. Landmann, *Pluralität und Antinomie. Die kulturelle Grundlage seelischer Kinflikte*, München-Basel, 1963, 82.
[43] J. Maritain, l.c., 268.
[44] A.D. Sertillanges, *L'art et la morale*, Paris, 1933, 33.
[45] E. Souriau, l.c., 87.
[46] J. Maritain, l.c., 123.
[47] Th. Haecker, *Dialog über Christentum und Kunst*, Hellerau, 1930, 22; cf. *Christentum und Kultur*, München, 1927, 50.
[48] Ph. Dessauer, l.c., 73.
[49] H.E. Bahr, l.c., 101; cf. Gadamer, l.c., 181.
[50] Cf. P. Bono, *La morale dell'artista. Discorsi sui fondamenti di etica estetica*, Milano, 1969, 275-299.
[51] Pius XII, Address to the International Congress of Catholic Artists, Sept. 3, 1950, in Utz-Groner (ed.), *Soziale Summe Pius XII*, n. 1954.
[52] Pius XII, Address to Authors and Artists, Aug. 26, 1945, l.c., n. 1979.
[53] Balthasar, *Herrlichkeit*, III/1, 28.
[54] G. Jacquemet, l.c., 873ff.
[55] Balthasar, l.c., 34ff.
[56] *Constitution on the Sacred Liturgy*, 122.
[57] Bahr, l.c., 186ff; R. Egenter, *Kitsch und Christenleben*, Ettal, 1958².
[58] *Consitution on the Sacred Liturgy*, 124.
[59] Pius XI, Address of October 27, 1932, AAS 24 (1932), 356.
[60] R. Régamey, *Art sacré au XX.e siècle*, Paris, 1952, 212ff.
[61] Quoted by J. Maritain, l.c., 140.
[62] *Webster's Seventh New Collegiate Dictionary*, Chicago, 1965, 892.

[63] G. Gurvitch, *Traité de sociologie*, Paris, 1963[3], 154.

[64] L. Gilkey, *Catholicism Confronts Modernity*, New York, 1975, 22.

[65] Cf. C.G. Jung, *Der Mensch und seine Symbole*, Olten-Freiburg, 1968; English tr. Collected works, vol. V, *Symbols of Transformation*, 1970[2]. Jung speaks above all of the archetypes, those symbols that seem to be common to all cultures although they manifest themselves in various modifications.

[66] Cf. E. Cassirer, *Philosophie der symbolischen Formen*, 4 vol., Berlin, 1923-1931 (English version: *The philosophy of Symbolic Forms*, 3 vol., New Haven-London, 1944-1953); R. Guardini, *Von heiligen Zeichen*, Mainz, 1949; M. Eliade, *Images et Symboles*, Paris, 1952; G.W. Ferguson, *Signs and Symbols in Christian Art*, New York, 1959; J.A. Jungmann, *Symbolik der katholischen Kirche*, Stuttgart, 1960; P. Ricoeur, *Finitude et culpabilité*, vol. II: *La symbolique du mal*, Paris, 1960; Id., *Le conflit des interpretations*, Paris, 1969; J. Daniélou, *Les symboles chrétiens primitifs*, Paris, 1961; J.F. Cirlot, *A Dictionary of Symbols*, New York, 1962; W. Heinen (ed.), *Bild-Wort. Symbol in der Theologie*, Würzburg, 1968; H.M. McLuhan, *From Cliché to Archetype*, New York, 1970.

[67] Cf. the interesting article of T. Goffi, "Linguaggio immaginoso per un'etica cristiana", *Studia Moralia* 15 (1977), 260-282 (with bibliography).

[68] Cf. E. Souriau, l.c., 243.

[69] Cf. Balthasar, *Herrlichkeit*, III/1, 25. He speaks frequently on "Erblickungslehre", that is the art to *see* and to discover the symbol more profoundly.

[70] K. Hemmerle, *Vorspiel zur Theologie*, Freiburg, 1970; cf. E. Fink, *Spiel als Weltsymbol*, Stuttgart, 1960.

[71] Cf. Gadamer, l.c., 66ff.

[72] Cf. M. Landmann, l.c., 83.

[73] Cf. Balthasar, l.c., III/1, 28.

[74] R. Bultmann, *Glauben und Verstehen*, II, Tübingen, 1958[2], 137.

[75] Cf. K. Kerényi, *Vom Wesen des Festes*, Paideuma, 1938; J. Pieper, *Zustimmung zur Welt. Eine Theorie des Festes*, München, 1963; H. Cox, *The Feast of Fools. A Theological Essay on Festivity and Fantasy*, Cambridge/Mass., 1969; J. Moltmann, *Die ersten Freigelassenen der Schöpfung*, München, 1971; English translation: *Theology of Joy*, London, 1976[2]; R. Schütz, *La fête sans fin*, Taizé, 1971; J. Mateos, *Cristianos en fiesta. Mas allà del cristianesimo convencional*, Madrid, 1975[2]; E. Otto, *Fest und Freude*, Stuttgart, 1977; J.J. Wunenberger, *La fête, le jeux et le sacré*, Paris, 1977.

[76] Cf. G.M. Martin, *Fest und Alltag. Bausteine zu einer Theorie des Festes*, Stuttgart, 1973, 9.

[77] Mateos, l.c., 262.

[78] Cf. J. Pieper, l.c., 81.

[79] l.c., 42, 50.

[80] H.E. Bahr, l.c., 79.

[81] H. Cox, l.c. Cox's starting point is the medieval "feast of the fools".

[82] Cf. G.M. Martin, l.c., 18-29.

[83] Mateos, l.c., 255.

[84] D.E. Jenkins, in Introduction to J. Moltmann, *Theology of Joy*, London, 1976[2], 25.

[85] Cf. J. Pieper, l.c., 93ff.

[86] Cf. Card. J. Ratzinger, "Ist der Glaube wirklich 'Frohe Botschaft'?", *Studia Moralia* 15 (1977), 531.

[87] Cf. G.M. Martin, l.c., 30.

[88] J. Moltmann, l.c., 36 (German edition).

[89] Cf. B. Häring, *The Eucharist and Our Everyday Life*, Slough, 1978.

[90] On the regular assistance at Mass cf. B. Häring, *Free and Faithful*, vol. I, 416ff; G. Troxler, *Das Kirchengebot der Sonntagsmesspflicht*, Freiburg/Schw., 1971; W. Thüsing, "Eucharistiefeier und Sonntagspflicht im NT", *Gottesdienst* 1971, 10-12.

[91] Cf. J.J. Wunenberger, *La fête, le jeu et le sacré*, Paris, 1977, 144ff.

[92] Chrysostomus, *De Sancta Pentecoste*, hom. 1, PG 59, 454; Jerome, *Epist.* 121, PL 22, 1031.

[93] Augustine, *En. in Ps. 41*, 9 PL 36, 470.

[94] H. Huber, *Geist und Buchstabe der Sonntagsruhe. Eine historisch-kritische Untersuchung*, Salzburg, 1958; J.A. Jungmann, *The Meaning of Sunday*, Notre Dame/Ind., 1961; Ch. Curran, "Catholic Convictions on Sunday Observance", in *Christian Morality Today*, Notre Dame/Ind., 1966, 100-119; W. Rordorf, *Sunday, the History of the Day of Rest and Worship in the Earliest Centuries of the Christian Church*, Philadelphia, 1968; P.K. Jewett, *The Lord's Day. A Theological Guide to the Christian Day of Worship*, Grand Rapids, 1972; C.H. Peschke, *Christian Ethics*, vol. II, Alcester and Dublin, 1978, 129-151.

[95] G.M. Martin, l.c., 49ff.

[96] Cf. W. Luijpen, *Existentielle Phänomenologie*, 181; G. Marcel, *Les hommes contre l'humain*, Paris, 1951, 43.

[97] G. Marcel, "Positions et approches concrètes du mystère ontologique", in *Le monde cassé*, Paris, 1933, 284.

[98] B.C. Hodgson, *New Birth of Freedom*, Philadelphia, 1976, 348.

[99] Cf. J. Pieper, l.c., 44.

[100] Cf. J. Mateos, l.c., 311ff.

[101] Cf. H. Rahner, *Der spielende Mensch*, Einsiedeln, 1952; F.G. Jünger, *Die Spiele. Ein Schlüssel zu ihrer Deutung*, Frankfurt a.M., 1953; J. Huizinga, *Homo ludens, Vom Ursprung der Kultur im Spiel*, Hamburg, 1956; W. Sorell, *The Dance Through the Ages*, New York, 1967; R. Kraus, *History of Dance*, Prentice Hall, 1969; J. Henriot, *Le jeu*, Paris, 1969; P.L. Berger, *Rumour of Angels: Modern Sociology and the Discovery of the Supernatural*, London, 1970; H. Jurgens, *Pompa Diaboli, Die lateinischen Kirchenväter und das antike Theater*, Stuttgart, 1970; W. Weismann, *Kirche und Schauspiele. Die Schauspiele im Urteil der Kirchenväter unter besonderer Berücksichtigung von Augustin*, Würzburg, 1972; R. Garaudy, *Danser sa vie*, Paris, 1972; H. Kutzner, *Erfahrung und Begriff des Spiels. Eine religionswissenschaftliche und metpsychologische Untersuchung*, Bonn, 1975; K. Hemmerle, *Vorspiel zur Theologie. Einübungen*, Freiburg-Basel-Wien, 1976; R. Bleienstein, S.J., "Der Christ und das Spiel", in *Stimmen d. Zeit* 196 (1978), 108-116.

[102] J.H. Henriot, *Le jeu*, 101.

[103] R. Garaudy, *Danzare la vita* (Italian tr. of *Danser sa vie*), Assisi, 1973, 175.

[104] l.c., 176ff.

[105] H. Rahner, l.c., 35.

[106] H.E. Bahr, l.c., 79.

[107] Gadamer, l.c., 97.

[108] H. Kutzner, l.c., 141.

[109] R. Guardini, *Vom Geist der Liturgie*, Freiburg, 1957, 102.

[110] G. van Leeuw, *Wegen en Grenzen. En Studie over Verhouding van Religie en Kunst*, Amsterdam, 1955³, 122.

[111] K. Hemmerle, l.c., 109ff, 125ff.

[112] M. Eigen - R. Winkler, *Das Spiel. Naturgesetze steuern den Zufall*, München-Zürich, 1975, 11.

[113] J. Moltmann, l.c., 49ff.

[114] Cf. H. Rahner, i.c., 21ff, 40.

[115] Bahr, l.c., 82.

[116] H. Küng, *Existiert Gott?*, München, 1968, 713.

[117] Cf. Garaudy, l.c., 179.

[118] Cf. A. and T. Schramm, "Heiterkeit und Spiel", in O. Betz (ed.), *Tugenden für heute*, München, 1973, 143.

[119] Cf. J. Heidemann, *Der Begriff des Spiels*, Berlin, 1968, 319ff.

[120] J. Moltmann, l.c., 42.

[121] l.c., 43.

[122] l.c., 44.

[123] Dr. med. E. Berne, *Games People Play*, New York, 1964; German tr. *Spiele der Erwachsenen*. *Psychologie der menschlichen Beziehungen*, Hamburg, 1967.

[124] Cf. W. Weismann, l.c., 211ff.

[125] F.G. Jünger, l.c., 226.
[126] G. Garaudy, l.c., 180-182.
[127] Cf. J. Heidemann, l.c., 223.
[128] F.J.J. Buytendijk, *Vom Wesen und Sinn des Spieles*, Berlin, 1933, 146.
[129] G. Bally, *Vom Ursprung und von den Grenzen der Freiheit. Eine Deutung des Spieles bei Tier und Mensch*, Basel, 1945, 104.
[130] H. Cox, l.c., 185-193; K. Hemmerle, l.c., 135-149.
[131] E. Bergler, *Laughter and the Sense of Humour*, New York, 1956, 2-41.
[132] Ph. Dessauer, l.c., 57.
[133] Card. J. Ratzinger, l.c., 533.
[134] Th. Haecker, *Dialog über Christentum und Kultur, mit einen Exkurs über Sprache, Humor und Satire*, Hellerau, 1930, 75.
[135] Cf. Lauer, *Humor als Ethos. Eine moraltheologische Untersuchung*, Bern-Stuttgart, 1974, 87, 228.
[136] l.c., 228.
[137] l.c., 342.
[138] l.c., 368.
[139] J. Ratzinger, l.c., 531.
[140] Lauer, l.c., 338.
[141] Ph. Lersch, *Aufbau der Person*, München, 1964[4], 345.
[142] Lauer, l.c., 167.

Chapter Three

Ethics of Communication

Just as conscience can be understood and lived only in the reciprocity of consciences, so truth can come to life and become our truth only in communication. Our shared search for truth, our joy in truth found, and the common effort to discern what is true and good, all belong to our very nature. In the previous chapters we have addressed ourselves to these matters; but here we have to do so more systematically, in view of the new situation of a changed society and the new mass-media.

I. THEOLOGY OF COMMUNICATION

1. Christ, the Communicator and the Communication

The papal instruction on communication, May 23, 1971, points to Christ as the saving communicator and master of communication.[1] He, who is the Word of the Father in whom all things are made, is the Father's supreme gift and message to man. In him the Father communicates his design, his wisdom, his love. If we speak on Christ, communicator and communication, we never forget that he is the Word that is in the Father from the beginning, and through him all of creation is communication addressed to those who are created in his image and likeness.

All the works of God are communication, a sharing of life-giving truth. Christ gives us the interpretation, the clear vision of creation as communication. He reveals, above all, the eternal dialogue with the Father. "Everything is entrusted to me by my Father; and no one knows who the Son is but the Father, or who the Father is but the Son and those to whom the Son may choose to reveal him" (Lk 10:22). Through Jesus Christ, the Father inserts himself in the dialogue between men. Jesus reveals himself and the Father as friends; his communication is a sign of his friendship. "I call you servants no longer; a servant does not know what his master is about. I have called you friends because I have disclosed to you everything that I heard from the Father" (Jn 15:15).

Jesus Christ is both Word and Image.

As the Word, he is also the listener; he reveals what he has heard (Jn 15:15). He also reveals what he has seen: "No one has ever seen God; but God's only Son, he who is nearest to the Father's heart, he has made him known" (Jn 1:18). But Jesus not only lives by the word that comes from the mouth of the Father; he listens to those to whom he communicates himself and his message. He fulfils the great prophecy on the servant of God: "The Lord God has given me the tongue of a teacher and skill to console the weary with a word in the morning; he sharpens my hearing that I might listen as one who is taught. The Lord God opened my ears and I did not turn away" (Is 50:4-5).

He who is the Word and the Image of the Father speaks in human words and in images and symbols. For a better theological understanding about audio-visual communication, it seems to me important to give particular attention to the fact that Christ is also presented as the image of God. Paul preaches "the gospel of the glory of Christ who is the very image of God" (2 Cor 4:4). Christ the communicator is "the image of the invisible God" (Col 1:15), "the effulgence of God's splendour and the stamp of God's very being" (Heb 1:3). Therefore he can say, "anyone who has seen me has seen the Father" (Jn 14:9).

Christ speaks in parables and makes his words visible by symbolic action, not only because of the temperament and tradition of the Orientals but also because images and symbols are most suitable for communicating the mysteries that transcend all concepts and words.[2]

2. *The trinitarian dimension of communication*

Jesus, the Word incarnate, reveals the divine life as communication, sharing. He prays, "All that is mine is thine, and what is thine is mine" (Jn 17:10). His sharing of himself and of all the truth arises from the total sharing between the Father and the Son in the Holy Spirit. The Holy Spirit *is* sharing, communication. "When he comes who is the Spirit of Truth, he will guide you into all the truth; for he will not speak on his own authority, but will tell only what he hears. He will glorify me, for everything that he makes known to you he will draw from what is mine. All that the Father has is mine, and that is why I said, 'everything that he makes known to you he will draw from what is mine' " (Jn 16:13-15).

Communication is constitutive in the mystery of God. Each of the three Divine Persons possesses all that is good, all that is true, all that is beautiful, but in the modality of communion and communication. Creation, redemption, and communication arise from this mystery and have as their final purpose to draw us, by this very communication, into communion with God. Creating us in his image and likeness, God makes us sharers of his creative and liberating communication in communion, through communion, and in view of communion.

3. *The truth of communication and the communication of truth*

"The disposition to communication belongs to the very essence of the Holy Trinity and of the Christian. Therefore, communication of truth and love on earth, in whatever form, is something divine and forms us in the image and likeness of God".[3] Being redeemed means to be redeemed for truthful communication, for sharing truth and love in a creative and liberating way. Disciples of Christ cannot be in the truth and grow in liberated truth without receiving and gratefully communicating truth.

Those who want to be active communicators in the image and likeness of Christ will be, first of all, good listeners. A teaching Church that is not, above all, a learning, listening Church, is not on the wave-length of divine communication. This is true not only in relationships within the Church but also in those between the Church and the rest of the world. The papal instruction on communication emphasizes this dimension. Information must not only go out from the Church but must also flow back in such a way that "Church authorities may be instructed".[4]

The Church can be a prophetic voice in the great currents of communication if she is also willing to accept secular prophecy and to share in the joys and hopes, the anguish and fears of all people.[5] Communication in the Church and through the Church is for the sake of community, of unity among humankind. But communication, even that of the Gospel, does not automatically bring about community. There is need for dialogue, for conversation, for being with and for each other.

The kingdom of God manifested in Jesus Christ is for the whole world. The power and authority given to Jesus Christ, the Lord, obliges his disciples to preach the Gospel, to be communicators everywhere, even to the ends of the earth (Mt 28:18). The Spirit who has anointed Christ to proclaim the Gospel urges Christ's disciples, the Church, to use all possible means to spread the Good News. This is one of the themes of the Acts of the Apostles. The kingdom of God is a public reality. "What I say to you in the dark you must repeat in broad daylight; what you hear whispered you must shout from the housetops" (Mt 10:27). Are not the modern mass-media today's housetops?

4.   Communication and humanness

In all the created universe there is a certain resemblance to divine communication. This is so because all exists through interaction, communication. The atom is a marvellous system of interaction. Mineralogy, biology and zoology give privileged attention to the systems of interaction within minerals, organisms and so on, and the interaction between them and the milieu. Each being is distinguished by its type of interaction of communication.

All this points to the distinguishing characteristics of humanness. These can be grasped best by their manifestations; and the medium of their manifestation is human communications.[6] The human being is so totally marked by communication that even the consciousness of selfhood depends on it. Man cannot live without communication; he cannot *not* communicate. Even the refusal to communicate is a message, a communication.[7]

Action is communication and communication is action, with repercussions on the communicator and on the world around him.[8] Each communication influences all the participants. Man has always developed means of communication: non-verbal sounds, gestures, oral and written words, facial expressions, signs, symbols, monuments, drums, carvings, paintings, and so on. "The easier communication between men becomes, the greater the opportunity for human beings to be human".[9]

We distinguish between that communication which is beneficial to man, and the media of communication, which are mere instruments and can be used for good or for evil. Man is at his best when communication becomes communion, and for that he needs not only language and symbols but, above all, mutual trust between communicators and recipients, and trust in the language and symbols. In each communication we find an element of content and an element of relationship. The healthier the relationship is, the less it calls for attention; and the more it is disturbed, the more it comes to the foreground of conscience.[10] Even before communicating, the person himself is somehow influenced by the expected response, and afterwards he is still more influenced by the kind of feedback he has received. To understand ourselves we need to be understood by others, and to be understood by the others, we must understand them.[11]

Disturbed communications can be understood only in the total human context. Pathologies of communication are not static but change with the whole human situation which depends on each participant. Many pathologies can be understood only as response or reaction to bad relationships.[12] The "sin of the world" becomes visible in unhealthy and misleading communications. "Along with the sense of self has gone a loss of our language for communicating deeply personal meaning to each other".[13]

We have to think about the pathologies of our age. Although it has developed such accurate concepts and symbols for technical questions, yet when it comes to communicating the highest values such as freedom, fidelity, love and personhood, there we stumble and do not easily find a common language. Commercial and technological communication can be so pre-eminent and aggressive that persons unlearn how to share their intimate selves and to communicate on the level of personal relationships. Pope Paul VI insists that communication manifests and strengthens communion only to the extent that it is inspired by loving sympathy and solidarity. Only thus can it promote true human development.[14]

Man communicates more by what he is than by what he says. He speaks not only with words that reach the ears of fellowmen; he speaks also to their eyes and to all their senses. He communicates by art, by feasts, by song, dance and play, and by the manifold symbols that reach the depth of human grasp. But only where symbol, word or action manifests the person's sharing himself or herself does humanness come to its fullness, to the image and likeness of God.

II. THE NEW SITUATION

1. Planetarian dimension

The public addressed by the Jewish priests were the Jewish people only, but Jesus enlarged the public by addressing Samaritans as well as Jews. This process, which led to his condemnation, involved the Roman Empire. But the public for which Jesus destined the Gospel included all people unto the ends of the earth.

The public forum in which information and opinions are exchanged is not something static, well defined from the beginning. It is the sum of the various "worlds" with which we can compare our immediate environment, the world in which we were raised and which we knew. Today we can compare our small world with many other cultures, our history with the total history of humankind.

Vatican II considers the awareness of this changing world as fundamental for understanding our task. "History itself speeds along on so rapid a course that an individual person can scarcely keep abreast of it. The destiny of the human community has become all of a piece, where once the various groups of men had a kind of private history of their own".[15]

For those who believe in one God, Father of all, and in Jesus Christ, Redeemer of all the world, this development is a wonderful event. However, it is marked by profound tensions that reveal sin to us in a new fashion and call to conversion in a new dimension. "Although the world of today has a very vivid sense of its unity, and of how one man depends on another in needful solidarity, it is most grievously torn into opposing camps by conflicting forces. For political, social, economic, racial and ideological disputes still continue bitterly, and with them the peril of a war which would reduce everything to ashes. True, there is a growing exchange of ideas, but the very words by which key concepts are expressed take on quite different meanings in diverse ideological systems".[16]

The printed word has greatly contributed to the experience of one history. But through the modern mass media, history "speeds along on a rapid course" while the breadth and intensity of the participating public steadily increase. "New and more efficient media of social communication are contributing to the knowledge of events. By setting off chain reactions they are giving the swiftest and widest possible circulation to styles of thought and feeling".[17]

2. *The new dimensions and dynamics of pluralism*

In the so-called primitive cultures all shared the same world view. The customs and ideas were shaped by the same myths and the same traditions. And normally this situation continued without much coercion. People knew no other models of world views and societies. For many, the transition to pluralism was a shaking experience. Many things that had seemed certain were no longer so.[18] In the primitive environments individuals could be in conflict with tradition and society, but they realized that they had made themselves marginal people with no support. The new pluralism, however, implies not only that each individual thinks for himself but that also diverse groups make their choices of cultural, political and religious ideas.

The phenomenon of today's pluralism is strongly underlined by its coexistence with political systems, especially

Marxism, that tend to impose one world view, one ideology against all others, and use for that purpose all the modern means of mass media and manipulation. If Communism in several western countries succeeds in affirming pluralism not only as a traditional system while striving to come into power, but in a permanent frame of thought and society, this will be a historical development of enormous relevance.[19]

Pluralism finds its modern political expression in democracy where, on principle, the different groups have the same chance, and where freedom of expression is guaranteed to all as long as they remain on the basis of democratic freedom. But for proper functioning, democratic pluralism needs to respect the other forms of pluralism and to understand their meaning and purpose.

The aspect of pluralism that particularly interests us here is a new way of approaching truth in general and, in particular, the use of the modern mass media towards that end.

According to Sir Hugh Greene, general programme director of the BBC, a pluralism, in order to have a chance to survive, needs "an ability to combine the deepest scepticism with the most profound faith, and an obligation towards tolerance and towards the maximum liberty of expression".[20]

Pluralism starts with Socrates' approach, "I know that I do not know", which for him implies an ongoing search for truth. John Milton expresses the same idea: "Where there is much desire to learn, there, of necessity, will be much arguing, many opinions, for opinion in good men is but knowledge in the making".[21] In Socrates it was a person's search for truth. In the modern pluralistic society it becomes more and more a collective search for truth, and that implies both freedom and conflict.

Pluralism is healthy if the opinions of other peoples and groups are taken seriously, and if nobody tries to stifle others by coercion or pressure, as long as they respect the basic freedom and rights of all. Pluralism presupposes a culture in which every group is willing to learn and to unlearn, where all are eager to know each other better and thus also to know themselves better, so that through common effort they may come to a deeper and broader knowledge.

Pluralism is not at all anarchy of ideas and a structureless society. Democracy needs mutual respect and agreement on basic values. But tolerance does not imply neutrality of thought. Rather, each group will bring home its insights and experience into the co-reflection of all, and everyone is urged to respect the rules that are indispensable for the proper functioning of pluralism. Sir Hugh expresses this clearly: "Although, in the day-to-day issues of public life, the BBC does try to attain the highest standards of impartiality, there are some respects in which it is not neutral, unbiased or impartial. That is where there are clashes for and against the basic moral values — truthfulness, justice, freedom, compassion, tolerance. Nor do I believe that we should be impartial about certain things like racialism or extreme forms of political beliefs. Being too-good 'democrats' in these matters could open the way to destruction of democracy itself. I believe a healthy democracy does not evade decisions about what it can never allow if it is to survive".[22]

A truly pluralistic culture presupposes and requires a sense of solidarity and respect for each person's dignity and conscience. It excludes both extreme individualism and totalitarian tendencies. In such a truly pluralistic culture and society people who claim a monopoly on truth, and are more interested in reassurance than in a courageous and sincere search for truth, have and should have a hard time.

The renewal of the Catholic Church inaugurated by Pope John and the Second Vatican Council, and especially the new élan of ecumenism, cannot be understood without attention to the new pluralistic society. Pluralism in the Church is a service to unity when the various approaches to truth and the practice of truth never forget the basic unity in diversity and diversity in unity. Remembering the event of the first Pentecost, when all heard the Gospel in their own language, we realize that a legitimate pluralism is never a threat but rather an indispensable condition for catholicity in truth and truth in catholicity.[23] Just as the Church realizes that the Latin language for liturgy, philosophy and theology is all too narrow for a universal Church, so we must also realize that some truths, especially the mysteries of faith, are too great and too deep to be expressed in a single philosophy or theology.

Pluralism in theology requires global intercommunication.

The Second Vatican Council was a great experience of pluralism, for it presented more than any previous council the various cultures and a diversity of theologies within the same faith. The experience was broadened and deepened by the presence of observers from almost all non-Catholic Churches and by a willingness to listen to them. The life of the Church, its way of presenting doctrine, and especially its approach to ethics, will be henceforth more marked by the awareness of unity in diversity.

The Roman Catholic Church is catholic only by emphasizing more its catholicity than its "Romanity", and by never allowing the Romanity (or a Roman way of philosophizing and Roman tradition) to diminish the equality of cultures other than the Roman or the Occidental ones. "Among all the nations of earth, there is but one people of God which takes its citizens from every race, making them citizens of a kingdom which is of a heavenly and not an earthly nature. For all the faithful scattered throughout the world are in communion with each other in the Holy Spirit ... The Church does foster and take to herself, insofar as they are good, the abilities, the resources and customs of each people ... In virtue of this catholicity, each individual part of the Church contributes through its special gifts to the good of the other parts and of the whole Church. Thus, through the common sharing of gifts and through the common effort to attain fullness in unity, the whole and each of the parts receive increase".[24]

Pluralism is never to be thought of as a consequence of sin or as a threat but as a gift that, through the Holy Spirit becomes most fruitful for the very unity of the Church. "There is in Christ and in the Church no inequality on the basis of race or nationality, social condition or sex, because 'there is no such thing as Jew and Greek, slave and freeman, male and female; for you are all one person in Christ Jesus' (Gal 3:28) ... In their diversity all bear witness to the admirable unity of the body of Christ. This very diversity of graces, of ministries and works, gathers the children of God into one, because 'all these things are the work of one and the same Spirit' (1 Cor 12:11-25)".[25]

As one of the outstanding "signs of the times", pluralism invites a courageous and generous ecumenical spirit and action.

For this, the decree on ecumenism counts on a respectful dialogue as the way to unity, with the hope that all parts of Christianity will come to a deeper knowledge of the common faith and of their own particular charisms. The pluralistic culture, sociology of knowledge, sociology of customs have all helped us to understand that many differences between the separated Churches are not at all contradictions but rather beneficial complementarities. "While preserving unity in essentials, let all members of the Church, according to the office entrusted to each, preserve a proper freedom in the various forms of spiritual life and discipline, in the variety of liturgical rites, and even in the theological elaborations of revealed truth ... Catholics must joyfully acknowledge and esteem the truly Christian endowments from our common heritage which are to be found among our separated brethren. It is right and salutary to recognize the riches of Christ and virtuous works in the lives of others who are bearing witness to Christ".[26]

To sum up: the full recognition of pluralism and methods of dialogue, the common search for truth, and reciprocal communication not only do not threaten the consistency and unity of a united Christianity but can greatly help to strengthen and deepen them.

An approach to ecumenism based on full awareness of the nature of pluralism will succeed and find trust among all parts of Christianity only if the Catholic Church becomes a model of pluralism within her own community. This means, for instance, that there should be no pressure whatsoever on Catholics to belong to one political party rather than another. Both the Church and political society will gain greatly by a spirit of freedom regarding the temporal options in the fields of economics, politics, culture, society and so on.[27]

A delicate test for the spirit of pluralism will be the approach of the official Church and of her moral theologians to urgent questions about natural law. We can come to a deeper knowledge only by sharing the experiences and reflections of all cultures, and by uniting with all people in the Church and outside of her in the search for what is true and good, and for truthful solutions to the problems arising in ever new forms in the individual and social contexts.[28]

An ethics of social communication has to give particular attention to the way a pluralistic society allows and fosters the search for truth. For this, we must be aware of the history of our Church in which, before the advent of the printing press, a small number of people has managed to keep a monopoly of authority about the diffusion of opinions. Not without great tensions have the Church and her authorities come to realize the right and duty of all to make their contributions to the formation of a healthy public opinion and to aid in the search for fuller truth.[29]

We live in a time of transition when great patience is needed. Theologians have to learn a new style and a new sense of responsibility, discernment and courage in offering their ministry in a pluralistic Church and society. While Church authorities are to some extent rightly concerned about people who are extremely vulnerable if their "certainties" are questioned or shaken, many — including theologians — have to be freed from that kind of concern for "security" that implies a neglect of honesty in searching for truth. Leaders in the mass media field tell us that they consider "breaking down the barriers" as necessary "so that those of different views may come to know and to better understand each other's attitudes", and that in this process, "shocking may be good, provocation can be healthy and indeed imperative".[30] In this new situation, the traditional distinction must be rethought between "scandal" taken by pharisees, and actual scandal given to the weak. While the weak must be treated with care and kindness, a one-sided focus on their immaturity may be conducive to a general paternalism that keeps more and more people in a state of immaturity and locked in security complexes.

The problem is especially acute for theologians who respond to questions raised everywhere in a pluralistic society and, for the sake of authentic communication, use not the usual ecclesiastical formulations but the vocabulary of those who question them. If Christians are to be "light for the world", then those who warn too readily against "unsafe opinions" must become more aware of the "signs of the times": the new situation, the new dimensions of pluralism, and as a consequence the need for a different strategy and a different vocabulary. Pluralism requires a maximum of liberty and honesty in the search for truth. And in view of this, it also requires great vigilance in the matter of political, ideological and commercial powers that, under the guise of pluralism, try to impose their interests or their narrow visions.

3. *Unmasking the powers*

Pluralism is beneficial to the search for truth and for communication in the building up of communion, *if* the realm of freedom is guaranteed for these noble purposes. For an ethics of communication, we have to deal with the "if" by first unmasking the hidden or open powers that try to manipulate freedom or pursue commercial, or political forms of "freedom" other than that which we have in mind, namely, the common freedom for truthful communication and the search for further truth.

The most dangerous powers are those ideologies which are generally accepted uncritically and with the inertia typical of recipients of the mass media's messages.

We live in a world of producers and consumers, a world constantly tempted to evaluate people more according to what they own, produce, and consume than to what they are and what their relationships with others are. It is a technocratic world in which the growth of technological power tends to impose itself as law in itself, instead of being measured by the service it renders for the growth of persons and communities. Everything possible has to be done to overcome the ideology of the technocrats if we do not want technology-for-its-own-sake to become the new opium of the people or for the people.[31]

In the democratic capitalistic world, there is a deep, though hidden, antagonism between the freedom of opinion — free communication of opinion through the mass media — and, on the other hand, commercial freedom. If those in authority have no definite political concept regarding the mass media, they practically favour the commercial freedom of the wealthy and powerful to the detriment of genuine freedom of opinion.[32]

Because of the high cost of modern mass media, there is a trend in the East and West that allows the leading class, the wealthy and politically powerful people, to exercise undue influence. Wherever this situation is uncritically accepted by the masses, it is even more dangerous for freedom. In the Communist countries, the bureaucratic power of the party prevails over all, and people are constantly indoctrinated to believe in it. In the democratic capitalistic countries, however, it is primarily the financial powers, frequently allied with political power, that prevail.[33]

The pastoral instruction, *Communio et Progressio,* appeals to the owners and administrators of the powerful mass media never to forget that the means of communication are not mere commercial enterprises but have to fulfil important social and cultural tasks; therefore they should respect the independence of the communicators, collaborators and recipients.[34] But an appeal to the individual conscience of the rich and powerful is not enough. All too often, an individual approach to ethics forgets or ignores the power of established structures favoured or tolerated by law, while they could and should be changed for the better.[35]

In most of the western countries, there are anti-trust laws to prevent monopoly of the mass media by individuals, groups or corporations. Frequently, however, these laws are ignored in favoured cases, or transgressions are condoned. René Berger gives considerable documentation about this situation and warns of "a monstrous love" between the mass media and multinational companies.[36]

Kyle Haselden draws our attention particularly to the combined power of politicians and media owners, and he strongly requests that those who have political responsibility and power should be forbidden any kind of ownership in the mass media.[37] The danger may be even greater when the politician is not the owner but the "owned". The power of media owners to "make or break" politicians and political candidates, especially on the local levels, is a hidden force that escapes recognition by the ordinary reader or viewer of the news media. Yet it can take a heavy toll in frightened legislators and biased legislation.

Wherever the mass media are commercial enterprises, advertising is a mighty and frequently dangerous power.[38] Since in many countries the press, radio and television depend mostly on income from advertisements, powerful advertisers can use their influence to shape the media. They decide which kind of programmes they want to sponsor. And not only can they manipulate people to buy their products but, what is worse, they can indoctrinate uncritical people, inculcating the ideology that coveting, purchasing and consuming are the most important commandments.[39] Sir Hugh Greene is right in saying that "the system of licence fees paid by our viewers and listeners is one which makes us financially independent not only of the government but also of commercial pressures".[40]

In the pluralistic capitalist world, where the mass media generally follow the rules of the market, the buyer, the consumer, is majesty: he has the power to identify and unmask the dangerous powers only if he has a critical mind and the will to do it.

4. *The new mediators*

The time when priests had a kind of monopoly as mediator and communicator of information is past. Today the journalists have a leading role as informers and solicitors of thought. People listen to them much more than to priests. In view of this, the journalistic profession is one of the most important. In the eyes of faith, it is an arduous and great vocation. Indeed, journalists take up a considerable part of the traditional role of the priest. Hence they are also tempted to become a social class with a nimbus similar to that of priestly classes of the past thousands of years. But if one truly understands his vocation, he can have a role similar to that of the great history of prophetism. He can not only denounce the great evils, he can also help people to discover the most urgent signs of the times, the greatest opportunities and the main dangers.

While the journalist can be manipulated by the powers, and be tempted to manipulate others, his vocation is to inform people properly, to make them think and to search for discernment. Highly qualified journalists can be mediators between the most noble achievements of science and the populace. And this is true even for religious thought. Not all bishops and professional theologians have the ability to find the wave-length of the public. If a journalist is familiar with the best of theology, he may be better able than most theologians to communicate it to the many people who are interested but who would never read or properly understand papal encyclicals and books written by theologians. Thus the Church as well as secular society is interested in the best possible professional training for the journalists.

Our specific interest is a spirituality that befits this arduous and important vocation. In his more than one hundred communications, addresses and meditations for journalists and about their profession, Pope Paul VI gave main attention to the professional ethos and the ethics of communicators.[41]

The journalist's ethos implies service and absolute loyalty to the search and sharing of truth, concern for the common good, wisdom and discernment, a burning zeal for justice and truly human progress. He is not only bound to the just norms laid down by society; above all, he is bound by his conscience. He needs time for reflection and examination of conscience. On the one hand he needs a critical distance from the events and the powers, and on the other hand a nearness to people and sensitivity for the greater needs of the silent majority. There is no doubt that he can greatly help to change the world for the better if he encourages interest and enthusiasm for the positive opportunities, the good in people, and all the encouraging events and achievements while, in thoughtful proportions, denouncing the evils, hypocrisy and cowardice.

III. THE MASS MEDIA AND THE MAKEUP OF A NEW HUMANITY

The basis of moral theology is the knowledge of God and the knowledge of man. Before we can intelligently speak about our responsibility in the use of modern mass media, we must ask how modern man is already influenced by them and how, therefore, ethical reflections can reach and influence him.

1. *The positive-negative influence of the mass media on people*

Based on a number of studies, Kyle Haselden makes a reasonable guess that "radio, television, films and reading consume 35 hours a week of the average American's time; and television increasingly gets the lion's share of this time".[42]

The same is true for most of the western countries and probably will eventually be true also in the Third World. At the time of graduation from college, the young person has spent many more hours with the mass media — especially television — than in the classroom and in contact with his teachers. Many children are exposed very early to television's incisive influence. It becomes almost a new kind of parent. We might compare it with the way the young grey goose depends upon the animal, person or object with which it had the closest contact in the early days of life.

The mass media brings nothing less than a psychological and cultural revolution to the world. Whether in the long run it will be beneficial or negative is still under discussion. There can be no doubt that they give humanity a marvellous positive chance. We can hope that they will exercise an ever more integrating effect on our whole society and eventually on the world.[43] A proper use of the media tends to make people more conscious of their oneness, of their common problems and mutual perils. People's horizons are broadened. Distances between cultures and nations are overcome. We are becoming contemporaries of all people, and are learning to understand them better, to sympathize with them and, if needed, to help them. And while learning about the diversity of cultures, we learn also to discern more carefully between the abiding truth and time-bound realizations.

If people only make up their mind, the mass media can have a liberating effect freeing great masses of people from the prison of ignorance, from isolation and from tribal bias. Thus sectarian allegiances can gradually be diminished and transformed into enrichment and complementarity. Through the media, oppressed and underdeveloped peoples can be helped to overcome fatalism. They can learn that situations could be quite different and could, indeed, be changed. For speeding development in the Third World, the media can become an enormous factor.[44] The richness of imagination and fantasy, especially of the audio-visual media, allows a quicker grasp of the message, and through them, millions of disinherited people could share in cultural progress.

But while Marshall McLuhan leads the chorus in optimistic or even over-optimistic evaluations, there is no lack of apocalyptic pessimism. There are dangers, no doubt; and only if we face them can we hope to reduce or overcome them.

Many people live constantly in a condition of over-information. They expose themselves so long, so frequently and so uncritically to the messages of the media that they become confused and end up in a state of passivity.[45]

We may ask if our identity is not threatened through the constant input of information and impressions, while we lack similar opportunities for creative participation. Through the mass media we can live in so many different worlds and share in so many experiences that our primary and direct experiences may be somehow devoured.

A too long exposure to the imaginary world of some of the mass media can cause regression in a person's capacity to reflect and to face life realistically. We are exposed to so many new conditionings that, unless we prepare ourselves properly, our freedom may be jeopardized.

Pessimism will do no good. If we make the best use of the present opportunities offered by the mass media and face the dangers sensibly, there will be not so much reason for pessimism as for gratitude that we live in this age when new possibilities of searching for truth and sharing it challenge our creative freedom and fidelity.

2.   Understanding the mechanism of the mass media

Marshall McLuhan's slogan, "The medium is the message" has frequently been criticized. "He takes a partly true premise — media influences us apart from their content — and moves toward a wholly false conclusion, i.e., we should concentrate our attention and our study on the media rather than on their content".[46] But the fact of exaggeration does not dispense us from proper attention to the mechanism of the media.

An ethics of the mass media has to take into account the relative autonomy of this realm. The way it tends to operate and to influence the individual and the collectivity has to be studied from a technological, sociological, and especially psychological point of view.

Whether we are faced with a western capitalistic society or with the state capitalism of the Communist countries, the fact remains, as we have seen above, that the expensive mass media offer by their own mechanisms a great temptation to the powers. But if we act in co-responsibility, we can to a great extent get hold of the various mechanisms and determinisms. Then we shall be able to apply to the realm of the mass media the Lord's words, "The Sabbath is for man, and not man for the Sabbath". Their mechanisms do not, of themselves, keep us from putting them thoroughly at the service of persons and communities. Indeed, the mass media constitute an enormous challenge to apply the ethical principle of absolute respect for the dignity of each human person.[47]

The problems presented by the mass media cannot be properly approached by a merely or mainly individualistic ethics. Of course, we all have to ask ourselves how we make use of the media, how to become a discerning person, and so on. But in view of the enormous influence they exercise on the whole of society, on each community and person, it is an urgent duty for all to find the proper structures and to offer the kind of education that is indispensable for both individual and social responsibility in this field.

Some of the mechanisms or tendencies of the new media entail a very positive ethical appeal if they are rightly understood. McLuhan notes that "the new electronic interdependence recreates the world in the image of a global world".[48] If people in an era of such opportunity withdraw into an ethics of self-fulfilment, the mass media will still work in the direction of a global world, but one miserably tortured by collective egotism, the harvest of the egotism of the many. Our moral tasks must be measured by the chance offered by this opportunity to make the new global world more humane.

a) The Press

Though the use of both sign and word as expression of human thought belongs to the essentials of human nature, the first written record of human thought (ideogram) appears only about the year 5000 B.C. Alphabetical writing dates from about 1200 or 1000 B.C., which is after the time of Israel's patriarchs. Alphabetical writing has surely played a great role in keeping the memory of the great events of sacred history, and in a form that will refresh the memory of all people in the same way throughout the ages.

But only the invention of the printing press by Gutenberg made the holy Scripture accessible to all those interested. The Psalter was printed for the first time in 1447, and the Bible in 1455. The printed word played a great role at the time of the reformation.

From the beginning, the printing press served religious culture, but it also broke the quasi-monopoly of the Church as mediator of thought. The development of pluralism in public opinion is intimately linked with the printing press. The first daily paper was printed in Leipzig in 1660. In 1751, the first volume of the famous French encyclopedia was printed: a signal and powerful instrument of the Englightenment. The Daily Universal Register — called, since January, 1899, The Times of London — was founded in 1785. But the widespread development of the daily paper began only in the second half of the last century. Without it, today's culture, lively public opinion, international information, would not be even thinkable. Now, each year more than 200,000 books are printed, serving the dissemination and progress of science, imagination and entertainment and, last but not least, the spreading of the Gospel.

The printed word invites the reader to critical reflection. The combination of the printed word, drawings and pictures both facilitates comprehension and gives the word a deeper impact. The news agencies, including Christian ones, render an enormous service to the societal dialogue, and can exercise a great power for good or for evil. The Catholic press serves well the circulation of public opinion within the Church.[49] But the educated Catholic today will not confine his reading to a typical Catholic press.

Christians have a right to be represented by a press which observes events in the light of faith and contributes to a valid judgment of things in this light. But to aim the Catholic press in a pluralistic society at an exclusively Catholic readership would only reinforce a "ghetto mentality". Catholic journalists work within the secular press, and Catholic newspapers, if they are competent, will reach a readership far beyond the Church membership.

b)   Film

After five decades of experimentation and progress, one of the most influential media reached its peak with an annual moving-picture attendance of more than twelve billion throughout the world. This included two billion, five hundred million in the U.S.A. alone, and one billion three hundred million in England.[50]

In spite of the enormous competition of television, and especially of movies shown on television, the motion picture industry still exercises a great attraction and influence on its millions of spectators. The film is motion: moving pictures. The intimate bond between the acceptance of the film's message, made graphic and vivid to the senses, and the inner emotional life of the beholder, give the film its extraordinary power to impress. This singular impact on the imagination and emotions, far reaching as it may be, is often entirely unconscious. This is the language of the motion pictures. In a film, the spoken word possesses a unique power — through the artistic unity of the picture, colour, music and motion — to address the whole person. The film, as such, has in a sense become a new world language, for it is comparatively easy to synchronize the filmed picture with the sound track of various languages.

In this newest of the generally recognized "fine arts", the contribution of artists of the different branches unite to present a collective product of new artistic dimensions. Through the motion of impressive pictures and all the technological contributions, the film reaches a degree of nearness and suggestive power which goes beyond the influence of other arts.

The film can respond to a great diversity of expectations: it can offer the musical, drama, comics, news, the documentary. Through all these, it can convey a powerful message of human values and conflicts, broadening horizons and deepening the vision, often more than the traditional theatre. Most frequently it serves mainly as entertainment.

The law of the market poses the most serious problems in regard to the motion pictures. No doubt there are great artists who, because of their extraordinary competence and vision, can reach a considerable audience. Success (including commercial success) depends on the cooperation of the authors, the story, the star, the studio and the national film industry. But much depends on the creative initiative of the director.

The industrialized studio system in the United States is an example of enormous economic power. At its peak, the Hollywood studio produced over five hundred feature films each year for over seventy-five million weekly customers. It also owned most of the film theatres. And because of financial interests, it became practically an entertainment factory.[51] The local theatres not owned by the studios practically lost their freedom of choice through the system of "block booking", the selling of an entire season's output under one contract. Even when this became unlawful in the United States, it continued to be standard practice of some American companies outside their own country.

Today, television is the principal competitor of theatrical films, but at the same time it is an economic ally. Film companies produce programme series for television and thus sometimes lose their own identity, for a film made for television is different from an original movie.

Because of the commercial interests, the predominant film product today is frequently "raw sex without love, and crass violence: sex without love and violence without redemptive purpose".[52] It seems that the industry has found out, or rather decided, what the public wants.

In a democratic world there is, no doubt, much manipulation through the great trusts. But political power can be even greater. Hitler, Mussolini and the Communist regimes used films for political indoctrination. But even before the dictators came to power, film influenced somehow the political development. In the years before 1933, an excessive percentage of German movies had as their theme pessimism, discouragement, cynicism, despair. No doubt this was partially caused by the total situation, but the movie themes deepened and exacerbated the situation.

A new science, sociology of the media, studies the various interdependencies, and can be of great importance to a better understanding of the mechanisms of the film market and of other powers. This better knowledge can give a broader space for freedom.[53]

A special problem manifested over the whole world is the idolatrous star cult. Film stars are frequently better known and remunerated than the highest officials of the greatest nations. And it seems that more often people go to see a motion picture because of its stars than for any other reason. Some viewers, in their dreams and even in their conduct, identify themselves so closely with their favourite star that they undergo a kind of identity crisis.

Film stars usually tend to appear as themselves manifesting their well-known individuality in all the different roles, for people expect it. Thus they play quite differently than the stage actor who simply presents the role given him by the theatre. To be a movie actor/actress is an arduous vocation. From this, however, the pastoral instruction on the mass media does not conclude, as earlier manuals of moral theology did, that one should keep away from all this "proximate occasion of sin". Rather, it suggests that representatives of the Church should enter into a constructive dialogue with the media.[54]

People learn more from the film by absorption than by indoctrination. The movies can speak even to illiterates and, through the international language of the motion picture, can contribute to a better understanding among people of different cultures. However, no one can deny that the more than eighty years of motion picture history could have served humanity better if everyone had shown a spirit of co-responsibility. The Churches, too, could have done much more by sensitizing both the spectators and those involved in the motion picture industry.

The supreme pontiffs have taken, indeed, a very constructive approach to motion pictures. Classical examples are the two discourses (June 21 and October 28, 1955) of Pius XII on the ideal film. The Pope's point of departure is the assumption that the film is to serve the moviegoers. The basic prerequisites are therefore esteem for man, and the effort to turn to him with sympathy and to fulfil his reasonable desires as far as possible.

The ideal motion picture should show the spectator a profound understanding of reality. Cinema can have a truly emancipating and elevating effect only if it takes seriously the canons of art and the realities of life. The Church surely does not expect pietistic and moralistic films. Just as in the other arts it is permissible and often unavoidable to choose sometimes the evil and the scandalous as its vein, so it is for the film, but in the right proportion to its endeavour, to present the good, the beautiful and the joyous aspects of life. "Surely human life would not be understood, at least in its great and momentous conflicts, if our eyes were closed to the faults which often cause these conflicts ... Even the sacred books of the Old and the New Testaments, faithful mirrors of real life, contain in their pages stories of evil, of its action and influence in the lives of individuals as well as in families and peoples ... Let us grant then that an ideal film can also represent evil, sin and corruption. But let it do so with serious intent and in a becoming manner, in such a way that its vision may help deepen knowledge of life and of people, and improve and elevate the soul".[55]

The Second Vatican Council takes the same viewpoint: "Finally, with the help of the media of social communication too, the narration, description or portrayal of moral evil can indeed serve to make man more deeply known and studied, and to reveal and enhance the grandeur of truth and goodness. Such aims are achieved by means of appropriately heightened dramatic effects. Still, moral norms must prevail if harm rather than spiritual profit is not to ensue. This requirement is especially needed when the subjects treated are entitled to reverence or may all too easily trigger desires in man, wounded as he is by original sin".[56]

c) Radio and television

In the very year (1895) in which Louis Lumière exhibited his 65-foot filmstrip in Paris, the brilliant Italian physicist Guglielmo Marconi began the transmission of wireless flashes. On the basis of research by Hertz and Braul, he developed the system which enabled him to send the first wireless communication across the English Channel. From such auspicious beginnings, wireless radio developed with singular rapidity and perfection. Equally amazing is the progress made by television, which bids fair to surpass all other communication media in importance.

The pastoral instruction succinctly describes the function of radio and television: "Radio and television have given society new patterns of communication. They have changed ways of life. Broadcasting stretches out farther and farther towards every corner of the earth. Instantaneous transmissions break through political and cultural barriers. What they have to say reaches men in their own homes. Broadcasters have access to the minds and hearts of everyone.

"Rapid technological advances, especially those that involve satellite transmissions and the recording and storage of programmes, have done still more to free the media from the restrictions of time and space, and these promise still more effectiveness and influence. For the listener and viewer, radio and television open up the whole world of events, of culture and of entertainment. Television, especially, brings individuals and events before the general public as though the viewers were actually present. And besides the established forms of artistic expression, broadcasters have created art forms of their own which can affect man in new ways".[57]

Combined with recordings, film, radio and television help to form a new culture in which are decisive not the printed word or the abstract symbol but direct speech and vivid picture. Man's talent develops predominantly through a mingling of hearing and seeing.

Radio and television enlarge and supersede the press in their threefold service of information, education and entertainment. As far as entertainment is concerned, they offer considerable competition to the movies. However, they foster more an "encyclopedic spirit" than the formation of judgment.[58]

In comparison with the film theatre, television has the special advantage of helping to keep families together in the home. Radio and television are guests in the home and should fulfil their role as servants of the family. As such, of course, they give rise to quite serious problems. Guests tend, in general, to accommodate themselves to the family. But in the case of television, the very converse is frequently true. The family becomes the guests in the television room and accommodates itself to the powers behind the tube. The family is thus faced with no small task in being true to itself, to family ideals, and to turning the services of this communication media to the good.

René Berger, in his aptly titled book "The Telefission" ("fission": splitting up), shows particular interest in whether and how television fosters creativity. For this purpose he distinguishes macro-television (the television of the masses, in Europe the official or national television, and in the United

States the commercial or so-called "free" television), the meso-television (the local stations serving a limited community by cable), and the micro-television whose main tool is the video.

He does not ascribe to macro-television a high measure of creativity, since it does not solicit a dialogue and thus normally does not allow the viewers to be creative partners. When polls look for the reaction of the public, numbers are counted but not reasons. With many other authors he thinks, however, that regional stations and particularly micro-television greatly foster the spirit of creativity, active participation, dialogue and democratic expressions.[59] In many countries macro-television clings so strongly to its monopoly that everything is done to eliminate cable television. If we believe in creativity we should oppose that spirit of monopoly.

3. *Advertising*

Of itself, advertising is a good thing, an important service to the public. For what would all the accumulated products serve if those who need them were not informed about where and under what conditions they can obtain what is useful or necessary. The pastoral instruction on mass media describes the positive aspects first: "The importance of advertising is steadily on the increase in modern society. It offers real social benefits. It tells buyers of the goods and services available. It thus encourages the widest distribution of products, and in doing this it helps industry to develop and benefit the population".[60]

We have already seen that advertisers can be also inimical to the independence of the mass media. On this point the pastoral instruction is very outspoken: "The vast sums of money spent in advertising threaten the very foundations of the mass media. People can get the impression that the instruments of communication exist solely to stimulate man's appetites so that these can be satisfied later by the acquisition of the things that have been advertised. Moreover, because of economic demands and pressures, the essential freedom of the media is at stake. Since advertising revenue is vital for this media, only those can ultimately survive which receive the greatest share of advertising outlets. Consequently, the door is open for monopolies to develop in the media, which may impede the right to receive and to give information, and inhibit the exchange of views within the community".[61]

In countries where commercial television (already the name is indicative) dominates the field, the powerful companies choose the programmes they want to sponsor. Thus cultural problems, entertainment and so on can become a means for commercial purposes. But this is only one aspect; others are no less serious.

Advertising is a privileged arena for the "hidden persuaders".[62] Mass psychology offers itself willingly to the production of skilled manipulators in this field. The media not only seduce people to buy things that are not necessary or useful but, what is much more serious, they shape a whole consumer mentality, creating artificial needs and distorting, in people's hearts, the scale of values. The present system of advertising, and the manipulative methods used, suggest that the person is what he buys. People who expose themselves three, four or more hours each day to such advertising gradually begin to measure everything, including their own values and preferences, in a quantitative way, just as consumer goods are measured.

Modern advertising has its power through the mass media but has it also from a culture of consumerism to which it lends its own dynamics. Thus the manipulating power of advertisement goes far beyond the field of production and consumption.

Haselden writes: "The invasion of privacy is one of the most serious problems of our society, but there is a more pernicious threat — the electronic invasion of man's subconscious being. It would be a great mistake to ignore what advertising does to our freedom, our tastes, our moods, our conduct and our morality. Particularly dangerous is the heavy advertisement of psychotropic drugs by the drug industry. Not only are many people therefore over-medicated, but the advertisement also strengthens the trend towards drug addiction. The drug industries' wilful manipulation, done to maintain profits, has created social consequences that are only now becoming fully understood".[63]

The constant exposure of children to television advertisements has a negative influence on their whole education. Many children "have a much closer identity with commercial symbols than with biblical characters. The values exalted by mass advertising are youth, sexual attraction, romance, prestige, affluence and power".[64] Before children know the ten commandments, the three commandments of advertisers occupy their conscious and subconscious life: "Thou shalt covet; thou shalt buy; thou shalt consume".[65] Advertising is an enterprise that shapes and spreads the myth which our society needs in order to function as it does as a consumer society.[66]

No less serious is the harm that can be done to developing countries if advertising is not judicious but rather uses manipulating methods whereby communities are "persuaded to seek progress by satisfying wants that have been created artificially. The result of this is that they waste their resources and neglect their very needs, and genuine development falls behind".[67]

Frequent use of sexual imagery to keep the viewers' interest alive for the advertisement suggests that sexual desirability is the highest human value and the decisive criterion not only for purchasing but for life together. Haselden suggests that the buyers should unite to make clear to the advertising industry that "commercials that exploit and inordinately glorify sex will fail to sell products".[68] The same author is even more outspoken against the advertisers' use of symbols of violence and cruelty. "Cruelty is a consumption of suffering ... Brutality is a spiritual cannibalism by which we feast on the other person's suffering".[69]

4. Mass media and manipulation

The supreme law for the mass media is respect for the freedom of the communicating partners. Whatever unjustly or even heinously diminishes the freedom of the partners can be called manipulation. As criteria for discerning manipulation we can look closely at the language used. Has it an authoritarian tone? Does it label those who do not think as the communicators do? Plain falsification is more evident, while the methods of partial information, over-emphasis on one aspect while ignoring important factors, distorting the proportions and so on are not so easily discovered. Very frequently the trouble lies with manipulated manipulators who are unaware that they are being manipulated or that they are manipulating others.

Since entertainment plays a major part in today's life, much attention must be given to what kind of worldview it insinuates. What is the style of life, the ideals it presents. Style and content of entertainment can be as seductive as advertisement.

One of the most serious threats to human integrity is the constant exposure to scenes of excessive cruelty. This abuse of mass media, which suggests that the normal solution of human conflict is violence and even cruelty, is called by Haseldon "the most monstrous obscenity of our time". Particularly dangerous to humankind is the glorification of war and "the glamorizing of the military tradition".[70]

In the United States, a national commission studied the problem of violence and cruelty so frequently shown on television. Its conclusion, published September 23, 1969, was that this does great harm to youth and can promote a worldview in which people all too easily recur to violence. The main recommendations were: first, that parents should do all in their power to see that their children are not exposed to negative problems, and to educate them in a spirit of responsibility and not violence; and second, that the public should let the television stations know that they disapprove certain kinds of programmes.[71]

Not only can people be manipulated by the mass media; the media themselves are exposed to the dangers of manipulation. Journalists are, as we have seen, frequently restricted in their freedom and manipulated by the political and commercial powers. Ideologies expose all those involved to the danger of being manipulated. Relatively small groups have a disproportionate influence on the mass media: the advertisers, the teenagers demanding superficial entertainment and noisy music, the politicians who have economic interests in broadcasting, and especially political and religious extremists. "The rating agencies are the gods of American television. They are the makers and breakers of TV stars, the authorities before which advertisers bow".[72]

The predisposition for being manipulated is the passivity of the viewers, readers, listeners. They allow others to tell them what is true and what has to be done.[73] A certain kind of people is especially inclined to accept uncritically almost anything just because it is presented by television.

However, it is an error to think that the mass media have an absolute power over people's thinking and feeling. Sociology of the mass media has broken the myth of the faceless masses. The influence of the media on different groups varies greatly according to the socio-economic origin, the religious belonging, the identification with certain groups and the level of education. The recipient is in no way delivered to the mass media. People have their own way of reacting and thinking. In the United States, Roosevelt was elected a third time as president although 75% of the press opposed his re-election.[74]

5. Presence of the Church in the mass media

In accordance with the leitmotif of this moral theology, we ask ourselves whether the official Church and Christians in general were and are present in the mass media in a creative, liberating and faithful way.

Because of the alliance between throne and altar, the defence morality taught by so many manuals of moral theology, and not least because of the besieged mentality of the Church-state and partially the Church itself, the attitude of the official Church towards the modern press was not at all constructive. The emphasis was on the "good press", and that meant the same as the Catholic press, informing the people accurately about the pronouncements of the official Church.

The discipline of the Index of Forbidden Books was strict in its intention to protect the Church's monopoly on information. On November 25, 1766, Pope Gregory XIII published the encyclical *Christianae Reipublicae Salus*, denouncing the bad press and appealing to "priesthood and empire" to "eliminate these elements of perdition". No less defensive is the encyclical *Diu Satis* of Pius VII (May 15, 1800). In his first encyclical, *Mirari Vos*, August 15, 1832, Gregory XVI condemns again the "modern liberties" with a sharp warning addressed to "the Catholic liberals". Pope Pius IX, in his first encyclical, *Qui Pluribus*, November 9, 1846, condemns "the licence to think, to say and to print everything". The Syllabus of 1864 concludes (proposition 80) by condemning those who assert that "the

Roman pontiff can and must reconcile himself with progress, with liberalism and the modern culture".

Leo XIII speaks on the press in forty documents. The fact that the Church had lost the Church-state and its political power allows an opening. The appeal to state control is lessened. In his encyclical *Libertas* (June 28, 1888) Leo reforms to some extent the condemnation of "modern liberties" by presenting positively the nature of "true freedom". The much more constructive approach to the modern mass media during the pontificate of Pius XII was somewhat prepared by his immediate predecessors. His discourse of February 18, 1950, on the role of the Catholic press with regard to public opinion, stresses strongly the importance of public opinion in Church and society and of the necessary freedom to contribute to it. Pope John XXIII warmed the heart of the journalists. He was a great teacher of constructive presence in the world of today, especially by his optimism and his capacity to recognize everywhere first what is good, right and true. Pope Paul VI whose programme was dialogue, explicitly recognized a healthy change in the Catholic Church regarding freedom of communication and a constructive presence of Christians in all the mass media.[75]

The change concerns, above all, the understanding of the relation between truth and liberty. For Pope Gregory XVI, Pius IX, and to some extent their immediate successors, the Church seems to have a monopoly on truth, and this monopoly is within the circle of the hierarchy. The others, in order to be free, have to accept this truth uncritically, passively. The "sacred alliance" between Church and state seemed to guarantee that the state, as controller, would have the vital task of suppressing or forbidding everything that was not in correspondence with the truth communicated by the hierarchy. Leo XIII realized more fully that there is a broad field not determined by the dogmas of the Church, and that there the journalists and others have the right to search for truth in freedom.

Pius XII initiated a great breakthrough by emphasizing the need for freely searching and freely circulating a healthy public opinion in society and Church. The profound change of understanding is to be seen in the light of the declaration of the Second Vatican Council on Religious Liberty. Liberty in the search for truth is a condition for genuine dialogue and for opening oneself to the liberating truth. Leo XIII, in his encyclical *Libertas*, already anticipated future development, saying, "In questions in which God or the Church have not spoken a final word, in questions which God has left to free expression, everyone may think as he wills; what he judges as right may be spoken out, and this is not forbidden by nature. This freedom will not seduce man to suppress truth but rather helps us frequently to find the truth and to bring it to the light".[76] However, in most of the official documents of the Vatican prior to Vatican II, the relationship of the dialogue is a one-way-street and vertical. Journalists are admonished time and again to think, to speak and to write in all things as the official Church does.

The pastoral constitution on the Church in the Modern World synthesizes briefly the present approach of the Catholic Church: "All these considerations demand, too, that within the limits of morality and the general welfare, a man may be free to search for the truth, voice his mind, and publicize it; that he be free to practise any art he chooses; and finally that he have appropriate access to information about public affairs. It is not the function of public authority to determine what the proper nature or forms of human culture should be".[77]

The pastoral instruction on the mass media follows faithfully the spirit of Vatican II. It emphasizes both the responsibility of all those involved in the process of communication and of the public authorities. The emphasis, however, is on co-responsibility and the greatest possible freedom and creativity, as long as the freedom of all and the basic rights of all are observed.[78]

A careful study about the approach of the Catholic and Protestant Churches in Germany shows that the attention to forming responsible and critical minds in all participants in social communication is not one-sided; there is at least equal care for healthy structures.[79]

In her best tradition, the Church especially encourages artists to use the mass media for their creative work. "In a very precise and lucid way, the creative arts are more revealing than conceptual descriptions of people's character, their aspirations, emotions and thought. Even when the artist takes flight from the tangible and solid world and pursues his creative fantasies, he can give priceless insights into the human condition".[80] "It is a fact that when you writers and artists are able to reveal in the human condition, however lonely or sad it may be, a spark of goodness, at that very instant a glow of beauty pervades your whole work. We are only asking you to have confidence in your mysterious power to open up the glorious regions of light that lie behind the mystery of man's life".[81]

6. Who controls the controller?

In authoritarian societies, those on the top control everyone and everything without being controlled. On the contrary, in a pluralistic society, the main force is not control but co-responsibility, patient dialogue, trust in arguments and responsible use of freedom. But there is also need of control. However, this takes on manifold forms. It is always reciprocal. Those in authority are controlled through free elections and through the forces of public opinion. It is important to ask ourselves, time and again, who controls the mass media? Who makes the choice of the journalists' programmes and so on? Is the power of choice exercised responsibly, openly, in view of the common good? Or are there particular interests militating against the common good?

Haselden addresses himself first to the kind of control the various Churches have exercised, and he dares to state: "Almost without exception the Churches have been wrong in their censorship and control, and they have been wrong not only in restricting human freedom but in their evaluations of what knowledge is valid, useful and beneficial to man. Over the years, the Churches, with occasional exceptions, have taken wrong positions on new theories of the cosmos, the continuing process of creation, the justification of war and slavery, the inerrancy of the Bible. They have not only tried to keep the people from discovering the truth for themselves, but have insisted that the people accept and profess error".[82] This is the evaluation of a Protestant author regarding the various Churches.

Regarding the Catholic Church, a Catholic author, Giselbert Deussen adds a further problem. He thinks that, until recent times, papal utterances ascribed to state control "a dangerous kind of infallibility that all too easily could imply the temptation to impose on the mass media a moral system that could eliminate the right to information, the truth and liberty of it".[83]

An open control by the state authorities that submit themselves willingly to democratic rules can be much better than control by financial powers or a group of élitists. A democratic state will be happy about decent self-control exercised by the professions and their partners, and will intervene only when there is special need. Control through state authority should cling to the following rule: "Freedom to receive and to utter ideas should not have to defend itself; censorship should".[84]

Regarding the responsibility of the legislator, there are two opposite trends. The first says, "You can't legislate morality"; the other insists, "There ought to be a law". Our response is: "The purpose of law is not to make man good, not even to make him just, but to protect him from injustice".[85]

The modalities of control will greatly depend on the different models of the organization of the mass media. In the democratic countries there are two quite different types, the one prevailing in the United States, the other well-functioning in England. The first is commercial broadcasting. There the recipient pays indirectly to the advertisers who, on their part, finance the mass media and therefore exercise disproportionate influence on them. The British system, also prevalent in the democratic countries of Europe, is public broadcasting or pay-broadcasting. The recipient pays a fee and the broadcasting organization is directly under public control. It is an institution that administers itself according to principles and rules laid down by the legislator and/or worked out through experience.

In several countries there is no state monopoly. Pay-television is side-by-side with commercial television stations and networks. But whatever the system, public authority has to guarantee some basic rights: first, to protect children in their formative years against programmes with a highly dramatic effect on their life; second, to oblige the owners or directors of the mass media not to prevent programmes of good quality; third, to protect recipients from inundation by commercials, to the damage of desirable programmes; fourth, to guarantee the rights of minorities (ethnic, religious, cultural); fifth, to protect persons and organizations against slander.[86] Control through sanctions and detailed rules are the last resort. Much more can be done by persuasion and by stimulating ideas. There must be special care not to provoke "frustration of creative people".[87]

7. *Creating the discerning and responsible person and community*

In 1963, the Council of Churches declared: "The whole public is responsible for the functioning of the mass media; and the individual Christian, as citizen, is impelled to exert what influence he can to have television and radio operate for the public good". [88] For this purpose it is necessary that the Churches themselves and all other educational agencies concentrate their energies to help form the discerning and responsible person and community. "It is never too early to start encouraging in children artistic tastes, a keen critical faculty and a sense of personal responsibility based on sound morality. They need all these so that they can use discrimination in choosing the publications, films and broadcasts that are set before them ... This is why parents and teachers should urge children to make their own choice even if, at times, the educators should reserve the final decision to themselves. And if they find themselves forced to disapprove of the way their children are using some aspect of the media, they must clearly explain the reasons for their objections. Persuasion works better than prohibition, and this is especially true in education".[89]

Families and communities should come together and discuss the various problems and ask themselves explicitly by what kind of criteria they are judging. The small-group dialogue should, time and again, include or inform the communicators, of course in a constructive way, not offering only negative critique but also praise and expression of appreciation.

The Church's main contribution is conscience raising, education to personal and social responsibility.[90] In this field, ongoing adult education is particularly urgent. And one of its main purposes is thereby to form the discerning, responsible person, offering proper criteria and a vision of wholeness. The Christian should know, above all, the dimensions of true freedom, for in Christ he has received the truth that makes people free.[91]

It is my conviction that we can avoid becoming manipulated manipulators only to the extent that we cultivate the contem-

plative dimension of our existence. Without education for the
right kind of contemplation and prayer (integration of faith and
life), our hope to see a discerning generation arising is in vain.
For Christians, it is contemplation in the Word incarnate.
We have to be aware of the audiovisual character of today's
mass media and of the whole mindset of modern man. Therefore
we turn to Christ, who is the Word and the image. But the
viewer, glutted by an endless stream of rapidly passing moving
pictures and an insatiable curiosity for all kinds of information,
may well damage his contemplative power.[92] And finally,
Christian contemplation makes us ever more aware that we are
not merely spectators but co-creators in this world entrusted
to our responsibility.

8. *Ascetics regarding mass media*

Today's world offers man, if he knows how to exercise
moderation, more leisure time than any previous generation.
These added hours open greater possibilities for relaxation,
entertainment and meaningful cultural development. Obviously,
active participation is required by the free creative spirit for
positive use of leisure time rather than for mere passive consumption of prefabricated programmes.

As far as individual morals are concerned, three norms
should regulate our conduct: 1) select with discretion; 2) use
with discrimination; 3) limit enjoyment in the spirit of Christian
freedom.

a) Selective discretion

In the cultivation of mind and spirit, there is undoubtedly
a grave obligation to select judiciously what fosters our psychic,
moral and religious development, and to shun all that jeopardizes
our mental and spiritual health, and especially our faith. To
this purpose, we have to pay proper attention to the practical
directives given by the Church concerning the mass media.

That the Church has abolished the Index of Forbidden Books
does not dispense with but rather demands more personal
responsibility and, if necessary, the help of people more competent than ourselves.

Committees set up by Church authorities or other ecclesiastical agencies for film classification provide help for proper selection, which one should not discard unless one is already well informed through other sources. Our care in selecting our reading, radio programmes, motion pictures and television offerings should be not less but more sensitive than in selecting our food, for moral and spiritual health is more important than physical health.

b) A critical spirit

It is not enough to make a judicious selection among the many offerings of the mass media. Equally important is it to develop a critical spirit in the reception of the offerings chosen. If we were to have millions of people with clear discernment and sound judgment, this would spontaneously influence the mass media everywhere. The Christian is guided by the words of the Apostle, "Bring them all to the test and then keep what is good in them and avoid the bad of whatever kind" (1 Thess 5:20).

c) Ascetic frugality

To preserve or regain moral independence, a resolute and ascetic frugality is required. This means, besides the judicious selection of programmes, a right-ordered moderation. The western world has frequently been characterized as a consumer society. A powerful and efficient advertising industry and a great part of the mass media look upon individuals and groups only as potential consumers of their products.

The flood of sentiment and sensation in our entertainment, the hum of the machine in our technical society, the rush of the assembly line, and the weekend traffic jam all make it difficult for people to possess themselves in peace today. In spite of all this, people who have chosen inner and outer freedom as an absolute norm learn to reflect thoughtfully and to ponder the message of things and events with freedom and discernment. Therefore, even in regard to useful and serviceable offerings, they will exercise moderation with sharp awareness. There must be time available for prayer, for meditation and reflective reading. Precisely where there is no objectionable content — let us say in an illustrated magazine, a screen offering, a telecast — the law of freedom enunciated by the Apostle holds good: " 'I am free to do anything', you say. Yes, but not everything is for my good. No doubt I am free to do anything, but I, for one, will not let anything make free with me" (1 Cor 6: 12).

The freedom of the children of God, bought with the great price of the blood of the covenant, constantly demands also the price of voluntary renunciation. The best opportunities for exercising this "being free for others" are presented in that solicitude for neighbour which is essential for genuine communication. For instance, we suggest that the father of the family should not bury his face in the sports page if his wife and/or children are wishing for his companionship in the evening after he has returned from work. Or the avid listener or viewer will turn off the radio, television or stereo in a spirit of community if the programme disturbs others. In countless ways one can and must exercise the moderation of ascetic frugality. Only thus does one avoid becoming a mere consumer of the mass media.

Spouses who know the genuine meaning of conjugal love and sexual endowment will not allow their home to be flooded with programmes that directly contradict their ideals. Priests and religious and, in general, all those who are called in a special way to bear witness to their free commitment in celibacy, will bind themselves by strict standard. They will avoid any kind of "input" that militates against their vows or state of life. Obviously, this applies not only to the specific choice of reading or screen and television fare but also as a comprehensive rule of moderation in all areas. Everything will be scrutinized as to whether or not it enhances their freedom for the Lord and for their fellowmen, and their fidelity in Christ.

IV. MASS MEDIA AND PUBLIC OPINION

Social communication is, above all, an exchange of opinions, news, worldviews, intended to promote mutual information, so that all may understand better not only what is happening but also what the happenings mean. In this communication, the consciences of all people should be united for the search of what is true, good and beautiful.

1. *Meaning and function of public opinion*

The individual, human groups, and society at large are never in full and uncontested possession of all truths. They can come closer to them through the shared effort of social communication. In a planetarian society, this communication occurs particularly through the mass media.

The pastoral instruction on the mass media of 1971 gives the following explanation. "Public opinion is an essential expression of human nature organized in a society. This opinion is formed in the following way. In everyone there is an innate disposition to give vent to opinions, attitudes and emotions in order to reach a general acceptance on convictions and customs. Pius XII describes public opinion as 'the natural echo of actual events and situations as reflected more or less spontaneously in the minds and judgments of men'... If public opinion is to emerge in the proper manner, it is absolutely essential that there be freedom to express ideas and attitudes".[93]

The pilgrim Church should have no fear of knowledge or of public search for knowledge through communication. Only undigested knowledge or supposed knowledge of those who dwell in ivory towers, or knowledge that is never to be put into practice can be futile and even dangerous.

Communicators play an essential part in forming public opinion. They should not try to impose their own opinion, however, but rather should give objective information "to gather up different views and compare them and transmit them so that the people can understand and make a proper decision".[94]

In this important task of forming healthy public opinions, nobody should be a bystander or simply a passive receiver. Even those who cannot directly influence the communicators can share their reflections and partial insights with their close associates. The communicator should not hide his convictions, but he has to distinguish carefully between firm convictions and tentative opinions; and he will use no trick to impose his convictions on others, for whatever does not arise from a convinced conscience is falsehood.

The free flow of communication and respectful participation in the formation process of public opinions is basic for the survival of a democratic free society. And democracy can make a very positive contribution to reaching more informed public opinions. However, one must be warned against the tendency simply to join the majority opinions. Even when a critical mind can join with them for common action, there must be an ongoing effort to bring home one's further or qualifying insights and convictions.

2.   Freedom and truth

Between freedom and truth, if both are rightly understood, there can be no conflict. God decides in his absolute freedom to share life and truth with us, and he calls us in freedom to receive truth, to search for more truth, and to share it with our fellowmen.

In the last century the dictum "truth will set you free" was frequently used not only against excessive libertinism but also against the desire for greater freedom in the search and utterance of convictions. The present teaching of the Church has overcome this kind of opposition between "truth" and "freedom". It carefully teaches the faithful, and through them the world, what our understanding is of freedom and of the search for truth and acting on the truth. "In order that men may carefully co-operate and further improve the life of the community, there must be freedom to assess and compare differing views which seem to have weight and validity. Within this free interplay of opinions there exists a process of give and take, of acceptance or rejection, of compromise or compilation. And within this same process the more valid ideas can gain ground so that a consensus that will lead to common action becomes possible".[95]

As we have seen in the first chapter of this volume, truth can be corrupted by using it for selfish interests or by proposing it in a loveless way. Genuine freedom is the freedom for others, freedom to love and to discern what builds up and what can only disrupt communion. There is a right to privacy and to that social honour without which one cannot play his full role in society and in the search for truth.

Not all news is useful for a civilized society. For instance, giving disproportionate attention to acts of terrorism gives terrorists a public forum that they do not deserve. Of course their attacks can and sometimes must be communicated, but this should be done as briefly and unsensationally as possible, except for the "sensation" of prompt action against them and the dignified conduct of people faced with this problem.

Genuine freedom, so necessary for building up healthy public opinions, includes the courage promptly to correct one's views or one's information about facts.[96] For a communicator to acknowledge an error is not a humiliation. We are all learners, and none is guaranteed to be always right. Our freedom is in many ways freedom for truth in the making. We all realize, too, that the professional job of the communicator often does not allow the amount of research and reflection that would be ideal.

3. Public opinion within the Church

The Church founded by Jesus Christ is much more than an opinion-forming forum. She has more to offer than mere opinions based on maximum probabilities. Taught by Jesus and the Spirit of Truth, she unfailingly communicates to us truth revealed in Jesus Christ, and the life-giving law of the Spirit in Christ Jesus.

The deposit of faith that has to be faithfully transmitted unto the end of history is not present in the Church as dead capital. Only in lively evangelization, in sharing truth, and in the common effort for a better understanding of salvation truth in order to live it more faithfully, does the Church remain "in the truth".

The Second Vatican Council has freed the people of God from a merely vertical communication from the top to the bottom, whereby the communicators were only channels to spread what those in authority had said. The pastoral instruction on the mass media is very explicit about the character of public opinion in the Church, both in the search for a deeper understanding of the common faith and in public opinions that do not belong to the deposit of faith. All of God's people have to contribute, each according to his competence and charism. This means much for an efficient exercise of authority. "The normal flow of life and the smoothest functioning of government within the Church require a steady two-way flow of information between the ecclesiastical authorities at all levels and the faithful as individuals and as organized groups. This applies to the whole world. To make this possible, various institutions are required".[97]

Of course, the first thing is to capture this spirit of dialogue on all levels, this solidaric commitment to the search of truth in order to join hands for common action in the communication of the Gospel and of new insights about history.

In regard to secrecy in the Church, we have the following courageous statement: "On those occasions when the affairs of the Church require secrecy, the rules normal in civil affairs equally apply ... Secrecy should therefore be restricted to matters that involve the good name of individuals or that touch upon the rights of people, whether singly or collectively".[98] We have to see this two-way relationship of information in the light of what we have explained about "the reciprocity of consciences". Everyone should participate in absolute sincerity and with a conscience as informed as possible.[99] Even this very sharing should tend to deepen one's own conscientious judgment.

The Church is fostering not only ecumenical dialogue as one of its main concerns but equally a dialogue with the world. Hence the circulation of public opinions, and the participation of all members of the Church in freedom and earnestness of conscience, makes the Church a servant for today's world.[100] In this participation and dialogue, very imperfect concepts and formulations in regard to faith will come into the open. They are not the result of this participation but of the earlier times of passivity. Active participation in a spirit of freedom and mutual trust, arising from trust in the "Spirit of Truth" will bring the faithful to greater maturity of faith and to a better deciphering of the signs of the times.

Everyone who is aware of the importance of this exchange of information and the common effort to form healthy and viable public opinions will also recognize his co-responsibility for the proper functioning of the mass media. We all have some measure of power to influence this function, and it is our duty as Christians, to use it intelligently.

Not only in matters concerned with a better understanding of the faith, but even more in religious and moral questions not defined by dogma and not belonging to the deposit of faith, and especially in the discernment of the signs of the times, the communicators should listen also to the voice of the humble people. That may sometimes make them more critical but generally less critical and more constructive in regard to the voice of the hierarchical Church and the voices of the great prophets of each age. Pope Paul VI invited journalists to make their journal "the voice of the people", the voice that comes from the people, voices that reach the heart of the people.[101]

V. THE MASS MEDIA AND EVANGELIZATION

The Council document on social communication, *Inter Mirifica*, concentrates mainly on the Church's mission to evangelize and to use the modern mass media to "tell out the Good News from the housetops" in a new and more effective way.[102] However, the scope of the Church's reflection on the mass media was broadened in the Council, especially in *Gaudium et Spes*, and even more through the pastoral instruction *Communio et Progressio* of 1971. Before the Church tries to use the mass media for evangelization, she tries first to understand the mechanics in the diverse societies, to see how people are influenced by the mass media, and to show great concern for people's integrity, dignity and freedom: a concern that flows from the Gospel and leads to the truth of the Gospel.

It seems to me that the Church's primary use of the mass media in a pluralistic society is a dialogue with other Churches, with other believers and religions, with the humanistic world. If this dialogue removes prejudices and leads to a better understanding, then the way is paved not only for an attractive evangelization but also for a common commitment to justice, peace and truth. We have already seen that the mass media offer effective means of presenting our faith and our moral convictions in an integrated and, so to speak, "incarnate" way.

The Church would not be faithful to her own identity and calling, did she not heed the urgent command to bring the Good News to all people. "Indeed, it would be difficult to suggest that Christ's command was being obeyed unless all the opportunities offered by the modern media to extend to vast numbers of people the announcement of his Good News were being used".[102] "Of course the mode of presentation has to suit the special nature of the medium being used. The media are not the same as a church pulpit. It cannot be overstressed that the standard of such presentation must at least equal in quality the other productions of the media".[103] Happily, the mass media force us to acknowledge a pluralism of cultures and customs. Their functioning also requires us to speak always respectfully about other people's convictions.

The people of the Church should not restrict themselves to the means of communication owned by the Church, or to programmes sponsored by the Church.[104] The use of mass media can be particularly effective when Christians act responsibly not as official or authorized representatives of their Church, but simply speak out faithfully and joyously their personal vision arising from faith.

Social communication in the service of justice and peace, and for the Gospel message should be given much greater emphasis and attention in the formation of all people, but especially of Christian educators and priests.[105]

Harvey Cox makes some pertinent suggestions for evangelization through mass media: first, a prudent limitation of those media that make dialogue difficult; second, the use of the media for the Good News, in such a way that people are invited to participate actively and to express themselves; third, Christians should unite with all people of good will to break the monopolies of the mass media; fourth, the whole education should lend itself to the virtue of discernment and constructive critique; fifth, the Churches have to develop a dialogical style that invites everyone to participate trustfully; sixth, the development of those mass media that are most accessible to the community; and finally, the use of the actual mass media through the Church in such a way that lends her voice to those who seem to have no voice to make themselves present in society.[106]

I might add the suggestion that Church prelates should not be seen too frequently in their full garb and dignity, for this can give a distorted picture of the Church as a whole. The Church should make known the Prophet, Jesus Christ, by being a prophetic voice helping people to discover all the possibilities to grow in justice, peace and compassion, and by denouncing the greatest evils, for instance, the arms race and hostile references to other groups and peoples. At the heart of the Christian Gospel is the message of peace.

NOTES

1 *Communio et progressio*, n. 11.
2 Cf. V. Schurr, *Das Wort Gottes und seine Verkündigung heute. Zur Theologie der Massenmedien*, Nürnberg-Eichstädt, 1962, 12.
3 l.c., 8f.
4 *Communio et progressio*, n. 175.
5 B. Häring, "Theologie der Komunikation und theologische Meinungsbildung", in F.J. Eilers and others (eds.), *Kirche und Publizistik*, München-Paderborn-Wien, 1972, 38ff.
6 P. Watziawick, J.H. Bevin, D.D. Jackson, *Menschliche Komunikation. Formen, Störungen, Paradoxen*, Stuttgart-Wien, 1972³, 22 (original English title: *Pragmatics of Human Communication. A Study of Patterns, Pathologies and Paradoxes*, New York, 1967).
7 l.c., 50.
8 Cf. R. Berger, *La telefission, Alerte à la télévision*, Tournai, 1976, 176.
9 K. Haselden, *Morality and the Mass Media*, Nashville, 1968⁴, 52.
10 P. Watziawick, l.c., 53.
11 D.D. Jackson, "Family Interaction, Family Homeostasis and Some Implications for Conjoint Family Therapy", in J. Massermann (ed.), *Individual and Family Dynamics*, New York, 1959, 237.
12 P. Watziawick, l.c., 48.
13 R. May, *Man Searching for Himself*, 64.
14 Paul VI, *Populorum Progressio*, n. 20; cf. G. Deussen, *Ethik der Massenkomunikation bei Papst Paul VI*, München-Paderborn-Wien, 1973, 216ff.
15 *Gaudium et Spes*, 5.
16 l.c., 4.
17 l.c., 6.
18 Cf. J. Magli, in D. Basili (ed.), *Pluralismo*, Roma, RAI, 1976, 194-198.
19 I refer to "Eurocommunism". Cf. L. Coletti, in D. Basili, l.c., 89ff. Everything will depend on to what degree these parties will foster a genuine dialogue within themselves and allow that extent of pluralism which is indispensable for seeking truth freely.
20 Sir H. Greene, *The Conscience of the Programme Director*, BBC, London, 1965, 5.
21 Quote in Greene, l.c., 5.
22 l.c., 12.
23 Cf. L. Giusani, in Basili, l.c., 172; B. Häring, l.c., 177ff; B. Sorge, l.c., 290-295; K. Rahner, Preface to K. Rahner (ed.), *Befreinde Theologie. Der Beitrag Lateinamerikas zur Theologie der Gegenwart*, Stuttgart, 1977, 6.
24 *Lumen gentium*, 13.
25 l.c., 32.
26 *Decree on Ecumenism*, 4.
27 B. Sorge, in D. Basili, l.c., 290-295.
28 Cf. *Gaudium et Spes*, 16; cf. K.W. Bühler, *Die Kirchen und die Massenmedien. Intentionem und Institutionen in Rundfunk, Fernsehen, Film und Presse*, Hamburg, 1968, 17f.
29 G. Deussen, l.c., 22f.
30 Greene, l.c., 4, 10.
31 J. Habermas, *Technik als Ideologie*, Frankfurt, 1969², 49-183.
32 Cf. H. Holzer, "Politik in Massenmedien. Zum Antagonismus von Presse — und Gewerbe-Freiheit", in R. Zoll (ed.), *Manipulation der Meinungsbildung*, Opladen, 68-108; E. Domay (ed.), *Manipulation in der Kirche*, Gütersloh, 1977.
33 H. Pross, *Moral der Massenmedien. Prologomena zu einer Theorie der Publizistik*, Köln-Berlin, 1967, 187-235.
34 *Communio et progressio*, n. 80.
35 Cf. Deussen, l.c., 280. The author thinks that most of the documents of the Church on the mass media appeal almost exclusively to the individual morality, leaving out the structural problems.

[36] R. Berger, l.c., 90-98.
[37] K. Haselden, l.c., 183.
[38] Cf. E. Henning, "Die Abhängigkeit der Massenmedien von den Werbeeinnahmen und dem Anzeigenteil", in R. Zoll, l.c., 27-67.
[39] Cf. Communio et progressio, 59-62.
[40] H. Greene, l.c., 10ff. (He speaks about the BBC system.)
[41] Cf. G. Deussen, l.c., 141-194.
[42] Haselden, l.c., 59.
[43] Cf. l.c., 66-70.
[44] Communio et progressio, 92-95.
[45] Cf. R. Berger, l.c., 33.
[46] Haselden, l.c., 63.
[47] Cf. Communio et progressio, 14.
[48] M. McLuhan, The Gutenberg Galaxy, The Making of a Typographic Man, Toronto, 1962, 31.
[49] Communio et progressio, 136-141.
[50] Cf. Enc. Britannica, 12, 497-511: "Art of Motion Pictures" (with bibliography).
[51] l.c., 12, 529.
[52] K. Haselden, l.c., 157.
[53] Cf. A. Silbermann, Mediensoziologie, vol. I, Dusseldorf, 1973.
[54] Communio et progressio, 147.
[55] Pius XII, "Address to Delegates to the Congress of the International Union of Theatre Owners and Film Distributors", October 28, 1955, in Catholic Mind 54 (1956), 104ff.
[56] Decree on the Media of Social Communication, 7.
[57] Communio et progressio, 148.
[58] Cf. R. Berger, l.c., 193.
[59] l.c., 191-205.
[60] Communio et progressio, 59.
[61] l.c., 62.
[62] Cf. V. Packard, The Hidden Persuaders, New York, 1957.
[63] K. Haselden, l.c., 144.
[64] J. Pekkanen, The American Connection. Profiteering and Politicking in the "Ethical Drug Industry", Chicago, 1973, 14; cf. B. Häring, Manipulation, Ethical Boundaries of Medical, Behavioural and Genetic Manipulation, Slough, 1975, 25-27.
[65] K. Haselden, l.c., 151.
[66] Cf. R. Berger, l.c., 74; K. Horn, "Zur individuellen Bedeutung und gesellschaftlichen Funktion der Werbeinhalte", in R. Zoll, l.c., 201-241.
[67] Communio et progressio, 61.
[68] K. Haselden, l.c., 110.
[69] l.c., 116.
[70] l.c., 117.
[71] Cf. G. Guardia, La televisione come violenza, Bologna, 1970, 194-211.
[72] Haselden, l.c., 131, cf. 129.
[73] Cf. H. Pross, Moral der Massenmedien,, Köln-Berlin, 1967, 235.
[74] Cf. Deussen, l.c., 148, 273ff; H. Zöller (ed.), Massenmedien, die geheimen Führer, Augsburg, 1965, 27.
[75] Deussen, l.c., 83; C.J. Pinto de Oliveira, Information et propagande. Responsabilités chrétiennes, Paris, 1968, 315-323; 399-411.
[76] Leo XIII, cf. Deussen, l.c., 44-47.
[77] Gaudium et Spes, 59; Decree on the Media of Social Communication, 5.
[78] Cf. Communio et progressio, 78, 108ff.
[79] K.W. Bühler, l.c., 64.
[80] Communio et progressio, 56.
[81] Paul VI, Address of May 6, 1967, to Artists and Communicators, AAS 59 (1967), 509.
[82] Haselden, l.c., 85.
[83] Cf. Deussen, l.c., 137.

84 Haselden, l.c., 93; cf. P. Casillo, *La morale della notizia*, Roma, 1974, 122ff.
85 Haselden, l.c., 174.
86 l.c., 180-182.
87 H. Greene, l.c., 8; cf. B. Häring, *Manipulation*, 83-84.
88 Quoted by Haselden, l.c., 135.
89 *Communio et progressio*, 67, cf. 81-83.
90 l.c., 102.
91 Cf. vol. I, ch. IV, esp. pp. 121-143.
92 Cf. J. Pieper, "Kann der Zeitgenosse ein kontemplativer Mensch sein?", in *Herderkorrespondenz* 31 (1977), 400-405.
93 *Communio et progressio*, 24-25.
94 l.c., 27.
95 l.c., 26.
96 l.c., 41.
97 l.c., 120.
98 l.c., 121; cf. F.P. Schaller, *Zum Informationsrecht im kirchlichen Raum*, Freiburg/schw., 1970.
99 Cf. vol. I, ch. VI.
100 Paul VI gives special praise to this emphasis of *Communio et progressio*, esp. of the dialogue and participation: *Address to Journalists*, L'Osservatore Romano of Jan. 25, 1973.
101 Address to the weekly "La Voce del Popolo", Sept. 20, 1969, quoted by Deussen, l.c., 193.
102 *Communio et progressio*, 126.
103 l.c., 128.
104 When I had to make a choice between different invitations for broadcasting stations I generally gave preference to participation in cultural (not church-related) programmes, because there we can reach many people who never show up under our pulpits and normally do not tune in on church-related programmes.
105 *Communio et progressio*, 134.
106 H. Cox, *The seduction of the Spirit*, Wildwood House, London. (Italian tr., *La seduzione dello Spirito*, Brescia, 1974, 285-359.)

Chapter Four

Salvation, Liberation Through Faith

The search for and sharing of truth, and especially life in truth, has its summit and centre in faith. Through faith we receive Christ and open ourselves to his liberating truth. Christ is the Truth. In him, the triune God has revealed himself as love. Whoever sees him sees the Father. And whoever receives him abides in him who is Truth, the truthful witness of the Father's love, and the way to him and to the fullness of life.

We speak here of faith in the biblical perspective, especially that of John and Paul. We do not mean only faith in a formulated creed, but faith as adequate response to God's revealing himself and sharing his life with us; faith as joyous, grateful reception of him who is truth and love, and to whom we freely entrust ourselves. This is the faith that bears fruit in love.

Very early, St Paul synthesized Christian life as a fully human life that shares in Christ through the three theological virtues. "We call to mind, before our God and Father, how your faith has shown itself in action, your love in labour, and your hope of our Lord Jesus Christ in fortitude" (1 Thess 1:3; cf. 1 Thess 5:8; 2 Thess 1:3-4).

Sometimes Paul sees this fullness of life altogether as an expression of faith that justifies those who turn to Christ. For him, faith is filled with hope and trust, and opens to the Holy Spirit who produces the fruits of love, peace, joy and so on. But he can also synthesize all three virtues in the dimension of love. "There is nothing that love cannot face; there is no limit to its faith, its hope and its endurance" (1 Cor 13:7). "There

are three things that last forever: faith, hope and love; but the
greatest of them all is love" (1 Cor 13:13).

Without hope and love, faith is practically dead, like a
comatose body. We may, however, hope that the body can
still be resuscitated, reanimated, as long as a sinner is still
somehow longing to put his trust in the Lord and to love him.

Here we speak of faith in its dynamics towards fullness,
in its saving and liberating power.

I. THE CONSTITUTIVE DIALOGUE

1. *Revelation through creation*

In theology there are different ways of speaking about
creation. Apologetics and a part of modern fundamental theology
speak about it first from the viewpoint of mere natural reflection.
Here in moral theology we speak of it in the full light of revelation,[1] giving particular attention to those fundamental dimensions that are relevant for the understanding of our moral life.

"The Word was with God at the beginning, and through him
all things came to be. No single thing was created without him.
All that came to be was alive with his life" (Jn 1:2-4). All of
created reality is radically marked by the Word. Through all
of creation God speaks to man whom he has created in his
image and likeness, and to whom he has given the most essential
quality, the ability to listen to the Word, to decipher it, and to
utter a word by which he gives a total response to God. The
whole world is a message, a word, a gift to that privileged
creature who comes to the fullness of his truth only in the
Thou-I relationship with God.[2]

Creating man in his image and likeness, God freely decides
to call each person by a unique name, and to call them all together
in his Word. Creation belongs to the great deeds of salvation.
It is God's free sharing of being, of life, of truth, of the capacity
to accept love and to love in return. Our relationship with God
is not something added to our being; his word is constitutive.
But we come to our fullness of being only by receiving his
word, gratefully treasuring it above all things, and responding
with all our being. We are in the truth only if we understand

and honour our own existence and all of creation as a word and gift, as a radical call to respond.

The superficial person, who never thinks of his coming from God and being destined for God, ignores not only the fundamental truth but fails to come to his own truth. The sinner who, by his word and his life denies God, disinherits himself from basic truth. By closing his mind to the truth of being created by God and called to him, he decides to live in radical contradiction to the constitutive word by which he still lives. He expresses himself in total self-contradiction. It is the mystery of sin that one can live in spite of this self-contradiction. But in reality, he does not live at all on the level of humanity as God wills it. Those who adore God and those who disown him are fundamentally two different species. The latter belong to the true human species only in the way of contradicting it.

In our reflections on existential truth, we have frequently spoken about man's search for truth. It is essential, however, to keep in mind that the question does not arise first from man. Rather, it is God's initiative. By creating man in his image, he makes man's truth dependent on how he responds to this constitutive word and question.

A transcendental theology that stresses the essential constitution of man through God's own creative word does not forget the psychological constitution that results from our communication with our fellowmen. Our being for each other and with each other is the psychological and historical recognition of our existence in the Word of God. It is the spectrum and condition that enables us to live in that Word by a life-response.[3]

As believers, we reflect on creation in the light of the mystery of the Holy Trinity. With Thomas Aquinas we think that "the knowledge of the divine persons is necessary for us in order to think rightly on created reality".[4] In everything that the triune God creates there are vestiges of the divine life, of the Father who speaks out himself in his Word, and of the Spirit who is the gift between the Father and the Son. The inner sharing in a communion of truth, love and life within the Holy Trinity determines, in absolute freedom, the bringing forth of creation.[5]

Holy Scripture teaches us to look on creation in a Christological perspective. All of creation, of evolution and history, has its finality in the coming of the Word of God in human flesh, thus bringing history to its fulfilment. The Word in whom all things were created "became flesh; he came to dwell among us, and we saw his glory, such glory as befits the Father's only Son, full of grace and truth" (Jn 1:14).

Paul is emphatic in this Christological vision of history. "There is one God, the Father, from whom all being comes, towards whom we move; and there is one Lord, Jesus Christ, through whom all things came to be, and we through him" (1 Cor 8:6). In one great vision Paul sees Christ, the Word incarnate and the Word pre-existent: "He is the image of the invisible God; he is the primacy over all created things. In him everything in heaven and on earth was created, not only things visible but also invisible ... He exists before everything, and all things are held together in him" (Col 1:16-17).

Creation and history have their identity and oneness in Christ. "In this, the final age, he has spoken to us in the Son whom he has made heir to the whole universe, and through whom he created all orders and existence: the Son who is the effulgence of God's splendour and the stamp of God's very being, and sustains the universe by his word of power" (Heb 1:2-3).

Hence, our relationship to the world is marked by our faith in Christ. And our devotion to Christ is therefore a commitment to world and history.

2. *God's self-revelation throughout history*

The believer, and especially the believer in modern times, who says "creation" is saying at the same time "evolution" and "history". Creation is not a static concept. All of creation throughout evolution and history speaks of the dynamic, active, creative, caring presence of God. Thus creation and history transmit a constant message and appeal to man to respond as co-actor with God.

In all that God does he reveals his glory, his holiness and his ineffably great and wonderful name. Man, on his part, cannot claim a right to learn and experience God's name, to call God by his name. When Jacob asked God, "What is your name?", the Lord answered, "Why do you ask my name?" (Gen 32:30; cf. Jgs 13:17ff).

In a tremendous historical moment, when God chose to communicate the marvel of his mystery to his chosen people, he disclosed his name to Moses: He is Yahweh, fullness of Being, sovereign in his freedom to be with his people as saviour, liberator. "Yahweh" means, "I am who am" (Ex 3:14). He is not only fullness of Being and the source of all being; he is, for his people, "being-with". He is the God of the covenant.

The monotheism of Israel is faith and trust in a God who alone can save (cf. Is 43:10ff). Through revelation, Israel comes to know, in faith, that there is only one God and that her being chosen in the covenant is a gift of the one God for all nations and all times.

In the revelation of his name, his glory, his holiness, God lays stress on his supreme and transcendent dignity. But at the same time he reveals his loving, saving design for humankind. "And God spoke further to Moses, 'Thus shall you say to the Israelites: the Lord, the God of your fathers, the God of Abraham, the God of Isaac, the God of Jacob, has sent me to you. This is my name forever; this is my title for all generations'" (Ex 3:15).

The revelation of God's glory is both awesome and beatifying. God lives in the midst of his people; through his glory he shelters them, lends his ear to their petitions. He is the Liberator, so that the people may be finally permitted to behold his glory in all its fullness (cf. Is 66:11ff).

On the one hand, God teaches his people that they can be saved only as true adorers; but on the other hand, in the light of Israel's faith-experience, it seems that God subordinates his own glory to salvation history. God glorifies himself precisely in bringing salvation to man. While revealing himself as absolute freedom to love, to save, and to reject those who contradict him, he simultaneously reveals the mystery of man. "God is love" is the revelation of man's supreme dignity in and through a love that utters God the Creator and Liberator.

In the light of the marvellous unity of God's self-disclosure and the communication of his salvific plan for humankind, there can be only one truthful response on man's part: praise and thanksgiving and, at the same time, fidelity to God's design to unite all people in mutual respect, love and fidelity.

Thus religion and morality meet each other in a wonderful synthesis of loving God with all one's heart and loving one's neighbour. "It is evident that the love of God is the one thing important. One is to think of nothing else. Nor is there anything else of which to speak. This is man's unique, lifelong occupation, his agapé that includes faith, worship of God, and the whole moral life".[6] Faith in the one God, Creator of all and Lord of history, is coherent only in and through all-embracing love, justice, solidarity.

Israel was not always open to the love of God. She did not always return his love with full faith. Consequently, Israel as a whole did not attain that justice which has its source and summit in Christ. "Israel made great efforts to follow a law of righteousness but never attained it. Why was this? Because their efforts were not based on faith but (as they supposed) on deeds" (Rom 9:30-32). For Paul, it is clear that God's revelation in Christ, Emmanuel, made it impossible to seek any way of salvation other than that of faith in him.

3. *Revelation and faith in Christ*

God's self-revelation and gift of self reaches its fullness in Christ. "Last of all in these days he has spoken to us by his Son" (Heb 1:2). In and through Jesus, the Father turns his countenance towards us with all his glory and love. And this is the truth for us: that in Christ and through Christ mankind can, in turn, truly honour and please God in a manner worthy of his supreme dignity. In Christ we are saved, and through faith we share in his life. "This life is found in his Son. He who has the Son has the life. He who does not possess the Son has not the life" (1 Jn 5:12).

Jesus Christ is the ultimate and definitive word of God's love for us. He is also man's sole worthy response to God's love. He lives the truth of man and for man, giving in the name of all a response of infinite value to the infinite love. In faith we listen to him as the Truth and the Life. This listening-in-faith is total, cordial, solidaric; a listening to him who is the Word and the Response. Therefore we listen in readiness to respond with him to the Father through all of our life.

"In his goodness and wisdom, God chose to reveal himself and to make known to us the hidden purpose of his will (cf. Eph 1:9), by which, through Christ, the Word made flesh, man has access to the Father in the Holy Spirit and comes to share in the divine nature (cf. Eph 2:18; 2 Pet 1:4). Through this revelation, therefore, the invisible God (cf. Col 1:15; 1 Tim 1:17), out of the abundance of his love, speaks to man as his friends (cf. Ex 33:11; Jn 15:14-15) and lives among them, so that he may invite and take them into fellowship with himself. This plan of revelation is realized by deeds and words having an inner unity. The deeds wrought by God in the history of salvation manifest and confirm the teaching and reality signified by the words, while the words proclaim the deeds and clarify the mystery contained in them. By this revelation then, the deepest truth about God and the salvation of man is made clear to us in Christ who is the Mediator and, at the same time, the fullness of all revelation".[7]

The summit of the revelation that illumines everything else is the death and resurrection of Christ and the final sending of the Spirit of Truth.[8]

Jesus exults in his mission. "I have manifested thy name to those whom thou hast given me out of the world. They were thine, and thou hast given them to me, and they have kept thy word. Now they have learned that whatever thou has given me is from thee; because the words that thou hast given me I have given to them" (Jn 17:6ff).

The Father has bestowed on Jesus, who has made his love visible to all, "the name that is above every name" (Phil 2:9). In this inexpressible name, the apostles rejoice to suffer (Acts 5:41).

If we are united with Christ through faith in his name, our prayer and our actions reach the Father's heart. "Whatever you do in word or in work, do all in the name of the Lord Jesus, giving thanks to God the Father through him" (Col 3:17). We can do this through the Spirit of Love who is the Spirit of Truth. He gives us an ever deeper experience of faith that we are reconciled and therefore can enter into a trustful relationship with God. "You have been through the purifying waters; you have been dedicated to God and justified through the name of the Lord Jesus and the Spirit of our God" (1 Cor 6:11).

The Spirit whom the Lord has sent us from the Father cries out in our hearts, "Abba, Father!" (Rom 8:15). Consequently our life is one in Christ Jesus, through faith, and thus is taken into the mystery of the triune God. The baptismal invocation of the Trinity, "In the name of the Father, the Son and the Holy Spirit" entitles us to this lofty vocation.

All this is a reality, indeed the central reality in the midst of history. The revelation of the Father in Jesus, his death and resurrection, is a reality in itself, otherwise it would not be a reality for our life. Although Jesus reveals to us more than our limited intellect can grasp, we believe in him and therefore believe all that he reveals. "Lord to whom shall we go? Your words are words of eternal life. We have faith and we know that you are the Holy One of God" (Jn 6:68-70).

Man's sinful self is shattered whenever it is confronted by the power and holiness of God. In Christian faith, Christ mediates the confrontation of the self by God, for it is faith in Christ, and in him "all that sense of the divine which human life never loses is crystallized into a revelation of the divine mercy and judgment".[9] Even the confession of sin is, for believers, a decisive act of profession of faith. We believe in him who reconciles, and therefore we can face our weak self.

The reconciliation theme is central in our faith. Proclaiming Christ, our peace and our reconciler, we also profess our faith in the task to be, in Christ and through him, operators of peace and reconciliation. These two aspects are inseparable as the self-revelation of God and the revelation of man's salvation.

The Paschal Mystery reveals how humankind becomes one as it was intended by creation through the triune God. The redeemed live wholly on the merciful love flowing from the heavenly Father in Jesus Christ, and they can return the gift by the loving offering of themselves in commitment to unity, solidarity, justice: that is, to redeeming love. Through the Paschal Mystery which we celebrate in the Eucharist, we are sharers of Christ's adoration of the Father and of his own love for the community of the brethren. His adoring love is likewise a sacrificial, reconciling love for them: "There is no greater love than this, that a man should lay down his life for his friends" (Jn 15:13).

For those who are reconciled in Christ, even suffering —

indeed, particularly suffering — can enter into the adoring faith-response which is, at the same time, active faith in saving solidarity. "It is now my happiness to suffer for you. This is my way of helping to complete, in my poor human flesh, the full tale of Christ's afflictions still to be endured for the sake of his body which is the church" (Col 1:24).

In Christ we are reconciled with God and among ourselves. We are all one body, members of one another (Eph 4:25). Through faith, the love of Jesus Christ can prevail in us even over hatred of enemies. And this liberation is the harvest of faith and our own manifestation of faith. "If your enemy is hungry, feed him; if he is thirsty, give him a drink; by doing this you will heap live coals on his head. Do not let evil conquer you but use good to defeat evil" (Rom 12:20-21).

Through the grace of faith, the Holy Spirit enables us to give a life-response to both the self-revelation of the all-holy God and the revelation of the mystery of man redeemed. Thus faith becomes the integration of our life in the fellowship with God and in the community of brotherly love and justice.

The strength of this synthesis, this integration of faith and life, arises from our awareness that faith is an undeserved gift of God which is lost where there is no active gratitude. By faith, active in justice and love, we render thanks to God who has saved us by grace and calls us to himself beyond all our powers. The constant consciousness of God's initiative in his self-revelation and in our salvation is a sign of the genuineness of our faith, and assures a favourable condition for a truly Christian morality.

4. Faith as self-commitment

a) The explicit faith of the Christian

At this point we consider faith as fundamental option. Although we can never leave out the content of faith, we turn our attention here primarily to the act and attitude of faith (*fides qua creditur*).

Faith in its full meaning is the weightiest act of conscience, the most radical fundamental option, a total self-commitment to Christ, the revealer of truth. He, who reveals himself as love totally committed to us, cannot accept any faith that is less than a total self-commitment to him and, through him, to the Father and to his brothers and sisters.

What we said in our first volume about fundamental option receives its full light in our understanding of faith. But on the other hand, our understanding of fundamental option can also deepen our understanding of the act and attitude of faith. "Faith in Christ is the acceptance of oneself in the knowledge that God has already accepted him in the sacrifice of Christ".[10] Although we are consoled by being accepted in all our weakness, we also, in faith, believe that this acceptance is for us God's calling to holiness. Thus our faith expresses itself through all our life, in all our relationships.

The calling to faith gives us the greatest chance of a deep self-understanding, according to the depth of the freedom by which we respond to God's grace. Without a radical self-commitment, a mere intellectual assent to the content of faith and the credibility of God does not reach the depth of a fundamental option. Any assent without commitment is a totally inadequate response and contradicts the very content of faith. Already in the Old Testament, faith is understood as a response to the covenant, and the prophets did everything to make the implications of the covenant clear. No one can be a subject in this covenant without a commitment both to the Lord of the covenant and to the people of the covenant. It is a covenant sealed by blood.

This becomes even more awe-ful and blissful for the Christian who, in faith, gives first attention to the Paschal Mystery, where Christ has sealed the everlasting covenant with his blood, and the Father has given his seal by the power of the resurrection. Anyone who believes that God has so committed himself to his people, and yet refuses to respond by a total self-commitment, does not give a genuine and saving assent of faith.

Faith is a commitment to the covenant offered us in Jesus Christ, a commitment to him and his *basileia*, his coming kingdom. At the same time it is a decision and commitment for what we essentially are and therefore ought to be. In faith we understand ourselves radically as a free gift of God's love. This self-understanding and decision can arise only out of grace.[11] In faith we know that we win our life if we give ourselves totally to the Giver of all good gifts, and to his cause, his kingdom.

The cause of Christian unity and common service to human-kind would enormously gain if all Christians were clearly aware that faith is infinitely more than a mere assent to a creed. We find ourselves, our true name and that of our fellow Christians, in the purpose to join in the following of Christ, a life with Christ. The awareness that faith is a wholly undeserved gift in which God commits himself to us in an all-embracing covenant, calls for a decision that, by necessity, includes the dimension of fellowship and fidelity in the covenant.[12]

Faith, understood in a biblical sense, is an act and attitude of the heart, a decision of the spirit in the depth where self-knowledge and freedom to love join in a unique integration of all our faculties, the intellect, will, memory and affection.[13] We cannot even reach that depth of knowledge that essentially belongs to faith without a clear intention to commit ourselves totally to God who is our Lord and Saviour.

In faith we expect and accept everything from God, and are therefore ready to give everything to him who has revealed to us the depth and height of his love. That means faith as joyous and grateful acceptance of him who is the saving Truth, the absolute Love, and who is calling us in order to be fully our life.

For St John it is all too little to say that faith is necessary to be saved. For him, there is no true life without faith, and faith is already the beginning of eternal life. It gives us the right to be children of God (Jn 1:12; 3:5, 7, 16; 6:47; 11:25; 1 Jn 2:24).

St Paul identifies faith with obedience of faith, that is, total acceptance of the Gospel and free embracement of the economy of salvation in Christ Jesus (Rom 1:5; 10:16; 2 Cor 9:13). In faith the believer renounces human glory and dedicates himself to the glory of God, with an ever increasing desire to know the Lord better.

By definition, a fundamental option reaches the depth of conscience, and this is particularly true of faith in its full sense. In all stages of the development of faith, there is a call to con-science. As soon as a divine message reaches the person, his or her conscience is called for earnest inquiry. But conscience also forbids us to accept as certain and give firm adherence to any alleged revelation whenever there is reasonable doubt in the mind of the sincere inquirer. Preceding the act of faith there must be a judgment of conscience about what he may and must believe.[14]

Whether one comes to fullness of faith and remains faithful has much to do with fidelity towards one's conscience. The "shipwreck of faith" follows the violation of conscience (1 Tim 1:19). The pure and faithful conscience is the guardian of "the mystery of faith" (1 Tim 3:9).

For the believer who has truly made a total self-commitment to the kingdom of God, faith is an ever-present reality in all decisions of conscience. But conscience is particularly challenged when faith itself is at stake.

Faith is a call to conversion. But we can also say that faith itself is the most radical conversion, a total turning to God and his kingdom. This is probably the meaning of Mark's 1:15: "Be converted and believe the Gospel". Turning in faith to God by a self-commitment (fundamental option) is the most decisive act of conversion in both a religious and moral sense. However, the believer who is justified by faith still experiences temptation and partial sinfulness. But if he is truly a believer and somehow faithful to his fundamental option, he will, even in the midst of sin, acknowledge the claim of faith and the verdict of guilt for conduct that contradicts the Gospel. Thus he also acknowledges the need of further conversion.

We have to distinguish between an initial faith that is already open to further and total conversion (although the total self-commitment is not yet consolidated) and, on the other hand, "dead faith" that has lost the dynamism towards conversion, the dynamism to bear fruit in love and justice. The Church teaches that loss of the friendship of God through mortal sin does not necessarily imply the loss of faith as assent to truth.[15] Man can be at the same time a sinner and believer. However, his imperfect faith is a bridge towards conversion only if he suffers under his sin, and is willing to accuse himself before God, and prays for the grace of conversion.

Faith that is like an aborted fundamental option, with no dynamism towards conversion, is not worthy of this noble name. It is simply dead. For if there is no longing for conversion to God and to good, faith no longer has the quality of experience or commitment. Heidegger says that, "To have an experience of something, be it man or God, means that it moves us, it strikes us, it meets us, turns us around and changes us".[16]

b) Implicit faith

On the one hand, we have to stress emphatically the truth that salvation does not come through good works but through faith, while on the other hand, we firmly believe that God wants the salvation of all people and that nobody will be rejected by God unless he has first rejected God. The point of departure for our reflections cannot be good works as such, but God's grace and the upright conscience. We can hope that those who search for truth in order to put it into practice are recognized by God as his children, surely not on the basis of works but on the basis of this commitment which, implicitly, is a commitment to him, the source of all truth and goodness.

Whoever has made a sincere self-commitment to truth and goodness, and hungers and thirsts for more truth and for a greater configuration with the good, is on the road of salvation. This salvation comes from God. The self-commitment, which is true self-transcendence, is not possible without the grace of the Holy Spirit, who proceeds from the Father and the Son. Those saved by the grace of the Spirit will, at the end, recognize him as the Spirit given in view of Christ's death and resurrection.[17]

A self-commitment to truth and goodness is an experience of conscience similar to that of faith. It is holistic, seizing the person in all his energies; and it will bear fruit in love and justice. And if, because of their fraternal love, Christ also calls into the Father's kingdom many who have not come to an explicit knowledge of him, he will honour his grace by which he has saved them.

5. *Faith and knowledge*

Genuine self-commitment in faith is that profound love arising from an incipient knowledge of him who reveals himself as our saviour, as our Father. From commitment (fundamental option) there arises a greater hunger and thirst to know him who calls us so wonderfully to know what he reveals to us. There is no genuine faith that does not seek understanding of its content and, above all, of the Revealer himself.

Faith searching for a deeper understanding is not a matter only for learned theologians; it is the attitude of every believer, even the simpler ones. This does not mean conceptual knowledge only. St John presents to us the knowledge of faith as an existential loving grasp: "This is eternal life: to know thee who alone art truly God, and Jesus Christ whom thou hast sent" (Jn 17:3). John's faith does not come from a study of philosophy but from meeting Christ who called him and allowed him to live in his company. It is a gift that comes from the risen Christ who revealed himself to his disciples.

The apostles have no doubt that, for them, faith has a content: Christ is the Son of God; he died for us and is risen, and sends us the Holy Spirit. He is saviour of the whole world. Already at the very beginning, Paul's faith is expressed in clear formulas (1 Thess 1:10; 4:14; 1 Cor 12:3; Rom 1:4; 10:9; Phil 2:5-11). In the celebration of Baptism and the Eucharist, the Church professes not only a self-commitment to Christ but also a knowledge about him and his salvation message. Not only the will and affection but also the memory and intellect of the believer seek the Revealer and his revelation.

The emphasis on the *fides qua* in the education of faith by no means detracts attention from the content of faith. A better understanding of the fundamental option shows that the contrary is true: basic freedom in self-commitment, through faith and basic knowledge of faith, coincide in the depth of the human person and in the community of believers. The loving knowledge (determined by the depth of the self-commitment) is what brings the believer into the wave-length of the message of faith. It is not only the intellect that hungers for greater knowledge of the faith to which the believer is committed; it is the believer in his wholeness who yearns to come into deeper contact and to a better knowledge of him who can give life and beatitude.

The knowledge of faith develops in three circles: first, in that basic knowledge that goes hand-in-hand with the self-commitment; second, this basic knowledge and experience find expression in symbols and concepts; third, at the same time, one is learning what faith says about the different realms of life.[18]

It would be misleading to present the knowledge of faith first or mainly as a collection of individual propositions and concepts. The knowledge of faith is characterized by *wholeness*. Therefore the knowledge of the individual truths can contribute to wholeness (salvation) only as part of the whole.

A Catholic Christian acquires his knowledge of faith by sharing in the worship and life of the Church, which is a communion of faith in Jesus Christ. Karl Rahner insists that this does not mean that the individual Catholic would be obliged to learn all the definitions of faith in their objective distinctions and historical development. He feels that frequently too much detail is imposed without vision of wholeness, so that the details are not only fruitless but even an impediment to growth. Hence he suggests that there can be a legitimate way of partial recess or bypass into implicit faith. This means that the individual will not have the same existential interest in all parts of the Church's doctrine. While he acknowledges her authority and mission, he may simply postpone some specific questions while focusing all his attention on coming to know Christ, to know the Father in him and through him, to learn how to live according to the grace of the Holy Spirit, and to live the synthesis of love of God and love of neighbour. Thus he comes to true adoration in the integration of faith and life.[19]

An untimely insistence on doctrines that are not revealed, or on time-bound formulations that are no longer in touch with the existential experience and culture, can handicap both the joy of faith and the true knowledge of faith.

The conceptualization and expression of faith in symbols is possible only to those who live intensely with the Lord of history in the pilgrim Church. The knowledge of faith is an integrating part of the total faith-experience, and can never be lived and shared as something totally severed from historical experience. But a knowledge of faith, lived and deepened by practice in the faith community, interrogates and challenges all forms of knowledge offered by people who think they know themselves, history, and the universe apart from faith.

The Gospel is a light that searches and shakes the self-sufficiency of philosophy and the natural sciences. But at the same time, faith gives a profound openness to all dimensions of human knowledge and brings them home into an existential synthesis. The Gospel is the yeast in the dough of human search for truth. Faith, therefore, needs a constant encounter and dialogue with all forms of human knowledge.[20]

The knowledge of faith is more urgent than any other kind of knowledge. To neglect it is a sign of grave ingratitude. Modern professional people know how important is ongoing formation. It should be clear to every believer that ongoing education in faith is even more urgent. In a world where there is so much learning, and where so many objections arise against our faith, there is a great need for adult education. Regular assistance at the weekly celebrations and homilies is less than a minimum. We need to reserve time, energy, personal and shared effort to deepen our knowledge of faith.

Growth in this knowledge requires a profound and abiding truthfulness in all of life's dimensions. It is a terrible misunderstanding to think that Christian faith contradicts or qualifies absolute sincerity. Merleau-Ponty represents this misunderstanding when, simultaneously accusing and excusing Christians, he says, "The faith in things not seen is an allegiance that goes beyond the guarantees. Therefore it excludes a sincerity at all moments. The Christian will not deny God and the Church even if he does not understand their decrees. He will not doubt the sacraments even though they do not bring him happiness".[21]

Our response is: we accept the truth of faith by trust in God's authority. We know that the mystery of God and man is always infinitely greater than our limited understanding. But we equally know that profound dedication to truthfulness is the condition for any growth in faith and the knowledge of faith. Therefore we will not hesitate to challenge, sincerely and courageously, unauthentic teaching and practice.

6. *Faith as history of creative liberty and fidelity*

It is in faith and through faith that the history of creative and redemptive liberty and fidelity is carried on. In faith, God's saving action is received and responded to. It is in faith that man becomes co-actor in the history of salvation, and in faith that the new creation comes into being in us and around us, and awaits completion. The history of faith is the history of covenant fidelity, which is never mere repetition but opens ever new horizons on the road to the heavenly Jerusalem. The history of hope, vigilance and discernment is grounded in faith, a faith active in love, in justice, in peace. Through faith our memory is stirred by the passion, death and resurrection of Christ. And faith brings our own life history and the history of the past (including that of the dead) into the present history of our life with God.

The more faith is experienced and lived as an undeserved gift of God and as our own free response, the more religious liberty, liberty of conscience and liberty of all people will be promoted.[22] It is through faith that the fundamental option reaches its highest level of consciousness, freedom and strength. The best opportunity for the reciprocity of consciences is in the community of true believers. And the highest form of responsibility and co-responsibility flows from authentic obedience of faith.

In faith we find the true meaning of history, and overcome our identity crisis. We say "Yes" to the history which God has initiated in creation and brought to the summit in the incarnation, death and resurrection of Christ. Faith does not allow a shallow historicity that ignores the great historical events and facts because, for us, it is true and decisive that the Son of God has become man, has suffered for us and is risen for us and has sent us the Holy Spirit. Through faith we have the promises as the clear direction for our own life history as a part of humankind's total history.[23]

In his revelation, in the demonstration of his own faithfulness to his own name and to his promise, in his creative act and his involvement in the suffering of man, God makes possible the free act, the faithful response of man as co-actor in the history of salvation.

Faith brings home personal and communal experience and makes it fruitful as a part of Christ's redemptive presence.[24] Whether Church leaders, theologians and the faithful intend it or not, the understanding and practice of faith have an impact on history and society. Hence it is most important to focus on the creative and solidaric dimension of faith.[25]

II. THE COVENANT DIMENSIONS OF FAITH

1. *Christ, the Covenant, the Mediator of faith*

Christian faith is faith in Christ, the living Gospel, who shows us the Father, and faith in the Father who, through his only begotten Son and by the gift of the Spirit, calls all to be his adoptive children, one family.

Christ reveals monotheism in a new way. He tears down all the man-made walls that separate cultures and nations. In him, the covenant relationship between God and his people comes to completion. "I, the Lord, have called you in justice and taken you by the hand; I formed you and set you as a covenant of the people, a light for the nations" (Is 42:6). In the God-Man, Jesus Christ, there is a unique and indissoluble covenant between the divine and human natures. Jesus knows that this privilege is his so that he might be servant to all nations and bring all people home into the unity of adoration of the one God and Father. This is the heart of the Gospel of St John and St Paul.

The calling to faith is a calling to that profound union with Christ that makes all his disciples one: "That they may be one, even as we are one... I pray also for those who, through their witnessing word, put their faith in me; may they all be one: as thou, Father, art in me and I in thee, so also may they be one in us, that the world may believe that thou didst send me" (Jn 17:11-21). Like the credible proclamation of the Gospel, so faith, too, is inseparable from brotherhood, from the solidarity of believers in Christ.

The covenant relation is not an addition to faith but an essential component of it. All truths of faith call for this covenant faith and covenant morality. "Spare no effort to make fast with bonds of peace the unity which the Spirit gives. There is one body and one Spirit, as there is also one hope held out in God's call to you; one Lord, one faith, one baptism; one God and Father of all, who is over all and through all and in all" (Eph 4:3-6).

A special motive for this covenant faith is the fact that there is "one baptism". We are baptized in Christ and share in his baptism. When he was baptized in the Jordan during a general baptism, he presented himself as the servant who bears the burden of all. He is baptized by the Spirit to be the covenant of the people, incarnate solidarity. And in the power of the same Spirit he accepts the baptism in his blood, the blood of the new and everlasting covenant. Believers all participate in this one baptism, making them one in Christ.

2. Faith in the Church

Living our faith as members of the Church is an essential expression of the covenant dimension of faith. "We believe in the Church". This does not mean exactly the same as "in Christ". In Christ we put all our faith, all our trust; he is the only mediator. But in and through Jesus Christ, the Church also has an important mission to communicate faith not only by the proclamation of the Gospel but also by witness and orthodox teaching.

a) The Magisterium of the saints

"We believe in the communion of saints". This means first that we believe in God's design and call for an all-embracing solidarity of humankind, for all are called to faith and holiness. But it implies also that the saints, through their faith and their consequent covenant morality, are teachers and models of faith in Christ.

History shows that office-holders are not always the best teachers of faith. Neither are they always the best theologians or the holiest men. MARY, the Queen of the apostles and prophets is, in a higher and more authentic way than the apostles, model and teacher of our faith. Gratefully we join in Elizabeth's paean, "How happy is she who has had faith that the Lord's promise would be fulfilled" (Lk 1: 45). Her *Magnificat* is the total witness of her life, disclosing the main dimensions of the history of salvation.

The saints speak to us the witnessing word of faith and of love, justice, peace and solidarity arising from faith. Those who have come to a profound and radiating faith are, indeed, also teachers of the office-holders, and the latter are bound to listen to them. Mary Magdalen not only came before the apostles to faith in the risen Lord; she is also sent to the disciples to give witness of this faith.

Of course, for the offices of bishop, priest, deacon and so on, those should be chosen who are outstanding in faith, in knowledge of faith and holiness, and in the capacity to render witness. They should be men and women able to say with St Paul, "In Jesus Christ you are my offspring, through the preaching of the gospel. I appeal to you, therefore, to follow my example. That is the very reason why I have sent Timothy, who is a dear son to me and a most trustworthy Christian. He will remind you of the way of life in Christ which I follow and which I teach everywhere in all our congregations" (1 Cor 4:15-17).

We can follow the faith witness only of those who, like Paul, draw all our attention to Christ. "Follow my example as I follow Christ's" (1 Cor 11:1). The letter to the Hebrews calls attention to the outstanding examples of faith which we can follow, and warns, "Do not become lazy, but imitate those who, through faith and patience, are inheriting the promises" (Heb 6:12). It also points to the leaders of the community and invites all to follow the example of their faith (Heb 13:7). Paul is particularly happy to call attention to the faith example of outstanding communities (1 Thess 2:14). It is, above all, through model communities of faith that the Church is an effective teacher of faith.

b) The charismatic leaders

In the Old Testament we see that God, time and again, reawakens and strengthens the faith through prophets and other charismatic leaders. They interpret the signs of the times and help people to discover God's presence in the events and in their hopes and anguish. The people of the covenant is in great misery if God sends no prophets or if the voice of the prophets is not listened to, if their faith is not followed.

Equally, the history of Christian faith points to the great charismatic leaders, to religious genius, to prophets who gather disciples for faith-sharing and actions arising from faith. Among others, we think of the founders of religious orders and congregations like Sts Basil, Benedict, Francis, Dominic, Ignatius, Alphonsus, Theresa of Avila, and others. We think also of prophets like St Catherine of Siena, like Martin Luther King who gave witness to faith by calling to action. We think of holy priests and bishops who did not tolerate mediocrity of faith and Christian life. We think of Pope John who helped Christians to decipher the signs of the times and called courageously for unity and for new ways to be explored. We think of great theologians like Origen, Augustine, Thomas Aquinas, Rosmini, Cardinal Newman, who bring home the message of faith in their respective cultures, and combine theological learning with holiness and great vigilance for the signs of the times.

c) Faith of the humble ones, and popular religiosity

Christ praises the faith of the lowly people. "I thank you, Father, Lord of heaven and earth, for hiding these things from the learned and wise and revealing them to the simple. Yes, Father, such was your choice" (Lk 10:21).

The teachers in the Church, bishops and priests as well as theologians, have normally received their faith through humble parents and through the total expression of popular religiosity which is never perfect but is frequently a very vital integration of faith and life. Alas for the theologians if they learn only through books while not listening to the humble ones. "Must not the theologian like to speak to the people? Must he not be committed to help people to be active partners and to find their language?... Faith that comes from listening (*fides ex auditu*) implies also a listening to the language of the simple ones to whom 'it is given'. Not only do the people need theology; much more does theology need the message of the people. The symbols and stories of the people cannot be replaced by anything else".[26]

d) Allegiance to the Magisterium

There is but one master, Christ. In Christ, and never without him, there is the Magisterium of the Church. We never should see the pope and his advisers and the college of bishops outside of the total Magisterium which includes the saints, the prophets and the humble people. The successor of Peter and the other apostles are outstanding teachers of faith insofar as they are outstanding listeners and learners. And of course, they are on the wave-length of the Gospel only to the extent that they are willing to put it into practice.

The clamorous conflicts of conscience of many theologians and lay people — for instance in the case of the encyclical

Humanae Vitae — and the much more shocking conflict of St Paul and St Peter in the case of Antioch (Gal 2:11-14), the oppressive reactions of high Church authorities against Thomas Aquinas and against other great theologians of past centuries, as well as of our own time, are part and parcel of the pilgrim Church. But this must not mislead us to see conflict and fight as the normal relationships. The normal reality is that all of us, theologians and lay people, are profiting from the official Magisterium, from the faith of the humble ones and the hard work of dedicated and creative theologians.

The Magisterium of the Church honours the upright conscience of the faithful even where they have difficulty in grasping the meaning of a doctrine or where they question the validity of non-infallible doctrines. The purpose of the Magisterium is both to illumine the conscience and to protect its sincerity. "The conscience of the faithful gives credence to the Magisterium for, because of its competence, it has always to be open to the word of truth. The conscience has the right to be illumined, for it has the right to decide according to its own knowledge and conviction".[27]

The successor of Peter, as well as the faithful, know that, as Cardinal Newman so well phrased it, "conscience is the original vicar of Christ".[28] Therefore the exercise of the teaching office has to be understood within the realm of reciprocity of consciences. Authentic teaching is thoroughly pastoral and therefore will, at all times and in all places, use the most appropriate means to reach the faith and conscience of the people. Care will be taken that they can realize concretely "that the Magisterium considers itself organ and function of the Church as a whole, and that it tends not only to offer a doctrine to man but to put him in contact with the reality of salvation itself and its saving power".[29]

On the one hand, we know that the Church is a pilgrim and has therefore constantly to search for better knowledge and a more vital expression of salvation truth, and that she is always in need of further conversion to truth. On the other hand, we have faith that Christ will protect his Church from falling totally out of truth. Through the assistance of the Holy Spirit, he guarantees the basic indefectibility of the Church, its infallibility not only in decisive solemn moments but in the over-all of her faith. Hence the Catholic Christian is confident that he will never be faced with the radical dilemma of "either to fall away from the truth of Christ or to be radically disobedient to the Church authority to the point of denying and rejecting the concrete authority of the Church".[30]

Only those who, in their own mind, separate the Magisterium of their bishops or of the pope from the total Magisterium of the communion of saints, the prophets and the humble ones will be tempted to defect from the Church when faced with some scandal given by office-holders, or some doctrines inadequately proposed. Grateful docility towards the Magisterium of the successors of Peter and the other apostles, combined with a highly developed sense of discernment and co-responsibility, may sometimes lead to conflict; but this conflict will not undermine the conscience or endanger the covenant faith as long as all are fully dedicated to Christ, to his Gospel, and to the service of his people. Conflict has its authentic role and can be beneficial only within the solidaric search for a better grasp of salvation truth.

3. The covenant-dimension of the faith of non-Christians, and implicit faith

Both faith and salvation are covenant realities in the vertical and horizontal dimensions. Whoever believes in one God, the Creator and Lord of all people, will know infallibly that no man may exploit another person, that no group may oppress another group. Wherever one's faith or talk about conscience does not reach this vision and decision, there is great doubt about whether there is given an implicit or explicit faith as fundamental option for God and the good.

There were times, however, when the inhabitants of one place knew only their nearest neighbours as belonging to them, to their clan. Even later in history, solidarity seems sometimes limited to one tribe or one nation, since people can so self-righteously and arrogantly look down on others as not belonging to the same human species. In such an environment, it might well be that the individual person, although believing in God or making a fundamental decision for the good as expressed in the "golden rule", may not reach the universality that is inherent in faith in one God, creator of all.

If, however, sincere Christians do not reach this universality, this covenant-dimension of faith and of fundamental option, it is a shocking sign of the weakness of the faith community and of a lack of the prophetic spirit which should awaken the conscience of all believers.

Wherever the Christian faith is strong and deep, there will be found a living Church. And where, even outside the Christian community, monotheism is a fundamental option of persons and groups, there will be a strong commitment for universal solidarity. The more faith and moral commitment outside the Church manifest unrestricted solidarity with all of humankind, the closer it comes to the Christian covenant faith.[31]

Universal solidarity and respect for each person's dignity create the divine milieu in which individuals and groups can exist as subjects before God, as co-actors in the one human history.[32] In a secular society like ours, the sense of the sacred will be recognized and honoured only to the extent that it leads to the experience of the sacredness of every person within the one human family. This is a basic question for today's Christian, for the Christian community, and for secular societies. Those who claim to be persons and actors within the one human history, while denying God by refusing to acknowledge the dignity of other people and ignoring human solidarity, are unmasked by those who have made an authentic fundamental option for a total human brotherhood and for respect for each individual's dignity.

III. THE SACRAMENTS OF FAITH

1. *The Church as primordial sacrament of faith*

Through her union with Christ and faithful acceptance of her mission, the Church is and can become ever more a great sacrament of faith. All that she is and has, all her dimensions and structures should manifest to the world her faith in Christ, and awaken and strengthen the faith of all. She is a sacrament of faith, above all, if in all her life she is visible as a great and effective sign of union with God and, at the same time, of unity of mankind.[33] Christ, who is *the* Sacrament of Salvation, extends his sacramentality to the Church, sending her as the Father sent him, to make visible his all-embracing love, his Gospel, and thus to make God known as the Father of all.

I think that the best model of self-understanding of the Church is the sacramental one.[34] This includes and informs the other models as the servant-Church, the pilgrim-Church, the community gathered by the Holy Spirit. It also gives the proper meaning to the Church as institution, testing whether or not she reveals Christ and his Gospel, and call to unity and peace through her institutional structures. The Church's mission is to help every believer and each community to become ever more an image and likeness of God, a living Gospel, an effective sign of faith in the one Father of all, in one Lord Jesus Christ, in the one Spirit who creates unity through the very diversity of his gifts.

2. *The privileged signs of faith*

The seven sacraments do not monopolize sacramentality. Rather, they are destined to open the eyes of believers to all the signs of God's active presence that call people to saving faith. However, the sacraments are privileged signs instituted by God as efficacious signs of grace and faith.[35] They are signs of the covenant sealed by the blood of the Redeemer. As signs of faith, they call us and introduce us ever more into this covenant in the faith-community. In the sacraments, God speaks to us in the covenant-community with words, with signs, and with his gracious gifts of the alliance which he offers to us. In receiving the signs of Christ's covenant with the Church, we share in the faith of the people of the covenant in Christ and through him.

The biblical idea of covenant, and the continuous living experience which the liturgy gives, instruct the faithful on the true nature of Christian life. As expressed by the privileged signs of faith, Christian life is a dialogue which is fully personal and, at the same time, fully communitarian.

The grace-filled signs (sacraments) of the covenant call us together in the ecclesial community so that we all, through our faith, may be a gracious call for all people to oneness before God. The liturgy, by its very essence, teaches us that there is no opposition between the fundamental social-communitarian aspect of salvation and the true personalism of faith. We become persons before God and in the covenant through our capacity to listen and to respond in Christ and in his Church.

The covenanted dialogue in the liturgy, being a dialogue of faith and adoring love, is a profound expression of the uniqueness of each person. However, the faith and the depth of identity of each person depend on the reciprocity of consciences in faith, hope and love. The dialogue of faith, as expressed and fostered by the liturgy, is in the We-Thou-I dimension. We are persons before God in, through and in view of the community.

The liturgy is one of the privileged schools of these truths. If we wilfully neglect it, we have little hope of learning the fundamental components of Christian life since, in Christ's intention, the Eucharist and the other sacraments are favoured sources of growth in faith and in the undivided love, justice and peace that are fruits of genuine faith.

St Augustine expresses the best of tradition about this covenant dimension of faith as we experience it in the sacraments of faith: " 'The bread which I will give you is my flesh for the life of the world'. The faithful recognize the body of Christ if they do not neglect to be the body of Christ. They become the body of Christ if they want to live in the Spirit of Christ. It is the body of Christ that draws life from his Spirit. My body certainly draws life from my spirit. Do you too want to draw life from the Spirit of Christ? Be the body of Christ... Therefore, the Apostle Paul, in presenting this bread to us says: 'There is one loaf of which we all partake' (1 Cor 10:17). O sacrament of piety, o sign of unity. O bond of love. Whoever wants to live has where to live, has the source from which to draw his life; so draw near, believe, do not move away from any member, do not be a gangrenous member deserving of amputation; do not be a deformed or disgraceful member but a fitting, a well-formed and healthy member; do not detach yourself from the body".[36]

3. Salvation through faith and through the sacraments

Often in the past, the reformed communities have accused the Catholic Church of a sacramentalism detrimental to the preeminence of faith. The Second Vatican Council, following the authentic Catholic tradition, excludes, through a reformed liturgy of the signs of faith, any kind of ritualism opposed to faith. As much as the reformed Churches, we profess that we are saved through faith. But faith refers to Christ, the visible sign of reconciliation. We are saved, not as separate individuals, but in the community of faith. Hence we can say that we are saved through faith and the sacraments of faith. If it is a matter of individual sacraments, we may also say that we are saved through faith and the sacraments, but more through faith. St Thomas Aquinas teaches, "We are saved by means of faith in Christ who was born and has suffered; the sacraments, then, are signs which attest to the faith through which men come to justification".[37]

The sacraments are to be seen thoroughly in a perspective of faith. "They not only presuppose faith but by words and signs also nourish, strengthen and express it; that is why they are called sacraments of faith".[38] At the heart of the sacramental celebrations is the incarnate Word of God. Indeed, the sacraments altogether are signs/words of Christ; it is he himself who speaks when the holy Scriptures are read in the church.[39]

Faith is, itself, a sacramental reality; never should it be misinterpreted as only intellectual adherence to a catalogue of beliefs. Its saving efficacy comes from Christ alone who is the Sacrament. In the words and the sacramental signs, Christ himself reassures us that he came to us, died and is risen for us and is sending the Holy Spirit to sanctify us. By his sacraments in the community of faith and by the light of his graces, he gives to our mind and heart, to our will and intelligence, the experience that the mysteries of salvation save us, bring us together in his love, if we loyally open ourselves to them in faith. And through faith he makes us signs of his saving presence for the world.

The sacraments are saving events only for those who believe and long for an increase of faith. For those who do not believe and do not long for the grace of faith, the sacraments are empty rituals. If these unbelieving people receive them, they use the sacred signs for lying. They disparage the faith which has God himself as witness. Those whose fundamental option contradicts faith, but who nevertheless approach the sacraments without the firm purpose to live according to faith, receive the sacraments fruitlessly.

Those who receive the sacraments in a spirit of faith and with a desire for an increase of faith, which includes the longing to bear fruit in love and justice, are justified by that faith which God himself has awakened and brings to fuller life by these sacred signs and symbols. They come to a deeper communion with the Church, the community of faith. It can be expected that the more fervently the ecclesial community celebrates the signs of faith, the more fervent will be each individual participant's profession of faith. On the other hand, the individual believer's profession of faith, in the liturgy as well as in daily life, will not be fruitful or pleasing to God if he does not want to live in saving solidarity with the faith of the whole Church.

The fecundity of the sacraments for Christian life depends above all on gratitude. The sacraments make it particularly visible that salvation through faith is an undeserved gift of God; it is grateful and joyous acceptance of God's loving self-revelation and of his saving power.

Although everyone is saved by his own faith, this is always sharing in the faith of the Church. The universal Church is actualized for the believer in the local Church which arouses and sustains the faith of the individual members. Although the grace of God is not at her disposal, and although God distributes it whenever and wherever he wants, nevertheless, the Church, both universal and local, contributes to the disposition of every person according to her degree of faith. Therefore much depends on the quality of faith of the celebrating community and priest, and of the quality of celebration as a visible expression of faith and love. To participate in sacramental celebrations in a way that manifests sloth, formalism or a frightening lack of faith and charity can be the cause of defections, even if all the rubrics and other conditions for "validity" are scrupulously observed.

With equal insistence, the Gospel teaches the regenerating power of both faith and sacraments. It is said: "In truth, I tell you, no one can enter the kingdom of God without being born of water and the Spirit" (Jn 3:5) and "whoever eats my flesh and drinks my blood dwells continually in me and I dwell in him" (Jn 6:56).

The same saving power is recognized for faith: "To those who received him, to those who put their faith in his name, he gave the right to become children of God" (Jn 1:12-13). "The Son of man must be lifted up as the serpent was lifted up by Moses in the wilderness, so that everyone with faith in him may in him possess eternal life" (Jn 3:14-15).

These two aspects of the one faith reality — faith in its inner power and the *gift of faith becoming visible in the sacraments* — ought never to be separated. "The problem is easily resolved if the two masterly lines of the theology of John are distinguished, that of gift and that of acceptance. The perspective of gift extends to all providential dispositions which the Spirit has given to the world, and encompasses the mysteries of the Incarnation and Redemption. The sacrament of Baptism is inscribed in their prolongation, but confronted by the gift, the individual remains free in his decisions. To accept the gift, he needs to believe in the Donor by virtue of an interior grace which is already thoroughly a gift, but an initial gift already ordained to a yet greater one".[40]

We have special reason to praise God for giving us visible, tangible signs of his gifts which correspond with human nature and with the Word incarnate. "When the word pronounces the gift of grace in the form of a sacramental act, the obedience of faith is acceptance of the gracious gift which becomes visible in the sacraments".[41]

A genuine sacramental morality dynamically opens us to new and radiant horizons, to a sacramental vision of all the works of God, the signs of the times, and the concrete opportunities of the *kairos*. A sacramental spirituality creates a grateful memory and a trustful acceptance of God's gifts in generous correspondence with the needs of our fellowmen.

4. *Salvation through faith, and infant baptism*

With great gratitude, the pious Israelites celebrated the circumcision of their children as thanksgiving for the gift of the covenant. The sign of circumcision should constantly reawaken the grateful memory of liberation and covenant, to the praise of

God's goodness. God said to Abraham, "I will establish my covenant between me and you and your descendants after you through their generations, for an everlasting covenant, to be God to you and to your descendants after you... This is my covenant which you shall keep between me and you and your descendants after you; every male among you shall be circumcised... This shall be a sign of the covenant between me and you" (Gen 17:1-11).

Even more is baptism of infants celebrated as thanksgiving for the covenant, a sign of the faith of the people and a pledge to share this faith with the descendants.

Today, however, a more personalistic understanding of faith and the sacraments of faith, and the realization that Christ, speaking on conversion and baptism, has primarily in mind the adult, have brought theology to new reflections. One of the first great theologians to cast doubt on the practice of infant baptism was Karl Barth. He felt that in reality this "bad custom" separated baptism from the personal act of faith and from the call to conversion.[42] The long discussions have found a balanced response by one of the most authoritative Lutheran theologians, Edmund Schlinck.[43] Based on holy Scripture and tradition, he favours infant baptism, but with discernment.

The following arguments are used against infant baptism.

a) While infant baptism makes sense as thanksgiving for God's undeserved grace, one cannot easily see how it expresses the faith of the recipient. We are no longer living in an era of compact Christianity. Rather, we are entering an epoch of Christianity by personal choice. Infant baptism is all too frequently sought without intention to educate the child in faith; hence it is not followed by a post-baptismal catechumenate and by a personal affirmation of the faith.

b) Infant baptism was frequently justified mainly by the theory of limbo, which seemed to exclude from redemption all the innocent infants who, without any fault, died without being baptized. This theory can hardly be reconciled with the dogma of God's universal will for salvation, manifested in the truth that Christ died for all. It leads to a shocking pessimism, as if the sin of the first Adam reaches farther than redemption brought by Christ. "Where sin was thus multiplied, grace immeasurably exceeded it, in order that, as sin established its reign by way of death, so God's grace might establish its reign in righteousness, and issue in eternal life through Jesus Christ, our Lord" (Rom 5:20-21).

But infant baptism, as such, does not at all depend on the untenable theory of limbo and its assertion that all the infants not baptized (or circumcised before the coming of Christ) are refused eternal life with God. There are good theological and pedagogical reasons for continuing infant baptism, however, under certain conditions that should help modern man to perceive its true significance.

a) Normally, the celebration of infant baptism ought to take place as a community celebration of the extended family and/or the parish. It is a celebration of thanksgiving for the life of the child, and even more, for the gift of eternal life promised to it. It celebrates the covenant and the active *belonging* to it, praising God's all-embracing salvific will, and giving thanks for the special grace given to this child in being born into a community of believers. Those participating in the celebration should express their renewed commitment to share the joy and knowledge of their faith with the infant as it grows up.

b) A child's baptism ought never be considered as an isolated moment but rather as an intense and privileged hour in the whole series of developments in which the baptized child gradually receives and responds to the good news of God's graciousness. All of education should be conceived in the light and perspective of Baptism as a sacrament of faith that calls for consciousness and growth in faith. This catechumenate should be particularly intensified in preparation for the sacraments of the Eucharist, Confirmation and Matrimony. Confirmation should be received only by those who are ready for a genuine self-commitment.

c) Except in the case of imminent danger of death, there should be firm refusal to baptize those infants who are not in any way inserted into the community of faith. Official Church legislation forbids one to be baptized if there is no hope of a post-baptismal catechumenate. However, baptism should not be refused if, by granting it, there results a greater chance that the child will eventually come in contact with the Church and be evangelized. The faith of the parents and of the family is a fundamental criterion but not the only one. Even if the parents are undependable as pillars of faith, there can be a community of lively faith into which the child can be integrated with the assent of the parents who ask for baptism. The weaker the solidarity of salvation in the local community, the less lively will be the liturgy and expression of faith and of praise of God, and the less justified can be the baptism of infants whose parents are either not able or not willing to educate the child in faith.

IV. ORTHODOXY AND ORTHOPRAXIS

1. *True orthodoxy*

Christian faith is not adherence to a philosophy or a system of ideas. God reveals himself not by mere words. His word is deed. He reveals himself, gives us a share in his life and calls us to a total commitment to him. It is his action that becomes intelligible.

What God is and what he does through his almighty word, the testimony Christ gives by his life and death: all this is fundamental in Christian faith. Therefore we can rightly speak on the primacy of praxis. But we must be quite precise by insisting that it is an intelligent practice, a practice inseparable from acceptance of and dedication to him who is the truth, but the truth breathing love. "Faith is the global response of man to God, unfolding itself throughout the whole existence; hope, love and Christian praxis are not really consequences of faith but a constitutive part of it".[44]

Faith is never a merely intellectual assent if it is truly saving faith. The gratuity of faith as saving action of God cannot be responded to by mere words or mere ideas. "What, then, of the man who hears these words of mine and acts upon them? He is like a man who had the sense to build his house on rock" (Mt 7:24). Those will be called, at the end, the blessed ones who have acted according to the main message of love, namely, that God is love and wants us to be active sharers of his love. And since his love is gratuitous even to those who do not deserve it, those are truly orthodox people who show love to those who cannot remunerate them (cf. Mt 25:31-46). "The unloving know nothing about God" (1 Jn 4:8). They cannot teach orthodoxy in the full sense.

The message of salvation brought by Christ's word, life, death and resurrection is uprooting and irritating to the sinner who lives in self-righteousness or superficiality. The message of the kingdom of God contains in its very heart the possibility and obligation of conversion. It is a history of the exodus. Christian theology is not narrative in a superficial sense. It is a story that concerns us and that we can tell truthfully only to the extent that we unite our own history with that of Christ. "The praxis of following Christ belongs constitutively to Christology".[45]

A faith that remembers the history of the passion of Christ and the victory of his love, is completely involved in the history of suffering and the battle for justice and peace. In that history, faith gives a meaning to suffering and transforms it by fighting against all useless and senseless suffering. Whoever, in faith, rejoices about freedom received from Christ will remember the price Christ has paid, and no price will be too high for genuine orthodoxy; that is, for orthodoxy which essentially implies orthopraxis.

Faith has a content, a message that is universal, but this message is accessible only to loving knowledge, the knowledge of those who are involved in the praxis of following Christ. The celebration of the sacraments of faith inseparably includes the mission to be witness to this memory by one's own life. The faith of Christians is a liberating practice, a practice of creative liberty and fidelity in history and society, in a soldaric hope that includes the living and the dead, and especially those whom the self-righteous world likes to forget.

All the key concepts of Christian faith such as faith, justice (*dikaiosyne*), redeemed and redeeming love (*agapé*), peace (*shalom*), reconciliation (*katallaghe*) are characterized as undeserved gifts of the one Father, received gratefully only by those who accept their solidaric character of being gift of the one Father *in view of the needs of all.*

The crisis of faith today is not so much a cognitive or intellectual crisis but rather a consequence of an intellectualism that separated a collection of doctrines under the name of orthodoxy, while forgetting or even denying that faith cannot be spoken of, cannot be given witness to without personal and communal involvement in the daily life and in the institutions, structures, customs of social and ecclesial life.

2. Plain heterodoxy

Heterodoxy or heresy is a selective approach to truth revealed by God. Consequently, it is a lack of truthfulness. Heterodoxy means holding or teaching doctrines contrary to the standard of faith. It means making arbitrary choices or selection in matters of doctrine. The classical case of heresy is intellectual arrogance. The heretic relies more on his own intellect than on the trustworthiness of God's revelation and the community of faith. Intellectual difficulties do not lead to the sin of heresy as long as the believer submits to God's authority and acknowledges before God that his mysteries are always infinitely greater than our intellectual grasp and all our thoughts.

Heresy is frequently a troublesome form of escapism from faith commitment into quarrels about mere words and concepts. The first letter to Timothy describes well this kind of heresy. The heretic there is called "a pompous ignoramus". "He is morbidly keen on mere verbal questions and quibbles, which give rise to jealousy, quarrelling, slander, base suspicions and endless wrangles: all typical of men who have let their reasoning powers become atrophied and have lost grip of the truth. They think religion should yield dividends" (6: 3-5). The second letter to Timothy is even more precise in unmasking the heresy of superficial intellectual "orthodoxy". "Go on reminding people of this, and charge them solemnly before God to stop disputing about mere words; it does no good and is the ruin of those who listen" (2: 14).

Heterodoxy is never confined to mere intellectual errors. It has its roots in a heretical attitude. God is not truly chosen as one's highest good, not sought with all one's heart. Some other value takes first place. For instance, a person who wants to make a diplomatic career in ecclesiastical service or in positions that will allow him to exercise great influence, may make an ostentatious display of orthodoxy. But if, in all his thinking, talking and acting, his first concerns are his selfish interests, then in whatever attention he gives to religious matters and questions of orthodox doctrine, he will see only what these interests allow. He is not committed to truth, to the God of Truth because of Himself. He is selective in a very dangerous existential way. And of course he will hide this very tendency from his own superficial conscience. He disturbs his depth-conscience by repression, concealing from himself the main motive that leads to falsified vision.

Certain traditionalist movements arise today from a political concern to keep the *status quo*, to preserve inherited privileges. As a consequence, they are against all changes, whether in liturgy or the methods of catechesis and preaching. They cling to words. Disputes with them will not help until they realize the deeper existential deviation. The fanatical or scrupulous attitudes towards formulae appear on the superficial level as orthodoxy, but it is plain heterodoxy as long as all these disputes and quarrels and displays of obedience are in the service of idols, of alien gods. It is not impossible that plain heterodoxy can take the form of the most intolerant orthodoxy, leading to inquisition, persecution, torture of those who think differently, especially of those who, by the authenticity of their faith and life, hurt the evil consciences of these people. Those who are unwilling to accept the call to ecclesial and social reforms will persecute the saints on behalf of seemingly orthodox formulations, while the real reason is the negative reaction to their call to conversion and reform.

3. *Heterodox orthodoxy*

As long as the self-commitment (fundamental option) in faith is not yet firmly rooted and has not yet transformed dispositions, there can be and, indeed, are all kinds of ambiguous mixtures between a genuine concern for the right faith and dangerous selective attitudes. Basic or initial orthodoxy will take on many shades of heterodoxy, at least on the existential level as long as the fundamental option shows abortive tendencies, for instance, unreadiness for ongoing conversion or for solidaric action.

Regarding teachers who more or less unconsciously neglect the social and communitarian dimensions of their doctrinal formulations, J.B. Metz speaks on "mendacious innocence".[46] These theologians or officeholders tend to speak on "truth in itself" while proposing doctrinal formulations and promoting Church structures that somehow "serve God and mammon". It might well be the "truth" of the ruling class, the truth of a clergy in alliance with the high nobility, the truth-approach of the bourgeoisie. It may be the half-truth of an intellectualism that betrays a lack of total commitment to do the truth.

We are not speaking here of plain hypocrisy or total unwillingness to be converted but of a lack of authenticity of faith because, side by side with the not-fully-consolidated fundamental option for God, there are still evil tendencies or dispositions that can be less or more dangerous and can gradually undermine the self-commitment in faith. A choice of mediocrity in matters of religion and morality produces a strange mixture of true orthodoxy and more or less hidden tendencies that can lead to any of the forms of plain heterodoxy.[47]

A certain form of apologetic theology can be a special brand of heterodox orthodoxy, a self-defensive "faith" that refuses to accept the challenge coming from the conscience of others, a more or less futile exercise of "proofs" where the true sense of God is lacking because of lack of love and genuine interest in the kingdom of God. There can be a way of proving God's existence by a rationalistic approach that is totally severed from all experience in history and society.[48] All this can be a cause of gradual apostasy of masses of people from the Church or from other religions, since the doctrines offered to them seem to be unrelated to their real life. They are not helped by those rationalistic teachers to find integration of faith and life.

4. The sin of apostasy

The code of canon law (can. 1325, § 2) defines apostasy in this way: "If one, after having received Baptism, totally defects from Christian faith, he is an apostate". In view of the fact that so many are baptized but never have received the message of salvation and the witness to faith, and have never become believers, we have to be more cautious. The sin of apostasy is committed only if one, through baptism and evangelization, had the real opportunity to come to faith and was a believer, and yet turns totally away from Christian faith. If he was baptized and evangelized and, through his own fault did not make a fundamental option for faith, then we would speak of the sin of infidelity rather than of apostasy.

The First Vatican Council teaches that God gives grace that helps those who are in error, "that they can come to know the truth (1 Tim 2:4), and he confirms through his grace those who, from darkness have come into his wondrous light (1 Pet 2:9) that they persevere in this light, never abandoning anyone unless he has abandoned him". The emphatic conclusion is: "Should anyone assert that the condition of believers and of those who have not yet come to the only true faith is the same, so that Catholics could have a just reason to doubt the faith which they have accepted under the Magisterium of the Church, and to suspend their assent until they come to a complete scientific demonstration of the credibility and the truth of faith: he be excluded".[49]

The text includes both heresy and apostasy. It is disputed whether the Council wants to say only that nobody can ever have objectively a sound reason to abandon the Catholic faith, or that subjectively there is always also grave personal guilt. What the Council directly teaches is obvious: a person who has received the faith, lives in the Catholic faith community and is solidly instructed, is in a quite different situation than others whose mind, heart and will have never yet been touched by faith. Even if one holds that the First Vatican Council speaks also of the subjective guilt of those who abandon the Church, we human beings can never make a judgment about our fellowmen. We never know whether they were sufficiently instructed or whether they ever made a genuine act of faith (in the sense of a fundamental option). And even if great sin is involved, we do not know whether it is a sin directly against faith. Before one leaves the Church or wavers in faith, he might have polluted his conscience and obscured its vision of truth through other sins not directly opposed to faith.

Those who have abandoned the Church will hardly be touched by the teaching of a Council. However, for many Catholic friends and relatives there is an anguishing question about the chance of salvation for beloved ones who have abandoned the faith; and the way they look at this problem will greatly determine their relationships.

In the first place, we have to say that we never know the degree of personal accountability. Human psychology is enormously complex. Karl Rahner is surely not alone when he says, "It is not unthinkable that someone frees himself in the depth of his conscience from formal guilt, and even if he has truly lost the faith, as such, he can regain an attitude of faith and yet be unable to overcome the prejudices against ecclesial Christianity and, like another person who has never been a Christian, remains in an invincible error without new guilt".[50]

In our age we are faced not only with individual cases of apostasy but even much more with collective apostasy. It happens on a local level frequently because of an all-pervasive formalism and ritualism and because of a thoroughly inadequate pastoral ministry. But it also happens on the broader level. In various countries, the faith of entire groups and social strata is in jeopardy. On the one hand we should be sharply aware of great deficiencies on the part of Christian communities; on the other hand, however, we are dealing with a "sociological mechanism".[51]

An individualistic thinking in matters of faith, and particularly an individualistic moral teaching, was not aware of the interdependence between the total structures of culture and society on the one hand and, on the other, the manifold expressions of religion. Modern sociology, particularly empirical religious sociology, shows clearly that the important structures of social life and the public opinions were not formed by believers but rather are the result of an unchristian philosophy of life. The Christians and the Christian Churches were not sufficiently the "yeast in the dough", the "salt of the earth".[52] The scandal that the Church lost a great part of the working class does not allow us to throw stones at those whom we have lost. Rather, we should accept it as a challenge to live our faith more consistently, especially its dimension of solidarity, and be more dedicated to the spreading of the Gospel.

NOTES

[1] Cf. E. Jüngel, *Gott als Geheimnis der Welt*, Tübingen, 1977. Jüngel makes a firm and well-pondered choice to speak on the world in the light of faith.

[2] Cf. R. Guardini, *Welt und Person*, Würzburg, 1950², 113; W. Kern, "Zur theologischen Auslegung des Schöpfungsglaubens", in *Mysterium Salutis* II (Einsiedeln, 1967), 464-545.

[3] Cf. J.B. Metz, *Glaube in Geschichte und Gesellschaft*, Mainz, 1977, 61ff; W. Kern, l.c., 473ff.

[4] S.Th., I, q 32, a 1 ad 3.

[5] S.Th., I, q 45, a 6.

[6] C. Spiq, *Prologomènes à une étude neo-testamentaire*, Paris, 1955, 94.

[7] Vatican II, *Dogmatic Constitution on Divine Revelation*, 2.

[8] l.c., 4.

[9] R. Niebuhr, *The Nature and Destiny of Man*, New York, 1941, II, 109.

[10] Ch. R. Stinnette Jr., *Anxiety and Faith*, Greenwich/Conn., 1955, 12.

[11] Cf. P. Tillich, *Biblical Religion and the Search for Ultimate Reality*, Chicago, 1955, 67.

[12] Cf. Beschluss der gemeinsamen Synode der Bistümer der BRD, N. 6, on Pastoral cooperation of the Churches in the service of Christian Unity (3.25).

[13] Cf. P. Evdokimov, *La conoscenza di Dio secondo la tradizione Orientale*, Roma, 1969, 16; H. Bahrs, *Die göttlichen Tugenden. Glaube, Hoffnung, Liebe*, Aschaffenburg, 1963, 29.

[14] Cf. Denz. Sch., 2121, 2253.

[15] Denz. Sch., 1578, 3010, 3035.

[16] M. Heidegger, *Unterwegs zur Sprache*, Pfullingen, 1959, 159.

[17] K. Rahner, *Grundkurs des Glaubens. Einführung in den Begriff des Christentums*, Freiburg, 1976, 308.

[18] Cf. O. Händler, *Angst und Glaube*, Berlin, 1953; H. Schär, *Was ist Wahrheit?*, Zürich, 1970, 217ff.

[19] K. Rahner, l.c., 370ff.

[20] Cf. E. Schlink, "Die drei Grundbeziehungen zwischen Glauben und Erkennen", in *Kerygma und Dogma* 23 (1977), 172-187.

[21] M. Merleau-Ponty, *Sense et non-sense*, Paris, 1966⁶, 312.

[22] Cf. *Declaration on Religious Liberty*, 10.

[23] Cf. M.D. Meeks, *Origins of the Theology of Hope*, Philadelphia, 1974, 66ff about the sharp criticism of Bultmann's existential concept of historicity by Pannenberg and Moltmann.

[24] R. Egenter, *Erfahrung ist Leben*, München, 1974.

[25] Cf. J.B. Metz, l.c., 50ff.

[26] l.c., 130ff.

[27] H. Diederich, *Kompetenz des Gewissens*, Freiburg, 1969, 334.

[28] J.H. Newman, *A letter addressed to His Grace the Duke of Norfolk on occasion of Mr Gladstone's recent expostulation in "Certain Difficulties Felt by Anglicans in Catholic Teaching"* (Christian Classics, vol. II), Westminster/ Md., 1969, 248. Cf. B. Häring, "Coscienza e Magistero", in *Magistero e morale*, Bologna, 1970, 319-345.

[29] K. Rahner, l.c., 191.

[30] l.c., 368.

[31] Cf. E. Klinger (ed.), *Christentum innerhalb und ausserhalb der Kirche*, Freiburg-Basel-Wien, 1976 (on K. Rahner's concept of "anonymous Christianity").

[32] J.B. Metz, l.c., 58.

[33] *Lumen gentium*, 1.

[34] Cf. A. Dulles, *Models of the Church*, Garden City, N.J., 1974.

[35] Cf. B. Häring, *The Sacraments in a Secular Age*, Slough, 1976, 93-179.

[36] Augustine, *In Joannis Ev.* XXVI, 13 PL 35, 1612ff.

[37] S.Th., III, q 61, a 4.

[38] *Constitution on Sacred Liturgy*, 59.

39 l.c., 7, 21, 33.
40 F.M. Braun, "La vie d'en haut", in *Revue des sciences phil. et théol.* 40 (1956), 19.
41 S.Th., III, q 48, a 2.
42 K. Barth, *Kirchliche Dogmatik* IV/3, 595; cf. 1000.
43 E. Schlink, *The Doctrine of Baptism*, St. Louis, 1969. Regarding the discussions within the Catholic Church, see A. Winklhofer, *Kirche in den Sakramenten*, Frankfurt, 1969, 302-308.
44 A. Schmied, "Wahrhaftigkeit und Glaube", in *Studia Moralia* 15 (1977), 554.
45 J.B. Metz, l.c., 48. In the following reflections I rely to a great extent on Metz, cf. l.c., 70ff, 128, 147.
46 l.c., 69.
47 Cf. Schär, *Was ist Wahrheit?*, Zürich, 1970, 231ff.
48 Cf. J. Ratzinger, Commentary to Gaudium et Spes, art. 19, *LThK, Das Zweite Vat. Konzil* III, 345.
49 Sessio III, cap. 3 and can. 6, Denz. Sch. 3014; 3036.
50 K. Rahner, "Der Christ und seine ungläubigen Verwandten", in *Schriften zur Theologie* III, 419-439, quote p. 435.
51 Cf. P. Schmid-Eglin, *Le mécanisme de la déchristianisation*, Paris, 1952.
52 Cf. B. Häring, *Macht und Ohnmacht der Religion*, Salzburg, 1956²; V. Schurr, *Seelsorge in einer neuen Welt*, Salzburg, 1959³; cf. chapter VII of this volume.

Chapter Five

Faith-Education and Evangelization in a Critical Age

Christ has consecrated the Church in his truth. He has bestowed on his disciples eternal life through knowledge of him who, as the living Gospel, makes known the Father (cf. Jn 17:3). Through the Gospel entrusted to the Church, Christ builds her up in the power of the Holy Spirit, who introduces her into all truth.

The saving truth and faith are wholly undeserved gifts of the one Father; and unless we realize that they are gifts of the one God and therefore *destined for all*, we cannot live in this saving truth and rejoice in the Gospel.

The evangelization of all people and the ongoing faith-education of the members of the Church belong to the very essence of the Church. Faith is not only rooted in the faith community; it is also destined to build up the community of all people in faith, and thus make visible the kingdom of God.

We speak here on evangelization, including always the ongoing faith-education. This "finds its reason in the will of God who wishes all men to be saved and to come to the knowledge of the truth. For there is one God and one mediator between God and men, Jesus Christ, himself man, who gave himself to win freedom for all mankind" (1 Tim 2:4-5). "There is no salvation in anyone else" (Acts 4:12)[1].

The traditional moral treatise on the duty to confess one's faith has to be restudied in the light of this universal mission of the Church and of each believer to give testimony to the Gospel, thus to call all people to the saving truth. Anyone who, by living faith, experiences the liberating power of the Gospel truth (cf. Jn 8:32) will also realize that he cannot rejoice in this freedom without desiring that the possibility be open to all people to know this truth and be converted to it.

I. THE MORALITY OF EVANGELIZATION

The Apostle of the Gentiles, who deeply experienced the absolute gratuity of the faith and its saving power, realized how ungrateful he would be if he did not proclaim the Good News whenever he could. "It would be misery to me not to preach" (1 Cor 9:16). Although not all have the unique mission to dedicate their whole life to the spreading of the Gospel, every Christian, as a member of the faith community, shares in the essential mission of the Church. So it is "misery" when one spouse does not help the other to come to faith or to a deeper faith, "misery" when parents do not share the Gospel with their children, "misery" for every believer who does not deepen his knowledge of faith and increase his joy of faith, to the detriment of his wonderful task to share this greatest gift with his fellowmen.

1. Evangelization and the Eucharist

The disciples of Christ celebrate the mystery of faith, the Gospel of the reconciling and liberating truth in the Eucharist. It is the height of faith expression and faith education, the grateful celebration of the gift which, by its very character, arouses the desire to render thanks for it by sharing it with others.

In the Eucharist, Christ continues to proclaim to us the good news that he lived, suffered, died for us, and lives for us as the risen Lord. He also inspires in us that joyful gratitude which makes our faith overflow into evangelization, in grateful response to the Word who gives us life.

Jesus of Nazareth lives gratefully by the Word that comes from the Father. The hypostatic union of his human nature with the eternal Word is the Father's gift, destined for all humanity. Therefore, Jesus joyfully and gratefully accepts his mission to bring the Good News and to work for salvation. And he praises the Father when he first experiences that his disciples share in his mission to preach the Father's kingdom. "I thank thee, Father, Lord of heaven and earth, for hiding these things from the learned and wise while revealing them to the simple. Yes, Father, such was thy choice" (Lk 10:21). In the Eucharist and the other sacraments, Christ not only gives us communion with his life but also a share in his mission to be the living Gospel.

Great attention should be given to Marcel Legaut when he says that the future of Christianity, and especially of evangelization, depends fundamentally on our capacity, as disciples of Christ, to celebrate the Eucharistic memorial.[2] The Church that finds its centre of life and mission in the Eucharist will not be seen so much as an institution preoccupied with its own conservation but as, rather, the grateful servant of the Gospel to the very ends of the earth. With overflowing gratitude, she will translate her eschatological hope and her invocation, "Come, Lord Jesus", into communication of this thankfulness and hope to all nations.

2. *The Lordship of Jesus Christ*

Jesus of Nazareth made himself totally the Servant, and thus has credibly and forcefully proclaimed the kingdom of God. He is *the* prophet who is unmasking and overcoming all the powers inimical to the kingdom of the Father. He proclaims the kingdom of saving justice and merciful love "even unto death, death on a cross. Therefore God raised him to the heights and bestowed upon him the name above all names, that at the name of Jesus every knee should bow, in heaven, on earth and in the depths, and every tongue confess, 'Jesus Christ is Lord', to the glory of God the Father" (Phil 2:9-11).

If, in the power of the Holy Spirit, we confess that Jesus is Lord (cf. Rom 1:4; 10:9; 1 Cor 8:6; 12:3), we also experience a burning desire to see him recognized and honoured by all people and in all conditions of life. Evangelization, and particularly moral teaching, is an interpretation of the relation between what God has accomplished in Jesus Christ and the complex conditions of human life.³ We cannot truthfully embrace the kingdom of God and profess the lordship of Jesus without an intense and active zeal to see his lordship acknowledged, and to give honour by our faith and our life, to the Father who has manifested his kingdom in Jesus.

3. *The irrenounceable priority in the preaching of the Gospel*

Moral theology must caution against the great temptation to reduce Christianity to a morality, with disastrous consequences for morality itself as well as for faith-education and evangelization. Christ has come to save us by faith and grace. Proclaiming the Good News, he enables us and obliges us above all else, to be converted to the kingdom of God, to honour God as God. Man alienates himself from salvation if he adores God only or mainly for saving himself. One who does not first give glory to God builds an image of God and of himself according to his own erroneous ideas of salvation and becomes entrapped in individual and collective egotisms.

Emmanuel Kant rightly fought against any ethics that makes one's own perfection the ultimate goal while not recognizing the inner majesty of goodness and truth. But his reflection did not reach ultimate conclusions, since his whole idea of religion is one-sidedly based on its relation to morals.⁴

Christianity cannot possibly become the yeast for culture and the light for social and international justice if it is reduced to horizontalism, to a mere *Kulturchristentum* or a social gospel.⁵ This would be the radical denial of the basic truth that salvation does not come first through work but through faith. The conversion to the kingdom makes us, above all, true adorers of God, attentive to his love, and thus orients our moral life to his praise.

Faith and evangelization include, of necessity, the call to justice, peace, reconciliation, fidelity and other moral values. But they do so only by bestowing on us saving justice, peace, reconciliation, liberation and the covenant, all coming from God as undeserved gifts. The moral imperative retains its vigour and identity in faith and evangelization only through the indicative which proclaims God's initiative, his gracious love, his kingdom.

For faith itself to generate new life, it is of prime importance to recognize the priority of existential acceptance and experience of the Gospel, of prayer, of listening to God and praising him. We should avoid the expression "faith and works" and speak rather on faith that is active in love and justice. And the more active it is in love and justice, the more it is adoring faith. Only thus does it become also the greatest humanizing force.

The proprium of Christian morals, if we want to be exact, is not the *humanum* as such, but its arising from faith, from loving acceptance of the kingdom of God. It is not fraternal love in itself, but the sharing of the believer in that love by which God, in Christ, unites us with his own life and thus enables and sends us to love the world with his own love, in order to save it.

4. *Evangelical poverty and evangelization*

The Sermon on the Mount shows us where the foundation of a living faith, faith-education and authentic evangelization is to be found: in the blessedness of those who know that they are beggars before God, and receive everything gratefully as a gift to be shared. "Theirs is the kingdom of God" (Mt 5:3).

Christ, the living Gospel, recognizes everything as a gift of the Father, giving himself to the Father in the service of his brothers and sisters. In all things he seeks the glory of the Father and honours him, the source of the Gospel and all good things. "For I have taught them all that I learned from thee, and they have received it: they know with certainty that I came from thee" (Jn 17:8).

Vatican II speaks of this spirit of poverty when announcing the programme of the Church to renounce every privilege, even justly acquired, whenever a privilege could disrupt evangelization or compromise her credibility.[6] In this spirit, all those involved in faith-education and evangelization ought to be most careful to respect and to enhance the conscience of those whom they serve. The main concern will never be success or, what is worse, self-importance, but only fidelity to the Gospel. "The apostles, their successors, and those who assist these successors have been sent to announce to men Christ, the Saviour of the world. Hence, in the exercise of their apostolate they must depend on the power of God, who very often reveals the might of the Gospel through the weakness of its witnesses. For those who dedicate themselves to the ministry of God's word should use means and helps proper to the Gospel. In many respects these differ from the supports of the earthly city".[7] This demanding programme is not only for the structures of the Church, the officeholders and those totally dedicated to the Gospel, but for every Christian who wants to witness to the Gospel and to strengthen and deepen the faith of his brothers and sisters.

The people of God admit and honour the lordship of God and the gratuity of reconciliation also through the confession of sins, whether they concern personal acts or the alienating structures, institutions and centres of ecclesiastical power. Only such a confession, truthful and serene, can fill the gap between the normative ideal of the Gospel and the inadequacy of the evangelizers.

The substantial infallibility of the Church can be affirmed only by admitting that she has made mistakes many times, compromising herself by declarations in fields in which the officeholders had no competence and for which she has no mission, as well as by claiming earthly power which was forbidden her by the Lord himself.

The Church strengthens and spreads the faith if each one is satisfied with his own charism, happy to cooperate with all, so that the various competences and charisms make known the giver of all good gifts. The spirit of poverty allows faith to be active in love and to build up the community of evangelizers. "Where the love of God reigns, no one wants anymore to dominate over others; there is created an ambiance free from domination; people accept each other in turn, pardon each other, carry each other's burden. There they celebrate and rejoice together and there also is constituted a space where the saving events in Christ can become present witness".[8]

5. *The absolute novelty of the Gospel and of moral life in Christ*

Whoever wants to share his faith and help others to grow in faith needs a profound experience of the utter newness of the Gospel of Christ. The true evangelist is so seized by gratitude for faith that he can — indeed, must — communicate the truth that the Gospel in Christ is the fulfilment of the whole history of the world and the hope of the future. "I tell you, many prophets and kings wished to see what you now see" (Lk 10:24). One who truly receives Christ, the living Gospel, has the experience, ever renewed by the Spirit, of the novelty of the saving message. And this absolute novelty of the faith-experience cannot be proclaimed while neglecting the novelty of the moral life in Christ.

Faith in the kingdom of God is given to us together with the gift of the Spirit who renews our hearts and the face of the earth. Whoever believes the Gospel wholeheartedly will experience a conversion on all levels in relationship with God, with fellowmen, with oneself and the whole of life (cf. Mk 1:15). The proclamation of the Paschal Mystery is not complete without presenting, by witness and word, the new life that arises from it. "The life I now live is not my life but the life which Christ lives in me; and my present bodily life is lived by faith in the Son of God, who loved me and gave himself up for me" (Gal 2:20). "Live in love as Christ loved you" (Eph 5:2).

The newness of the Gospel that engenders and strengthens faith and a life according to faith is greatly damaged not only by a moralism that emphasizes works before faith, but also by the various forms of confounding our ethos and our historically conditioned norms with the firm and essential exigencies of faith.[9] Where the newness of both faith and moral life is rightly presented, it will be easier to bring home all the cultural values into the light of faith, and find the integration of faith and life.

Certainly faith-education and evangelization will appraise very highly the values and the moral sense of genuine humanism, but we shall be able to unmask and avoid the traps of human self-sufficiency only by adoring God in spirit and truth, and witnessing to that morality which springs from faith and blossoms in gratitude for the undeserved grace of God.

The novelty of faith implies always a call to conversion. But we shall not forget that the proclamation of faith will frequently meet a fundamental option already formed for the good, which implicitly is an option for faith and Gospel morality — a fundamental option, however, that still needs unfolding, fuller consciousness and the consequent ongoing conversion.[10]

6. Evangelization and pre-evangelization

Those dedicated to share faith and to proclaim the Gospel will carefully watch for the *kairos*. Christians who speak with *parrhesia* (courageous confidence), whether timely or untimely as far as their own interest is concerned, will speak at the right time as far as the fecundity of the word is concerned.

Whatever prepares for evangelization and faith-education can be called pre-evangelization. Thus, the activity of Christians who dedicate themselves to social, charitable works, to instruction and the spreading of culture, are pre-evangelizing to the extent that they are inspired by the love which the Gospel teaches us and by the desire that all may know the love of God revealed in Jesus Christ. Not only will missionaries in some non-Christian countries not always be able to proclaim faith directly, but even parents and others may sometimes realize that those entrusted to their special responsibility will, at this moment, not yet be open to an explicit dialogue on faith. The witness of faith, active in love and justice, ought to precede the word of faith.[11] Social action and good human behaviour, as such, are not pre-evangelization by themselves, but only by the burning desire to communicate the full liberating truth.

It therefore becomes clear that idols and ideologies can easily hide under the term "pre-evangelization". For example, one thinks of those who hold that making underdeveloped people literate, turning nomads into farmers, teaching technical progress, imposing the adoption of certain political systems, is more urgent than evangelization, or at least an indispensable condition for it. People who think this way are still prisoners of their culture transformed into an idol. In the same category are those who think that they must first teach a certain philosophy, a determined ethical system, or a theory of natural law before "adding" the Gospel. They hide the Gospel, having not yet been liberated by it and for it. Or the Gospel is, for them, no more than an "addition to" instead of being the yeast in the dough.

Things are different if we help others to make a firm fundamental option for the good and for truth, and for searching even more earnestly for a better understanding of what is good and true. This can be called pre-evangelization.

II. EVANGELIZATION AND THE SIGNS OF THE TIMES

One who communicates faith is a co-worker with the Lord of history. Therefore he has to be most attentive to what God says through events. The whole of history has the character of a word-event and of an event-revealer. The same Lord who has revealed his most active presence in the Incarnation, Passion, Death and Resurrection is present in the whole of history. The Spirit renews the face of the earth and the hearts of people, especially by giving them discernment so that they can grasp the present opportunities, the hopes and the risks.[12]

1. *How can the signs of the times be discerned?*

Discernment is one of the eschatological virtues, and will not emerge without the others: with gratitude for all that God has done in the past and does even today, with hope that praises God's promises by a life of trust and fidelity, with vigilance for the present opportunities, and with readiness to greet the Lord when he comes to call or to challenge us. We must live with the Lord of history by solidarity with his people if we are to understand his voice in the events.

Discernment is a gift of the Holy Spirit given to those who praise and honour him and have accepted the law of grace in view of the needs of people. The Spirit teaches us to see everything in the light of Christ, his mysteries, his words and his presence. In this light, creation and history take on the perspective of sacramentality, as signs of God's gracious presence.

To be vigilant and to know how to discern require rootedness in the community of believers and in a personal and communal prayer life that allows the Spirit to cry out in us, "Abba, Father!" Such an intimate prayer fosters spontaneity, creativity, openness, liberty and courage. Only a community of persons that lives this prayer — which is consciousness of the presence of God who calls and gathers all together — is capable of listening to the voice of the times and discerning the true prophets who interpret the signs.

Trust in the Spirit of God does not permit us, however, the least intellectual or spiritual laziness. The community that is guided by the Spirit will use all the means which Providence puts at its disposal today — at this hour, this moment of *kairos* — to know better today's people, the course of history, the social processes and relations, the various interdependencies between religion, family, economy, culture, politics, and so on.

The Spirit inspires trust and courage, and disallows both superficial optimism and pessimism. The spiritual people will always give attention first to the positive signs of the presence of God, but then will also face the challenging signs that call for a strong decision to fight the evil by the good.

In and through the eschatological virtues, faith becomes fully alive and active, a power for evangelization. Faith-education based on discernment of the signs of the times will never be abstract, alienated talk but a manifestation of saving solidarity, of integration between life and culture, faith and life.

Not everyone and every community can, by themselves, decipher the important signs of the times. But inserted in the universal, prophetic Church, all can come to the necessary vision of the main signs, and learn to discern the particular opportunities and dangers in personal and community life.

2. *The encouraging and alarming signs of the times, and the challenge they present*

a) The encouraging signs

To honour God, the Lord of history, it is necessary to give attention first to the encouraging signs. One who looks first at the discouraging, negative signs, and magnifies them, gives more honour to the Evil one and his followers than to the Creator and Redeemer of humankind. Thus he will be thoroughly unable to evangelize the world and to help others to grow in faith.

Throughout the whole treatise we have discovered, as one of the most urgent signs of our times, the experience of unity and solidarity in a manner unknown until now. We are, in a new way, conscious of the fact that we are all in the same boat, and we either liberate ourselves from the tendencies to violence and domination by promoting justice by non-violent action, or we will sink the boat.

For the first time in history, all the different cultures, races and religions can enter into fruitful communication. All the nations can enrich each other by the various aspects of development. All these new experiences and possibilities can and must become an integral part of faith-education and evangelization. Then the great truths of faith and the lives of believers can offer the true dimensions of human solidarity.

The ecumenical movement is one of the most important responses and a part of this sign of the times.[13] "Here is found the specific contribution of the Church to civilizations: sharing the noblest aspirations of men, and suffering when she sees them not satisfied, she wishes to help them attain their full flowering. That is why she offers men what she possesses as her characteristic attributes: a universal vision of men and of the human race".[14]

The modern means of communication and other social processes have opened an era of *worldwide dialogue*. More than ever in history we can free ourselves from tribal attitudes by being open to the values of others and ready to share with them, in full knowledge and appreciation, their own histories and cultures. In such a moment, the Church is called by God to broaden the horizon of natural law teaching, bringing home the experience and co-reflection of all cultures and religions.

It is a time of *exodus* for the occidental Church which, up to our time, has expressed universal truths with the concepts and experiences of only the western culture. All her life, and especially her approach to faith-education and evangelization must be characterized by consciousness that the centres of influence are shifting from the old western world to the so-called Third World, to Asia, Africa and Latin America.

Faith-education and evangelization have to give particular attention to the fact that we live in an extremely *critical* age, at least as far as that part of humanity is concerned which will be decisive in shaping the future. In this context, we see a new emphasis on sincerity in the search for truth, the respect for each person's dignity and conscience, and the demythologizing of authority.

There is growing a new consciousness and consciousness-raising about the personal and social dimensions of freedom, including liberty of conscience and religion. Faced with new threats of manipulation and oppression, new ways are being explored on how to increase the awareness of and the decision for freedom and the space for freedom. The people of God have to be a sacrament of liberty and liberation if they want to spread and to increase the faith in Christ, the Redeemer and Liberator.

Today's culture assumes an ever more *dynamic* character. Not only is the volume of knowledge growing immensely; life is seen in a perspective of development. Human psychology is studied as life history, with the chance for growth and the threat of decay for those who refuse to grow. Faith-education is called to give the proper vision of growth. We shall overcome the dangerous imbalance and demythologize the idol of economic growth only if faith and morality are presented with the dynamics of the Gospel, as ongoing conversion and growth in the knowledge and love of God and man.

We shall give particular attention here to the critical temper of our age, for it offers a unique opportunity and tremendous challenge for education to a mature faith and a mature morality.

b) The challenge of the alarming signs

Christ, who is the living Gospel, is also the prophet who interprets history and thereby unmasks the idols, the many disguises under which the Evil one presents his plans. Our purpose to give prime attention to the gladdening news and to the hope-inspiring signs of the times does not allow us to act naïvely. In the light of the Gospel and the positive signs of the times, we shall be better able to face the negative signs.

The greatest challenge to faith and faith-education in our era is atheism in its various forms. (We dedicate Chapter Seven to this problem). All that we are saying here about evangelization and faith-education has to integrate the reflections on the encounter of faith with today's atheism.

Today's believers are challenged by the fact that in western culture, which traditionally was under the influence of Christendom, there are, besides atheism, powerful idols such as success in an exclusively material development, the idol of power, and the idol of sex in a thoroughly disintegrated approach. All believers and the Church as a whole can be asked why we are not more "light for the world". Why are we Christians so vulnerable to these idols?

In spite of a new consciousness of solidarity, there are developing sharper polarizations and conflicts both in the secular city and in the Church. We cannot avoid asking ourselves whether we have preached and lived the Gospel of reconciliation actively enough. Are all Christians taught to know Christ, the Reconciler, the Prophet and the Servant? Do they realize that much of their life directly contradicts their faith?

If we speak of faith-education and evangelization, one of the most challenging signs of our times is the fact that a great segment of the baptized are either not at all evangelized or have less and less contact with the Church, or only a negatively critical one. All this has to be kept in mind if we address new and old questions about difficulties in faith and faith-education.

III. THE GRACE AND THE CHALLENGE OF A CRITICAL AGE

In the following pages we speak of "crisis" and "critical attitude" in the original sense of the Greek word *krisis* and in the way Erik Erikson understands the crisis that characterizes each phase of human development. But we are concerned not only with the crisis in the life of the individual but, at the same time, with a crisis forced upon humanity or offered to humanity by the present historical development.

"Crisis" has not a negative sense but can have a negative outcome if the positive challenge is not accepted. The crisis we speak of here is meant as an opportunity to acquire the virtue of critique, for without this, there is a danger of bondage in vicious criticism or the proclivity to surrender uncritically to manipulation.

1. *The new situation*

Faith-education has to be sharply aware of the epochal transition taking place in our time. From an age in which Christianity, in spite of all its imperfections, was profoundly incarnated in the culture in which one was born and educated, we are moving into an age where faith becomes more and more a personal choice, often in conflict with the environment.

In the past era, not only were all baptized but they normally accepted Christian doctrine and discipline without any criticism and without personal crisis. Of course there are still people today who grow up under the ambiguous conditions of the old "Christendom" or — what is much better — who are favoured by a truly Christian environment and receive such a convincing testimony of faith that they are spared their share in the collective crisis. However, not only the social élites but also great segments of the masses — especially those decisive for the future of Christianity — are conscious of the necessity of having to make a clear personal choice of faith, often after having gone through a more or less long and profound crisis.[15]

In almost every part of the world there is a considerable group, sometimes even the majority of those registered in our Church statistics, who can be described as "on the fringe".[16] These are not completely cut off from the Church or from a religious tradition. Some of them are firmly dedicated to Christ but are not so sure whether allegiance to the Church is part of this dedication. Others are lukewarm and are gradually losing their interest in both Christ and the Church. However, very many want to remain Christians and belong to the Church, although they cannot or do not accept the doctrines and moral norms of the Church as "a package deal" to "take or leave" in its entirety. They have decided to search personally for a synthesis in an existential way, distinguishing what they can accept and integrate in their conscientious plan of life from what does not seem to fit into their vision or at least is not convincing to them.

To understand this sometimes frightening phenomenon, we must remember that each of us behaves selectively towards information and truth. Some things do not touch our interest and therefore do not come to the surface. But beyond this mostly unconscious cognitive reality, there is something more. The history of dogmatic theology, and especially of moral theology, shows that rigorists, laxists, and people sworn into a certain school, have always chosen parts of scripture and tradition somehow unilaterally. Often they were absolutely blind in the face of explicit and consistent doctrines of the Bible, such as evangelical poverty, simplicity, absolute truthfulness and fidelity to an infinitely merciful God, while being extremely sharp and rigorous in selecting and explaining a few words (proof-texts) of the Bible, for example, in favour of their rigoristic, undiscerning sexual morality or their emphasis on private property, to the detriment of social responsibilities. Today the selective attitude manifests itself in a different way. It is no longer restricted to theological schools but extends to numerous persons of all social strata and whole social groups and classes. And while the theologians, whether lax or rigorous, were frequently more or less unaware of their extremely selective attitude, today's people are becoming much more conscious of it. It is an expression of a critical attitude.

In earlier times, the theological disputes did not reach the masses. Today the mass media publicize their theological pluralism and the public takes part in the discussions. Average people read books and articles, and are quite aware that not only their local pastor but Church authorities on all levels have made grave mistakes and committed errors. And whenever ecclesiastical documents reaffirm, without qualification, that the Church has never erred in her moral and doctrinal teaching, a whole orchestra of mass media reminds people of errors committed.

In the past political choices by Church authorities — by the Pope as head of the Church-state and by princes of the Church — frequently caused anticlericalism which is still alive. Today's world has a much sharper consciousness that the "sacred alliances" between clergy and high nobility, between the Pope as political leader and other powers, influenced also, almost by necessity, certain doctrinal positions. Because of historical experience and the influence of the behavioural sciences, many people no longer believe in a "political innocence" of the Church.[17] Only a new practice and a conversion incarnated in new structures can dissipate doubts that frequently go far beyond a balanced evaluation.

For its own internal use, theology always paid great attention to theological qualifications, distinguishing sharply between truths revealed by God, truths defined as dogmas, truths that might probably be defined as dogmas (*fidei proximas*), doctrines considered certain in theology, doctrinal opinions more common or less common, and so on. However, in preaching and in catechesis, these distinctions were often not kept in mind. A whole package including doctrines like that of limbo (discussed earlier) was presented as if it were, altogether, a matter of faith. Even political questions such as the sacredness of the Church's state and political privileges were frequently proposed as if they were sanctioned in virtue of faith.

While people earlier responded to these matters simply by anticlericalism, accusing the clergy of domineering attitudes and political interest, the response today is even more radical and sometimes more confused. The general authority crisis in the civil and political spheres extends all too easily to the Church authority, especially when the structures and exercises of authority follow older patterns which, meanwhile, have been eliminated in the secular world.

Another cause of criticism has been the militant attitude of the Roman Catholic Church towards other parts of Christianity or against modern science, modern culture, and especially against the modern world's desire for liberty and the affirmation of progress.[18] A suspicious or self-defensive attitude, expressed in generalizing terms against modern science, in our century especially against behavioural sciences, made the Church appear, in the eyes of many, as an enemy of progress and scientific thinking.

Although the Church as communion of saints, as the Church instituted and preserved by Christ and assisted by the Holy Spirit, is a very important reason for credibility, an over-emphasis on her authority and sanctity does not help to overcome the crisis of faith if her practice and way of teaching are not, of themselves, convincing.[19] An authoritarian style of leadership by priests on the various levels becomes a symbol of authoritarianism in society, contradicting the basic symbol of Christ the servant, the attitude of the humble, gentle poor ones.[20]

Apologetics, without humble confession of shortcomings, faults and sins, and without acknowledgment of past errors, had frequently a paradoxical effect.[21] The heavy control that hit especially the creative theologians, bishops and pastors not only increased suspicion among people but also impoverished the Church in its task of faith-education.

With the slogan, "the world come of age", Dietrich Bonhoeffer described the reaction of the laity against traditional methods of control and the paternalistic style of their respective

Church authorities. He surely did not think or assert that today's man is always mature, but rather that the laity is longing for an adult relationship, a partnership between laity and clergy. And if the clergy accuses the laity of immaturity, refusing partnership on that ground, the laity will answer a paternalistic clergy in the same tone and with the same weapons.

It would be a great error, however, to assume that the sharpness of the crisis arises only from faults on the part of the clergy and the higher Church authorities. We have to take into account the generally critical attitude which, in a pluralistic society and culture, is necessary to protect one's liberty of choice and to preserve integrity against all the dangers of being manipulated. We are aware, too, of the impact of a better knowledge of history, including the history of religions, and of a mentality formed partially by the natural sciences but especially by the behavioural sciences which became more antagonistic to theology when theology did not come to an appropriate appreciation and full acknowledgment of the diversity of methods.

Recently a number of empirical studies have been made about the degree of people's partial identification with the Church or partial distance from her: from her structure, her doctrine and her moral norms. I mention two studies, one sponsored by the Central Committee of German Catholics about the situation in Western Germany,[22] and another by Andrew Greeley about the situation in the United States of America.[23]

These two studies came to similar conclusions. The increasing critical distance from the Church authority expresses itself mostly through decreasing participation in the sacraments of the Church. However, an only partial identification with certain doctrines, or especially with certain moral norms of the Church, does not at all exclude a strong dedication to the Church and a lively interest in her life. A critical attitude can be a suffering with the Church and a testimony of solidarity with and love for her.

Greeley states, "There has been a substantial decline in acceptance of the legitimacy of ecclesiastical authority. In 1963, 70% thought it was 'certainly true' that Jesus handed over the leadership of his Church to Peter and the Popes; ten years later, that proportion had fallen to 42%. Only 32% think it is 'certainly true' that the Pope is infallible when he speaks on matters of faith and morals". Greeley concludes that "loyalty to the Church remains but it is being transformed".[24] He is convinced that, according to his data, the Council increased trust in and dedication to the Church, but that the post-conciliar era, especially since 1968, led to a sharp decrease. A main cause seems to be non-identification with certain norms taught by the Church about sexual morality.[25]

The study about German Catholicism mentions as a cause of distance the conflict regarding ethical norms but does not pursue the question of how far the moral teaching, through an impression of regression or of exaggeration, has caused an alienation of Christians from faith and Church.[26]

A widespread dissent concerns canon law and the effort on the part of ecclesiastical officials to impose on the conscience of the faithful certain laws and precepts of the past, as if nothing had happened in the Second Vatican Council. For example, there is strong dislike and disagreement shown against the existing system and practice of the marriage tribunals although the pioneering example of some of them is recognized.[27] While canonists in some nations have become a spearhead of renewal, it is well known that others indulge in a cult of the written law which contradicts both the Gospel and the present pastoral needs.

Another pertinent fact is that, especially before the Council, liturgical renewal has often been able to make headway only by ignoring or violating established norms untimely reaffirmed by authorities, and that official acknowledgment of good changes finally came only in view of the accomplished fact. That a part of Church authorities introduced liturgical renewal with only a lukewarm interest and frequently without explaining its deeper meaning, sharpened the authority crisis.

There is particularly profound criticism of a concept of sin still prevailing among those of the clergy who lament a disastrous loss of the sense of sin among the people, when this often concerns only a change of perspective, that frequently goes hand in hand with greater sensitivity for high values and a prophetic emphasis on justice and peace.[28]

Regular confession is in crisis because some confessors still act as controllers who want to know accurately numbers, species and all the details of sins in order to assess whether they were mortal or "only" venial, frequently with no relation to salvation and conversion. A particularly sharp reaction is caused by their too detailed and sometimes disrespectful interrogations about the sixth commandment, especially since the encyclical *Casti Connubii* (1930). This author knows many persons who, very early in their lives, have abandoned the sacrament of Penance and, as a consequence, the sacramental life, because of excessive rigorism about masturbation and similar things.

2. Response in education of faith

a) Special emphasis on discernment

In its decree on the Church's missionary activity (n. 39), Vatican II orders theologians to bring to the fore the missionary aspects of their disciplines. To my mind, one of the most important aspects is the gradual education to faith, especially through discernment.

Those in authority who are mainly concerned for order and discipline, and for reassuring people who care more for security than for courageous search for truth, are easily tempted to consider all critique as destructive, a sign of lack of loyalty. Conscientious people who suggest that some norms should be better formulated or that greater fidelity towards the Lord's commandment of mercy should be shown are all too often accused of wanting to make Christian life cheaper. John Baptist Metz feels that "the crisis of the Church of today is not caused by too much critique but rather by a lack of training for genuine critical freedom. Those who try to correct the attitude of the faithful, who expect an authoritarian reassurance of knowledge, do not work for the destruction of the Church. They do not act lovelessly against the simple people of the Church, but labour for the chance of a firm ecclesiastical spirit of tomorrow".[29]

Faith-education includes education for that discernment which allows people, after infant baptism, to come to an adult faith and to accept the crisis that leads to it with as much serenity as possible. Pastors and educators have to expect that the transition to an adult faith will pass through some creative crisis while the young person strives for his or her identity.[30] Special attention must be given to avoid bitter criticism and to teach by example and word a loving critique of the Church, a loving understanding of her difficulties in a time of profound cultural changes and of deep contrast between the mission of the Church and the value system of a great part of society.

The educator must not only teach with discernment but also must elicit a discerning faith. Teachers and disciples have to search together for "more suitable ways of communicating doctrine to people of their times. For the deposit of faith or revealed truth is one thing; the manner in which it is formulated, without violence to its meaning and significance, is another".[31]

People should learn about the time-bound character of dogmatic formulations and their partial conditioning by the changing worldview and cultural circumstances. Even where it is a matter of truth, of faith or explicit dogmas, we cannot possess formulas which are and remain perfect and communicable to every culture and each new age. In comparison with other documents of the Holy See, the declaration *Mysterium Ecclesiae* (July 5, 1973) from the Congregation for the Doctrine of Faith, constitutes notable progress because it openly recognizes the necessity of discernment in the presentation of formulations, insofar as they depend on a particular culture, language or philosophy.[32]

Already in the New Testament, the kerygma manifests a noticeable diversity according to the circumstances of the writer and his audience. And throughout the ages there were many direct and indirect approaches to faith in poetry, in art, in music, in popular religiosity, liturgy and theology.[33]

Discernment in faith-education entails not only criteria for discerning the abiding truth from time-bound formulations and similar aspects, but also an education in faith-experience and the purity of motives. We look to the experience of faith in the saints whom we meet and whom we know from history, and thus we come closer to experiencing Christ, which is the basis of the faith of the apostles (cf. 1 Jn 1:1-3).

Time and again we must be reminded that we cannot make progress in discernment and faith unless we are willing to act on the truth. "The man who lives by the truth comes out into the light so that it may be clearly seen that God is in all he does" (Jn 3:21). We can help others to grow in faith and discernment only if we are confident like Paul: "I know who it is in whom I have trusted" (2 Tim 1:12). But at the same time we must respond to intellectual difficulties with intelligent questions and not try to attribute all difficulties in faith or crises of faith to existential shortcomings.

Faith-education must know about the history of faith in the life of each individual. In his essay on the history of faith and doubt of faith, Romano Guardini insists that we must know more about the specific forms of the faith of the child with its basic trust, of the critical mind of the adolescent searching for personal convictions, and of the wise and simple faith of older people.[34]

An important criterion that can help adolescents and adults in their crises of faith is the question, "Is the search for truth and the readiness to act according to it the most important concern in your life?"

b) Emphasis on absolute sincerity in the search for truth

The words of St John, "The unloving know nothing of God, for God is love" (1 Jn 4:8) are help and consolation to the person who is searching for better knowledge of what love truly is, and striving for healthy relationships, especially if, in spite of troubles with faith, the person is growing in sincere love. We all need to realize ever more keenly that a sincere conscience is the best way to gain light. We can help others in their difficulties only if they know that they can speak to us with absolute trust and sincerity, whatever may be their problem. Since trust is a basic element of faith, we have to create an atmosphere of mutual trust if we want to promote authentic faith.

The document of the Congregation for Catholic Education, dated July 5, 1977, exhorts Catholic educators not just to propose ready-made answers but to foster the desire to search for and to discover the truth.[35] Religious education has a chance only if it is allowed to be creative and can create an atmosphere in which sincerity, trust and creativity can blossom.[36]

c) Hierarchy of truths in a genuine synthesis

Genuine faith-education does not present a code of dogmas and norms, side by side, but brings people into contact with Christ, the living Gospel, in an inspiring synthesis that gives direction to our life, to the glory of God. We can synthesize the whole in three aspects: (1) To know God as he has revealed himself in Jesus Christ; (2) to know man in the light of God's design revealed in the God-Man, Jesus Christ, and in the light of the total human experience and co-reflection; (3) to know how to pray, prayer being understood as integration of faith and life. Faith-education is impossible if we split dogma and morals into two separate pieces. Salvation truth gives guidance to life. We conceive morality as it is rooted in faith.

Theology itself is concerned with a hierarchy of truth. The essential task of scientific theology is to present an attractive picture of Christ at the centre. In faith-education, a new aspect enters. It is not only a question of the absolute hierarchy of truth but of gradually helping the person to find an inspiring leitmotif and to bring the truths home into an existential synthesis to be lived and witnessed to.

Living faith cannot be confined to the truths of faith revealed directly by God; it embraces everything that gives meaning to life in the light of Christ and the whole ministry of salvation. Everyone will try to see all of his life and all life in history and society in a vital synthesis. This needs a high level of maturity and an awareness that each person has to reach his or her personal synthesis in a way that enriches the community of faith, manifesting unity in diversity and diversity in unity.

Superficial talk on faith by people who are not truly striving for full integration can lead to a dangerous pluralism that would contradict unity and solidarity. On the contrary, the dialogue of faith between people thoroughly committed and concerned for the best possible integration between faith and culture, and faith and life will lead to a genuine pluralism.[37]

d) The law of growth in faith

Through faith, the kingdom of God takes hold of us and becomes active in us and through us. The parables on the kingdom of God, explaining the dynamics of growth, apply to faith. "Faith is like a mustard seed, the smallest of seeds, which grows into a tree large enough for birds to roost among its branches" (Mt 13:31-32). "It is like yeast which a woman mixes with half a hundredweight of flour until all is leavened" (Mt 13:33).

Through faith, the whole of Christian life is a manifestation of the dynamics of the kingdom of God. Faith is grace and calling to an ongoing conversion that allows the Gospel to transform the whole way of thinking and living. It calls constantly for greater depth and for all-inclusive breadth. A believer can accept the partial blindness and lack of depth of his faith only if he can say sincerely, "I press on, hoping to take hold of that for which Christ once took hold of me" (Phil 3:12). Then, in our mutual help, we can be patient and steadfast. "There is nothing love cannot face; there is no limit to its faith, its hope and its endurance" (1 Cor 13:7).

e) Creative doubt

For faith-education in one man's life, and for help offered to others, it is most important to discern what the expression "doubt in faith" really might mean.[38] On one extreme it might be arrogant doubt, an obstinate refusal of faith commitment. On the other hand, it might be a creative doubt as expression of the most earnest and sincere search for fuller light, either on the road to the first faith-commitment or in the ongoing conversion to a deeper and more illumined faith. In between, there can be all kinds of shades and mixtures of good and bad. The doubt can concern the credibility of revelation in Jesus Christ; it can touch essential dogmas such as the divinity of Christ and his resurrection; it can be a doubt about whether a certain doctrine really belongs to faith and, if it is known as an authentic doctrine of the Church, whether it is irreformable or not. The doubt can touch a taboo or a superstition which one has considered as belonging to the Christian religion, so that the doubt is the way to overcome a striking imperfection in one's religiosity.

We do not speak here of "heretical" doubt, insofar as is meant a merely objective opposition to a truth of faith (material error). Although such an "objective" consideration may have its value, here we approach the whole problem from the subjective disposition of the individual person.[39] This perspective is essential for a moral theology that has made the "turn to the subject".

Doubt as conscientious and humble search, and question about certain points of the Christian doctrine, can help faith to remain genuine.[40] Open and sincere questions do not touch the faith-commitment as long as one concentrates on the central aspects of the Christian message while remaining open for all the truths in the ongoing effort for more knowledge and integration. As long as our doubt expresses our humble readiness to revise our opinions and to improve our knowledge, it is a sign of the sincerity of our overall faith.

The whole Church is a pilgrim. Throughout the ages the Church has come to a deeper understanding of many aspects of faith and has met the need to eliminate some doctrines that once were proposed as certain or almost certain theological propositions. Our own development in faith is analogous to the pilgrim road of the Church. The wholesome doubt can unmask the most unwholesome attitude, fanaticism in holding certain theological opinions and doctrines, or fanaticism in denying them. The creative doubt increases in us the openness to the whole of the revelation in Jesus Christ.[41]

Romano Guardini follows the vision of Cardinal Newman, holding that a strong faith is able to give positive value even to doubts. The doubts of a true believer do not arise from mere intellectual lack of insight, nor are they the result of moral defects. Rather, they are an inner possibility of faith itself, a faith that realizes our pilgrim situation and accepts the need of further purification and progress.[42]

f) Sinful lack of doubt

If one agrees with this analysis of faith and doubt, it will be easy to realize that a total lack of doubt in a believer may be a shocking sign of unwillingness to learn and to unlearn, to grow and to be purified in one's vision of faith. The external appearance of firmness of faith can be either a security complex or a stubborn refusal of openness for more light.

g) Sinful doubt regarding faith

Until the believer is converted to total humility, to the purity of full sincerity, there will always be the possibility of sinful doubt arising from spiritual laziness or even from contemptuous arrogance. There are all kinds of doubt that urge us to remember more humbly that faith is an undeserved gift, and we have constantly to pray, "Lord, I believe; help me where my faith is falling short".

If we are faced with fellow Christians who emphatically deny certain doctrines of the Church, the least we should try to do is to invite them to suspend their judgment, to renew their basic faith commitment, and to be open for further search.

IV. EVANGELIZATION IN A DYNAMIC AGE

Many tensions and conflicts within the faith community arise from two opposite mentalities, a static one with a static worldview, and a dynamic attitude corresponding with the dynamic worldview and a dynamic character. For the dialogue with today's world, Vatican II has given great emphasis to the rapid transition from a rather static to a more dynamic worldview.[43] One should consciously make one's choice for a more static or more dynamic outlook, or at least should become sharply aware of one's psychological trend. Only then will a dialogue be profitable.

If we want to be light for the world, we have to express our faith radically as the history of God with men, in full awareness of evolution and the unity of human history.

The growth of population, the worldwide encounter, the new experience of solidarity, cannot be thought of without the almost incredible development of science and technology. Humanity today does not only make chance discoveries; it has practically invented the art of invention. And this has an enormous impact on all future history.

There are at this moment probably more trained scientists than the sum of all generations that lived before us. There is an ever increasing professional specialization. In the Third World nations, which have an enormous population increase, there is need of economic growth. But there is at the same time a harmful expansion of economic production and consumption in the western world, with terrible risks for ecology. The ruthless exploitation of the irreplaceable resources is a shocking sign of irresponsibility for the future.

The most horrifying dynamism is in armaments, with the invention of ever new weapons. Humankind has not much time left to overcome these trends if it is not to destroy itself.

All these things challenge theology. Faith-education has to take into account this reality. Only if we succeed in living our faith in the dimension of the eschatological virtues, of ongoing thanksgiving, firm orientation, trust and hope, vigilance, readiness and discernment, the spirit of poverty and serenity, only then can we unmask the ideologies and proclaim the saving power of the Gospel.

Man's spiritual forces have not kept pace with his economic, technical and scientific development. The dynamism which belongs to the whole man and the whole humanity is exhausted one-sidedly in the technical, productive and commercial fields. Many lose the sense of wholeness and their own most noble and fundamental capacities for admiration, adoration, spiritual awareness and responsiveness, creative liberty and fidelity.

Evangelization, or perhaps pre-evangelization, must convince man he will remain or become ever more underdeveloped if he does not know how to impose limitations on himself and on unwise practices in technical, material development. To man, who already feels an existential vacuum, we should offer by example and word the value of true leisure and the sense of silence, so that he can enter into the sanctuary of his own conscience and discover in its depths the presence of God.

The Church, which lives in a time of exodus, is in need of profound adjustments. However, psychological and spiritual health demands serenity, and especially a profound sense of continuity of life.

The most profound energies of faith and testimony to the world are arising from the experience of the gratuitousness of faith. And in the light of all of God's gifts, a keen awareness that we are saved by grace and faith will increase in us the praise of God's saving justice and love. From that source, and only from that, arises the true dynamism of faith, active in love. This is the vision of true morality which Paul calls the "law of faith" (Rom 3:31).

If all could experience the convincing witness of love and justice, given by faith communities that, in the midst of all the unrest, produce the harvest of the Spirit (love, peace, joy, serenity, gentleness, kindness, benevolence, generosity, creative liberty and fidelity), then our dynamic age would learn to impose on itself proper moderation and see where the right growth of history belongs. All of our religious and modern education must manifest this true dynamism of grace and faith, this creative liberty and fidelity. Only then can we help others to come to fullness of faith in Christ, the Lord of history.

V. EVANGELIZATION IN A TIME OF EXODUS

In the Bible, the exodus paradigm goes hand in hand with the liberation theme. Noah, Abraham, Moses, the people of Israel, and finally Jesus, have to leave everything behind in the great event of liberation and redemption.

Faith as liberating event includes always an exodus. But particularly in our time, evangelization and faith-education imply a profound exodus, the courage to leave behind an age that will never return, and to enter trustfully into the new era in which not only the cultures of the Third World will be more decisive than those of the western world, but in which there will also be, and in fact already is in the western world, a new generation that needs a new language and a new way of testimony.

Each believer, and the Church as a whole, have to live in a new modality the great exodus of the Paschal Mystery that leads to the new life of resurrection, but only by way of Mount Calvary. We have to leave behind man-made security to make room for the firmness, trust and fidelity that come through faith in Jesus who is the new leader of the exodus to freedom and fidelity.

In many ways and in many places, the Church has lived in serfdom to the wealthy and the powerful who turned to her, not so much to serve the Gospel as to use her influence for their own interests. And although the accusations that the Church is seeking power are still coming from all corners today, the powerful and the greedy have not yet stopped using the Church.

The ongoing exodus, with the firm purposefulness necessary today, is that we opt for the poor, the downtrodden, the powerless people, the modest cultures, the poor nations. This choice is an absolute condition for the exodus that brings the full freedom of evangelization. Each Christian has to make this choice for his personal life and his social commitment, but also the Church as a whole has to make this choice.

As we have already seen, much depends on how we celebrate the memorial of the exodus throughout the history of salvation, especially that of Jesus of Nazareth and his disciples. The celebration of the memorial, with our own grateful memory, must be a shaking and liberating event, just as the preaching of the kingdom by Christ was.

Faith-education and evangelization is, by necessity a clear option for non-violent action. Leaving behind the trust in armaments and wars, the Church turns radically away from any thought about "holy wars". Only the radical exodus of the Church in the choice for the poor and in commitment to non-violent means of liberation can help humanity to the so necessary exodus from violence and ideologies that glorify the sharpening of tensions, conflicts and terrorisms.

The Church can be the critical conscience of today's world only by her total readiness to live the exodus as required by the signs of the times. In order to be a prophetic voice and a true liberating witness, the people of God, and especially those in authority, must be continually alert so that they may not become instruments of or be manipulated by any faction of society. As a prophetic voice, the Church does not enter into "sacred alliance" with any system, but helps people to discern sharply and make their own options with an upright conscience and sincere motives.

The exodus morality will prevent the Church from speaking on actual questions of political, economic, social and cultural problems beyond her competence. Frequently she will reach people more effectively if she speaks interrogatingly instead of trying to give solutions that have not yet matured in people's consciences. While we believe in the prophetic nature of the New Testament priesthood, we do not expect that all those in authority are both prophets and competent analyzers of the situation. The official Church will speak only after serious reflection and after having brought together all the competences. But if she fulfils her prophetic role as educator of faith and morality, there will be Christians who can speak, if not in the name of the official Church, at least with great conviction and persuasion.[44]

The apostolic Church had to make a most difficult exodus from Jewish culture and Jewish law in order to evangelize all nations. It needed a prophetic man like Paul, the Apostle of the Gentiles, to force the Church to make the breakthrough. This was not possible without tensions and suffering.[45] The outcome of Paul's prophetic ministry in the Church and to the Church was the solemn pledge of the Council of Apostles: "It is the decision of the Holy Spirit, and our decision, to lay no further burden upon you beyond the essentials" (Acts 15:28).

The evangelization of those who are baptized but who are more or less alienated from the Church, of the young generations, and especially of the cultures of the Third World, calls for a decision from the official Church no less courageous than that which the apostolic Church made to become the Church for the Gentiles. And just as it was not easy at that time for Jewish Christians and Gentile Christians to live together in harmony, while recognizing the diversity, so it is not easy today to allow that diversity that is the condition for incarnating the Christian faith in all cultures and all generations.[46]

VI. THE ROLE OF THE THEOLOGIANS

We have touched frequently on the role of the theologians. Here we do it in the perspective of faith-education and evangelization. To offer a theology for a time of exodus, marked by creative liberty and fidelity, is an enormous task. However, theologians do not have to do it all by themselves. They can draw upon a great tradition of courageous theologians, and can receive guidance and help from those in authority and from others who have a prophetic vision. They are helped by all those who have experience in evangelization and faith-education. Therefore the theologians will be, above all, listeners, listening to the past and the present voices, listening to those who are in authority and to the most humble ones, listening through constant contact with the pastoral ministry. Theologians need team work in order to bring all their experiences and co-reflections together in the service of evangelization. And the more explicitly they reflect on their task in the light of faith-education and evangelization, the more fruitful will be their whole theological work.

Today's theology is still searching for its identity, and it will find it only in a perspective of theologians as communicators of salvation truth.[47] Although the presence of theologians at Vatican II was strongly felt, the Council did not say much about the function of theology in the Church. Nevertheless, some precious indications are given. "Theologians are invited to seek continually for more suitable ways of communicating doctrine to the men of their times".[48]

Bishops are exhorted to take care "that some persons dedicate themselves to a more profound knowledge of theological matters".[49] I feel that it is particularly important that the young Churches of the Third World should have enough indigenous theologians who remain rooted in their own culture, yet keep enough contact with other parts of the Church. Western theologians are urged by the Council to take full advantage of the great heritage of Oriental theology.[50] No doubt, theologians of all Churches will have to pray and to work hard to make their contribution for Church unity, always also in view of evangelizing all nations.

VII. THE ROLE OF THE MAGISTERIUM FOR KERYGMA

Although the whole Church is obliged to spread the faith and to educate people to mature faith everywhere, the successors of the apostles have, collegially, a particularly urgent responsibility to see that the Gospel is announced to all nations, all cultures, all generations. They have to watch for the right teaching because of the high importance of salvation truth, but preserving orthodoxy in teaching is inseparably one with the kerygma, with the proclamation of the Good News. Indeed, the Church cannot be orthodox in the full sense unless she is totally dedicated to communicate the truth in the right way. To conserve it without full attention to how it is communicated would already contradict the truth and full sense of orthodoxy.[51]

We can distinguish the teaching office from the pastoral ministry of the successors of the apostles, but the deeper unity of both is rooted in the pastoral ministry, since revealed truth is salvation truth and must be so communicated that it serves the salvation of all people. The Magisterium's way of teaching must make particularly manifest that, and how, the Spirit teaches teachers and faithful alike, and that all together are learners (cf. Mt 23:8-12) who honour the Holy Spirit who teaches us the faith and the new law.[52]

There is a noticeable difference between the Catholic and Protestant concepts of the teaching office in the Church. Paul Althaus gives a characteristic presentation of a Protestant position: "The promise of the Spirit given to the Church means this: God will never permit that the Church dies because of herself, because of her own sins and weakness; but the Holy Spirit will, somewhere in the Church, bring forth a new breakthrough of truth and life; somewhere he awakens prophets and reformers. This is the evangelical concept of the guidance of the Spirit and of the 'infallibility' of the Church".[53]

Magnus Löhrer expresses the Catholic position: "Where the Church of the New Testament, in her authoritative Magisterium, says the final word on a doctrine binding the conscience of all, she cannot err". She has this conviction and firm trust "not because of any kind of arrogance but solely trusting in the guidance of the Spirit".[54] The same author insists, however, that it would be a one-sided view to think that the mission to teach could be confided exclusively to the office-holders. It must not be forgotten that the prophetic element in the Church has a profound meaning for the ever new actualization of the word of God and of the effective authority of God over the Church.[55]

The First Vatican Council made clear that the Pope, acting as supreme teacher of the Church, does not do so in isolation or without adequate information. "The Roman Pontiffs called ecumenical councils or explored the sense of the Church spread over the earth, sometimes through particular synods, sometimes through other means as divine providence offered it, as the condition of the times and of the situation suggested, and then defined the doctrine which they knew in accordance with sacred scripture and the apostolic traditions".[56]

Vatican II endorsed the definition of the First Vatican Council and explained its limits and conditions in the same sense: "This infallibility with which the divine Redeemer willed his Church to be endowed, in defining a doctrine of faith and morals, extends as far as extends the deposit of divine revelation, which must be religiously guarded and faithfully expounded".[57]

Speaking on the infallible teaching of the Church, and particularly of the successor of Peter, without indicating its clearly defined limits and without mentioning that there is a broad area of non-infallible teaching, causes unnecessary temptations against faith in the Church, and contradicts truth. While the formulations of explicit dogmas can never be contradicted by future doctrines, they can be improved through more understandable formulations and a broader integration into the whole vision of faith. Non-infallible teaching can be partially corrected and sometimes must be corrected. The readiness to do so gives witness to the docile discipleship of the Church.

The Catholic will give his allegiance to the Magisterium not only by the assent of faith to defined doctrines but also through a most attentive listening and humble openness to all that the Church teaches. But such a listening and docility "has its gradations. To a non-infallible proposition of the Church, an assent of divine and Catholic faith cannot be given".[58]

Through the ecumenical spirit, through respectful and open-minded dialogue between the different parts of Christianity, through easier communications, the greater number of well-trained theologians, the broader participation of a highly competent laity, and full attention to the Spirit of faith of the humble ones, the exercise of the teaching office of the Church can improve in authenticity and effectiveness, especially in view of the proclamation of faith. The collegial exercise of the teaching office is particularly important in matters of morality, since there is always a danger of not discerning sharply between moral norms binding all people of all times and cultures, and particular moral norms that authentically incorporate customs so that they are the best possible norms for a certain culture or a certain time.

Attempts to over-extend the realm of infallible teaching, even to the point of including every detail of papal encyclicals, have caused dangerous crises in the consciences of many people and in public disputes regarding the teaching office in the Church.[59] But these disputes should not let us forget gratitude towards the Lord who has given us the teaching office in the Church, without which there can be no unity. And a special thanksgiving should be offered for the infallible realm of the teaching office that suffices to give us the necessary firmness of faith in the essential parts of our faith.

This gratitude will increase if we understand the doxological dimension of each dogma. The Church's teaching is proclamation of Good News to the praise of God. Doctrinal formulations will be the more fitting for evangelization, the more they manifest this doxological dimension.[60] And it is equally true that the doctrine of the Church honours and praises God for his revelation the more its expression is joyous communication and convincing witness.

NOTES

[1] *Ad Gentes* (Decree on missions), 7.
[2] M. Légaut, *Introduction à l'intelligence du passé et de l'avenir du Christianisme*, Paris, 1970, 290-370.
[3] Cf. L. Newbegin, *La Chiesa missionaria di oggi*, Roma, 1968, 39.
[4] Cf. B. Häring, *Das Heilige und das Gute*, Krailling, 1950, 111-135, 219-270.
[5] Cf. H.R. Niebuhr, *Pious and Secular America*, New York, 1958; Id., *Radical Monotheism and Western Culture*, New York, 1960.
[6] *Gaudium et Spes*, 76.
[7] l.c.
[8] R. Zerfass, "Herrschaftsfreie Kommunikation: Eine Forderung an die kirchliche Verkündigung?", in *Diakonia* 4 (1973), 343; cf. H.D. Bastion, *Theologie der Frage: Ideen zur Grundlegung einer theologischen Dialektik und zur Kommunikation. Kirche in der Welt*, München, 1969.
[9] Cf. B. Häring, "Die Neuheit des sittlichen Lebens", in *Die gegenwärtige Heilsstunde*, Freiburg, 1964, 25-33.
[10] Cf. K. Rahner, "Glaubenszugang", in *Mysterium Salutis*, II, 414-420.
[11] Cf. M. Cornelis, *Sortis du ghetto: spiritualité de la pré-évangelisation à la lumière de Foucauld, Teilhard, Perguère*, Paris, 1964; A.-M. Nebreda, Pre-evangelisaciòn, *Missiones Extranjeras* 15 (1968), 1-15.
[12] Cf. M.D. Chenu, *L'Evangile dans les temps*, Paris, 1964; Id., "Les signes des temps: réflexions théologiques", in *L'Eglise dans le mond de ce temps*, Paris, 191-194.
[13] Cf. E. Lange, *Menscheneinheit - Kircheneinheit*, Stuttgart, 1973; J.R. Nelson, W. Pannenberg (eds.), *Um Einheit und Heil der Menschheit*, Frankfurt, 1973.
[14] Paul VI, *Octogesima adveniens*, n. 40.
[15] Cf. M. Bellet, *La crisi della fede*, Roma, 1971; H. Fries, *Glaube und Kirche auf dem Prüfstand: Versuch einer Orientierung*, München/Freiburg, 1970.
[16] P. Lippert, "Die Fernstehenden. Theologische Deutung eines praktischen Problems", in *Theol. d. Gegenwart* 16 (1973), 154-164; R. Zerfass, "Die 'distanzierte Kirchlichkeit' als Herausforderung an die Seelsorge", in *Lebendige Seelsorge* 22 (1971), 249-266.
[17] J.B. Metz, l.c., 78, 82.
[18] Cf. the *Syllabus* of Pius IX (Dec. 8, 1864) concluding with the summary condemnation of the following opinion: "The Roman Pontiff can and should reconcile with progress, with liberalism and with modern civilization" (Denz. Sch. 2980). What is particularly striking here is the lack of distinctions.
[19] K. Rahner, "Die Kirche in säkulrisierter Umwelt. Ein Gespräch mit K. Rahner", in *Herderkorr.* 31 (1977), 606-614.
[20] Cf. G. Baum, *Religion und Alienation*, 234, 249. Vatican II was quite aware of this problem: cf. *Ad Gentes*, n. 25.
[21] A.J. Niij, *Secolarizzazione*, Brescia, 1973, 332-341.

22 Cf. A. Seeber, "Kirchendistanzierte Religiosität. Zu einer Studie der Pastoral-kommission des Zentralkomitees der deutschen Katholiken", in *Herderk.* 31 (1977), 444-449.

23 A. Greeley, *The American Catholic. A Social Portrait*, New York, 1977.

24 l.c., 128.

25 l.c., 138ff.

26 D.A. Seeber, l.c., 449.

27 Cf. M. West and R. Francis, *Scandal in the Assembly*, London, 1970.

28 Cf. B. Häring, *Sin in the Secular Age*, Slough, 1974.

29 J.B. Metz, *Reform und Gegenreform heute*, Mainz, 1969, 20.

30 Cf. H. Bars, *Göttliche Tugenden heute*, Aschaffenburg, 1963, 42.

31 *Gaudium et Spes*, n. 62; cf. opening discourse to the Second Vatican Council by John XXIII, AAS 54 (1962), 792.

32 Cf. A. Dulles, "Infallibility Revisited", in *America*, Aug. 4, 1973, 55-58; K. Rahner, "Mysterium Ecclesiae: Zur Erklärung der Glaubenskongregation über die Lehre von der Kirche", in *St. d. Zeit* 191 (1973), 579-594, esp. 588ff.

33 K. Rahner/K. Lehmann, "Kerygma und Dogma", in *Mysterium Salutis* I, 622-707, esp. 702ff.

34 R. Guardini, "Glaubensgeschichte und Glaubensweifel", in *Glaubenerkenntnis*, Würzburg, 1949, 107ff; Id., *Die Lebensalter*, Würzburg, 1957[4]; O.F. Bollnow, *Krise und neuer Anfang*, Heidelberg, 1963; P. Schmidt, "Gaubenserfahrung und Glaubenskritik. Der Beitrag R. Guardinis zu kritischen Theologie des Glaubens", *Theol. u. Glaube* 64 (1974), 323-337.

35 Document on "The Catholic School" of the Congregation for Catholic Education, July 5, 1977, n. 27 (Herderk. 31, 1977, 407-417).

36 H.G. Koch, "Religionsunterricht - Last oder Chance?" Herderk. 31 (1977), 436.

37 Cf. M. Légaut, l.c., 151-289; E. Gautier, *La foi nue selon Marcel Légaut face à la foi de l'Eglise*, Dinan, 1974.

38 Cf. W. Wunderle, *Glaube und Glaubenszweifel moderner Jugend*, Düsseldorf, 1932; J. Pieper, *Über die Schwierigkeit heute zu glauben. Aufsätze und Reden*, München, 1974; W.-J. Bausch, *Do You Believe? Contemporary Insight on the Question of Faith*, Grand Rapids, 1975.

39 Cf. K. Rahner/K. Lehmann, l.c., 646.

40 A. Schmied, "Wahrhaftigkeit und Glaube", in *Studia Moralia* 15 (1977), 441. In the following pages I have greatly profited from this article.

41 P.W. Schefe, "Kirchliches Dogma und persönliches Gewissen im Widerstreit", in *Alles in Christus*, Paderborn, 1977, 32-49.

42 Cf. R. Guardini, *Unterscheidung des Christlichen*, Mainz, 1963[2], 290; P. Schmidt, l.c., 335.

43 *Gaudium et Spes*, 5.

44 P. Ramsey, *Who Speaks for the Church?*, Nashville, 1967.

45 Cf. J. Bligh, *Galatians*, Slough, 1969.

46 B. Häring, *Evangelization Today*, Notre Dame/Ind. and Slough, 1974, 141-163; W. Bühlmann, *The Coming of the Third Church*, Slough and Maryknoll, N.Y., 1976; Kath. Akademie in Bayern, *Das Ende der Exportreligion*, München, 1976.

47 Cf. B. Studer, "Träger der Vermittlung. 5. Theologen", in *Mysterium Salutis* I, 600-605; K. Rahner/K. Lehmann, "Kerygma und Dogma", in *Mysterium Salutis* I, 622-707 (with bibliography).

48 *Gaudium et Spes*, 62.

49 *Decree on Priests*, 19.

50 *Decree on Ecumenism*, 17.

51 Cf. M. Löhrer, "Das besondere Lehramt der Kirche", in *Mysterium Salutis* I, 555-587; A Dulles, *The Resilient Church: The Necessity and Limits of Adaptation*, New York, 1977.

52 Cf. A. Jonsen, *Responsibility in Modern Ethics*, Washington-Cleveland, 1968, 227.

53 P. Althaus, *Christliche Wahrheit*, Gütersloh, 1958[4], 526.

54 Löhrer, l.c., 559; cf. Vatican I, Denz. Sch., 3074.

[55] Löhrer, l.c., 560.
[56] Denz. Sch. 3069.
[57] *Lumen gentium*, 25; cf. *Constitution on Divine Revelation*, n. 10 (on the meaning of "deposit of faith").
[58] Löhrer, l.c., 561.
[59] Cf. J. Beumer, "Sind päpstliche Enzykliken unfehlbar?", in *Theol. u. Glaube* 42 (1957), 262-269; R.A. McCormick, "Notes on Moral Theology: The Church in Dispute", *Theol. Studies* 39 (1978), 76-138.
[60] Cf. K. Rahner/K. Lehmann, l.c., 691.

Chapter Six

Faith and Ecumenism

In Christian faith we adore God, the Father of all, we greet Jesus Christ as the saving truth for all, and we entrust ourselves to the Spirit of Truth who leads us simultaneously into truth and unity. The endeavour for Christian unity is a constitutive part of our faith.

By its own nature, God's revelation is a gratuitous gift and a binding call for unity. Genuine ecumenism may threaten security complexes but it holds no danger for truth. On the contrary, it unites us all in greater openness to truth. Pope Paul VI addressing the observers to the Council, expressed this very clearly. "It is necessary that we should unceasingly endeavour to deepen and possess divine truth better and to live it more fully. 'Seek to find and find to seek again' — this phrase of St Augustine, which we had the pleasure to hear you quote, concerns all".[1]

Openness to each other gives the Christian communities a greater chance to come to a more profound knowledge and realization of truth. "We shall therefore strive in loyalty to the unity of Christ's Church, to understand better and to welcome all that is genuine and admissible to the different Christian denominations that are distinct from us ... For that fullness of truth and charity will be made the more manifest when all those who profess the name of Christ are reassembled into one".[2]

Ecumenism is an indispensable expression of our faith in one Lord, and a necessary way to come to a deeper understanding of the history of salvation and of salvation truth.

275

I. OUR FAITH AND OUR COMMITMENT TO CHRISTIAN UNITY

1. *We believe in the Holy Spirit*

Ecumenism can flourish only if it manifests unreservedly that "We believe in the Holy Spirit". We can say that the basis and starting point of our common search for unity and greater fullness of truth is holy Scripture. But immediately we must add that this is so because we believe in the Holy Spirit who not only has inspired the sacred authors but who will also guide us in our common search if we trust in him. "The witness of Scripture reveals to us that the unique communion open for us is entirely God's gift ... The most adequate way may be the joint act of thanksgiving and praise. The communion we have received is primarily communion with the Father through the Son in the Holy Spirit".[3]

Although, as Catholics, we have special reason to praise the Holy Spirit for never having abandoned our Church, we can wholeheartedly agree with the Anglican Canon A.M. Alchin when he says, "The gifts of the Spirit have never scrupulously observed canonical boundaries".[4] Faith in the Holy Spirit does not allow a monopolistic attitude. By mutual openness, we adore the Spirit's freedom to work in all, through all and for all. It is faith in the Holy Spirit that brings into a synthesis our personal faith in a triune God, our devotion to him and the suprapersonal element of the content of our faith.[5]

The future of ecumenism does not lie in our hands. "Whatever may be this future, it will be the work of the Holy Spirit".[6] We honour the Holy Spirit by praise and thanksgiving for all that is achieved in ecumenism, and by great trust regarding our future. We adore him by putting all his charisms, all our capacities, all our creativity into the service of Christian unity.

Knowing that she is called to be and to become ever more a visible sign of unity, the Church is obliged to make visible her manifold charisms in her whole way of life and in all her structures, so that the fullness of humanity redeemed in Jesus Christ may become ever more manifest in its diversity.[7]

The contribution of the Second Vatican Council to the cause of unity lies not first in the splendid decree on Ecumenism — itself a gift of the Holy Spirit — but even more in a renewed pneumatology.[8] Only in the Holy Spirit can we acknowledge the lordship of Jesus Christ in our hearts, in our lives and in our joint endeavours. It is through the grace of the Holy Spirit that not only individual Christians but also the Christian communities and Churches receive the call to conversion and to greater openness to each other. "Nor should we forget that whatever is wrought by the grace of the Holy Spirit in the hearts of our separated brethren can contribute to our own edification".[9]

The dynamic unity of the Church, whose heart is the Eucharist, is essentially the harvest of the Spirit. It is to be seen in the great vision of Pauline theology as expressed in Ephesians 4 and Galatians 5.[10] In the pioneering groups of ecumenism, it has become ever more clear that strong faith in the Holy Spirit does not allow a recess into a merely personal faith. While it strengthens both the joy and the depth of personal faith, it gives also a deeper understanding and appreciation of the sacraments of unity, especially of the Holy Eucharist. With many other groups and movements, the charismatic renewal expresses the hope that "union in the Spirit will lead to union in the Eucharist".[11]

It is the Holy Spirit who enables God's people to combine holy patience and holy impatience. Faith in the Holy Spirit disallows equally disorder and spiritless routine. It calls for prophetic realization.[12] It is also the power of the Holy Spirit that gives Christians and Christian Churches that inner freedom to meet each other, to listen to each other, and to seek at the same time both truth and unity.

2. *We believe in one holy, catholic and apostolic church*

Since the Holy Spirit calls Christians to unity through the very diversity of his gifts and ministries, we must qualify our faith-expression when we say, "We believe in one, holy, catholic and apostolic church". It rejects that kind of militant ecclesiality that makes some people forget their Christianity while confessing their Roman catholicity. If we confess one, holy, catholic and apostolic church, then it must be done in a way that we confess the lordship of Jesus Christ who reveals to us the one Father and guides us, through his Spirit, towards unity.

"Today, it is a conviction common to all Christians that there has to be one Church, and that the question whether there is one Church or any number of Christian religious communities is not for Christians to decide as they will ... Looking at Christianity as a whole, today there is a conviction which is experienced as an element of Christian faith, a conviction that there has to be *one* Church, and moreover that in the concrete situation of Christianity as a whole today, the unity which Christ willed and which follows necessarily from the essence of the Church is not yet realised sufficiently".[13]

It is impossible for us Catholic Christians, as for any other Christian community, to reflect on the identity of the Church without deep pain about our separation. Realizing that the very notes of holiness, catholicity and apostolicity depend also on a genuine manifestation of unity, we are forced to join in a humble and courageous search for a more authentic identity. We can say that the commitment to Christian unity belongs to the very identity of our Church and our faithfulness to it.[14] Our first faith and faith-commitment is not to the actual form of our Church as it has developed historically after all the separations, but is a commitment to Christ himself who wants his Church to be one, holy, catholic and apostolic in an all-inclusive sense.

It is precisely our faith in the one Lord Jesus Christ and our trust in the Holy Spirit that commit us to the visible Church as we know her in the Catholic Church. "They are fully incorporated into the society of the Church who, possessing the Spirit of Christ, accept her entire system and all the means of salvation given to her, and through union with her visible structure are joined to Christ, who rules her through the supreme pontiff and the bishops. This joining is effected by the bonds of professed faith, of the sacraments, of ecclesiastical government and of communion".[15]

Vatican II has, however, made clear that this full acceptance of the basic structures of the Church includes a firm commitment to conversion and renewal; a faith-commitment to unite with our Church and all Christians in striving for a better realization of unity, holiness, catholicity and apostolicity.

The Second Vatican Council does not simply identify the

concrete form of today's Roman Catholic Church with the Church as willed by Jesus Christ to be one, holy, catholic and apostolic.[16] "This Church, constituted and organized in the world as a society, subsists in the Catholic Church, which is governed by the successor of Peter and by the bishops in union with that successor, although many elements of sanctification and of truth can be found outside of her visible structure".[17] The decree on Ecumenism expresses, in a dynamic, hope-filled way, this trust in the abiding givenness of the notes of the Church. "This unity, we believe, dwells in the Catholic Church as something she can never lose, and we hope that it will continue to increase until the end of time".[18]

When the ten tribes of the north (Israel) separated from Judah, the promises and the Davidic kingdom "subsisted" still in Judah. However, it was almost as gravely affected by this schism as Israel was. We can see this as an analogy for the situation of the Church after the various schisms. Hence, Catholic ecumenists do not think that the separate parts of Christianity can simply be invited to return to the Roman Catholic Church. Rather, it is a matter of reintegration. As the first words of the decree on Ecumenism indicate, it is a matter of a more thorough-going conversion of all parts of Christianity to the one Lord, and a conversion to each other.

The special role of the Catholic Church regarding the notes of unity, holiness, catholicity and apostolicity imposes on her the responsibility to be outstanding in zeal for reintegration, for unity. No part of separated Christianity can heal itself without recurring to mutual healing through dialogue, mutual encounter, reciprocal forgiveness, cooperation and integration.[19] The break between East and West, and similarly the separation of the reformed Churches from the Catholic Church, were mutilating for all concerned, and all have suffered ever since.[20]

3. *On the history of ecumenism*

At the very heart of the history of Christianity in our century is the ecumenical movement that has brought astonishing changes in the relations between separate Christian bodies.[21]

In its first phase, the ecumenical movement was mainly a cordial meeting of revivalists, mostly fundamentalist evangelicals,

marked by distrust of the big Church institutions, especially of
Rome. For a considerable time, the Churches, and particularly
the Roman Catholic Church, responded with similar distrust.
A major role in the growth of the ecumenical longing for unity
was played by the mission Churches who, more than the Churches
in Europe and the United States, suffered under the Christian
division.

The second ecumenical movement grew gradually. The most
important dates were of the Edinburgh Conference of 1910, the
Stockholm and Lausanne Conferences in the twenties, and the
Amsterdam Conference that led to the formal foundation of
the Ecumenical Council of Churches in 1948. The most important
forces that drew together in the World Council of Churches were
especially the International Mission Council and the Faith and
Order Commission.

A great development came when the major ecclesiastical
institutions caught the ecumenical fervour and earnestly tried
to become the spearhead of further evolution. A major and
astonishing event was the entry of the Orthodox Church into the
Ecumenical Council. There the various Churches have created a
forum for dialogue and common endeavour, for mutual healing
and encouragement on the road towards greater unity. Gradually,
the longing for Eucharistic communion among the member
Churches has come to the foreground.[22] There is constant cross-
fertilization between the ecumenism of enthusiastic believers
and the ecumenism of the denominations.

The most surprising and decisive event was the vigorous
awakening of the Catholic ecumenical movement under Pope
John and Pope Paul, particularly through the Second Vatican
Council. The Council's ecumenical effort is crowned by the
decree on Ecumenism, *Unitatis Redintegratio* (1964), and by
the strong ecumenical expression in almost all of the Council's
decrees and constitutions. Since then, there have been not only
cordial relationships between the ecumenical patriarch in
Constantinople and the Roman See, but also friendly relations
between Rome and Geneva (World Council of Churches). The
Catholic Church participates in the "Faith and Order" commission, and in many other shared ecumenical endeavours.

Although the charismatic personality of Pope John XXIII
made the greatest contribution to the Roman Catholic ecumenical

awakening, it should be remembered also that a whole generation of theologians and other churchmen worked and suffered to prepare this possibility.[23] As a result, we have seen a great era of the ecumenism of such charismatic Church leaders as Pope John, Pope Paul, Archbishop Ramsey, Patriarch Athenagoras, and leading men of the World Council of Churches. Theologians of all Churches and denominations have begun to study theology mainly in the perspective of the Lord's testament, "that all may be one". And through the interdenominational theological dialogue in commissions constituted by the official Churches, great progress has been made in understanding better the mystery of the Church, authority in the Church, ministry and the Eucharist.

The decree of the Second Vatican Council on Ecumenism served as a basis and point of departure for further progress, as the Churches came to know each other better and were ready to reintegrate the truth found in other Churches, in view of a final reintegration of the Churches themselves in the hoped-for "one Church".[24]

Looking back on the past nine hundred years, the great progress made in the relationship between the Roman Catholic and the Orthodox Church seems to be miraculous.[25] One need not wonder that tensions and temporary difficulties arise on various levels and that the evaluation of the progress of ecumenism shows a great diversity.[26]

4. A new look at sins of heresy and schism

Jesus the Prophet shakes the concept of the Jews about schismatics and heretics, especially with the parable of the Good Samaritan. In contrast to the higher and lower clergy who fail to fulfil the law of universal love, the Samaritan appears as the holy man. In the present hour of ecumenism, this teaching of Jesus should prevent us from looking down on all those outside our Church as heretics and schismatics.

Already in 1937, Yves Congar proposed in his book, *Divided Christendom*, that the present-day Protestant should be considered a "dissident" rather than a "heretic". Although he found opposition in Catholic quarters, his view has become common. In a survey carried out in 1962 when Catholics were asked how they considered Lutherans and Reformed Protestants, the answer was overwhelmingly for "Christian brothers" (47.6%) or "separated brothers" (47.2%). Only 1.2% opted for the word "heretic".[27] Due to Pope John XXIII, other Christians are now designated in the official language of the Catholic Church as "Christian brothers" or "separated brothers".

The decree on ecumenism (Art. 3) gives compelling reasons for the change of mentality behind this more respectful expression: "At times, men of both sides were to blame. However, one cannot impute the sin of separation to those who at present are born into these communities and are instilled therein with Christ's faith".

We realize ever more that judgmental attitudes and formalistic talk about heresy may betray a dangerous self-righteousness. As soon as we confess our own sins, we come to a more balanced vision of the other's situation. Pope Paul VI expressed this beautifully. He said: "We have recognized certain failings and common sentiments that were not good. For these we ask pardon of God and of you. We have discovered their unchristian roots and have proposed to ourselves to change them, on our part, into sentiments worthy of the school of Christ; to abstain from pre-conceived and offensive controversy and not to bring into play questions of vain prestige".[28]

Reviewing the many ambiguities of the situations, and the partial accountability of Catholic authorities, we wonder whether those who were involved in the terrible event of separation committed, subjectively, the sin of heresy. Some would even doubt that they were involved in an objective grave sin of schism or heresy.[29] However, truth and the cause of unity would be served poorly if we were to stop here. We have to take another look and ask ourselves if, in the light of a covenant morality, a morality of grace and faith, we have always done our utmost in the common search for truth. Have we done all that is in our power to tear down man-made barriers opposing Christian unity? Have we not sometimes indulged in disputes about secondary things, observing man-made traditions, like the clergy in the parable of the Good Samaritan, while neglecting the essential truths of the Gospel?

5. *Non-theological causes of separation*

The grace and task offered us by the Lord's prayer "that all may be one" equally forbids escapism into idle self-accusation and a dangerous moralism, especially regarding the fault of those on the other side. While we all must have the courage and humility to shoulder our responsibilities, a realistic evaluation demands also a closer look at the non-theological, sociological, psychological and other causes of Christian disunities.

There are the tendencies of cultures and sub-cultures to absolutize themselves. There is the most dangerous temptation of those in power to use religion, including Christian religion and Church organization, for their political interests. There is a universal trend to absolutize one's own linguistic concepts. So we have to study more how language can unite us and how it can separate us. We need a profound philosophy and psychology of knowledge and language. "It contributes, before the thought is expressed, to the very formation of the mechanics of thought and to that kind of inner mirror wherein our inner perceptions are 'refracted'; it really constitutes the climate which is called 'the mind' ".[30]

Language is a part of the total culture influenced by all sociological factors, economy, politics, structure of society and family, and the whole fabric of traditions. By itself, the diversity of languages within the larger diversity of cultures can be an enrichment. But human sinfulness and narrow-mindedness, and especially the abuse of power, tend to absolutize one's own way of thinking.

The diversity of Latin culture and Greek culture is not, by itself, the cause of disunity, but the unawareness of these factors, together with cultural arrogance, have greatly contributed to the evil of separation between East and West. A similar conflict happened in the sixteenth century between the predominantly Latin world and the Germanic world. "As we enter the ecumenical movement, little can be more important than to recognize the existence of these factors called non-theological. And this because they are not theological at all. They are hidden and therefore do not belong to conscious theology, but they are material with which theology must be concerned".[31]

We have to study inter-confessional psychology to discover not only how all these things contributed to separation and its persistence, but also how it can help to promote the cause of Christian unity. Sociology cannot make a final judgment on the Church's organization, but it can help us to understand how sociological conditions, relationships and processes contributed to shape the actual structure of hierarchy, priesthood and so on, so that we can see better what is the abiding mission entrusted by Christ and what is the time-bound expression in the Church's institutions. Sociology can also help us to discover the various psychological types that hinder or foster the cause of unity in diversity. Since God's plan for humanity is revealed not only through what is going on in the Church, but also through what is going on in the whole world, we have to be aware of the global sociological processes.

Our greater awareness of the oneness of human history and the solidarity of all humankind, and the fact that we have the scientific tools — study of history, comparative cultures, social psychology and sociology — are signs of the times that cannot be neglected without sinning against God's design for Christian unity and the world's unity.[32]

II. ALLEGIANCE TO ONE'S NATIVE CHURCH WITHIN THE ABSOLUTE FIDELITY TO CHRIST'S TESTAMENT "THAT ALL MAY BE ONE"

1. *Theological and psychological reasons for our allegiance to our native Church*

Absolute allegiance to the Church in which one is born contradicts our creed that God alone is holy and deserves absolute allegiance. Indeed, such an absolute allegiance to time-bound forms can be one of the greatest obstacles to fidelity to Christ's own testament "that all may be one", a fidelity that has to be absolute. However, if there are dangers in absolute allegiances, there are, on the other hand, great risks of unrootedness if Christians are not committed to their respective Churches.

In traditional apologetics, the starting point was objective truth; and the conclusion was clear-cut that Catholics owe absolute allegiance to their Church, while the others have to abandon their separated or schismatic, heretic Church and return to the Roman Catholic Church.

The Orthodox Christians were supposed to be converted at least to the oriental "United" Churches which, however, were practically Roman Catholic also in the sense of being latinized. To the honour of the Orthodox Churches it must be said that, on the whole, they did not try to make individual converts or to erect Orthodox Churches in the West; they were always sharply aware that the only road to unity is through reunion of the Churches.

But Protestants took generally the same absolutist stand as Catholics. Douglas Horton, reporting the controversy between Cardinal Bellarmine and William Ames (the author of Bellarminus Inervatus), gives us a classical example: "Here are two men — Ames and Bellarmine — each one an exemplary Christian, who nonetheless give the impression of being more concerned with winning the argument than with anything else".[33] On the conscious or unconscious level, in both Ames and Bellarmine, absolute loyalty to their respective Church plays a decisive role.

In John Henry Cardinal Newman, a convert from the Anglican to the Catholic Church, we see a quite different attitude. He is always deeply grateful to the Anglican Church that made him a Christian, and he expects from all Anglicans this type of loyal attitude. "The Church of England has been the instrument of providence in conferring great benefits on me ... And as I have received so much good from the Anglican establishment itself, can I have the heart, or rather the want of charity, considering that it does for so many others what it has done for me, to wish to see it overthrown?"[34]

Karl Rahner's approach to the question is probably typical for the new ecumenical age. After giving so many good arguments for Catholics to remain in their Church and to work there for Christian unity, he has the courage to give a number of psychological reasons (considered, however, in a theological historical perspective) why Protestants, too, can presume that they have to be loyal to their Church and to work there for Christian unity. "In the first instance, therefore, every Christian has the right to accept, as something whose legitimacy is presumed, the Christian and ecclesial situation which was bestowed on him in history and which he has appropriated. This is undoubtedly a proposition which is hardly reflected upon and is not expressed explicitly in the usual abstract and theoretical fundamental theology in the Catholic Church. But this basic and general fundamental theology does not deny, in itself and in the abstract, the fact that we are bound to a particular situation, nor does it deny that we are justified in presuming the legitimacy of our historically conditioned situation. This is true, of course, not just for Catholic Christians but for everybody. Obviously we recognize that, for example, an Evangelical Christian or an Orthodox Christian or a member of some sect will have an antecedent trust in the meaning of his existence, and will accept the situation which has been given to him and in which he finds himself. He will think from this situation and rightly so. No Christian has the task and the obligation, because he is a Christian, to step out of the historical situation of his existence, and to want to ground the concreteness of his existence exclusively by means of reflections".[35]

Of course, Karl Rahner does not deny the obligation to reflect responsibly upon our separated situation and to ask whether one's Church corresponds to the design of Christ the founder of the Church; but he takes into account the historical nature of the human person and communities, especially one's trust in his parents. We have to think about the deep gratitude of the pious Protestant Christian for his Church because he has learned there to live with the word of God. And this gratitude normally prevails psychologically over and above the questions about ecclesial structure and institutions. Rahner rightly points to the danger for the Catholic Church and the cause of unity if one takes as starting point "militant ecclesiality as the specific distinction of Roman Catholicism".[36]

2. *A main motive for questioning the legitimacy of one's Church*

In an ecumenical age and in this historical hour when humankind so greatly experiences its solidarity, and where we are guided by hope for the future, a main motive for questioning the legitimacy of one's Church is if she refuses to be a pilgrim Church. If she refuses to search together with others for greater fullness of truth and unity, if she is boasting more in the flesh than in the Lord, or is marked more by individual and collective self-righteousness than by the *confessio laudis* that is the humble confession of sins to the praise of the Lord's mercy, then there is good reason to look for alternatives. A Christian community that turns away from concern for Christian unity is not a place where an open-minded Christian can live with tranquillity of conscience. Either he will try to change the mentality in his community or will consider conversion to a Church that is more a pilgrim Church on the road towards fuller Christian unity. Wherever a Church, enslaved in security complexes and in a false concept of continuity, refuses to be a pilgrim Church and to take the possible steps towards unity, she greatly risks alienating the most fervent Christians and especially the youth.

The question is one of finding the right synthesis between historical continuity and creative fidelity. "The fidelity of God is concrete. It manifests itself in the continuity of history. Whoever, all too quickly and all too one-sidedly, speaks on the necessity of ever new beginnings, diminishes the certainty of God's fidelity and in consequence also the capacity for renewal in continuity with the past. It seems to be a decisive matter that all Churches understand anew the continuity of God's fidelity. Each Church is already shaken in her identity. Quite aside from the ecumenical movement, each Church has to examine to what extent she is the same as she was in the past ... A new consciousness of the continuity of the Church will facilitate the structuring of a provisional communion".[37]

Fidelity to God's design and to the Lord's testament "that all may be one" will not only look to the past but will raise the more fundamental question of our fidelity regarding the future. A pilgrim Church is surely concerned with continuity but always in the sight of God's fidelity that calls to conversion. However, she is more concerned with grasping the present opportunity and marching faithfully into the future than with explaining all the problems of the past.[38]

3. A *"double membership"*

There are ecumenical communities like Taizé in France, the "Church of the Saviour" in the area of Washington, D.C., and numerous charismatic communities, where Christians from various denominations keep membership in their original Church but feel themselves together much more as members of the hoped-for unified Church. Roger Schütz and other theologians of Taizé describe this as "double membership". It is a most demanding idea. To use this title and to draw conclusions, for instance in regard to sharing the Eucharist, one must be most gratefully rooted in one's own community, do all possible to move this Church towards Christian unity, and be thoroughly committed to this goal in all his life and constantly watchful for every opportunity to manifest this hope in a concrete and prophetic manner.[39]

This double membership of which we speak does not imply that the various members already have exactly the same concept regarding the constitution of the hoped-for Church. It is an undeniable fact that in the New Testament, while the unity of the Church is clearly required and presupposed, there are different ecclesiologies, for instance in the Synoptics, in Paul, and in John.[40] Wherever the Eucharist is celebrated in firm faith in the Lord's presence, and with equally firm commitment to the cause of unity, there is church and there is a substantial outline of unity. But this requires also an ongoing process of search, interrogating and being interrogated, and readiness always to take the next possible step to bring this unity to greater fruition and visibility.

I conceive "double membership" in the Church as the highest form of gratitude for what we have received through our respective Churches and as ongoing praise of the Holy Spirit. The Holy Spirit is glorified in his gifts and charisms if they are used for greater unity in diversity and for diversity only in view of greater unity.

Eastern theology points to the mystery that the Holy Spirit does not manifest his person directly. He comes, not in his own name, but in the name of the Son, and to bear witness to the Son whom he has anointed to bear witness to the Father.[41] Similarly we honour our Church and show gratitude for what we have received from her by pointing faithfully to God's design for unity and by living in the hope that it might be manifested in history.

4. The quest for greater apostolicity

a) A demanding vision of apostolicity

Christianity can remain faithful to the grace and task of unity only by striving at the same time for greater holiness, greater universality (catholicity) and, above all, for a fuller realization of apostolicity.

All the institutional parts of Christianity have a share, although imperfect, in apostolicity. We all have received the faith in Christ proclaimed by the apostles. Through holy Scripture we receive the apostolic tradition in a very privileged way. For apostolicity to be a mark of the Church, there must be great dedication to the preaching of the Gospel to all nations, to all cultures, according to the Pentecost event which made the apostles speak in all languages.

The Orthodox Churches can claim apostolicity in a special way, for they gather around the episcopal sees founded by the apostles and their direct successors. They have always preserved the episcopal constitution, with close contact among the various bishops under the leadership of their patriarchs. Although their apostolicity is shaken by their separation from the Roman see, they have never ceased to recognize a certain primacy in the Roman bishop. They have never denied the necessity of offices, including the Petrine, for guaranteeing a greater unity.

With the Orthodox Churches, the Roman Catholic Church emphasizes the apostolic succession. Through the sacrament of episcopacy, today's bishops are in uninterrupted succession from the apostles. However, a one-sided or almost exclusive emphasis on apostolic succession would greatly weaken the apostolicity of the Church. If every bishop were to look back to all those bishops of the past with whom he is connected through ordination, the list would not look much better than that of the kings of Judah and Israel. There were ordaining bishops who knew little about the charism and duty of a bishop and gave little sign of being filled with the Holy Spirit. This remark should not be misunderstood as denying the importance of apostolic succession. Our point is rather that all the signs of apostolicity have to be seen together. In that perspective, it becomes clear that each part of Christianity has something to offer, while the Roman Catholic Church can surely offer a very large portion, particularly the Petrine office of unity.

Apostolicity includes the institutional dimension. "From the encounter of the human social bonds and the instituting Word, through the unifying power of the Holy Spirit, there results the Church. The conclusion is unavoidable that the Church is, by essence, institution, while at the same time being the event of salvation in history".[42] But in the concrete case, as far as apostolicity is concerned, the institutional element must also be sacramental: that is, an effective sign that makes present and visible Christ who sends apostles and sends his Church to preach his Gospel in unbroken continuity. The vocation of each bishop and all the bishops together, with the clergy and the faithful, is constantly to become an ever better sign of Christ gathering the apostles around himself, praying for them, that they may be one and, through their witnessing word, may be sacraments of unity for all believers.

The World Council of Churches, in constant dialogue with the Roman Catholic Church, has assumed the mission of leading the various traditions into dialogue and into an ongoing examination of whether their traditions keep them within the limits of apostolicity and develop in a way that apostolicity becomes ever more visible.[43]

b) Apostolicity and episcopacy

As we have already seen, it is the common conviction of the Roman Catholic and the Orthodox Churches that apostolicity necessarily includes the episcopal body: not only the individual bishop, but also bishops throughout the world, united with each other collegially. The dissent is rather on how they should be united through collegial exercise, through councils and through the Petrine office.

Less than fifteen years ago, Bernard Lambert could write that outside the Roman Catholic Church there is little readiness, except in the Orthdox Churches, to recognize an episcopal authority.[44] Today, many separate Churches realize that they have practically an office similar to the bishops' office, and that they are obliged to bring their authority into harmony with that of the apostles and their successors who exercised episcopal authority throughout history.

For the Anglican Episcopalian Church, there is no doubt about episcopacy which they, too, see in continuity with the office of the apostles. Progress in theology, in ecumenical dialogue, along with a better understanding of our own history of episcopacy and that of the Anglicans, should bring closer the moment in which the Roman Catholic Church recognizes the Anglican episcopacy. Pope Paul set a great prophetic sign when in 1965, during a common prayer service, he took his own fisherman's ring and put it on the finger of Archbishop Ramsey, the head of the Anglican constituency. It was a symbolic gesture which could not mean less than "You too are bishop and thus united with the bearer of the fisherman's ring". In 1958 Bishop S.C. Neill observed that about half the Anglican episcopate had the Anglican episcopal succession from that of the Old Catholics, and that before long all Anglican bishops would have it.[45]

A greater openness to the Spirit, and a sharing between the Roman Catholic bishops headed by the Pope with all the bishops and Church authorities, should be able to resolve the question of apostolic succession by mutual acknowledgment and appropriate imploration of the gifts of the Holy Spirit.

c) The Petrine ministry for unity

In ecumenism, the understanding of the ministry of unity is a cornerstone or a stumbling block. All those Churches and Christians who believe that Christ truly wanted a visible unity believe today, much more explicitly, that there is need of such a ministry. The discussion is not so much on whether it is needed as on how it should look in order to be faithful to Christ and effective in a divided world and a not yet fully united Christianity.

We have no chance to reach out to the still separated brethren and the sister Churches if we present the ministry for unity simply and solely as given to the papacy. First, we should not equate the ministry of Peter simply with the papacy as it has developed historically during the Constantinian era and especially in the Avignon exile. It is better to speak of the *Petrine ministry* whereby we Catholics express our faith that the ministry evidently entrusted to Peter should continue in the Church "in the successor of St Peter".

The Petrine office must be thoroughly liberated from all

considerations of prestige, all rivalry, and from any kind of careerist promotions and titles that resemble the diplomatic world and powers. Speaking to our Christian brothers and the sister Churches, we must accept their insistence on a sharp distinction between the Petrine ministry and the actual historical shape of the Roman Curia.

There are many signs that allow us to hope that in the not-too-distant future the Petrine ministry will be accepted by the still separated Churches. Among these signs is surely the Second Vatican Council's effort towards collegiality, and the decentralization that began with the return of many functions to the episcopal conferences, to the Eastern United Churches and to the regular synods of bishops in Rome. All this has awakened great hope, although our interlocutors among the other Churches tell us, time and again, of their frustrations and fears when, as in the dogmatic constitution on the Church and in the *Notae Explicativae*, it is reiterated a dozen times that the college of bishops can act only with the Roman bishop and never without him, with no explanation of what occurs in situations like that resolved for instance in the Council of Constance. There, the bishops were forced to act without the Roman bishop since no one knew who he was. And how would the bishops all over the world have to act if a Roman bishop were to become senile or lose his mind? While such questions may remain open and left to the Spirit, an insistent inculcation that all the powers are in the Roman bishop is at least psychologically inappropriate in view of the ecumenical movement. On many occasions Pope Paul VI found the right language, especially in symbolic actions such as his visiting twice the Orthodox Patriarch in the East before inviting him to Rome. We are and always should be in a learning process.

Luther went as far as he could in cursing the papacy, yet even in the midst of fighting, he did not forget important values inherent in the Petrine ministry, even in its historical shape. He still could utter such words as, "Much Christian good, nay all Christian good is to be found in the papacy and from there it descends to us".[46]

A leading Orthodox theologian tells us about the vision of the primacy: "The one, holy, catholic and apostolic Church must necessarily exist in the world as an orderly and visibly united Church, Church Universal, and it is the function and charism of the primacies to serve as centres of communion, unity, coordination. There exist local and regional primacies (metropolitans, patriarchs) and a universal primacy. Orthodox ecclesiology has never denied that, traditionally, the latter belonged to the Church of Rome. It is, however, the interpretation of this primacy in terms of a personal infallibility of the Roman pontiff and of his universal jurisdictional power that led to its rejection by the Orthodox East".[47] Note that the Eastern Orthodox Churches lived through centuries in union with Rome without ever fully agreeing with all the claims the Popes made about primacy and universal jurisdiction, while still accepting the fact of primacy.

If all leaders of the separated Churches, with the successor of Peter and all of God's people, unite in responding to the pressing needs of our time, and help each other to accept more radically the Christian message and to answer the questions which a non-Christian age is posing to Christianity, "there will be the best chance that this new theology being done by people who belong to different Churches will slowly develop a theological unity from out of the questions which are being proposed to all of them in common. This unity will then move beyond many of the controversial theological problems which at the moment are insoluble, and will render them to a certain extent odious".[48]

But let us be sure that the question of an effective ministry of unity in a united Christianity is not and will never become an odious problem. The exercise of God-given authority in the service of unity is a burning question. The Petrine ministry can be exercised in creative fidelity in a way that fosters not only unity but also creative liberty. Douglas Horton, a Protestant observer of Vatican II, comes close to this opinion or, rather, conviction. "I can imagine that the Pope can be elected for a period, with place for retirement ... The Pope might become for the Church more and more what the President is for the United States; that any shadow should be cast on papal primacy rests upon speculative illusion ... Protestant groups must ask themselves quite simply if acceptance of the primacy of the Pope robs them of any essential freedoms, and those within the papal system will have to ask whether the allowance of such freedom to groups diverse from themselves would break down the essential order and unity of the Church".[49]

Yves Congar is convinced that Pope Paul VI, by repeatedly calling the Orthodox Churches "sister Churches", has taken a great step towards renewed acceptability of the Petrine office by the Orthodox Churches and eventually also by the Churches that issued from the sixteenth century reformation if they too in due proportion, will be called and honoured as sister Churches.[50]

A genuine reunion of the Orthodox and reformed Churches with the Roman Catholic Church would not only enrich them and the whole catholic Church but would also bring the Petrine office to a more creative and attractive functioning. "We must not let the Orientals believe that they are tolerated with their diversities as an annoying necessity; no, the Catholic Church loves them for themselves, for what they are, and she would not want them to be otherwise".[51] The Catholic Church in the Third World would then be able to profit more from the Petrine ministry for the sake of their own creative fidelity and their contribution to an effective catholicity.

To fulfil all the roles that the papacy has historically accumulated is impossible for one man. He needs a great diversity of help in the exercise of his authority. As a local bishop of Rome and the metropolitan area, he might have his Roman cardinals, a pastoral council. For the exercise of his particular jurisdiction for the Italian Church — which has a right to be an adult Church — he might have a synod of Italian people. As Patriarch of the West, the successors of Peter in the future will never call themselves "monarchs". For an effective exercise of such a great responsibility, they will use the best possible structures for being helped by all the experiences and co-reflections of creative and courageous believers. In the case of a provisional and even more in a definitive reunion of Christians, why should not the successor of Peter and the college of the Catholic bishops enter into a very humble and sincere dialogue with the sister Churches, to find out the best possible ways to guarantee cooperation for the sake of unity? They will look both to the biblical teaching,[52] and to the signs of the times.

In order to make the Petrine ministry ecumenically acceptable, all the changes in the structures and in the day-by-day exercise of the primacy which will help to convey the right image of Catholic understanding should be made as quickly as possible. It is for this reason that a moral theology of today has to treat these questions, for the changes can be made only if they find a lively echo in the Catholic community and are prepared by strong convictions and shared reflections.

c) Papal infallibility

The ecumenical dialogue of the last twenty years has made much more progress in the matter of papal primacy than of papal infallibility. Even among Catholics this dogma finds serious difficulties because it is so seldom known in its clear-cut definition, which includes also its clear-cut limitations. Yet we have good reason to believe that it will be accepted by a united Christianity when it is more fully integrated into a vision of the Church and her faith which corresponds with the best of Orthodox tradition and with some of the great concerns of the reformed Churches. The dogma which, as Catholics, we cannot disown, can be more clearly expressed and presented in a more pastoral way, so that the right exercise of Church authority is at the same time guaranteed. In other words, a future formulation can better prevent misinterpretations and make clearer that infallibility has nothing to do with power in an earthly sense.

"The Catholic understanding of the Church says that when the Church in its teaching authority, i.e., in the whole episcopate along with the Pope, or in the personal head of this whole episcopate, really confronts man in its teaching with an ultimate demand in the name of Christ, God's grace and power prevent this teaching authority from losing the truth of Christ".[53] Protestants, too, recognize the need for a teaching authority, but many of them would not recognize an absolute and ultimately binding character of any specific teaching. But great parts of the Protestant Churches, and especially the Orthodox Churches, would recognize the absolute and ultimately binding declaration of ecumenical councils in the same, or almost the same, way as we Catholics do.

A sign that the ecumenical dialogue on papal infallibility is not a hopeless issue is Professor Lindbeck's proposal on how to understand it and accept it in a reunited Christianity. Lindbeck, a Lutheran theologian, was an observer at the Second Vatican Council. He sees some noticeable progress towards a better understanding and appreciation of this doctrine insofar as the historicity of doctrinal formulations is better understood,[54] but he also warns against the temptation to politicize any interconfessional discussion on infallibility. "The Catholic who ventures beyond the reiteration of past formulas to attempt a fresh understanding tends to be classified as an enemy of the Magisterium, and the Protestant who sees positive values in the doctrine risks being viewed as betraying both the cause of ecumenism and the reformation".[55]

Nevertheless, Lindbeck dares to propose an understanding of papal infallibility which, in his eyes, can be harmonized with the official Catholic doctrine as it emerged in the First and Second Vatican Councils. "An infallible Magisterium is one which never prescribes irretrievably erroneous (i.e., unchristian) usages or forbids usages which are essential, indispensable parts of Christian speech and action".[56] He finds himself in the company of many Catholic theologians when he insists that "in order for the Magisterium to act infallibly, it should act in a way which is not only formally or canonically but really and substantially universal or ecumenical".[57] He touches, however, a critical point — although with the greatest ecumenical sensitivity — when he raises the question of whether *Pastor Aeternus* and the Marian definitions were "really, substantially or theologically ecumenical in intent; and therefore it is not clear that they are infallible even in the qualified sense which we have described".[58]

Since the great schism, the Orthodox Church never thought of convening alone an ecumenical council. For them and for the reformed Churches, the difficulty remains about whether dogmas declared by the Roman Catholic Magisterium in time of schism can find the consensus of the sister Churches separated from Rome and therefore not involved in the process that led to the formulation of a dogma in the Roman Catholic Church. Professor Lindbeck raises one of the most urgent questions: whether differences on this point "need prevent the Churches from joining together in full communion in an ecumenical, conciliar fellowship".[59] Would not an essential openness to this question be sufficient, together with the hope that in due time a united Christianity will come to a better understanding?

III. FUNDAMENTAL DISPOSITIONS FOR ECUMENISM

For all Christian communities, Christian leaders, theologians and lay people, the self-commitment to Christian unity should be part of the fundamental option. It must be a decision at least on the level of fundamental option, and therefore must also gradually shape all our dispositions. Ecumenism is, above all, a request for ongoing conversion towards the one Lord Jesus Christ. We cannot say, in the Holy Spirit, "Jesus is Lord" without a faithful effort to bring our ecclesiastical communities into that unity which manifests this our profession of faith.

The guidance of the Spirit is assured to Peter, with all the Church, as long as they profess with their whole life, and especially by their endeavour for unity that "You are the Christ, the Son of the living God" (cf. Mt 16:16). It is useless to tell anyone that Jesus is the Lord, the Messiah, if we are not ourselves committed wholeheartedly to the unity of his disciples (cf. Mt 16:20). Jesus' promise for the Church, "that the gates of death shall never close upon it" (Mt 16:18) implies the grace and call to conversion towards ever-greater unity. Only if we Christians are fully converted to the Lord's testament "that all may be one", can we hope that the world, too, may be converted.[60]

The conversion of which we speak here is both personal and communal. The participants in an ecumenical study-week ten years after the decree on Ecumenism expressed the communal dimension emphatically. Confrontation of the Churches in dialogue should lead to "structural conversions" that would characterize the whole life of the Church.[61] And when we speak on "conversion", we must never lose sight of the essential truth that it is a conversion to Christ, so that the life of Christians and Christian Churches proclaim, "Thee, Christ alone do we know". The homily of Pope John Paul II at his installation exemplifies this best.

1. *Conversion to Christ the Healer, to Christ the Peace*

Just as the truth that Christ is the Reconciler is central to our faith, so is the whole endeavour of ecumenism. Indeed,

ecumenism is based on the right understanding of and full
commitment to reconciliation as grace and task.[62]

Christ's healing touches the Churches through mutual confession of their sins and mutual forgiveness. Pope Paul VI
expressed this forcefully: "Let us forgive and ask for forgiveness
mutually".[63] Ecumenists have always insisted that our commitment to Christian unity includes both prayer and repentance,
manifested in humble confession of our sins.[64] For instance, the
Orthodox cannot be freed from their fears and distrust until
the Roman Catholic Church humbly and explicitly regrets all
her efforts to impose latinization on the Eastern Churches.[65]

It is not enough to acknowledge that some members of the
Roman Catholic Church have been sinners, nor is it realistic
to say of the Church simply that "She is without blemish and
yet not without sinners".[66] It must also be acknowledged
that all the sins together have partially embodied themselves in
the structures, the mentalities, and even in the formulations of
doctrines. Protestants and Orthodox will hardly understand
language like this: "The covenant by which Christ gave all his
possessions to his bride, the Church, so that she might dispose
of them as she would, was a covenant effected once forever".[67]
Such language can only hinder the Roman Catholic Church from
asking herself humbly whether she disposes faithfully all the
treasures the Lord has entrusted to her. Only mutual confession
can repair all the loveless and unjust judgments on the other
traditions.

Of the schism between East and West, Congar says, "The
separation became marked by the fact that each of the two
positions of Christendom withdrew behind the barriers of its
own tradition and always judged the other from the point
of view of its own tradition".[68] By so doing, all parts of Christianity were deeply wounded. Hence it needs a mutual healing;
and, indeed, the wounds cannot be healed without mutual
forgiveness and reintegration of unity. Christian Churches can
celebrate Christ, the Prince of peace, and fulfil their peace
mission in the world only when they gratefully accept the grace
of reconciliation and peace among themselves and are willing
to pay the price necessary for it.

2.　*Conversion to Christ the Prophet, to Christ the Saving Truth*

Christ is the saving Truth by joyous sharing of the Good News and sealing it with the blood of the covenant. But he is also the saving conflict, the Prophet, who unmasks all the various forms of falsehood that oppose truth and unity, and who tore down the barriers that separated Jews and Gentiles.

Christ the Prophet continues his mission wherever, by the power of his Spirit, people and communities in the separated parts of Christianity protest everything that contradicts the Church's calling to be one, holy, catholic and apostolic. Such a protest is not against the Church but is a manifestation of faith in it, and is of humble service to it.[69] Those who know Christ the Prophet, and listen to him, will listen also to the voices that protest against all the tendencies of western Churches to absolutize their own traditions and time-bound expressions. Prophetic men have raised their voices in the East when slavophiles were "boasting in the flesh" by practically identifying religion with their national cultures.[70]

Many conservative people would not object to hearing about errors of the past and about sinners in the Church. But the problem becomes more acute if we assert that the accumulated sins against Christ the Prophet created structures, expressions of canon law, traditions, a style of authority and of teaching that at least partially contradicted the grace and calling bestowed upon the Church. However, if we do not have the courage to face these realities, then we make ourselves co-responsible for the past by allowing perpetuation of these faults and errors.

We cannot faithfully proclaim the liberation wrought by Christ from the powers unless we unmask all the connections with earthly powers and power-seeking that led to many conflicts in Christianity, and unless we face the fact that the various parts of Christianity still need ongoing liberation and healing from the wounds that power-seeking has inflicted on the Church.

Much protest against frozen structures in the life of the Church and in doctrinal formulations comes from the Third World which suffers greatly from the causes and consequences of the division of Christianity. In this situation "we would need a new Apostle for the Gentiles".[71]

The prophetic history described in the Bible and manifested in Church history should lead us all to Christ the Prophet. Then it becomes clear that an effective prophetic protest is possible only by a life in the Spirit and vigilance for the signs of the times. The ecumenical endeavour can never locate itself outside of the hopes and joys, the anguish and suffering of the people of our times.

3. Conversion to Christ, the Dialogue

The encyclical of Pope Paul VI, *Ecclesiam suam*, describes the life of the Church and the task of Christians in a perspective of dialogue. The World Council of Churches equally has chosen the method of dialogue, of patient listening to each other and patient raising of pertinent questions. This is possible only if we are gathered in the name of Jesus and know him as the servant of God, listening humbly to the Father while listening also to the needs of people. In the temple, the twelve-year-old Jesus is already characterized as one proposing questions and listening.

The Church understands herself as a pilgrim. In this perspective, ecumenical dialogue is a colloquium among various partners on pilgrimage, about their mutual relationships. But far more it is a confrontation with their Lord who is the Truth and the Way. Thus the dialogue among Christians becomes the dialogue of charisms.[72] The goal of this dialogue is always to find the other who is indispensable for our own existence in faith. Only through mutual acknowledgment and praise for the diversity of charisms bestowed on all the various parts of the Church, do we come to Christ who is the Listener and the One who responds, the One who praises the Father in all this.

There is, however, a distressing possibility that the separated parts of Christianity may go on and on in dialogue without finding the courage to draw the practical conclusions that result from dialogue. One reason is that frequently those who make the decisions are not partakers in the ecumenical exchanges; they have not experienced the climate of mutual listening and respectful interrogation, and therefore can hardly evaluate the concrete results.[73]

It would be wrong to think that the result of dialogue is a compromise, a watering down of doctrines. It suffices to read the documents of the Catholic-Anglican dialogue, for instance, on the Eucharist, in order to realize gratefully that both partners have brought home the wealth of their faith-experience and the treasures of their respective traditions. It is a good ecumenical practice that the partners in dialogue share with each other in the praise of God what the respective truth means to them in their life. Frequently, then, there is the great surprise of a wonderful convergence of their faith-experience and traditions.

Dialogue helps us to discover "Christian treasures of great value", and this will lead to a greater zeal for Christian unity, as Pope Paul VI expressed it: "Far from arousing our jealousy, this rather increases our fraternity and desire to re-establish the perfect communion between us desired by Christ. And this leads us to discover still other positive results on the road of our peace".[74]

4. *Conversion to Christ, the Covenant: Unity in diversity*

Hope for the reintegration of Christianity in one Church is not thinkable without allowing a certain pluralism or diversity in expression of faith, worship and institutional structures. Here we are mainly concerned with the fundamental disposition. It is not only a matter of tolerating diversity more or less unwillingly. Conversion to Christ, the Covenant, is rather a fundamental disposition to rejoice in the wonderful ways of the Holy Spirit, to build up the fullness of the Mystical Body of Christ by the diversity of charisms and ministries in the midst of the diversity of cultures, and to accept and promote all this in praise of the Holy Spirit, in remembrance of the Pentecostal events.

Christ is the Covenant of the people, solidarity incarnate, who is equally near to all cultures and traditions, bringing them all home into the one covenant. He who has made visible God's all-embracing love and the call to unity is the universal sacrament. "There is no other sacrament than Christ".[75] In him, all sacraments — above all, the Church — symbolize this unity in diversity. Sacramentality is not primarily ritual; it is making visible the one covenant between Jesus Christ and the Church whom he calls from all nations and places, from all traditions and cultures. This vision also has deep repercussions in regard to pluralism in the various rites, in the celebration of the sacraments in the various Churches.[76]

A positive disposition towards pluralism is also necessary for the search for truth and for abiding in truth. As a point of departure in our reflection, we can return to St Thomas Aquinas who considers doctrines as that kind of truth which points to Truth itself.[77] Theologians and churchmen who insist on one, and only one, formulation of salvation truth are leading themselves and others into great error. They are sinning not only against the ever greater mystery and against necessary tolerance but are sinning against Truth itself.

The claim of truth is absolute; however, truth is ever greater than our means of thought and expression. We always can point to truth itself from one direction or from another. If, in dialogue, we then learn to appreciate the various ways to point to the same truth from the various directions, we are respecting more the absolute truth and coming closer to it.[78] Dialogue is not only a means of promoting ecumenism; it belongs to the constitutive life of the Church in unity and in striving towards greater unity. However, we need appreciation of pluralism in our Church in order to come closer to the truth and to prepare for a fruitful pluralism in a united Christianity.

Salvation truth can become "salt for the earth" and "light for the world" only to the extent that it is incarnate in the diverse cultures and traditions. Wherever one local Church tries to impose its own rite, its own thought-patterns and formulations, its own institutional structures on the other Churches, with no concern for diversity, she becomes accountable for the sterility of such colonized Churches, accountable for having hindered a fruitful incarnation of truth in all cultures.

The joint synod of the dioceses of West Germany, insisting on this pluralism in view of genuine catholicity, reminds us that we can find a certain pluralism in the expression of the one faith even within the various parts of holy Scripture. Such diversity is not only possible but even necessary.[79] To the extent that this diversity is recognized and practised in one's own Church, one's capacity and readiness to perceive and to appreciate the wealth of diversity in other Churches and ecclesial communities is increased.[80] One who lives fully the covenant faith and covenant morality in Jesus Christ can frequently realize that disputes concern questions of minor diversities under major unities, even though the external appearances of the diversities sometimes may be great.

A positive disposition towards pluralism allows us the ardent hope that "in the whole vocabulary of ecumenism there are no such words as 'surrender' or 'compromise'. Not only the values that actually exist in the uniting Churches, but those also that are felt by any one of the uniting Churches, must be carried into the ensemble. In the economy of ecuminizing, there is no barter, no cancelling of one belief or procedure held dear if the negotiator on the opposite side will cancel one of his ... We are seeking unity and not uniformity".[81]

From all those involved, pluralism requests a great effort to pass over to the others in order to understand them from their points of departure, and thus return enriched in one's own vision, a vision of convergence. "Just as it is impossible to turn the West into East, so it is impossible to make the East into the West, or to interpret the East by the West. Whenever it has been tried it has led to failure".[82] "The difference of mentality between the East and the West can be characterized by the development of the eleventh century's western theology, a transition from exemplary causality to efficient causality, a transition from symbol to dialectic, from a synthetic perception to an inclination to analysis".[83]

Alexander Schmeemann draws our attention to a fundamental point for all ecumenism with the East and with the other Churches. "Since apart from the 'content' the 'form' has no meaning (cf. the reluctance of Orthodox theologians to discuss problems of 'validity'), Orthodox ecclesiology, rather than looking for precise definitions or forms, conditions and modalities, is an attempt to present an *icon* of the Church as life in Christ — an icon which, to be adequate and true, must draw on all the aspects and not only on the institutional aspects of the Church. For the Church is an *institution* but she is also a *mystery*".[84]

An immediate conclusion seems to impose itself: ecumenical concern and concern for the vitality of each Church in truth obliges the supreme Magisterium, in the exercise of its teaching office if it is offered to the universal Church, to bring home all the diverse experiences, thought-patterns and co-reflections. Theology should also clearly point out whether a document of the Magisterium speaks to the universal Church through these modalities or only to a part of the Church with one thought-pattern. The more this interrelation between unity and diversity becomes one of the basic patterns of a Church, the more she can serve the cause of reunion of a separated Christianity.

The Church grows in knowledge of the world and in the art of reaching out to the world as light for it if, in her own life and in that of all humanity, she positively appreciates pluralism, diversity in unity. We think not only of coexistence of diversities but of pluralism for each other. How shall the world learn to come to unity without being pressed into uniformity, if the Church does not set an example?[85]

The report of an ecumenical symposium gives a good picture of how pluralism, marked by different points of departure, can be fruitful if the various confessions complete each other. "Some of us would give first place to the proclamation of the Gospel as a means to awaken faith. Action would then be considered as the necessary fruit of such a faith. Others, however, think that proclamation and action must be interwoven, even identical. Both perspectives are conditioned through different theological convictions and through different situations in which Christians live. As long as both understand themselves as obedient to God's work of salvation, they should not think that they exclude each other but rather that they can be understood in a creative complementarity and tension".[86]

IV. ECUMENISM IN ACTION

Proper dispositions and a firm commitment must guide the action; and action appropriate to the grace of each hour will deepen the dispositions. The ecumenism of the World Council of Churches and the ecumenism fostered by Vatican II have led to manifold ecumenical actions. The decrees of the Second Vatican Council point to numerous areas of ecumenically shared responsibility: common enterprises such as translating and explaining the Bible,[87] common witness,[88] training of priests,[89] theological dialogue and religious education.[90] Since the Council, shared ecumenical action has increased in depth and has extended to new areas.[91]

1. Spiritual ecumenism: sharing the charisms

Perhaps we can apply to the ecumenical movement the observation of Gregory of Nazianzen: "The corporeal work of Christ is consummated ... The work of the Holy Spirit is only beginning".[92]

The unity of Christians in the full diversity of all that is good can only be the work of the Holy Spirit. Most important on our part is faith and trust in the Holy Spirit, and the kind of action that manifests our faith in the Spirit.

All the wonderful achievements and the frustrations have strengthened the conviction of many ecumenists in the various Churches, that spiritual ecumenism must take the first place. "The ecumenical spirituality must become a dynamic inspiration for all our ecumenical endeavours, so that the Holy Spirit can move us, and that, under his guidance, we can reach out towards our future as people of God".[93] Time and again, reports of ecumenical meetings say that the participants were "deeply concerned with spiritual ecumenism as the only framework for making fraternal understanding possible".[94]

A basic characteristic of ecumenical spirituality is a strong faith in the Holy Spirit and a new devotion to holy Scripture, which is seen as a book not only for the study of ecumenical problems but also as a source of strength and trust. It is the Holy Spirit who enables us to bring orthodoxy and orthopraxis together. To open ourselves to the word of God written in the Bible, and to the signs of the times, the Spirit gives us a new understanding of initiative, creative fidelity and liberty, shared meditation, common worship, intercession and praise. All these are signs of spiritual ecumenism.

In our dialogue, we shall be particularly attentive not to offend the Spirit. Only guided by the Spirit can we follow the ecumenical method outlined by Pope Paul VI: "Hope is our guide, prayer our strength, charity our method in the service of divine truth which is our hope and our salvation".[95]

2. Grace and strength of provisional union

Nothing would be more dangerous for the ecumenical movement than to try first to settle all things theoretically, and only then to move into a practical realization of unity. There is a special grace and strength in the courage to move towards unity by provisional solutions. Many members of the different Churches, and especially youth everywhere, feel that the time has come to take more concrete and courageous steps. "As an eschatological gift of grace, each *communio* lives in the tension between the 'already' and the 'not yet'. Therefore, our realization of communion is always provisional ... This should encourage us to seek provisional solutions and should, at the same time, incite us never to be content with them".[96]

Many consider the community of Taizé, and especially the youth council inspired by Taizé, as a prophetic model of provisional solutions. "The dynamic of the provisional allows one to rediscover the Gospel in its original freshness".[97] Taizé's programme is one of creative fidelity to Church institutions. It is designed to move people, not by protest, but by living the Gospel in freedom and fidelity to the common heritage.[98] "The Church suffers; therefore we cannot abandon her".[99]

There are numerous groups around the world similar to Taizé, as mentioned above, and many ecumenical "Houses of Prayer" (shared life and search for integration of faith and life). Tired of ecumenical discussions that did not lead to any practical results, people are convinced that "our living together may itself widen and deepen our togetherness in faith".[100]

On a larger scale, there are many provisional solutions, for instance, the World Federation of Lutheran Churches and federations of other reformed Churches, the United Church of Canada, the United Church in South India, all bringing a number of Churches into a communion. There were and still are great and hopeful efforts to bring forth a gradual and even complete communion between the Anglican Churches and the Methodist Churches. There is a partial intercommunion between the Anglican and Swedish Churches, with reciprocal acknowledgment of the sacred order of priests and bishops. Other types of provisional or gradual solutions are: (1) spiritual union, (2) union in cooperation in various fields, (3) union by federation, (4) union through reciprocal recognition and open intercommunion and intercelebration, (5) organic union.[101]

At the end of the Second Vatican Council, Pope Paul VI said to the observers, "We should like to see you with us always".[102] This word might give inspiration for further reflection on provisional solutions. There should be, for instance, regular consultation on common action and on urgent problems, exchange of consultative representations between the various Churches, a system of regular visits.[103] Would it not be more important for the Roman See to have apostolic delegates to all the major Churches in the East and West, and to have their delegates in Rome, than to restrict the system of nuncii and apostolic delegates to the earthly powers and the national conferences of bishops?

3. Ecumenism and mission

The ecumenical movement of this century received its first and strongest impetus from the missionary world, for messengers of the Gospel coming from various Churches experienced most painfully the separation which greatly diminished the credibility of their witness. "No doubt the Word of God finds so many obstacles in our world especially because, among Christians, there has not yet been realized a common meditation on the Gospel and a common consciousness of being sent to proclaim it. The voice of the Gospel is weak because the Spirit likes to manifest his power only through the unanimous profession".[104]

Much is already gained when the separate Churches manifest a spirit of friendship and mutual respect. When they move closer to each other, much more can be done in common. The decree of Vatican II on missions strongly emphasized the ecumenical spirit in mission activity. "The ecumenical spirit, too, should be nurtured in the neophytes. They should rightly consider that the brethren who believe in Christ are Christ's disciples, reborn in baptism, sharers with the people of God in very many riches. Insofar as religious conditions allow, ecumenical activity should be furthered in such a way that, without any appearance of indifference or of unwarranted intermingling on the one hand or of unhealthy rivalry on the other, Catholics can cooperate in a brotherly spirit with their separated brethren, according to the norms of the decree on Ecumenism. To the extent that their beliefs are common, they can make before the nations a common profession of faith in God and in Jesus Christ. They can collaborate in social and technical projects as well as in cultural and religious ones. Let them work together especially for the sake of Christ, their common Lord. Let his name be the bond that unites them, a sign of exhortation".[105]

If we preach the Gospel in a fresh way and try to incarnate it in the new cultures, we will not burden the new communities with our occidental quarrels. There is good hope that the Churches in the Third World can make a major contribution to the reintegration of the separated parts of Christianity. Provision should be made that they are well represented in ecumenical study-weeks and encounters.

4. Ecumenism and diakonia

It becomes increasingly clear that the various Churches cannot unite fully in faith and in one Church unless they are consistently united in service to the world. What God has entrusted to his Church is the Gospel of his love for his people, not only for their souls but also for their humanness, their dignity, health and daily bread. If the divided parts of Christianity join their efforts in manifesting the love of Christ to the world in all its dimensions, then the world can see that they are one in a love that embraces not only themselves but all people. Thus Christ's high-priestly prayer comes closer to fulfilment: "May they all be one, as thou, Father, art in me and I in thee, so also may they be in us, that the world may believe that thou didst send me" (Jn 17:21).

The ecumenical collaboration of the various Churches united in the World Council of Churches and the Catholic Church, has made great progress. Sodapax, a commission of the World Council of Churches and representatives of the Catholic Church for promoting peace and justice in the world, is one of the most lively signs of ecumenism in action. Christianity will always continue to give witness to the love of Christ by fulfilling the bodily works of mercy, feeding the hungry, healing the sick, visiting and, if possible, freeing the prisoners, teaching the poor. But today's conditions demand also a joint effort to promote better conditions of life, genuine development, a healthy and strong public opinion regarding justice and peace.

Christianity is not a political power, yet by its witness and as a prophetic voice, those Churches which do not seek any power or privileges can greatly help politics to serve the common good.[106] A Christianity that has freed itself from the power structures of the Constantinian era can become a visible sign and a witness to Christ the Redeemer, who is on the side of the poor and the downtrodden.

If, however, the divided parts of Christianity only discuss under what conditions and at what time they finally will celebrate the sacraments together, without becoming a sacramental service to the greatest needs of humankind, they will not win people for Christ. "For modern people, the first things to give attention to are not the sacraments but the action of the Church for human liberation and the communion of people and nations".[107]

During the past years, many zealous promoters of Christian unity have become wearied by unending disputes about doctrinal formulas, especially where the Church bodies failed to realize or did not implement the results of the ongoing dialogue in the official commissions. As a consequence, they emphasize somewhat one-sidedly a "secular ecumenism", the solidaric work of the Christian Churches for justice and peace, for helping the poor and oppressed. The tension between a missionary and the sociological-political task of the Church is the phenomenon that has characterized ecumenical life during the last decade.[108]

There is, however, a noticeable diversity of mentality and approach between the eastern Churches and western Christianity. The Orthodox Churches are not indifferent towards civilization, but the emphasis is on the transformation of the individual. The transformation of society is considered as a by-product of seeking the heavenly kingdom. It comes about by way of superabundance of faith, but is not sought for itself as a necessary step towards the universal establishment of the kingdom. In the western Church the emphasis is somewhat different. Protestants and Catholics see the Word and the sacraments also as a power for transforming the world. They are not only signs of Christ's presence for adoration but also the proclamation of Christ, the Redeemer of the world.

The anthropological interest is more direct in the West, whereas in the East it is more implicit. If the secular ecumenism were to be too one-sidedly stressed by western Christianity, it would cause new difficulties for the reunion of the East and

West. Moreover, the witness of secular ecumenism is authentic only if deeply rooted in spiritual unity. Common action cannot be a substitute for communion in faith and worship, but it can be a way towards unity if there is, at the same time, a deep desire for greater unity in faith and adoration. And the more collaboration there is in the field of diakonia, with peace and justice being illumined by faith and directed to the praise of the one God and Father, the one Lord Jesus Christ and the one Spirit, the more the collaboration will manifest a prophetic spirit.

5. Prophetic realization

The great pioneers of the ecumenical movement in all Churches have been men and women of a prophetic spirit and prophetic courage. They were not only far ahead of the institutions in their thinking but also in their gestures. It is most encouraging that the Spirit of the Lord inspired even the highest Church authorities to offer prophetic gestures that frequently mean much more than well-formulated words. I think of Pope John XXIII who, when he first received the observers of the other Churches at the Council, took a chair and seated himself among them instead of talking to them from a papal throne. And we have already noted Pope Paul's gesture in putting his fisherman's ring on Archbishop Ramsey's finger.

The community of Taizé seems to me to be a great prophetic sign, a prophetic anticipation of things to come. There we find a beautiful synthesis between a profound spirituality and a great openness to the yearnings of the world. No wonder that it attracts youth from everywhere! The Council of Youth, under the guidance of the Friars of Taizé is a prophetic realization and promise.

The late ecumenical Patriarch Athenagoras was not only himself a great prophet; he also called repeatedly for courageous prophetic realizations. "I am not a man of the sacristy and I do not see myself enclosed within an ecclesiastical milieu. I love people and observe their history. Men of the Church frequently lack the spirit of Christ, the humility, the renunciation of self, the capacity to discover the best in the other. They make the Church an organization like others. And after having used all our energies to build it, we consume ourselves to keep it going;

and this happens as if it were a machine and not life. Unity must make progress. Everywhere the laity is longing for it. Those in authority must feel the burning desire of youth for unity. This is of extreme urgency. How much I would like to see theologians seized by the impatience of youth and realize that they are not ready for any compromise. Alas for the theologians, alas for the Church leaders, if young people, in their burning zeal, gather secretly outside the Church to share wine and bread! ... The Holy Spirit is not only light; he is fire".[109]

Both spiritual and secular ecumenism, as expressions of faith, must be witness to trust in the Holy Spirit. They must be courageous and imaginative; signs must be set everywhere in the world. But it is important that creative and courageous realizations should never lose contact with those in authority. They must be signs that can be followed by clearsighted people in the various Churches. An outstanding Orthodox theologian tells us, "Theology has a prophetic dimension. It tests all traditions and, by exposing the true tradition, makes us time and again free children of God".[110]

Prophetic realization shies away from negative and bitter criticism that blocks energies and undermines trust. An ardent Lutheran ecumenist notes that "criticism, though allowable and sometimes mandatory, must remain loyal". The most dedicated sons and daughters of the Church may sometimes assume the role of being the "maternal majesty's loyal opposition".[111]

The future of ecumenism depends greatly on how Christians of the various Churches and traditions understand fidelity. Do we believe in the Holy Spirit who awakens imagination and enables creativity in fidelity?

6. *A central quest: Eucharistic communion*

One of the greatest concerns and longings of ecumenists in all Churches, and rightly so, is the re-establishment of Eucharistic communion. "The Church is fulfilled in the Eucharist, and each sacrament therefore finds its end, its fulfilment in the Eucharist".[112]

Here again there is the frequently half-conscious conflict between a static and dynamic vision. All ecumenically concerned Christians agree that the Eucharist is a sign of unity; therefore the longing and endeavour for Christian unity coincides with the longing for Eucharistic communion. However, for those who think more statically, Eucharistic communion is the final crowning of a complete unity, while for others it is a sign of a unity in progress and a sign requesting commitment to make further progress in unity until the Lord's prayer is completely fulfilled.

The decree on Ecumenism, speaking on common worship whose centre is the Eucharist, states clearly: "Such worship depends chiefly on two principles: it should signify the unity of the Church; it should provide a sharing in the means of grace. The fact that it should signify unity generally rules out common worship. Yet the gaining of a needed grace sometimes commends it".[113]

The Council continues: "The practical course to be adopted after due regard has been given to all the circumstances of time, place and personage, is left to the prudent decision of the local episcopal authority". Decisions cannot be made once and forever since, with the grace of God, ecumenism is progressive and therefore requires constant openness to new opporunities. For Catholics, there can be no doubt about the high degree of the bishops' competence. "The heart of ecclesial organization is the Eucharist, hence the expression, 'the sacramental order'. A certain right belongs respectively to the Pope or to the bishop according to his role with regard to presiding over the Eucharist. The Eucharist is truly the source of law in the Church, just as it is of love".[114]

Eucharistic communion has various degrees: (1) one-sided Eucharistic hospitality; (2) reciprocal but limited Eucharistic hospitality; (3) unlimited intercommunion, crowned by concelebration by bishops and priests of the respective Churches.

The lack of Eucharistic communion could, by itself, be a shock. A Lutheran bishop writes, "Everything that separates Churches in the profound sense, that is, what prevents brethren from participating in the common table of the Lord, must be challenged. If Eucharistic communion is once reached, then all the other questions concerning communion are, in a way, merely practical and of a subordinate character".

At the present stage of ecumenical progress, the question must be raised again whether there are still obstacles so great that Eucharistic sharing must be excluded. Throughout all the ages, Christians of quite different theologies and organizational principles have granted each other Eucharistic communion. "Unbreakable Eucharistic communion in the midst of diversities is a witness of the reconciling power of Christ, and therefore serves the proclamation of the Good News in the World".[115]

Not only individual Christians sometimes have urgent need of the grace of the sacrament; Church communities also, struggling for final reunion, seem to need most urgently the grace of common worship, especially of Eucharistic communion. Many ecumenists share the conviction expressed by a report of an ecumenical colloquium: "We have the hope that common sharing in the Eucharist will be for all a source of a deeper unity".[116]

The difficult question is how much unity must be reached in order to allow Eucharistic sharing to be a truthful sign of unity and grace for further unity. The official ecumenical commissions of Catholics and Anglicans and of Lutherans and Catholics have reached an astonishing degree of agreement about ministry and the meaning of Eucharist. Even the possibility of a renewed papacy exercising its unity-ministry in a communion of sister Churches is being seriously considered.[117]

A survey of newer Protestant publications on the Eucharist shows that most of the traditional difficulties are removed, and Protestants deeply affirm their faith in the real presence.[118] But we cannot acknowledge more validity to the Protestant ministries than they themselves do. There is no difficulty between the Catholic Church and the Orthodox Churches. Protestant Churches have begun to adjust their understanding of their own ministries to that of the Catholic and Orthodox Churches.[119] Congar suggests that in Thomas Aquinas there is an indication of an important route for solving the present difficulties regarding Eucharistic sharing. About those living in a separated Church, Thomas writes, "They are in the Church insofar as they observe the form of the Church".[120]

At the present moment, open communion between the Catholic Church and all the Protestant Churches seems not yet possible. There must first be mutual recognition of the validity of the ministries. It seems to me also that the Catholic Church cannot yet grant unrestricted Eucharistic hospitality to members

of Protestant Churches. There is not yet enough preparation
and not all fulfil the conditions that must be requested.

Quite different, however, is the situation of those Protestant
men and women who are most actively committed to the
ecumenical movement, who profoundly believe in the real presence
of the Lord in the Eucharist, and desire to share in the Eucharist
for further progress and stronger commitment to unity on all
levels. I have heard Presbyterian theologians and ministers professing their faith in the Eucharistic presence in the following
way: "We believe that the Lord is present in the same power of
the Holy Spirit in which he gave himself up for us on the
cross; he is present to give himself totally to us, and sends us
his Spirit, that we too can be totally present in him, surrendering
ourselves to him and thus to the work of Christian unity".

Here, one question cannot be avoided: Have all Catholics,
whom we have unrestrictedly admitted to the Eucharist, such
a deep faith in the Eucharistic presence of Jesus, and such a
strong commitment to the cause of Christian unity?

V. A BROADER ECUMENISM

Ecumenism, in the strict sense, embraces all those who believe
in Christ, the Son of God, and son of man, and call themselves his disciples. But the new explosion of mutual love
among Christians of different Churches has its repercussions in
a revised reflection and new attitudes towards non-Christian
religions.

Faith in the lordship of Jesus, Saviour of the world, and a
deeper understanding of the history of salvation, lead to a better
appreciation of the positive elements in non-Christian religions.
The declaration of the Second Vatican Council on the non-
Christian religions is a milestone in the history of religion. The
Secretariat of the Vatican for dialogue with non-Christian
religions has greatly contributed to reconciliation and mutual
enrichment.[121]

Fully in line with the declaration on Religious Liberty and
the pastoral constitution on the Church in the Modern World,
the Council insists: "We cannot in truthfulness call upon that

God who is Father of all if we refuse to act in a brotherly way towards certain men, created though they be to God's image ... As a consequence, the Church rejects as foreign to the mind of Christ any discrimination against men or harassment of them because of their race, colour, condition of life or religion".[122] The relation of the Church to people of other religions and their religious leaders must reflect the role of the Church as a sacrament of reconciliation. The first thing to communicate to them is the love of Christ through brotherly love. Only in that climate can the proper conditions for growth of knowledge, of salvation be hoped for.

A preface to a Latin translation of the Koran by Martin Luther in 1524 is a stream of scorn, ending with the warning, "If any reader, after all this, still has the courage to read this book, and then imagines that he has found something worthwhile, he should not forget that this is nothing else than pearls stolen by the Moslems in order to make them dirty in their dunghill". Most of the Catholics of the time did not think differently.

Against this sad background history, we can enjoy the words from the declaration on the Relationship of the Church to non-Christian Religions (*Nostra Aetate*): "Upon the Moslems, too, the Church looks with esteem. They adore one God, living and enduring, merciful and all-powerful, Maker of heaven and earth, and Speaker to man. They strive to submit wholeheartedly even to his inscrutable decrees, just as did Abraham, with whom the Islamic faith is pleased to associate itself. Though they do not acknowledge Jesus as God, they revere him as a prophet. They also honour Mary, his virgin mother".[123] The litany of praise about the values of Islam still continues in the declaration. The Church earnestly desires to join hands with the Moslem believers in the common cause "of safeguarding and fostering social justice, moral values, peace and freedom".

The Church has gone through a deep conversion about Judaism and the Jewish people. Anti-semitism, which so frequently in the past made the Jewish people suffer and in which many Christians shared, contradicts the very origin of Christianity. The declaration[124] follows the spirit of Pope Paul VI and the whole Second Vatican Council by putting in the foreground the many positive elements of Judaism, and exalting the common bond with the history of Israel. "The Church ever keeps in mind the words of the Apostle about his kinsmen, 'who have their adoption as sons, and the glory of the covenant, the legislation and the worship and the prophecies; who have the Fathers, and from whom is Christ according to the flesh' (Rom 9:4-5), the Son of the Virgin Mary. The Church recalls too that from Jewish people sprang the apostles, the foundation stones and pillars, as well as most of the early disciples who proclaimed Christ to the world". With the Apostle of the Gentiles, we hope that Israel will be, in its time of grace, a special object of mercy (cf. Rom 11:30-32).

The declaration expresses particular esteem for the great spiritual values found in Hinduism and Buddhism.[125] We surely can learn much from the great contemplative religions of Asia, and sometimes are ashamed, seeing them more zealous in contemplation and prayer than many Christians. A deeper understanding of the religiosity of the people of Africa, Asia, Oceania, and the Indians in America can only issue in the praise of God who never has abandoned his creatures and has helped them to seek him and to find a way to him. "The Catholic Church rejects nothing which is true and holy in these religions".[126] In the dialogue with representatives of all these religions, the Church has not only to give the great treasures of the Gospel but also can learn of and receive spiritual treasures and profound human experiences that help her to understand better the history of salvation preparing the coming of Christ.

VI. DIMENSIONS OF AN ECUMENICAL MORAL THEOLOGY

Dealing honestly with certain problems such as intercommunion, mixed marriages, and so on, is by no means all that ecumenism requires. More fundamental, and therefore more important, is the ecumenical spirit of all moral theology. Here, common efforts must surely be made on the level of official dialogue between the separated Churches. Promising beginnings and achievements have been prepared in this perspective.[127] It is, above all, a task of reintegration of the various dimensions and traditions.

1. Reintegration of dogmatic and moral theology

Before the great schisms of the eleventh and sixteenth centuries, Christianity had known nothing like the manuals of Roman Catholic moral theology which came into existence at the beginning of the seventeenth century and were used up to the Second Vatican Council.

Theology had disintegrated into a dogmatic, a moral and a spiritual-ascetical theology, to the detriment of each of them. It is my conviction that the schisms of the various parts of Christianity cannot be overcome unless, within the Roman Catholic Church, the schism of the various parts of theology is thoroughly overcome. The ecumenical discussions about dogmatic formulations will not be fruitful until the moral dimension is brought home, for God has not revealed abstract doctrines but salvation truth. That means dogmatic truth that guides our path in life.

All that God has revealed of his own mystery and of the mystery of man created in his own image and likeness is, by necessity, fruitful in and for Christian life. In our discussions about divergent doctrines we have to ask ourselves in common dialogue: What does this doctrine mean for my life in my community, and how does it fit into the Lord's testament and prayer "that all may be one"? In the tradition common to East and West until the schisms, and in the eyes of today's Orthodox theology, dogma is not a mere intellectual acquisition that requires nothing more than formal assent and obedience; it is a living and saving truth which must shape the life, thought and prayer of the Church, and assure the difficult and creative process of entering into the truth.[128]

The fruitfulness of salvation truth in the heart and mind of Christians and the Churches is best guaranteed if reflection arises from worship and is directed to the final question of how it contributes to the adoration of God in spirit and in truth. On this point, Orthodox tradition and our own ancient traditions can make a great contribution.[129] Orthodoxy of doctrine cannot be severed from doxology without losing its dynamic for life.

Nothing is more important for our own integration and integrity, and for the reintegration of the different parts of Christianity in the one Church, than the oneness of theology.

Even if, because of the magnitude of tasks, there are various theological disciplines, each of them must be aware, first of all, of the oneness of theology, a theology of life in Christ Jesus, a salvation theology to the praise of God.

2. Reintegration of eastern and western tradition

Until the fifth century the impact of the eastern tradition on the West was very deep. Christian life and its moral implications were still seen in a sacramental vision. The life of disciples of Christ was nourished, above all, by the celebration of the liturgy and the liturgical proclamation of the word of God. But gradually there developed in the West a moral preaching not always sufficiently rooted in the mystery, not always fully aware that Christian life arises out of our union with Christ. Yet the rich theology of the twelfth and thirteenth centuries still treated moral questions as much in the light of the mystery of Christ and the sacraments as in the light of creation. However, after the great schism in the eleventh century, the West went its own way and the East remained foreign to the three influences that shaped modern Catholicism (scholasticism, reformation, and sixteenth-eighteenth century rationalism).

Congar stresses the fact that after the thirteenth century, theological formation was fully integrated into a life of contemplation, mostly in religious life. But then there arose a new type of teaching and study "of an academic and rational nature". The East never accepted this new approach to theology. It was only F. Serge Bulgakov who combined all three kinds of theology in one undivided theology. "Sapiential knowledge was neither a separate philosophy nor a pure mysticism nor a 'scientific' theology, but all three combined".[130]

Roman theology felt a need to define faith in clear-cut concepts, while the Orthodox theologians feel the need to define it in a way that will not obscure the character of the mystery that transcends all concepts. They manifest and communicate faith chiefly in and through worship. They accept the definitions of the ecumenical councils of the time when East and West formed the one Church; but they will have great difficulty accepting definitions made later by Roman Catholic synods without participation by the East.

In order to attract the Orthodox Christians to union with the Roman See, we need a theology centred in the Eucharist, a theology that integrates contemplation and life. The dogmas of the Church can be communicated to the Orthodox in this kind of theology. Vatican II has given the directives on how to renew moral theology — thoroughly nourished by holy Scripture and understood as the lofty vocation of the faithful in Christ, with its inner dynamics to bear fruit in love and justice for the life of the world.[131] Such an integration, so necessary for the reunion of the Roman Catholic and the Orthodox Churches, would greatly enrich all parts of Christianity.

3. Reintegration of Protestant and Roman Catholic moral theology

Roman Catholic and Protestant theologians were always in dialogue with each other, although mostly in a negative form whereby everyone emphasized the opposite pole. When Catholic moral theology emphasized clear norms, sanctions and controls, Protestants would then even more emphasize liberty and spontaneity under the action of the Holy Spirit. While Catholic theology emphasized institution and objective truth taught by the Church, Protestant ethics turned to the subject of truth: to believers united with each other and searching freely for truth.

Thanks to the ecumenical movement, things have changed. Catholic moral theology gives close and loving attention to the best of Protestant theology, especially where it manifests great openness for the mission of believers in today's world.[132] Catholic moral theology has made great efforts in the area of its own tradition and in dialogue with Protestant Christian ethics, to see how conscience and law meet: how the liberty in the Holy Spirit can be harmonized with ethical guidelines and norms.[133]

Protestant ecumenical theology acknowledges fully the necessity of law not only in secular society but also in the Church which is, at the same time, a communion and an institution. "Law is essential to the order of a society so that the purposes of that society may be carried out, but once the law outruns that purpose, it is not only non-essential but positively harmful".[134] As Catholics we can fully agree with this explanation of law, and I would add that all ecclesiastical laws in all Churches have to be tested constantly on whether they serve the reintegration of Christian unity. Where this is not the case, the laws have outrun one of their main purposes, namely, to guarantee and to promote Christian unity.

James M. Gustafson, as writer and moderator for many Protestant and Catholic graduate students, sets an example for a truly ecumenical theology. It comes legitimately from the Protestant tradition but is constantly open to the positive in the Catholic theology of the past and the present. While North American Protestant ethicists tend frequently to concentrate on practical questions (unlike the Europeans, especially the German Lutheran moral theologians), Gustafson rightly insists that ecumenical dialogue must give particular attention to the basic principles, perception or outlook. "*Rapprochement* between traditions is easier to achieve with reference to more limited and special areas that can be tested for adequacy (as in the use of psychological information about homosexuality) than it is to achieve between the basic organizing principles or perceptions around which the basic points cohere".[135]

Protestant ethicists are in agreement in rejecting extreme perspectives which seemingly provided coherence in the past: namely, a static moral order suggested by Catholic manualists and, on the other hand, an actualist view of God's presence in the world, commanding persons in "the moment". Between the two there is more than sufficient space for disagreement, but the dividing lines are no longer denominational.[136]

No systematic approach is perfect; therefore other attempts are called for. For some, Christian ethics "is primarily guided by an eschatological principle or by one of a *logos* Christology". Uniformity is not desirable; it would impoverish the life of the Church. "Faith has never issued in uniformity of theological ethics".[137] Yet in important matters there must be constant effort to reach a consensus or at least a convergence of visions. Great progress has been made in this direction. "Whether these interesting beginnings develop significantly depends on many factors, not least of which is the effort to do so. If they develop with cogency, it will not be because ecumenical sentiment is embodied but because criteria of 'adequacy' and 'coherence' are better met".[138]

It seems to me extremely important that Catholic-Protestant

dialogue and common effort remain always fully aware of the great eastern Orthodox tradition. This can contribute greatly to resolving the traditional divergence between Protestant and Catholic theologies. I mention, for instance, the dispute about nature and grace, with Protestants asserting "grace alone". For the Orthodox, "creation, being creation by God, is in itself an act of grace".[139]

The believer sees everything as the gift of God. All of creation, being directed to Christ, the high-priest, is a call to man "to perform the sacramental task as king and priest of creation, and his whole life is to be one all-embracing Eucharist".[140] The Orthodox can offer us a synthesis (which corresponds to our own best tradition) that does not emphasize God's grace less than Protestant theology and, similarly, appreciates nature, the work of the Creator, not less than Catholic tradition.

The Orthodox offer us also a convincing vision of the much discussed relation between grace and freedom, since they do not consider grace as just something added to freedom but are convinced that a truly redeemed and free person considers and uses all his freedom as a gift of God. Because of their beautifully developed doctrine on the "synergy between grace and freedom, any idea of merit is totally absent from the Orthodox cult and understanding of the saints".[141]

In this age of secularization, both Catholics and Protestants of the West have to be reminded by the Orthodox that neither word nor work alone can help us to grasp the Christian message. We need a deeper understanding of the "icon". Christ is not only the incarnate Word of the Father; he is also the image (icon) of the invisible God. And in him all of reality, but particularly the human person created to the image and likeness of God, is to be seen in a thoroughly sacramental perspective. "The icon manifests Christ, man and the whole cosmos in the perspective of transfiguration, resplendent with the divine Presence and enveloped in the divine *energeia* of the Holy Spirit which was most vividly revealed at Pentecost".[142]

4. *Reintegration through creative liberty and fidelity in Christ*

While Protestants emphasized liberty, Catholic and Orthodox tradition cherished more the idea of fidelity. What I have tried

to do in this synthesis of moral theology is to show that creative
liberty, as expression of a life in Christ under the power of the
Holy Spirit, by inner necessity calls for equal emphasis on creative fidelity that flows from the life-giving law of the Spirit in
Christ Jesus. Liberty is truly creative only to the extent that it
manifests covenant fidelity in gratitude for God's wonderful
works in the past and for his promises.

The future of ecumenism would not be assured by a one-sided
secular ecumenism, particularly if this is not rooted in a common
faith. But the great concern for the quality of human life that
secular ecumenism has manifested during the last decade must
be brought home into the ecumenical Christian ethics. The
Church is meant to be the vehicle of Christian life, a life in
genuine freedom and fidelity to the Lord of history. We need
an ecumenical moral theology that makes tangible the living God
who calls us here and now to creative responses. But equally
to be witnessed to is the Faithful One who guarantees a profound
continuity of history.

What is most needed is that all Christians manifest to each
other and before the world a greater and more creative faithfulness to Jesus' prayer that "all may be one". All initiatives, laws,
formulations of doctrine, and the effort of synthesis, have to be
tested as to whether they serve that unity between the different
parts of Christianity that makes them a vehicle and sign of unity
in justice and peace.

VII. SOME ACTUAL ECUMENICAL PROBLEMS

1. *Common worship as expression of spiritual ecumenism*

We have seen how serious is the longing of all fervent ecumenists for the day when we can share the Eucharistic celebration
and thus praise the Lord for the gift of unity, and work harder
for ever-increasing oneness. Impatience about the fact that we
have not yet reached this point should not allow us, however,
to omit the many opportunities for common worship authorized
and recommended by the respective Churches. We can celebrate
together the word of God, learn together a prophetic prayer in
the hope to decipher the signs of the times and to respond

courageously to them. We can try to make our shared prayer
and paraliturgical celebrations more attractive. We can join in
the "houses of prayer", the schools for prayer in the prophetic
tradition. The prayer meetings of the charismatic renewal surely
have given witness and will give even more witness to the fruitfulness of shared prayer, especially the prayer of praise and
thanksgiving. Sharing prayerful study of the Bible and sharing
our religious experience in view of giving a common witness to
the world are decisive steps towards the hoped-for Christian
unity.[143]

2. Conversion in an ecumenical age

It is an undeniable fact that since the Roman Catholic Church
participated actively in the ecumenical movement, the number
of converts coming from active life in other Churches has greatly
diminished. Traditionalists use this as an argument against the
Second Vatican Council. We cannot share this opinion. Christian
unity cannot be reached through individual conversions to the
Roman Catholic Church. We all have to be converted individually
and corporately to the Lord's testament that "all may be one".
Have not men like the late Patriarch Athenagoras, Archbishop
Ramsey of the Anglican church, the Brothers of Taizé done more
for the cause of Christian unity than their individual conversions
to the Catholic Church could have done?

The whole problem of individual conversions has to be
thoroughly rethought in the light of the present experience of
how God calls us to Christian unity:

(1) Ecumenical dialogue between the Churches must not be
used as a means for making individual converts. Helping each
other to become fervent apostles of the cause of Christian unity,
to work within one's native Church may accomplish much more
than converting an individual to one's own Church just for "the
saving of one's soul".[144] We have to ask ourselves seriously what
the following teaching of the Second Vatican Council in this
ecumenical situation means: "Whosoever, therefore, knowing
that the Catholic Church was made necessary by God through
Jesus Christ, would refuse to enter her or to remain in her could
not be saved".[145] In my opinion, the paradigm of "double

membership" can best help us to respond to this problem. Those who remain in their native Church while praying, suffering and doing everything they can to move that Church towards the hoped-for fully catholic Church, remain truly in the Catholic Church built by Christ, or enter more effectively into it.

(2) Those who have reached the conviction of conscience that an immediate and external conversion to the Roman Catholic Church is, for them here and now, the best way of pleasing Christ, have to follow their conscience. Such a conviction seems to me objectively stringent if a fervent Christian realizes that the sect or Church to which he belongs does nothing to respond to Christ's prayer that "all may be one", after having made his contribution to enkindle the ecumenical fervour.

However, if one belongs to a Church that can be ecumenically awakened or is on the road of ecumenism, new forms of "conversion" might take place, in line with the classical example given by V.S. Solovyev who, after having been received in the Roman Catholic Church, continued to participate in the life of the Orthodox Church, as testimony that turning to the centre of Christianity, to Rome, does not alienate one from one's native Church.

At any rate, individual conversions to the Catholic Church should be performed in a way that is not offensive to one's native Church. All the good that one has received there should be gratefully acknowledged.

(3) In the past, many so-called conversions from one Church to another, particularly on the occasion of mixed marriages, did not come from conscience but from pressure. For those who have not found their home in the Church to which they turned, there should be pastoral help so that they can go back to the Church to which, according to their conscience, they still belong. It might be, however, that in today's ecumenical climate they may, with God's help, join those who are earning a "double membership", one in the Church to which they now belong and, by their longing, prayer and activity, in the one Church that Christ wants.

(4) Up to now we have spoken of conversions especially in relation to members of Churches that belong to the ecumenical

Council of Churches or the ecumenical movement in the broader sense. However, there is enough occasion and space left for making conversions among those who are not committed to any Church, or who belong to sects that are not at all moving towards Christian unity. As Catholics, we should not consider it a loss if a person baptized in the Catholic Church but never evangelized in the Church, receives the Good News from another Church and finds there, in an ecumenical climate, his home. The same should be thought about baptized people who are not at all active in any Church and then are won to the Catholic Church. These are truly conversions to the Church. Each Church should first try to evangelize fully those whom she has baptized before trying to make converts of practically non-evangelized people in areas where another Church is mainly represented. On principle, each Church's mission should be especially where Christ is not yet proclaimed.

3. Mixed marriages

Throughout history, the Church has frequently changed her policies about mixed marriage without changing her basic principles and pastoral concerns. The meaning and justification of the policy depends on the total situation.[146]

The Church's legislation and the applied principles of today's moral theology are quite different from the legislation before the Council and from the texts of the manuals of that time. The Church had to face a new situation. The old legislation and the corresponding treatises of moral theology were addressed to closed Catholic and non-Catholic societies and groups where a transference was the exception. Today, in our highly mobile society, marriage between Christians of various Churches is only a part of the general pattern of intermarriage.[147]

During the last century and until our time, mixed marriages suffered greatly under the sharp conflict between the respective Churches. Pastors and ministers frequently brought into these marriages not so much the peace of Christ as the striving between denominations.[148] According to the then existing canon law, many if not most mixed marriages were considered invalid, and whenever they broke up, the partners could enter a new marriage in the Catholic Church without difficulty. No wonder the statistics could show that mixed marriages were the most fragile!

The era of ecumenical openings has brought an enormous theological, canonical and pastoral endeavour to come to more appropriate solutions.[149] The March 31, 1970 *Motu Proprio* of Paul VI, "Mixed Marriages", is a gigantic step forward, although further development in ecumenical *rapprochement* will allow and request further adaptation.[150] This text is ecumenical not only by intent but also by giving the greatest possible attention to the diversity of situations in the various countries, and allowing the episcopal conferences to issue, within certain limits, their own legislation. Some bishops' conferences, for instance the German and French, have used this possibility most generously.

The new legislation repeats the unchanged and unchangeable principle that no believer, by entering into a mixed marriage, may expose his or her faith to the proximate danger of losing it.

While many canonists and moralists earlier thought that the obligation to guarantee the baptism and upbringing of the children in the Catholic Church to be absolute, this principle is now modified. The Catholic partner has to do this "as far as possible", and the partner from another Church should know about this obligation as pronounced by the Catholic Church. But it seems now to be clear that a Catholic, generally speaking, is not obliged to renounce the basic right to marry if he or she cannot effectively bring about the baptism and upbringing of the children in the Catholic Church.

One reflection seems to be pertinent: a mixed marriage can be a way of salvation much more easily than can celibacy inflicted on a person who does not feel a vocation to it. Furthermore, it is better for a child to be born and raised as a holy Anglican, Methodist or Presbyterian than not to be born. The new legislation continues to discourage mixed marriages, but there is a greater awareness that sometimes a mixed marriage can be the best marriage possible for the particular partners. While the document says that mixed marriages generally do not serve the cause of Christian unity, it adds, "except in some cases". But if the Catholic and Protestant pastors observe the urgent invitation to unite in caring for people in mixed marriages, in a spirit of openness, then these hitherto exceptional mixed marriages that actually foster Christian unity can become much more numerous.

Dispensation from the impediment of mixed marriage in the strict sense (between a Catholic and another Christian) is necessary for licit marriage celebration in the Catholic Church but not for its validity. In a mixed marrriage between a Catholic and an unbaptized person, marriage without a dispensation from the impediment is declared invalid.

All persons baptized in the Catholic Church are bound to observe, under pain of invalidity, the canonical form of marriage (before a priest who has the faculty to assist, and two witnesses). This is a very easy criterion for marriage tribunals. However, the question must be raised whether this legislation is not still too reminiscent of the "Church of the empire", a Church of statistics and control.

The Catholic Church becomes truly the mother of the baptized only by evangelizing the baptized. It seems to me, therefore, that only those should be counted as Catholics who are not only baptized in the Church but also evangelized in the Church and adhering to her in faith. The important difference in mixed marriages is not so much ritual baptism in a certain Church, or even statistically belonging to a certain part of Christianity, but the quality of faith in Christ and the firmness of commitment to the Church as willed by Christ.

It should be added, however, that canonically invalid marriages can now easily be convalidated by *sanatio in radice,* whereby the marriage now being registered in the book of the Church is considered as juridically valid from the very beginning. This modality of dispensation from canonical form can be granted whenever the couple continues to live the marriage covenant.

In its document on "Pastoral Cooperation of the Churches in the Service of Christian Unity", the common synod of the dioceses of West Germany made a statement on mixed marriages that beautifully embodies the new ecumenical spirit. It allows the spouses to decide, in common reflection and without anguish, about the baptism and upbringing of the child in one or the other Church, according to the greater chance to guarantee a true faith commitment. And if one of the partners later would like to change his or her decision, for instance because of a new fervour in faith, then the reciprocity of consciences should be guaranteed in a new, respectful reflection.

The education of the children should promote the cause of Christian unity. Therefore it is said, "The children's belonging to a certain Church must include openness to the other Church. This can manifest itself by taking the children occasionally to the worship and communal events of the other confession".[151]

NOTES

1 Paul VI, Address to the Observers, Oct. 17, 1963. quoted by D. Horton, *Toward Undivided Unity*, New York/Notre Dame, 1967, 74.

2 Paul VI, Address to the Observers, Sept. 14, 1964, l.c., 7; cf. Address of Sept. 29, 1965, a beautiful programme of joint search for greater fullness in truth, l.c., 77ff.

3 G. Békés and V. Vajta (eds.), *Unitatis Redintegratio 1964-1974. The Impact of the Decree on Ecumenism*, Rome, 1977; Observations and Reflexions of an International Colloquium on the Ecumenical Developments between 1964 and 1974, 163.

4 A.H. Allchin, "The Nature of the Catholicity: An Anglican Approach", in Békés, l.c., 115.

5 Cf. B. Lambert, *Ecumenism*, New York, 1966, 388.

6 "Bericht eines Kolloquium", in G. Gassmann, P. Lonning, G. Casalis, B. Häring, *Die Zukunft des Okumenismus*, Frankfurt, 1972, 97.

7 *Pastorale Zusammenarbeit der Kirchen im Dienste an der christlichen Einheit*. Ein Beschluss der gemeinsamen Synode der Bistümer der BRD, N. 6: 4.31.

8 *Lumen gentium*, 15; *Unitatis Redintegratio*, 1 b; 4 a; 3 d; cf. H. Mühlen, *Una persona mistica. Eine Person in vielen Personen*, Paderborn, 1964 (the title of the French translation is clearer: *L'Esprit dans l'Eglise*, Paris, 1969); P. Evdokimov, *L'Esprit Saint dans la tradition Orthodox*, Paris, 1969; A. Laminski, *Der Heilige Geist als der Geist Christi und der Gläubigen*, Leipzig, 1969; Ph. Ramillac, *L'Eglise, manifestation de l'Esprit chez Jean Chrysostome*, Beyrouthe, 1970; H. Cazelles, P. Evdokimov, A. Greiner, *Le mystère de l'Esprit Saint*, Tours, 1969.

9 *Unitatis Redintegratio*, 4.

10 *Nostra Aetate*. Nisiotis, in Békés, l.c., 38.

11 Card. Suenens, quoted in *Nat. Cath. Reporter*, June 30, 1978.

12 B. Häring, "Routine oder prophetische Konkretion", in Gassmann and others, l.c., 67-96.

13 K. Rahner, *Foundations of Christianity. An Introduction to the Idea of Christianity*, New York, 1978, 349; cf. W. Dietzfelbinger, *Die Grenzen der Kirche nach römisch-katholischer Lehre*, Göttingen, 1962.

14 Cf. Békés, l.c., 164.

[15] *Lumen gentium*, 14.
[16] Cf. Y. Congar, in Békés, l.c., 72, 96.
[17] *Lumen gentium*, 8b.
[18] *Unitatis Redintegratio*, 4 d; *Dignitatis humanae*, 1 d.
[19] B. Lambert, l.c., 31ff.
[20] l.c., 34.
[21] On the history of the ecumenical movement cf. above all: B. Lambert, *Ecumenism, Theology and History*, New York, 1966 (with abundant bibliography); C.F. Hallencreutz, *Dialogue and Community, Ecumenical Issues in inter-religious Relationships*, Uppsala, 1977; N. Goodall, *Ecumenical Progress: A Decade of Change in the Ecumenical Movement*, 1961-1971, London, 1972. The most complete bibliography on ecumenism is to be found in *The Journal of Ecumenical Studies; The Ecumenical Review* (ed. by the World Council of Churches); *The Ecumenist; Irenikon; Okumenische Rundschau; One in Christ: Una Sancta*.
[22] Cf. P. Lonning, "Von der Bewegung zur Institution? Eine kritische Bilanz der ökumenischen Bewegung", in G. Gassmann and others, *Die Zukunft des Okumenismus*, Frankfurt, 1972, 11-26.
[23] Cf. P.M. Minus, Jr., *The Catholic Rediscovery of Protestantism. History of Roman Catholic Ecumenical Pioneering*, New York/Toronto, 1976. (The book is written by a well-informed Methodist); cf. Y. Congar, *Divided Christendom*, Ann Arbor, 1962 (first published in French: *Chrétiens desunis*, 1937); Id., *Chrétiens en dialogue. Contributions catholiques à l'oecumenisme*, Paris, 1964; O. Cullmann and O. Karrer, *Einheit in Christus*, Zürich-Köln, 1964.
[24] G. Baum, *The Catholic Quest for Christian Unity*, Glenn Rock, N.J., 1965; B. Häring, *The Johannine Council*, New York, 1964; G. Bavaud, *Le décret conciliaire sur l'oecumenisme, l'evolution d'une théologie et d'une mentalité*, Fribourg/Paris, 1966; G. Thils, *L'oecumenisme du deuxième Concile de Vatican*, Paris, 1966.
[25] Cf. Y. Congar, *After Nine Hundred Years. The Background of the Schism Between the Eastern and the Western Churches*, New York, 1959; cf. N. Nisiotis, "Die Promulgation des Okumenismusdekrets: Erwartungen und Ergebnisse", in Békés, l.c., 36-62.
[26] Cf. H. Küng (ed.), *The Future of Ecumenism*, New York, Concilium, vol. 44; O. Cullmann, *Vrai et faux oecumenisme après le Concile*, Neuchâtel, 1971; P. Hebblethwaite, *The Runaway Church: Postconciliar Growth and Decline*, New York, 1975; Card. J. Willebrands, "L'avenir de l'oecumenisme", *Proche Orient Chrét*. 25 (1975, 3-15; W. Visser T'Hooft, *Has the Ecumenical Movement a Future?*, Atlanta, 1976; C.J. Peter, "Ecumenism and Denominational Conversion", *Communio (Intern. Cath. Rev.)* 3 (1976), 188-199; M.E. Marty, "A New Phase in Ecumenical Expression", ibid., 231-243; K. Lehmann, "Where Do We Stand on the Road Toward Church Unity?", ibid., 262-271; H. Fries, *Okumene statt Konfession? Das Ringen der Kirche um die Einheit*, Frankfurt, 1977; H. Mülen, *Morgen wird Einheit sein. Das kommende Konzil aller Christen: Ziel der getrennten Kirchen*, Paderborn, 1977; F. Heyer (ed.), *Konfessionskunde*, Berlin, 1978; R. Boekler (ed.), *Welche Okumene meinen wir? Eine Bilanz der Okumene seit Nairobi*, Frankfurt, 1978.
[27] P.M. Minus, Jr., l.c., 97, 219.
[28] Paul VI, Address to the Observers, Dec. 6, 1965, quoted by D. Horton, l.c., 81.
[29] B. Lambert, l.c., 498.
[30] Y. Congar, *After Nine Hundred Years*, 30.
[31] D. Horton, *Toward an Undivided Church*, New York, 1967, 16; cf. *Dokument 6 der Gesamtsynode der Westdeutschen Diözesen* (On ecumenical cooperation of the Churches for Christian unity), 8.11.
[32] Cf. B. Lambert, l.c., 339ff, 366ff.
[33] D. Horton, l.c., 15.
[34] J.H. Card. Newman, *Apologia pro vita sua* (1864), New York, Image Books, 1956, 371.
[35] K. Rahner, *Foundations*, 350.
[36] l.c., 324; cf. B. Lambert, l.c., 499.

[37] L. Vischer, "Wie weiter?", in Békés/Vajta, l.c., 156.
[38] Vajta, l.c., 23.
[39] Cf. B. Häring, Prospettive e problemi ecumenici della teologia morale, Roma, 1973.
[40] Cf. K. Rahner, Foundations, 335ff, 348; cf. V. Vajta (ed.), The Gospel and the Ambiguities of the Church, Philadelphia, 1974.
[41] Cf. V. Lossky, The Mystical Theology of the Eastern Church, London, 1957, 159.
[42] B. Lambert, l.c., 384.
[43] l.c., 333ff.
[44] l.c., 336.
[45] l.c., 243; cf. K. Rahner, Episcopate and Primacy, New York, 1962.
[46] WA 26, 146ff; cf. E. O'Brien (ed.), Convergence of Traditions. Orthodox, Catholic, Protestant, New York, 1967, 100.
[47] A. Schmeemann, "The Orthodox Tradition", in E. O'Brien (ed.), l.c. 11-38, quote p. 16.
[48] K. Rahner, l.c., 369.
[49] D. Horton, l.c., 54ff.
[50] Y. Congar, in Békés/Vajta, l.c., 93ff.
[51] Y. Congar, l.c., 87.
[52] Cf. R.E. Brown, K.P. Donfreid, J. Reumann (eds.), Der Petrus der Bibel. Eine ökumenische Untersuchung, Stuttgart, 1976 (with an Introduction by E. Hahn and R. Schnackenburg); J.-J. von Almen, La primauté de Pierre et de Paul, Fribourg, 1977.
[53] K. Rahner, l.c., 381.
[54] Mysterium Ecclesiae, AAS 65 (1973), 396-408.
[55] G. Lindbeck, "Problems on the Road to Unity: Infallibility", in Békés/Vajta, l.c., 98-109, quote p. 103. The road to further clarification is well presented by J. Feiner/L. Vischer (eds.), The Common Catechism, New York, 1975, 644-657.
[56] l.c., 105.
[57] l.c., 106.
[58] l.c., 106.
[59] l.c., 109.
[60] Unitatis Redintegratio, 1.
[61] Békés/Vajta, l.c., 9.
[62] G. Gassmann (ed.), Die Zukunft des Ökumenismus, 105.
[63] Paul VI, Address to the Observers, 29 Sept. 1963, quoted by Horton, l.c., 73.
[64] B. Lambert, l.c., 511ff.
[65] Cf. Y. Congar, After Nine Hundred Years, 37ff.
[66] B. Lambert, l.c., 213 (in practice, however, the author draws the same conclusions as we do, in spite of his different vocabulary).
[67] J. Daniélou, in E. O'Brien, l.c., 63.
[68] Y. Congar, l.c., 76.
[69] Cf. G. Weigel, Catholic Theology in Dialogue, New York, 1961, 27.
[70] Y. Congar, l.c., 45ff.
[71] Békés/Vajta, l.c., 9.
[72] l.c., 23.
[73] l.c., 24.
[74] Paul VI, Dec. 6, 1965, quoted by D. Horton, l.c., 81.
[75] Augustine, Epist. 187, 34 PL 38, 845.
[76] Cf. Y. Congar, in Békés/Vajta, l.c., 88ff; E. Theodoron, Glaubensgemeinschaft und Ausdruckvielfalt. Ein Weg zur Einheit, Innsbruck, 1976.
[77] S.Th., II II, q 1, a 6: "perceptio veritatis tendens in ipsam".
[78] Cf. O. Cullmann/O. Karrer (eds.), Toleranz ein ökumenisches Problem, Zürich, 1964.
[79] Dokument 6 der Gesamtsynode: 3.22; cf. 3.23 and 4.13.
[80] l.c., 4.31.
[81] D. Horton, l.c., 49.
[82] B. Lambert, l.c., 422.

83 Y. Congar, *After Nine Hundred Years*, 39ff; Id., "Pluralism et Oecumenisme en recherche théologique", in *Mélange offert au R.P. Dockx, O.P.*, Paris, 1976.
84 A. Schmeemann, l.c., 12.
85 P. Lonning, l.c., 22.
86 G. Gassmann and others, l.c., 100.
87 *Dei Verbum*, 22.
88 *Ad Gentes*, 15, 29, 36, 41; *Gaudium et Spes*, 88, 92.
89 *Optatam Totius*, 16.
90 *Gravissimum Educationis*, 11.
91 Cf. L. Vischer, *Okumenische Skizzen*, Frankfurt, 1972; E. Lange, *Okumenische Utopie. Oder was bewegt die ökumenische Bewegung?*, Stuttgart, 1972; R. Groscuth (ed.), *Wandernde Horizonte auf dem Weg zur Einheit*, Frankfurt, 1974; H. Fries, *Okumene statt Konfessionen? Das Ringen der Kirchen um die Einheit*, Frankfurt, 1977; J.J. Degenhardt, H. Tenhumberg, H. Thimmer (eds.), *Kirchen auf gemeinsamem Weg*, Bielefeld/Kevelaer, 1977.
92 Migne, FG, 36, 436-437.
93 Vajta, in Békés/Vajta, l.c., 35.
94 l.c., 8.
95 Quoted by D. Horton, l.c., 74.
96 Report, in Békés/Vajta, l.c., 164.
97 R. Schütz, *Dynamique du provisoire*, Taizé, 1965, 43 (new German ed.: *Dynamik des Vorläufigen*, Freiburg, 1978); J.-M. Paupert, *Taizé et l'Eglise de demain*, Paris, 1967; L. Hein, *Die Einheit der Kirche*, Stuttgart, 1977.
98 Békés/Vajta, l.c., 20.
99 R. Schütz, *La fête sans fin*, Taizé, 1971, 95.
100 P. de Letter, "Our Unity in Faith", *Theol. Studies* 38 (1977), 537.
101 B. Lambert, l.c., 132.
102 Quoted in D. Horton, l.c., 80.
103 Békés/Vajta, l.c., 166.
104 Vajta, l.c., 27; cf. J.K. Pollard, "Evangelization in an Ecumenical Age", in *Communio* 3 (1976), 200-214.
105 *Ad Gentes*, 15.
106 Cf. D. Hudson and others, *Okumene und Politik*, Stuttgart, 1970; Report: "Die Gegenwart Christi in Kirche und Welt. Gespräche zwischen den Reformierten und dem Römischen Einheintssekretariat", Text in *Una Sancta* 33 (1978), 1-29.
107 Cf. Mgr. R. Coffy, *Eglise, signe de salut au milieu des hommes*, Paris, 1972, 47.
108 Vajta, l.c., 16. Cf. Gassman and others, l.c., 27-66; 84-86; 98-100.
109 Interview with Patriarch Athenagoras, Paris-Match, 27 Dec. 1969, p. 1259. quoted in G. Gassmann and others, l.c., 65ff; as an example of theologians seized by this ecumenical impatience, see K. Rahner, "Die eine Kirche und die vielen Kirchen", in *Schriften zur Theologie*, Zürich, 1975, 531-546; Id., "Ist Kircheneinigung dogmatisch möglich?" l.c., 547-567; P. Brunner, "Reform - Reformation", in *Kerygma und Dogma* 13 (1967), 161.
110 A. Schmeemann, l.c., 27; cf. B. Häring, "Routine oder prophetische Konkretion", in *Zukunft des Okumenismus*, 67-93.
111 G. Lindbeck, l.c., 108.
112 A. Schmeemann, l.c., 31.
113 *Unitatis Redintegratio*, 8.
114 Cf. B. Lambert, l.c., 435.
115 P. Lonning, in *Die Zukunft des Okumenismus*, 23.
116 l.c., 106.
117 P. Minus, Jr., l.c., 246; cf. *Eucharist and Ministry: Lutherans and Catholics in Dialogue*, IV, New York (USA National Committee of the Lutheran World Federation) and Washington D.C. (Bishops' Committee for Ecumenical and Interreligious Affairs), 1970; for further development and reflection see: H. Fries, *Ein Glaube, eine Taufe - getrennt beim Abendmahl*, Graz-Wien-Köln, 1971; W. Pannenberg, "Einheit der Kirche als Glaubenswirklichkeit und als ökumenisches Ziel", in *Una Sancta* 30 (1975), 216-222; L. Swidler

(ed.), *The Eucharist in the Ecumenical Dialogue*, New York, 1976 (this is the most complete information of the development up to 1976); R. Boeckler, "Interkommunion und Einheit", in *Lutherische Monatshefte* 15 (1976), 421-423; Anglican-Catholic, Methodist-Catholic and Lutheran-Catholic Statements on the Eucharist and the Ministry, in Appendix to J. Feiner/L. Vischer, *A Common Catechism*, New York, 1976, 667-681.

118 J. Obronczka, "Die Eucharistie in neueren protestantischen Publikationem", in *Theol. d. Gegenwart* 19 (1976), 199-205.

119 Cf. Y. Congar, in Békés/Vajta, l.c., 89.

120 IV Sent. d. 25 q 1 a 2 ad 4: "sunt in ea (Ecclesia) quantum ad formam Ecclesiae quam servant"; cf. Y. Congar, l.c., 64.

121 *Nostra Aetate;* cf. P.M. van Buren, *The Burden of Freedom: Americans and the God of Israel*, New York, 1976; R.R. Hann, "The Undivided Way; the early Jewish Christians as a Model for Ecumenical Encounter", in *Journal for Ecumenical Studies* 14 (1977), 233-248; D.L. Berry, "Buber's View on Jesus as Brother", l.c., 203-218; M. Bormans, "The Doctrinal Basis Common to Christians and Muslims and Different Areas of Convergence in Action", l.c., 32-50; Z.M. Schachter, "Bases and Boundaries for Jewish, Christian and Muslim Dialogue", l.c., 407-418; M.K. Hellwig, "Bases and Boundaries for Interfaith Dialogue: A Christian View", l.c., 419-432; Z. Ishaq Ansari, "Some Reflexions on Islamic Bases for Dialogue with Jews and Christians", l.c., 433-447.

122 *Nostra Aetate*, 5.

123 ibid, 3.

124 ibid, 4

125 ibid, 2.

126 ibid, 2 and 1.

127 Two great initiatives mark the new cooperation: J. Feiner/L. Vischer (eds.), *The Common Catechism. A Book of Christian Faith*, New York, 1975 (German original title: *Neues Glaubensbuch*, Freiburg, 1973). This ecumenical "Catechism" for critical adults presents the common Christian vision and the still existing divergences. The second enterprise regards moral theology directly: A. Herzt, W. Korff, T. Rendtorff, H. Ringeling (eds.), *Handbuch der christlichen Ethik* (2 volumes), Freiburg and Gütersloh, 1978.

128 A. Schmeemann, l.c., 23.

129 l.c., 24ff.

130 Y. Congar, *After Nine Hundred Years*, 41.

131 *Optatam totius*, 16.

132 Cf. H. Köhler, *Ethik nach den Prinzipien evangelischer Theologie. Um die christliche Ethik in der Welt von heute und morgen*, Salzburg/München, 1975.

133 Cf. F. Boeckle, *Gesetz und Gewissen, Grundfragen theologischer Ethik in ökumenischer Sicht*, Luzern/Stuttgart, 1962².

134 D. Horton, l.c., 59.

135 J.M. Gustafson, *Protestant and Roman Catholic Ethics. Proposals for Rapprochement*, Chicago, 1978, 150.

136 l.c., 152.

137 l.c., 154.

138 l.c., 156.

139 A. Schmeemann, l.c. 34.

140 l.c., 32.

141 l.c., 37.

142 Y.E. Krekshovetsky, "The Holy Spirit and the Icons", in *Diakonia* (Quarterly Devoted to Advancing Orthodox-Catholic Dialogue) 13 (1978), 3-16, quote p. 13; cf. B. Häring, *A Sacramental Spirituality*, New York, 1965; Id., *The Sacraments and your Everyday Life*, Liguori, 1976.

143 A.M. Alchin, in Békés/Vajta, l.c., 114.

144 For a cautious pre-conciliar approach see J. Pfab, *Reversion und Konversion*, Freiburg, 1961; for a post-conciliar vision see B. Häring, "Konversion und Konvertitenseelsorge", in F.X. Arnold, F. Klostermann, K. Rahner, V. Schurr (eds.), *Handbuch der Pastoraltheologie* III, Freiburg, 1968, 510-517.

145 *Lumen gentium*, 14.
146 B. Häring, "Mischehe", *Lexikon für Theol. u. Kirche* (ed. by K. Rahner), Freiburg, 1962, VII, 440-444; cf. J. Halduk, *Mischehe. Eine pastoral-histori-Untersuchung von der apostolischen Zeit bis zum Konzil von Agde* (506), Düren, 1965.
147 Cf. M.L. Barron (ed.), *The Blanding American, Patterns of Intermarriages*, Chicago, 1972.
148 A.M. Kreykamp and others, *Protestant-Catholic Mixed Marriages, Interpreted by Pastors and Priests*, Philadelphia, 1967.
149 Cf. K. Müller and M. Zimmermann (eds.), *Mixed Marriage - mariage mixte: International Bibliography 1964 - June 1974*, Strasbourg, Cerdic, 1974; M. Colacci, *Christian Marriage Today: A Comparison of Roman Catholic and Protestant Views with Special Reference to Mixed Marriages*, Minneapolis, 1965.
150 Paul VI, *Matrimonia Mixta*, official English translation in *The Jurist* 30 (1970), 356-362; cf. B. Häring, "Noch nicht gelöste Probleme in der Mischehe", in *Orientierung* 34 (1970), 132-135. For mixed marriages between Catholics and Orthodox Christians there is a different legislation reflecting the deeper bonds of unity: *Crescens matrimoniorum* AAS (1967), 165-166; cf. "Orthodox-Catholic Statement on the Sanctity of Marriage", of Nov. 4, 1971. Text in *Diakonia* 13 (1968), 89-90.
151 *Pastorale Zusammenarbeit der Kirchen im Dienst an der christlichen Einheit. Ein Beschluss der gemeinsamen Synode der Bistümer in der Bundesrepublik Deutschland*, n. 7.9.

Chapter Seven

Faith in an Age of Unbelief

In the course of the Second Vatican Council, there was a growing consensus that the Council would fail greatly if it did not explicitly address itself to the most shocking problem of our age, post-Christian atheism, which challenges the Church and all believers.

It is my conviction that all of theology, and particularly moral theology, has constantly to be aware of this reality. We cannot treat any relevant problem of moral life without a sharp awareness of the crisis of faith and the existence and seductive powers of modern atheism. But it is also necessary to address this question more systematically in the context of faith and faith-education. A biographical survey indicates that this is the number one theme in today's theology and beyond it.[1]

In moral theology we are particularly interested in the problem of the atheistic lifestyle which is found also among those who profess the Christian faith, a lifestyle lived sometimes with and sometimes without atheistic philosophy. It is not only a matter of the lifestyle of individual persons, but also one that is incarnate in a great part of modern culture.[2] Hence moral theology cannot approach atheism from only an individualistic point of view; it has to be treated in the light of both the personal and the social dimension of all moral life.

The overall theme of this volume is, "Truth will set you free". Therefore, we look especially at what atheism may mean in view of the liberating truth and the bondage of falsehood. We therefore distinguish: (1) the pseudo-believer who explicitly

334

professes faith but has stopped seeking salvation truth in itself, and uses faith expression only for purposes other than God; (2) the pseudo-atheist who is existentially searching for truth and willing to put truth into practice; (3) the "authentic" atheist who consciously and in the reality of his life has made a decision against God.

Although God's existence is of paramount importance, our question is about faith in the true God, a question quite different from faith in God's existence. One can "believe" in God whom he defines as "prime causality" and have no idea or interest in communion with God.

The burning interest that guides us here is beautifully expressed in the Second Vatican Council. "An outstanding cause of human dignity lies in man's call to communion with God. From the very circumstance of his origin, man is already invited to converse with God. For man would not exist were he not created by God's love and constantly preserved by it. And he cannot live fully according to truth unless he freely acknowledges that love and devotes himself to his Creator. Yet many of our contemporaries have never recognized this intimate and vital link with God, or have explicitly rejected it. Thus atheism must be counted among the most serious problems of this age, and is deserving of closer examination".[3]

The truth with which we are concerned is that God is love and in his infinite love he calls us to communion. The affirmative response to this grace and call is what makes a person a believer in the Christian sense. One might acknowledge the existence of God, but as long as he ignores or even rejects the idea of being called to communion with him, he is an areligious person. The very word *religio* expresses a relationship of belonging to God, of being at home in the sphere of the sacred.

Atheism is a challenging "sign of our times". Of itself, it is something negative, a threat, a danger to the believer. But through the interpretation of this phenomenon by prophetic voices, it can become a challenge, an urgent call to be totally converted to the Gospel, to authentic faith.

Realism forces us to give particular attention to the oppressive atheism of Marxism (I) but it would be unrealistic to concentrate on it alone. There are many other forms of atheism besides Marxism, and even in Marxism there is a great diversity. We need a careful phenomenology of atheism, particularly in its relation to Christian faith (II). The hardest examination concerns the "hidden atheist" in ourselves, in the various forms of "organized religion", in moral teaching, and in the lifestyles of so-called believers. So a better definition of the "sin of unbelief" is necessary (III). Our interest is not apologetic. While the prime purpose is our complete conversion to fullness of faith, the important purpose of dialogue with the various forms of atheism must also be considered (IV). Finally, we have to question whether there can be, for atheists and in atheistic systems, an authentic morality and a valuable ethics (V).

I. MILITANT AND POWERFUL ATHEISM

1. *The old atheism and the new situation*

In all cultures and at all times there have been many forms of turning away from God, of practical denial of his presence in life, of turning to false gods. But the choice was normally not between religion and atheism but rather between faith in a living God and the various forms of superstition and idolatry. In his arrogance, man turned away from God and made his own gods, especially by idolizing power, kings and dynasties. Power-seeking nations magnified their military power and their kings as an embodiment of divinity. This kind of power manifested itself in the adoration of male power in a god. Female power found its priestesses and divinities of fertility. The world was filled with deities.

Even the defection from the living God took explicitly religious forms. It had its priests, its priestesses and its cults. In a sacral world in which man had not yet deciphered the natural powers, believers and sinners alike thought themselves surrounded by all kinds of "supernatural" powers. To doubt or deny the existence of a God or gods governing human life was the exception. Indeed, if one uttered such a doubt or denial in a sacral society, he made life almost impossible for himself. Socrates was accused of atheism because he challenged a superficial worship of gods; and Christians were frequently persecuted as if they were atheists, because they refused to adore the oppressive powers that were disguised as religions. However, it seems that already in pre-Christian times, there were some philosophers in Greece who taught a kind of atheism.[4]

Under the reign of Christendom and Islam, denial of the existence of God meant risking one's life. Even among the most liberal representatives of the Renaissance, such a denial of a personal God's existence was an exception. But Renaissance humanism removed God farther away from people's lives. The Enlightenment continued in the same direction, but some of its philosophers taught "deism" about a God who, robot-like, had started the world and left it to go on its own course. Thus each sector of life could claim its own autonomy. One could talk about God without existential involvement. Whether one would accept or deny such a God would change nothing in one's life.

The situation changed radically throughout the nineteenth century. Philosophy had already prepared the field for the prophets of atheism, Ludwig Feuerbach and Karl Marx. Very soon, atheists occupied key university chairs in Europe, and great masses of the middle class and even more of the proletariat were attracted by the new doctrines.

Since 1917, the date of the Russian revolution, organized atheism has become the official doctrine not only of the Communist party but also of the government of the Soviet Union and gradually of many other countries. The mass media of many Marxist countries are in the hands of militant atheists, and youth must undergo atheistic indoctrination as a part of the official educational programmes.

The oppressive atheistic states have far outdone the most intolerant religions and religious state powers of the past thousand years. The result is not a matter only of atheistic doctrine and an exercise of authority in favour of atheism. It is, above all, a moulding of society in such a way that atheism permeates everything, from the style of family life to the socio-economic-political structures of the whole of society. Lenin, then Stalin in Russia, and Mao-Tse-Tung in China inherited the "charism" of the prophets and became infallible interpreters of atheistic Marxist doctrine.

2. The Second Vatican Council and organized atheism

The Second Vatican Council avoided most carefully any position for or against economic and political systems, as such. In spite of some pressure from about three hundred bishops, the Council refused to condemn Communism, as such. It would have been impossible to offer adequate definitions of the various shades of Communism to describe the present state of development. A sweeping condemnation of the whole complex phenomenon of historical Marxism could have frozen the situation and confused it even more. The Council's response is sensitive to further developments in which socialist and communist theories of Marxist inspiration might gradually overcome the intolerance towards believers and eventually the confusion between economic and political systems and atheism.

The text of Vatican II concerning scientific socialism and Marxist atheism takes as its starting point the humanistic concern. "Modern atheism often takes on a systematic expression which, in addition to other arguments against God, stretches the desire for human independence to such a point that it finds difficulties with any kind of dependence on God. Those who profess atheism of this sort maintain that it gives man freedom to be an end unto himself, the sole artisan and creator of his own history. They claim that this freedom cannot be reconciled with the affirmation of a Lord who is the author and purpose of all things, or at least that this freedom makes such an affirmation altogether superfluous. The sense of power which modern technical progress generates in man can give colour to such a doctrine.

"Not to be overlooked among the forms of modern atheism is that which anticipates the liberation of man especially through his economic and social emancipation. This form argues that, by its nature, religion thwarts such liberation by arousing man's hope for a deceptive future life, thereby diverting him from the construction of the earthly city. Consequently, when proponents of this doctrine gain governmental power, they vigorously fight against religion. They promote atheism by using those means of pressure which public power has at its disposal. Such is especially the case in the work of educating the young".[5]

The first part of this conciliar article refers to points of departure which Marxism has in common with several other forms of atheism. It is, above all, the concern for human autonomy, man as the maker of his history, freedom creative in history and society.

The second paragraph is a short synthesis of the Marxist doctrine, but only insofar as atheism is concerned. The doctrine has no place for a theology of redemption and liberation, since Marx's scientific socialism sees the whole of man's history determined by economic processes and relationships, and therefore liberation does not come from above but from below, from a new shaping of the economic relationships and processes. This atheism rejects the idea of redemption for this life and for future life because it wants all human energies to be invested in economic and social emancipation. It believes that the religious outlook, by its very nature, produces an energy crisis to the detriment of the construction of society. The Council deplores particularly the intolerant approach of this form of atheism.

3. *Anti-theism as counterfeit of organized religion*

Karl Marx had no intention of creating a new kind of religion or of imitating religion. Hence, in its origin, Marxism is quite different from the "religion of blood and race" of Hitler and his ideologists. Marxism claims to be purely scientific, a scientific socialism based on the analysis of the economic, social, cultural processes, relationships, and interdependencies. However, dialectical materialism is a philosophy of history that implies a strong faith in teleology (meaningful development of history). It draws its attracting power especially from the hope and promise of a perfect society, quasi-perfect economic structures, relationships and processes that would produce the perfect man: a hope that can in no way be the product of scientific analysis.

There is in Marxism a strong tension between the original humanism of young Karl Marx — his hope for the coming of a perfect society with perfect men — stemming from an earthly messianism inherited from a part of Judaism and Christianity, and on the other hand, his emphasis on the scientific aspect of economic determinism that should produce finally the classless society.

Karl Marx's scientific analysis would never have had such an impact on the working class, and especially on the downtrodden and oppressed, without the messianic prophetic element in his philosophy of history and the promises which he made as if he were a prophet of old. Marx, and a part of Marxism with him, believe in the unity of the human race, and derive from that the obligation to fight for the socialist revolution until all of humankind is united. Following the same "faith", a part of Marxism — especially Soviet Marxism and the International Organization of Communist Parties — believes in the legitimacy of a supreme Communist authority that has to guarantee this unification of humankind in socialism.

Marxism is quasi-religious in the role it gives to the downtrodden for the final liberation. It is the earthly version of the Servant-Messiah, collectively understood. On one side it is vastly different from our Christian understanding of the Servant-Messiah who wins over humanity by his gentleness and his non-violence, while Marxism believes in unavoidable power struggle and hatred. On the other side Marxism believes that the final redemption comes through the oppressed. Karl Marx had a prophetic vein in his denunciation and unmasking of injustice and oppression, and especially of the misuse of religion for the purpose of the oppressor.

Classical Marxism, especially that of Lenin and Stalin, takes on the worst features of organized religion's intolerance in its religion of the state, in its fanatic fight for "orthodoxy" and in its cruel persecution not only of believers in God but also of socialists and Marxists judged as less orthodox. Frequently it has embodied other features of intolerant religions, identifying power with truth, and thus allowing or calling for ruthless abuse of power so as to impose uniformity in thinking and in ways of acting. While religion gradually found reconciliation with science and freedom, Marxism submitted the whole scientific world to its claim of orthodox interpretation of Marxism.

4. Is Marxism wedded to atheism?

The relationship between Marxist Communism and Christianity, indeed with the whole world of religion, depends greatly on how one judges the relation between the economic-social-political goals of Communism on the one hand and atheism on the other.[6] The Second Vatican Council conscientiously abstains from any statement that would preclude a further development in which Marxist Communism might liberate itself from atheism as a part of its doctrine.

There can be no doubt that the Marxist movement was strongly marked by an earthly messianism, the expectation of a kind of paradise on this earth. This strain had appeared time and again in Judaism and even in Christendom, but nobody can say that it is or was the very essence of Judaism or Christianity. While it was a main cause of the rejection of Jesus by a great part of his people, it cannot be regarded as a characteristic note of all of Judaism. Neither the hope for an earthly paradise nor a religious claim to power is essential to Christian faith or to the best of Judaism, but rather a passionate interest in justice and peace.

Today's Christianity strongly affirms, and on the basis of the Bible, that our other-worldly hope does not hinder but rather inspires us to order society in justice and with special attention to all that fosters human freedom. Might not a renewed Christianity help Marxism to overcome its prejudices?

There are Marxist thinkers who are quite aware of the shift in Christianity towards greater emphasis on responsibility, freedom and justice; yet they assert that Christians would do well to enter into dialogue with Marxists only with the realization that Marxists are and will remain atheists. Ernest Moss, a Communist journalist, writes: "Communist opposition to religion is not limited to a fight against political clericalism. There remains the conviction that the materialistic and atheistic character of Marxism-Leninism belongs to its very essence, since it is a scientific and absolutely coherent philosophy".[7] This is the party line not only of Russian Communism. When French Communist philosopher Garaudy asserted the possibility of dissociating atheism from Marxism, he was excommunicated by his party.

Marxism believes in class fight and class hatred as vehicles of all human progress, while we believe in the God of peace and forgiveness.[8] But we remind ourselves that Jesus put before us the paradox that he came to bring us peace and, on the other hand, also to disturb false peace. Perhaps if Christians better understand the role of conflict within the total message of re-conciliation, Marxists might also begin to rethink their one-sided emphasis on conflict.

It seems to me that all efforts to declare atheism as secondary in Karl Marx's own thought are in vain. He had already firmly opted for atheism before he developed his economic and social analysis. He was a wholehearted atheist. But this might not hinder Marxists of this and future generations from critically discerning what is essential for their efforts to build a socialist society fully respecting human dignity and freedom.

Communism cannot avoid looking critically at its past and acknowledging errors of the founding fathers. A critical genera-tion of Communists will not accept a whole "package deal". There are many voices among both Christians and Marxists who speak of a development already underway. Adelmann speaks for many Christians: "I believe that Marxism can be intrinsically revised so as to tolerate theism without ceasing to be a philosophy or a metaphysics, and yet retain its essential insight into human life on this planet. This revision is already occurring, to the chagrin of many world Communists".[9]

Ernst Bloch represents a whole group of unorthodox Marxists who think that faith in an other-worldly God is not essential for Christianity, and that Christianity could take the shape of atheism, or at least give to the exodus story and to liberation an emphasis so great as to build a strong bridge between Chris-tianity and Marxism. In his eyes, Marxism could be reconciled with a Christianity in which faith in an other-worldly God does not diminish but strengthens commitment to the earthly city; and Christians could be reconciled with Marxists who are atheists but not antagonistic to Christians who are equally committed to human freedom and social justice.[10]

While Christians never can abandon faith in the living God, the Lord of history, Creator and Liberator, it would mean tre-mendous progress for peaceful co-existence of Christians and Marxists if Marxists could appreciate the essential dimensions of Christian ethics and, at the same time, renounce militant atheism.

II. PHENOMENOLOGY OF ATHEISM

It would be a great error to be so one-sidedly interested in atheistic Marxism that we overlook the many other forms of atheism. In Marxism, various streams are already flowing together, and this is in interaction with religion as well as with other forms of atheism. And we should not forget that there may be many so-called believers, with strong anti-Communist and anti-Marxist feelings, who are no less a danger or challenge to Christians than Marxism.

In order to accept the many-faceted challenge, we need a careful phenomenology of atheism.[11] The Second Vatican Council was quite aware of the diversity of forms and causes of atheism and of the need for a careful phenomenology.

1. *Atheism in an age of science*

The Vatican Council sees a main cause of modern atheism in a certain methodological or practical reductionism in science. Thoroughly imbued by the empirical methods of science, some "use such a method so to scrutinize the question of God as to make it seem devoid of meaning. Many, unduly transgressing the limits of the positive sciences, contend that everything can be explained by this kind of scientific reasoning alone, or by contrast, they altogether disallow that there is any absolute truth".[12]

The Council Fathers were sharply aware that the reductionism occasioned by a one-sided development of empirical sciences now permeates the whole intellectual atmosphere. "Unlike former days, the denial of God or of religion, or the abandonment of them, are no longer unusual and individual occurrences. For today it is not rare for such decisions to be presented as requirements for scientific progress or for a certain new humanism. In many places these views are voiced not only in the teachings of philosophers, but on every side they influence literature, the arts, the interpretation of the humanities and of history, and civil laws themselves. As a consequence, many people are shaken".[13]

The way of thinking that finds the God idea irrelevant or outside of human experience has its own history. Long before atheism was taught, there was a trend in philosophy, and sometimes even in theology, towards a rationalism that practically eliminated the mystery of God and man. It accepted only what could be conceptualized. Such a rationalism has no place for the richest human experiences and the wealth of history.

Theological objectivism, in common with rationalism, manifested a great distrust about religious experience, and blindness towards holistic experience and thinking. Further, legalism built up so many borderline laws that it caused a loss of synthesis, of the holistic vision without which the God question does not make sense.[14] Where this rationalism, alienated objectivism and legalism went unchallenged, it could lead, in the case of an habitual and unreflective possession of faith, to a weakening of one's grasp of the prime truth that God is always greater than ourselves, our work, and our concepts.[15]

Basically, it was Christianity that enabled occidental man to become the scientific man and to study the chain of causes and effects within the world. It was the right understanding of God's transcendence and of the relative autonomy of the temporal sphere that allowed scientists to assert that the "God hypothesis is not necessary for explaining the world scientifically". This approved "scientific methodological atheism", as some called it, in no way excludes faith in the living God; it only excludes the idea of God as a gap-filler within the scientific fabric.

The danger arose from occidental man's gradual loss of the contemplative dimension of religion. With such a one-sided concern for knowledge of dominion, people gradually lost the sense to look for overall meaning; for scientific endeavour that is totally dedicated to dominion never raises the question of meaning.[16] Thus the one-sided effort of scientific explication, geared to the dominion of the earth, became the tragedy of the West, and through the West, of the whole modern world.

The idea that atheism is a requirement for scientific thinking and that scientific thinking is opposed to faith rests on a number of erroneous positions and presuppositions: (1) the limitation of "scientific" to verifiable, empirical research, with total neglect of philosophy (friendship with wisdom); (2) philosophy itself was sometimes reduced to language analysis and similar tasks without cultivation of a holistic vision or search for the total meaning of life; (3) the narrowly defined "science" allowed itself a grave transgression of its boundaries by drawing conclusions that are possible only by a kind of philosophy, a false philosophy; (4) the frequent unconscious prejudice or kind of "infallibilism" that made people unable even to suggest that science could be biased; (5) by the same kind of reductionism, religious faith was sometimes confused with vague opinion. All this contributed to the event that "methodological atheism" led to a denial of God's existence and to complete neglect of the total meaning of human existence.[17]

Natural science and mathematics became the prototype of "objective truth" in the sense that they could be studied without existential involvement. And through a false conclusion, the question of the ultimate meaning of religion and faith was considered mere subjective opinion. It was not understood that subjective truth, in the sense of a total existential commitment of the searcher and doer of truth, has nothing to do with a subjectivistic destruction of truth.[18]

2. *Affirmation of autonomy against heteronomy*

The Second Vatican Council was humble enough to recognize that some causes of atheism can be attributed to religion, and particularly to the Christian religion. "Believers themselves frequently bear some responsibility for this situation. For, taken as a whole, atheism is not a spontaneous development but stems from a variety of causes, including a critical reaction against religious beliefs and, in some places, against the Christian religion in particular".[19]

Organized religion has done "too little too late" in meeting modern man's emphasis on his own conscience, his own duty to search for truth and truthful solutions of social as well as individual problems. One of atheism's roots lies in an anticlericalism that violently rejected the alliance of organized religion with absolutism. Particularly detrimental was the role of those Popes who claimed supreme political authority, direct power over all spheres of temporal life and exercised a religious leadership in the same style as absolutist kings. The alliance between throne and altar in the Church-state led to abuse of religion for the purpose of stability in the given social and political order, the privileges and power of a minority. Any attack against the gods of the nation, the state, the powerful, was adjudged a subversive action and a sin against God.[20]

The way religious authorities brought God into play, and indeed into an evil game of dominion, frequently led anticlericalists into the counter-confusion of rejecting God because of the political authoritarian style of religious leaders. They saw religion (faith in God, as organized religion presented it) as condemning them to heteronomy, to renunciation of their autonomy in favour of guidance by alien forces that did not respect their own sincere and intelligent conscience.

3.   The freedom of man to be an end unto himself

The modern focus on affirming one's freedom, autonomy and independence goes far beyond anticlericalism. It is a rebellion against authority, especially against the father image, transferred to the image of God. A postulatory atheism stretches "the desire for human independence to such a point that it finds difficulties with any kind of dependence on God. Those who profess atheism of this sort maintain that it gives man freedom to be an end unto himself, the sole artisan and creator of his own history".[21]

One of the loudest exponents of this kind of atheism was Nicolai Hartmann, philosopher of the University of Berlin before and during the time of Hitler.[22] Hartmann was sharply aware of the different spheres of values and the conflict among them. His thesis was that if there were an almighty and all-holy God, man would not be free to choose between the different systems of values and duties; he could not be the independent artisan of his own life in his freely chosen sphere of values. An all-holy God could not put man into conflict in which, by necessity, he becomes guilty of offending against some values and duties while choosing the others.

A most radical proponent of postulatory atheism in the name of human freedom is Jean Paul Sartre. "If God exists, then I must content myself to be an object and not an autonomous free being. I exist alienated from myself and am guided by a kind of computer".[23] His philosophy is conceived in the mentality of natural science and, at the same time, in rebellion against all kinds of knowledge of dominion and control that would reduce the human person to a function within causality.

Although Merleau-Ponty is more realistic than Sartre in the assessment of human freedom, he too considers faith in God as irreconcilable with human freedom. For him it is inconceivable that man could be the subject of human history, the free actor in his life, in society and in history if there were absolute truth and an all-powerful God.[24] It is always man's fear of being treated by religion as an object and not as a subject in plain co-responsibility.

4. *The birth of a new humanism*

Among the signs of the times, the Second Vatican Council sees especially "the birth of a new humanism, one in which man is defined, first of all, by his responsibility towards his brothers and towards history".[25] An ever-increasing number of men and women are realizing that they themselves are the artisans of history and culture.

This humanism could well have been a great opportunity for Christianity which, by divine design, is the religion of the Incarnation, of God's total concern for man's responsibility. However, in reaction to a verticalist supernaturalism, many of today's humanists hold the wrong conviction that faith in man and his history is opposed by religion. In consequence, they think that they must oppose religion for the sake of man.

In 1949, Teilhard de Chardin, in a most candid statement, spoke of "an irresistible growth of atheism — or more exactly, of a mounting and irresistible dechristianization". He deplored the fact that not only the other-world religions of Asia but even the Christian Churches were missing the unique opportunity to strengthen the "upward movement" by "forward movement", and to strengthen faith in God by a more incarnate human faith. "By definition and principle, it is the specific function of the Church to christianize all that is human in man. But what is likely to happen (indeed is happening already) if, at the very moment when an added component begins to arise in a naturally Christian soul, and one so compelling as the awareness of a terrestrial 'ultra-humanity', ecclesiastical authority ignores, disdains and even condemns this new aspiration without seeking to understand it?"[26] By "ultra-humanity", Teilhard understands the vitality of a new humanism corresponding with the new shape of humanity, having a new consciousness of evolution and a new freedom to participate consciously and creatively in the future shape of humanity.

Since the second half of the nineteenth century, there has developed gradually a new form of atheistic humanism. "Christian revelation is no longer rejected out of hand, Christianity is now regarded as an authentic platform insofar as it envisions unity among men and brotherly love. But now the atheistic critic sets out to prove that this platform can only be realized if Christianity itself is eliminated. So long as the quest for universal love is directed by religion, it is doomed to the realm of abstract ideals".[27] More and more people became convinced that Christianity, by its very nature, is doomed to remain an unfulfilled hope. And this conviction grew especially from the condemnation, by the official authorities of the Churches, of all theories of evolution, and stern opposition to new ideas and new models of society. The new humanism did not throw away the Bible but began to read it in direct opposition to the vertical explications.

Ernst Bloch has received such wide attention because he gave to all these tendencies a coherent expression in his book, *Atheism in Christianity*.[28] He finds in the Jewish-Christian Bible and traditions the basic elements of a new humanism, one filled with hope, with faith in the humanity to come, with radical dedication to the exodus and the liberation. But he believes that official Christianity has betrayed the hope in humanity's future, the history of ongoing liberation, and faith in man's solidaric responsibilities. In the God of Christendom he sees the superstructure of all the oppressive authorities radically opposed to the hope of the "kingdom of freedom".[29] What Bloch proposes is an esoteric form of Marxism. For him, "atheism is meaningful only to the extent that it can help liberate man for self-fulfilment and aid him in his own formation... One can therefore understand it as an atheism for the sake of God and his kingdom".[30]

Bloch believes in creative liberty and even in creative fidelity. He believes in the meaning of history that is carried on by the creative dream that keeps the process going, "something still pending in latent hope, thrown into its vanishing point in the perspective of meaning, thrown to the gravitational centre of an as-yet-unrealized At-all which men used to call God; but with atheism as the utopian omega of the fulfilled Movement, the Eschaton of our immanence, the illumination of our incognito, the forward look has replaced the upward look".[31]

Bloch's humanism is a religion of hope and faith in the coming kingdom of freedom, a freedom to be incarnated in the whole of history and society. He is totally opposed to an individualistic bourgeois concept of freedom. His hope is for all creation, for all of humanity, and that gives it the quality of "religion": "Where there is hope there is religion, but where there is religion there is not always hope: not the hope built up from beneath, undisturbed by ideology".[32]

As Bloch sees it, "the prophetic impulse of Marxism and a humanism of hope and liberation from alienation is unquestionably rooted in the originally Christian groundplan for the kingdom of freedom itself".[33] This groundplan demands an ongoing exodus, leaving behind and looking forward. He speaks of a "leap of memory" whereby the clinging to the status quo is left behind and yields to the happy image of the Where-to, the What-for and the At-all to complement its morality.[34] Repeatedly he quotes a word of Karl Marx, "It will then become evident that the world possesses something in a dream of which it needs only to become aware to possess it in truth".[35]

For Bloch, the Bible belongs essentially to the memory of the past that must not be lost because this memory is "a radical, subversive dream which, far from being a haze or opium, stems from a profound wakefulness to the future, to the great dimension of light with which the world is pregnant".[36] The exodus and liberation history cannot be discarded but must be freed from the alienating "upward", freed from a god who would deprive humanity of its freedom and creativity. The religion of hope for a liberated and liberating humanity is "the anticipated presence of the kingdom of Freedom kept alive in the hope of those who walk with the labourers and heavy-laden, the degraded and despised, and available only to those who can stand up on their own feet".[37] Bloch accuses Christianity of having misinterpreted and domesticated the theme of revolt so evident in the Old Testament. He sees in Jesus the counterpart of Caesar. A Christ who disallows conflict with the powers is, for him, the worst of ideologies and misinterpretation of the Bible.[38]

The atheistic emphasis is very strong in Bloch. The non-existence of God must be postulated because, for him, God is nothing else than a power from above, and since this divine "Above" makes men servile, it makes them weak for their task to master history.[39] He sees Christian verticalism as not only an alienation but the very elimination of the horizontal and forward movement.

This atheistic humanism that is so forcefully expressed by Bloch could exercise a great power of attraction and seduction, for it is a reflection of people thoroughly concerned with the space of freedom for men, for all men, for their freedom to give themselves, their history and society a hope-inspiring vision.[40] The prophets of this hope-without-faith, or this faith that is radical hope in man's humanity and future, constantly inculcate that Christian religion, in spite of its beautiful Gospel, stands in its own way, stands in the way of freedom, and therefore must be either radically transformed into atheistic christianity or fade out.

Unfortunately, these enemies of Christianity were helped by those traditionalists who opposed any idea of evolution or of profound social and historical change. The situation was worsened by the general authority crisis and the reaction against authoritarian fathers. Since the name "father" is decisive for our God, our whole tradition could be misunderstood by a fatherless society where the father had become a sort of *boogeyman*. The crisis of religion has also much to do with those parents who have the capacity to give their children many things but are unable to give them love and respect.[41] They treat their children mainly as consumers, and if these parents speak to the children about God, he remains on the consumer level where, indeed, we have no use for "it".

Atheistic humanism is a continuation of the drama within theistic theology that did not find a genuine synthesis between theocentrism and the anthropocentric dimension of our faith.[42]

5. Lack of interest in God

Vatican II probably describes the situation of a large group when it says that "some never get to the point of raising questions about God, since they seem to experience no religious stirrings, nor do they see why they should trouble themselves about religion."[43] The reason for this complete lack of interest can be manifold. One is mentioned by the Council: "Modern civilization itself often complicates the approach to God, not for any essential reason but because it is excessively engrossed in earthly affairs".[44]

In a certain sense, this group seems to be less atheistic, since it does not make any statement about God's existence. But from an existential point of view, they are more god-less than those who are still vitally interested in the god question, although they express their interest by a denial of God's existence. Today's materialism and one-sided success orientation reduce people to the level of consumers and producers. Others simply have never reached that level of human development where the sense of admiration, the sense of mystery arises. Their underdevelopment might be also partially caused by a process of demythologizing in an excessive rationalism that practically teaches a religion without mystery.

The lack of interest in the god question can coincide with a total or almost total neglect of the question of the ultimate meaning of life. It is, as Viktor Frankl expresses it, a "life in an existential vacuum". That it produces manifold noogenic neuroses is a sign that humanness is not yet totally extinguished in these people. From their depths the need arises again and again to ask about life's meaning.

The Second Vatican Council does not seek all the causes and reasons for unbelief in the faults of the individual. On the contrary, it excludes an individualistic approach. It sees life positively in the perspective of covenant morality and negatively in man's shocking solidarity in sinfulness. However, individual accountability is not ignored: "Undeniably, those who wilfully shut out God from their hearts and try to dodge religious questions are not following the dictates of their consciences. Hence they are not free from blame".[45] As we noted earlier, the personal fault might not be directly committed in rejecting the religious question and faith; it can well be that conscience is gradually stifled and eventually becomes blind through a habitual way of acting against it.

6. *Protest against an unworthy image of God*

Vatican II faces the possibility and reality of a pseudo-atheism, one which is not so much a rejection of God as a protest against unworthy images of God. "Believers themselves frequently bear some responsibility for this situation. For, taken as a whole, atheism is not a spontaneous development but stems from a variety of causes including a critical reaction against religious beliefs, and in some places against the Christian religion in particular. Hence believers can have more than a little to do with the birth of atheism. To the extent that they neglect their own training in faith, or teach erroneous doctrine, or are deficient in their religious, moral or social life, they must be said to conceal rather than reveal the authentic face of God and religion".[46]

Some pseudo-atheists are closer to the worldview of the Bible than some Christian teachers. They approach all of human life and religion in a dimension of history and society. If, in the name of Christian religion or any other religion, a natural law doctrine portrays the image of a timeless human nature and thus of a God not present in the real history of mankind, then the reaction can be a denial of that false image of God. The god question has been concealed or blocked.[47] As an illustration, we can revert once more to the doctrine about the exclusion of unbaptized children from communion with God. This writer has met many people whose faith was shaken — at least, faith in a loving God or faith in the Church — by this teaching. Reading the most rigorous textbooks of moral theology, one wonders how different the whole book — and surely its effect — would have been if their authors had always consciously posed the question of what image of God their teaching portrayed.

7. *Atheism as a protest against the evil in the world*

Vatican II says, "Moreover, atheism arises not rarely from a violent protest against the evil in the world".[48] The kind of protest that underlies atheism can be of considerable diversity. It can be a false understanding of the relationships between God and creation, so that God would be directly accountable for all evils in the world, especially those of a moral character. It can be a theoretical inability to understand the almighty and all-holy God against the background of an imperfect creation that produces earthquakes, floods and similar catastrophes. Frequently the difficulties are made worse because there is no differentiation between physical and moral evil.

The prophets most violently protested against the great evils of injustice, war, hatred, mercilessness and so on. The moral evils can cause a breakdown of faith in the God which a specific religion teaches if the representatives of that religion make no realistic protest against sins, and even justify ruthless power and exploitation in the name of God. That Christians so frequently have justified slavery, nationalistic wars, armament, and hatred of other nations is one of the greatest scandals which, for many people, have caused a loss of faith.

Believers and religious bodies give scandal if they try only to explain the evil in the world without making any noticeable effort to remove such great evils as injustice, famine, war and the like. A merely theoretical approach to all this shows that there is no existential opening to the holy God. God does not guide human history without man's own effort to search for meaning and to give meaning. Therefore, we cannot meaningfully discuss the problem of evil, suffering and injustice without contributing our efforts to make the world a better dwelling place, and to shape history in justice and peace.

For some people, the existence of evil and suffering brings a breakdown of faith because theirs was never an adoring faith. God was for them a "necessary thing" for the functioning of their world. As soon as God does not function in this way, there arises an absurd protest. It may be that their faith has to be built upon the ruins of their false beliefs.

8. *Agnosticism and nihilism*

One of the most disheartening phenomena today is widespread agnosticism. Vatican II speaks explicitly on this: "While God is expressly denied by some, others believe that man can assert absolutely nothing about him. Still others use such a method so to scrutinize the question of God as to make it seem devoid of meaning. Many, unduly transgressing the limits of the positive sciences, contend that everything can be explained by this kind of scientific reasoning or, by contrast, they altogether disallow that there is any absolute truth".[49]

A frequent cause of agnosticism is not the progress of science, as such, and not the cultivation of the kind of knowledge that is meant to subdue the earth, but a one-sided education and a one-sided look at reality. "No doubt today's progress in science and technology can foster a certain exclusive emphasis on observable data, and an agnosticism about everything else. For the methods of investigation which these scientists use can be wrongly considered as the supreme rule for discovering the whole truth. By virtue of their methods, however, these scientists cannot penetrate the intimate meaning of things, yet the danger exists that man, confiding too much in modern discoveries, may even think that he is sufficient unto himself and no longer seeks any higher realities".[50]

A widespread form of this agnosticism argues against the God question with linguistic analysis, according to methods developed by Wittgenstein, a method that is not suited to solve the question but to dissolve it.

The agnosticism we are talking about must not be confused with the Socratic "knowing that we do not know", which is part of a fervent search for more truth or else the reverent silence of those who feel that the best response to the highest mysteries is silence, awareness that the mystery is too great to be expressed in human language. Silence can, indeed, be a positive response, at least for a certain time.

An extreme form of agnosticism not only arrogantly asserts that it can say nothing about God but denies practically every deeper meaning of life. Such a position practically leads to or implies nihilism, a position which makes impossible a life in common, because it makes impossible all communication on life's meaning.

The outspoken atheist is probably less common in cultural history than the agnostic, whose position may vary from something almost indistinguishable to one of genuine doubt.[51]

III.   CHALLENGE TO THE "HIDDEN ATHEIST"

The Church can never compromise with any form of atheism. It is her mission to be an effective sign of union with God and of the unity of humankind: two aspects that cannot be separated. For the very sake of human dignity and fellowship, the Church must do whatever she can to help humankind in order to overcome atheism. "She strives to detect in the atheistic mind, the hidden causes for the denial of God. Conscious of how weighty are the questions which atheism raises, and motivated by love for all men, she believes these questions ought to be examined seriously and more profoundly".[52]

The most religious persons and communities are shocked by the widespread phenomenon of atheism, but the more disturbing realization is not how adamantly so many reject the God in whom we believe "but how poorly we who believe present the faith-life and witness to its truth and power".[53] The response given by the Second Vatican Council is that of a humble Church. Thanks to her humility, she can decipher the prevalence of atheism as a challenging sign of the time. God has something very serious to tell us, something very challenging.

1. *The challenge to organized religion*

The fact that in the Second Vatican Council the Church had the courage to submit herself to a painstaking scrutiny of how much her own history has to do with the rise of massive atheism is the great drama of articles 19-21 and, indeed, of the whole pastoral constitution on the Church in the Modern World. This humble courage is a milestone in the history of the Church in our century which, in its relevance, comes close to the declaration on Religious Liberty.[54] It will have its impact on all of the Church's life and on all its theology.

For all the great religions, today's atheism is an interrogatory. As in the western world it is a post-Christian atheism, so in other parts of the world it is a post-Islamic, post-Hinduistic atheism, etc. Not only is it a general critique of the religious person but a critique of the particular religiosity and the particular form of organized religion.[55] Hromadka, a well-known promoter of Christian-Marxist dialogue, echoes one of the most frequent reproaches made to churchmen: "All too frequently Christians enclose the living, active presence of God in history within dogmatic systems and Church institutions. The creative action of the Holy Spirit, of the Spirit of the crucified and risen Lord was suffocated through a routine and conventional piety".[56]

The new countenance of God, reflected by a new Church, a renewed Christianity, is the most direct and most needed response to the problem of atheism. Without the challenge of atheism, the Church would probably never have come to this healing critique. This threat and challenge has helped the Church to make a sharp shift from knowledge of dominion to knowledge of salvation, from power to humble dialogue, from sanctions and imposition to witness within the reciprocity of consciences. "The Church passes from a position of power to one of animation and service".[57]

The Church is learning not only to respond gently to the critique of outsiders but also to educate believers towards discernment, towards a critical spirit. She will not renounce proclaiming the Gospel to all people but she realizes much more clearly that she can be a light to the world only if she trusts in the power of the Gospel and of Gospel-witness. She proclaims the transcendence of God by acknowledging fully the relative autonomy of the temporal sphere, and proclaims his immanence, his presence with us, by her humble service to people.

Much better than in past centuries, the Church now sees that she is not a part of the political game. "Christ, to be sure, gave the Church no proper mission in the political, economic or social order. The purpose which he set before her is a religious one".[58] "The apostles, their successors, and those who assist the successors, have been sent to announce to men Christ, the Saviour of the world. Hence, in the exercise of their apostolate, they must depend on the power of God, who very often reveals the might of the Gospel through the weakness of its witnesses. For those who dedicate themselves to the ministry of God's word should use means and helps proper to the Gospel. In many respects, these differ from supports of the earthly city ... Indeed, she stands ready to renounce the exercise of certain legitimately acquired rights if it becomes clear that their use raises doubts about the sincerity of her witness, or that new conditions of life demand some other arrangement".[59] This is a new language that manifests the Church as a holy penitent.

The fact that atheism reacts particularly against organized religion can be no motive or reason for the believer to abandon the Church institution. Rather, it challenges the believers to contribute in every possible way towards bringing the Church community to greater life. Only the faith community is able to give a convincing witness. "The subject of faith is 'we', not 'I'; it is through the 'we' that the transmission or the tradition in the literal sense of the word is carried on. The word arouses and stimulates man only when it continues to be transmitted, and the purpose of preaching is to be heard by many ... The dialectic of conviction and responsibility must be supported by the more profound dialectic of the ecclesial and the social".[60]

2. Challenge to moral theology

To fulfil its task today, all of theology, but particularly moral theology, has to be constantly aware of the threat and challenge of atheism. Each particular point and the synthesis have to be examined as to whether they are the message of the living God for the people of today. There has to be a full "Yes" to humanism, a radical turn to the subject of truth and of moral action, a new emphasis on the reciprocity of consciences in co-responsibility, a new synthesis between love of God and love of neighbour, in full awareness of historicity and the signs of the times.

No talk of God or his law, or sanctions of a religious nature can ever be used as a means for selfish individuals or collective egotism. Each moral imperative and norm, and the whole of systematization, have to be presented with great concern that there is no conflict between morals and religion. And if we speak on rebellion against God, it must be made clear that it is also rebellion against the dignity and full meaning of human life. We have to realize fully that atheism is not only a conceptual problem; it is a temptation incarnate in life's condition, and can be overcome only through a new incarnational approach.

a) A radical "Yes" to humanism

Vatican II responds to the challenge of atheism by a radical "Yes" to humanism: "According to the almost unanimous opinion of believers and unbelievers alike, all things on earth should be related to man as their centre and crown".[61]

To people marked by the secular era, the God question cannot impose itself unless it assumes all the authentic values of the human person, human history and society in all its dimensions.[62] This is no new doctrine. It is necessary in the light of the Incarnation and the whole history of salvation. Thomas Aquinas best sums up the philosophical reflection and Christian tradition on this point: "In the whole universe, only the intelligent nature is an end in itself and all the others are for its sake".[63]

By nature, man is an adorer, and he is to seek in all things the glory of God; but for St Thomas Aquinas, this theocentrism contains the most emphatic anthropocentrism. "God does not seek his glory for himself but for us".[64] This is the highest expression of God's freedom to love and to make us sharers in his work. The more we believe in creative freedom and creative fidelity as co-workers of God, the more we extol God's glory. The dogma of the Incarnation of the Word of God obliges us to incarnate salvation truth in all of our life, in personal relationships, in the social, cultural and political realm. It must be guaranteed that all the institutions serve the human person in his or her capacity to develop healthy relationships with others, in solidarity and co-responsibility.

Moral theology has to make the greatest possible effort to ensure that Christian life belies the aforementioned thesis of Ernst Bloch, who cannot accept a God because in his eyes "God is nothing else than the Above and because this divine Above keeps man subservient and makes him weak for the task of his life".[65]

b) The turn to the subject

The way Vatican II treats the problem of atheism sets a model for combining concern for objective truth with the most radical turn to the subject, to the person who is the actor. It avoids most carefully the empty label, "atheist". It looks at persons who are more or less concerned for what is good and what is true, and at the person's fundamental option and rectitude of conscience. It follows the example of Christ, the Prophet, who praises the Samaritan who lives the truth of love and shocks the priests who do not live it. The Council does not exclude the possibility that people who consider themselves atheists will be saved because of their good will to do what is right and good, while others who seem to be strictly orthodox will be rejected because they are unloving people.[66]

In the search for truth and goodness, we always have first to confront ourselves with him who is the Truth and all Goodness: with God revealed in Jesus Christ. We must be clear and outspoken about the subject of truth sought for and gradually found by the holy people of God, the believers who "in fidelity to conscience are joined with the rest of men in the search for truth and in the genuine solution to the numerous problems which arise in the life of individuals and from social relationships".[67] When speaking of objective truth, we shall be most careful about whose truth it is. Who has formulated it, and for whom was it formulated? Whose interests are served by formulating it in this or that way? Why does a certain group claim a monopoly in the formulation of truth and in the decision about what is good? What are the motives?

c) A new presentation of the synthesis: love of God and love of neighbour

By a lively synthesis of love of God with the love of neighbour, the Gospel message shows the organic unity of religion and morals. It is God who takes the initiative. By his love and his Spirit, he enables us to love him in return and to join him in his love for all his people. The synthesis of the Gospel has been presented, however, according to cultural background and the roles of the respective societies, with the emphasis on person-to-person relationships and on the love that flows from the human heart.

In an era when we realize that people can change the economic, social, cultural, political and international structures, and thus prevent much suffering and provide people with more favourable conditions for mutual respect, a new way of presenting this synthesis is necessary. We are keenly aware now that men grow "daily more dependent on one another, and the world becomes more unified every day".[68] Both the we-relationships and the they-relationships have new dimensions that must be brought home into the same synthesis of love of God and of neighbour. Today's world leaves no room for an I-Thou island. An individualistic concept of love that does not include a clear vision of social and international justice is, today, alienating. And even more alienating is a religion that concerns itself almost exclusively with the salvation of the individual soul. Indeed it is, above all, alienation from the biblical covenant vision.

However, Hans Küng is wrong when, aiming particularly at Blaise Pascal, he calls quite heroic acts like receiving poor people into one's own home, helping young people in their education, and giving to the poor more than what is superfluous, "socially irrelevant love of neighbour".[69] Love in the "we" relationships is the absolute condition for an effective change of the world through the "they" relationships. Especially Marxist humanism is greatly tempted to expect everything for the sake of humanity to come from structures and development, while ignoring the need of the individual to be honoured, to be loved, and to receive full justice. Even more alienating is it for people with a bourgeois style of life to confine themselves to calling for social upheaval and revolution elsewhere, while using in their own domain more earthly goods for themselves than is necessary. Yet the point Küng is making — that charity today must include a strong commitment for changing the world — is absolutely necessary. In view of the new experiences of history, our responsibility for the future takes on new dimensions.

That we look for life "above" is all right, but attention to the vertical is alienating if we are not at the same time seeking life "ahead". Teilhard de Chardin sees as the source of the modern religious crisis "a conflict of faith between upward and forward".[70] However, Teilhard is very clearsighted. He is convinced that all endeavour to shape the future must fail if it is severed from the source of all love. "With no supreme centre of personalization to radiate love among the human cells, it is a frozen world which in the end must disintegrate entirely in a universe without heart or ultimate purposes".[71] It is equally clear that Christian charity, in order to be effective, needs a sensitizing ingredient of human faith and hope: faithfulness to the earth and its future as a part of our fidelity to the Creator.

d) Conflict or synthesis between morals and religion?

The decision for atheistic humanism is frequently a decision in favour of morality and against religion, insofar as religion appears hostile to basic human values or is unable to bring home all of life in one inclusive vision. A moral theology with so many moral absolutes that contradict the good in its wholeness, and cause conflicts where higher values (or those considered by modern man as higher values) are sacrificed, can be a serious temptation to opt for atheism in order to save those values.

Conscience is the bridge to religion if it is rightly understood as the longing for wholeness, integrity and integration in the reciprocity of consciences. A legalistic teaching that ignores the nature of conscience destroys the bridge to religion. Those who experience wholeness in a sincere conscience and in a total openness to values are best prepared for religious experience. Religion, and particularly Christian faith, is not something for one sector of life. It is the experience of the whole, and dedication to it.

In a healthy milieu, man almost naturally develops a grasp of the whole, although he might be ignorant or might deceive himself about details. However, in today's world people are so surfeited with information about individual phenomena and details that they can lose the grasp of the whole. "In science as well as in the prescientific consciousness, there can be points of departure that lead towards atheism. Insofar as man severs the single phenomenon from the whole, he remains imprisoned in second-to-last questions, and he loses sight of the ultimate and consequently of God, on the slippery road towards atheism".[72] Moral and religious education must therefore be more concerned for the sense of wholeness, for vision of synthesis. Insofar as modern science and a great part of modern culture tend to give primacy to specific sectors of life over total meaning, people become ever less able to see in all events the whole of meaning, the whole of the picture.

In order to bring modern man home from exile and into the nearness of God for which his innermost being yearns, a re-structuring of human consciousness is necessary. The grasp of wholeness in the prescientific vision has to be rediscovered, and special reflection given to the whole of meaning, the ultimate meaning that embraces all of our life. Human liberation, creative liberty and fidelity make a common effort indispensable in this direction.[73] Especially human freedom must be presented in all its dimensions, individual and social, personal and institutional, the freedom to love and to order the conditions of life. Thus people would understand not only that rebellion against God is rebellion against the whole meaning of human life, but also that neglect of wholeness, of the total meaning of freedom implies rebellion against God.[74]

A vision of wholeness and the formation of conscience that allows the deepest experience of wholeness is not possible if our approach is too much on the level of abstractions. "The central question is whether Christianity is in fact doomed to the realm of the abstract and the unhistorical, or whether it is truly meant to transform history (even though it is not equated with this work of transformation)".[75]

Against the superficial consumer-attitude, it must be made clear that God cannot be used as a gap-filler for any human purpose, and that it does not make sense to believe in him only for the private sphere or for any other single sector of life. He is the Lord and giver of all good things, the One who gives meaning to everything. On the other hand, any kind of religion or cult, conceptualization or moral teaching, must be sure that, in all its dimensions, it is always in contact with the basis of human experience.[76]

3. The hidden atheist and the open unbeliever

The Bible frequently speaks of godlessness and unbelief. However, it is not speaking of theoretical atheism but of a life that practically discards God. The impious fool says in his heart, " 'There is no God'; how vile men are; how depraved and loathsome; no one does anything good" (Ps 14:1).

The godless fool of whom the psalmist speaks is one who does not follow God's claims in his life; he does not trust his promises; he scorns God in practice. In this sense, Paul speaks of "the godless wickedness of men. In their wickedness they are stifling the truth. For all that may be known of God by men lies plainly before their eyes; indeed, God himself has disclosed it to them. His invisible attributes, that is to say, his everlasting power and deity, have been visible ever since the world began, to the eye of reason in the things he has made. There is therefore no possible defence of their conduct; knowing God, they have refused to honour him as God or to render him thanks. Hence all their thinking has ended in futility, and their misguided minds are plunged in darkness ⋯ For this reason, God has given them up to the vileness of their own desires" (Rom 1:18-25).

Paul speaks not only about theoretical errors but about the interrelatedness of "stifling the truth" and terrible misconduct. Godlessness is to refuse to honour God as God; to refuse to render him thanks with one's life. The godless do not see fit to acknowledge God in their lives, and as a consequence their minds are plunged in darkness (cf. Rom 1:28).

The heart of Christian faith is God's love for people and his calling them to be a true image of their Creator and Redeemer in their own love. Hence the refusal to love neighbour is tantamount to unbelief. "If anyone does not make provision for his relations, and especially for members of his own household, he has denied the faith and is worse than an unbeliever" (1 Tim 5:8). This truth is presented also in the message about the final judgment. Those who have refused to love their neighbour, especially the needy one, have opted for eternal "godlessness" (cf. Mt 25:31-46).

One who does practically nothing throughout his whole life to promote mutual love, respect and justice, but on the contrary increases indifference, disrespect and hatred among men, travels far from God. He is existentially opting against God, and will stay in his godlessness as long as he remains imprisoned in his private and collective selfishness. "This kind of atheist-egotist can be found in all worldviews, among non-Christians and Christians. But even more: each man, as long as he practises egotism, moves in these zones of godlessness".[77] But godlessness in its full sense is present only where there is a fundamental option against God and against good.

In saving faith there is a synthesis between rationality and liberty, a blending of heart, mind and will. The unbeliever-at-heart may hide his godlessness under a cloak of religiosity, but he has lost his wholeness, his freedom; he is not enlightened and his reasoning does not lead to wholeness. Even to affirm God's existence while contradicting it by one's whole life is not only incoherent but shows a shocking loss of wholeness and integrity.

Both the negation and affirmation of God's existence, as well as the adherence, or the refusal to adhere, to a religious body are to be judged according to the basic motives. The one who opts for a religious belief because of individual or collective selfish interest is no better than the one who, with the same polluted motives, refuses to adhere to faith. Those who make their choice in deeply rooted egotism, whether for a set of beliefs or for unbelief, will not know God. Only the pure of heart, the blessed ones, will know God. Yet a person who may consider himself an atheist, "when he really knows about unconditional loyalty, absolute truthfulness, unselfish commitment to the good of others and similar basic human attitudes, knows something about God, even if not reflectively".[78]

Both professed unbelievers and people who claim to be unbelievers can dissolve the God-question in abstract conceptualizations; both, in a similar way, can be uncommitted to the good, can be in flight from the living God and his claims on man. Even a total control of orthodox expressions that does not allow the newness of faith to be proclaimed to each generation can be a manifestation of existential godlessness.

For those who speak and think of God only on the level of usefulness, there will be no great change in their life when they find out that God is not "useful" and therefore declare themselves atheists. And the person who clings to religion as long as it is useful is no better than his alternate who simply stops being "a religious consumer".

Where atheism is loudly proclaimed by the mass media and favoured by those in political power, the "hidden atheist" is easily induced to throw away the religious mask and profess his atheism publicly. For others, the new situation is a radical challenge. "A more critical ability to distinguish religion from a magical view of the world, and from the superstitions that still circulate, purifies religion and exacts day by day a more personal and explicit adherence to faith. As a result, many persons are achieving a more vivid sense of God".[79] Others, however, will become even more acquiescent in their indifference, which seems to be the most hardened form of godlessness.

IV. FROM DIALOGUE TO COOPERATION

The Church has entered into an era of dialogue of which the first encyclical of Pope Paul VI, *Ecclesiam suam* and the whole Second Vatican Council are typical. Both Pope Paul in his encyclical, and the Council in the constitution on the Church in the Modern World explicitly include the atheists in their readiness to dialogue.[80] Indeed, dialogue has already begun on the highest level, since the articles on atheism (GS 19-21) are themselves dialogue. The Council carefully listened to the atheists in their various shades, and speaks on atheism in response to what they tell us about their reaction to religion in general and Christianity in particular. The response is neither captious nor condemnatory. Rather, it is a sincere encounter, and even more sincere because the Church has alerted all believers about the possibility of a hidden atheism in themselves, an atheism that might well influence the structures of the Church at large.[81]

1. *The virtue of dialogue*

The fact that political powers of opposite ideologies possess enough weapons to destroy each other and the whole of humanity, forces upon all of them a readiness to dialogue and to work to overcome the dangerous defence mechanisms. It is within this situation that Christians and atheistic humanists must recognize the necessity of entering into a constructive dialogue with each other for the sake of Christian hope and the the humanists' hope.

We can call dialogue a virtue, since it sums up the most basic human virtues. By "dialogue" we understand an encounter characterized by mutual listening and readiness to respond in full freedom and total sincerity, an exchange of communications in which the participants act as partners. A dialogue, if it is to be fruitful, requires a minimum of common values as a point of departure. Its purpose is better mutual knowledge which is possible only if both parties are willing to learn and unlearn, and to enrich each other by their experience and reflection.

a) Discernment

By its own example, Vatican II teaches us discernment. It energetically withstood the pressures of those who wanted a sweeping condemnation of atheism and Marxism, without any distinction. The Council avoids most carefully a simplistic label. While there are, on the one hand, atheists who violently assert that there can be no God, and others who simply have no interest whatever in the God-question, there are, on the other hand, atheists who are seeking for the ever-greater God, and tell us, "If a God exists — and maybe he does exist — he is infinitely greater than the one you have shown us by your formulations and your life".

For the virtue of discernment, it is not enough to offer objective criteria and detailed distinctions. The most important condition is a loving respect for the other. We must be loving persons who accept the others unconditionally, as God accepts us, in order to better understand them and their positions. Moreover, we have to try to understand the atheist not as an isolated person but as a person in community. We look at the various causes, milieux, motives and mentalities involved.

The Church strives to detect in the atheistic mood the hidden causes of the denial of God. Conscious of how weighty the questions are that arise from atheism, and motivated by love for all people, she believes these questions ought to be examined seriously and more profoundly.[82] One of the main causes might well be that Christians and Christian communities frequently have not given the witness of a mature faith.[83]

Just as ecumenical dialogue must distinguish the non-theological causes from the theological ones, so dialogue with atheists must study the total milieu in which atheism arose, including the Church milieu as well as the economic, social and cultural conditions. Only after giving sufficient attention to these factors can we turn to the ideological questions which, on our part, are questions of faith.

We have to discern the various mentalities: our own and that of our partners in dialogue. Do we, for instance, have a more static outlook than our partner? Might we, perhaps, have too great a concern for security and certainties while he might have a more dynamic outlook, a more courageous mentality that appreciates more than we do the risk of life? Having sometimes to deal with atheists who seem arrogant, as if they had nothing more to learn, we might ask ourselves whether we somehow share such a mentality, at least in a partial unreadiness to learn. On both sides there can be a kind of pharisaism, a self-righteous stance of knowing everything.

We have to try to discern the hidden motives behind the atheism of individual persons, and the causes of particular kinds of atheism. But while we must be careful not to accuse individual persons, our partners in dialogue, "of evil motives", we have to examine painstakingly our own motives regarding our faith and everything we are saying and doing.

b) Seeking common ground

One of the secrets of Pope John's popularity was his coherent way of seeking first what unites us before confronting the divisive problems. In dialogue with atheists, we can find some common values among almost all the different types, especially those professing a kind of humanism. The whole constitution on the Church in the Modern World points carefully to this possible common ground. It includes the dignity of each human person, humankind's solidarity, responsibility on all levels, a solidaric hope for the future — although this hope might take quite different forms.

With various types of atheism we can find some common ground in the vision of creative liberty and creative fidelity. For a good part of humanism, the main idea is the coincidence between being and love. If we Christians understand this concern, and understand better our own faith, we can show the atheistic humanists that this identity is even more strongly rooted in our faith. For "God is love"; and since he created man to his image and likeness, we can find our own being and truth only as loving people. If our own faith shapes our life — our private and social life — then we can refute the objection that God is "the Above" that suffocates human initiative.

The Christian truth is that God came down from heaven to be "the son of man", that is, to be "one of us". And we can easily agree with humanists that it is pure alienation and imagination for one to say that he loves God while he is unloving towards his fellowmen and unconcerned for better conditions of life. If atheists show us a prime concern for the emancipation of the oppressed and downtrodden, we, if we are authentic Christians, can easily show them that this is at the very heart of Christian faith.[84] Moreover, if we are faithfully on the wave-length of the prophetism of the Old and New Testament, we can to a great extent agree about the dynamics of the "Forward". How could we, as authentic Christians, not agree with those atheists-humanists asserting that one cannot even dream of realizing his own freedom unless he is concerned for the freedom of all?

Last but not least, if we are sincere, we have some unpleasant common ground with our partners, namely, the atheist in ourselves, hidden in some corner of our thinking and desires, and in quite a few corners of our life. If, in some atheists, we find a lack of vision and wholeness, a departmentalism, while others more strongly emphasize the total meaning of man in history and society, we surely can find common ground on the basis of the Christian ideal as compared with our own shortcomings.

c) Readiness for conversion: humility

The Second Vatican Council notes that the Holy Spirit can call the Church to greater purification even through the hostility of unbelievers. "We include those who oppress the Church and harass her in manifold ways".[85] However, she realizes that not all are enemies. In many atheists there is something more: "For our part, the desire for such dialogue, which can lead to truth through love alone, excludes no one, though an appropriate measure of prudence must undoubtedly be exercised. We include those who cultivate beautiful qualities of the human spirit but do not yet acknowledge the Source of these qualities".[86]

The Church knows how fundamental is the readiness for ongoing conversion which by necessity includes conversion on the social and ecclesial levels. "The remedy which must be applied to atheism, however, is to be sought in a proper presentation of the Church's teaching, as well as in the integral life of the Church and her members. For it is a function of the Church, led by the Holy Spirit, who renews and purifies her ceaselessly, to make God the Father and his incarnate Son present and, in a sense, visible".[87]

Facing a partly intolerant and even fanatic atheism, the Church realizes how thoroughly she has to be purified from these tendencies. Here we see the enormous relevance of the new climate created by the declaration on Religious Liberty.

The Church's readiness to learn and unlearn can and must go so far as to invite the atheists to tell us frankly what irks them and what creates their distrust. In an interesting interview, Pope Paul VI said, "The problem of today consists in the fact that millions of men live without religious faith … The Church must open herself to the world. We must go towards the world in order to meet those who no longer believe and have mistrust of us. We must tell them, 'Look what we are! Tell us if you do not believe and why you nurture distrust' ".[88]

For a fruitful dialogue, Christians must meet with atheists on level ground. We will not teach them from above but we will recognize that we believers, too, have to search for more truth. A frank challenge to atheists may help them, but at the same time we should give them credit, presuming that they, as we, are looking for more truth and expect us to enrich them. The more frankly we admit our shortcomings, the more we can hope that the partners will likewise disarm themselves. A Christian who has a good measure of the virtue of dialogue will not only frankly and humbly acknowledge past and present failings, errors and partial abuse of authority; he will generally urge a more charitable judgment of the stranger while requiring of himself a harsher judgment.[89]

d) Full identity and partial identification

The Christian can conduct a dialogue only if he presents himself fully in his identity as a Christian believer. Otherwise it will never be a dialogue between a Christian and an atheist. The indispensable concern for our identity includes, however, the expression of identification in solidarity. Karl Rahner expresses this beautifully: "This faith must be such that even the unbeliever cannot deny that here a man believes who is like himself, a man of today who does not speak the word 'God' easily or frivolously, who does not assume that he has grasped this mystery, a modest, cool, sceptical man, a man of today like himself who, despite this — no, not despite this but just because of this — believes. Our faith must appear before the so-called unbeliever as fraternal love".[90]

The Christian partner must be one who has suffered in his (or her) quest for God, suffered on behalf of a partial alienation from him. The believer must know about his own latent "No" to God's grace, in order to meet the atheist partner realistically and respectfully, to suffer with his doubts and problems. He must realize his own vulnerability and how much his faith can be threatened by a disordered world unless he is committed to a common search for building a better world.[91] Only Christians who, with all their being, have a deep grasp of the biblical message can enter into a creative and meaningful dialogue with atheists, for only this faith is a genuine synthesis of the depths of human existence and the breadth of human history.[92]

2. Dialogue in view of common action

The Second Vatican Council sees dialogue explicitly in relation with a hoped-for cooperation. "While rejecting atheism, root and branch, the Church sincerely professes that all men, believers and unbelievers alike, ought to work for the rightful betterment of this world in which all alike live. Such an ideal cannot be realized, however, apart from a sincere and prudent dialogue".[93]

Marxism and several other forms of atheistic humanism are action-oriented. They cannot conceive of any meaningful dialogue that wants to remain forever on the theoretical level. If we are authentic Christians it should be easy to prove to our partners that our concept of truth is an even stronger call to action. At the heart of all our knowledge is salvation knowledge. This confronts us with God who is Love and who has created and liberated us to be creative sharers of his love and zeal for justice for all his people. "A more recent Marxism, which is no longer a monolithic block, emphasizes clearly that the Marxist alternative to religion is not properly a materialistic atheism as Christian scholastics have tried to confront and to refute it, but a humanism that is firmly decided to draw total and radical consequences to save the honour of men".[94] Our dialogue can indeed be fruitful if we Christians have fully decided to draw all the consequences from the dogma of the Incarnation and liberation.

V. MORALITY WITHOUT FAITH

Throughout this chapter, time and again we have met the phenomenon that atheists reject God in the name of morality. We have considered it a challenging sign of the times that believers are being interrogated about some parts of their moral doctrines and basic approaches to morality. Legalism and formalism in moral theology seem to need sometimes to be sharply interrogated by atheistic ethics.[95] Now we ask ourselves two questions: first, is atheistic morality possible as a matter of fact? Second, can an atheistic ethics give ultimate justification for its values and demands.[96]

1. *Atheism's moral principles and moral conduct*

It cannot be denied that people who declare themselves atheists can have strong moral principles and do frequently manifest admirable moral conduct. In his first encyclical, Pope Paul VI spoke explicitly of unbelievers who manifest noble motives and sentiments and high ideals of solidarity.[97] Atheists often insist on the coherence and sincerity of conscience. Ethical theories that are not put into practice are rejected as being alienating. They know that they would degrade themselves if they did not practise their basic convictions of human dignity, solidarity and freedom.

There are atheists who most emphatically, in word and deed, acknowledge that they cannot truthfully affirm their own dignity and freedom unless they are committed to promote the dignity and freedom of all. On this ground their moral conduct and principles can be far superior to both the principles and the conduct of many South African Calvinists who justify, with religious ideologies, racial segregation, refusal of the most basic civic rights, and all kinds of injustice as, for instance, the payment to black workers of salaries far lower than those paid to whites.

In humanity today there is a growth of moral sensitivity, as in the rejection of slavery, colonialism and racial discrimination, and the affirmation of freedom, freedom of conscience and of religious liberty. This growth is classically expressed by the declaration of the United Nations on basic human rights; but unfortunately, among those who trail behind this growth can be found not only atheists but also people who belong to various religious theistic beliefs.

It is an astonishing fact that sometimes believers can more easily agree and cooperate with atheists on matters of racial and international justice and peace than with members of their own religious group. All this points to the fact that there exists a relative autonomy of an ethics based on shared human experience and reflection.[98]

If we want to speak of atheists' moral principles and conduct in a more realistic way, then we have again to refer to a careful phenomenology of atheism. If we speak of the arrogant atheist who, in radical pride, has made a fundamental option against God, then it is evident that he also has jeopardized knowledge and practice of the good. But immediately we remind ourselves of the so-called believer who has made a fundamental option against the good and, as a consequence, has also darkened his knowledge of God. We need not discuss the moral principles and conduct of those who are totally indifferent to the God-question if they are equally indifferent about the ultimate meaning and value of life. But we have to think about the broad grey area of people who are non-believers because they have not yet reached the necessary level of identity and maturity. As a result, their moral life and their conduct lack coherence, possibly even more than that of believers who, because of the same lack of maturity and identity, have not yet consolidated the fundamental option. In both categories we can find partial knowledge and realization of moral values while a more or less chaotic scale of values can be evident.

We remind ourselves, however, that among atheists there can be people who have a consolidated fundamental option for the good in a very clear perception and realization of the dignity of all human persons, a commitment to the freedom of all, and self-transcending solidarity. Are they people without faith?

2. Can atheism offer an ultimate foundation of ethics

It would be grossly unfair to focus one-sidedly on those atheists who have no faith in God because they have no faith whatsoever, and to compare them only with Christians who have faith in God and that faith in human goodness which corresponds to a consolidated fundamental option. Teilhard de Chardin compares a neo-humanistic faith in the world, faith in the future of humanity, a faith entailing sacrifice and a final abandonment of the selfish self on the one hand and, on the other, that of Christians who have faith in the earth because they believe in the Word incarnate, and faith in man because they believe in God who has made man to his image and likeness. Teilhard is convinced that the humanistic faith in the world implies an element of worship, the acceptance of something 'divine'.[99]

The humanist Eric Fromm, who does not deny the existence of God but keeps the throne of God empty for the time being, so as not to see a legalistic rabbi or clergyman there, follows a similar line of thought. He does not speak of "worship" but he uses explicitly the word "faith". According to Fromm, a child develops authentic morality because of a basic faith in the goodness of the parents, faith in love, in justice. In the case that such a faith is shaken, there seems to be, as far as morality is concerned, no great difference whether one loses faith in persons or faith in God; the great loss is always that of faith in life and the possibility to have trust in it.[100] Fromm does not acknowledge Sartre's ideal of freedom as the equivalent of "faith"; rather, in his eyes this freedom coincides with an arbitrary egotism that rejects the most relevant conquest of theistic religion and the best humanistic tradition.[101] But Fromm discovers in men like Karl Marx, Sigmund Freud and Spinoza, in spite of their scepticism, at the same time "a deep faith" that allows for genuine moral concerns.[102]

In Karl Rahner's transcendental theology, freedom is always freedom either for God or against God. Only in a profound realization of one's freedom can there be the existential experience of what is meant by God and by good, and this realization leads either to an explicit or implicit "Yes" or "No" to God. The full actualization of human freedom for the good, as such, is identical with "faith" as such; it is the one and undivided totality of this faith.[103] "In his spiritual existence, man will always fall back on a sacred mystery as the very ground of his being, whether he admits this explicitly or not ... This mystery which has an ineffable and therefore not articulated circumference, lies at the very root of our being ... Where man accepts his existence in full responsibility, where man seeks and expects his final meaning trustingly, there he has already found God by whatever name he may call him, since his ultimate name can forever be spoken in a love that is speechless before his incomprehensibility".[104]

A careful discernment of the various types of atheism has allowed and obliged us to acknowledge not only some principles of atheistic ethics but also to discover a hidden faith in it. However, the acknowledgment of certain values in atheism, whatever kind it may be, is possible for a believer only in the context of a clear refusal of unbelief, just as a critique of certain positions of one's own Church is only possible in the context of a clear fidelity towards her. And truth that sets us free requires frank criticism of the weaknesses of atheistic ethics in our dialogue that aims at cooperation for the good of humanity.

We have to interrogate the atheistic humanism that believes in the one great aim: to bring forth the final kingdom of freedom. In this endeavour, does it truly respect the freedom of each person? The sad fact is that, for all its utopian hope of final freedom, historical Marxism has sacrificed the freedom and dignity, the happiness and life of a great part of the present generation almost everywhere. All too easily — indeed almost inevitably — the heartless pushing of the process of socialization without proper concern for the living persons and for personalization, and the growth of a ruthless technocracy follow the atheistic philosophy that rejects a personal God who is Love.

From its very beginning, atheistic Marxism has leaned towards a certain determination that, together with utopian hopes, can easily lead to a chaotic ethical theory and practice. At the Congress of the PCUA, in 1976, before representatives of almost all the Communist parties of the world, Mr Brezhnev declared: "We hold that everything that favours the progress and triumph of Communism is good and everything that is an obstacle to it is evil".

Not all atheists nor even all Marxist atheists would go

that far; but the historical experience should make Marxists critical about their ideology.

In our dialogue we cannot refrain from pointing to these inherent difficulties. How can freedom and dignity for all people be hoped for if, in the process, wherever this is useful for Communism that very freedom and dignity are denied to so many people? Even the unorthodox Marxist Ernst Bloch takes the question of human guilt and sinfulness all too lightly. If there is not a God who calls for love and justice by his very being, how can one so easily hope that a concrete humanity will, by necessity, gain "the kingdom of freedom"? Surely Bloch's hope of a final kingdom of freedom is a kind of faith. But how can his burning desire for hope, built on utopia, be sufficient to overcome the darkness and evil in humanity? How can we heal the wounds and act as reconcilers on the road to a kingdom of freedom and peace if we do not realize that we ourselves are in need of healing and reconciliation?[105]

No form of atheism can offer any convincing alternative as a solid basis for a hope-filled humanism. But by allowing themselves to be interrogated by atheism, Christians can better integrate the values they have neglected to the point of provoking atheistic protest.

NOTES

[1] The most comprehensive philosophical and theological work on atheism (containing also an enormous international bibliography) is the 4 vol. work *Ateismo contemporaneo,* a cura della facoltà filosofica della Pontificia Università Salesiana di Roma, Torino, 1967-1970 (French edition: G. Girardi et J.F. Six (eds.), *L'atheisme dans la vie et la culture contemporaine,* Paris, 1967-1970); E. Coreth/J.B. Lotz (eds.), *Atheismus kritisch betrachtet,* München/ Freiburg, 1971 (pp. 269-303: German bibliography 1960-1970); J. Reid, *Man Without God. An Introduction to Unbelief,* New York, 1971 (pp. 293-298: bibliography); C. Tresmontant, *Les problèmes de l'atheisme,* Paris, 1972; J. Figl, *Atheismus als theologisches Problem. Modelle der Auseinandersetzung in der Theologie der Gegenwart,* Mainz, 1977; E.F. Harris, *Atheism and Theism,* New Orleans, 1977. The most recent study on atheism is that of H. Küng, *Existiert Gott?,* München, 1978. It is one of the most profound treatises from a philosophical, psychological and theological point of view, and perhaps the best book of Hans Küng.
[2] Cf. R. Caporale/A. Grumelli (eds.), *Religione e ateismo nella società secolarizzata. Aspetti e problemi della cultura della non-credenza,* Bologna, 1972.
[3] *Gaudium et Spes,* 19 a and b.

4 Cf. J. Thrower, *A Short History of Western Atheism*, London, 1971.
5 *Gaudium et Spes*, 20. Regarding the historical development of atheism in Marxism cf. I.M. Bochenski, *Soviet-Russian Dialectic Materialism*, Dordrecht/ Holland, 1963; G.A. Wetter, *Soviet Ideology Today*, New York, 1966; Id., *Dialectic Materialism*, New York, 1968; G. Girardi, *Marxism and Christianity*, New York, 1968; Id., *Credenti e non credenti per un mondo nuovo*, Firenze, 1969; A. Auschieri, "The Christian-Marxist Encounter, in *Cross Current* 27 (1977), 279-297.
6 Cf. P. Ehlen, *Atheismus im dialektischen Materialismus*, München, 1961; R. Garaudy, *From Anathema to Dialogue*, New York, 1966; E. Bloch, *Atheism in Christianity*. *The Religion of the Exodus and of the Kingdom*, New York, 1972; W. Kern, *Atheismus - Marxismus - Christentum*, Innsbruck, 1976; P. Hebblethwaite, *The Christian-Marxist Dialogue. Beginnings, Present Status and Beyond*, New York, 1977; Le marxisme, l'homme et la foi chrétienne. Déclaration du conseil permanent de l'episcopat français, in *La doc. catholique* 74 (1977) 684-696.
7 E. Moss, "Gemeinsame Ziele", in H.J. Girock (ed.), *Partner von morgen? Zum Gespräch zwischen Christentum und marxistichem Atheismus*, Stuttgart, 1968, 25.
8 G. Jacob, "Möglichkeiten der Koexistenz", in H. Girock, l.c., 52ff.
9 F.J. Adelmann, S.J., *From Dialogue to Epilogue, Marxism and Catholicism Tomorrow*, The Hague, 1968; in the same sense: J. Malachowski, "Möglichkeiten der Koexistenz", in Girock, l.c., 44-49; H. Gollwitzer, *Die marxistische Religionskritik und der christliche Glaube*, München, 1967, 79ff. It is well known that J. Hromadka, in spite of bitter experience, always hoped that historical Marxism could free itself from its anti-theistic stand and be helped in this direction through Christians who combine faith in God with human experience in its depth and in its historical breadth; cf. J. Hromadka, "Unüberwindlicher Gegensatz oder Missverständnisse", in Girock, l.c., 9-17.
10 Cf. E. Bloch, *Atheism in Christianity: Religion of the Exodus and of the Kingdom*, New York, 1972; C.H. Ratschow, *Atheismus in Christentum, Eine Auseinandersetzung mit Ernst Bloch*, Gütersloh, 1970; H. Sonnzmans, *Hoffnung ohne Gott, in Konfrontation mit Ernst Bloch*, Freiburg, 1974.
11 Cf. W.A.M. Lujipen, *Phenomenology and Atheism*, Pittsburgh, 1964; Id., *Phenomenology and Humanism*, Pittsburgh, 1966; Id., *Religion and Atheism*, Pittsburgh, 1971; J. Lacroix, *The Meaning of Modern Atheism*, New York, 1965; A. Gibson, *The Faith of the Atheist*, New York, 1968; H.R. Burkle, *The Non-Existence of God, Antitheism from Hegel to Duméry*, New York, 1969; G.M. Gottier, *Horizons de l'atheisme*, Paris, 1969; V.M. Miceli, *The Gods of Atheism*, New Rochelle, 1971; P. Masterson, *Atheism and Alienation: A Study of the Philosophical Sources of Contemporary Atheism*, Notre Dame/Ind. and London, 1971.
12 *Gaudium et Spes*, 19c.
13 Ibid, 7d.
14 Cf. G. Girardi, *Credenti e non credenti*, 98, 106.
15 J. Reid, l.c., 2.
16 Cf. J. Feiner/L. Vischer, *A Common Catechism*, 52ff.
17 J.B. Lotz, "Von der vorwissenschaftlichen Gewissheit im Hinblick auf die Atheismusfrage", in Coreth/Lotz, l.c., 222ff.
18 Cf. l.c., 238; cf. chapter I of this our volume, on "existential phenomenology".
19 *Gaudium et Spes*, 19.
20 G. Girardi, l.c., 158; cf. Feiner/Vischer, l.c., 55ff: French philosophy influential on L. Feuerbach, K. Marx and S. Freud who accused the Church of "clerical deception", using God in an attempt to cling to power.
21 *Gaudium et Spes*, 20a.
22 On Nicolai Hartmann, cf. B. Häring, *Das Heilige und das Gute*, Krailling, 1950.
23 J.P. Sartre, *L'être et le néant* (Being and Nothingness), Paris, 1943.
24 G. Girardi, l.c., 114.
25 *Gaudium et Spes*, 55.

26 T. De Chardin, *The Future of Man*, New York, 1964, 265.
27 J.-Y. Jolif, O.P., "The Real Challenge of Atheistic Humanism" in Ch. Duquoc (ed.), *Opportunities for Belief and Behavior, Concilium* 29, New York, 1967, 6; cf. H. de Lubac, *The Drama of Atheistic Humanism*, New York, 1950 (*Le drame de l'humanisme athée*, Paris, 1945).
28 E. Bloch, *Atheism in Christianity*, New York, 1972; *Herderk.* 31 (1977), 447-448: "Marxistischer Denker der Hoffnung, zum Tod Ernst Blochs".
29 Cf. I. Lepp, *Atheism in Our Time*, New York, 1963 (*Psychoanalyse de l'athéisme modern*, Paris, 1961).
30 J. Moltmann, "Ernst Bloch and Hope Without Faith", in Moltmann, *Experiment Hope*, Philadelphia, 1975, 31.
31 E. Bloch, l.c., 265.
32 l.c., 266.
33 l.c., 269.
34 l.c., 271.
35 l.c., 265; K. Marx, *Letter to Ruge*, 1843.
36 l.c., 264ff.
37 l.c., 265.
38 Cf. C.H. Ratschow, l.c., 75ff.
39 l.c., 105.
40 Cf. W. Kern, "Uber den humanistischen Atheismus", in K. Rahner (ed.), *Ist Gott noch gefragt? Zur Funktionslosigkeit des Gottesglaubens*, Düsseldorf, 1973, 9-55, esp. 40ff.
41 Cf. J. Feiner/L. Vischer, l.c., 66ff.
42 G. Girardi, l.c., 160.
43 *Gaudium et Spes*, 19d.
44 ibid, 19e.
45 ibid, 19f.
46 ibid, 19g.
47 Cf. B. Welte, *Zeit und Geheimnis, Philosophische Abhandlungen zur Sache Gottes in der Zeit der Welt*, Freiburg-Basel-Wien, 1976; B. Häring, "Natural Law Thinking as a Possible Source of Unbelief", in *Morality is for Persons*, New York, 1971, 181-186.
48 *Gaudium et Spes*, 19g.
49 ibid, 19c.
50 ibid, 57e.
51 J. Reich, *Man Without God*, 23.
52 *Gaudium et Spes*, 21.
53 J. Reich, l.c., 236.
54 J. Ratzinger, *Lexikon für Theol. u. Kirche, Ergänzungsband III*, 343.
55 G. Girardi, l.c., 17.
56 J. Hromadka, l.c., 11.
57 G. Girardi, l.c., 60.
58 *Gaudium et Spes*, 42a.
59 ibid, 76.
60 P. Ricoeur, "Science humaine et conditionnement de la foi", in *Dieu aujourd'hui*, Paris, 1965, 142.
61 *Gaudium et Spes*, 12a.
62 ibid, 24c; cf. 25a.
63 S. *contra Gentiles* III, c. 112 in fine.
64 S.Th., II II, q 132, a 1 ad 1.
65 C.H. Ratschow, l.c., 105.
66 cf. *Lumen gentium*, 16.
67 *Gaudium et Spes*, 16.
68 ibid, 24b.
69 H. Küng, *Existiert Gott?*, München, 1978, 106-108.
70 T. de Chardin, l.c., 263.
71 l.c., 265.
72 J.B. Lotz, l.c., 226.
73 l.c., 238-241.

[74] Cf. C.H. Ratschow, l.c., 62.
[75] J.-Y. Jolif, l.c., 12.
[76] W. Kern, l.c.
[77] P. Bolkovac, "Atheist im Vollzug - Atheist durch Interpretation", in E. Koreth/ J.B. Lotz, l.c., 23.
[78] K. Rahner, "What Does Vatican II Teach About Atheism?", in Rahner (ed.), The Pastoral Approach to Atheism, Concilium, vol 23, New York, 1967, 22.
[79] Gaudium et Spes, 7c.
[80] In this section cf. D. Sölle, Atheistisch an Gott glauben. Beiträge zur Theologie, Freiburg, 1968; E. Bieser, Theologie und Atheismus. Anstösse zu einer theologischen Aporetik, München, 1972; L. Scheffczyk, Gott-loser Gottesglaube? Grenzen und überwindung der nicht-theistischen Theologie, Regensburg, 1974; S. Palumbieri, L'ateismo sfida della fede. Una scommessa dell'uomo, Napoli, 1974; H. Petri, "Der neuzeitliche Atheismus als Herausforderung des christlichen Glaubens", Theol. u. Glaube 65 (1975), 336-350; B. Balder, Der glaubenslose Christ, Darmstadt, 1975; G. Geffré, "Die Situation des Unglaubens", Theol. d. Gegenwart 19 (1976), 159-165; A. Paus (ed.), Suche nach Sinn - Suche nach Gott, Graz-Wien-Köln, 1978.
[81] Cf. G. Garaudy, From Anathema to Dialogue, New York, 1966; V. Miano, Ateismo e dialogo nell'insegnamento di Paolo VI, Torino-Leumann, 1970; L. Bogliolo, Ateismo e cristianesimo (Punti scottanti 61), Roma, 1971; R. Mate, El ateismo un problema politico. El fenomeno del ateismo en el contexto teologico y politico del Concilio Vaticano II, Salamanca, 1973; A. Grumelli, Ateismo, secolarizzazione e dialogo, Roma, 1974.
[82] Gaudium et Spes, 21b.
[83] Cf. ibid, 21d.
[84] Cf. E. Bloch, l.c., 353.
[85] Gaudium et Spes, 92.
[86] ibid, 92.
[87] ibid, 21e.
[88] Paul VI, Interview with the editor-in-chief of Corriere della Sera, Oct. 1st, 1965 (cf. H. Morley, The Pope and the Press, Notre Dame/London, 1969, 79).
[89] H.W. Richardson, Foreword to F.J. Adelmann, From Dialogue to Epilogue, XII.
[90] K. Rahner, Im heute glauben, Einsiedeln, 1966², 21.
[91] Cf. K. Lehmann, "Some Ideas from Pastoral Theology on the Proclamation of the Christian Message to Present-day Unbelievers", Concilium 23, New York, 1967, 87ff.
[92] J. Hromadka, l.c., 10.
[93] Gaudium et Spes, 21, towards the end.
[94] J.B. Metz, "Gemeinsame Ziele", in Girock, l.c., 35.
[95] E.B. Ballard, "A Use to Atheism in Ethics", Journal of Religious Health 2 (1962), 151.
[96] Cf. M.D. Chenu, "Morale laïque et foi chrétienne", in Evangile dans le temps, Paris, 1964, 311-330; A.C. MacIntere, The Religious Significance of Atheism, New York, 1969; B. Häring, "Morale e religione in una prospettiva cristiana", in Ateismo contemporaneo, vol. IV, Torino, 1970, 201-220; C.J. van der Poel, The Search for Truth, New York, 1971, 11-38; J. Magno, The Christian, the Atheist and Freedom, New York, 1973; E. Krocker, "Der Sinn der menschlichen Existenz in der maoistischen Lehre", Stimmen der Zeit 195 (1977), 683-693.
[97] Ecclesiam suam, n. 108; cf. Gaudium et Spes, 92e.
[98] G. Girardi, l.c., 168.
[99] T. de Chardin, l.c., 266.
[100] E. Fromm, The Heart of Man. Its Genius for Good and Evil, New York, 1962, 28ff.
[101] l.c., 15.
[102] l.c., 147.
[103] K. Rahner, Ist Gott noch gefragt?, Düsseldorf, 1973, 131ff.
[104] K. Rahner, "In Search for a Short Formula of Christian Faith", Concilium 23, New York, 1967, 76ff.
[105] J.B. Metz, in Girock (ed.), l.c., 41.

Chapter Eight

Hope Assured By Faith

The three theological virtues must not be considered side by side. Wherever they are set apart even partially, there is a striking imperfection. They are fully alive only as one reality with various moments. As we saw earlier, there is a kind of *perichoresis* that turns our thoughts to the mystery of the triune God: a movement from one to the other within a wonderful unity.

Following St Augustine, the general trend of the Middle Ages was to make love the synthesis (*ordo amoris*), love being the integrating centre of which faith and hope are two inseparable moments. Luther integrates all of Christian life in faith, with a strong emphasis on the hope structure of faith itself. But our time, moving so quickly and in so much hope towards a new future, tends to synthesize everything in hope. This is why Ernst Bloch's vision of hope in a secular world found such a strong echo among theologians like Moltmann, Metz and Rahner.

My earlier work, *The Law of Christ*, followed mainly the Augustinian tradition. Without denying that basic approach, the present work, especially this volume, puts *faith* at the centre. However, I trust that the reader has realized that it is always a faith that gives substance to hope, a faith thoroughly structured by hope and, of course, a faith active in love and justice, as faith in God who is Love.

The scope of this chapter is to show that it is impossible to present faith as adherence to the liberating truth without being sharply aware that Christian faith cannot even be thought about without its dynamism of hope. We shall follow generally the line of Hebrews Chapter 11, where the synthesis between faith and hope strikes the reader immediately. "And what is faith? Faith gives substance to our hopes and makes us certain of realities we do not see" (11:1). Teilhard de Chardin chose to translate this thus: "Faith is the element that stabilizes and divinizes our future".[1]

All of God's work is a promise, a revelation that awakens and strengthens hope and sets us on the road. Therefore a synthesis of Christian life in faith is essentially a theology of hope marked by creative liberty and fidelity.[2]

I. HOPE IN THE BIBLE

1. *Hope of God's people*

To understand the message of hope in the Bible, it is not enough to look just for texts mentioning the word "hope". The Old and New Testaments in their entirety are a message of hope, including warnings not to jeopardize this hope.[3] In both Testaments, most of the prayers express, in one way or another, hope and trust as response to God's covenant fidelity, thanksgiving and praise that God's faithfulness will save even sinners and sinful nations if only they turn to God and put their trust in him.

Israel's faith is based on historical experiences. Its hope is directed towards a future whose horizons are constantly broadening, bringing ever new surprises. What unites the past and the future in the present is Yahweh's fidelity. Hope is kept alive in thanksgiving and praise; and this hope-filled faith enables the people, as a whole, to take the risks of history with God, in full awareness that the future depends on their free and faithful response to his wonderful fidelity.

The subject of hope is God's people. During the time of exile, each individual becomes more prominent, while in the past much more emphasis was given to the patriarchs and the charismatic leaders who were the representatives of the people's response to God's fidelity. The people's final decision is whether they put their trust in God as a sign of their faith, or sin against hope by putting their trust in earthly powers or in themselves. Hope of things to come, important as they may be, never has the quality given to hope *in God*, hope of people entrusting themselves to God, honouring his fidelity by unshaken trust and hope. Having experienced oppression and the threat of destruction, Israel's hope in God was for liberation and salvation. Her hope was for the saving presence of the God of the covenant.

In the New Testament, hope in God's presence comes to the fore immediately and completely, since the basic experience is the Emmanuel, "God with us". Christ, who experiences on the cross the anguish of forsakenness, is the guarantor of final salvation by his trust: "Father, into thy hands I entrust my spirit". Already in the Old Testament, stemming from the basic experience of hope in God's saving presence, hope had developed for abiding presence with God in resurrection.

Christ's resurrection gives his disciples the divine assurance of their being always with God, beyond death, by the hoped-for resurrection. This does not, however, diminish the emphasis on God's saving presence as the source and object of hope throughout our earthly life. The breadth and height of hope is expressed by the words, "Christ in you, the hope of a glory to come" (Col 1:27). But all narrow individualism is excluded here. God's glory will manifest itself for all the world. All of creation yearns for a share in that glory which is guaranteed in the glorification of Christ (cf. Rom 8:22ff). "We have been saved, though only in hope" (Rom 8:24). We have experienced and shall further experience God's saving presence and his faithfulness that makes his promises sure.

Hope has no end, and therefore the believer yearns for the final glory of being totally with God. But the emphasis in the Scriptures is still more frequently on hoping *in* him and expecting everything *from* him than on the definition of what we are hoping from him (cf. 1 Tim 4:10). Already now the believers can "exult in the hope of the divine splendour that is to be ours" (Rom 5:2; cf. Rom 8:18; Eph 1:18ff.).

The quality of Christian hope is marked by patience, endurance, fidelity, and readiness for the coming of the Lord. "Let us exult even in our present sufferings, because we know that suffering trains us to endure, and endurance brings proof that we have stood the test, and this proof is the ground of hope. Such a hope is no mockery, because God's love has flooded our inmost heart through the Holy Spirit he has given us" (Rom 5:3-5). The firmness of the believer's hope is in the work of the Holy Spirit.

The features of hope are much clearer in the New Testament than in the Old. Since Christ is our hope, through him the promises also are becoming clearer, especially the promise of the abiding presence of the living Lord through his Spirit, and the assurance that we will forever be with him in glory if we are faithful to the covenant.

There can be no doubt, however, that in the New Testament hope takes on different forms and different emphases according to the underlying models of the various writings and especially of the types of eschatology.[4]

2. Faith in hope and hope in faith as history

Hope makes it quite clear that the Christian religion cannot be understood as an adherence to a system of unchanging formulae or as an ideology. It is the history of God with man, the ongoing experience of God, the Artist and Lord of history calling men to be co-actors and co-artists.

The truth of faith can be grasped only in the perspective of hope. For hope not only indicates the goal of faith but, more importantly, hope is the inner force of faith that makes people walk with God, seek his presence and his glory, and dedicate themselves to the ongoing work and event of his kingdom. Just as revelation and promise are inseparable, so are hope and faith. Dogmas are indications of the truth which is Christ, the One who was, who comes and will come; they are not the truth itself.[5]

Most of the treatises on hope were influenced mainly by Thomas Aquinas' *Summa Theologica*, II, II questions 17-22, which, however, is not all that Thomas had to say on hope. This particular writing is mainly speculative, and what is distinctly Christian — the Paschal Mystery, the lordship of Jesus, the covenant dimension, the historical dynamics — is not brought to the foreground. Hope seems to be a rather private matter concerning the salvation of individuals.

Moltmann stresses the point that a theology of hope can and must bring forth a dehellenization of the whole of theology.[6] The Greek worldview emphasized the unchangeableness, the immutability, the impassibility of God. History was a mere repetition with no surprises and no call for creative liberty. Moltmann instead speaks of "progressive revelation". Through the events of salvation history and prophetic interpretation, the experience and content of Christian hope is enriched.

On the one hand, Moltmann takes distance from that kind of earthly messianism that sees the promises of God as being in continuity with the innerworldly dialectic. His starting point, the death and resurrection of Christ, and his emphasis on prophetic history make such an interpretation absolutely untenable. Christ the Prophet and his prophets radically contradict a world closed on itself. On the other hand, Moltmann criticizes Karl Barth and others for whom the future, including the Parousia, are only unveiling what already is. The history of hope is more: it is always the revelation of God's creative fidelity through the synthesis between new and old (*nova et vetera*). This historical event of the cross and resurrection of Christ brings forth ever new realities, similar to a new creation (*ex nihilo*).

Christ will never be contradicted by history. The Son of God, Christ Jesus, proclaimed by the apostles, "was never a blend of 'Yes' and 'No'. With him it was and is, 'Yes'. It is a 'Yes' pronounced upon God's promises, every one of them. That is why, whenever we give glory to God, it is through Christ Jesus that we say 'amen'" (2 Cor 2:19-20). Christ alone, and no one else, is our hope; he is the faithful one. But he is also the Lord of history who continues his work. Therefore "Christian hope expects from the future of Christ not only the unveiling but also fulfilment".[7] We do not expect from Christ eternal repetition but the fidelity of our Creator and Saviour who has still great surprises in store.

Jesus promises the coming of the Holy Spirit, the Advocate who will make his disciples witnesses and co-actors in history. Through them he will do new things. "In truth, in very truth I tell you, he who has faith in me will do what I am doing;

and he will do greater things still because I am going to the Father" (Jn 14:13-14). The disciples of Christ will be co-actors in the history of God's creative liberty and fidelity, and not people who only draw away the curtain from history when God wants to unveil things already done. The unveiling of the future is revelation in action and action in revelation. One cannot live hope-filled faith without acting in this history, in the ongoing Christ-event until Christ hands everything over to the Father. "When all things are thus subject to him, then the Son himself will also be made subordinate to God who made all things subject to him and God will be all in all" (1 Cor 15:28).

Insight into salvation history is unfolding not only through theological reflection; it is something more. The history of salvation itself, the fulfilling of God's promises, is unfolding a mysterious relationship between God, the Faithful One, and human persons called to be partners.

The promises of God are irrevocable; the one and undivided history of salvation. "Here and now, dear friends, we are God's children; what we shall be has not yet been disclosed, but we know that when it is disclosed, we shall be like him, because we shall see him as he is. Everyone who has this hope before him purifies himself as Christ is pure" (1 Jn 3:2-3). We can hope for the new earth and the new heaven only as co-actors in Christ, and our actions can never be routine; we are always called to honour God creatively and faithfully. That is a requirement of faith itself, for faith is filled with hope.

Karl Rahner speaks on the "freedom of creative hope". Freedom that is faithful to the Lord of history can "never be repetition, never copying of the same models ... Finite freedom, too, is creative freedom in authentic history".[8]

Hope energizes faith and preserves the faithful from timidity. It is the full "Yes" to our call to be active in the history of salvation. The liberating truth of faith can be grasped only in the perspective of hope. Hence only those can grasp it who, by the inner force of faith, manifest their hope creatively and faithfully.

In the light of eschatology, only such a vision of faith and hope, active in love, can respond to the basic vision of the Bible as well as to modern man's full awareness of evolution and history. Teilhard insists that "nothing is comprehensible except through its history".[9] The human spirit is still in the process of evolution, and the most important aspect of this ongoing evolution is the growth of human consciousness as awareness of being called to greater freedom and responsibility in hope. There are two inseparable dimensions, the genesis of humanity in the world and the genesis of Christ in mankind. The great message and event that hope spells out is this: "Life for man, man for Christ, Christ for God".[10]

Heidegger defines human existence (*Dasein*) as "the Open", the radical openness to the future by which the person lives on the horizon of transcendence.[11] If Christians understand and live hope in active orientation and radical openness to the future, then they will surely be light for the world in this time of a new consciousness of evolution and history.

3. *Trustful and faithful response to God's promise*

As Christians we have the most compelling reasons to respond to God's promises by firm and active hope. We have the unique Promise, for Christ is promise fulfilled, the supreme revelation of God's plan of salvation (Col 1:25-27; Eph 1:3-14). We have the divine Presence and the Spirit who, flooding our hearts with love, is promise and beginning fulfilment (cf. Rom 5:5; 8:17ff.). Christ, who is the Way, the Truth and the Life, is both the Promise and our Hope.[12] In him, God reveals himself as the One who is faithful to the covenant forever (Ps 88:14).

Christ is also the Faithful One who, in our name, responds in covenant fidelity to the Father. Therefore we can be trustful and faithful in Christ. The acceptance of revelation in Christ is the commitment of faith and hope to the future, for it is commitment to Christ. Through responsible hope we are on the road with Christ who is the Way. And this hope is a "Yes" to creative detachment from all individual and collective egotism, a "Yes" to all that is entailed in suffering with Christ in his liberating love for all people, in his zeal for justice.

Hope responds to God's promise (*pro-missio*) and the mission it implies.[13] In hope we expect not only the final coming of Christ at the end of time but also his ongoing coming to the world in and through the Church and beyond the visible boundaries of the Church. Hope is a promise and a mission to all humankind, a promise and mission, however, entrusted directly to the believer.

Christian hope has a trinitarian dimension.[14] It is responsible praise of the Father who continues the work that he began in creation and will bring to completion. It praises the Father for the resurrection of Christ as a sign of his might and fidelity, and praises the crucified God in Jesus Christ in whom God "as one of us" (the son of man) bears the burden of humankind and conquers all enemies including death. And it praises the Holy Spirit who enables us to be faithful and creative partners in carrying out God's design.

Christian hope has its dimensions through the mystery of the Incarnation, the cross, the resurrection and Pentecost. It honours Christ the Prophet and the Holy Spirit who has spoken and is speaking through the prophets, always in view of Christ the Prophet. Believers meditate on the charismatic sayings and the words and deeds of the prophets in the light of Pentecost, trusting in the Holy Spirit. Thus the charismatic sayings that predict future events have their influence on the present, and the words of the prophets that interpret the present have their effect upon the future.[15]

Teilhard de Chardin emphasizes, above all, the Incarnation as the great event that should guide all our responsible hopes for the transformation of the world, always of course, in the light of the other mysteries of salvation. "In essence, Christianity is the religion of the Incarnation: God uniting himself with the world which he created, to unify it and in some sort incorporate it in himself. To the worshipper of Christ, this act expresses the history of the universe".[16]

4. *The exodus and the kingdom*

Ernst Bloch is right when he sees basic themes of hope expressed in the Bible, in the themes of exodus and kingdom, although we cannot accept the whole meaning he attributes to them. Salvation history as interpreted in holy Scripture allows no liberation theology without exodus. The acceptance of the saving reign established in Christ requires a radical "No" to the reign of collective sinfulness (cf. Rom 5:17).

Abraham's exodus derives its meaning from the hope enkindled in him by God's promise and mission. He is setting out for an unknown land, for new ventures. Through the promise that he receives in faith and trust, the exodus is a creative covenant that makes him free to walk with God. The promises which Moses received for his people give meaning to the exodus, the leaving-behind, the risk and courage to walk forward with no assurance other than the divine promise and no other passion than freedom and liberation. The exodus from Babylon is the condition for liberation from exile and for the joy of living in the promised land.

The exodus paradigm is already essential in the infancy story of the Gospel. In Christ, the historic exodus is relived in his birth, his extreme poverty, in the flight to Egypt. The forty days in the desert memorialize the forty years the people of the exodus lived in the desert. But the supreme exodus is that of Calvary, the most creative detachment, the absolute rejection of earthly power, of this-worldly messianism.

The lordship of Christ cannot be separated from the fulfilment of the promises about the Servant of God. God has ways of establishing his kingdom. There can be no real understanding of his kingdom and reign without a firm "Yes" to the exodus that has to be lived by Christ's disciples and the whole community of the Church.

The Church cannot proclaim God's kingdom and reign unless it follows Christ the Servant in his exodus. Particularly at this crossroad of history, the Church has to leave behind all the earthly splendour which the Constantinian era imposed on her. As mission Church, she can and must live the exodus in a shift to the Third World, free from the enclosure of the old western culture, free to meet all nations. Only in the freedom which the exodus manifests and gives can she humbly and courageously proclaim Jesus' lordship.

The exodus is much more than mere modernization. It is the freedom for the mission that is entailed in the promise, a mission that has to be fulfilled in faithfulness to the covenant. To refuse the exodus would make the Church a "fossil Church" and theology a "fossil theology". But without faithfulness, adaptation would mean only a "chameleon theology".[17]

The hope for glory with Christ the Risen Lord implies an

irrevocable "Yes" to the following of Christ on the path of the cross, to a living out the exodus and thus becoming fully free to say "Yes" to his kingdom and reign.[18] A Church that clearly understands the relation between exodus and the proclamation of the lordship of God in Jesus Christ will find the courage to face the uncertainty of history.[19] Without any false desire for security, she will be free to decipher the signs of the time. The exodus attitude will by no means be hostile towards tradition but will liberate it from particular traditions. Time-bound traditions will be seen in the light of the exodus and of the universal reign of God. Full recognition of the provisional character of the pilgrim status will preserve the Church from the sin of triumphalism and of immobilism.

The promise of the kingdom, in which all people will be united under the reign of God's love, is the basis for the mission of love to the world that can be carried out patiently and creatively.

Those who live the exodus will experience ever more the freedom that arises from one's total subjection to the absolute demands of the love and power of God, and this freedom gives a new perspective. One grasps more readily the all-embracing quality and demand of the kingdom of God, including its cosmic dimensions. Evolution and history, particularly insofar as it is history of liberty and liberation, are seen in the light of these two paradigms, the exodus and the kingdom. In this light, all of life can proclaim, "Jesus is Lord to the glory of God the Father".

5. Hope and ongoing conversion

Christian hope enables people to live healthily in the tension between the "already" and the "not yet", in the sometimes painful tensions between the spirit and the letter of the law, between freedom and law. A theology of hope has to teach us how to discern the true gateways of exodus to the promised future from the wrong expectations that can only cripple our future.[20] Relying on the guidance of the Spirit, Christian hope will find the synthesis between the two dimensions of the same mission, one being, "Change your heart and your conduct", and the other, "You are salt to the earth". Individual conversion and social involvement cannot be two separate realities; they are two facets of the one vision that arises from divine promise.

The kingdom of hope is not a matter of automatic growth; it is grace, and has to grow in liberty through ongoing conversion. Teilhard de Chardin is frequently criticized as not distinguishing evolution from history and consequently not seeing the main road to liberty. I consider this criticism unjust. While he sees the one great reality of evolution preparing history, he sees it in the light of divine freedom to create and to love; and indeed he sees as the hidden goal and eventual reality of evolution, freedom in the image and likeness of God. "Evolution, by the very mechanism of its synthesis, charges itself with an ever growing measure of freedom".[21] As the insight develops that all of evolution and history have their centre in Christ, who is totally free for God and for man, there arises ever new hope and even the experience that true freedom is not only possible but is "also the essential impulse without which nothing can be done. A passionate longing to grow, to be, is what we need ... Life is ceaseless discovery; life is movement".[22]

Such a noble vision could never reduce growth and hope to the mere individual dimension. Hope is held in common. And because it is held in common, everyone experiences the grace and appeal to be converted and to work together in ongoing renewal for the growth of genuine freedom. On both the individual and social levels, hope demands detachment for the sake of forward movement, acknowledgment that there is a time to tear down in order to build up.[23]

Christian hope as well as the desire to grow in the kingdom of freedom have to face the possibility that freedom may be misused for evil and self-destruction. But the fight against evil is possible only for those who have hope and are able to offer the world greater hope. The hope that is based on divine promise and mission is the only hope that can strengthen us in the never-ending fight against evil in ourselves and in the world around us. It also allows us a constructive dialogue with unbelievers, since the courage to grow and to be converted frees us from illusions and helps us to discover and unmask the hidden atheist in ourselves.

The reader can only wonder how Ernst Bloch can indulge in such a lighthearted yet militant optimism that promises the coming of a perfect humanity in spite of all the evil we experience. It is true that Bloch mentions Auschwitz; yet he does not face the dimensions of evil that come from the abuse of freedom. Are self-made utopias truly sufficient to exorcise the darkness of sinful mankind?[24] All the optimistic efforts based only on changes in economic and social structures have led to failure whenever they refused, as ground and motive, the promises of God and people's readiness for conversion of heart and mind.

6. *Memory and hope*

Today's psychology as well as the theology of hope have rediscovered the importance of a healthy, grateful memory that energizes both the individual and social consciousness. For Teilhard de Chardin, the chief effect of evolution today is the growth of consciousness that, by necessity, includes consciousness of the past from which we have come. Such a consciousness also broadens the horizon of the here-and-now and increases responsible hope for the future. Only by a free "Yes" to this broadening consciousness, that enables and demands increase in liberty and responsibility, can man hold in his hands all his future and his past, and make the choice "between arrogant autonomy and loving excentration".[25] To make the false choice is "nothing less than sin and damnation".

Theologians of hope are giving ever increasing attention to the memorial of the event of creation, the incarnation, death and resurrection of Christ as an absolute condition for well-grounded hope. Moltmann writes, "I was concerned then with the remembrance of Christ in the form of hope, and now I am concerned with hope in the form of remembrance of his death".[26]

Both the remembrance of the past and the remembrance of Christ in the form of hope are celebrated in the here and now. They are genuine remembrances only to the extent that they engender and strengthen the celebration of the here and now through preparedness, readiness, vigilance. For it is through our response to today's situation that we effectively give thanks for the past by moulding the richness which we have received from it in active responsibility for the future.[27] A healthy memory that prompts us to celebrate the Eucharist truthfully disallows any kind of flight into the past. "The story of the past becomes a parable and a sign of God's continuing purpose".[28]

Everyone can look to the future, but only those whose trust is grounded in the divine promises and the memorial of the experienced fidelity of God can march towards the future with that freedom that can decipher God's will in the present in view of his abiding fidelity. The memory of the community of faith is therefore future-oriented. "As memory is prophecy in reverse, hope is memory projected to the future".[29] Just as history is one in its dimensions of past, present and future, so a grateful memory combines inseparably responsible hope and readiness for the call of the here and now. Where they are not united there is decay in each of the dimensions. In this light we see the enormous importance of the celebration of the memorial of the Lord until he comes. "If our life is consistent with right worship, then and only then do we adore God in faith and truth and can we be a sign of hope for the world".[30] This synthesis sets free the greatest and most admirable energies of creative liberty and fidelity.

II. THE NOTES OF CHRISTIAN HOPE

1. *Grace-filled hope versus hope without grace*

If we Christians speak of hope we are speaking also of grace, gracious and undeserved gift, the gift of God's self-commitment to us, the commitment of his creative and redemptive fidelity. We celebrate the feast of hope and celebrate hope as an ongoing feast until we enter into the everlasting feast, for it is a gift of God. "To surrender unreservedly to the grace of God, to believe: all this is radical openness to the future; this radical openness to the future is the Christian's freedom".[31]

The Christian vision is radically opposed by Ernst Bloch.[32] The hope which he proposes is not only hope without faith but, even more, hope without grace. He has a kind of "faith" in humankind's future, in the inborn power of man and matter, without anything above and beyond. For him there is nothing that can qualify as grace. Utopias, self-determination, dream and wishful hope eliminate all kinds of gracious gifts that come from elsewhere. The person in Bloch's philosophy of hope cannot accept anything as a gift, a grace. But in the final analysis, can man be grateful to an abstract humanity and trust in his own utopia for his perfect future?

The Christian knows the source of his hopes: a gracious God. Through humble recognition, joyous praise, unceasing prayer, he keeps himself on the road of Christian hope. He has the courage to acknowledge and accept his frailties and failures as long as he looks to and draws energy from the fountain of his hope, a gracious Creator and Redeemer.

Work as an expression of one's creative liberty, especially when it is performed in the service of humanity, gives one a healthy self-trust, an indispensable element in hope. But if man works only for self-actualization or devotes all his energies to work and places all his trust in it, then his confidence wavers with each failure.

There is joy and expectation in study and reflection, in scientific inquiry, and especially in sharing in the process itself and the results of research. All this can greatly enrich one's life. But all too often the fragmentation characteristic of modern science, and the lag in the implementation of the findings constitute a source of frustration.

Reflection, meditation and dialogue about the great questions of life serve to undergird hope and life itself; for where there is hope there is life. They demand a depth of thought that arises from man's deepest heart; otherwise, reflection and dialogue remain on the theoretical plane that can become an insurmountable obstacle to faith and hope in a living God. Even theological theory can degenerate into futile disputes, as it has often done in the past in the quarrels between theological schools and the separated Churches. Even an interior contemplation that pursues only peace of mind cannot fully open one's heart to the God of hope and faith.

In Christian hope, man turns to his innermost depth while at the same time being at home, "being with". It is there that he entrusts himself to God. This is the very heart of the process of prayer. Hope attains maturity when there is a constant acknowledgment of the truth that everything is a gift. This, then, is hope in adoring love of God and active love of fellowman.

Rooted in God, the source of our life, it leads to a deepening awareness of his gracious presence.

One's capacities, energies and achievements can be a source of affirmation of self and of others, inspiring a natural optimism. But unless all this is acknowledged as undeserved gift of a gracious God, it is forever threatened by misgivings and failings that undermine a self-made hope.

The more a person truthfully reaches out for the courage to be, the more he allows himself to recognize his limitations. This awareness helps to create a healthy insecurity. And there is no other path to abiding hope than this "holy insecurity". It can lead — but only through God's grace — to a life trustfully lived in the presence of God who gives his frail creature the courage to be and to hope in the midst of his human insecurity. One's hope is assured in total reliance on God after one has learned the wholesome way of self-doubt and mistrust of the world, insofar as it is a world ungraced, ungrateful, filled with self-importance.

In prayer, life and hope have their source, whether it be the prayer of praise and thanksgiving, the prayer of sorrow or the prayer of petition and intercession.

Thanksgiving increases in the believer the blessed consciousness that good things are more than material realities; they are gifts from a gracious God, signs of his loving presence and care. But they are also a constant appeal to entrust ourselves to him and to radiate hope by making them signs and means of solidarity among all men, for God.

The prayer of sorrow can give even the greatest sinner the courage to be and to hope, while he experiences the dawning of a creative transformation. The prayer of contrition is genuine if it is filled with trust and praises God, the source of reconciliation and peace.

The prayer of petition reflects hope and increases hope insofar as we place unconditional trust and confidence in God. By faith we are assured that God will grant us whatever we ask in the name of Jesus. Faith illumines us about the gifts God wants to grant his children: increase in wisdom and love, fellowship in the Holy Spirit, and all the harvest of the Spirit. In the prayer of petition, the believer knows that God will grant him more than he is asking for; therefore he is prepared to receive trustfully whatever comes as a surprise. "God is a generous giver who neither refuses nor reproaches anyone. But one must ask in faith, without a doubt in his mind; for the doubter is like a heaving sea ruffled by the wind" (Jas 1:5-6).

The Lord himself tells us clearly in his prayer what we should long and hope for. In the "Our Father" he teaches us the prayer of the new family. There, hope asks first for the courage to live so authentically as children of the one God and Father that we can truthfully say, "Our Father". And by the courage with which we believe that we are named, in Christ, as children of God, we can hope that even on earth we can honour the one Father by promoting brotherhood among all people. This implies a resoluteness to do so patiently, trusting in God's fidelity and knowing full well that final and complete manifestation awaits the end of history.

The Lord's prayer introduces us to the salvific tensions between the "already" and "not yet" that makes of us untiring pilgrims. We are on a journey during which we can neither expect a perfect anticipation of the heavenly dwelling in God's love nor stop to "look lazily at the skies". We know that God's will is done on earth as in heaven by Jesus Christ, and that, if we are open to him in faith, we are, with God's grace, on the way towards the heavenly way of doing his will in a spirit of praise and thanksgiving and in solidaric hope with all of his family.

If we kneel before God in prayer, we realize that it is not possible to pray truthfully if, at the same time, we long selfishly for our own bread alone or if we forget that people crave for more than bread. Prayer extends our hope to all people so that we may learn to gather to share our bread given by the one Father, and to coordinate all our skills and organize all our talents not only to feed those who need it, but also to allow them self-respect and participation in the work and its results. As children of God, we can eat our bread together only while acknowledging the dignity and freedom of all and allowing them a creative co-responsibility in all the dimensions of this-worldly life.

When trustfully praying for our own needs, we realize more and more that sharing our daily bread takes place at the common table of life. Partaking together of the Word of God and the Eucharistic bread, we realize that we can effectively hope for the heavenly banquet only in that solidarity of hope with which our whole life cries, "Our Father".

Prayer that brings us to the source of hope makes us realize also how ardently we should hope for peace and reconciliation. We are unholy liars uttering sacred words when we express hope for the gift of *shalom* without showing serious willingness to be peacemakers. If, as members of God's family, we pray to be freed from the bonds of sin-solidarity, then we come to the existential understanding that we cannot escape the dark powers in our own life and in our environment unless we commit ourselves both to our own purification and to the building up of a divine milieu of peace, goodness, kindness, sincerity. Those who pray in this way need not fear the evil one.

Prayer is hope in action because it is hope at the very source of all creative and redemptive history. Being trustfully at home in God's loving design means being a part of his promises for the world. Thus we become bridges of hope capable of spanning the gap between faith and life. If our hope in prayer is truly Christian, then the whole world attains, with us and through us, the source of its hope, since we pray in the name of Jesus and pray with him for the well-being and salvation of all the world. Prayer that is at the source of hope follows the prophetic tradition that excludes any dichotomy between religion and life, between faith and hope, between love of God and love of neighbour.

Formalism is one of the greatest threats to prayer and hope. Of course some structure is needed for common prayer, but there must always be a space and encouragement for spontaneity and creativity. Prayer is a sign of hope if it allows the Spirit freedom to renew our hearts and, through us, the face of the earth. The prayer of active hope makes men and women sharers of God's sabbath repose that gives light, peace and strength to their creative and liberating presence in the world.

The prayer of the prophetic tradition arises when experiencing solidarity with outcasts, the poor, with those who are discriminated against, with people in trouble. It brings this vital solidarity before God in Jesus Christ, "the hope of the world". The more hope remains an experience through genuine prophetic prayer, the more its messengers can bring a sense of wholeness that combines the expectation of the final coming of the Lord and his coming in daily events. Hope for "the new earth and the new heaven" is thus synthesized in a solidaric commitment to work for the kind of world that invites people to trust in God.

In prayer, grace-filled hope becomes responsible hope.

2. Hope held in common: solidaric hope

Among the motives to "make fast with bonds of peace the unity which the Spirit gives" is above all solidaric hope. "There is one body and one Spirit as there is also one hope held out in God's call to you" (Eph 4:4). Without a radical conversion to solidarity in hope and hope in solidarity, the conditions for creative liberty and fidelity will never be created.

Christian hope is covenant hope. God keeps his covenant which calls to covenant fidelity. The hope of the Church is absolute. She will be saved, and there will always be in her a remnant of saving fidelity. The individual is assured in hope insofar as he belongs to the covenant. The Christian's hope is, in the first place, a hope for all, and thus for each of those who shares effectively this solidaric hope.

An individualistic hope that forgets about the covenant dimension will always be filled with fear and scrupulosity. Our salvation has to be worked out with trust but also with fear, in view of the possibility of falling out of the covenant relationship. We can overcome the fear about our salvation only by trustful prayer marked by covenant hope.[33] Our hope and our prayer are supported by the communion of saints gathered around Christ who is solidarity incarnate. In gratitude, each of us is called to support the common hope.

It is a sign of the times today that humankind has reached a crucial point of social organization and of consciousness that the future of humanity is one and undivided in good and evil. Still greater unification is unavoidable.

Here we have to make two profound decisions. The first is to say "Yes" to this historical movement; the second is to choose the kind of unification for which we hope. In this situation, few are as clear-sighted as Teilhard de Chardin. He sees, in the hope held in common, the only direction that can lead upward: " ... that which, through increasing organization, leads to greater synthesis and unity. Here we part company with the wholehearted individualists, the egoists who seek to grow by excluding or diminishing their fellows, individually, nationally or racially. Life moves towards unification. Our trust can only be realized if it finds expression in greater cohesion and greater human solidarity".[34]

Nothing can hinder the process towards unification. However, for Teilhard de Chardin, the decisive issue here is for freedom. Humanity is at the crossroad where we have to make a purposeful choice either for — God forbid! — compulsory unification or for unanimous solidarity as an expression of genuine freedom and conviction. Coercion can lead only to pseudo-unity. "It materializes instead of spiritualizing".[35] And since man is not an insect he must not be guided by the "blind devotion of a kind of ant-hill".[36]

Teilhard goes so far as to say that unification by free consent, in full justice to the uniqueness of each person, is the only "biologically valid" choice.[37] His conviction is that the whole of evolution, and especially that of life, is yearning for this kind and only this kind of unity among human beings. He sees in the biological processes a presence of the Spirit who renews the face of the earth in this and only in this direction. And the Spirit is honoured finally through human freedom that alone "can work miracles of causing heightened personality to emerge from the forces of collectivity. It alone represents a genuine extension of the psychogenesis that gave us birth. Therefore it is inwardly that we must come together and in entire freedom".[38]

Solidarity is a matter of a common aspiration and unity that is characterized as "heart-to-heart". In this vision it is evident that to love God and to love our neighbour is not something imposed or "merely an act of worship or of compassion superimposed on our other individual preoccupations" For a Christian it is "life itself, life in the integrity of its aspirations, its struggles and conquests that he must embrace in a spirit of togetherness and personalizing unification".[39]

The great betrayal that Christians can commit is an individualistic refusal of the process of unification, as well as yielding to a process of unification marked by collective egoism. The Christian must know that his contribution to the salvation of all, even in its cosmic dimension, is the realm in which his own salvation is realized. "True union, the union of heart and spirit, does not enslave nor does it neutralize the individuals which it brings together. It super-personalizes them".[40]

Early in his life, Teilhard had already grasped clearly what this process of growth, this "super-personalizing" means. It is total dedication to unity that demands the highest form of purity of heart. "One can only be terrified at the crying need for purity the universe suffers from, and almost beside oneself in longing to do something to supply it. What a wonderful object on which to focus our interior efforts! "[41]

3. *Courageous hope: hope and suffering*

Christian hope is the courage to be, to grow, to take risks in the midst of uncertainty and suffering. This is possible by turning our eyes and heart, in faith, to the Paschal Mystery of the death and resurrection of Christ. The courage to hope, to suffer and to take risks in freedom and fidelity has its foundation in God's promises and covenant faithfulness.

Hope does not at all guarantee that we will not have undesirable experiences. On the road of history, hope contains risk and partial disappointment and many surprises. Therefore Moltmann speaks of "experiment hope"; but he sees the whole of history as God's experiment with his creation and Christianity's experiment with history. The great experiment, arising from the absolute freedom of God's love, is allowing the creature to respond and to act in freedom. This entails man's capacity to bring immense suffering into history by his refusal to cooperate with God's faithfulness.

Christians know that God's faithfulness will report a final victory. "Christian hope is learning hope, in that it knows concretely the overwhelming power of the negative and of the judgment over all beings and its possibilities, and yet it still hopes. As 'crucified hope' it can be resurrection hope".[42] It takes great hope, a courageous hope to believe in the God of history and draw from this faith the conclusions. "Without a revolution in the concept of God there will be no revolutionary faith. Without God's liberation from idolatrous images produced by anxiety and hybris, there will be no liberating theology".[43]

An evolutionary-revolutionary hope like that of Julian Huxley[44] need not at all be grounded in atheism. Christians can fully integrate it provided they free themselves from a hellenistic concept of God and return to that of the Bible, the God of history, the God of "experiment hope". This, however, requires a courageous hope and an education to it, a liberation from a false desire for security. Only those Christians who are strongly rooted in the faith and hope community can live this courageous hope that gives meaning to all the shaking experiences of history.

For Teilhard de Chardin, evil in all its frightening forms — injustice, inequality, suffering and death — "ceases theoretically to be outrageous as soon as we see the whole of evolution and history in the light of the final triumph of God's fidelity to his freedom to love, God's victory present in the midst of history through Jesus Christ".[45] But all this remains *practically* outrageous unless Christians find the courage to withstand evil in a responsive and solidaric hope. This is the lesson we learn through faith in "the crucified God".

Disciples of Christ who believe in his cross as the way to the resurrection, and draw the meaning of suffering from it, will be the antithesis and contradiction of a godless and forsaken world. Faith in the cross not only makes sense of their way of accepting suffering; it also deepens their sensitivity to the suffering of the oppressed, the downtrodden, the sick, and leads to a free acceptance of all the forms of suffering that are inherent in a prophetic role against injustice and lovelessness.[46]

Nobody can teach a theology of hope unless he or she is involved in the suffering necessary to withstand evil and to eliminate as far as possible the suffering caused by sin. It is in the school of suffering (Heb 5:8) that the disciples of Christ have constantly to learn obedience to God understood in the perspective of faith active in love and in responsible hope.[47]

Living the morality of the Paschal Mystery, Christians learn a hope that is totally different from superficial optimism. An optimism that tells us "Take it easy; everything will be all right" contradicts our faith in the Paschal Mystery and provides no preparation for confronting life in its realities. When the day comes — as it will — when illusions collapse, then nothing will be left but scorching bitterness. Today's pessimism arises from yesterday's superficial optimism. Those people who look only for success and self-made happiness are lacking in depth and denying Christian hope; consequently they are traumatized when they have to go on living in the midst of setbacks, failures and disillusionments.

Pessimism prepares the way for the most deceitful of all doctrines. Afraid of suffering, the pessimist flees from the battlefield of life and betrays life's deepest meaning. Lacking the courage to *be*, he renounces the fullness of life. He refuses to learn unselfish love in the school of suffering.

For many people it is not so much suffering itself as a seeming senselessness that makes life unbearable. But as Viktor Frankl and many other men and women have shown us by example and word, one can bear up under the most terrible sufferings when one discovers some profound meaning or purpose in them. This presupposes that man yearns for a total grasp of life's significance even though he may come to this knowledge only gradually and painfully. The meaning of suffering in union with the crucified God is love that hopes and a hope that gradually discovers the dimensions of true love. And that love brings forth the readiness to pay the price.

The courage to be and to hope, to find one's true self in the midst of suffering — not only in spite of it but especially by confronting it — manifests the height of human freedom. Freedom comes into its own only when it accepts the mightiest challenges in life and love. Seeking a life on earth in which there will be no suffering or frustration is a coward's way of escaping from freedom's choice and its highest realizations. Creative faithfulness and freedom grow with every courageous "Yes" to the real conditions of life, in full knowledge of the complexities of the present situation, including its many possibilities and its limitations.

One who dares to face one's own need for purification and the cry of the universe for greater purity knows that suffering can offer unique opportunities for freedom. I refer especially to those sufferings that test unselfish love and fidelity in the school of the divine Master. In such a freedom, one can not only endure suffering without hurt but can even see it as a royal path to still greater freedom. Having opted for its saving meaning, one gradually comes to understand the beatitude, "How blessed are the sorrowful; they shall find consolation" (Mt 5:4).

4. *Joyous hope*

Grace-filled hope, hope held in common, hope that accepts the mystery and reality of the cross, discovers increasingly the power of the resurrection. It is basically a joyous hope.[48]

Christian hope enables the believer to live the morality of the beatitudes and therefore to taste and see ever more how good the Lord is. To be "saved in hope" implies that true life, life in Christ, has already begun although there is still need to be tested. The Spirit is already poured out in the hearts of the believers who "press towards the goal to win the prize which is God's call to the life above, in Christ Jesus". Paul can say, "I count everything sheer loss, because all is far outweighed by the gain of knowing Christ Jesus my Lord, for whose sake I did in fact lose everything" (Phil 3:8, 14). This is because "the peace of God, which is beyond our utmost understanding will keep guard over hearts and souls, in Christ Jesus" (Phil 4:7).

Paul's hope is solidaric. "It is now my happiness to suffer *for you*" (Col 1:24). Those who, individually and collectively, have put to death their selfish self will enjoy the harvest of the Spirit: love, joy, peace (Gal 5:22). For the believer, the future has already begun: Christ is his life here, now, and forever. The response can only be a joyous hope.

III. CHRISTIAN HOPE AND RESPONSIBILITY FOR THE WORLD

One of the leitmotifs of Teilhard de Chardin's whole thought is, "The world belongs to those who can offer it the greater hope". We can offer the world the message of our hope, and invite all to cooperation in this hope, only if we also listen to the hopes of the world. The Second Vatican Council insists on this point: "The joys and the hopes, the griefs and anxieties of the men of this age, especially those who are poor or in any way afflicted, those too are the joys and hopes, the griefs and the anxieties of the followers of Christ".[49] It is impossible to profess faith and hope in Christ and, at the same time, be unconcerned for the future of the world. This would betray the hope that Christ brings as the Saviour of the world.

The Church teaches that "a hope related to the end of time does not diminish the importance of intervening duties but rather undergirds the acquittal of them with fresh incentives. By contrast, when the divine substructure and the hope of life eternal are wanting, man's dignity is most grievously lacerated, as current events often attest".[50]

This teaching characterizes the Church's response to modern atheism. Where religions propose a thoroughly other-worldly hope while this world's hopes are either glossed over lightly or judged negatively, we should not wonder that a deep schism occurs between religion and evolution, between Church and enlightenment, between reliance on salvation of souls and, on the other hand, responsibility for the world.[51]

Far more than our anti-religious world, it is Christ himself who calls us to greater fidelity to the legitimate hopes of the world. He who revealed himself as the Resurrection, is also the Word incarnate who brings to completion the work of creation. He preaches the everlasting kingdom of the Father and, as part of this preaching, he also heals the sick, liberates the anguished and oppressed, feeds the hungry and urges all to be converted to brotherhood in justice and peace. As the Apostle Paul teaches, those who, through the Holy Spirit, experience the freedom of the sons and daughters of God, are most sensitive to the cry of the created universe as it waits with eager expectation for God's children to be revealed: "Yet always there was hope, because the universe itself is to be freed from the shackles of mortality and enter upon the liberty and splendour of the children of God" (Rom 8:21).

The legitimate hopes of humankind do not stand side by side with the Christian hope; the hope that Christ brings includes them all. We can speak to the world and join in its legitimate hopes only if we focus on our own identity. As Christians, we must know what Christ has promised and what we may hope for. This allows us to discern among the manifold hopes awakening in our era.

For the sake of the future of hope, Christians have to unmask false hopes as, for instance, the Marxist hope that a future paradise of peace can be built by conflict and hatred. "Alas, it is a forlorn hope ... a kind of death — death of the individual, death of the race, death of the cosmos ... A more realistic and more Christian view shows us Earth evolving towards a state in which man, having come into the full possession of his sphere of action, his strength, his maturity and unity, will at last have become an adult being".[52]

Our hope is not outside the present history, for our trust is in the eternal Love, in God who is present in the midst of human history and guides it to fulfilment. For us Christians, the divine promises are incarnated now in our midst, in all the universe; and we know that we have received the pledges of hope and the mission not only for the Church but for all the world.

We also know that if we live according to the Gospel, we can transform the world radically and fill it with the right hope. Only the witness of Christian hope can unmask the dangerous ideologies about hope. If we are salt for the earth, people will understand that the hope of the future is not just "well-being" but above all, more-being.[53] This can be achieved only if we live fully the synthesis between Upward and Forward, between Above and Ahead.

Teilhard de Chardin pleads for a better vision of the relation between matter and spirit — "the terrestrial synthesis of the Spirit" — which would allow a more incarnated synthesis between love of God, love of neighbour, and our commitment to progress in its entirety.[54] If we are truly faithful to the earth, as we see it in the light of evolution and even more in the light of revelation, we can bring home everything that is good and hope-filled into the one Christian hope. Mere material progress and success, even an education marked by an integrating hope "is but dross except inasmuch as it becomes the most precious and incorruptible of all things by adding itself to an immortal centre of love".[55] Christian education has the privilege of communicating this all-embracing hope.

Although the Christian knows that "the new heaven and the new earth" will come to completion only through divine intervention, we envision it in continuity with all the investment of genuine hope in this history. Thus no one has a right to look hopefully for the promised new heaven and earth except those who have done their best to make our earth a better dwelling place for all humanity.

"Christians have little sympathy for the despairing views of history that see human society as inevitably moving towards decline ... In such an intellectual climate, Christians must affirm, on the strength of the divine promises, that history remains open to human freedom and creativity, open to the unexpected".[56] This Christian hope summons us to action for significant changes in public opinion, in the understanding and creation of culture, in the economic system and the power structures of the wealthy nations. But Christians have no special promises apart from the divine promise and their corresponding commitment to human freedom.

IV. THE SACRAMENTALITY OF HOPE AND THE SACRAMENTS OF HOPE

1. A broader vision of sacraments

God gives his promises not only by words; above all, he gives them by his works. The prophetic word explains what the work itself means and what it makes present to us. Creation is a word-work and a work-word. By its very nature it is a promise, for it bears in itself the active presence of God. Evolution and the history of humankind belong together in God's one design.

Creation and history are hope-filled by the very presence of God in his faithfulness. He who has begun the work will complete it. In the light of holy Scripture, the ancient Church — and up to now the Orthodox Churches — see no gap between natural and supernatural. Creation as the word-work of God, and creation as made in the divine Word and in view of Christ, is truly a great sacrament by the presence of the Creator and Redeemer in it.[57]

This, too, is one of the great concerns of Teilhard de Chardin. Christ, and Teilhard's own deep knowledge of evolution, open his eyes to the cosmic liturgy. He sees the marvellous relation between matter and Spirit. From the very beginning the Spirit of God hovers over the earth (Gen 1:2). Matter, of itself, is not opposed to the Spirit; it became involved only in the frustration that comes from sin. While there is not a separation between nature and supernature, there is a great disparity between creation in God's design and creation distorted by sin. Yet the distortion cannot reach the point where creation and history lose their fundamental goodness, their quality of promise and hope. God's glory, the splendour of his might and love, continues to shine in all his works. Only to the unbeliever is his promising presence hidden.

Christians see the sacramentality of creation and history consciously in the light of Jesus, the promised Messiah, the embodied promise of final fulfilment, "He is the image of the invisible God; his is the primacy over all created things. In him everything in heaven and on earth was created, not only things visible but also the invisible ... the whole universe has been created through him and for him" (Col 1:15-16).

2. Christ the Sacrament of Hope

There is no sacramentality apart from Christ. From the beginning he is the promise to creation, the promise for man. In his coming, he is the fulfilment of all previous promises and, at the same time, the promise of final fulfilment. Christ is more than what creation could dream; yet this dream, this hope and promise, was in creation from the beginning, since it is made in him, the Word of the Father, made in view of his coming.

Christ's first coming in the Incarnation is the summit of prophecy and promise of God's faithfulness, and a summons to a trustful and creative fidelity. He is not only the sacrament of the Father's love by making visible "the full extent of his love" (Jn 13:1), he is also the promise that his disciples — to whom he promises the Holy Spirit — will also be able to make that love visible by loving each other as he has loved them. He has shown the Father to his disciples so that they, by their love, will in turn show him to the world, and the world will know him and the Father by their love. In Jesus Christ, and only in him, all those who bear fruit in love and justice are a sign of hope, the promise of the things to come.

In his whole being and conduct, Jesus is a visible sign, a word-sign of promise and a call to hope. He fulfils the keenest prophecies of the Old Testament as the Servant of Yahweh and of man, and he is acknowledged by the Father as this promise fulfilled, with all the promises in store. "Thou art my Son, my Beloved; on thee my favour rests" (Lk 3:22).

When Jesus meets sinners, he does so in such a way that he awakens new hopes and brings forth a new creation. To the sinner who washes his feet with her tears of sorrow, he gives the assurance that her "great love will prove that her many sins have been forgiven" (Lk 7:47). His last words on the cross, while sealing the covenant with his blood, are human and divine promises that make hope possible for everyone, and thus calling to hope.

3. The sacramentality of the Church

The Second Vatican Council has given priority to the sacramental model of the Church's self-understanding. By her relationship with Christ, the Church is a kind of sacrament of intimate union with God, and of the unity of all mankind; that is, she is a sign and an instrument of such union and unity.[58]

The word of Leo the Great about the continuing presence of Christ's sacramentality has to be applied first of all to the Church, a pilgrim, a sign of love and docility to the Spirit. "What has become visible in our Redeemer has now passed into the sacraments".[59] The Church has the divine promises and, to the extent of her creative fidelity to the word and grace of Christ, she is and will become ever more a great sign of hope.

Therefore, the Church has to re-examine constantly all aspects of her life — the worship, evangelization, institutional structures, administration and the handling of finances — in this one great perspective. Does she reveal Christ, the Sacrament of Hope, to all of humanity in relation to the hopes of humankind? Is she a great sign of hope for those whom the world would write off as "hopeless cases"? Does she herself put all her trust in Christ and thus teach all people to do so? Does she work so courageously and hopefully for the unity of all Christians that the world can hope for peace and unity? The Church as a whole, and each community within the Church, exists "as a symbol of the divine, providential purposes when its being, as just and human, shows forth the divine rule and manifests the divine

Being; and such is the eschatological dimension of the kingdom".[60]

The individual sacraments and the whole of worship in and through the Church have their *sitz-im-leben*, their vitality and whole meaning within the whole life of the Church. As institution, as pilgrim, as servant, as evangelizer, the Church must speak out the same message as that of the sacraments, and the sacramental celebration must speak out the whole life of the Church.

To point to Christ in absolute humility but with great trust: this is the Church's understanding of her unique mission, expressed in the Second Vatican Council. For this she finds her model in Mary who, with all her life, sings the song of Christ the Servant and thus exalts the majesty of the Lord. By turning her eyes to Mary, the Church will understand better her role to be and to become more fully a great sign of hope for the world. Just as Mary, the humble handmaid, the model of the Church, is lifted high while the dragon (symbol of arrogance) is thrown down to the earth, so will the Church be lifted up as a sign of hope by following Jesus, the Servant, with Mary, the handmaid (cf. Rev 12: 1-9).

In its constitution on the Church, the Second Vatican Council presents Mary as a sign of sure hope: "In the bodily and spiritual glory which she possesses in heaven, the Mother of Jesus continues in the present world as the image and first flowering of the Church as she is to be perfected in the world to come. Likewise, Mary shines forth on earth until the day of the Lord shall come (cf. 2 Pet 3: 14) as a sign of sure hope and solace for the pilgrim people of God".[61]

It is the purpose of the Church as a whole, as well as of the sacraments, to form all Christians and Christian communities to be signs of hope for each other and for the world, thus to offer to the world Christ, the greatest hope.

4. The seven privileged signs of hope

After Christ and the Church, the most privileged sign of hope is the human person *in* Christ, created in the image and likeness of God. That person has come to live this truth in a way that his or her whole life shares in the prophetic role of Christ, pointing to him who is the Promise and our Future.

We see the role of the seven sacraments of hope and salvation especially in this perspective: to help all Christians to become what they are meant to be, living signs of the hope that is in us, the hope for the whole world. This meaning and dynamism of the sacraments is beautifully expressed by St Augustine. When the faithful asked him how the heathen can be saved while the Church is hiding from them the great sacraments of initiation — Baptism and the Eucharist — he responds, "The sacraments of Baptism and the Eucharist are hidden in the Church. But while the sacraments remain hidden to the heathen, your good deeds can be seen by them. What is visible arises from that depth which they cannot perceive, much as from the hidden part of the cross there arises that part which is visible".[62] Thus the sacraments can shape not only the conduct but the very character of Christians so that they can become the salt of the earth, visible and effective signs of hope to the world.

This vision is a programme for the Church's worship and evangelization, a programme never completely fulfilled but always to be better fulfilled. Langdon Gilkey makes some highly relevant suggestions in this direction. In order to form Christians who are signs of hope for the world, "liturgy must express the sacred quality of the secular if it is to be meaningful".[63] Worship needs symbols as much as it needs appropriate words. However, religious symbols lose their reality if they are separated entirely from the life-world; yet they lose their integrity if they are simply identified with the social symbols that structure that world. Symbols that once were a special promise and call to hope can, under changed cultural conditions, lose their meaning and become less promising than the present cultural realities.

The whole worship and use of symbols must be faithful to the prophetic mission of the Church. "A church using the remnants of its sacrality to bless instead of transforming all the most oppressive elements of our culture cannot be a sign of hope and cannot raise Christians to be sacraments of hope".[64]

Christian worship must never allow a split between culture and life, between religion and life, a false separation between natural and supernatural. Every creature is potentially a symbol. "Humans achieve humanity when they are images or reflections of God, when their autonomous freedom unites with grace".[65]

Not only the Church community but each community exists as a symbol of the divine providential purposes whenever the human qualities like love, justice, discernment show forth the divine rule and the divine presence: "and such is the eschatological conception of the kingdom".[66] Unless the symbols of our tradition and our worship reawaken in us our role as symbols of the divine activity, there is no vital experience of the holy.[67]

But while it is urgent to bring into worship and evangelization symbols that are understandable and vital for modern people, we must realize that many of our cultural and social symbols actually participate in the estrangement of collective sinfulness. They are not simply "natural" but rather partially contradictory to man's true nature and vocation. Hence symbols need to be chosen judiciously and to be purified.

The Church is constantly in need of guidance by the prophetic spirit in view of Christ, the Prophet. Thus the worshipping and evangelizing Church responds to the yearning of creation to share in the Redemption and to become ever more keenly aware of the hope in which we are redeemed.

With Gilkey we can conclude that "Worship, therefore, is primarily related to this presence of the divine throughout the human creature's existence. Its central purpose is to bring to awareness and to celebrate that universal presence, to shape that awareness into Christian form, and throughout that shaping of our natural existence by sacrament and word, to elicit gratitude, contrition, recommitment and transformation of that natural existence".[68]

In the light of these reflections, we have to respond to urgent questions. Why does not our baptismal rite gratefully celebrate the gift of life as such, the gift of a child to a human family as well as to the Church? Would not such a change contribute more to *generous* responsible parenthood than a legalistic imposition of prohibitions? A giant step in the right direction is taken whenever parents and the whole community make solemn promises to teach the child by word and example the hope which it has received in *Baptism,* and to do so throughout the whole process of education and in all human relationships.

Why do we not bring home to the sacrament of *Confirmation* the symbols of growth into adulthood, maturity, and the acceptance of various responsibilities in family, economic, social, cultural and political life? Why does not the Church celebrate an equivalent to the ordination of priests by bringing home to all the genuine human professions the full meaning of that maturity which is the gift of the Spirit? By doing all this, we would be celebrating the rebirth into the community of faith, the new life given by the Spirit, and better manifest the special role of ordained ministers.

Marriage is brought into worship by the celebration of the sacrament. Until the liturgical reform, canon law, which saw the sacrament of marriage merely as a contract about acts fit for procreation, reduced to a minimum the worship accompanying the sacrament, and that minimum could not attain its beauty while isolated from the broader aspect of the covenant. Much more could and should be done to bring home to the sacrament the prophetic role of the spouses and the family. The Second Vatican Council indicates the direction. "That state of life which is sanctified by a sacrament is obviously of great value, namely, married and family life. For where Christianity pervades the whole way of life and ever increasingly transforms it, there will exist both the practice and an excellent school of the lay apostolate. In such a home, husband and wife find their proper vocation in being, for each other and for their children, witnesses of faith in Christ and love for him. The Christian family loudly proclaims the present virtues of the kingdom of God and the hope of a blessed life to come".[69]

The whole liturgy should make everyone more alert to the participation of all of God's people in Christ's role as The Prophet. "Christ, the great Prophet who proclaims the kingdom of his Father by the testimony of his life and the power of his word, continually fulfils his prophetic office until his full glory is revealed. He does this not only through the hierarchy who teach in his name and with his authority, but also through the laity. For that very purpose he made them his witnesses, gave them understanding of the faith and the grace of speech (cf. Acts 2:17-18; Rev 19:10), so that the power of the Gospel might shine forth in their daily social and family life".[70]

The newer theology of hope has become sharply aware that social involvement is no reason not to celebrate feasts, and that the theology of hope for a better future needs the theology of feast and worship.[71] The social concern must be brought home into worship and back to life as a share in Christ's prophetic role.[72]

V.　THE HUMAN BODY AS SIGN OF HOPE

The spirited human body is a promise fulfilled and a promise of even greater things to come. As organ and manifestation of the spirit, the body fulfils a promise given to all evolution. It reaches its highest peak in the incarnation of the eternal Word of the Father. "Thou hast prepared a body for me. Then I said, 'Here am I; as it is written of me in the scroll, I have come, O God, to do thy will' " (Heb 10: 5-7). This body, in its entirety, is the language of truth and love. Even if sinful humanity crucifies it, the outstretched arms and open heart speak with supreme eloquence of the all-embracing and saving love.

Jesus' body, shedding the blood of the covenant, tells us the truth about creation and history. And the glory of the Father shines on this body of Jesus who has so wonderfully glorified the Father. The risen body of Jesus is the promise fulfilled that was foreshadowed in the first human body alive by the Spirit. The resurrection of Christ is the promise to be fulfilled in all those whose body, in its entirety, speaks the truth of love.

A widespread mystique, born of thought patterns in Greek philosophy, considers the body as the prison of a fallen soul that pre-existed in immaterial purity. The hope is for the immortality of the soul liberated from the body. But this vision of immortal souls finally escaping the disaster of matter and biological life leaves the world without hope. John, in his first letter, called such gnostic tendencies "godless world". The focus of the Christian hope, which has its central symbol and reality in the risen body of Christ, is on the body of each human person and on humanity *as* body. Thus the whole of creation, the whole universe receives a share of the promise and hope.

The hope of resurrection from the dead is central to Christian faith. "Now if this is what we proclaim, that Christ was raised from the dead, how can some of you say that there is no resurrection of the dead?" (1 Cor 15: 12). Death, painful as it may be, can no longer restrain the body but is the door of hope not only for the life of the soul but for the life of the embodied spirit; for the body. "The seed you sow does not come to life unless it has first died. What is sown in the earth as a perishable thing is raised imperishable. Sown in humiliation, it is raised in glory; sown in weakness, it is raised in power; sown as an animal body, there is also a spiritual body ... When our mortality has been clothed with immortality, then the saying of Scripture will come true: 'Death is swallowed up; victory is won'" (1 Cor 15:35-55).

Faith and hope in the resurrection allows no escapism from this world. Christ's promise "to transfigure the body belonging to our humble state, and give it a form like that of his own resplendent body" (Phil 3:21) is a liberating and demanding law of hope and an effective inducement to "honour God in the body" (1 Cor 6:20) during our earthly existence. God's design is that "in this body also life may reveal itself, the life that Jesus lives" (2 Cor 4:10), and not only on the day of the resurrection but during our earthly pilgrimage.

As all the longing of the universe has reached its peak in the resurrection of the body of Christ, so our life in the body, looking forward to the resurrection, is a commitment to radiate in all the relationships of our bodily existence this hope, that the world — the whole earth — may have a share of it. The glory that will shine on our body depends on how we discharge our responsibility to this world. "The universe itself is to be freed from the shackles of mortality and enter upon the liberty and splendour of the children of God. Up to the present, we know, the whole created universe groans in all its parts as if in the pangs of childbirth. Not only so, but even we to whom the Spirit is given as first fruits of the harvest to come, are groaning inwardly while we wait for God to make us his sons and daughters and set our whole body free" (Rom 8:21-23).

When we look up in hope to the risen Lord we cannot forget how, in his corporeal life on earth, he manifested the Father's love for us. As the divine Healer he was present to the blind, the crippled and the paralytic. He taught us by his word and example to make the earth a hopeful dwelling place. As the divine Master radiated peace, joy, mercy, hunger and thirst for justice, so can and must his disciples do in their bodily life.

A Christian who is aware that his body is a sign of hope will never be tempted to throw away or denigrate his bodily life as worthless but will be willing to follow the divine Master: "There is no greater love than this, that a man should lay down his life for his friends" (Jn 15:13).

As Christians we will never split soul and body. Ours is a spirited body created in the image and likeness of God, and if we cooperate with the divine Artist, this spirited body can become for many a real promise of goodness, compassion and passion for true justice. The fundamental attitudes of the eschatological person are gratitude, praise, trust, peace and purified passion, vigilance and joy, and they are inscribed in the human physiognomy. The spiritual is incarnated while the body is spiritualized.

A human countenance that radiates goodness and cordiality is a reflection of God's graciousness, and helps us to understand God's grace (*charis,* grace pointing to God's attractive countenance). It is through Christ and through his true disciples that God reveals his loving countenance to people.

The human hand is far more than a marvellous instrument for handling things. Jesus' hands healed, comforted, served, and accepted the nails on the cross. So our hand, too, can serve and soothe, can confirm an alliance, and be a sign of reconciliation. Hands resting in one another's communicate confidence and trust.

In the four sacred books of Confucius one can read, "The most precious gifts which heaven has bestowed on the wise man are the fundamental attitudes of benevolence, gentleness, justice and prudence. All of these have their roots in the heart but their effects shine through the face, are revealed in the bearing of the shoulders and in all the members of the body". In the best Chinese tradition, Confucius holds in particular esteem politeness as a manifestation of one's innermost thoughts and feelings.

The human body in its entirety is communications, a hope-filled sign that people should turn to each other and so make themselves known to one another in the reciprocity of consciences, in reverence and friendship. Thus they come to understand better the hope for final communion with God. Human sexuality, which is an essential dimension of bodily existence, has to be seen in this perspective. This is the most demanding but also the most promising view of sexuality. It not only awakens hope but also keeps promises.

VI. HOPE FOR THE "HOPELESS"

Without Christ, the great Sacrament of Hope, sinful humanity would be a "hopeless case". The Church, each of the disciples of Christ and all of them together, is given to the world as a sign of hope. By their hope and courageous love they can broaden the world's horizons. In fidelity to the liberating love and promise of the Master, they can break out of the narrow circle of friendship with only those who are right enough to respond with rewarding love, and bring new life and freedom to the hopeless, the handicapped, the sick, the oppressed, and those who have become guilty.[73] Hope must open the prisons filled by collective selfishness and despair.

The Church's faithfulness to her mission as a sacrament of hope will constantly be tested by her attitude towards those who are, in one way or another, outlaws. I particularly mention homosexuals, who need so much to be helped to discern between sin and suffering. Very often the afflicted person needs to be helped to accept the suffering implied in sex deviancy. The painful experience is made worse by the harsh judgments of others and the personal inability to distinguish between the extent of guilt and the degree of illness. They must therefore be comforted and encouraged for any display of good will. Their initial effort, along with their acceptance of suffering, is a basis for hope, a sign of God's saving presence.

Appropriate motivation and more positive attitudes in deal-ing with psychologically impaired persons will make Christian morality more credible to people than harsh judgments and stereotyped imperatives based on inadequate knowledge of man and his world. The shocking problems of drug addiction, wide-spread sexual deviancy, and other psychopathological tendencies call for a more constructive approach based on painstaking scientific study of the causes, and supported by Christian hope. We have to turn our eyes constantly to how Christ brought hope to public sinners, to offenders against public morality, the tax-gatherers and prostitutes.

Millions of people around the globe who, without personal guilt or with faults no greater than ours in our state of life, have failed in a first marriage and live in a second canonically invalid one, are testing the Church to see whether she is at the same time a sacrament of faithfulness and of mercy: faithfulness to the covenant and faithfulness to the great command, "Be merciful like your heavenly Father".[74]

VII. SINS AGAINST HOPE

Traditionally, the sins against hope were classified under two headings: (1) despair, anticipating final failure and (2) arrogance, anticipating final victory without putting one's trust in God, without praying humbly, and/or without making the necessary effort on the road to final freedom and victory.

But sins against hope are of great diversity. One can sin against the divine gift of hope not only by direct opposition to hope and trust but also by failing to become a sign of hope in the world and failing to work with others for a hopeful milieu.

Those who look only for their individual salvation, while neglecting the hope of all the others for salvation and wholeness, contradict the divine promises and threats.

There are attitudes and ideologies that are enemies of the hope structure of faith. "Fundamentalism petrifies the Bible, conservatism makes liturgy inflexible, and Christian morality becomes icebound by rigid legalism".[75]

Enemies of hope are the wealthy and powerful who look only for their own *now*, their own privileges and power, their unjust Mammon, while depriving the underprivileged and the oppressed of their this-worldly hope. Their sin is even greater when they try to console the oppressed by other-worldly hope, while renouncing for themselves that hope which is given only to those who hunger and thirst for justice and for love.

People and communities who refuse to act compassionately towards others are enemies of hope.

Those who, by their apathy, sloth and non-involvement, make themselves unable or unwilling to be grateful to God for all the compassionate love and saving justice he has offered them, also make themselves unable to be signs of hope for others. They offend God and his promises and deprive themselves and others of Christian hope.[76]

People who refuse to take the risk inherent in human life, who look more for security than for the saving truth, and cling too fearfully to the past instead of committing themselves to the future, offend against the gift and task of hope.

Probably the largest number of sinners against hope are those who sin by irresponsible hope, by hoping for the wrong reasons or for the wrong things as, for instance, for political, economic or social success over and against the capacity to love, to help others and to act justly.

They also sin who hope for things never promised by God, while refusing all the promises given to those who accept the call to holiness.

Likewise sinning against hope are those who, although hoping for the right things, refuse to act responsibly and thus refuse to express and communicate their hope to others.

Is our world of today aware of one of its most dangerous sins against hope? It is the overcommitment to activity, to success, to progress and development, while cutting off the fountains of hope: contemplation, prayer, repose before God.[77] Those who will not bother to keep the wellspring of creative liberty and fidelity clean and strong are sinning against their own hope and the hope of the world.

NOTES

[1] Cf. P. Teilhard de Chardin, The Making of a Mind, New York, 1965, 232.
[2] The theological literature on hope is vast. I mention here only those publications that are relevant to a theology of Christian life: H. Bars, Faith, Hope and Charity, New York, 1961; Ch. A. Berard, Théologie de l'espérance, Paris, 1961; J. Bouillac, The Hope that is in Us, Glen Rock, N.J., 1965; J. Moltmann, A Theology of Hope, New York, 1967; Id., Experiment Hope, Philadelphia, 1975; J. Pieper, Hoffnung und Geschichte, München, 1967; Id., Uber die Hoffnung, München, 1975; A. Edlmaier, Horizonte der Hoffnung, Regensburg, 1968; F. Kerstiens, Die Hoffnungsstruktur des Glaubens, Mainz, 1969; Id., "Hope", in Sacramentum Mundi III (New York, 1968), 61-65; L. Boros, Living

in Hope. Future Perspectives in Christian Thought, New York, 1970; Id., *We are Future*, New York, 1970; Id., *Geborgene Existenz: Christliches Leben als Hoffnung*, Freiburg, 1975; R.A. Alves, *A Theology of Human Hope*, New York, 1971; B. Häring, *Hope is the Remedy*, Garden City, N.J., 1972; H. Rotter, "Freiheit durch Hoffnung in der Sicht einer theologischen Anthropologie", *Zeitschrift f. Kath. Theol.* 95 (1973), 174-185; W.D. Marsch (ed.), *Dibattito sulla teologia di speranza di Jürgen Moltmann*, Brescia, 1973; J.M. Diez-Alegria, *I Believe in Hope*, Garden City, N.J., 1974; P. de Surgy (ed.), *Recherches et réflexions sur l'espérance chrétienne*, Paris-Montreal, 1976; Gesamtsynode der Bistümer der BRD: "Unsere Hoffnung", in *Offizielle Gesamtausgabe der Beschlüsse*, Freiburg/Basel, 1976, 84-111; cf. "Evangelische Stellungnahme zum katholischen Synodenbeschluss 'Unsere Hoffnung' ", *Una Sancta* 32 (1977), 228-233; K. Rahner, *Meditations on Hope and Love*, New York, 1977; J. Galot, S.J., *The Mystery of Christian Hope*, New York, 1977; L. Gilkey, *Reaping the Whirlwind: A Christian Interpretation of History*, New York, 1977; W.P. Frost, "A Decade of Hope Theology in North America", *Theol. Studies* 39 (1978), 139-153.

3 N. Zimmerle, *Man and His Hope in the Old Testament*, London, 1973; A. Voss, "Neutestamentliche Worte und Zeichen der Hoffnung", *Una Sancta* 1974, Heft 4; A. Flecha, *Esperanza y moral en el Nuevo Testamento*, Leon, 1975.

4 Cf. F. Kerstiens, *Sacramentum Mundi* III, 62.

5 Cf. l.c., 64.

6 J. Moltmann, *Theology of Hope*, 140, 259.

7 l.c., 225-228.

8 K. Rahner, *Grace in Freedom*, New York, 1969, 258.

9 T. de Chardin, *The Future of Man*, 12.

10 l.c., 34.

11 M. Heidegger, *Uber den Humanismus*, Frankfurt, 1947, 35.

12 Cf. K. Lehmann, *Jesus Christus unsere Hoffnung, Meditationen*, Frankfurt, 1976.

13 J. Moltmann, l.c., 287.

14 M.D. Meeks, Introduction to J. Moltmann, *Experiment Hope*, XI.

15 J. Feiner/L. Vischer, *The Common Catechism*, 534ff.

16 T. de Chardin, l.c., 33.

17 J. Moltmann, *Experiment Hope*, 3.

18 Cf. J. Coburn, *The Hope of Glory*, New York, 1976.

19 K. Rahner, l.c., 259.

20 J. Moltmann,, l.c., 8.

21 T. de Chardin, l.c., 72.

22 l.c., 72.

23 Cf. J. Sarano, *Le defi de l'espérance: "Arracher et planter"*, Paris, 1973.

24 Cf. C.H. Ratschow, l.c., 119.

25 T. de Chardin, l.c., 19; cf. 15ff.

26 J. Moltmann, *The Crucified God. The Cross of Christ as the Foundation and Criticism of Christian Theology*, New York, 1974, 5.

27 Cf. A. Bord, *Memoire et espérance chez Jean de la Croix*, Paris, 1971.

28 P. Minear, *Eyes of Faith*, Philadelphia, 1946, 216.

29 R.A. Alves, l.c., 162.

30 Cf. J.M. Gustafson, *Can Ethics be Christian?* Chicago, 1975, 140.

31 R. Bultmann, *Primitive Christianity*, Median Books, 1956, 320ff.

32 Cf. E. Bloch, *Das Prinzip Hoffnung*, Frankfurt a.M., 1959.

33 Cf. C. Kramer, *Fear and Hope According to Saint Alphonsus Liguori*, Washington D.C., 1951; World Council of Churches, *Uniting in Hope*, Genève, 1975.

34 T. de Chardin, l.c., 72.

35 l.c., 73ff.

36 l.c., 40.

37 l.c., 74.

38 l.c., 74ff.

[39] l.c., 79.
[40] l.c., 119.
[41] T. de Chardin, *The Making of a Mind, Letters from a Soldier Priest 1914-1918,* New York, 1965, 252.
[42] J. Moltmann, *Experiment Hope,* 36.
[43] l.c., 69.
[44] J. Huxley, *Touchstone for Ethics 1843-1943. Ethics and the Dialectic of evolution,* New York, 1947.
[45] T. de Chardin, *The Future of Man,* 90.
[46] Cf. J. Moltmann, *Theology of Hope,* 222, 21; W.H. Capps, *Hope Against Hope. Moltmann to Merton in One Decade,* Philadelphia, 1976, 159.
[47] Cf. J. Ellul, *Hope in Time of Abandonment,* New York, 1973.
[48] M. Müller/H. Pfeil, *Hoffnung und Freude. Das Diesseitserleben und die Jenseitserwartung des Christen,* Aschaffenburg, 1974; N. Beaupère, *San Paolo e la gioia. Il messaggio della speranza,* Roma, 1975.
[49] *Gaudium et Spes,* 1.
[50] ibid, 21c.
[51] Cf. E. Fromm, *Revolution of Hope. Toward a Humanized Technology,* New York, 1968; G. O'Collins, *Man and His New Hopes,* New York, 1969; E.H. Cousins (ed.), *Conference on Hope and the Future of Man,* New York, 1971; D.G. Miller and D.Y. Hadidion (eds.), *Jesus and Man's Hope,* Pittsburg, 1971; H. Descroche, *Sociologie de l'espérance,* Paris, 1973; G. Gennari, *Cristo speranza della speranza umana,* Modena, 1973; R. Garaudy, *Le projet de l'espérance,* Paris, 1975; G. Bauer, *Christliche Hoffnung und menschlicher Fortschritt,* Mainz, 1976.
[52] T. de Chardin, *The Future of Man,* 19; cf. P. Masset, "Espérance Marxiste, espoir chrétienne", *Nouv. Rev. Theol.* 99 (1977), 321-339.
[53] T. de Chardin, l.c. 303.
[54] l.c., 93-95.
[55] l.c., 36.
[56] G. Baum, *Religion and Alienation,* 286.
[57] A. Schmeemann, *Sacraments and the Orthodoxy,* New York, 1965; to this section cf. B. Häring, *Hope is the Remedy,* Slough and Garden City, 1972, ch. 7 and 8; Id., *The Sacraments in a Secular Age,* Slough, 1976 (American edition under the title *The Sacraments and Your Everyday Life,* Liguori, 1976).
[58] *Lumen gentium,* 1.
[59] Augustine, *Sermons,* 74, 2, PL 54, 398.
[60] L. Gilkey, "Symbols, Meaning and the Divine Presence", *Theol. Studies* 35 (1974), 256.
[61] *Lumen gentium,* 68.
[62] Augustine, *En. in Ps. CIII,* PL 37, 1348.
[63] L. Gilkey, l.c., 249.
[64] l.c., 252.
[65] l.c., 256.
[66] l.c., 256.
[67] l.c., 260.
[68] l.c., 257.
[69] *Lumen gentium,* 35.
[70] ibid, 35.
[71] Cf. W.H. Capps, l.c., 151ff.
[72] For the individual sacraments as signs of hope see my book *The Sacraments in a Secular Age,* 139-152.
[73] J. Moltmann, *Experiment Hope,* 189.
[74] Cf. B. Häring, *Hope is the Remedy,* ch. 15.
[75] J. Moltmann, l.c., 2.
[76] J. Moltmann, *The Crucified God,* 5ff.
[77] Cf. W.H. Capps, l.c., 134; J. Moltmann, *Experiment Hope,* 69-84: "The Crucified God and the Apathetic Person".

Chapter Nine

Actualizing the Truth in Love

"God is Love" (1 Jn 4:8). This is the truth from which all human freedom comes and towards which it tends. God is absolute freedom to love. The Father speaks out his Word in love, and in the same love the eternal Word breathes the Spirit, the Spirit of truth. He is the truth of love.

In the superabundance of his triune life and love, God creates the human person. His creative and redemptive presence is the freedom of love to be with us and to be for us when we, in turn, respond with adoring love and accept the sublime vocation to share in his divine love for all people. Only by accepting this vocation to join God in his love can we reach a liberating knowledge of the truth that God is Love. "The unloving know nothing of God" (1 Jn 4:8).

There is no liberating truth apart from the love of God and love of neighbour. Man can accumulate a great deal of knowledge of essences (abstract ideas and definitions), and "knowledge of domination", but all this can contribute nothing to his growth in liberty and genuine responsibility without knowledge of the truth that God is Love, and that only those who actualize truth in love are set free.

In this chapter we treat of the love with which God loves us and by which he enables us to respond lovingly to him and, at the same time, to share his love by loving each other in his own love. We distinguish love of God and love of neighbour but we do not separate them.

The reader will find repetitions in this chapter. This seems

419

to me unavoidable in a moral theology that gives special attention and emphasis to synthesis, to the vision of the whole. The liberating truth of the divine love and our vocation to share in it are present in all parts of a Christian ethics. Here, our theme is one of reflection on the heart of the matter, on the architectural centre of the whole of Christian life.

We cannot speak on faith, hope or adoration without having in mind him who is love. Faith and hope have their inner truth and authenticity in the love that God bestows on us. It is only as loving people that we are on the wave-length of faith in God who is love. St Augustine explains this well: "He who does not love believes in vain even if he believes in what is true; he hopes in vain even if the things he hopes for are thought to pertain to true happiness, unless he believes and hopes that the gift of love can be given to him if he asks for it".[1]

If we say "love", we must be aware of the richness but also of the ambiguity of the word. Especially because it is a central word in human history, it takes up much of the historical context and its various shades and nuances. Hence a careful hermeneutics is necessary. Our focus must be, above all, on the specificity of Christian love. We can know what love is in the full sense only through its revelation in Jesus Christ.

I. THE TRUTH OF LOVE REVEALED IN JESUS CHRIST

1. The truth of divine and human love

The whole of history, especially the history of humankind, is an ongoing revelation of love, for God is Love, and he creates man for the one great purpose of having, as Duns Scotus says, "sharers of his love". In their best attributes, human persons and human communities are revelations of God's love, since they are created in God's image and likeness.

The special revelation of God in the word, as we find it in holy Scripture, is interpretation of human history in the main perspective of love. But love in its full truth is revealed to us in Jesus Christ, true God and true man. In his humanity and co-humanity, he reveals the highest possibilities of human love, and even more, the love of God himself, and human love as participation in it. In him, the love of God the Father becomes visible. Being one with the Father, he loves us as the Father has loved him (Jn 15:9).

All the best of human history is a kind of pre-incarnation according to God's design, a promise of the full incarnation of his love. Christ is not only the Word incarnate; he is also Love incarnate. In his warm, pure and passionate love, in his humanity and co-humanity, the divine love is present and visible. Therefore, only by knowing Christ can we truly know what God is Love means.

Jesus also tells us that the history of divine love, visible in human beings, will continue in his disciples. He prays for his disciples at the climactic moment of his life, asking the Father "that the love thou hast for me may be in them and I may be in them" (Jn 17:26). Discipleship is possible only as life in Christ, whereby we share in the divine love through the power of the Holy Spirit.

Jesus manifests the Father's love, not by abstract words but by his whole life, by the way he meets people in their uniqueness, disclosing to them their dignity in being called to live a life with him, to the honour of the Father. His words are one with the total testimony (sign) of his life. They interpret his life and, at the same time, are interpreted by his life and death.

With the incarnation of Jesus Christ, the divine and human love takes on the dimension of history. Jesus loves as an Israelite, a carpenter's son and a man of his time. He enters history, acts historically, and shapes history by the manifestation of his divine and human love. After him, history will never be the same, nor will it be a mere repetition of his actions and words. He has initiated a history of love to be lived in ever new forms, but a history that, as it unfolds, must be constantly interpreted in the light of the life, death and resurrection of Christ.

Christ does not make the human love of mothers and fathers, brothers and sisters, friends, prophets and priests, physicians and wise rulers dispensable; rather, he brings home all the experiences and qualities of human love into the great vision of God. What the prophets said before him about the tender love of God — more tender than a mother's love (cf. Is 49:15) — and what wise men and inspired poets have said about the love of spouses and of betrothed couples (cf. The Song of Songs) all receives its final meaning and criterion in the love of Jesus Christ and in his interpretation of love. His parables, for instance, that of the prodigal son and his merciful father (Lk 15:11-32), will be repeated in ever new forms since Jesus Christ, as the beloved Son, has fully revealed the mercy and fidelity of his heavenly Father (Mk 1:11 and par.). These stories, along with our own and the life stories of others, are now brought home into the great history of love that reached its summit in the incarnation, death and resurrection of Christ.[2]

2. Covenant love

a) In union with Christ, the Covenant

God has made visible in his covenant the reality and quality of his love. Time and again, from Adam to Abraham, Moses, David, Solomon, he offered a covenant to man. His love is faithful, merciful and holy. It is a most serious love, requesting nothing less than a total response in love, with all one's heart, energy and fidelity.

The covenant between Yahweh and Israel implies partnership as an undeserved gift. Israel is called to make God's holiness and mercy visible to all nations. In spite of Israel's many sins, God has not rejected her but has brought everything to fulfilment, by choosing Jesus, the new Israel, the Servant, to be the covenant of the people, and revealing himself in him as "the God of love and peace" (2 Cor 13:11).

Jesus is the supreme manifestation of the Father's and his own solidarity with us sinners. "Christ was innocent of sin and yet, for our sake, God made him one with the sinfulness of man so that, in him, we might be made one with the goodness of God himself" (2Cor 5:21; cf. Rom 8:32; Heb 2:11-18).

The call to apostleship and discipleship implies friendship with Jesus and, at the same time, friendship among all the disciples of Christ. One cannot be Christ's friend without being a friend of his friends. The I-Thou relationship between Jesus and the disciples is, by necessity, a we-relationship, for Christ is the Covenant. He calls his disciples to be one in him, so that all people may come to know that he is the saviour of the world, the covenant of the people (Jn 17:20-23).

The covenant dimension of love is already clearly present in the synoptics but is deepened in the writings of Paul and John. They see all of Christian life as a life in Christ, and from that life there arises the covenant love: "If then our common life in Christ is anything to stir the heart, any loving consolation, any sharing of the Spirit, any warmth of affection or compassion, fill up my cup of happiness by thinking and feeling alike, with the same love for one another, the same turn of mind, and a common care for unity ... Let your bearing towards one another arise out of your life in Christ Jesus" (Phil 2:1-5).

The great experience of the disciples after the Easter event is a community built on love and depending on love. John synthesizes the whole of Christian life as faith in Jesus, leading to a profound union with him and a sharing of his love with all his disciples and, indeed, with all for whom Christ died.[3] The community of disciples is the quasi-sacrament of the love of Christ, to be responded to in mutual love. But this in no way means a limitation of love to the actual community of believers. Rather, it is the basic covenant experience of love in view of all the world for which Christ has given himself up.[4]

The love that God reveals in Jesus Christ and in the community of the disciples, is not only fatherly but also fraternal and a call to community. Wherever the disciples love each other in the love of Christ, the God of love is present in a special way. And wherever there is authentic love and a building up of community, Jesus is the hidden partner in this reciprocal love.[5]

The new experience of the disciples should lead to a new consciousness about the origin and purpose of love in all the world. The Second Vatican Council has underlined this covenant dimension of Christian life and love. "Indeed, the Lord Jesus, when he prayed to the Father 'that all may become one ... as we are one' (Jn 17:21-22) opened up vistas inaccessible to human reason. For he implied a certain likeness between the union of the divine Persons and the union of God's children in truth and charity".[6]

In one of his richest books, Henri de Lubac has shown that it is authentic Catholic tradition — indeed, the nature of Catholicism — that the covenant dimension is present and all-pervading in all the dogmas.[7] Unity, solidarity and redeeming love are inseparable dimensions. "A charity that is not willing to pay a high price for unity is not authentic and, equally, unity is only an illusion where love does not reign. 'Charity is the unity of the Church. Whether we call it charity or unity it is the same, for unity is charity and charity is unity' ".[8]

In many parts of the world, small communities strive to relive this experience of love and unity as an expression of our life in Christ and our dedication to the unity of humankind.[9] The goal of these communities is to personalize, in observable relationships, the life of Christ in each individual and the community as a whole, so that one and all can communicate this message to society as a whole. Life in Christ Jesus, actualized in discipleship communities, gives the ego-strength so necessary for responsible participation in the building of unity and peace in the world.

b) In the power of the Holy Spirit

Jesus is anointed by the fullness and power of the Spirit to be the covenant of the people, the servant and friend of all. In his human nature, Jesus is one with that divine Word that breathes love, the Holy Spirit. Through the same Spirit he gives us a share in his redeeming and unifying love. The Pentecost event brings forth the new family of God that can work and testify to the new heaven and the new earth, the communion of saints.

Not only has God loved us before we loved him (1 Jn 4:10; 4:19) but, through the Holy Spirit, he also makes us sharers of both his inner wealth of love and his love for the world. This very love enables us also to share in the redeeming suffering of Christ and in all his efforts to build up a new family, the family of God. "Let us exult in the hope of the divine splendour that is to be ours. More than this, let us even exult in our present sufferings because we know that suffering trains us to endure, and endurance brings proof that we have stood the test, and this proof is the ground of hope. Such a hope is no mockery, because God's love has flooded our innermost heart through the Holy Spirit he has given us" (Rom 5:3-5).

The loftiest gift of the Holy Spirit is *agapé*, the love that unites us with Christ and enables us to build up a redeemed and redeeming community. In this inspired love, the gift of the Spirit, we become allies of the apostles in the battle against evil and in bearing testimony for Christ (cf. Rom 15:30). Life in Christ Jesus is love within fellowship of the Spirit (cf. Ph 2:1). The Spirit not only assists us in our needs but also enriches us by that gift-love which becomes our new law to work for peace and unity. "Spare no effort to make fast with bonds of peace the unity which the Spirit gives. There is one body and one Spirit, as there is also one hope held out in God's call to you" (Eph 4:3-4; cf. 1 Cor 12, and Rom 12).

Covenant-love is the supreme charism of the Spirit that enables and obliges us to bring home to the community and society all the charisms of the Spirit and all our capacities. Charisma is not so much a distinction for the individual as a gift given in view of all. Persons and communities who live their charisms in this covenant-love give witness that the Holy Spirit is poured out over all flesh.[10] Baptism in the Holy Spirit and prayer in the Spirit are manifested in this covenant-love.

3. *Unity of divine love, love of neighbour and love of self*

a) Unity and distinction between love of God and love of neighbour

Christ himself has synthesized his moral message in the twofold yet single commandment of love of God and love of neighbour. "Love the Lord, your God, with all your heart, with all your soul, with all your mind. That is the greatest commandment. It comes first. The second is like it: love your neighbour as yourself. Everything in the law and the prophets hangs on these two commandments" (Mt 22:37-40; Mk 12:28-31).

Jesus affirms this dual commandment as the main teaching of the Old Testament. In Luke 10:27-28, it is a lawyer who quotes the commandment in response to Jesus' question, "What is written in the law?" Jesus replies, "That is the right answer", and then elucidates the point with unique originality. First he makes clear the indissoluble unity of the two commandments; secondly, he transcends the Old Testament words by showing us that love of God and neighbour is, above all, a gift of God, a sharing in his divine nature; thirdly, there is a clear consciousness that the whole of religion and morality is contained in the love of God and love of neighbour, and that there is nothing apart from it; fourthly, Jesus teaches us how universal and comprehensive the love of neighbour is.[11]

The great new theme in the moral message of Jesus, as explained by John and Paul, is the mystery of God's sharing his own love with his people: the gift of participation. In the New Testament, "love of God" means God's own love, the love with which he loves us; but at the same time, it also means the mighty presence of the love of God who, by the power of the Holy Spirit, gives us life in Christ Jesus and thus enables us to love him and each other with his own love. His children are sharers of his love (condiligentes).[12]

According to traditional Catholic theology, justification enables God's children to love each other with the theological virtue of love. St Augustine is very explicit on this point. "With one and the same love, we love God and neighbour, God for God's sake, ourselves and our neighbour, however, for the sake of God".[13] Thomas Aquinas, too, insists that this love includes the love of neighbour.[14] One cannot love the God who has revealed himself in Jesus Christ without joining him in his love for all people.

Since God has revealed himself as "the God of love", the response to his love is at the same time loving him and loving with him, as he teaches us through his Spirit. The message that the chosen "come to share in the very being of God" (2 Pet 1:4) means that they share in the love of the triune God: the love with which the Father speaks out his Word, the love with which the Word turns totally to the Father, and the Father's love which the Spirit (who is the sharing) breathes through the Son.

b) Distinction between ontological and psychological priority

Since both the love of God and the love of neighbour have their source and goal in God, the first precept of God's saving justice is the love of God with one's heart, soul and mind. But since his love for all of us is totally undeserved and by its very nature tends to unite us in his love, the second commandment is included in the first. God, who is Love, infinitely deserves and wants the love of those whom he loves. Not only does he want to be loved in his children; he wants first that his love be honoured and responded to. We have always to keep in mind the ontological priority of the love of God, for otherwise we cannot be adorers of God in spirit and truth.

However, on the psychological level of development, first there must be some experience of true love of neighbour before we can love the invisible God. "He who does not love the brother whom he has seen cannot love God whom he has not seen" (1 Jn 4: 20). The great psychologist, St Augustine, is quite clear on this: "The love of God is first in the order of precept but the love of brother is the first in the order of action ... Love, therefore, your neighbour, and look into yourself to see where this love of neighbour comes from. There you will see God insofar as you are capable. Begin, therefore, by loving your neighbour, share your bread with the hungry, open your house to the roofless, clothe the naked and despise no one of the same human race".[15] Thomas Aquinas is equally clear. "In the order of perfection and dignity, love of God comes first before love of neighbour. But in the order of origin and disposition, love of neighbour precedes the act of loving God".[16]

Even on the psychological level there is a reciprocity. Love of neighbour does not come to its perfection without love of God. But we must not love God only to increase our love of neighbour. God must be loved for himself. In the Christian experience, the religious dimensions have priority over the moral. God-experience and worship must not be sought in order "to prop up moral character". God-experience and the adoring love of God in Jesus Christ, both engender and require "the moral character that embodies fraternal love".[17]

c) Fraternal love as fundamental option for God

"He who abides in love abides in God, and God in him" (1 Jn 4: 16). From the inseparable unity of love of God and love of neighbour, and from the psychological priority of fraternal love, Karl Rahner concludes that whoever truly loves his neighbour has already made and lives implicitly his fundamental option for God.[18] St Augustine comes close to this position at least from a pedagogical if not from a systematic point of view. "When we love the brother with true love (*dilectione diligimus*) then we love the brother through God, and it is impossible not to love, above all, that very Lord by whom we love the brother. It follows that the two precepts cannot be separated from each other. Since God is love, he who loves true love surely chooses God in love. However, it is necessary that he who loves the brother be a lover of true love (*dilectione diligat*)".[19]

In the Gospel of St John there is the great experience of the friendship of Jesus who, by his infinite love, deserves all our love. In Chapter 15, the first reality explained by Christ is that we abide in him through faith and love. Without responding to his love, we cannot share in his life. But then follows, with equal emphasis, the truth that fraternal love is the test of our abiding in him. Without this love our life would be sterile, like a tree ready to be cut down. It is unthinkable to live in Christ, to abide in his friendship, and not to bear fruit in fraternal love and justice. This is stressed even more in the first letter of John.[20]

d) Love of self and love of neighbour

No biblically grounded person would speak of the "true self" outside of a genuine relationship with the other, with the Thou. Man exists in word and love; he becomes a spiritually conscious and free being only by opening himself to the love and acknowledgment coming from others and by responding in acknowledgment and love, by work and action.[21]

The behavioural sciences make it even more evident that a legitimate self-affirmation, ego-strength and genuine love of self goes hand-in-hand with love of neighbour, just as the Bible teaches.[22] We can have the courage to be and to accept ourselves serenely and creatively only because we are accepted and affirmed by others and, equally, are willing to affirm and to love others. We consciously affirm that we are affirmed.[23] The Bible emphatically teaches us, moreover, that only to the extent that we love our neighbour and serve willingly those who cannot repay us, can we overcome the tendency to destroy ourselves by selfishness.

"All the commandments are summed up in the one rule: 'Love your neighbour as yourself' " (Rom 13:9; cf. Lev 19:18; Mt 19:19; Mk 12:31). The Second Vatican Council expresses the same truth. "Everyone must consider his every neighbour, without exception, as another self".[24] We cannot honour and love ourselves as persons if we honour only those who are rich, who can reward us. If we despise other people or refuse them honour and love because of their colour, culture, social status or religion, we become unable to affirm our personal dignity and to love ourselves.[25]

e) Love of God and love of self

Just as love of neighbour and love of self are inseparable, so are the love of God and love of self. We must hate our selfishness, our sins and sinfulness, but loving God, our Father, we can and must love ourselves as God loves us. God's love for us is the basis and motive for our legitimate self-esteem. The more our love of self is rooted in God's love for us, the healthier and stronger it will be, and the more it will be united with the love of neighbour. "Only those who love themselves truthfully love themselves for the sake of God. In order to love themselves, they must love God".[26]

Throughout history there has been much discussion about the relation between a selfless love of God (*amor benevolentiae*) and need-love (*amor concupiscentiae*). It is unrealistic to separate a disinterested love of God from an interested one. God takes interest in us; therefore, in our love of God, there is a profound gratitude for this interest. While a redeemed love of God is, above all, thanksgiving and praise for his loving us, it is always an acknowledgment that we are in need of him. The humble need-love in no way devalues the gift-love. The New English Bible translates the first beatitude: "How blest are those who know their need of God; the kingdom of heaven is theirs" (Mt 5: 3).

There is a kind of *perichoresis* between love of God, love of neighbour and love of self. As long as there is tension or conflict between them, it is a sign of striking imperfection. An asceticism that does not have the courage to give the proper place to self-respect and self-love within the triad of love of God, neighbour, and self, does not lead to spiritual health. But it is equally true that our legitimate self-interest is best fulfilled through growth in the love of God and of neighbour.

f) Its relevance for moral theology and pedagogy

A synthesis of the whole of moral theology in the light of what we have said about the *perichoresis*, the inner dynamic unity of love of God, neighbour, and self, is vitally important for the whole of moral theology and education. It makes evasion, flight, and non-involvement, as well as over-involvement to the detriment of worship impossible. It liberates us from sterile ritualism and formalism, it fosters unity and coherence, and makes it possible for all Christian life to become a song of songs like that envisioned in Chapter 13 of Paul's first letter to the Corinthians.

Karl Rahner points out that this synthesis is particularly important in view of modern atheism which may not be absolute atheism. A self-giving love of neighbour implies love of God, even if one's interpretation does not bring this home to explicit consciousness and conceptualization. Absolute atheism, rejection of the God of love, is rejection of love of neighbour and leads to inability to love oneself.[27]

A juridical way of defining and distinguishing love of God, love of neighbour and of oneself leads to a religion of evasion under the pretext of loving God, and/or to a reductionism in love of neighbour, and loss of the centre of life.

g) Its relevance for worship and prayer

All worship and prayer must reflect and foster the indissoluble triad of love of God, neighbour, and self. There must be present the synthesis between gift-love and need-love, between praise of God and watchfulness for the needs of neighbour. "Persevere in prayer, with mind awake and thankful heart" (Col 4:3). There is nothing that cannot be brought home in prayer, and there is no happening that is not in need of being illumined by worship.

Prayer is sharing in the mystery of Christ who is one with the Father and one with us, who reveals to us the love of God and the love of neighbour, and who enables us to love ourselves. Prayer is the supreme expression of the mystery of man in the light of God's love. It is a dialogue with God nourished by the dialogue between people, purifying and ennobling it. In origin, dynamics and orientation, Christian prayer is trinitarian; it is prayer in the Spirit (Eph 6:18). The trinitarian dimension is reflected by prayer that is governed by the triad of faith, hope and love, but a love of God that includes love of neighbour and love of self. It is an expression of gift-love and need-love and, at the same time, an expression of apostolic love.[28]

4. Characteristics of love

Revelation of the God of love through Jesus Christ and throughout the whole of history does not allow us to build moral theology on a vague concept or on the mere sentiment of love. The whole of revelation is a revealing of the characteristics of true love. Love has an entrancing and impelling countenance. Stemming from faith in all its richness, it clears our eyes and lights our way to an ever better knowledge of the saving truth.

St Paul, who made it his purpose to know nothing apart from Jesus Christ, speaks on the qualities of Christ-like love. "Love is patient; love is kind and envies no one. Love is never boastful, nor conceited, nor rude; never selfish, not quick to take offence. Love keeps no score of wrongs; does not gloat over other men's sins, but delights in the truth. There is nothing love cannot face; there is no limit to its faith, its hope and its endurance. Love will never come to an end" (1 Cor 13:4-8).

That love which is life in Christ is sovereign in its gift and demand. Disciples of Christ will never be content with anything less than loving God and neighbour with all their heart and energy. Although they will never reach perfection, they will always reach out in the impelling direction, "Let your goodness have no limits, as your heavenly Father's goodness knows no bounds" (Mt 5:48). And since God's goodness is merciful love, the disciple will strive always in the same direction: "Be compassionate as your Father is compassionate" (Lk 6:36).

Since the human person, in his or her goodness, comes forth from God's love, all our life is intended to manifest and foster love. Love wants to fill our innermost being and to be present in all our deeds.

The history of humankind is pre-incarnation and incarnation of divine love. This love is the most powerful and decisive reality of history. Therefore it must be rooted and incarnated in all of human life; and man is called to incarnate it throughout all time. St Augustine saw this as the main purpose of human history: "The two kinds of love have produced two states: the perishable, produced by self-love to the extreme of disdain for God; the heavenly, produced by divine love to the point of renunciation of selfishness for God".[29]

God's people are his co-actors, his partners in the building up of the city of God by their love. There is no other way to unmask and overcome the wicked counterfeits of love than to incarnate in all of life this redeemed and redeeming love. Those who believe in the God of love will at all times join hands and efforts to overcome individual and collective selfishness by fully incarnating love in their own lives and in the world around them.

Christ-like love is marked by creative liberty and fidelity. All that we have said about Christ's liberating action can be said again about love; for it is through his love, active in us, that Christ wants to continue his liberating action and the revelation of his creative fidelity. Belief in the Holy Spirit whom Jesus Christ has sent us, the Spirit who renews the hearts of men and the face of the earth, means creative and liberating participation in ongoing history.[30]

If we believe wholeheartedly in the Word incarnate who breathes love and sends out the Spirit of truth, then we know that "all creativity is love and all love is creative".[31] Like true love, true creativity cannot exist apart from Christ. Freedom without Christ the Liberator is the counterfeit freedom of the old Adam, and all talk and involvement for this kind of freedom-without-love leads to chaos and slavery.

Persons imbued by the Spirit and his love discover the real opportunities for good. Love is a way of doing things which descends from God himself; therefore we know that we cannot learn the inventions of love from rules alone. We need first, loyalty and faithful love, and intelligence, discernment and imagination besides.[32]

The question at the heart of all liberation theology is whether man loves in freedom and is thus free to love. True love sets all the energies free for the kingdom of freedom. "Freedom becomes significant only through love".[33] By redeemed love we are set free from anguish, scrupulosity and slavish fear (cf. 1 Jn 4: 17). If we accept Christ's gift and love each other as he has loved us, then we are no longer slaves but friends in freedom (cf. Jn 15: 15).

Freedom and friendship, granted by the Son, replaced the old order. They built up the new creation of liberating truth (cf. Jn 8: 32-36).[34] At the beginning of history, there is neither hatred nor selfishness but only love. It has a history, it is history, and it shapes the truth of history for humankind, the history of freedom and reconciliation. The calling to share in God's own creative and liberating love gives courage and strength to build the hoped-for community — the kingdom — where all will share in the love of Jesus Christ, our Lord, and in the love of the Father, knowing that the God of love calls us by his Spirit. We are assured that his calling is creative, for God creates through his Spirit. Giving us a share in the hoped-for blessed communion with God, he urges us to work for a new heaven and a new earth.[35]

Grateful love discovers the possibilities for the innermost good. Love that hopes gives to the sinner new dignity and hope, and restores the distorted image of God to new splendour. When people are united before God in his gift-love, they discover not only their urgent needs but also their creative capacities. Love gives the courage to accept the other and to enter into a commitment of love. Love is the force that builds up the human person.[36] It is an ever new creation, affirming God's own creation. "What being loved makes being do is precisely: be".[37] By affirming each other in reciprocal love, we let each other know that it is good to be. Thus we are able to grow to a greater fullness of being.

In a human and religious peak experience, we know in a new way that everything is a gift of love. We appreciate God's initiative and the initiative and generosity of others, and thus find true spontaneity. Our creativity is awakened, and we make ourselves more worthy of all this wonderful love that we have received.

Reciprocity in love brings forth the highest form of reciprocity of consciences, and fosters creative co-responsibility.

II. LOVE IS MORE THAN A COMMANDMENT

Parents fail who try to educate their children for love by just telling them that they must love their parents and each other. Wise and loving parents let their children experience the attraction of genuine love and thus learn to discern the true nature of love. This follows the example of God, our creator and redeemer. He who is Love and the source of all goodness cannot put the commandment of love first. That would demand from creatures the greatest creation. God first manifests and shares his own love, and from there, he leads people by his fatherly command.

1. The sacramentality of love

All of creation and history is a visible sign, a powerful revelation of God's love and his loving presence. While all things are a gift of the loving God, love on earth is the very image and likeness of God. It therefore has a kind of sacramentality. We say this in view of Christ, sent by the Father to make visible to us the height and depth, the length and breadth of his love. To Philip's request, "Lord, show us the Father and we will ask no more", Jesus answered, "Have I been all this time with you, Philip, and you still do not know me? Anyone who has seen me has seen the Father" (Jn 14:8-9). And the prologue of the Gospel of John exults, "We saw his glory, such glory as befits the Father's only Son, full of grace and truth ... No one has ever seen God; but God's only Son, he who is nearest to the Father's heart, he has made him known (Jn 1:14-19; cf. 1 Jn 1-3).

It is not enough to point to the sign value, to the visibility of testimony to understand the sacramentality of Christ's love. Christ radiates love; he shares it with his disciples. He is the source who shares the living water of his love by sending the Holy Spirit (cf. Jn 7:37-39). He has brought the fire of love to the world, and those who know him in love know also that it is possible to love God with Jesus and to join God in his saving love.

Christ's glorification of the Father coincides with his bringing the disciples home into the Father's love. It is in this sense that Jesus is the sacramentality of love.[38] As the Sacrament, the effective sign of love, Christ is the adorer in spirit and truth.

The sacramental model chosen by Vatican II for the self-understanding of the Church has always to be seen in view of Christ from whom all sacramentality comes.[39] The effective presence of the Church in the world depends on the intensity and breadth of the visibility of love in all her relationships: evangelization, celebration, and the institution itself. To the extent that she is a sacrament of union with God and unity of humankind she is a sacrament of salvation. Unity and solidarity, seen in the sacramental dimension, need to be incarnated in the whole of life for the sake of all people, to the glory of the one God and Father.

2. *The sacraments of unity and love*

The farewell discourses and the high priestly prayer (Jn 13 — 17) present love as the great mystery revealed in Jesus Christ and to be revealed in his disciples. The new commandment, "Love each other as I have loved you" (Jn 15:12) is grounded in the mystery of union with Christ, life in Christ Jesus. "I am the vine, and you the branches; he who dwells in me as I dwell in him, bears much fruit; for apart from me you can do nothing ... As the Father has loved me, I have loved you. Dwell in my love" (Jn 15:5-9).

Through faith and the sacraments of faith, the disciples are born to a new life. To those begotten of God, it is connatural to love God and to observe his all-embracing command to love our neighbour (cf. 1 Jn 5:1-4). Biblical scholars agree that the Johannine Gospel and the first letter of John have to be seen in a sacramental dimension. The rejoicing about the full visibility of God's love in Jesus Christ continues in the rejoicing about the power of faith. The sacraments of faith enable the disciples to make the same love visible in their oneness and love.

The sign value and special grace of all the sacraments, but particularly of baptism, confirmation, eucharist and reconciliation, point to the unity of the disciples in Christ and in the Church, making visible their union with God. Henri de Lubac insists that this is not a marginal truth but is at the very heart of the Christian mysteries. "The sacraments, insofar as they effect, renew or strengthen union with Christ, also effect, renew and strengthen unity within the Christian community".[40] If all the sacraments are seen rightly in the light of the Eucharist, then this becomes even more evident. "The central sacrament, the Eucharist which contains the whole mystery of salvation, is simply the sacrament of unity".[41]

St Augustine explains the deep meaning of the "Amen" response when the priest offers the faithful the body of Christ with the words, "the body of Christ". "If you are the body of Christ and members of each other, your mystery is on the table of the Lord: you receive your mystery and this is the meaning of your response, 'Amen', for with your response you commit yourself. For you hear, 'the body of Christ', and you respond, 'Amen'. Be a member of Christ and your 'Amen' will be truthful. We of the many are one bread, one body (1 Cor 10:17); understand and rejoice; unity, truth, piety, charity. Be what you see and receive what you are".[42]

"If you receive in the right way you are what you receive, for the Apostle says, 'We, the many, are one bread, one body'. In this bread you are taught how much you have to love unity". Augustine continues to explain that the bread, the Mystical Body, is baked by the fire, by the sacrament of confirmation. Thus, by baptism in the water and the Holy Spirit, Christians are prepared to receive the body of Christ and to be the body of Christ. "To the water comes the fire, that is, the Holy Spirit, and you become the bread that is the body of Christ". And here Augustine teaches the faithful that their response at the Preface is a commitment to the truth that those who receive the body of Christ are called to be the body of Christ by their fraternal love and unity, whatever may be the sacrifice. Thus those who receive "having unity in mind, have their heart lifted up to the Lord".[43]

Following the patristic tradition of East and West and the emphasis of the Orthodox, de Lubac sees the *epiclesis* in the Eucharist in view not only of the consecration of the body and blood of Christ but also as a consecration of the faithful to *be* the body of Christ and to live what the cup of the covenant means.[44] We are truthful to our baptism, our confirmation and to the Eucharist only if we are thoroughly committed to the unity of all Christians and of all humankind to the glory of the triune God.

The Second Vatican Council has greatly stressed this signification of the sacraments as a basic motif for all of Church life and the believers.[45] It is important for the right celebration of the sacraments and especially of the Eucharist, and for the understanding of the dual commandment to love God and love neighbour.[46] Without it, even a morality based on the commandment to love can become another kind of moralism which would not offer the most effective motives or give the necessary honour to the source of all life and love.

Neither the universal priesthood of the faithful nor the ministerial priesthood can be understood without giving attention first to this mystery of unity.[47] It is a very demanding vision, requiring a deeper understanding of the sacrificial aspect of the Eucharist. "If I celebrate fraternal love at the Eucharistic meal and refuse to translate its meaning into concrete life, I either mock God or God alienates himself from me by allowing me to live in imagination what is never lived in fact".[48]

If the ministry of bishops, particularly in their collegiality and the role of the successor of Peter, is thoroughly understood and realized in the light of the Eucharist, then there is a solid basis for unity and renewal of the Church and for the greatly desired union of all Christians. But if it is buried in a juridical context and envisioned in a perspective of power, it will be not only inoperative but also alienated.[49]

The mystery of unity which we celebrate becomes visible only if we ourselves are gratefully united with Christ's total sacrifice of himself, offered in our name. There will be no worthy and fruitful memorial of his supreme sacrifice unless those who celebrate and receive the Eucharist are, themselves, wholeheartedly united and willing to bear the sacrifices necessary for unity and love. It is the one sacrifice and the one love that builds up the body of Christ.[50]

This vision of the sacraments and particularly of the Eucharist, as the main motif of worship and life, leads us by necessity to the morality of the Paschal Mystery of death and resurrection with Christ, and of Pentecost, a life in the Spirit in the unity which the Spirit gives. Then it will be evident that the goal-commandments, "Abide in me" and "Love each other as I have loved you" are in no way optional but are truly normative: that is, normative for a morality understood as ongoing conversion and growth. It is a normativeness given by grace.

If the deepest sacramental experience is translated into life, then it becomes evident that Christian love is not just a matter of being nice to those who are nice to us, or just following sociological trends; it is love that comes from the innermost heart, a love that transcends limitations, overcomes discrimination, is ready to accept sacrifices, and includes the down-

trodden, and difficult people. Only thus can we hope that the
experience of the pneumatological presence of Jesus will be given
to many.[51]

This vision will allow Christians and the Church to present
the Gospel morality with all its gentle rigour and, at the same
time, to jettison useless ballast.[52]

3. The meaning of the commandment of love

Although we warn against the danger of considering love of
God and love of neighbour merely as a commandment or
primarily as a commandment, we also have to be realistic and see
clearly that there *is* a commandment; that we sinners on earth
still need law and obedience to law. There are several aspects
of love that can be considered under the heading
"commandment".

Disciples and friends of Christ need, above all, to learn all
they can about the nature and demands of love, to know it as a
gift, and to know all the tasks it entails. We need to give
attention to the direction of the goal commandments, and to
see also the boundaries that can never be consciously overstepped.
And we need to see how all the other commandments flow
from the gift and commandment of love.

For the sinner who has transgressed the basic command,
"Abide in my love", the most urgent demand is one of total
conversion: to pray to God, to remove obstacles, and to open
himself again humbly and gratefully to the gift of divine love,
without which we cannot fulfil the commandment of love. For
all of us, the commandment requires an ongoing conversion.

The commandment demands that we do all we can to nurture
in ourselves profound and strong sentiments of love that inspire
action, the fruits of which the fifteenth chapter of John's Gospel
speaks so eloquently. As pilgrims on our earthly sojourn, we
cannot merely rest in the love of God and in our feelings of
friendship. We must pass continually from repose to action
and from action to reflection. Love in our hearts will incite us
to act and, conversely, loving action will deepen the inner disposition to love. The more we understand love as gift, the more
will we be ready to embrace generously those aspects that still
have the character of law and precept.[53]

III. LOVE IN THE COMMUNITY OF SAINTS AND SINNERS

Since love is a universal reality in historical diversity, it includes many forms. There is the love marked by family solidarity: the father's love for his sons and daughters, the mother's love for them, the children's love for their parents and for each other. There is, besides, possibly a typology according to the family structure: patriarchal, matriarchal, partnership. All these structures reflect in their way the type of family spirit (in Latin, *pietas;* in Hebrew, *chesed*). There is the sexual dimension of love in man and woman, in courtship and marriage, and the masculine and feminine diversities that enter somehow in all the various forms of love between man and woman, even in the most religious. There is the *eros,* differently expressed and structured in the various cultures.[55] The eros can take up all shades of need-love and friendship. There is, finally, love coming from God, the pure source of all love, leading back to him and yet fully incarnated in human love.

1. *Friendship love and universal love*

One of the names we can call Jesus by is "friend". He calls his disciples "friends" (Jn 15:13). Jesus gives to friendship a new character, a new depth and dignity. He gives his life for his friends (Jn 15:13). Indeed, giving his life for all people, he shows friendship-love to all and calls them all to his friendship. For all his apostles and disciples, the men and women who follow him, his friendship is total; and from that experience, he opens their hearts and himself to all. He is the friend of tax-gatherers and sinners (Lk 7:34 and par.). He sits with them at table in a friendship that is an expression of the messianic banquet which he anticipates with them.[56] This friendship is the sign of grace and reconciliation.

Jesus extends his friendship even to the disciple who is at the point of betraying him. He calls him "friend" and thus assures him that he is still called to true friendship. Jesus' friendship with the downtrodden and sinners restores dignity and assures the capacity to love. He teaches that his most intimate friendship with his mother extends also to his disciples who, in turn will win many people to this kind of open friendship. There are no boundaries. This is the revelation of Jesus' absolute freedom in the power of his love.

Friendship has a character of totality, of freedom of choice. It is *dilectio* (from *diligere*, to choose). The friend is a chosen one; there is freedom to give preference beyond the boundaries of flesh and blood. Moltmann emphasizes the need to speak more on friendship-love, for the expression "brotherly" or "fraternal" love seems to include women only indirectly.[57]

A friend is dear to us (*carus*, from original meaning of *caritas*). There is here an element of respect, of high evaluation, reverence. But it also includes the joy of being with the friend. Augustine says that the reward of friendship-love is the friend.[58]

In friendship-love there is a profound recognition that we are in need of affirmation and love from the other. This kind of need-love does not at all diminish the gift-love. Even Jesus, true man as well as true God, asks of Peter the poignant human question, "Do you love me?" And for all time this remains the central question for all his apostles and disciples.

There is always reciprocity in our giving and receiving love. "To make ourselves capable of loving and ready to receive love is the paramount problem of integration; indeed, the key to salvation". Friendship-love is "a delight in the presence of the other and an affirming of his or her value and development as much as one's own".[59]

Without the capacity to give and receive friendship-love, there is no way to universal love. The sign of true friendship, of a redeemed and redeeming friendship, is its liberating effect for universal love. Of this psychological experience, Goethe says, "A heart that loves one person can hate no one".[60] A highly developed friendship-love discovers the design for goodness in the other, and having discovered it in one person, the friend is eager to discover it in all.

Jesus has schooled his disciples for universal love in a group of close friends. And this seems to be a rule also from the psychological point of view. The Quakers call themselves "the Society of Friends". Fostering friendship among their members opens them to an inclusiveness that has generous and sincere concern for all. Friendship is the source of *diakonia*, of service and ministry.

The Second Vatican Council speaks emphatically on this broadening of the horizons of love.[61] The declaration on Religious Liberty has to be seen in this perspective.

Teilhard de Chardin sees in this universal love a special sign for our times. "We are often inclined to think that we have exhausted the various natural forms of love with man's love for his wife, his children, his friends, and to a certain extent for his country. Yet precisely the most fundamental form of passion is missing from the list". Teilhard is aware of possible objections and real difficulties, as long as one is imprisoned in an abstract or collective idea. To this he responds, "It is impossible to give oneself to an anonymous number. But if the universe ahead of us assumes a face and heart and, so to speak, personifies itself, then in the atmosphere created by this focus, an elemental attraction will immediately blossom". And he further explains, "Not, of course, by becoming a person but by charging itself at the very heart of its development with the dominating and unifying influence of a focus of personal energies and attractions".[62]

Teilhard is especially fascinated by the development of the universe towards unification because this vision is Christic and mystic. In a passionate love he sees how everything issues from divine love and is attracted by him who is Love. Everything that is less than personal enters, for him, the great believer, into the dialogue of love between God and humankind, which is the great history of love, and to which all of evolution tends. "The universe is a collector and a conservator, not of mechanical energies, as we suppose, but of persons, All, one by one, will find final conversion by the very nature of Omega".[63]

The message of universal love rooted in the God of love is meaningful only if believers manifest "solidarity with the doomed of the earth".[64] If we honour the least of our brothers and sisters as friends in Christ, then and only then can we speak of universal love.

2. *Eros and Philia*

In his extreme concern for the purity and absolute gratuity of gift-love (*agapé*), Anders Nygren fails practically the incarnational aspect of redeemed and redeeming love.[65] Joseph Pieper considers Nygren's work to be not only tainted by a discarnate supernaturalism but also by a plain denigration of the *eros*. The eros is, point by point, presented as the enemy of agapé; it is neither creative nor spontaneous.[66] C.S. Lewis hits the mark by describing the person who hopes only for a love that is totally gift-love as a vain and stupid creature who, before his Creator, is boasting that he comes not as a beggar but with selfless love.[67]

While Nygren is concerned for supernatural purity, the pure gift character of love, Emmanuel Kant is concerned with the purity of motivation understood as recognition of duty. Love based on affection and attraction is for him a "pathological love". The moral man's love must be a "practical love" as "a mere love of law".[68]

God, being himself the great attractive power of love, has made the good attractive; and since Christ has come to draw all to himself and to the Father, he surely does not exclude the drawing-power of inclination and affection for his attractive love. "Since love is the basic power of man expressing his whole self, there must be a place for emotion, imagination, affection" not only in persons but also in the Church and in lofty desires and ideals.[69]

Following Aristotle and the great tradition of Church Fathers and scholastics, Johann Baptist Lotz ascribes an important role within the *philia*, the friendship-love, to the eros. Although by itself eros is not yet friendship, it does yearn for it if it is not alienated. It can remain on the level of that spontaneity which is not yet controlled by the higher freedom, yet it is not excluded from the realm of freedom. Once a person has clearly made his or her fundamental option for philia and agapé, eros can come to its fullness. This full development and integration of the eros is not a matter of despotic precept against the nature of the eros; on the contrary, it is "the completion that is designed for him by man's totality".[70]

Karl Rahner goes ever further. He sees in the eros a *potentia obedientialis*, that profound openness in the human person and that innermost yearning that makes the person able to receive the gratuitous love of God.[71] The deepest longing of need-love is for gift-love, the agapé, although this yearning is recognized as such only when it is fulfilled.

All human love, insofar as it is truly human love, can be redeemed and wants to be redeemed. It is surely not to the honour of the one God, the Creator and Redeemer, to belittle and even to bedevil the energies of human love. These cannot be totally destroyed by original sin but come gradually to strength and purity wherever the fundamental option for the good is made.

3. *Eros and agapé*

Since Jesus Christ is the incarnation of *agapé*, he is also the redeemer of *eros* and brings *philia* to completion. The growth of redeemed and redeeming love is, in final analysis, the ongoing incarnation of this same apagé.[72]

We see agapé, above all, in the perspective of God's initiative, of his absolutely free and undeserved love. In this perspective we also praise him for our need-love, for the eros, and for those degrees of friendship that somehow make us more receptive to the divine love. All this comes to its truth when it is considered as a gift of the Creator and in the light of the highest form of his gift, his love.

When the believer, in response to God's love (agapé), has committed himself in a fundamental option to the God of love, then all the prior dispositions, especially eros and friendship, are gradually transformed, purified and raised to a higher level. This does not mean that they lose their own character; on the contrary, they find their greatest fullness and authenticity. In the agapé-friendship with Jesus, the disciple learns friendship with fellow-disciples, where receiving and giving love are inseparable. Both are marked by gratitude and thus can be brought home into the Eucharist.

In the reciprocity of gift-love, we find the freedom to recognize our own and the other's needs and to praise God for the capacity to complete each other. In this reciprocity with the human partner, there is a presence of the divine Partner who gives to human friendship its wholeness. The more the human partners communicate to each other their experience of the divine Partner, the stronger and purer will be their mutual love.[73]

Agapé opens the horizons of the sacred in the midst of human experience. It is in this love that we come closer to the fundamental knowledge that the God of Love is the Holy One. Man comes closer to salvation to the extent that his grateful and truthful love invites him to put all his trust in Christ and his Spirit, thus making his whole life adoration in spirit and truth. An adoring love makes the person a sharer in God's own love, and in that love the person gratefully makes himself a free servant of all God's children.

To this redeemed and redeeming love, and only to this, St Augustine ascribes the freedom and capacity to find the proper expression and action for love. "Have true love and do what you want".[74] This is the most courageous expression of the hope that man, in all the powers of his love, can be transformed by the divine love.

4. Love of enemies

The poor and the enemy are the two great tests of the authenticity of one's love.[75] No one can imitate God's love and share in it if he is unwilling to be a peacemaker, to forgive and to heal both on the individual and on the collective level. God establishes his kingdom of love and freedom by calling sinners (who by their very sin are his enemies) to become his friends and children. "Christ died for us while we were yet sinners, and that is God's own proof of his love towards us ... When we were God's enemies we were reconciled to him through the death of his Son" (Rom 5:8, 10).

From God's example, we learn to love the "enemy", inasmuch as he is called to the love of God and to universal friendship under God. Love of enemy is a healing love in the power of agapé, the love of benevolence which we experience in Christ.

The commandment to love our enemies is absolutely central in the Christian economy of salvation, and is truly binding. It is already repeatedly stressed in the Old Testament (Lev 19:17; Job 31:29ff; Prov 25:21ff; Sir 28:1ff). One of the most striking examples of love of one's enemies is the tender solicitude of Joseph of Egypt towards his brothers who had sold him into slavery. The Old Testament nowhere says, "Thou shalt hate thine enemy" (cf. Mt 5:43) but some of the rabbis of Jesus' time interpreted the Old Testament texts in a sense of mere non-binding counsel, as if it might mean, "You shall love your neighbour but you may hate your enemy". Jesus, however, made it solemnly clear that all people are our neighbours and that love of enemy is the supreme test of our love of God and of our gratitude for his forgiveness. "What I tell you is this: love your enemies and pray for your persecutors; only so can you be children of your heavenly Father who makes his sun rise on good and bad alike" (Mt 5:43-45).

Forgiveness is healing only when it comes from the heart. The readiness to forgive, to heal and to reconcile must even be given before the offender begs for pardon, just as God meets us with his grace to enable us to repent before we have asked him for forgiveness. A wholehearted forgiveness is the condition for God's peace reigning in our hearts and for confidence that we shall be forgiven and be called his children (cf. Mt 6:12ff). Those who live the Eucharist in ongoing praise and thanksgiving for God's healing forgiveness will set no limits for their goodness and readiness to forgive (cf. Mt 18:21ff).

A love of enemy is serene, yet it is the most aggressive and effective power of love. We can overcome evil only through good. "If your enemy is hungry, feed him; if he is thirsty, give him a drink; by doing this you will be heaping live coals on his head. Do not let evil conquer you but use good to defeat evil" (Rom 12:20; cf. Prov 25:21ff).

Christian forgiveness is a part of the beatitude proclaimed for the peacemakers (Mt 5:9). Forgiveness and reconciliation concern the salvation of all. Those are truly reconciled who show merciful love for the other. The Christian suffers with his neighbour whose anger is aroused against him. We are unable to offer worship to God in spirit and truth if this anger contaminates our relationship. "If, when you are bringing your gift to the altar, you suddenly remember that your brother has a grievance against you, leave your gift where it is before the altar. First go and make your peace with your brother and only then come back and offer your gift" (Mt 5:23-24).

Redeemed and liberating love makes it imperative for us to wish our enemy well, and forbids us to rejoice in his distress and failures. "Love keeps no score of wrongs; does not gloat over other men's sins" (1 Cor 13:5). Job enjoyed a special peace of conscience because he never exulted over the misfortune of an enemy (Jb 31:29ff).

A sincere and effective love of the enemy is sometimes

very difficult to achieve; but the disciple of Christ sets himself decisively on the way. He does wholeheartedly what he can, and prays for what he cannot do. Love of enemy is patient with the other and patient with oneself. But patience has nothing to do with inertia; it is the collected energy of a love that is filled with hope.

The offending party or the one with the greater guilt is, absolutely speaking, obliged in justice to take the first step towards reconciliation. But in the light of divine justice and under the law of grace, the one who has received the greater gift of God, the greater capacity to heal and to make peace, is obliged by this very law of grace to take the first step. One who claims that he cannot forgive because the other is wrong and has not yet asked forgiveness should put himself before the saving justice of God and see how wrong his reasoning is. St Alphonsus warns, "Love of justice is only too readily made a cloak which hypocritically masks a spirit of revenge".[76] However, sincere love can and must sometimes be reconciled with a moderate and restrained insistence on justice, especially when the rights of third parties and the common good are involved.

IV. LOVE AS MINISTRY OF SALVATION

Nothing is more prominent in the Second Vatican Council than the Church's self-understanding of being a "sacrament of salvation".[77] Practically, the main purpose in all the documents of this "pastoral council" is the right understanding of and the motivation for the apostolate of the Church. But what is most characteristic is the emphasis that the Church as a whole, as people of God, is founded for this apostolic purpose. The fact that there is a special ministry of apostolate must never darken but rather should illumine the universal vocation to be disciples of Christ and to live in him the essential vocation of all to share in his redemptive task in the apostolate.[78]

1. A vocation for all who love the Lord

Christ came to reveal the Father's love to us, to make us sharers in his own love, and thus to bring us to salvation. For this same purpose he has founded the Church. All who rejoice in knowing him and the Father, and who call themselves disciples of Christ, share in this common vocation. "By its very nature the Christian vocation is also a vocation to the apostolate. No part of the structure of a living body is merely passive but each has a share in the functions as well as in the life of the body. So, too, in the Body of Christ, which is the Church, the whole body 'according to the functioning in due measure of each single part, derives its increase' ... The laity, too, share in the priestly, prophetic and royal office of Christ and therefore have their own role to play in the mission of the whole people of God, in the Church and in the world".[79]

The vocation to holiness is a call to perfect charity and coincides with the noble task of spreading the Good News, of making the love of God known so that all may join with Christ in adoration of the Father. "Every exercise of the apostolate takes its origin and power from charity".[80] In the apostolate, saving love is everything. The point of departure is Christ in his paschal communion with the Father, glorified by the Holy Spirit who is Love. Its purpose is to extend the kingdom of God, the kingdom of saving love. The strength of the apostolate is the Holy Spirit who has empowered Christ to give himself up for our salvation and it is he who continues this same work in the disciples of Christ.[81]

Christ's mission to make all people partakers of God's saving love is not something added to his coming from the Father and returning to the Father. He returns to the Father by giving himself up on the cross for the salvation of all. Thus he has glorified the Father, and the Father responds by glorifying his Son. It is therefore impossible to separate the vocation of the Church and of every disciple of Christ from their mission to join in the Paschal Mystery of Christ, in his saving love and his zeal to bring all people to salvation.

The Church as a whole is apostolic. First, she is expected to be faithful to her origin with the twelve apostles, and secondly, to be wholly dedicated to the apostolate. These two aspects are, indeed, one, for the Lord has built his Church on the apostles so that all may continue the apostolic mission. The apostles and their successors do not, by themselves, take up the whole mission: they form disciples of Christ who will associate themselves with the same task, in adoration of God in spirit and truth.[82] Although there is a special priesthood in the Church, and a hierarchical structure, this by no means infers a monopoly of apostolate. Rather, it is the special task of the priests and the hierarchy to live and to spread that love of Christ which makes us all sharers in the apostolate.

The mission to manifest saving love is not a superimposed commandment but is inborn in the grace and the very dynamism of the holiness to which we are called. Every disciple of Christ has been granted the wonderful task and call to share in his redemptive love and work, "in the One and through the One saved and saving".[83]

Salvation is an indivisible reality. A disciple of Christ cannot receive life in Christ without sharing Christ's zeal for the salvation of all. The three main aspects — the glorification of God, universal salvation and individual salvation — cannot be separated. The disciple comes closer to salvation by the very manifestation of the love that brings the other closer to salvation. Apostolic love assures us in a special way that we are sharers of Christ's saving love (cf. 1 Cor 9:19-23).

The social dimension of saving love requires solidarity in the exercise of the apostolate. Each disciple is expected to make full use of his or her special charism, and to do so in a spirit of solidarity. "For the exercise of this apostolate, the Holy Spirit who sanctifies the people of God through the ministry and sacraments gives to the faithful special gifts as well (cf. 1 Cor 12:7), 'allotting to everyone as he wills' (1 Cor 12:11). Thus may the individual, 'according to the gift that each has received, administer it to one another' and become a 'good steward of the manifold grace of God' (1 Pet 4:10), and build up thereby the whole body in charity (cf. Eph 4:16)".[84] There is, however, a special need for leadership, in order to help in the discernment of the charisms and the ongoing effort to use all of them in harmony.

2. The sacraments and apostolate

In the Eucharist the Church celebrates her union with Christ, the source of all sacramentality and salvation. At the Last Supper, Christ instituted the messianic banquet, celebrating it with the twelve apostles. Does this not signify that the Church consists forever of disciples and apostles?[85] The apostles are not only the beginning of the sacred hierarchy but also and above all, "the first members of the new Israel".[86]

The Last Supper is the abiding image of the Church. The sacrament of the kingdom is Christ and his apostles and disciples celebrating together the saving Paschal Mystery. They all learn from Christ to give themselves wholly to the saving love that always has its centre and summit in his death and resurrection. "Through the sacraments, especially the Holy Eucharist, there is communicated and nourished that charity towards God and men which is the soul of the entire apostolate".[87]

The Eucharist should bring all the disciples to an ever-increasing awareness that they share in the priesthood of Christ and therefore also in his saving charity. The Eucharist is grace and calling for all to render thanks always for the gift of salvation and to offer "the immaculate Victim not only through the hands of the priest but also with him, offering themselves too".[88] Only by uniting with the sacrificial love of Christ which is completed in the Paschal Mystery, do the faithful enter truthfully into the mystery of redemption; and this is not conceivable without an ever intensified participation in the apostolate for which Christ founded the Church. The emphasis on the faithful's active participation in the Eucharist is very important, but this means activation not only in the external forms but, above all, in renewed commitment to the redemptive work of Christ.

Tradition has always affirmed that baptism and confirmation impress indelibly in the Christian the sacred commission of participation in the high-priestly concern of Christ for the salvation of man, to the glory of God. The Second Vatican Council emphasizes this doctrine and its practical consequences. "Incorporated into Christ's Mystical Body through baptism, and strengthened by the power of the Holy Spirit through confirmation, the believers are assigned to the apostolate by the Lord himself. They are consecrated into a royal priesthood and a holy people (cf. 1 Pet 2:4-10) in order that they may offer spiritual sacrifices through everything they do, and may witness to Christ throughout the world".[89]

The Holy Spirit is already given in baptism. Where the Spirit is, there is salvation — not only received but also active through charity. Confirmation means an advance characteristic of the new life of love. The expansion, through confirmation, of the priestly participation in Christ imparted in baptism, manifests the basic line of supernatural growth. The Christian grows into Christ and into redemptive love in whatever measure he realizes that his individual salvation is only a radiation of the total fullness of salvation in Christ and in the Church. "Bound more intimately to the Church by the sacrament of confirmation, the faithful are endowed by the Holy Spirit with a special strength. Hence they are more strictly obliged to spread and defend the faith by both word and deed as true witnesses of Christ".[90]

What is new in the character of confirmation, in contradistinction to the mark of baptism, is that the confirmed person is qualified and obliged to act as a mature member of the Church through responsible initiatives. He or she is to "participate in the priestly and royal action of Christ by publicly cooperating in the spreading of the kingdom of God and withstanding the obstacles and difficulties which contradict the growth of the kingdom".[91]

The gifts of the Holy Spirit are imparted in view of the spiritual combat of saving love against the destructive powers. As Christ has conquered the godless world by his love and surrender unto death, so those who are baptized in the Holy Spirit will trust that the final victory is for love.

For the believer who follows the call of the apostolate, endowed as he is with the pentecostal spirit of love and fortitude through the sacrament of confirmation, two predominant types of participation in the redemptive love are open. The first is the individual engagement granted him in his own position and in the hour of grace, and the second is the organized action of the Catholic laity who follow the direction of the hierarchy. We may not assume that there is a universal obligation to participate in this latter form of apostolate unless there is a special need. But no one will neglect the social dimension of the apostolate.

Vatican II speaks eloquently on marriage and the family as an opportunity and a school for the lay apostolate. "Since the Creator of all things has established the conjugal partnership as the beginning and basis of human society and by his grace has made it a great mystery in Christ and the Church (cf. Eph 5:32), the apostolate of married persons and of families is of unique importance for the Church and civil society. Christian husbands and wives are cooperators in the grace and witness of faith on behalf of each other, their children and all others in their household. They are the first to communicate the faith to their children and to educate them; by word and example they train their offspring for the Christian and apostolic life".[92] "The family is, so to speak, the domestic Church. In it, parents should be, by their words and example, the first heralds of the Good News to their children".[93]

The family's apostolic riches will radiate far beyond its own realm. Its apostolate will give particular attention to the many interdependencies between family and religion, family and culture, family and society, and so on. Families will join together in their efforts to create human conditions and public opinions more favourable for the development of healthy marriage and family life.

Consecration to Christ through the vows of poverty, obedience and celibacy for the kingdom of God is not a sacrament in the strict sense, but the public vow in religion binds one in the saving union between Christ and the Church in a way similar to the sacrament of marriage. Through its special grace it imposes a most pressing obligation to bear witness to the universal call to holiness which is, by necessity, also a call to the apostolate. A life according to the vow of poverty makes authentic and visible the vocation of all to seek first the kingdom of God, and all other things only in view of the kingdom. The vow of religious obedience should lead to a radiant witness of docility to the Holy Spirit and the generous use of all of one's capacities and charisms for the good and salvation of all. Celibacy for the kingdom of God means freedom for Christ and a total readiness for that love which seeks first the salvation of others.

3. *Basic expression of active zeal for the salvation of fellowmen*

The general obligation that binds all Christians to concern themselves and to care for the salvation of all for whom Christ died includes the following positive obligations: prayer and sacrifice, good example, the work of Christian instruction, encouragement and correction. Of course there is also, negatively, the obligation to shun all that could imperil the salvation of others, such as scandal and complicity in the sins of others.

a) The apostolate of prayer

Holy Scripture makes it evident that prayer is of prime importance in the redeeming work of Jesus. His prayer gives meaning and strength to all that he does, says and suffers for our salvation. It is the prayer of the Prophet, the Mediator and High Priest. "In the days of his earthly life he offered up prayers and petitions with loud cries and tears ... Because of his humble submission his prayer was heard; Son though he was, he learned obedience in the school of suffering and, once perfected, became the source of eternal salvation for all who obey him" (Heb 5:7-10). He teaches his disciples the prayer for the coming of the kingdom, which is the salvation of all to the glory of God.

The apostle's life is, above all, a life of apostolic prayer and of teaching the faithful to pray apostolically also. "First of all, then, I urge that petitions, prayers, intercessions and thanksgiving be offered for all ... Such prayer is right and approved by God, our Saviour, whose will it is that all should find salvation and come to know the truth. For there is one God, and also one Mediator between God and man, Christ Jesus, himself man, who sacrificed himself to win freedom for all humankind" (1 Tim 2:1, 3-6).

If our prayer is apostolic, it is offered with a great willingness to work and to suffer everything for the salvation of our fellowmen. Then we are sure that we offer prayers in the name of Jesus, and that this prayer will not be fruitless.

In the life of Christ, his prayer and his suffering are one. They are offered to the Father for our salvation. Our prayer follows his if we, too, are willing to shoulder our cross and to offer our suffering for the salvation of the world. "Let each one remember that he can have an impact on all and contribute to the salvation of the whole world by public worship and prayer as well as by penance and voluntary acceptance of the labours and hardships of life. By such means does the Christian grow in likeness to the suffering Christ" (cf. 2 Cor 4:10; Col 1:24).[94]

The Apostle of the Gentiles manifests with great fervour this readiness to offer his suffering for the redemption of all. "It is now my happiness to suffer for you. This is my way of helping to complete, in my poor human flesh, the full tale of Christ's afflictions still to be endured, for the sake of his body which is the Church" (Col 1:24). "And I endure it all for the sake of God's chosen ones with this end in view, that they too may attain the glorious and eternal salvation which is in Christ Jesus" (2 Tim 2:10). For Paul, this is an expression of our "being in Christ". We conceive salvation not in a juridical form, as merits earned by Christ and then to be merely distributed. We see it as Christ's life permeating his disciples, conforming them and associating them with his own salvific life and work.

It is not as though the prayer and suffering, death and resurrection of Christ is in any way inadequate for the salvation of all; but the salvific economy of the kingdom of God allows and calls for participation with Christ. He who is seated at the right hand of the Father and interecedes for us lives in the Church and in all his disciples until his work is completed. We should see also the role and privileges of Mary in this perspective. They do not separate her from us but show us how to be united with Christ in his redemptive work.

b) The apostolate of good example

Our prayer and expiation are directed immediately to God; we affect our fellowmen only through the mysterious solidarity of salvation in Christ. Good example and fraternal encouragement are directed immediately to our neighbour in a psychologically experiential way. And it is here, in this immediacy, that we see how effective and constant is the power of an exemplary personality. First, then, we look at the significance of the model in Christian morality.

Christ, who is the visible image of the Father, is the exemplary cause of our salvation (cf. 2 Cor 4:4; Col 1:15). Reborn in him, we can become for each other a true image of God. If we speak of good example, it is not so much a calculated good action or gesture as an effort to become for each other truly a model, an image in Jesus Christ. Discipleship means "being constantly renewed in the image of the Creator and brought to know God" (Col 3:10). God has chosen us to be "shaped to the likeness of his Son, that he might be the eldest among a large family of brothers" (Rom 8:29). We become, as it were, a revelation for each other of God's goodness and saving presence.

Being light in Jesus Christ who is the Light, the disciples draw their fellowmen's attention to Christ who is the model Person. This is more important than laws, precepts and individual acts of good example, for the person of Jesus Christ as the model of the new man is more central than law and norms, and gives meaning to them. The supreme calling of the disciple, then, is to become, in Christ and through him, an image of the very goodness and compassionate love of the Father (cf. Mt 5:48; Lk 6:36). Only Christ, who comes from the bosom of the Father can show him to us: "He who sees me also sees the Father" (Jn 14:9). Discipleship is configuration with Christ. Therefore we have to learn not only from his words but, above all, from his being the image of the Father: "I have set you an example; you are to do as I have done for you" (Jn 13:15).

In Jesus, the ultimate pattern is revealed for all times, and thereby the likeness of the children of God. Similarly, the saints, all in their own time, are visible reflections of Christ and guides leading to him. Though by comparison with Christ the reflection is faint indeed, nevertheless the image of Christ comes closer to us and touches us more immediately when we see him in his saints. This is one of the reasons why veneration of the saints is so significant in the Church. The humble saints in our own environment are like beacon lights pointing to the prototype of all morality, to Christ. As sunlight is reflected in a prism in many rays, so in each of the saints Christ the Light is reflected for us. Like Paul and his co-workers, those are true apostles who, by their whole life, invite us to follow and to imitate Christ (cf. 1 Cor 4:16; 11:1; Phil 3:17; 1 Tim 4:12; Tit 2:7ff.).

The exemplary life and the apostolic word fit together like sign and word in the sacraments. As the ministry of the word must never be without witness, so the witnessing life prepares the word spoken at the right moment. "The very testimony of their Christian life and good works done in a supernatural spirit have the power to draw men to belief and to God; for the Lord says, 'And you, like the lamp, must shed light among your fellows, so that when they see the good you do, they may give praise to your Father in heaven' " (Mt 5:16).[95]

This significance of the exemplary person is fully appreciated by present day psychologists. They distinguish, however, between the conscious and unconscious following of a model. A person should be fully conscious of the exemplar who influences him or her. But here we are speaking of persons who deserve to be models or patterns for our own way of life. The merit of a model lies in the concrete and vivid appeal that invites trust and a healthy relationship, and awakens us to an appreciation and deeper knowledge of ethical and religious values. The person who incarnates mature love, responsibility and creative fidelity enkindles a profound knowledge of and a great attraction to these same values. Max Scheler is right when he asserts that "the principle of the pattern of conduct exemplified in the model is everywhere the primary vehicle of all transformations in the moral world".[96]

If such is the power of an exemplary person, then it is obvious that the responsibility for the salvation of others imposes a serious obligation to give good example. This, of course, implies much more than the duty to perform individual exemplary acts. Rather, it is the comprehensive obligation to try to become model personalities, loving persons who can attract others to the good. Yet concern for the salvation of our fellow-men can and should be also a motive for specific exemplary actions and for avoidance of other specific actions.

Many things may be good and lawful as far as the individual Christian is concerned, but consideration of the effect they might have on others can forbid us doing them. Similarly, a special need to encourage others may be a reason to perform actions which are not in themselves mandatory but are, here and now, the best way to act because of their beneficial influence on others. In brief, the main motive for our actions is their intrinsic goodness, from which naturally follows their attractiveness in general or in special circumstances. The practical effectiveness of good example does not consist in the particular acts alone but rather in the attraction for good in the personality itself.

Those in authority, whether in the Church or in society, and those who are looked up to in any group or community, should especially be models of conduct, carefully weighing their actions in view of their impact on others. The weight of authority and the beauty of example combine to produce an overwhelming effect on people that can result in setting free the energies of creative liberty and fidelity. A winning exemplary character in parents furnishes the very foundation for the children's early moral formation. Before a child can understand the reasons behind parental guidance and particular rules, it can intuit the value of the good that shines forth in the parents. If the child can trust that they are good and loving, and also are willing to correct their own faults, then there grows in the child a basic faith in the good, and love for it.

Whoever has gained the love of his fellowmen is particularly bound to give good example, for the reciprocal love that makes the good example more effective also makes poor or bad example more dangerous. Noble friendship, especially wedded love, can be a precious additional motive for trying to become an exemplary person and thus a witness to Christ's redeeming love.

c) Fraternal encouragement and correction

In a traditional list of spiritual works of merciful love — to instruct the ignorant, to counsel the perplexed, to console the sorrowing, to correct the erring, to forgive injuries, to bear wrongs patiently, to pray for the living and the dead — fraternal encouragement and correction occupies a prominent position. For St Paul, the attempt to rescue others from dangerous sins is at the very heart of "the law of Christ" (Gal 6:2). He considers it as an expression of our being of the same family; therefore he requires "friendly advice" (2 Thess 3:15).

Christ did not come primarily to correct us or to blame us, but first to proclaim the Good News by his word and his whole life and death; and only in this context does he admonish and warn us. Fraternal correction can have its meaning and efficiency only in such an ambience of constructive friendship. It is a privileged way of coming together in the name of Christ (cf. Mt 18:15-20). But only those who are aware of their own need for further conversion can fulfil the command given by the Apostle, "You must live at peace among yourselves. And we would urge you to admonish the careless, encourage the faint-hearted, support the weak, and to be very patient with them all" (1 Thess 5:14).

The more the love of neighbour grows under the impulse of grace, the more the believer will feel himself obliged to help the other, insofar as he can, on the road to salvation, the road to holiness. But under certain conditions there is a particular and grave obligation to do so: (1) when the salvation of the neighbour is in serious peril; (2) when there is reasonable hope that help will be accepted and will prove fruitful; (3) when, in one's own prudent judgment, admonition is the sole means of averting the evil.

On the first point, it is not the fault of the other, as such, that justifies or demands correction, but the danger which threatens him. We are not meant to be judges but healers. It is better to prevent a fault by assisting one's neighbour by judicious and timely intervention than to await actual commission of sin. However, only parents or those in a similar position would be obliged to investigate the existence of spiritual hazards that endanger those committed to their care. There will be careful avoidance of any distrustful attitude in matters relating to the other's conduct, for it would jeopardize the mutual confidence so necessary for mutual encouragement and correction. Where there is great mutual trust, an honest question might prove sufficient to alert the neighbour to possible spiritual perils.

On the second point, everyone, on principle, is obliged to offer fraternal correction when the neighbour is in great need of it. However, for people who have not yet acquired the self-control and gentleness necessary for this help (cf. Gal 6: 1), there is an added motive and obligation first to acquire these qualities. Should there be no danger of scandal caused by our non-intervention, and no other good at stake except the salvation of the individual who is in error or sin, there can be no obligation to act in a cause which is futile. *A fortiori*, there is no obligation to correct the faults of others if there is reason to anticipate more harm than good as a result of such endeavours. On the other hand, if no harm is in prospect but rather some hope of success despite possible misgivings, we do not have sufficient reason to omit the correction.

In some instances, one who is obliged to correct another realizes from past experience that he himself is not likely to succeed. If he knows someone else more qualified and more acceptable to the one in need, he may ask him to undertake the task. Even parents or superiors who ordinarily have a special obligation might sometimes have recourse to others who, in their opinion, are more qualified or more acceptable.

The occasion or moment chosen for correction is not without its importance. It is better to wait for an opportune time than to risk a complete failure, even though new faults may be added to the old, assuming, of course, that the common good is safeguarded. Ordinarily, however, it is better to correct evil in its very inception than to wait until it is strong and obdurate in its hold on our neighbour. Those who admonish others out of personal resentment, or demean those in their charge for every petty failure, are themselves often accountable for the failure of fraternal admonition.

Traditional theology considers the omission of fraternal correction particularly grave when those in authority are in need of it and there is reasonable hope that its being given might help. The reasoning is that particular love is due to those who bear the burden of authority, but even more urgent is the concern for the common good.[97]

As to point three, follow-up criticism of faults is contrary to charity. Once the sin is corrected and our neighbour has amended his fault, there is neither need nor excuse for further correction. Of course, in the event of a new danger it may be pedagogically sound to remind the neighbour kindly of his frailty in this regard; but if he is aware of his weakness, positive encouragement might be more necessary than a reminder of past faults.

As a matter of principle, scrupulous persons do not incur the obligation of fraternal correction, especially if some of their mental torment is centred precisely in this sensitive area.

Reporting faults to superiors is permissible only if those in charge are best qualified to help the one who is in need, or if the common good is at stake. A fault corrected may never be reported to those in authority.

d) Creating a favourable environment

Fraternal correction can be like medicating fish in polluted waters; it may be much better to clear the water. The behavioural sciences and modern conditions of life, as well as a deeper understanding of the mission of the Church for the world, have alerted our consciences about our responsibilities not just for souls but for the wholeness of persons and communities in the world in which they live with many interactions. The first task of the Church, as well as of all the faithful, is to cooperate in making the Church ever more a divine milieu, a living Gospel. It is not just a matter of correcting a Church leader who might be at fault; rather, it is a collective task for all the faithful in the various parts of Christianity to work together to make the Church ever more holy, catholic, apostolic, and one in holiness.

Individually and collectively, the Church leaders are obliged to share their apostolic efforts with the laity, especially with those of particular holiness and competence, in order to promote the renewal of the Church and its incarnation in the various cultures. The mission of the Church requires the cooperation of all.

Christ, the Prophet, continues his work of renewing the face of the earth and of the Church, through those whom he has called to share in his prophetic office. That includes all believers who let themselves be totally guided by the Spirit. The laity shares in this prophetic office of the Church and therefore, according to each one's special gifts and capacities, they must be concerned for the renewal of the Church as well as for the ordering of the temporal world for the benefit of all. "A layman, by reason of the knowledge, competence or outstanding ability which he may enjoy, is permitted and sometimes even obliged to express his opinion on things which concern the good of the Church. When occasions arise, let this be done through the agencies set up by the Church for this purpose".[98]

Both the hierarchy and the laity must be concerned for the whole human environment, that it may be ordered to the honour of God and for the wholeness of human persons, which always has to do with salvation. But the laity has a special competence and obligation in this sphere. Christ is the Redeemer not only of souls but of the whole world, and Christians share in this redemptive task. "Through the members of the Church, Christ will progressively illumine the whole of human society with his saving light. Moreover, let the laity also, by their combined efforts, remedy any institutions and conditions of the world which are customarily an inducement to sin, so that all such things may be conformed to the norms of justice and may favour the practice of virtue rather than hinder it. By doing so, lay people will imbue culture and human activity with moral values. They will better prepare the field of the world for the seed of the Word of God".[99]

The Second Vatican Council has made a great and systematic effort for a better understanding of the mission of the Church as a whole, and how each part and member can be "salt for the earth", making the world a divine milieu in which Christ's redemptive work becomes ever more visible and operative. For this task we need an urgent spirit of initiative and freedom, and of solidarity wherein the faithful can see ever more clearly God's creative and redemptive presence in the Church. "The laity should also know that it is generally the function of their well-formed Christian conscience to see that the divine law is inscribed in the life of the earthly city. From priests they may look for spiritual light and nourishment. Let the lay people not imagine that their pastors are always such experts that to every problem that arises, however complicated, they can readily give a concrete solution, or even that such is their mission. Rather, enlightened by Christian wisdom and giving close attention to the teaching authority of the Church, let the lay people take on their own distinctive role".[100]

4. *The official apostolate of the Church*

a) Ordained ministers

The affirmation that charity makes all the disciples of Christ apostles is not the whole truth although it is one important aspect of it. The apostolate does not arise from charity alone but, above all, through institution by Jesus Christ.

Christ founded his Church on the apostles. He not only instructed them and made them his friends but he also celebrated the Last Supper with them, and prayed for them, that they might be consecrated by the truth as he had consecrated himself for the work of redemption (Jn 17:17-19). The risen Lord makes them his messengers and fills them with the Holy Spirit: "As the Father has sent me, so I send you. Then he breathed on them saying, 'Receive the Holy Spirit' " (Jn 20:21-22).

Christ "appointed twelve as his companions whom he would send out to proclaim the gospel" (Mk 3:14). With them he celebrates the messianic banquet and calls them friends (Jn 15:15). They are the germ of the Church and symbolize her future. It is decisive that they are companions and friends of Christ, totally dedicated to him, and that they consecrate themselves for the work of redemption as he did. Therefore the consecrated ministry "presupposes an identification with Christ".[101]

These chosen friends are called and, by the power of the Holy Spirit, are enabled to be dedicated wholly to the service of the Gospel and thus to the kingdom of God and the salvation of humankind. They are to be friends of Christ and friends among themselves, united with him in the same love for the salvation of all people. They can be called "vicars of Christ"; and it is their wonderful privilege and mission to make Christ present with all their being, their love and their devotion to the spreading of the Gospel. Being authorized as his vicars, they guarantee the presence of Christ. Even Karl Barth can say, "To deny on principle the vicar of Christ would entail denying the *Christus praesens*".[102] He insists that his dissent from the Catholic dogma concerns only the "how" of this vicarship: that as vicars of Christ they cannot take his place but must most humbly point to him, and that they should not think that Christ is bound to their office but rather that their office is bound to Christ. As good Catholics we can only thoroughly agree on this point.

The apostles are dedicated to the Easter mystery by a death similar to that of Christ, which puts to death all selfishness so that they may live in Christ and for his Gospel. They are sent as witnesses who must be ready to shed their blood for Christ and to manifest this readiness by their whole style of life. No wonder, then, that the third century Canons of Hippolyte determined that a confessor who has proved his readiness to give his life for Christ is, without formal ordination, empowered to preside at the Eucharist![103]

At the Last Supper, Christ did not say to his apostles, "Consecrate the bread and the wine", but "Do this in memory of me". This implies total dedication to Christ; they give themselves wholly to proclaim his saving death and the Gospel of the resurrection. It is the "consecration in truth" of which Christ speaks (Jn 17:17-19).[104] Their apostolate cannot be separated from their communion with Christ. Not to be his friends contradicts their very mission. To be with Christ, to join him in his love for the redeemed, and to be sent by him are two inseparable aspects. "The apostle is sent as much as he is in Christ".[105] As Christ is "consecrated and sent into the world by the Father" (Jn 10:36), so the apostles are sent as friends of Christ, wholly consecrated to him and with him.

Christ has not come to perfect the priesthood of the Jews and the Gentiles; rather "he has abolished it; he has created apostles. Indeed, he is creating nothing else than apostles. Here we find the basic truth of the theology of the Christian priesthood, of that of the priest and that of the lay people".[106]

The true word for the mission of the priest is "apostolate". His supreme task is to preach the Gospel to all people.[107] This, too, is the principal task of bishops. "Among the principal duties of bishops, the preaching of the Gospel occupies an eminent place. For bishops are preachers of the faith who lead new disciples to Christ".[108] The words of the Apostle, "Woe to me if I do not preach the Gospel", must be in the mind of every bishop and priest. He lives the truth of his calling to the extent that, filled with charity and united with Christ, he makes the apostolate his first task at all times and in all events. This is the first offering he makes to God, which he can bring home into the Eucharist and derive from it. He should be able to say with the apostles, "God is my witness, the God to whom I offer the humble service of my spirit by preaching the Gospel of his Son" (Rom 1:9). He intends to offer, with Christ to the Father, those who are his "offspring" through the Gospel (1 Cor 4:15). "My priestly service is the preaching of the Gospel of God, and it falls on me to offer the Gentiles to him as an acceptable sacrifice consecrated by his Holy Spirit" (Rom 15:16).

The priest is a minister of reconciliation (2 Cor 5:18). He can fulfil this task only if he himself is reconciled and lives as a saint-penitent. He can be a messenger of peace only if he gratefully rejoices in the peace of Christ.

One of the greatest dangers for priests is to become a separate caste rather than being friends of the faithful and totally dedicated to them as friends of Christ. It is shocking to read in Max Weber that the modern Catholic priest and chaplain is as typical a representative of bureaucracy and dominion as the employee of a bank, the manager of a big capitalistic enterprise, or a state official.[109] The power to guide (*potestas dominii*), the jurisdiction of the successors of Peter and the other apostles, must be seen in intimate connection with their being conse-crated to the apostolate.[110]

The distinction between the universal priesthood in which all the faithful share, and the priesthood of the priest in collab-oration with the bishops, is not only one of function, for he is not a mere functionary. The priesthood of Christ is one, and all his disciples share in it but in various ways. "The baptized, by regeneration and the anointing of the Holy Spirit, are con-secrated into a spiritual house and a holy priesthood. Though they differ from one another qualitatively and not only quanta-tively, the common priesthood of the faithful and the ministerial or hierarchical priesthood are nevertheless interrelated. Each of them, in his own special way, is a participant in the one priesthood of Christ".[111]

The apostolate of bishops and priests is therefore not some-thing added to the apostolate of the laity. "The apostolate of the bishops and priests is primordial; it is fundamental".[112] As at the Last Supper, so in the whole reality of the Church's life, the apostle represents the new people of God who are meant to be apostolic. Hence, we should say that the sacrament of priest-hood is not added to that of baptism and confirmation. It is new not by addition but by its fullness.

While all Christians, by their very union with Christ and urged by his love, are apostolic-minded, the priest exercises the apostolate by the commitment of his whole person. Other-wise, he does not exercise it in truth. His action is true and effective only in faith filled with hope and active in love. Since the priest is priest as a Christian, he lives his Christian life and gives witness to it by the very dedication of his apostolate which implies a fullness of saving love. He finds his holiness and sal-vation in the apostolate.[113]

Bishops and priests have no monopoly on the apostolate. Priests and lay people exercise their mission in the Church and in the world for the whole people of God. Both priests and lay people are rooted in the earthly realities, and both are signs of eschatological hope. "The difference is in a greater concen-tration on the ultimate realities in the life of the priest".[114]

There is a distinction in the Church between teaching office and docility, but there is no separation between the teaching Church and the learning Church. "Those who share in a special way in the apostolic succession have, more than others, the role to teach. But they also have more than the others the duty to let themselves be taught by God in the Church".[115]

Priests can and, according to historical circumstances, sometimes must exercise also another profession; but they remain faithful to the truth of their priesthood only if the apostolate always visibly occupies the first place in their lives. Like all other Christians, they are called, above all, to follow Christ in his redeeming love. But if a priest becomes unfaithful to his priesthood and does not live fully a life of faith, hope, love and dedication to the apostolate, he contradicts the sacramental character which he has received in his ordination.

The Eucharist is the source and summit of evangelization, and it is the noble task of the priest to lead the faithful to the redemptive consecration of Christ. It is essential for the priest's celebration that he receive communion. That implies that he cannot truly celebrate the Eucharist unless he is united with Christ and unites himself ever more with his redeeming love, for the salvation of the world.

b) The religious and the apostolic life

What we call today the "life according to the evangelical counsels" was traditionally called "*vita apostolica*", the apostolic life or life of the apostle. This need not mean that the witness of this style of life is the principal motivation for the apostolate; on the other hand, the great freedom for apostolic activities may motivate this style of life. In either case it implies a total consecration to Christ and his redeeming love. It is a life with Christ for his apostolate, to the glory of the Father who is glorified by the salvation of his people.[116]

With the opening words of the decree on Religious Life, *Perfectae caritatis*, the Second Vatican Council underlines the centrality of a constant striving for perfect love. The intent is to give witness that all Christians should seek first the heavenly kingdom, knowing that growth in the love of God and of neighbour is the source of all apostolic fruitfulness.

The availability of the religious communities and secular institutes for preaching the Gospel and carrying out the various forms of charity where there is the greatest need is of great importance for the whole apostolic mission of the Church.

Through religious vows, religious are "more intimately consecrated to divine service. This consecration gains in perfection since, by virtue of fervour and of steadier bonds, it serves as a better symbol of the unbreakable link between Christ and his spouse, the Church. By the charity to which they lead, the evangelical counsels join their followers to the Church and her mystery in a special way".[117]

The religious state belongs inseparably to the life and holiness of the Church. And since religious communities are approved and guided by the successors of the apostles, they belong in a special way to the Church's official apostolate.

Besides the religious orders and congregations, there are the more recent "secular institutes" which offer a form of life open to the common life of lay people. All these testify to the sincere conviction that the evangelical counsels can be fully realized even in the midst of the world and in secular vocations. Such being the case, they are well able to attest to the holiness of the laity in the world and in the married state, for all Christians are called to live the spirit of the evangelical counsels in the depth of their heart, in radical interior freedom, and in total dedication "to the things of the Lord" (1 Cor 7:29ff.).

Added to all these, there are countless members of orders and of secular institutes devoted to charitable and cultural tasks which give significant evidence that the Church is thoroughly concerned for the terrestrial order, realizing that earthly things are indissolubly bound up with people's salvation. Thus the testimony of the holiness and love of Christ and his Church assumes flesh and blood in earthly matters.

c) Lay people participating in the official apostolate

Paul ends his epistle to the Romans with a long list of men and women who toil with him in the Lord's service and are "eminent among the apostles" (Rom 16:1-15). Through the centuries there have been men and women who, without being ordained, have given themselves wholly to the apostolate and were officially acknowledged by bishops and priests as precious collaborators. Today, hundreds of thousands of lay women and men are engaged officially, full or part time, in the apostolate of the Church. There are not only sacristans, organists, choir directors, administrators of church property, artists and writers, but above all, catechists, directors of religious education and pastoral assistants chosen from the laity and given canonical mission.[118]

In a certain sense, these people belong to the clergy. Although they are not ritually ordained, they are sent and assisted by the prayer and blessing of the Church which highly appreciates their dedication to her apostolate. This is a special, quasi-official activation of the sacramental mission which all lay people receive through the sacrament of confirmation, to profess the faith in Christ.[119] Through this greater diversity of lay ministries that somehow belong to the tasks of the apostles and their successors, the Church is now able to respond to many of the new needs in today's world.

In our time, a special way of associating lay people, both individually and communally, with the official apostolate of the Church is Catholic Action in organizations created or officially approved by the hierarchy. They exercise their communal apostolate directly under the auspices and to a certain extent under the responsibility of the hierarchy. This does not at all imply, however, that there is no room for initiative and creativity by the lay organizations themselves, but only that the initiatives should be under the eyes of the hierarchy. The hierarchy does not look upon the lay people in Catholic Action as mere instruments to carry out orders or designs placed before them. Much more is expected: they are to act as mature cooperators in the vineyard of the Lord. The role of the hierarchy is to guarantee the effective cooperation of all the energies, the harmonious orchestration of the vast diversity of gifts and grace, in thoughtful responses to the signs of the times.

Side by side with the Catholic Action groups, there are numerous Christian lay organizations that carry out their social and charitable initiatives on their own responsibility. Especially if the activities and decisions concern political questions, it is better that the accountability should not fall on the official Church.

V. LOVE AND JUSTICE

The constitution on the Church in the Modern World classically synthesizes the forces and dimensions of a redeemed and redeeming community. "The social order must be founded on truth, built on justice and animated by love; in freedom it should grow every day towards a more humane order".[120] The truth of love must shine forth not only in the person-to-person relationships but also in the life of the community and society.

1. We-relationships and they-relationships

Love expresses itself more specifically in I-Thou-We relationships where everyone is accepted, affirmed and loved as a unique person and in a direct relationship. We-relationships are appropriate to friendships and to natural communities like marriage and family and their immediate extensions.

They-relationships are those based on mutual service, on functions and offices. There, love expresses itself chiefly in righteousness and justice. Conduct and activities must not be casual, hence not isolated. They receive stability and reliability by institutional structures and laws. "The beginning, the subject and the goal of all social institutions is and must be the human person which, for its part and by its very nature, stands completely in need of social life. This is not something added to the person. Hence, through his dealings with others, through reciprocal duties, and through fraternal dialogue, man develops all his gifts and is able to rise to his destiny. Among those social ties which man needs for his development, some, like the family and political community, are related with greater immediacy to his innermost nature. Others originate rather from his free decision".[121]

Love becomes a history through its incarnation in customs, traditions, institutions and laws that regulate the they-relationships and strengthen justice. On the other hand, traditions, institutions and laws receive their vitality and meaning through the constant input of love. Loving people are, as it were, the soul of the world by enriching life with the warmth and strength of their love. It is through love that all the other realities become truly creative and redemptive. God's relationships with us are "thou"-relationships, and build up first the we-relationships.

God's love, speaking to us directly through Jesus Christ and by the grace of the Holy Spirit, touches our heart. If we enter into this dialogue by responding to God in adoring love and joining him in creative and redeeming love for our fellow-men, then we also realize that his love and fatherly care speak to us through all of created reality and history. We can consider this as a kind of they-relationship which, through faith, becomes transparent in the Thou-I-We relationships.

If we follow a merely individualistic morality limited to the Thou-I-We relationships, we have not yet entered into the full dimensions, the height and depth, the length and breadth of the mystery of God and his creative and redemptive love.[122]

2. Love and the saving justice of God

To understand better the relation between love and justice, we cannot confine ourselves to psychology and sociology. Above all we must see how, in God's revelation, love is related to his justice. "The content and form of what men seek from each other in a given civilization is adapted by the content and form of that which they seek from heaven, and vice versa".[123]

God reveals his justice in a way that always reveals at the same time, his love. The revelation of Yahweh's justice is almost synonymous with the salvation he grants. In the Bible, "God's justice manifests itself especially as enactment of the covenant in communion with his people".[124] The sinful creature can make no claims on God. But God has revealed his name as Saviour, as Love. Therefore, in fidelity and justice to his own name and his own holiness, his justice reveals itself as fidelity to the covenant, as mercy, as saving justice. The deeds of God's justice are manifestation of his graciousness, of pure mercy.

Before God, there can be no other justice than grateful acceptance of his saving justice, praise of his mercy, and com-mitment to act always with the same justice and mercy. God, who justifies us sinners by his undeserved grace, enables us gradually to conform our attitudes and conduct to his own justice. But in order to receive this gift we must hunger and thirst and humbly implore God for this share in his saving justice (cf. Mt 5:6).

To accept the kingdom of God is to accept gratefully, as the kingdom's rule, God's saving justice which coincides with love and mercy. To refuse this saving rule of God by acting mercilessly and neglecting the salvation of one's fellowmen is to call down disaster upon oneself. The merciless man excludes himself from God's saving justice; he condemns himself.

This concept of saving justice comes through with particular clarity in Matthew's Gospel and the letters of Paul. By opposing a sterile orthodoxy with the truth of life expressed in mercy and justice (cf. Jas 2:23), James in no way contradicts Paul's doctrine on justice by faith. The very awareness that God justifies the sinner because of his own name and by sheer grace is, for Paul, the strongest motive to conform our life with this divine rule of saving justice and merciful love. Those are found to be just who have fulfilled the great commandment of merciful love (Mt 25:31-46). Christ is our saving justice. Therefore a life in Christ bears fruit in love and justice, in compassion and generosity.

In the concept of God's saving justice and the truthfulness of a just life enabled by it, there is an encounter with God's holiness and judgment. Man is so called to respond that he is put under judgment if he refuses to accept the saving justice and to act accordingly (cf. Jas 1:20; Rom 14:4; 14:10; 1 Cor 4:4). Boasting of one's own justice and acting in merciless "justice" calls directly for God's judgment. The vision of God's saving justice is at the same time experience of God's holiness.

Love (agapé) and saving justice (dikaiosyne) coincide insofar as both are equally God's saving action and gift, enabling and requesting that total response that unites the believer with God's own love and justice. However, the biblical concept of justice, in its diversity, includes also what is objectively man's duty. It points to the content of love, while love itself is what primarily constitutes the bond of the Thou-I-We relationship with God, and consequently with people. In this perspective, the *ordo amoris* (that order which is born of love and serves love) coincides with justice but not with love itself. By redeemed love, people sense the order of justice and fulfil law and justice beyond the letter.

The relation between love and justice looks different if it takes as its point of departure the mere justice among people not yet transformed by the dynamics of God's saving justice. Justice among men, especially commutative justice, distributive and legal justice, can somehow be defined and enforced. But pure love cannot be enforced; it is simply a liberating event and attitude that generates a freedom that goes far beyond the human definitions of justice. Love can never be measured quantitatively.

The believer, seized by God's saving justice, recognizes that the new justice includes, above all, love for one's fellowmen, a love according to the measure of God's grace bestowed on each. This measure of the divine gift is hidden from the public eye and can therefore not be enforced by law or by concepts of human justice. Yet for the sake of peace among humans, the minimum requirements of justice must somehow be defined and sometimes be enforced. Redeemed love does not cling to the lowest limit; it is always on the road towards greater love, in the image and likeness of God's saving justice. Psychologically and theologically we can say with Justinus, "Justice is grounded in love".[125]

Life according to God's saving justice is in a special way reflected in social justice that goes far beyond commutative justice and group interests. It is a social life that accords with the truth that God has created us as a social unity, as if we were his family. This solidarity must be constantly increased until the coming of the Lord, when it will be brought to perfection. Then, saved by grace, man will offer flawless glory to God as a family beloved of God and of Christ, their brother.[126]

It is a characteristic sign of the Church of our time that she does not confine her social doctrine to the relationships between social classes but includes equally those between rich and poor nations. "Development help" is a new name for social justice and for peace.[127]

Today, love must also translate itself into political activity, for politics can be an effective way to improve social relations and the conditions of people's lives. So love and justice cannot ignore the need for power. If power is not brought into the service of these noblest human qualities and goals, it will become disruptive. Political power must always be at the service of the whole and never yield to unjust group interests. "The centre of power is only centre of the whole as long as it does not degrade its centrality by using it for particular purposes. In the moment in which the representatives of the centre use the power of the centre for their particular self-realization, they cease to be the actual centre; hence the whole being, without a centre, disintegrates ... Finally, the loss of the power of the whole, through internal and external causes, is unavoidable".[128]

3. Works of charity and justice

While love is the foundation of justice, in a certain sense the involvement of justice in creating happy human conditions precedes the works of charity. We must never be satisfied to offer alms-help where we can assist people by way of a justice that allows them to satisfy their needs by their own participation in the social process. If those who act unjustly offer alms to the damaged instead of repairing their injustice, it is not love but an offence against the dignity of their neighbour.

Yet however great may be our political endeavour for justice, there will always be the needy, the handicapped, the sick, suffering, and imprisoned, the alcoholics, drug addicts and many others. The world will always be in need of the works of mercy and charity. It is a particular duty of the Church to be present as healer in a wounded social life, and present to those who need charitable assistance. And if the Christian has understood what the saving justice and mercy of God mean for all of us, he will never offer his charitable help condescendingly.

VI. SINS AGAINST LOVE

To describe the sins against love of God and love of neighbour, we would have to repeat all that has been said up to this point, for falling short on any of these points incurs sin whereever we do so in freedom. One of the sources of many sins against love is negligence in meditation, in reflection, in exploring the height and depth, the length and breadth of the love of God and love of neighbour. In the following pages we shall mention some sins which, in a particularly striking way, offend the commandment of love.

1. Sins against the love of God

All sins manifest a lack of love of God. Mediocrity and laxity contradict the fervour of the love of God, the serious desire and endeavour to love him with all our heart. While venial sin shows "only" the momentary lack of this fervour of love, mortal sin is the ruin of one's friendship with God, a striking contradiction to our basic vocation.

The most drastic contradiction to love in its very essence is the sin of hatred of God. This is also indirectly the most drastic contradiction against our very being. It is a perplexing mystery how man, created in the divine image and totally dependent on God, can hate his Creator and Redeemer. Here we are at the very heart of the "mystery of iniquity" (2 Thess 2:7). While every mortal sin is a fundamental option against the love of God, the actual hatred of God is direct opposition to and rebellion against him (odium personae). Jesus speaks of this terrible hatred of a godless world against the Father, against himself, the Father's own ambassador, and against his disciples (Jn 15:18-27).

Of course, there is frequently a "hatred of God" which in reality is not directed against the true God at all, but rather against an idol or false image of God. It may be no more than a violent rejection of religion falsely conceived or presented.

Those who have invested all their freedom in the option against God consequently see in God their great enemy. Unless they succeed in repressing their hatred by escaping into atheism, their whole conscious life will be marked by conscious enmity.

The full revelation of the love of God in Jesus Christ has forced people to a more radical decision either for him or against him. Jesus is destined to manifest the full extent of God's love. For those who reject this revelation and his very love, he is "destined to be a sign which men reject ... Many in Israel will stand or fall because of him, and thus the secret thoughts of many will be laid bare" (Lk 2:34-35).

It is false to assert that the sins in the Church are entirely responsible for all the hostility against her. It may well be that the holiest members and communities of the Church provoke the sharpest opposition by godless people. "As they persecuted me, they will persecute you; they will follow your teaching as little as they have followed mine" (Jn 15:20). Of course where, individually and in community, the disciples of Christ are totally guided by the Spirit and bring forth the fruit of the Spirit, many will be converted to Christ. But the Spirit, through the disciples, will convict of wrong the enemies of God: "He will convince them of divine judgment by showing that the prince of this world stands condemned" (Jn 16:8-11). However, judgment does not belong to us. The disciples of Christ will always continue to win the hearts of men for God.

2. Direct sins against love of neighbour

Most sins against love of others consist of omissions of the positive duties of love. But the sharpest conflict with the "royal law" is in attitudes and acts of hostility, enmity against fellowmen, and any conduct which directly hurts others' welfare. The principal sins of this kind are: enmity against individuals, whole groups, or nations; hatred and hostility towards the person of another (in contrast to hatred of his sins which, of itself, is good); diabolic hatred consciously directed against another's spiritual good or salvation, against his or her friendship with God; envy which begrudges one's neighbour the goods he possesses, and which becomes diabolic envy if it begrudges him the good of divine love. It is from hatred and envy that discord and quarrels, destructive conflicts and wars flow. In an unjust war, the defection of love in a whole populace swells up and bursts into vile fury. The most dreadful concomitant of preparation for war is the widespread and systematic sowing of the seeds of hatred against foreign nations and their citizens.

As love of others is realized in the many virtues that manifest charity, so the violation of these virtues is indirectly a violation of the love of others. It is impossible to give a full list of all these sins like lack of consideration, disrespect, injustice, and so on. In the following paragraphs we are concerned only with those sins which are in direct opposition to loving concern for the salvation of neighbour: seduction, scandal, and complicity in the sins of others.

3. Seduction

Seduction (*scandalum directum*) is the deliberate effort to lead others to sinful thoughts, desires and actions. The seducer lays a trap, a snare (*scandalum*) designed to bring about the fall of another. Seduction can be by means of direct persuasion, advice or command, or of calculated suggestive actions. The most insidious form of seduction places the snare in such a way that the victim is entrapped without being aware of the evil intent of the seducer. In such a case the tempter may avoid being externally involved in the matter, in order to escape accusation of evil or recognition as a servant of evil. Such covert enticement is at least as unjust as the overt seduction, and consequently must be equally repaired.

Seduction is a twofold sin. It contradicts love and responsibility for the salvation of the neighbour, and it equally violates the particular area of values which one induces others to violate. The success or lack of success of the evil design does not alter the guilt of the tempter, although it may be significant in the matter of reparation which is demanded for the temporal or eternal damage inflicted by the successful seducer.

Tempting others is usually due to sinful self-interest or to a craving for companionship in evil attitudes and actions. The deliberate effort to pervert someone spiritually, to turn him or her away from God, is the great sin of diabolic seduction (cf. Jn 8:44).

Jesus is stirred to wrath by the sin of seduction. "If a man is a cause of stumbling to one of these little ones who have faith in me, it would be better for him to have a millstone hung around his neck and to be drowned in the depths of the sea. Alas for the world that such causes of stumbling arise. Come they must, but woe betide the man through whom they come" (Mt 18:6-7). The text applies not only to seduction but also to indirect scandal.

It would be erroneous to think only or mainly of seduction as unchaste action and/or sinful talk or thinking about sex. The most disastrous seduction is to hatred, to enmity, to group egotism, to collective injustice and, last but not least, to war. Perhaps those who try to manipulate public opinion and glorify the freedom to abort, and who make abortion one of the big national industries, are more guilty than the individual victim who, under stress or under pressure of public opinion, commits an abortion. Seduction of public opinion causes the downfall of many, of whole groups, cultures and societies. Seduction and scandal can undermine the basic values without which a society cannot prosper.

Organized aggressive atheism intends directly to destroy faith and hope in eternal life. In various forms it also intends to destroy faith in love as the heart of history. Aggressive atheists know how faith and morality are interrelated; therefore they try to undermine people's personal integrity and those moral values that protect faith or arise from faith.

4. *Scandal*

The use of the word *skandalon* in the Bible differs considerably from its use in moral theology,[129] where it means a simple lack of responsibility for the salvation of one's neighbour; it places a culpable occasion of sin in his path. The inspired authors used the word "scandal" to characterize something that can provoke a shock, either dangerous or wholesome: a way of acting or speaking that can be irresponsible or can be an extreme effort to shake the other and force him to decide either for good or for evil.

a) Christ and scandal

Christ himself, according to Simeon's prophecy, is a great "scandal" for a sinful and self-righteous world. "This child is destined to be a sign which men reject" (Lk 2:34). By himself, however, he is a sign of salvation. That a considerable group of his hearers react so violently against him lays bare the secret thoughts of those who are not willing to accept the rightful rule of God. It is in this sense that he becomes "a stone to trip over, a rock to stumble against; but he who has faith in him will not be put to shame" (Rom 9:33; cf. Is 8:14; 28:16; 1 Pet 2:6ff; Mt 21:44).

Christ knew that his prophetic words and actions would cause a shock that for some would be wholesome but for others could cause a hardening of an already obdurate heart. To the timorous objection of the disciples he gives a very tart response: "Then his disciples came up to him and said, 'Do you know that the pharisees have taken great offence at what you have been saying?' His answer was, 'Any plant that is not of my heavenly Father's planting will be rooted up. Leave them alone; they are blind guides, and if one blind man guides another they will both fall into the ditch' " (Mt 15:12-14). Those who take umbrage at Christ are blind because they are unloving. Christ must open their eyes even at great risk, since the purpose of his "scandal" is their conversion.

Christ realizes that his Eucharistic promise, with all its implications, is a shaking experience for all who hear him, even for his disciples; but he must be faithful to his salvific mission, whatever the result. "So Jesus asked the twelve, 'Do you also want to leave me?' " (Jn 6:67). He sets forth the scandal of his teaching, his person and his cross, surely not to be an occasion of another's fall, but that the sharp antithesis of his "scandal" might shake up people about their shameful blindness and alienation. The incipient shock should make them realize the malice of certain attitudes and prepare them for a total conversion to God. This explains Jesus' words, "Happy is the man who does not find me a stumbling block" (Mt 11:6). This is said in the context of Christ as bringer of the Good News for the poor. There can be no other Messiah than Christ the healer, Christ the prophet and the servant.

Most strikingly, Christ places before the High Priest the great "scandal" of his claim to be the Son of God. He formulates his response with such clarity that, knowing the mentality of Caiphas, it seems almost designed to lead to condemnation. It was Christ's mission to give this response in all its sharpness so that it was impossible for the Great Council and all future generations to avoid the decision. Thus, ultimately, the faith of the ages could be based specifically on this "scandal" of his response.

Following the example of the Master, and quite contrary to the attitude of the Gnosis, the apostles in no way softened the scandal of the Gospel of the cross. Paul places the cross of Christ at the very centre of his preaching. "Jews call for miracles, Greeks look for wisdom, but we proclaim Christ — yes, Christ nailed to the cross; and though this is a stumbling block to Jews and folly to Greeks, yet to those who have heard his call, Jews and Greeks alike, he is the power of God and the wisdom of God" (1 Cor 1:22-24).

As Christ revealed himself progressively and tried to win over the minds and hearts of his hearers, so Paul proceeds with great caution. He wishes to allow both Jew and Gentile converts ample time to mature, so that they might appropriate certain

difficult insights. For instance, he circumcised Timothy to facilitate the acceptance of the Gospel by the Jews who otherwise
might have prejudiciously closed their hearts to his teaching. He
tries to become all things to all men, becoming weak for the
weak so that he "might save some" (1 Cor 9:20ff).

The Apostle of the Gentiles knows that there can be sinful
ways of giving scandal, provoking others by an unwise use of
the newly gained freedom. He warns the enlightened of Corinth
not to eat meat offered to the idols whenever this can be an
occasion of downfall for the others. "If food be the downfall
of my brother, I will never eat meat any more, for I will not
be the cause of my brother's downfall" (1 Cor 8:13).

With a heavy heart, Paul takes upon himself the "scandal"
of confronting Peter publicly when he sees that Peter's conduct
would block the spreading of the Gospel among the Gentiles
(Gal 2:11-16).[130] But the same Paul warns the Christians
of Rome, especially the Gentile Christians, not to use their liberty
about traditions and food in a way that might make impossible
the unity of Gentile and Jewish Christians. "Do not ruin the
work of God for the sake of food ... It is a fine thing to abstain
from eating meat or drinking wine, or doing anything which
causes your brother's downfall" (Rom 14:20-22).

b) Discerning sinful and wholesome scandal

It is clear that the Christian must avoid all sinful actions
not only because of their sinfulness but also because by their
very nature they oppose the fullness of salvation and sometimes
give very dangerous scandal to fellowmen. Here, however, it is a
question of discerning, in the light of the Bible, what is sinful
and what is wholesome scandal.

Christian individuals and communities can give a most
dangerous scandal by assimilating themselves to the evil and
mediocre spirit of this world. By their very vocation, Christians
must continue the vocation of Christ to call the world to a
clear decision. If, for instance, in a legalistic era Christians
confine the great commandment of love of God and neighbour
to a legal minimum, and as a consequence live a life of mediocrity
by putting the lamp of faith under a bushel (Mt 5:14), then
prophetic voices must speak out against these dangerous attitudes and trends.[131]

We increase the scandal if, on the one hand we accuse the official Church of her defects while, on the other, we continue to live personally on a mediocre level. At all times, prophets have been a wholesome scandal for "the king's priests" and for a weak or careless Christianity. It seems that the Church suffers much less from the so-called "imprudences" of the prophets than from the inaction of those who do little more than call for cautiousness. Emile Mounier notes, with Kierkegaard, that "The combatant of faith presents to the men of our century not so much the scandal of the heroic as the scandal of the evasive middle-class existence. But it seems that we must be tried in our very hearts by such deficient appearances".[132] By this kind of sad scandal the Church stands to lose the most dynamic persons and communities. There must always be loving attention for the weak, and great care not to request things at an inopportune time; we must allow others as well as ourselves a time to grow; but in all this we must never betray the law of grace and the goal commandments that imply the universal vocation to holiness.

A scandal given frequently in the past has been rigorous insistence on small details, on secondary questions of discipline, while betraying the spirit of wholeness and of ongoing conversion. A particular scandal is given by those who quarrel about uncertain laws while ignoring the great law, "Be merciful as your heavenly Father" (Lk 6:36).

c) Reparation for sinful scandal

One who has given scandal culpably must, to the best of his power, repair the evil he has done. For those in authority this obligation is particularly urgent. One who has given scandal publicly must make public reparation insofar as this is possible. The fact that the scandal is given through thoughtlessness or because of a sleeping conscience does not excuse one from reparation but should provide an additional motive for deepening one's own conversion.

The seducer, insofar as it is possible, must attempt to exert direct influence for good upon the one whom he has misled. However, a direct contact is not always advisable. The weakness on one side or the other may cause a new danger of sin.

Writers, artists, actors, theatre owners, politicians, and others in similar positions who have given scandal should look to the very area where they have been active to make good the evil they have caused. Only if the level of their competence and moral strength does not match the difficulties may they give up the activity in which they have given scandal and which now demands their reparative effort.

4. Complicity in the sins of others

God has called us to be collaborators in his kingdom, sharers and witnesses of his saving love. As such, how could we permit ourselves to be misused as "accomplices of the rulers of this dark world"? (Eph 6: 12). Yet we all occasionally discover to our horror that what we have done with the best of intentions has been used by others to carry out their nefarious designs. What conclusions does Catholic moral theology draw from this accidental tragic connection of good actions with the machinations of the spirit of darkness?[133] Surely we cannot withdraw to the point of missing our calling to be yeast in the dough, salt to the earth.

In the following pages we deal only with a specific kind of cooperation, namely, cooperation in the execution of a sinful deed by another who is the principal agent and who has already determined the course to be followed in the evil project. This distinction marks the essential differentiation between cooperation and scandal as such. Whereas scandal furnishes the occasion for another's sin, cooperation, as we treat it here, enters into the actual execution of a sinful action already determined. Of course cooperation also poses the question of scandal.

a) Formal cooperation

The distinction between formal and merely material cooperation is basic to our entire appraisal of complicity in the sins of others. Formal cooperation in another's sin is every cooperation which, by its inner purpose and meaning (*finis operis*) or by deliberate intent (*finis operantis*) is characterized as complicity in the other's sinful action. That means that the formal cooperator places himself directly in the service of evil. Through his own intention or by inner approval of the principal sinful deed, or through a cooperation which, by its very nature, is approval of the action, he formally makes the deed his own.

Formal cooperation is always sinful. The degree of malice has to be judged according to the malice of the sin in which one cooperates, according to the degree of one's actual cooperation, and according to the measure in which another's malice is confirmed. The cooperator's responsibility is especially greater if he has a particular duty to hinder the other's sinful action or if the execution of the evil deed would have been impossible without his cooperation.

Formal complicity in the sins of others is always a violation of charity as well as a specific offence against the virtue violated by the sinful deed itself. In the sins of injustice, formal complicity bears with it the obligation of restitution *in solidum* with the principal agent, although secondarily and according to the degree of cooperation. This means that if the principal agent does not make restitution, the cooperator is obliged to do so in full; otherwise he must provide his share according to the degree of his complicity.

b) Material cooperation

In material cooperation, the act of the cooperator contributes to the sin of another neither in itself nor by the intent of the agent, but it is misused or misappropriated and thus placed at the service of sinful activities. This is a moral question insofar as the cooperator foresees with certainty or at least with probability that his act will be misused. The presumption or the awareness that another will make evil use of one's good or indifferent action may arise from the special circumstances or from one's own or others' unfortunate experience, or perhaps the evildoers themselves may reveal the facts.

The significance of special circumstances creates a knotty problem. At times they can pave the way to evil, making an otherwise indifferent action serve the very purpose of evil. Circumstances can so penetrate the structure of the action as to qualify it unequivocally as direct complicity in another's sin. This is surely the case if the special circumstances, by themselves, abstracting from the evil intent of the other party, make the action illicit. But many times the situation is not at all clear.

A word of caution is in order. We must avoid any extreme position in this matter. If each and every circumstance and even the mere foresight of evil used by another would make the action inwardly evil, then all distinction between material and formal cooperation would collapse.

The mere foreseeing of incidental evil effects does not enter so intimately into the action as does the sum total of circumstances that motivate the action or directly accompany it. A controversial example may illustrate the problem. A master charges his servant to break into a house and thus assist in his plan of robbing or abducting a person. The master's evil intent is obvious from all the circumstances. Someone might argue that to help break open a door or to help a person through a window is not by its own nature evil, that indeed, under certain circumstances such as in rescuing someone from a blazing home, it can be a work of generous love. However, in our case, the circumstances are such that the action surely does not serve a good purpose. What the servant does under pressure or someone does under serious threats is, in the opinion of some authors, no more than material cooperation. As a consequence, the very grave reasons might be considered sufficient for excusing the cooperation.

But to me it seems more to the point to reason as follows: the action in the concrete case is so unequivocally determined as contributing to another's sin that it can be conceived only as formal cooperation. It is not the abstract crashing through a door but the actual concurrence in robbery, rape or other crime.[134] I prefer the opinion which holds that an act may be appraised as merely material cooperation only if a clear-thinking person can, without wrestling with abstractions, simply say, "what I am doing is in itself good. I act with worthy motives. It is only the human malice of others that takes advantage of it".

Faced with a serious case of cooperation, one may come to the following conclusion: "I have no other reason to perform this act than the requested cooperation in another person's sin. In fact, under the actual circumstances, I can think of no morally good purpose for which I should do it". In other words, the person can no longer assume that his own good act is being perverted only by the other person. Rather, he must concede that his act has no meaning at all except insofar as it contributes to the other's sin. This is what we call formal cooperation. If one does something that normally serves the good of persons, but in the concrete circumstances is abused by another, the presumption is that it is simply a material cooperation.

That an action materially contributes to an evil effect planned by another person is a serious matter for our conscience. It is all the more serious the more proximately it serves the evil purposes. A most decisive point is whether or not it is an indispensable condition for the execution of the evil design.

First principle: the virtue of responsibility for our own actions, and the love of neighbour which the principal agent proposes to violate, obliges us to keep our actions as far as possible from being diverted to an evil end.

Second principle: there are reasons, however, which sometimes justify material cooperation and may even suggest and recommend it. These reasons must be the more weighty the greater the evil to which our actions are diverted, the more proximately our action is drawn into the sinful action of others, the greater the certainty that our work will really be misused, the higher the probability that our refusal to cooperate could prevent the sin, and finally, the greater the danger of scandal to others.

Merely material cooperation is lawful if, through such concurrence, a higher good is assured and safeguarded or a greater evil is averted. However, according to the principle of double-effect,[135] no evil deed may be made the means to further the good, for the end does not justify the means.

The moral conviction of the principal agent has to be taken into account. The concurrence of my good action with that of another who is convinced that his action is good is not formal cooperation although one might be convinced that the other's action is wrong. This happens frequently in our pluralistic society. We think, for instance, of situations where the sincere conviction of the main agent is supported by that of a considerable number of good people.

In evaluating the "greater good" or the "lesser evil", it is to be noted that no private gain or loss or fear of personal hurt justifies proximate cooperation in an act which inflicts grave damage on a community. The reason is evident: evil afflicting a community is always greater than harm accepted by any individual in a spirit of sacrifice. Remote cooperation on which the execution of the evil deed in no way depends is permitted for any proportionally good reason.

Material cooperation in an action that causes unjust damage to a third party is permitted only for the prevention of greater damage to others or to the cooperating person. In this we assume, of course, that the concurrence to the evil action does not, of itself, cause harm to others but only by misuse by another.

Third principle: material gain is never an acceptable motive for any cooperation, nor should a dread of material loss or damage be the first consideration in a moral evaluation. The primary motive for sometimes agreeing to cooperate "materially" should be the prevention of spiritual hurt to oneself and others, and the possibility of effective action in the world for the good.

The discerning judgment will always take into account the mission of the disciples of Christ to be light and salt to the world. An overly rigorous stance with respect to material cooperation simply renders the exercise of the lay apostolate in many areas of life, for instance in politics, totally impossible. Christ prayed for his disciples that, while remaining in the world, they might be preserved from evil (Jn 17:15-18). To sustain this polarity in a truly Christian manner, we must be both as "guileless as doves" and "wary as serpents" (Mt 10:16).

c) Examples of licit and illicit cooperation

Each area of life presents common and special problems of cooperation. We can refer to a few only in a kind of typology to illustrate the general principles. However, the concrete solutions can be attained by the individual only by taking into account all relevant relationships and circumstances. The conclusions we arrive at in the typology may, in their actual applications under different sets of circumstances, require the consideration of some new principles and values to which we have not yet given particular attention.

(1) *Cooperation in politics*

In politics, the attitudes of the leaders, the parties and their platform are frequently neither black nor white but grey. Most parties have some points in their platform, or at least in their practice, that merit disapproval. By electing the party that seems to be, under the given circumstances, the best one, frequently offers concurrence in some particular points that the conscience cannot approve. This kind of concurrence is licit and necessary, for withdrawal would simply favour the greater evil.

A person running for office with sincere intentions, but foreseeing that in the elective process others who promote him will use dubious means, can tolerate this concurrence if it is unavoidable and he is convinced that his option is for the greater good of the community. When one is elected by a party which he considers best under the prevailing circumstances, and he is bound by party discipline sometimes to support unjust legislation, he should normally express his dissent and oppose that kind of party discipline. A member of a legislative body who simply votes in favour of legislation that is unjust or hostile to religion is a formal cooperator in sin. If, however, he has only the alternative, either to vote for a less evil legislation or to let pass a more pernicious one, he may well have sufficient or even stringent reasons for his material cooperation. In order to avoid scandal, however, he must explain his motives and express disapproval of what is unjust in the bill.

Members of a police force, in executing an unjust law or order, cannot be readily excused from sin when arresting an obviously innocent individual. It may be that an ordinary policeman who has no power to make decisions and no oversight of the circumstances might more easily be excused. But if officials who possess a degree of discretion in carrying out the unjust law or the orders of superior officers track down the innocent, ferret them out or arrest them, they are by that very fact formally guilty in conscience as accessories of the unjust laws or orders, and as persecutors of the innocent. The sin is greater if they go beyond an explicit order.

A soldier who, following orders, cooperates in the mass murder of innocent people (for instance in the deliberate bombing of residential areas), or in killing a patently innocent person, is guilty of formal cooperation. He cannot be excused even though his crime is usually subjectively less heinous than that of the official who commands the actions.

(2) *Complicity of managers and employees*

A taxi driver may fulfil his ordinary service although he might suspect that his customer wants to go to a brothel. But if the passenger asks where the nearest brothel is, and then orders him to drive him there, he should refuse complicity gently and firmly.

If a manager realizes that his otherwise correct services are used for concurrence in tax frauds or other injustices, he must do his best to correct the situation or at least express his clear dissent.

Owners or managers of a drug store commit the sin of formal complicity when selling drugs destined exclusively for evil goals such as for procuring abortions or illegal sale to addicts to their great detriment. It seems to me that a pharmacist or drug clerk who deals directly with a customer, and is quite aware of the immoral purpose for which the item will be used, is also guilty of formal cooperation in every such sale. The excuse that he merely does what he is told is insipid. Such excuses have been alleged in defence of the most abominable crimes. However, I doubt that a cashier or wrapping clerk can be accused of formal cooperation even if, by chance, he learns that items destined for evil use are among the things he is dealing with. Proportionate reasons may excuse this remote material cooperation.

The drug store owner, manager, pharmacist or clerk who sells contraceptives which he considers as being against the doctrine of his Church, realizing however that many of the customers are convinced in conscience that for them the use of these contraceptives is morally good, commits, in my opinion, no formal or material cooperation with a sin of another, due to his conviction that the customer is in good conscience. If there is no sin on the part of the other, there is no cooperation to sin. If, however, the pharmacist himself feels in conscience that these means are intrinsically and absolutely evil, it can be disputed — especially in view of differing opinions on this point even within his own Church — whether respect for the other person's conscience allows him to serve the customer of good conscience. In this case tolerance may be better for peaceful relationships and for avoiding hard reactions against the Church. This reasoning can, of course, not be applied to cases where unjust damage to third persons must be avoided.

(3) Complicity in abortion

No conscientious person will take a job in an abortion agency or abortion clinic. This kind of complicity would be extremely scandalous even if the activity might not involve direct participation in abortions or in advertising for abortion.

No physician may carry out in any hospital a direct abortion (i.e. an intervention that is not life-saving). It seems to me that the same strict evaluation applies to the assistant physician. However, interns, technicians and nurses in the operating rooms, who have duties of a permanent nature such as sterilization of instruments and administration of anesthesia, cannot be accused of formal complicity if the illicit operation is something exceptional and accidental in relation to their routine work. Normally they are not competent to judge in any way what the physicians are going to do and what the real situation is. On the contrary, if the immorality of the intervention, for instance of a non-therapeutic abortion, is evident to their conscience before it happens, there are frequently good reasons and even a duty to refuse any kind of cooperation, even mere material cooperation (which is what normally is the case for this category).

It is very much disputed and can be disputed whether Catholic hospitals must in all circumstances refuse cooperation (for instance by offering their facilities) for sterilization when in the eyes of the doctors and patients, it can be qualified as therapeutic in a broad sense. A good reason for allowing doctors who, in conscience, are convinced that this is a positive health service in the particular case, and are ready to offer it only to those patients requesting it in good conscience, can be taken from a broad understanding of tolerance and respect for a sincere conscience, especially in questions and situations where the givenness of an objective moral evil is doubtful.[136]

NOTES

1 Augustine, *Enchiridion, sive de fide, spe et caritate,* c. CXVII, 31, PL 40, 286.
2 Cf. Th. Ohm, *Die Liebe zu Gott bei den nicht-christlichen Völkern,* Krailling, 1950; V. Warnach, *Agape. Die Liebe als Grundmotiv der neutestamentlichen Theologie,* Düsseldorf, 1951; H.U. von Balthasar, *Glaubhaft ist nur die Liebe,* Einsiedeln, 1963; K. Rahner, "Liebe", *Sacramentum Mundi* III, 234-252 (Bibliography); W. Molinski, "Nächstenliebe", *Sacramentum Mundi* III, 669-675 (Bibliography).
3 Cf. R. Schnackenburg, *Das Johannesevangelium,* III. Teil, Freiburg, 1975, 91ff; cf. R. Rinker, *Sharing God's Love,* Grand Rapids/Mich., 1976; G. McGregory, *He Who Lets Us Be. A Theology of Love,* New York, 1976.
4 Cf. R. Schnackenburg, l.c., 124.
5 Cf. K. Rahner, l.c., 250; R. Schnackenburg, *Die sittliche Botschaft des Neuen Testamentes,* München, 1962², 75ff.
6 *Gaudium et Spes,* 24c.
7 H. de Lubac, *Glauben aus der Liebe,* Einsiedeln, 1970² (*Catholicisme: Les aspects sociaux du dogme,* Paris, 1938).
8 l.c., 70, quoting Cyprian, *De Ecclesiae catholicae unitate,* c. 7; c. 15; R.I.C., *Supplement,* 6, 1974, *Bibliography on Love and Community* (published by Université des sciences humaines de Strasbourg; it lists 507 titles for the years 1970-1974); *Orientamenti pastorali,* nn. 2/3, 1975: Bibliography on Love for the years 1970-1975.
9 Cf. Ph. Warnier, *Le phénomène des communautés de base,* Paris, 1973; *Laity Today* (Rome: Secretariat for Lay Apostolate), "Towards Responsible Christian Communities".
10 E. Käsemann, *Exegetische Besinnungen,* I, Göttingen, 1963, 118; J. Moltmann, *Kirche in der Kraft des Heiligen Geistes,* München, 1975; H.U. von Balthasar, *Spiritus Creator,* Einsiedeln, 1967.
11 Cf. R. Schnackenburg, *Die sittliche Botschaft des NT,* 68.
12 Cf. C. Spicq, *Agape dans le Nouveau Testament,* I, Paris, 1958, 156ff; 303ff; III, 313ff; Paris, 1959; H.-M. Féret, OP, "Brotherly Love in the Church as Sign of the Kingdom of God", in Ch. Duquoc (ed.), *Opportunities for Belief and Behavior,* Concilium, vol. 29 (New York, 1962), 15-37; N. Lofink, *Das Hauptgebot,* Rom, 1963; J. Ratzinger, *Die christliche Brüderlichkeit,* München, 1960; M. Nédoncelle, *Love and the Person,* New York, 1966; H. Rotter, *Strukturen sittlichen Handelns. Liebe als Grundprinzip der Moral,* Mainz, 1960; S. Lyonnet, "L'amore del prossimo: pienezza della legge alla luce delle interpretazioni dei Padri", *Rassegna di teologia* 15 (1974), 174-186; 241-256; 450-460.
13 Augustine, *De trinitate,* VIII, 12, PL 42, 959.
14 S.Th. II II, q 44, a 2; cf. l.c., q 23, a 5.
15 Augustine, *Tract. XVII in Jo. Ev.,* XVII, 6ff, PL 35, 1531.
16 S.Th. I II, q 68, a 8 ad 2.
17 J.M. Gustafson, *Can Ethics be Christian?,* 73.
18 K. Rahner, l.c., 245.
19 Augustine, *De trinitate,* VIII, 12, PL 42, 958.
20 Cf. R. Schnackenburg, *Das Johannesevangelium,* III, 123ff.
21 Cf. F. Ebner, *Das Wort und die geistigen Realitäten,* Innsbruck, 1921; Id., *Wort und Liebe,* Regensburg, 1935; Id., *Schriften,* 3 vols., München, 1963/65; M. Buber, *I and Thou,* Edinburgh, 1971³; R.O. Johann, *The Meaning of Love,* Westminster, Md., 1959.

22 Cf. R. Völkl, Selbstliebe in der Heiligen Schrift und bei Thomas von Aquin, München, 1956; Id., Frühchristliche Zeugnisse zu Wesen und Gestalt der christlichen Liebe, Freiburg, 1963; Id., Botschaft und Gebot der Liebe nach der Bibel, Freiburg, 1964.

23 P. Tillich, Der Mut zum Sein, Stuttgart, 1954; cf. J. Pieper, Uber die Liebe, München, 1972, 77ff.

24 Gaudium et Spes, 27a.

25 ibid, 27b.

26 Augustine, Retractationes, I, 83, PL 32, 594.

27 K. Rahner, l.c., 248.

28 Cf. D.M. Stanley, Boasting in the Lord, New York, 1973, 179-183. On Prayer: J. Pieper, Happiness and Contemplation, New York, 1958; R. Guardini, The Lord's Prayer, New York, 1958; Id., Prayer in Practice, Garden City, N.J., 1963; H.U. von Balthasar, Prayer, New York, 1961; B.C. Butler, Prayer. An Adventure in Living, London, 1961; F.M. Moschner, Christian Prayer, St. Louise and London, 1962; M. Quoist, Prayers, New York, 1963; R. Maritain, Notes on the Lord's Prayer, New York, 1964; M. Nédoncelle, God's Encounter with Man, New York and London, 1964; H. Schürmann, Praying with Christ. The "Our Father" for Today, New York, 1964; J.H. Newman, Reflections on God and Self, ed. by L. Barmann, New York, 1965; Archbishop A. Bloom, Living Prayer, London, 1966; J. Jeremias, The Prayer of Jesus, London and Nashville, 1967; Id., The Lord's Prayer, Philadelphia, 1969; K.H. Miskotte, The Road of Prayer, New York, 1968; J.B. Lotz, Interior Prayer. The Exercise of Personality, New York, 1968; J. Sheets, The Spirit Speaks in Us. Personal Prayer in the New Testament, Wilkes-Barre/Pa., 1968; R.J. Heyer and R.J. Payne, Discovery in Prayer, New York/Paramus, 1969; P. Himelbush, OP, Dynamic Contemplation, Inner Life for Modern Man, New York, 1970; F.C. Happold, Prayer and Meditation, Baltimore, 1971; M. Gibbard, Why Pray? Valley Forge, 1971; B. Häring, Prayer: Integration of Faith and Life, Slough and Notre Dame, 1974.

29 Augustine, De civitate Dei, 14, 28, PL 41, 436.

30 R. Coste, Pour une charité liberatrice, Paris, 1974.

31 N. Berdyaev, Destiny of Man, 141.

32 Cf. A. Royce Gibson, The Challenge of Perfection, Melbourne, 1968, 20.

33 M. Nédoncelle, God's Encounter with Man, New York and London, 1964, 179.

34 R. Schnackenburg, Das Johannesevangelium, III, 126.

35 Cf. F.X. Durrwell, "Vous avez été appelés", Studia Moralia 15 (1977), 355ff.

36 Cf. R. Johann, Building the Human, New York, 1968.

37 F.D.W. Wilhelmsen, The Metaphysics of Love, New York, 1962, 139; cf. J. Pieper, Uber die Liebe, 52ff.

38 Cf. R. Schnackenburg, Die Johannesbriefe, Freiburg, 1953, 202ff; Id., Christliche Existenz im Neuen Testament, München, 1962, I, 81.

39 Lumen gentium, 1.

40 H. de Lubac, Glauben aus der Liebe, 74.

41 l.c., 79. De Lubac proves this thesis by an enormous amount of texts from Tradition and the Magisterium.

42 Augustine, Sermo 272, PL 38, 1247.

43 Augustine, Sermo 227, PL 38, 1099-1101.

44 H. de Lubac, l.c., 99.

45 Cf. Lumen gentium, 3, 9, 10, 26; Unitatis Redintegratio, 15.

46 Cf. B. Häring, The Eucharist and Our Everyday Life, Slough, 1978; R. Schäffer, "Fähigkeit zum Kult. Ihre Bedrohung und Wiedergewinnung", Theol. pr. Quartalschrift 126 (1978), 105-121; V. Eid, "Die Sakramente und christliches Ethos", Studia Moralia 15 (1977), 139-153.

47 Cf. Presbyterorum Ordinis, 5, 14; cf. K. Rahner, Knecht Christi, Freiburg, 1967.

48 Ch. Duquoc, Opportunities and Behavior, 2.

49 Cf. H. Riedlinger, "Die Eucharistie in der Ekklesiologie des II. Vaticanum", in E.C. Suttner (ed.), Eucharistie, Zeichen der Einheit. Erstes Regensburger Okumenisches Symposium, Regensburg, 1970, 75-85.

50 Chrysostomus, *In ep. ad Hebr.*, hom. XVII, 3, PG 130ff; cf. G. Saphiris, "Eucharistie als sacrificium und commemoratio", in Suttner (ed.), l.c., 69.
51 G. Koch, "Theologie der Erfahrung-Sackgasse oder Weg zum Glauben?, Ein Gespräch mit Prof. E. Schillebeeckx", *Herderkorr.* 32 (1978), 292-297.
52 Cf. H. de Lubac, l.c., 266.
53 V.P. Furnish, *The Love Commandment in the New Testament*, Nashville, 1972; M. Hopkins, *The Law of Love and Love as Law, or: Christian Ethics*, New York, 1974.
54 *The Idea of Love*, New York, 1967; M. Balint, *Die Urformen der Liebe und die Technik der Psychoanalyse*, Frankfurt, 1969; J. Eibl-Eiberfeld, *Liebe und Hass. Die Naturgeschichte elementarer Verhaltensweisen*, München, 1970.
55 Cf. H. Marcuse, *Eros und Kultur*, Stuttgart, 1957; A. and W. Leibbrand, *Formen des Eros. Kultur- und Geistesgeschichte der Liebe*, Freiburg-München, 1972.
56 l.c., 242ff.
57 The literature on friendship is quite abundant. I mention only some works directly related to our theme: E Fromm, *The Art of Loving*, New York, 1952; M.C. D'Arcy, *The Mind and Heart of Love. A Study in Eros and Agape*, London, 1954; E. Walter, *Wesen und Macht der Liebe. Beiträge tur Theologie der Liebe*, Freiburg, 1955; C.S. Lewis, *The Four Loves*, London, 1960; M.M. Laurent, *Réalisme et richesse de l'amour chrétien. Essai sur Eros et Agape*, Paris, 1962; C.F. Kelley, *Der Geist der Liebe nach der Lehre des hl. Franz von Sales*, Paderborn, 1963; J. Schneider, *Das Gute und die Liebe nach der Lehre des hl. Albert des Grossen*, München, 1967; J.B. Lotz, *Drei Stufen der Liebe. Eros - Phylia - Agape*, Frankfurt, 1971; J. Pieper, *Uber die Liebe*, München, 1972; P. Lain Entralgo, *Sobre la amistad*, Madrid, 1972; B. Welte, *Dialektik der Liebe. Gedanken zur Phänomenologie der Liebe im technologischen Zeitalter*, Frankfurt, 1973; A. Ilien, *Wesen und Funktion der Liebe bei Thomas von Aquin*, Freiburg-Basel-Wien, 1975; A. Riva, *Amicizia: integrazione dell'esperienza umana*, Milano, 1975.
58 Augustine, *En. in Ps.* 118, XXII, 2, PL 37, 1563: "Praemium dilectionis ipse dilectus".
59 R. May, *Man's Quest for Himself*, 241.
60 Goethe, *Die Laune des Verliebten*, 5. Szene.
61 Cf. *Lumen gentium*, 7, 8; *Ad Gentes*, 9; *Gaudium et Spes*, 21, 24, 27, 39, 93; *Unitatis Redintegratio*, 24.
62 T. de Chardin, *The Phenomenon of Man*, London, 1959, 266.
63 l.c., 272.
64 K. Rahner, *Sacramentum Mundi* III, 245; cf. R. Follereau, *Revolution der Nächstenliebe*, Freiburg, 1968.
65 A. Nygren, *Eros und Agape*, 2 vols., Gütersloh, 1930, 1939; E. Brunner, *Eros und Liebe*, Berlin, 1937.
66 J. Pieper, l.c., 97ff.
67 C.S. Lewis, l.c., 12; cf. J. Pieper, l.c., 109.
68 *Kritik zur praktischen Vernunft*, II/I, 3.
69 Cf. V. Warnach, "Liebe", in H. Fries (ed.), *Handbuch theologischer Grundbegriffe*, München, 1963, 69.
70 J.B. Lotz, l.c., 79.
71 K. Rahner, l.c., 238ff.
72 Cf. G.H. Outka, *Agapé: An Ethical Analysis*, New Haven, 1972; M. Lattle, *Einheit im Wort. Zur spezifischen Bedeutung von "agapé", "agapan" und "filein" im Johannesevangelium*, München, 1975.
73 Cf. J.B. Lotz, l.c., 87, 105.
74 Augustine, *In ep. S. Joannis*, tract. VII, 8, PL 35, 2033.
75 P. Helwig, *Liebe und Feindschaft*, München, 1964; cf. P.F. Sladek, "Liebet eure Feinde", (Mt 5:44), in *Festschrift für Weihbischof Dr. Adolf Kindermann*, Königstein-München, 1969, 30-46.
76 Alphonsus de Liguori, *Theol. mor.*, lib. II, n. 28; *Homo Apostolicus*, Tr. IV, cap. II, n. 17.
77 *Ad Gentes*, 5.

78 Cf. F.X. Durrwell, *Le mystère pascal source de l'apostolat*, Paris, 1970; F. Klostermann, *Das christliche Apostolat. Idee und Problematik*, Innsbruck, 1961; V. Schurr, *Seelsorge in einer neuen Welt. Eine Pastoral der Umwelt und des Laientums*, Salzburg, 1959³.

79 *Apostolicam Actuositatem*, 2; cf. *Lumen gentium*, 30-42.

80 *Apostolicam Actuositatem*, 8.

81 F.X. Durrwell, l.c., 180.

82 l.c., 76ff.

83 Clement of Alexandria, *Stromateis*, VII, 2, PG 9, 413 (quoted by the encyclical *Mystici corporis Christi*), AAS 35 (1943), 221.

84 *Apostolicam Actuositatem*, 3.

85 F.X. Durrwell, l.c., 77.

86 *Ad Gentes*, 5.

87 *Lumen gentium*, 33; *Apostolicam Actuositatem*, 3.

88 *Sacrosanctum Concilium*, 48.

89 *Apostolicam Actuositatem*, 3; *Lumen gentium*, 10.

90 *Lumen gentium*, 11.

91 M. Schmaus, *Katholische Dogmatik*, München, 1957⁵, IV/1, 196.

92 *Apostolicam Actuositatem*, 16.

93 *Lumen gentium*, 11.

94 *Apostolicam Actuositatem*, 16.

95 ibid, 6.

96 M. Scheler, *Der Formalismus in der Ethik und die materiale Wertethik*, Halle, 1927, 599.

97 Medieval theologians and canonists called this omission *peccatum taciturnitatis* (sinful silence); cf. *Summa fratris Alexandris* II, B., n. 396-398.

98 *Lumen gentium*, 37.

99 ibid, 36.

100 *Gaudium et Spes*, 43. The constitution on the Church in the World of Today is the most creative text of the Magisterium on apostolate through creating a healthy world around us.

101 D. Bonhoeffer, *Gesammelte Schriften*, I, München, 1965, 413.

102 K. Barth, *Die Kirchliche Dogmatik* I/1, Zürich, 1964⁸, 99.

103 Cf. Canon 43 of Hippolyte; cf. Achelis, *Die Canones Hippolyti. Texte und Untersuchungen*, Vol. VI, Leipzig, 1891, 68; Durrwell, l.c., 224.

104 F.X. Durrwell, l.c., 201.

105 l.c., 207.

106 l.c., 194.

107 *Presbyterorum Ordinis*, 2, 4.

108 *Lumen gentium*, 25, 28; *Ad Gentes*, 20.

109 M. Weber, *Gesammelte Aufsätze zur Religionssoziologie*, Tübingen, 1922, I, 272.

110 *Lumen gentium*, 10.

111 ibid, 10.

112 F.X. Durrwell, l.c., 211.

113 Cf. *Lumen gentium*, 41; *Presbyterorum Ordinis*, 13.

114 F.X. Durrwell, l.c., 227.

115 l.c., 227.

116 Cf. B. Häring, *Acting on the Word*, New York, 1968.

117 *Lumen gentium*, 44.

118 Cf. ibid, 33, 41; *Apostolicam Actuositatem*, 16, 17.

119 Cf. V. Schurr, *Seelsorge in einer neuen Welt*, 65.

120 *Gaudium et Spes*, 26c.

121 ibid, 25.

122 Cf. ibid, 30.

123 M. Nédoncelle, *God's Encounter with Man*, New York, 1964, 180; cf. E. McDonagh (ed.), *Moral Theology Renewed*, Dublin, 1965; E. McDonagh, "The Primacy of Charity", l.c., 130, 150; D. O'Callahan, "The Meaning of Justice", l.c., 151-172; W.A. Luijpen, *Existentielle Phänomenologie*, München, 1971, 22-256: "Phänomenologie der Liebe und der Gerechtigkeit"; R.

Laurentin, *Die neuen Forderungen der Liebe*, Graz/Wien/Köln, 1971; K. Thekkinedath, *Love of Neighbour in Mahatma Gandhi*, Alwaye/Kerala, 1973; J.M. Dias Alegria, "Gerechtigkeit", *Sacramentum Mundi*, II, 261-275; B. Häring, "Gottesgerechtigkeit und Lebensgerechtigkeit", in J. Feiner and M. Löhr (eds.), *Mysterium Salutis*, Zürich/Einsiedeln, vol. IV (1976), 259-284 (bibliography).

[124] G. Schenk, "dikaiosyne", *Th.W.z.NT*, II, 197; cf. W. Eichrodt, *Theologie des Alten Testamentes*, Stuttgart, 1959⁶, I, 155-162.

[125] Justin, *Dialogue with Tryphon*, 93, 3.

[126] *Gaudium et Spes*, 32.

[127] Cf. Paul VI, Enc. *Populorum progressio;* L.J. Lebret, *Dynamique concrète du dévelopment*, Paris, 1967.

[128] P. Tillich, *Love, Power, and Justice*, London/Oxford, 1954, 45.

[129] G. Stählin, *Skandalon. Untersuchungen zur Geschichte eines biblischen Begriffes*, Gütersloh, 1930; W. Schöllgen, *Soziologie und Ethik des Argernisses*, Düsseldorf, 1931; A. Humbert, "Essay d'une théologie du scandale dans les synoptiques", *Biblica* 35 (1954), 1-28; G. Stählin, "Skandalon", *Th.W.z.NT*, VII, 338-358; W. Molinski, "Argernis", *Sacramentum Mundi*, I, 318-327.

[130] Cf. H.M. Féret, *Pierre et Paul à Antioche et à Jerusalem. Le conflit de deux apôtres*, Paris, 1954; J. Bligh, *Galatians*, Slough, 1969.

[131] Cf. *Gaudium et Spes*, 19-21, and chapter VII (on Atheism) in this volume.

[132] E. Mounier, *L'affrontement*, Paris, 1948, 36.

[133] Cf. P. Knauer, "The Hermeneutic Function of the Principle of Double Effect", *Natural Law Forum* 12 (1967), 132-162; R. Roy, C.Ss.R., "La coopération selon St. Alphonse de Liguori", *Studia Moralia* 6 (1968) 377-435; R.A. McCormick, *Ambiguity in Moral Choice*, Milwaukee, 1973; Ch. E. Curran, "Cooperation: Toward a Revision of the Concept and its Application", *Linacre Quarterly* 41 (1974), 152-167; Id., "Cooperation in a Pluralistic Society", in *Ongoing Revision. Studies in Moral Theology*, Notre Dame/Ind., 1975, 210-228.

[134] However, St Alphonsus holds that it is a merely material cooperation and therefore can be sometimes justified, e.g., by fear of being killed. I do not dare to deny that the opinion of St Alphonsus has its probability; cf. R. Roy, l.c., 415-421.

[135] Cf. R. Bruch, "Die Bevorzugung des kleineren Ubels. Moraltheologische Beurteilung, ein problemgeschichtlicher Durchblick", *Theol. u. Glaube* 48 (1958), 241-257; Ch. E. Curran, "The Principle of Double Effect", in *Ongoing Revision*, 173-209.

[136] Cf. Ch. E. Curran, *Ongoing Revision*, 223ff.

Chapter Ten

The Liberating Truth in Sexual Language

Our inquiry into the liberating truth has found its summit in faith active in love. The essential truth of the living faith is "God is Love". He has created us in his image and likeness in order to have sharers of his own love. We issue from the creative love of God. He has redeemed us for this love, and we find the truth of life only in loving him and, with him, our fellow travellers.

The truth of sexual love has much to tell us about being free and faithful in Christ. We would not be able to conceive any truths about the creative and redeeming love of God our Father, and Christ our brother, without the basic experiences of love that have come to us through the institutions of marriage and family. God not only compares his own love with the love of fathers and mothers and with spouses living the covenant of love; he also has given marriage and family as an effective sign of grace in the ongoing revelation and communication of his own love.

The Church recognizes as part of holy Scripture the *Song of Songs* that simply exalts the love between spouses who come to know each other in mutual love. The love of the betrothed that leads to the highest freedom of self-commitment in mutual fidelity and self-bestowal is, by itself, a song to the praise of God's love.

Here we treat human sexuality and its manifestations in the full light of Revelation, of historical development, and of human experience in the search for ever fuller truth in sexual relationships.

492

We approach this dimension of human life and relationships in full awareness of its complexity: the goodness of sexuality as a gift of the Creator, its involvement in sin solidarity and, last but not least, its role in the light of redemption, which allows believers to be free and faithful and to live the sexual dimension of their lives as life in Christ.

Our treatment of human sexuality is influenced not so much by a defence morality as by a covenant morality with its own dynamics and its proper protection. Our specific approach is to consider sexuality in its dimension of "language", a language of love which, in the life of sinners, is sometimes disturbed and confused and even falsified. But even here, where the sexual "language" unmasks a lack of liberty and fidelity and even speaks in plain lies, its very misery is crying out for the liberating truth, for communication in true love.

This whole volume has explored the different ways to reach out for and to live in the liberating truth. We have seen the various accesses to ever fuller truth: beauty, art, feast and play, sense of humour, the art of communicating the truth, and the grace of the loftiest sharing in truth by faith and hope active in love. Our inquiry would not be complete, however, without also considering human sexuality and its chief manifestations as a way towards fuller truth, a way of knowing each other in love and leading each other into the fullness of truth, into a community that reflects the love of a triune God.[1]

I. HUMAN SEXUALITY AS LANGUAGE

Nothing is more futile than to speak on sexuality by beginning with norms and prohibitions. Norms do not help anyone who does not first understand meaning. So, as in other areas, we begin by searching for meaning. It is the meaning that can articulate itself in beneficial norms and protective prohibitions.

The understanding of human sexuality depends greatly on how we look at the human body and relate it to the whole of human communication. As a gift of the Creator, renewed by the Redeemer, sexuality is a message that God speaks to us in love. And it is an essential part of the total human language and its truth.[2]

1. *Embodied language: spirit and body*

The human person is an embodied spirit and a spirited body. Each of us is a word spoken by God in a unique love, a word that has taken flesh and blood. And God calls us to transform all of our bodily being into glorification of his name: "Then honour God in your body" (1 Cor 6:20).

Our body speaks a language, a communication of meaning and purpose. Especially in its sexual dimension, it calls for relationship with the other; it appeals to the other, speaks to him or her. Our countenances speak, manifest joy, affection, acceptance or rejection, openness or withdrawal. Our arms can stretch out in supplication or reach for embracement. Our hand can rest in another's hand; we can shake hands and become a sign of the covenant. We speak with the sound of our voices almost as much as with the words formed by the sound. Indeed, the tone makes the music.

Although human language has its dimensions in the polis, in all our culture, society and politics, its original locus is the family, and at its centre is the total word of love spoken between husband and wife and then between parents and children. "The child understands the depth and meaning of love through the actions of mother and other people rather than by words".[3] If the children have learned the language of love, if they have seen how father and mother love each other in all the dimensions of their life together, and if they have been allowed to share in the abundance of the love and the word of their parents, then they, in turn, will pass on the language of love to their own children. They are privileged if they have been called into life by that unique and most incarnate word by which their parents have expressed their total mutual self-giving. "This concept of the body as the agent by which love is constantly renewed and deeper insight conveyed, is one of Christianity's great contributions to human relationships".[4]

When the spouses, in their bodily union, speak out and deepen the irrevocable "Yes" of the covenant, then they speak a word that re-echoes somehow the life of the triune God. "At the beginning was the 'Yes', and the 'Yes' was with love and the love was the 'Yes' ".[5] In the totally free mutual self-bestowal of the spouses in irrevocable fidelity, sexuality points to the incarnate Word who is the embodiment of the covenant and in whom "was never a blend of 'Yes' and 'No'. With him it was and is 'Yes'. He is the 'Yes' pronounced upon God's promises, every one of them" (2 Cor 1:19).

The language of the body that becomes language of love participates in the mystery of the Word of the Father breathing love.

When silence and the word that arises out of it speak out the being-with and being-for each other, then the spouses participate in the creation of a world that is an echo of God's word calling us and being with us.[6]

Human sexuality is a fundamental modality of how we relate to other people, to ourselves and to God. It is therefore a modality that reaches its full truth only through its integration in the total truth of our life. This is particularly true for the sexual "language" of husband and wife.[7] Its liberating truth depends on how genuine and trustworthy our expressions are, how open we are to the gift of the other in his or her otherness, how attentive we are to the message we convey and the message we receive. "The wonder of sexuality consists in the capacity of the body of the one seized by love to express this very love in a kiss or in a movement of the hand … so that the body, by itself, speaks, it becomes the word of love".[8]

In Freud and Marcuse, the eros takes the place of the logos; and thus the eros loses a great part of its meaning. It is bereft of its liberating truth. Eros and logos will not exclude each other. In true humanity they belong to each other essentially. The eros is embodiment of the logos, and through it the logos is embodied and takes strength.[9] The redeemed eros and logos participate in *agapé*.

"God created man in his own image; in the image of God he created him; male and female he created them" (Gen 1:27). The meaning and purpose of sexuality is visible in the human body; and it is the art of man to intuit the message and meaning of this image. Only if we have discovered the unity of the human person and have realized that the body is communication; only then is it clear to us that bodily reality, including its sexuality, is an image speaking of God.[10]

Sexuality manifests its purpose in a truly human way only to those who look first for its meaning. And its meaning is communication in truthful love. This is also the vision of the Second Vatican Council when speaking of the dignity of conjugal love and this bodily expression. "This love is an immensely human one since it is directed from one person to another through an affection of the will. It involves the good of the whole person. Therefore it can enrich the expression of body and mind with a unique dignity, ennobling these expressions as special ingredients and signs of the friendship distinctive of marriage".[11]

The human body, including its sexual dimension, is not just an image of the universe in its various compositions. It is, rather, the focal point of transformation, meaning, unto the dimension of adoration.[12]

Human language comes to its summit when one person speaks out himself or herself for the other in a covenant of love. Human sexuality, insofar as it is human, seeks the word that befits its meaning. It comes to its full truth only if we communicate with each other in all our reality, and so communicate that we speak out our belonging to each other or at least our being for each other. Only an integrated person can bring sexuality fully home into the dimension of communication of the full truth of love. To bring it home into this dimension is a part of the ongoing redemption.

Both spiritualism and sensualism have befouled sexuality; they have bereft it of its dimension of communication. Spiritualism considers sexuality as humiliating, and therefore the conjugal act as in need of justification by the direct intention of procreation. Thus the highest sexual expression is reduced to an animal operation "whereby the male impregnator mounts and dismounts the female as quickly as possible. This is the final ransom paid for identifying nature with biology and sex with genitality".[13] "To explain sexuality in terms of its procreative function alone is to reduce it to pre-human sexuality".[14]

The naked sensualists who disown both the unitive and the procreative meaning of sexuality do even worse. They talk a lot about sex; they know no barrier. "The most common problem now is not social taboos on sexual activity or guilt feeling about sex in itself, but the fact that sex, for so many people, is an empty, mechanical and vacuous experience".[15]

It is true that expressions of sexuality can be fallacious and degrading; but this is no more reason to defame sexuality itself than to defame language even though it frequently does not reach its full meaning and it is not seldom deceptive.

"And Adam knew Eve" (Gen 4:1). The Old Testament speaks of the conjugal act in terms of "knowing" (*jadac*). When man and woman truly love each other, they speak a most valid word of love that calls for eternity and opens new vistas for knowing the God of love and fidelity. But whatever the quality of the conjugal act may be, truthful or untruthful, manifesting the depths of heart and mind or superficiality, it is a way of "knowing" each other: either knowing the truth of love or unmasking each other by behaviour that contradicts the very meaning of sexuality. "Even in the most callous coital act, there is an element of honesty in which the mask slips and the true self is revealed to the partner".[16]

2. *Male and female he created them*

Sexuality is a relational concept; it points particularly to the bipolarity between men and women.[17] (In the use of language, I try to follow a suggestion by Baily: "The scholar at least should endeavour as far as possible to restrict the unqualified use of 'sex' and 'sexual' by relating them strictly to the being of Man, and not to his behaviour or biological functions".[18] Holmes makes another good suggestion: to write "Man" with a capital when it means man and woman without discerning the gender, and to write "man" with a small "m" whenever it relates to a male.) [19]

God's word is solemn: "So God created Man in his own image; in the image of God he created him; male and female he created them" (Gen 1:27). It is not my intention to give the impression that this text points only to sexuality; it speaks also about the image of God in man's and woman's vocation to be co-creators in ordering the world around them. But sexuality cannot be excluded from the concept of "image of God".[20] "Men are simply male and female. Whatever else they may be, it is only in this differentiation and relationship. This is the particular dignity ascribed to sex relationshp".[21]

The Yahwistic narrative of creation insists, far beyond and even against the spirit of that era, on the equal dignity of man and woman. God gave Eve to Adam (man) not only as a helpmate but rather as a counterpart, a partner. "Then the Lord said, 'It is not good for man to be alone. I will provide a partner for him' " (Gen 2:18). Adam (man) exults in the equality of the woman: "Now this at last — bone from my bones, flesh from my flesh — this shall be called woman (ishshah), for from man (ish) was this taken. That is why a man leaves his father and mother and is united to his wife and the two become one flesh" (Gen 2:23-24).

"Man" means simply man and woman, male and female: "On the day when God created Man, he made him in the likeness of God. He created them male and female, and on the day when he created them, he blessed them and called them Man". "Mankind is neither a men's club nor a women's club".[22]

We cannot speak on the human person without giving proper attention to the bi-polarity or reciprocity between man and woman in the whole of creation and redemption. The reciprocity is fundamental and presupposes, by necessity, equality in relational diversity.[23] Only in their mutuality can they find and communicate to each other the fuller truth. Wherever equal dignity is denied in this relationship, truth is jeopardized. The equal dignity of man and woman, translated into respect for the equal dignity of the child, may well be understood as an image and likeness of the Holy Trinity. "The Christian view derived from the creed on Trinity proclaims that personhood is constituted by loving relationship. This, to my mind, is perhaps even the most profound reading of the man-woman structure of humanity".[24]

Whenever equal dignity is denied to woman, Man ceases to be a fitting image of God. The story of the Fall points to male centredness as a main sign of a world and a relationship disordered by sin. God said to the woman: "Your yearning shall be for your husband, yet he will lord it over you" (Gen 3:16).

The frustration caused to the woman by a domineering husband will perpetuate the disorder in the very heart and mind of the children. "Sex is the mainspring behind maternal love. Thus when a mother is happy and well-adjusted as a wife and mother, her love for her child is selfless and geared to the needs of the child. Where her relationships, particularly with her husband, are unhappy, consciously or unconsciously, she finds her own emotional satisfaction through her children, either by rejecting them or by loving them possessively or destructively".[25]

Most modern languages, particularly English, are deeply marked by sexism: by male-centredness. There is an interdependence between language and the sexual dialogue. If one side is disturbed, it will have its repercussions on the other.

Max Scheler has already raised the question of whether our occidental languages do not reveal "the victory the male spirit has reported over the spirituality of woman".[26] He feels that this damages the growth of wisdom in favour of an unbalanced growth of technocracy. But most harmful of all is that the image of God is also distorted by such a language and such a disturbed sexual relationship.

This cultural bias has also influenced theology. Thomas Aquinas, for example, writes, "In the generation of the divine Word there is no relationship to motherhood but only to fatherhood".[27] Of course the divine relationships (*relationes subsistentes*) are beyond sexuality. But in human language they should be reflected by the reciprocity of father and mother, man and woman. Pope John Paul I left us this message: speaking of divine tenderness and compassion, he insists that in God there is even more of the motherly tenderness than of a certain father image.

The modern male sexist outstrips by far the bias of past theologians. In the Kinsey report on the human male, malehood is presented in a perspective of a fellow seeking "sexual outlets", and woman is appreciated only insofar as she is responsive to his desire for the "outlet". This leads Kinsey also to ignore the difference between human and animal sexuality. "The elements that are involved in sexual contacts between the human and animals of other species are at no point basically different from those involved in erotic responses to human situations".[28] Male-centredness reveals itself here particularly in the tendency to reduce sexuality to the animal level and especially to those species of animal where the male overpowers the female animal.

The male superiority asserted by a certain type of philosophy and theology was frequently reinforced if not partially caused by the erroneous biological ideas of the times, as well as by a biological outlook on sexuality. Until 1827 the existence and function of the ovule was not known. The male was simply considered as the procreator and the female only as the passive recipient.

Now we know that in each ejaculation there are about three hundred million spermatoza. And only one meets with the ovule, which is biologically a much more developed entity. During the first fourteen days, the whole life process is directed by the RNA (rebonucleic acid, the active messengers of the DNA) that has developed in the ovum alone prior to ovulation. The new DNA and its RNA will be operative only about fourteen days after fertilization.[29] The female's sex chromosome is composed of two X chromosomes. The male contains one X and one Y gonosome. The X gonosome bears much richer information than the Y gonosomes.

All this biological information will shock only those whose understanding of the male-female sexual relationship was based mainly on biology. They will either have to give up their biological outlook or change radically their view about the roles of male and female. In my opinion, the new information does not entitle us to attribute to man a role inferior to woman. They are equals in their diversity and reciprocity.

As long as equality in partnership is recognized, the very diversity of man and woman will enrich all human relationships and not only their sexual modality. But the summit of this enrichment, in which the children will share, is in the becoming-one-flesh, the *henosis* between man and woman (Gen 2:18; cf. Mt 19:5; Mk 10:7). The richness of the two people will flow into one. The presence or absence, the full acceptance or the refusal of the other party will determine the course of all the processes of life. The integrity and integration of each partner and the quality of this *henosis* condition each other.[30]

The unity and stability and, above all, the integration depends on the quality of the "sexual dialogue" which, of course, includes the whole life, not only the conjugal act. Man and woman, just because they are man and woman, come to this dialogue from two different experiential worlds. They can fully understand each other and live truth together only insofar as they both speak the same language of love in total openness to each other. This requests the great art of passing over to the other, of being "at home" in his or her innermost feeling, and from there, coming to understand better one's own identity.

This enriching mutuality is made possible by the increasing integration of *animus* and *anima* in the man, and of *anima* and *animus* in the woman. The human person becomes more himself or herself by bringing home into his or her own life-experience the qualities of feeling and expression of the partner. The honest and respectful communication between man and woman fosters inner integration, the being-in-the-truth that "as it is gradually learned and spoken — both learning and speaking influencing each other — sensuality and tenderness should achieve an ever greater harmony in the very intimate communication of one's self to the other. This is what chastity means".[31]

In this honest encounter between the sexes, two minds, two embodied spirits, meet in growing self-knowledge and mutual knowledge, and in an integrated outlook on life. But once more it has to be emphasized that this process of acquiring and sharing vital knowledge and integration depends both on the acceptance of diversity and full acknowledgment of equality.[32]

The biological basis of this enriching diversity in reciprocity should not be minimized, but we should be fully conscious that we are speaking of human biology. "The evidence strongly suggests that at the outset males and females are 'wired-up' differently. Social factors thus operate on already well-differentiated organisms, pre-disposed towards malehood and femininity".[33] Nevertheless, it seems that the total cultural conditioning exerts great influence on the modality of the sexual roles.

3. *Cultural incarnation of sexuality*

Man is a cultural being also in his sexuality.[34] He has a history, he is a history, and he shapes history. Tradition reaches him in the present culture. He is a part of this history by becoming conscious of it, grateful and critical at the same time, and he makes his history as a social being in personal and collective responsibility.

Sociology of marriage and family, and sociology of sexuality in general, study the ideas and expressions of sexuality in interdependence with the economic, cultural, social and political structures of life, and with the whole worldview predominant in a certain era. We have already referred to this interdependence in the roles of man and woman and their total self-understanding. Everyone is born into this stream of tradition and interdependence. With typical acumen, Simone Beauvoir insists that "no one is born a woman".[35] Surely one is born female, but then, in order to become fully a woman, she has the task of living her femininity. She cannot do so without taking into account the models and images provided by concrete civilization. The question is how far she is a passive product of the given models, and how far she enters into a creative dialogue with them.

An urgent task of moral theology is to make people, particularly those in teaching and education, fully aware of the social dimensions of human sexuality and, in consequence, of sexual ethics.

Referring to Ephesians 5:16 and Colossians 4:5, the Second Vatican Council warns us that we can give convincing testimony and make a constructive contribution only if we learn to discern. "Redeeming the present time and distinguishing eternal realities from their changing expressions, Christians should actively promote the values of marriage and the family, both by the example of their own lives and by cooperation with other men of good will".[36] And the Council makes it quite clear that for this purpose, theologians have to profit from the contribution of the behavioural sciences.[37]

In order to fulfil our roles as educators and counsellors, we not only have to be aware of how a society's attitudes, conventions and codes mould a child's sexual make-up and influence his or her sexual behaviour; we also must study the whole tradition of sexual ethics in the context of the various cultures. Only thus can we fully understand sexuality as an incarnated reality, and promote a critical spirit that challenges harmful sexual attitudes in given cultures.

Legalism and a simplistic use of past doctrinal formulations deprives the moralist the opportunity of exercising a beneficial impact for a genuine incarnation of sexual ethics. It is an undeniable fact, for instance, that through a long period of tradition — even Christian tradition — the cultural situation and the worldview did not allow the proper role to be attributed to love in the understanding of sexual attitudes.[38]

Biblical scholars have alerted moralists to the need for careful hermeneutics when using the Bible for an understanding of the meaning of sexuality, and even more for the understanding of sexual norms.[39] Even within the Bible there is evidence of a certain pluralism that corresponds to the cultural standpoints of the various texts. We cannot expect, for instance, that St Paul's letters, written within a particular culture, would indicate to us the accurate pattern of behaviour in an era when partnership family is the prevailing model. The Bible itself has set in motion a dynamic transformation that allows and requests new and frequently more demanding models of sexual ethics.

Not only the Gospel but also sexual ethics must be proclaimed to all nations in the diversity of their languages. Christians will observe the sexual "language rules" of their given cultures, but they are not imprisoned in them. The more they are attentive to a creative incarnation of sexual patterns, the more they will be speaking a truly Christian and fully humane "sexual language".[40] "Sexuality is not a 'dead language' like classical Greek or Latin, expressing things which *were* or 'universal ideas' which, as such, never exist. The sexual language is ever young with every new human being — and filled with hope which characterizes youth. Rooted in our own bodily and spiritual tradition, inspired by eternal vision, it is made to sing ever new modulations of love. Made wiser through trials and successes, formed through creative and uncreative pleasures, each one of us elaborates more or less skilfully the language with which he will write a unique sexual poem, that of his own intimate self in search of other selves".[41]

4. *The morality of the learning process*

To evaluate sexual behaviour, we have to consider the developmental process. Just as a tailor cannot make a garment in abstraction — that is, without knowing whether it is for a child, a youth, an adult man or woman, a short or tall person — so we cannot evaluate sexual ethics abstracted from the developmental process. For instance, as we shall see later, we cannot first propose the abstract norm that masturbation always is a mortal sin, and only then consider the difference between masturbation by infants, masturbation by adolescents, and others.

We need to consider here the contribution of developmental psychology and the dynamics of the social learning processes.[42]

Everyone knows that learning languages, including the child's learning of the mother tongue, necessarily entails the right to make mistakes. Dramatizing a learner's grammatical errors or ridiculing a child's mispronunciations inhibits the learning process. There is something similar in sexual development. The sexual language has to be learned gradually, and dramatizing the imperfections and mistakes of childhood and adolescence leads to alienation of sexuality.

The word "chastity" came into bad repute through those representatives of spiritualism who combined an abstract and static approach and imperative tone with an asexual, antisexual, or at least desexed vision of reality.

The process of coming to the right understanding and expression of the sexual modality of our being requires a "body-spirit integration and sexual identity to be realized gradually through a long man-woman dialogue".[43] Man never comes to the full realization of his chastity. It is not only a process of growth and struggle but also an opening of new vistas and a new adjustment in each phase of life.[44]

The relation to one's own body and to that of others is quite different for the infant, the adolescent and the adult. At the beginning, the infant sees everything as an extension of his own body, and pursues an experimentation, a learning process with his or her own body, in an egocentric relationship to others. Later, in the so-called "latency period" there gradually emerges the ability to care for and to love, to win distance from others, and to recognize their otherness more fully. Only gradually does the first autoerotic phase lead to growing specialization. "Sexuality becomes mature when it becomes a task for two rather than one, when it becomes social".[45]

The learning process in sexual integration goes hand-in-hand with the person's general development and integration. It is a work of reason, of love, of freedom, of art and of culture of all those involved.[46]

In the declaration on Christian Education, the Second Vatican Council, referring to "advances in psychology", insists that youth, "as they advance in years, should be given positive and prudent sexual education".[47] And the constitution on the Church in the Modern World urges that this sexual education be given especially in the youths' own families and in view of the dignity and expression of married love.[48] Sexual education must be a part of the whole process of education and well integrated into it.

It seems to me that the traditional doctrine on "parvity of matter" in the domain of sexuality should be thoroughly reformulated in the light of individual development and social dynamics.[49]

II. LOVE IS THE ANSWER

A Christian moral theology would be thoroughly unfaithful to the whole vision of revelation if, in the treating of sexual ethics, its purpose, ends and norms were defined apart from love. Here is a special test of whether we believe wholly in the great truth that God is love and Man is created in his image. The love of God and neighbour illumines the domain of sexuality. But sexuality, too, opens gateways for better understanding of what love is.[50]

1. *The true meaning of love*

Sexuality is integrated and reaches the quality of creative liberty and fidelity when it finds its meaning and purpose in human and divine love. The biological reality is only the material that receives its form (*causa formalis*) by love.[51]

The human biological reality is not indifferent to love. In love it finds its completion, its truth. Love is not only important for the married person, it is essential in whatever state of life the person may live. Conjugal intercourse is important but not, in the strict sense, essential. Love requires expressions that are best fitting and, in the given situation, possible and true. Conjugal love does not suppress any natural values but purifies them and integrates them.[52]

According to the design of the Creator, the sexual energies have to be formed, energized and elevated not only by *eros* but also by *philia* (friendship) and by *agapé*, the love that comes from God as gift and enables people to conceive themselves as a gift and to actualize this vision in mutual self-bestowal.[53]

The power of the sin of the world menaces this integration and will not allow it unless the person has made a firm and clear fundamental option for integrity and integration in divine and human love. The fundamental option opens the person and personal relationships to the power of divine grace, so that the integration willed by the Creator and the Redeemer becomes, as it were, "natural". Disintegration is unnatural, unnature. To bring home all one's energies into the truth of love is a precious grace and a noble art.[54]

To say that sex and eros are in need of redemption implies that they need to be assumed by that love that has the character of gift, and is lived in gratitude and mutual appreciation. Nothing makes people so joyous and so free as this integrated love, even though it demands the sacrifice of everything that opposes integration.

Humanist psychology gives strong and clear emphasis to this vision of integration as required by the true humanness of sex. Love is as primary a phenomenon as sex. Normally, sex is a mode of expression of love. Sex is justified, even sanctified, as soon as but only as long as it is a vehicle of love. Thus love is not understood as a mere side-effect of sex, but sex is understood as a way of expressing the experience of that ultimate togetherness that is called love.[55]

In today's occidental culture it is not good to speak of love as a "purpose" along with other purposes. For modern technical man, "end" or "purpose" has not the same meaning as *"finis"* had for medieval theology. There, it meant inborn dynamics, inborn meaning. Marriage is neither a contractual relationship for purposes nor a communion for purposes (Zweckgemeinschaft); it is a covenant of love.[56]

In all states of life, healthy sexuality depends on the strength of love; but above all, marriage is constituted as a community of love in mutual self-bestowal that, by its specific nature, is a bearer of fecundity. This fecundity is seen by Christians as a sharing in the creative love of God. Genuine human fecundity is the superabundance of love. Vatican II did not speak of conjugal love as a "primary goal" or a "primary purpose". Nor did it speak of procreation and education as a "secondary purpose". It seems to me that the formulations of Vatican II somehow suggest conjugal love as the surpassing form and inborn meaning, the overall grace and the spouses' response, which allows them to see parenthood as a crowning fruit and a most noble vocation, but a vocation that arises from love and leads to love.

For Christians who have found their centre and summit of life in the Eucharistic banquet, it is "normal" to bring home all their ideals, their involvements, their commitments into the great feast of love. For married people who consider their union as sharing in the saving covenant between Christ and the Church, their marriage is a feast of love from which everything else receives its meaning.

The Second Vatican Council says about married love: "It involves the good of the whole person. Therefore it can enrich the expressions of body and mind with a unique dignity, ennobling these expressions as special ingredients and signs of the friendship distinctive of marriage. This love the Lord has judged worthy of special gifts, healing, perfecting and exalting gifts of grace and of charity. Such love, merging the human with the divine, leads spouses to a free and mutual gift of themselves, a gift proving itself by gentle affection and by deed. Such love pervades the whole of their lives. Indeed, by its generous activity it grows better and grows greater. Therefore it far excels mere erotic inclination which, selfishly pursued, soon enough fades wretchedly away".[57]

It is the truth of love that brings forth as fruit creative fidelity, liberty, joy and healing.

Traditional moral theology spoke much about marriage as a "remedy for concupiscence", which means healing the restlessness of sexual desires that threaten disintegration. All this makes sense only if we see clearly that it is through the genuineness of integrated love that grace produces the healing.

The indissolubility of marriage and all the qualities of an ordered sexuality can only be understood as qualities and fruits of true love. As we have seen, the specificity of conjugal love implies that all the energies of sex and eros are assumed in the friendship sealed by redeeming love. Spouses are not allowed to let the energies of eros fade away, or to degrade the powers of sexuality.

If married people knew every hidden truth but not that of love, they would be nothing. If they have not conjugal love, they are nothing. They may dole out all they possess or even let their body be burned, but if they have no love, they are none the better. Love is faithful, joyous. Love is patient and has the powers of healing forgiveness. Love is affectionate and kind; it does not envy. Love is never boastful, but gratefully acknowledges the good in the other. Love is not conceited nor rude; it puts to death selfishness, and in consequence is not quick to take offence. Love keeps no score of wrongs but has a healthy memory for all the good. Love does not gloat over other people's sins. It delights in the truth that love, by its goodness, can overcome evil. There is nothing that love cannot face. It is above all in a saving solidarity that there is no limit to its faith: faith that all of creation issues from love, and that love will report the final victory. Hence there is no limit to its hope. And knowing that redemption flows from the death and resurrection of Christ, there is also no limit to its endurance. Love will never come to an end (cf. 1 Cor 13:1-8).

It suffices to compare this song of love, this feast of redeemed conjugal love with sex-consumerism, where the other is viewed as a sexual "outlet". Then we know what redemption means and how great is the misery of unredeemed sex. The sex-consumer renounces his human countenance; he meets the other not as a person but as a means. Not seeing the other in his or her uniqueness, he himself has no identity. Such a sexuality will never free anyone from the prison of self-centredness. The sex-consumer is unreal, for he does not know the supreme truth: Love is the heart of the matter.

2. *Love and growth in love as ultimate criterion for norms in sexual ethics*

Until now we have concentrated our attention on meaning grounded in the true nature of redeemed and redeeming love, and on sexuality and eros integrated into this highest heavenly gift. This vision allows us now to face the problem of norms.

It is our thesis that norms flow from love's meaning and from a realistic understanding of the realms of life.[58] But it must be added that the unloving know nothing about the real meaning of norms that arise from love's meaning and protect love. One needs a conversion to the Gospel of love in order to understand what the true countenance of love is.

It cannot be denied that different norms are proposed by people who all speak about love. Therefore we must give attention first to discovering what truly integrated love means for Christians, for all full human beings. The more people grow in this love, the better will they understand what love requires.

Christian faith has the courage to propose the very qualities of a love-integrated sexuality, as norms for thinking, speaking, learning and practising sexual language. For we know that God's grace calls us and his love guides us to a total conversion to redeemed love. As Christians we know that we are not redeemed by law and norms. But being "under grace" means also that we allow the Spirit to guide our lives along the lines of true love.

From all this flows a basic norm for educators and teachers of sexual morality. They are expected to show, sensitively and lovingly in the light of redeemed love, all the values and all the duties of the various domains of life and how each domain makes its particular contribution. They must, however, know that just as learning needs time, so also growth and ongoing conversion towards ever fuller integration in love needs time. They must clearly define the goal and direct the norms towards this goal; but there must also be an allowance for one step to be taken after the other.

Deficient forms of sexuality and even sexual perversions are not, in themselves, sinful. The sin is in the lack of love, in the accountable "No" to true love and the search for true love. Yet we should be aware also that the cause of deficiency and disorder might well be in the lovelessness of others and the lack of responsibility of those who could have built up a better and more helpful environment.[59] The misery of our time is not in the growth and exaltation of sexuality but, on the contrary, in its decay because of being alienated from true love.

A loveless sexual act, even though the motive might be to beget or conceive a child, is missing the mark, is sinful. And people should know that their sexual encounter will not express love unless their love is active in all domains of their life.

The loss of many earlier functions of the family, the many hours spent in frequently cold and impersonal working conditions, and "the withering away of the harsh physical and economic necessities by which marriage was dominated, has enabled our own generation to decide more firmly that marriage is primarily about human relationships, and that it is in the service of love".[60]

All this calls for greater attention to the dialogue between the spouses. Their sexual encounter cannot easily be love unless they are united by shared ideals and commitment.

The sexual union has its rightful home only in marriage, which we understand with Vatican II as "conjugal covenant and irrevocable personal commitment, as the intimate partnership of married life and love".[61]

Healthy sex is also play and feast, but the main source of this feast and play is fruitful love, and that is a firmly committed covenantal love.

For Playboy's man, others — especially women — are for himself. They are his leisure accessories, his playthings. But in the Bible, man becomes man only by being *for* the other.[62] Being for the other implies acknowledgment of the other's history, projects, feelings, and especially of his or her conscience. The other is allowed to be truly himself or herself.

An auto-erotic quest rooted in basic selfishness depersonalizes sexual relationships, makes them insignificant and, at the same time, harmful for oneself and for the other person.

Love entails a responsibility, and responsibility requires a knowledge of life. One must know how relationships affect others. Young people are sinning against love if they are unwilling to learn from tradition, from past experience, if they are claiming the "right" to experiment. Experimentation in the field of sexuality, especially experimentation with others, neglecting all traditional history, is grossly irresponsible.

Responsibility, that indispensable associate of love, requires knowledge of and respect for a given culture, but also a critical attitude towards it. Not only our subjective understanding of love but also the acceptable manifestations of love change colour over centuries and from culture to culture. All that is good and acceptable, and a proper step towards growth in a given culture must be respected. Ruptures or sudden changes that do not take into account the interdependencies and the rules of genuine development are detrimental even if the intentions for change are good.

The Second Vatican Council shows acute awareness of this dimension. "Many men of our own age also highly regard true love between husband and wife as it manifests itself in a variety of ways, depending on the worthy customs of various peoples and times".[63]

Christians are both grateful to and critical of their specific culture; but their critique is never destructive. Here again we can note the connection between language and sexual attitudes, for instance, in the sexist bias of our occidental languages. By a more creative use of our language, we can promote the gradual elimination of this bias. And as we recognize a responsibility to improve our language creatively, we also should recognize a shared responsibility to make our given culture more favourable for the ideal sexual morality.

A fuller awareness of the interdependence between sexual morality, marriage and family, and the total culture — the economic, social and political conditions — becomes for the Christian an appeal to join with all people of good will to improve both the quality of marriage and family and, indeed, the whole of sexual morality. The Second Vatican Council begins the chapter on marriage with a scrutinizing the signs of the times, and ends the chapter by calling for joint responsibility both for marriage and for the conditions of life that favour it.[64]

3. *Is there a distinctively Christian sexual ethics?*

Sexuality, as designed by the one God and Creator, allows a pluralism but also calls for basic unity. The creative and redemptive love of God is present to all people in all ages; yet there is a specific gift in the knowledge of Christ and in the community of the disciples. We not only know that men and women, in their reciprocity and bi-polarity, are created in the image and likeness of God; we know also him who is the perfect image of the invisible God, Jesus Christ. Moreover, the Bible and the witness of the saints and sages of the Judeo-

Christian tradition have made precious contributions to our seeing sexual life fully in the light of redeemed love. I do not dare to assert that Christian theologians and teachers have always taught a specifically Christian sexual ethics, but there is something specific in the mainstream of Christian tradition that is faithful to the Bible.[65]

The incarnation of the Word of God, his glorification of the Father in his body, faith in the resurrection of the body, the teaching of Christ and the apostles, and the lives of so many holy spouses and parents: all this directs our intuition to the specificity of a Christian sexual morality. We come to an integrated vision illumined by the truth that God is love and that the sexual dimension of men and women will find redemption and completion in the light of this truth.

As Christians, we believe that sexuality, fully accepted and lived according to God's design, is a part of our way of salvation. And married people know that their state of life is an effective sign, a sacrament of salvation. They believe that they can love each other in a fully humane way in God. "Only in God can I love the other as I want to love him for his, the other's sake, and only with God can I love myself as I should desire to love myself. If this is so, then we also are called to love God together with all our hearts, for his sake, that in such a gratitude we become one as he wants it for our sake".[66]

A better knowledge of the cultural context in which the pilgrim Church lives can help us to understand somehow that some aspects of what is specifically Christian in sexual ethics were darkened, here and there, even by such great thinkers as St Augustine.

Clement of Alexandria, who so forcefully defended the goodness of marriage and family against Gnosticism and Manicheism, and so beautifully praised the spiritual unity of the spouses, "never quite reconciles his belief in marriage as a gift of a good Creator with his conviction that sexual intercourse is a sign of imperfection".[67] This is no reason to look down on these giants of Christian tradition but rather to be more aware of the seductive power of erroneous cultural patterns which become stronger than ourselves unless we creatively and constructively try to shape the world around us.

4. *Love and pleasure*

Throughout tradition and up to the manuals of moral theology, the problem of pleasure in the sexual act occupied a great deal of space in sexual ethics.[68] In the Bible there is not the slightest indication that pleasure, as such, in ordered sex could be wrong. But there is a good deal of warning against pleasure-seeking in disordered sexual life.

The Church Fathers were faced with an overly sensuous world, especially in the great cities in which they lived. They saw the need to warn against a tedious hunting for sexual pleasure, with no attention to meaning. Today we find ourselves in a similar situation. It suffices to read the boring book, *The Sensuous Woman* by "J" (New York, 1971), to form an idea of how tedious a world can be when senseless and selfish pleasure-seeking is considered the highest "value".

However, Christian theology can fulfil its prophetic role and denounce deviations only against the background of meaning and the full acknowledgment of whatever is good. The Manicheans and Gnostics built their worldview and their radical condemnation of sexual pleasure and of sexuality itself on the experience of disorder. But by doing so, they did grave injustice to the many good people who lived their marriage in love and with genuine joy.

Asceticism is good in the service of love. Renunciation and sacrifices offered for the sake of genuine love cannot be praised enough. But asceticism and sacrifices become sour when God's gifts are suspected and degraded. False asceticism, combined with pastoral concern, produced a flagrantly unhealthy suspicion of all forms of venereal pleasure. The more the fear of pleasure took over the less central and constructive was the role of love seen in sexuality. Some moralists spoke of the marriage act almost exclusively as "marital duty", forgetting the joy of love while warning against all kinds of pleasure. And when speaking of marital love, they almost presented the ghost of joyless love.

Under the impact of Manicheism, Gregory of Nyssa developed the theory that sexual differentiation derives from a "second creation" decided by God only in view of sinfulness.

In this view, the exercise of sexuality becomes essentially a consequence of sin.[69] In his early writings, St Augustine followed the same theory and never could free himself from a view that saw pleasure in conjugal life as wholly contaminated by concupiscence. For him, the evil of concupiscence and the dreadful consequences of sexual pleasure made the conjugal act a shameful act held excusable only by the direct purpose of procreation. And even then he warned spouses not to affirm pleasure but to disdain it. "Desire the physical union only for the begetting of children, since this is the only way by which you can beget children; but condescend to it only with regret, for it is nothing else than the punishment of Adam from whom we all descend: let us therefore not boast of our punishment".[70] He thought that it would be an unspeakable joy of the spirit if spouses could have children without the pleasure of cohabitation.[71]

Explaining a frequently quoted text attributed to Gregory the Great, according to which spouses could commit venial sin if they were not successful in eliminating all pleasure in the conjugal act, Hugo of St Victor says that this is true only if they seek disordered pleasure.[72] This can be considered the healthy tradition that is common doctrine today. Vatican II acknowledges the conjugal act as a source of joy.[73] In the context, this surely does not mean a purely spiritual joy. When spouses celebrate their love before God in their bodily union, they are reaffirming the covenant of love. They give and receive together not only love but also joy in spirit and body.

The conjugal act would become distasteful if one of the spouses were to try to refuse its pleasure and thus kill the joy of the being-together, being one flesh. The deeper the meaning in true love in mutual self-bestowal, the greater is the joy and pleasure also. St Thomas Aquinas, refuting sharply the theory of Gregory of Nyssa, teaches not only that conjugal coitus would have been God's will in the earthly paradise, but also that pleasure would have been greater in the state of innocence.[74]

We do not praise all sexual pleasure but we do praise the pleasure that is joined with the joy of genuine love, the pleasure that praises the goodness of God's creation and the joy in a redeemed way of living. We distinguish the boring pleasure of sex-consumerism from the joy of loving spouses, a joy that pervades spirit and body, whereby pleasure is the real symbol of the total joy. Pleasure comes to fullness only in mutual self-bestowal, where the other person is honoured and loved.[75]

The great humanist psychologists have observed how intimate is the connection between meaning and joy and how they give dignity and enrichment to pleasure. Abraham Maslow writes, "It is certainly fair to say that self-actualizing men and women tend on the whole not to seek sex for its own sake or to be satisfied with it alone when it comes ... They would rather not have sex at all if it came without affection ... In self-actualizing persons, the orgasm is simultaneously more important and less important than in average people. It is often a profound and almost mystical experience, and yet the absence of sexuality is more easily tolerated by these people ... They do not need sensuality; they simply enjoy it when it occurs".[76]

Victor Frankl speaks in the same sense. According to him, the frustrated libido mushrooms in the existential vacuum that produces a sexual inflation. "Truly human sexuality is always more than mere sex, as far as it is manifestation of love. If this love is missing, then there is no real sexual delight ... Even if we would not have other reasons, we would even, in the interest of the highest possible delight, insist how important it is to incarnate the full human potential inborn in sexuality, namely the capacity to love that unites two people most intimately and personally".[77] Rollo May says it more directly: "So much sex and so little meaning or even fun in it!"[78]

Delight in spirit and body comes on the shoulders of mutual love; it is the bright light of meaning and commitment to it. In his present condition in a sinful world, Man needs the courage given by faith in redemption, the courage to resist the temptation to seek pleasure for itself. Everything that becomes too cheap brings nothing more than boredom and tedium. This is the traditional doctrine of temperance. Too much exposure to sex arising from lack of tender respect and responsibility makes sex meaningless and even a source of sadness, while temperance arising from the strength of love, even while requesting self-discipline and sacrifices, brings genuine delight, joy and pleasure in an integrated life.

III. FECUNDITY AS INTRINSIC PART OF THE SEXUAL LANGUAGE

1. *Fecundity: an abiding quality of conjugal love*

Love's fecundity is a reality totally different from biological fertility and any productivity of technical man. God has created men and women in his image and likeness, and blessed them so that, in their mutual self-bestowal, they may be sharers of his creative love. God's calling and blessing is given not just for producing children but for "knowing" each other, for making the world richer in love and, if it is his will, for having children from the superabundance of their love.[79]

Conjugal love has its value in itself. Its proper fecundity is in love and for love itself. It enriches not only the spouses but all whom they meet who become sharers of the overflow of their love. Persons who are truly in love become beautiful, intuitive, insightful, attentive, caring, generous and gracious.

What is predominant in the transmission of life is love's own fecundity.[80] Conjugal love, by its own truth and specificity, is open to the parental vocation. The encyclical *Humanae Vitae*, says beautifully, "This love is fecund for it is not exhausted by the communion between husband and wife, but is destined to continue, raising up new lives".[81]

In the pastoral constitution on the Church in the Modern World, the chapter on marriage and family insists that it is conjugal love itself that makes marriage truly and, in a human way, fecund. This fecundity arises not just from an institution or purpose. "Marriage and conjugal love are, by their nature, ordained towards the begetting and educating of children ... The true practice of conjugal love, and the whole meaning of the family life which results from it, have this aim: that the couple be ready, with stout hearts, to cooperate with the love of the Creator and the Saviour who, through them, will enlarge and enrich his own family day by day".[82] But only insofar as they are loving spouses can they be both cooperators and interpreters of God's love.[83]

Today, the grounds for desiring children for any utilitarian motives are falling away. The truth of love is the abiding wellspring of this desire. But even if, for grave reasons, the spouses have to renounce the desire to have children, their covenant has its full value.[84] Their love will enrich others and all of society in manifold ways. It is quite different, however, if spouses refuse their parental vocation for egotistic reasons. Only through their power to love together can parents create the necessary space and education in which their children can grow in the image and likeness of God, enriching the world by their capacity to love and to discern genuine love.[85]

Sexuality that is not integrated in mutual love is alienating and alienated. If it is activated only for the biological purpose of fertility it will remain most vulnerable to all kinds of abuses, to the exercise of power over the other, or to base sex appeal.[86]

The difference in the language describing the essence of matrimony, on the one hand in the code of canon law and in Vatican II on the other hand, is striking. Canon 1012 says, "Christ the Lord has elevated the very marital contract between baptized persons to the dignity of a sacrament", and Canon 1081 describes the contract performed by the consent in the following way: "Marital consent is an act of the will through which both parties hand over and receive a perpetual and exclusive right over the body, in view of acts which of themselves are fitting for the procreation of offspring". The cold word "contract" is quite appropriate for this transfer of rights defined by a purpose: rights and duties to acts for the sake of procreation.

The language of Vatican II is thoroughly different. "The intimate partnership of married life and love has been established by the Creator and qualified by his laws. It is rooted in the conjugal covenant of irrevocable personal consent ... Thus a man and a woman who, by the marriage covenant of conjugal love 'are no longer two but one flesh' (Mt 19:6) render mutual help and service to each other through an intimate union of their persons and of their actions. Through this union they experience the meaning of their oneness and attain it with growing perfection day by day. As a mutual gift of two persons, this intimate union, as well as the good of the children, imposes total fidelity on the spouses and argues for an unbreakable oneness between them".[87]

This vision surely does not belittle the parental vocation. Conjugal love itself discovers its innate dynamics towards sharing life and love with children, who can truly be called the "ultimate crown of matrimony and conjugal love".[88]

2. Historical and cultural diversities, development and decay

Theologically, the relation between love and fertility depends on whether sin or redemption prevails. As long as sin manifests itself in the domineering power of man and/or in woman's envy for similar power, biological fertility will take precedence as long as fertility is socially advantageous. Where humanization progresses under the power of redemption, mutual love and partnership in mutual respect will come more and more to the foreground. And this will radically change the relational aspect of the children. They are not an economic or social commodity; they are participants in the feast of love.

Throughout about four million years, biological fertility stood, by necessity, in the foreground, because it filled the most urgent need for survival both of humankind and of the family and clan units. Generally speaking, the biological fecundity of woman had to be used to the full because of the high rate of infant mortality and the frequent epidemics that decimated the population. To live out old age with dignity, there was no other hope than to have enough offspring. Further, in a culture of sustenance farmers, children were important helpers for they returned to the family, in material help, all that they had received.

Within this context a great love for children could and did frequently develop which, in turn, could strengthen the affection between the spouses. They honoured each other gratefully as father or mother of their children.

In city cultures like that of Babylon, and later of Rome, the physical work was performed by slaves, and help came from the tribes submitted to the power of the warrior. Children became less important. And when these city people, in their decadent luxury, lost the meaning of life, a drastic restriction of offspring was one of the main signs of decay. While it contributed to the decay of the national power, it was even more the sign of a deeper cultural decay.

In comparison with old rural society modern industrial and urban society has a quite different attitude towards the begetting and upbringing of offspring. Infant mortality is drastically reduced. The life of the aged is assured by social security, pensions and so on. Children can be playthings, which is bad enough, but they will not be an economic commodity. Their upbringing and education in a highly specialized society is most expensive. And if they are well prepared professionally, society and not the family directly will receive the benefits. The old patriarchal family, with three generations living together, has yielded its place to the nuclear family where the relationship between the spouses has become more and more that of partners.

That these personal relationships between the spouses have developed is a fact Christians should rejoice about in view of the centrality of the message of love. The growth of consciousness and shared reflection about the begetting of offspring seems to be an irrevocable conquest. It can, however, and frequently does degenerate into a utilitarian calculation.

In urban society, with its lonely crowd and depersonalizing economic and political conditions, it is normal that people feel a greater need for intimacy in sexual relationships; but stability in marriage is not always fostered. Frequently faith and the sense of ultimate meaning are lost. There are all too high and wrong expectations about sex. Artificial means of contraception and easily accessible abortion has made possible the severing of unitive and procreative goals.

In this atmosphere, human fertility may be drastically reduced by sex-consumers, people who have lost the true meaning of life. Not needing children for social status or for security's sake, they have no motive for begetting offspring. It seems to me that the present situation is moving towards a profound separation of humankind into two species. On the one hand are those who have no ground or motive to transmit life; or if they do transmit it they only increase the number of competitors and rivals in a consumer society. On the other hand there will be those who firmly make their commitment to genuine love and, moved by their mutual love and sense of life, desire as many children as they can well prepare for life's combat, for this life and the other.

The situation in the so-called "third world" is again different. The large family unit is still operative; the transmission of life has still a transcendental right. Life beyond the grave and the desire to be always honoured by the offspring still form a synthesis. And although infant mortality is already reduced, there is no system of social security; hence only offspring can give security. This great difference between the outlook in the occidental world and in the southern hemisphere may well be a profound cause of long-lasting imbalance. The Church, too, has to give specific attention to the different culture stages and value systems.[89]

3. Responsible parenthood

Profound cultural and psychological changes, the population explosion in some parts of the world, an all too low birthrate in other parts, and many other reasons make the transmission of life a matter of serious and direct reflection for most people.

Although we cannot ignore the burning problem of population and its regulation,[90] we concentrate our main attention here on the problems of married people in the matter of family planning.

Almost all nations show a positive approach towards family planning. The spouses' right to decide the ideal number of children and their capacity and duty to educate the children are well recognized. But more and more nations are fashioning elaborate policies regarding the regulation of population growth. The Church is fully aware of this need but also of the great problems involved.[91] It is my conviction that the right solution to family planning throughout the world will indirectly affect the population problem in the best way.

a) Conscious transmission of life

Although a tradition issuing from Clement of Alexandria, Gregory of Nyssa and Augustine taught that the conjugal act is fully justified ("excused") only when procreation is directly desired and actually possible, today's official doctrine of the Church, prevalent at least since St Alphonsus, allows conjugal intercourse for sterile persons and during times of pregnancy, which means in circumstances where the conjugal act is not suited to the transmission of life. Nevertheless, Catholic doctrine has always asserted and still asserts the need of a synthesis between the unitive and the procreative purposes or dimensions of the conjugal union. However, the various currents of tradition do not all understand this in the same way.

Contrary to Augustine, Alphonsus de Liguori teaches emphatically that the conjugal act does not at all need an "excuse" As expression of genuine conjugal love and indissoluble faithfulness, it is in itself (*per se*) honourable (*bonus et honestus*). He even dares to say, "This is a matter of faith (*Hoc est de fide*)".[92]

Alphonsus offers an interesting explanation of the synthesis between the various purposes of marriage and of the conjugal act. "Three kinds of purposes can be considered in marriage: (1) the innate *essential* purposes, (2) the innate *incidental* purposes, (3) the incidental extrinsic purposes. The innate *essential* purposes are two: mutual self-bestowal (and as a consequence the due rendering of the conjugal act) and the indissoluble bond. The innate *incidental* purposes are equally two: transmission of life and remedy of concupiscence. The incidental extrinisic purposes can be manifold. From this follows: (1) it is certain that, by excluding the innate *essential* purposes, one does not only sin but also nullifies the marriage ... (2) it is certain that, by excluding the innate *incidental* purposes, one might in some cases not only validly but also licitly contract the marriage".[93]

Of course St Alphonsus considers any *arbitrary* exclusion of the two innate *incidental* purposes, and particularly the exclusion of the procreative meaning of marriage or the marital act as illicit, and if it concerns the marital contract, this would be nullified.

I do not consider this systematization of the relation between the unitive and procreative ends of marriage to be the only possible one. However, I find it extremely interesting and a worthwhile effort to explain how the unitive and the procreative dimensions are related as innate purposes of marriage, forbidding any arbitrary separation.

Marriage between persons who are sterile can be valid and good even though the spouses, while rejoicing in the unitive meaning, cannot really fulfil a procreative role. When the partners truly love each other as spouses, in a way that would keep them open for the parental vocation if this were within the range of possibility, the true functions of marriage are not arbitrarily sundered. One who sincerely loves the other as his/her spouse would not refuse to have the spouse as a parent of his or her children if the responsible choice were truly given.

In a marriage where fertility is naturally and responsibly given, the very unitive function will keep loving and responsible spouses open to the desire for children, and make them more able to give the children a harmonious education based on their own unity and harmony.

The project of fecundity is so much a part of the marriage covenant and of conjugal love that those acts in which a new conception is explicitly desired have a special fullness and devotion. When, then, a new pregnancy cannot be looked for, the act participates somehow in that same fullness and dignity. Conjugal life has to be looked upon as a whole.[94] Any arbitrary separation of the two functions affects also the unitive goal in a negative way.

b) Responsible parenthood; shared reflection and decision

That the transmission of human life transcends biological fertility and instinct, and is entrusted to the shared reflections and decision of the spouses, has been an established approach in Catholic doctrine since Pius XII.[95] It has been thoroughly explained in the Second Vatican Council's constitution on the Church in the Modern World, Article 50, and by Pope Paul VI's encyclical, *Humanae Vitae*.

Two things have to be thoroughly distinguished: first, the decision to transmit life, to observe certain intervals and/or to limit the number of children desired, and second, the question of method. I want to make it clear to the reader that on this point I do not at all speak on methods, just as Article 50 of the pastoral constitution does not at all speak on methods. This was not fully understood by bishops and many leaders who approached the whole problem from the perspective of methods.

It has to be understood that the question of responsible transmission of life makes sense only for those who consider the parental vocation as an innate meaning or purpose of the conjugal covenant and marital love. Responsibility is understood here not merely as accountability but as the basic ability and readiness to respond to God's gifts and calling. The spouses have to reflect together and make a shared decision on how many children they should desire and at what intervals. It is Christian responsibility if they make a decision that they can offer to God as a grateful response to his calling and to all his gifts. "They will thoughtfully take into account both their own welfare and that of their children, those already born and those which may be foreseen. For this accounting they will reckon with both the material and spiritual conditions of the times as well as of their state in life. Finally, they will consult the interests of the family group, of temporal society and of the Church herself. The parents themselves should ultimately make this judgment in the sight of God. The spouses should be aware that they cannot proceed arbitrarily".[96]

Nobody but the spouses can make this decision. Only they, united before God, can somehow evaluate the strength of their mutual love, their pedagogical capacities, their physical and mental health. It would, for instance, be a grave injustice and a loveless procedure if a husband would request from his wife a new pregnancy when this would overburden her and jeopardize her health. However, in common decision before God, they can accept a proportionate risk. The greatest tasks on earth sometimes allow and even demand a reasonable risk. But trust in divine providence does not authorize spouses to act inconsiderately.

c) Harmonizing responsible transmission of life with the requirements of conjugal love [97]

The angle and perspective of one's approach to the question of methods for regulating conception are decisive. Even the choice of words is very important. For instance, the various planned parenthood societies usually speak of "birth regulation". The very words intentionally include abortion which prevents a normal birth. We prefer the expression "regulation of conception" or even "contraception", in order to make clear that abortion is thoroughly excluded from our theme and, indeed, rejected as a means of responsible parenthood.

Many moralists and, following their tradition, the encyclical *Casti Connubii* treated the question of methods exclusively without giving attention first to the basic decision of responsible transmission of life. It seemed that the method alone would decide the morality. The same harsh words of condemnation were used for those who already had fifteen children and, for instance, used interrupted intercourse to prevent a further conception, as for those who rejected their parental vocation altogether and decided arbitrarily and selfishly not to allow a pregnancy.

It must be said firmly and clearly that if the motives for excluding the transmission of life are selfish or vicious, the method alone, be it total or periodical continence or not, does not save the morality of it.

Many writers and other people approach the matter of methods with a thoroughly contraceptive attitude. They, too, do not at all consider the basic moral question of responsible parenthood, of generous acceptance of the parental vocation and a judicious decision about the number of children and at what intervals. We understand a "contraceptive attitude" or "contraceptive culture" as a trend of the modern technically oriented person and sex consumer to think that technical methods alone can resolve the problem. This kind of person decides on the number of children in a utilitarian attitude, and so approaches the problem and methods of regulation of conception or birth regulation as a consumer.[98]

The fact of mutual exploitation will always hang over the heads of those who, instead of respecting the sexual language of love, look only for technical methods and pleasure. Officers and leaders of other Christian Churches, who are more lenient than the official Catholic doctrine about the solution of difficult situations, are fully aware of this trend. Beckmann, the former president of the Evangelical Church in the Rhineland, said, "Contraception because of a need is more seldom than contraception because of other motives, for instance, avoidance of hardship or for the sake of mere pleasure".[99]

The Second Vatican Council approached the problem on the highest level of principles, in a personalistic vision but without going into details on methods. The question of methods is not approached at all until the more basic principles about responsible parenthood are thoroughly explained. Then it is presented under the heading, "Harmonizing Conjugal Love with Respect for Human Life". Before "dishonourable solutions", especially abortion, are firmly rejected, the Council recognizes how unrealistic it would be to propose total abstinence as *the* solution of the problems involved in responsible parenthood.

"As a result, the faithful exercise of love and the full intimacies of their lives are hard to maintain. But where the intimacy of married life is broken off, it is not rare for its faithfulness to be imperiled and its quality of fruitfulness ruined. For then the upbringing of children and the courage to accept new ones are both endangered".[100]

The Council is convinced, however, that there must be an honest solution, since "a true contradiction cannot exist between the divine laws pertaining to the transmission of life and those pertaining to the fostering of authentic conjugal love". While all that we would like to know about this solution cannot be said immediately, a purely biological approach is excluded: "The sexual characteristics of man and the human faculty of transmitting life wonderfully exceed the dispositions of lower forms of life".[101]

The positive approach of the Council in this matter, as in the whole constitution on the Church in the Modern World, is taken from the dignity of the human person. This dignity must also and particularly be applied to conjugal love. "Hence the acts themselves which are proper to conjugal love and which are exercised in accord with genuine human dignity must be honoured with great reverence. Therefore, when there is a question of harmonizing conjugal love with the transmission of life, the moral aspect of any procedure does not depend solely on sincere intentions or on an evaluation of motives. It must be determined by objective standards. These, based on the nature of the human person and his acts, preserve the full sense of mutual self-giving and human procreation in the context of true love".[102] Then follows a text added at almost the last hour: "Such a goal cannot be achieved unless the virtue of conjugal chastity is sincerely practised".

In the whole perspective of the Council's text, chastity can surely not be meant as simply renouncing the intimacy of married love; but it does imply renunciations required by the very dignity of conjugal love. And once chastity and its deference are understood as a requisite of love, then a great and illumined love is also able to accept the necessary renunciations. Particularly Christians, who see their earthly life and love bound up with the love of God, will be best prepared to do what love bids and to renounce what love forbids.

The encyclical *Humanae Vitae* (nn. 7-11) takes up the Second Vatican Council's basic vision of married love. Then, from its own approach to natural law, it reaches the conclusion: "Nevertheless the Church, while she warns men and women concerning the observance of the precepts of the natural law as it is interpreted by her unchanging doctrine, teaches that it is necessary that any act of intercourse in marriage remain, of itself, aimed towards procreating human life" (11). The Latin text can also be translated "of itself open to procreation". I think that the most acceptable (interpreting) translation might be, "of itself, pointing towards procreating human life".

Pope Paul VI was thoroughly convinced that in those situations where life cannot be responsibly transmitted, spouses who use the infertile period with the intention of avoiding a new pregnancy, can still say that their conjugal intercourse is "of itself aimed towards procreating human life", although this is not the case when other methods of preventing conception are used. Paul VI sees here an essential qualitative difference: "Therefore, it is a great error to think that the act of intercourse in marriage, intentionally deprived of its fertility and thus inwardly disfigured, can find justification from the fertile acts of intercourse of the whole life of husband and wife".[103] It seems that the Pope wants to explain the difference between the natural act of intercourse during the infertile period — this act still pointing towards procreation — and the external manipulation that visibly points towards depriving the act of its fertility.

Humanae Vitae does not request total but periodical abstinence only. Paul VI is convinced that this method keeps the marital act really open to the procreative function while effectively preventing conception through the mere choice of the infertile period. But this calculation must never be arbitrary. "There are just reasons for spacing subsequent births, reasons which originate from physical or psychological conditions of husband and wife or from external circumstances. The Church teaches that it is then permitted for husband and wife to follow the natural cycles coursing the regenerative faculties, in having intercourse only at those times which lack fertility".[104]

The French Jesuit Gustave Martelet tries to explain by the paradigm of language the difference between calculated use of the infertile period and other means of blocking conception. And since Pope Paul VI repeatedly praised Fr Martelet, it is worthwhile to look at his interpretation.

He first accurately describes the doctrine of the Second Vatican Council, where the whole problem is sharply set forth. "The spouses can sometimes see themselves as painfully torn between the unifying values of the sexual language of love and, for them here and now, an undesirable fecundity". Then, regarding fecundity, he speaks of "the structures, the functions and the rhythms which condition man's truth in this domain".[105] The periodical rhythm between fertile and infertile days is, for him, the very structure and language of fecundity; and if love expresses itself within this language of fecundity, it is true to life. "The analogy of the word in its relationship to the truth can serve us as guide to understanding the vision of a love which, in itself, is dialogue and language, and we ask: Could one fulfil the duty to say the truth by speaking while trying to mask it?"[106]

The language rule whereby sexuality expresses itself in a rhythm of fertility and infertility seems to be, for Martelet, an absolute one. His conclusion, therefore, is that if the natural rhythm is disturbed, "love participates here in the drama of language where sometimes it becomes terribly necessary to be silent in order to avoid a lie by speaking".[107] From this follows that those who rely on the natural rhythm to avoid an undesirable pregnancy are truthful to the sexual language, while others who use a method that does not rely on this language structure are "betraying life" by not observing the law of the sexual language.[108]

One may ask whether such an absolutizing sacralization of one phase of a biological function, with accusations as severe as "betraying life" is convincing. The whole conceptive process needs further analysis, and the "language" argumentation needs both a deeper exploration of the psychology and sociology of language[109] and, of course, a careful synthesis between the total meaning of sexuality and faithfulness to life as gift and call.

Our physical processes are inherited from prehumanity. Of themselves they have no moral responsibility and can command none. But this does not mean that the human conceptive design has no message for man; it only means that, as morally responsible beings, we have to interpret its message into our own language of responsibility.

When we look at the human conceptive system as a whole, rather than at this or that detail, we receive a quite coherent message. We find that the structures, functions and rhythms of the human conceptive process which, for Martelet, "condition man's truth in this domain", compose a system which gives free rein to the unitive dimension of human sexuality but carefully monitors its conceptive power. It refuses all conceptive power to women before puberty and after menopause, during a pregnancy and frequently during lactation, as well as during two-thirds of all days of their fecund years. Beyond that, it refuses, in overwhelming proportion, the opportunities for conception during the fertile periods. Yet this same system grants and invites the unitive expression of human sexuality at all times from puberty until long after the normal age of menopause.

It is true that one part of this biological "language" is spoken on certain days of the month; but partial messages are not dependable. If we are to reach man's full truth in this domain, then we must first listen with the utmost care to the total message, and only then offer a translation in the language of our own moral responsibilities.

This does not imply that better knowledge of the natural rhythms between fertile and infertile days in the monthly cycle are of no value. On the contrary, periodical continence, based on ever better knowledge that may eliminate some hazards, if practised by a highly motivated couple who can apply it, has distinct advantages over all the other methods of controlling conception.[110]

Pope Paul VI, in *Humanae Vitae*, invokes "the unbroken tradition". The encyclical bases its conclusion on tradition and on natural law. It therefore tries to give convincing reasons, since "natural law" is what is open to the eyes of reason after shared experience and reflection. If the reasons do not convince fully, this does not prove the doctrine wrong. Competent people should probe the possibility of finding more convincing ones.

Regarding tradition, there is surely something abiding. André Guindon expresses it thus: "The tradition fears that when sexuality is not lived within the whole project of fecundity, of that 'historical love' which marriage stands for, then it is betrayed in its very nature because sexuality is played against tenderness".[111]

The basic concern of tradition must be upheld, first against the contraceptive "use" of sexuality outside of marriage, and secondly against a contraceptive mentality in marriage where spouses, refusing the parental vocation, seek sexuality apart from that unitive function that opens up to the parental vocation. All methods of controlling conception must be thoroughly rejected whenever sensuality is played against tenderness. However, many married people and marriage counsellors hold that spouses who are truthfully living the parental vocation are able to use, with a high degree of tenderness, contraceptive methods other than periodic continence. It seems to me, however, that married people should be warned against possible pitfalls.

The reading of tradition needs hermeneutics in full understanding of the total cultural context and worldview of the past and present. The condemnation of contraceptive methods in past centuries was convincing for many reasons. Frequently magic practices were invoked; the sperm was considered as a "little man" (*homunculus*), so the voluntary waste of sperm was almost equated with abortion; the concept of responsible transmission of life was not yet clearly conceived; the approach to life was generally not reflexive; the direct intention to procreate was considered necessary in order to "excuse" the conjugal act; the unitive function as such of the conjugal act was frequently not considered and hence the alternatives seemed to be either procreation or the mere search for lust. The "openness" of the conjugal act in the calculated use of the infertile period, asserted by *Humanae Vitae* is not the same as that which tradition has asserted. It is an important modification.

In view of all this it is no wonder many bishops and even more theologians, pastors, confessors, and particularly married people and marriage counsellors have difficulty in accepting the absoluteness of the new norms. Confessors and counsellors have to bear in mind that married people are generally aware of all these difficulties and of the various declarations of the episcopal conferences.

What is necessary is openness in the search for truth, readiness and effort to listen to and to understand the Magisterium, honesty and sincerity in thinking about these grave problems and, above all — what is particularly underlined by the declarations of the episcopal conferences and by theologians — respect for the sincere conscience.[112]

A Catholic couple will not form their judgment of conscience without giving proper attention to the total Magisterium of the Church. The common synod of the diocese of the Federal Republic of Germany says on this point, "The judgment of the methods regulating conception, for which decision the conscience of the spouses is competent, may not be taken arbitrarily, but must make the objective norms proposed by the Magisterium of the Church a part of the conscientious evaluation. Thereby, the methods applied may not be those which hurt a partner psychologically or diminish him or her in the capacity to love".[113] The footnote to the document refers to the following texts to be taken into account: The pastoral constitution on the Church in the Modern World, 51c; the encyclical *Humanae Vitae*, nn. 10-14, and the declaration of the German Episcopate regarding the pastoral situation after publication of the encyclical, issued August 30, 1968. The encyclical of Pope Paul VI must be read and interpreted in the context of the total Magisterium of the Church.[114]

No one should be shocked about the difficulties in the Church on this point. It is a search for truth imposed by profound and shaking changes in human history and in the face of an unprecedented impact on the whole of humankind. If there is dissent on some limited details of the doctrine, one must not overlook the broad consent on the most basic values and principles.

IV.   THE COVENANT OF LOVE: MARRIAGE AND FAMILY

I hope that the foregoing reflections have shown how impossible it is to grasp the meaning of sexuality without concentrating our attention on marriage as a covenant of love, as vocation and as institution.

In all cultures, we find marriages and families within which the spouses are called and enabled, and sometimes also ordered to fulfil their high vocation as spouses and parents. The functions and concrete structures of marriage never arise from the mere realm of sexuality or from sexual hygiene; they have not only to do with a relationship between husband and wife. An historical and actual understanding of marriage has to see it in the light of the total family structure, of the exigencies of education, the interdependence with economic life, structure of property, social security, and last but not least, the interests of society as a whole.

1. Marriage as institution

Marriage as vocation and saving mystery cannot be understood outside of its institutional, cultural, historical context. Hence, the incarnational vision of Christian life demands proper attention to these various dimensions.[115]

On the institutional level, marriage and family belong together. They are the oldest and most basic institutions that guarantee human culture and the growth and security of the human person. They are the living cell of human society and of the Church. Throughout history, marriage exists, prospers or suffers in interdependence with the social, cultural, political, and economic structures of the whole of human life.

If we speak of marriage as "institution", our first thought, as believers, is that it is instituted by God, and that he has a design for it which humankind has to respect. Marriage, as we have seen, is willed by God as a community of love and as a life-giving community. We do not know God's design in the abstract, but only as he has revealed it in the unfolding history of salvation.

The holy texts and the doctrine of the Church on marriage are "situated", but they illumine the ideal in the prevailing culture and structure. The inspired authors challenge the domineering attitude of man over woman, but they do not outline marriage as partnership when the existing culture produces only the patriarchal type of family. Yet the ideal proposed by sacred Scripture can revolutionize the existing structure of patriarchalism as it did the structure of slavery, for growth also is a basic ideal and value understood by faith.

Marriage and family need society to guarantee its security, stability and the fufilment of its inalienable functions. Christian marriage needs the Church to uphold its ideals and to help spouses and families come to an ever better understanding of their vocation. The Church that proclaims marriage as a saving mystery cannot be uninterested in how society relates to marriage, protects it, fosters it or causes it handicaps and obstacles.

In its own interests, the state must examine all its activities and legislation, its economic planning and cultural programmes in view of their influence on marriage and family. A state or society that is careless about the stability of marriage and family, and about allowing and helping parents to educate their children properly, is undermining its own health and prosperity.

In the first centuries the Church, wherever she preached the Gospel, relied greatly on the customary marriage and the state regulations about marriage and family. She helped spouses and families to live the faith, to give witness and to render service within the given institutions. But from the very beginning, she developed some elements of ecclesiastical law about Christian marriage. Only in the last millenium has there developed (perhaps overdeveloped) Church regulation by canon law of multiple details concerning marriage. Much is time-bound, tied up with the cultural conditionings of Christendom.

Martin Luther challenged Church legislation about marriage, insisting that marriage is an earthly reality and therefore under the state's right and duty to legislate. However, all parts of Christianity show themselves interested in marriage as institution, partly by their own legislation and partly by admonishing Christians to work within society and state to uphold and promote marriage as an institution.

The Second Vatican Council, fully aware of the institutional dimension of marriage, was particularly concerned that no split should be accepted between marriage as institution and marriage as covenant of love. The following quotations are typical. "By their very nature, the institution of marriage itself and conjugal love are ordained for the procreation and education of children, and find in them their ultimate crown".[116] The Council deplores the fact that "the excellency of this institution is not everywhere reflected with equal brilliance".[117] The Church expects the spouses to "do their part in bringing about the needed cultural, psychological and social renewal on behalf of marriage and the family".[118]

While courageously facing the imperfections of and threats to the institution of marriage in today's world, the Council is basically optimistic. "Yet, the power and strength of the institution of marriage and family can also be seen in the fact that, time and again, despite the difficulties produced, the profound changes in modern society reveal the true character of this institution in one way or another".[119]

The profound cultural changes of which the Council speaks have forced and helped many people, including ethicists, moral theologians and canonists, to give greater attention to discerning what is abiding truth and what are changing realities, and to discovering how marriage and family life can be more truthfully incarnated in the various cultures and subcultures.

However, it cannot be overlooked that during the past decades there has developed an increasing crisis concerning marriage as an institution. The general anti-institutional complex has also partially affected marriage. Many young people refuse not only ecclesiastical celebration but also civil marriage. They live their sexual union in plain protest against institution. They seem to be blind to the social dimension of sexuality and of the sexual "community of life". "Living as a couple without legal recognition nearly always implies, in the long run, a series of lies destructive of the social bond".[120]

When people refuse to make a marriage commitment before society and in view of it, they deny an essential dimension of the sexual community of life and deprive themselves of the support of society while refusing to give their own support to society.

The modern nuclear family is quite different from the traditional patriarchal family whose strong social bonds united several generations in special solidarity with the clan. The nuclear family can be healthy only if it is open to and united with other families in shared ideals and commitments. Marriage Encounter, the Christian Family movement, the family groups of Notre Dame and others respond to this new need. Margaret Mead and Harvey Cox suggest the need of "cluster families", where several families living in the same neighbourhood own a few things for common use, and help each other in mutual solidarity and friendship.[121]

It can be hoped that the new code of canon law will present

the institutional dimension of marriage in a language, style and content that will make immediately clear that marriage is for the sake of the true covenant of love, and thus and only thus, able to fulfil its role also for the sake of the Church, and society at large.

2.   Marriage as vocation

The Second Vatican Council is forthright in praising marriage as a "lofty vocation". It speaks of "the dignity of the marriage state and its superlative value".[122] Nothing has remained of the tradition of St Augustine and others who considered marriage, or at least the marital act, as a necessary evil for the sake of procreation and the prevention of fornication.

In view of this vocation, Christians will examine themselves before God as to whether they are called to marriage and have the necessary qualities. They will most earnestly prepare themselves for it, and will make their choice of the future partner in view of this lofty vocation. The main criteria of choice will not be wealth, social prestige or external beauty, but those qualities that allow one to hope for faithful love, for mutual respect of conscience, and for freedom from all kinds of manipulation that would diminish one's inner freedom and particularly the freedom of conscience. Of course a very essential question in making marriage a vocation is whether or not the partner will be a good parent of the expected children.

Marriage will have, even in a particular sense, the quality of vocation if the persons have asked themselves before God whether they are called to marriage or to celibacy for the kingdom of God, having only one intention: to seek that state of life to which God, by his gifts and their inner connaturality, calls them.

3.   The sacramentality of marriage

The one vocation of all the faithful in Christ is to become ever more a visible image of God's love and to guide others towards the same goal. Marriage as sacrament has to be seen in this light, where the two persons become one flesh, one in a community of life and love, helping each other in their complimentarity and reciprocity. Together they come to a true image of God's fatherly-motherly love, and an image at the same time of the covenant of love and fidelity between Christ and the Church.

Wherever and whenever in the world and throughout history, a redeemed and redeeming love is lived in marriage and family and thus becomes a sign of covenant fidelity, there, in a true sense, is given a sacramentality, a way of salvation. Not without a profound reality of experience did the prophets of old compare the covenant of God with his people to the covenant of marriage. They also likened the infidelity of Israel towards God to adulterous or prostitute relationship. But the comparison of God's covenant with marriage was possible only because there were true marriages filled with the grace of God.

Since we reject the idea that the Christian marriage has a monopoly of grace and sacramentality, we have to ask what is the specific quality of matrimony between two Christians.

If a marriage of two Christians manifests the love of God, mutual love, growth in maturity, creative freedom and fidelity less than a good marriage between two non-Christians, it deserves the noble title of "sacrament" less than the one between two holy non-Christians. But the comparison must be between the good marriage of Christians and other marriages. Christians, if they are true believers, are aware of the grace and call of God as given in Christ Jesus and in view of his covenant with the Church. The Christian marriage is a special grace and opportunity to reach a grateful consciousness of Christ's presence and an explicit trust in the grace of the Holy Spirit. It is lived in gratitude for the support it receives from the Church and which it can give to the Church in Christ Jesus.

The Second Vatican Council has beautifully presented the true meaning of the sacrament of marriage. "Christ the Lord abundantly blessed this many-faceted love, welling up as it does from the fountain of divine love and structured as it is on the model of his union with the Church. For as God of old made himself present to his people through a covenant of love and fidelity, so now the Saviour of man and the Spouse of the Church comes into the lives of married Christians through the sacrament of matrimony. He abides with them thereafter so that, just as he loved the Church and handed himself over on her behalf, the spouses may love each other with perpetual fidelity through mutual self-bestowal. Authentic married love is caught up into divine love and is governed and enriched by Christ's redeeming power and the saving activity of the Church".[123]

The disciples of Christ who are called to marriage know that the grace of marriage is marked by its source, the cross of Christ. They know that they can share in Christ's glory forever, and even now in the joy that flows from the resurrection, only if they are willing to walk in the footsteps of Christ who has suffered for us. The grace of marriage enables and obliges the spouses in a particular way to put to death selfishness, individual egotism and dual egotism, and to live the fecundity of their covenant of love in openness to their parental vocation and the service of humankind.

They know that redeemed married love takes part in the all-embracing love of God and neighbour. The spouses will consider themselves mutually as the first pastors, ministers of salvation for each other and their children. And knowing that life in Christ is an ongoing reconciliation, they will be forebearing with each other and, by bearing each other's burdens, will fulfil the law of Christ.

4. Monogamy

Once the full equality of man and woman and the partnership structure of marriage are recognized, it cannot easily be denied that monogamy is normative for marriage among Christians. When monogamy is once reached in a culture, any return to polygamy would be a lamentable regression. It seems to me that the declaration of the Council of Trent on this matter can or must be understood in this way. Contrary to Martin Luther who had approved polygamy for his benefactor, Count Philip, the Council of Trent says bluntly: "If anyone would say that is not forbidden by any divine law, he should be cut off (anathema)".[124]

The messengers of the Gospel during the first centuries met only with cultures where monogamy prevailed — often a miserable monogamy that, at the same time, allowed or tolerated concubinage and prostitution. The problem of polygamy therefore was not raised by those cultures.[125] In Israel, certain forms of polygamy were tolerated, but ruthless polygamy by domineering men was sharply disapproved (cf. Gen 4:19-24). David was not blamed for his rather extensive polygamy but for his adultery. Solomon did not lose the grace of God because of polygamy but by marrying pagan wives for political purposes and building pagan temples for them, thus seducing the people. But at the time of Jesus and the apostles, polygamy in Israel had generally yielded to monogamy except in the case of the levirate, which imposed on a brother or other heir of the deceased husband, the care of the widow, to raise up with her children to the name of the dead brother. This, apparently, caused no problem in the community of Jerusalem.[126]

The problem of polygamy is raised again today, most sharply by the situation of Africa and parts of Asia.[127] The Catholic biblical scholar, J.L. McKenzie urges theologians to re-examine "the question without prejudices and with attention to the study of cultures".[128] It seems to me, however, that Harvey Cox goes too far by stating that "the Africans remind us that neither the Bible nor Christian history can be read to endow monogamy with exclusive or eternal validity".[129]

It is true that some African theologians and pastors and some western missionaries who have studied the problem would state the question in these terms. However, most African theologians plead only for respectful (temporary) tolerance of an institution that is deeply rooted in the worldview and in the total economic, political and cultural structure of most African tribes. The African theologian, St Augustine, would probably agree with them. In a time in which the Latin Church did not know the problem of polygamy, he wrote: "For the patriarchs of the Old Testament, it was no fault to have several wives. They were sinning neither against natural law, for they used marriage not for lust but in order to have children, nor against custom, for polygamy was approved at that epoch, nor was it against a precept, for no law forbade it".[130]

The "classical" missionary, who did not know anthropology and the strong interdependence of polygamy with the total culture, gave African men the alternative either to divorce all but one wife, sending away the other mothers of their children, or to be refused baptism. In the last few decades, in most of the African Churches — Catholic, Anglican and others — almost nobody dared to propose this disastrous "solution":

disastrous for all the persons involved and disastrous for the stability of marriage in Africa. Instead, many pastors now console the polygamist man who comes to faith, by saying that salvation comes always through faith and only exceptionally also through the sacraments. But this is contrary to the validity of the sacramental order and most contradictory for the Africans with their very high evaluation of the sacramental symbolism and realism. For them, this solution means a cautious "Yes" and a loud "No" at the same time.

After innumerable discussions in twenty African countries and a careful study of the literature, my own tentative conclusion is this: the Church must strive to bring the normative ideal of monogamy to bear, but she also should imitate God's patient pedagogy with Israel. She must take into account the interrelatedness of the marriage structure with the totality of life's structures.

Where polygamy was and unto now is the preferred system, the Church has to fight against new forms of polygamy which are socially disapproved and are unacceptable. But I suggest that the Churches admit to baptism and full participation in the life of the Church the polygamous families who find themselves in a socially approved and lawfully contracted marriage of this type when they come to faith. I do not think, however, that the Church should allow her members who are fully evangelized and baptized to enter into a polygamous marriage, although she can be temporarily tolerant in exceptional cases such as in the levirate, where the woman and the deceased husband's brother cannot refuse it without grave harm to the persons involved, or in a case similar to Abraham's where a man is urged and forced by his environment to take a second wife when the first is sterile.

5. *Fidelity and indissolubility of the marriage covenant*

a) Indissoluble by law or by grace?

The right understanding of the indissolubility of marriage is of paramount importance for a moral theology in which creative freedom and fidelity in Christ are the leitmotifs.[131]

Christian marriage is a sacrament not only as an external image of the covenant between Christ and his Church but also and even more so as participation in this covenant reality. By faith and grace, the self-commitment of the spouses to each other is, at the same time, a grace-filled self-commitment to Christ and his covenant.

Throughout the Old Testament there is a growing understanding that, according to God's intention, marriage should be indissoluble. However, concessions were made to human frailty. The Mosaic law protected the woman from being arbitrarily dismissed. The husband had to write out a writ justifying his action before the elders. "Supposing a man has married a wife, but she does not win his favour because he finds something shameful in her, and he writes her a note of divorce, gives it to her and dismisses her; and suppose, after leaving his house, she goes off to become the wife of another man, and this next husband turns against her and writes her a note of divorce which he gives her and dismisses her, or dies after making her his wife — then, in that case, her first husband who dismissed her is not free to take her back to be his wife again after she has become for him, unclean" (Deut 24: 1-4).

The dismissal was not so much a permission as a kind of compromise, a step forward after a period in which men had dismissed their wives without any legal procedures. The Mosaic compromise wants to prevent a divorce for disproportionate reasons: "The error of the Jews was that they understood Deut 24: 1 not as a request to care for the wife but as a permission, a relaxation to make life more comfortable".[132]

The prophets constantly inculcated fidelity to the wife as a part of covenant morality. "Why do we violate the covenant of our forefathers by being faithless to one another? ... The Lord has borne witness against you on behalf of the wife of your youth. You have been unfaithful to her, though she is your partner and your wife by solemn covenant. Did not the one God make her both flesh and spirit? ... If a man divorces or puts away his spouse, he overwhelms her with cruelty, says the Lord of hosts, the God of Israel" (Mal 2: 10-16). When Jesus sharply rejects those interpretations that make divorce a legal right of the husband against his wife, he can rely on a previous tradition.[133]

What Jesus said against divorce has been the object of numerous studies and diverse interpretations.[134] The three synoptics report the words of Jesus with interesting nuances (Mt 5:32; 19:3-9; Mk 10:2-12). Luke probably comes closest to the original saying: "A man who divorces his wife and marries another commits adultery; and anyone who marries a woman divorced from her husband commits adultery" (Lk 16:18). The words of the Lord, "What God has joined together man must not separate" (Mk 10:9) forbids not only divorce and remarriage but also separation, for it contradicts fidelity in loving mutual care.

In Jesus' time, the school of Schammai allowed divorce only in the case of unchastity of the woman, but according to the school of Hillel, divorce was fully at the husband's discretion. But what Jesus insistently teaches by his response is that man, not less than woman, is bound by fidelity. "The obligations formerly onesided are now mutual. Man and wife are shown to be equal partners with equal rights".[135] What Jesus says is surely a moral directive, an obliging goal commandment. But it is not so much a law as, rather, a promise that this indissoluble fidelity will be possible to believers who trust in God. "Mark is hinting that Jesus' revelation is only accessible to the believer".[136]

One of the central questions is whether Jesus laid down a law that allows undiscerning application. Biblical scholars respond: "He reveals the reality of a human relationship in which God lays direct claims to man's response, and he frees this relationship from the straitjacket of law".[137] Cardinal Ratzinger says on this point: "Jesus reaches behind the plane of the law to that of the law's origins; so his words must not in their turn be taken directly and simply as law".[138]

Jesus points to the original design of the Creator: "It was because your minds were closed that Moses made this rule for you; but in the beginning, at the creation, God made them male and female. For this reason, a man shall leave his father and mother and be made one with his wife; hence the two shall become one flesh" (Mk 10:6-8). Original intention or order of creation does not mean exactly the same as "a natural law". In a sinful world, a legislator like Moses cannot impose indissolubility as an absolute law. And Jesus' proclamation of God's original design does not change the situation much for those who have no faith in him and do not trust in his grace.

b) The relevance of law and casuistry

While Luke and Mark understood Jesus' word as an ethical norm that has all its power for the believer who puts his full trust in God's grace, it seems that Matthew understood it more as a law adjusted to the mentality of his community. Thus he was the first to take into account the reality of human frailty, for he added an explanation: " ... except for unchastity" (Mt 19: 9), "except on the ground of unchastity" (Mt 5: 32).

Today, most of the biblical scholars of the various Churches tend to interpret this addition (which we do not find in the other synoptics) as giving freedom in an intolerable case where the wife has broken the marriage covenant by unchastity, probably not understood as a single act of adultery but as a whole attitude of infidelity.[139] So if the Lord's word can be applied as law manifesting the power of grace and faith, the particular situation has also to be taken into account in order to avoid inhumane legalism.

Paul considers the Lord's word surely as an ethical directive for believers, as a normative ideal (cf. 1 Cor 7: 10-16), but not as an absolute law that would allow no exceptions. The particular situation faced by the apostle was marriage between a believer and a non-believer. Paul insists that the believer makes the non-believer holy, and may therefore not abandon the marriage if the spouse is willing to live with him or her in peace. What he has in mind is above all *shalom*, the order of peace reaching out to all levels of life, especially to the most basic human relationships like marriage. Thus he reaches the conclusion: if the non-believer refuses to respect the faith and conscience of the believer and, as a consequence, makes impossible any reciprocity of conscience, the believer is declared free from an enslaving marriage bond.

Paul does not explicitly speak on the right of the believer to remarry. We might think here on Paul's expectation of the near second coming of Christ. "But the principle of the revocation of marital obligations is so strongly formulated that the Christian partner may well in fact be free to enter a second marriage if he wants to".[140] Distinguishing clearly his own solution given for an extraordinary situation on the one hand, and the Lord's saying, on the other, Paul feels free to give attention first to the peace and freedom of conscience of the believer. His concrete solution explains best how he understands the Lord's words and intention.

At all times, the Church has first to proclaim the Lord's grace and promise, and, in that light, the actual directive strengthening fidelity; but she also has to pass laws fitting to the concrete historical situations, laws that always point to the highest normative ideal, but also manifest the Lord's compassion and patience.

Regarding civil laws, it is in the interest of the states themselves to do everything they can to foster the stability of marriage, including protective laws. However, no less than Moses, the modern states have to do with many people of closed minds and hardened hearts and people who are injured by unfaithful, cruel partners. The Church cannot expect the modern pluralistic state to do much more than Moses, which is to reach out for the possible and to protect, above all, the innocent party.

c) Pastoral care for the divorced

The Church of today faces a new situation no less in her legislation, than in her teaching. In many countries a high percentage of believers are abandoned by their spouses or are divorced. The Church must ask herself how she can be faithful both to the particular strong saying of Jesus about divorce and to his all-embracing law, "Be merciful as your heavenly Father" (Lk 6:36). Biblical scholars, theologians, pastors and canonists are raising questions from their various disciplines.[141] Their disputations should not let us lose sight of basic principles which can never be ignored.

Opportunely or inopportunely, the Church must proclaim Jesus' saving grace and promise and ethical directive. The Gospel of fidelity, made possible by faith and grace and through the support of the community, must be preached hand-in-hand with the Gospel of reconciliation and generous forgiveness. Marriage preparation and marriage counselling must help Christians to be better prepared for fidelity in difficult times. Further, it must be clearly understood that the Church has no right to dissolve any true marriage, whether of non-Christians or Christians of other communities.

Quite different, however, is the question of whether the Church can allow remarriage if the earlier marriage is hopelessly dead and if the one who requests permission has grave reasons not to remain celibate (difficulty with chastity, with education of children from the first marriage, and so on). It is also not an indifferent matter whether the Catholic who wants to remarry has been abandoned against his or her will.

It is important not to use the label "divorced" for totally different situations. On the one hand, there are those who have frivolously divorced their spouse, while on the other hand there are people who have most generously forgiven and have constantly tried to preserve the marital unity. It is not in the spirit of the Gospel to put both exactly under the same law and to judge an eventual marriage by the same yardstick.

Legislation and the practice of marriage tribunals, at least in many dioceses, have greatly improved. Better criteria are used in judging the validity of a prior marriage. If the marriage has already hopelessly failed and there are good reasons to presume that it was doomed to failure from the very beginning — for instance because of psychological immaturity or complete lack of sincerity of one of the partners — then it is right and just to grant an annulment. However, the official Church will have to make great efforts to respond to the new insights of biblical theology, tradition, the behavioural sciences, and the various situations in different parts of the world.

Pastoral theology and pastoral practice have come more and more to the conclusion that spouses who live in a second marriage — the destruction of which would be a disaster — should be admitted to the sacraments of Penance and Eucharist if they are longing sincerely for regular participation in the sacramental life of the Church, live in good faith regarding their new situation, have forgiven the wrong they have suffered, and are trying to give their children a good education.

V. SEXUALITY AND CELIBACY

The Church believes that the mystery of the covenant of love between Christ and the Church, between God and humankind, are symbolized in two vocations that illumine each other:

marriage, and celibacy for the heavenly kingdom. The supreme purpose of both is the growth of a Christlike love that gives testimony to the presence of the kingdom of God and of the hope of things to come.

St Thomas Aquinas explains the unity and complementarity of marriage and virginity in the following way: "In the Church, the spiritual realities are symbolized by bodily realities. But since the spiritual realities are so much richer than the visible signs which express them, sometimes there is need of several visible realities to symbolize the one and the same spiritual reality. This is the case with the union between Christ and the Church: she is fecund, for she engenders us as children of God. But she is also virginal, being 'with no stain or wrinkle' (Eph 5:27), 'a virgin to her true and only husband' (2 Cor 11:2). Now, in the corporeal realities, fecundity is incompatible with virginity. Therefore the need for the two earthly images to express the total meaning of the union of Christ and Church: one for her fecundity, and this is the sacrament of marriage; and one for her virginity, and this is the consecration of virgins".[142] I would like to say that both symbols have their specific fecundity and their specific way of being consecrated to honour the covenant of love between Christ and the Church.

It is not my intention here to explore all the dimensions of celibacy for the sake of the kingdom of God. The main question is how the celibate person regards the sexual endowment, his or her sexual dimension. Is it a mere hindrance, a cause of frustration and temptation, or is it, for him or her, a precious gift of the Creator and Redeemer?

How the celibate understands the values of sexuality is greatly determined by the prevailing anthropology and theology. If sex is presented as degrading, how then can renouncing marriage be an acceptable sacrifice? Celibacy is not a valuable Christian symbol and testimony if it is extolled to the detriment of marriage and the goodness of sexuality.

On the other hand, in a culture in which sex seems to be at the top of the scale of values, the celibate will not easily find his or her identity. But marriage, too, will be negatively affected by unrealistic expectations from sexuality as such. There are good grounds for assuming that one of the chief reasons for the failure of so many marriages in our occidental culture is the high expectations about sex satisfaction. This is something quite different from high expectations about marriage as a community of love and a way of salvation.

It seems to me very important that the celibate consciously face his or her sexuality and ask what it means in the particular state of life.[143]

a) Celibacy for various reasons

Speaking of celibacy, we should not think only of the Roman Catholic priest, brother, or nun who, in the first place, has renounced marriage for the kingdom of God. The reasons for celibacy are of enormous diversity.

There are celibates who have not accepted their sexuality and, in one way or another, deny its goodness. There is the homosexual who emphatically affirms and activates his homosexual trend and therefore renounces marriage, not truly accepting and understanding the dignity of the other sex. There are celibates who are totally dedicated to a noble cause or ideal for which they are willing to forego marriage although they may have a high appreciation of it. And there are, on a different level, celibates who are simply wedded to their competitive career in which they are determined to "get to the top" at any cost.

In the ranks of Roman Catholic priests and religious, there are celibates who have explicitly chosen this state of life for such intrinsic values as total dedication to the service of the Gospel, of the sick, the downtrodden or the handicapped. There are others who find enough meaning in priestly or other religious ministries to renounce marriage if this is made a condition for the service, although they would like to marry if Church law or conditions would allow these ministries for married people. We should be honest enough to face also the possibility that a priest can be so "wedded" to an ecclesiastical career involving power and prestige that his sexual energies are dangerously sublimated into aggressiveness or similar dispositions. But our main concern here is with celibates who have freely chosen this state of life for an ideal which they consider proportionate to the renunciation of marriage. These celibates grasp the Lord's word, for they are among those "for whom God has appointed it" (Mt 19:11). In the words of St Paul, "we have been given from God this gift" (1 Cor 7:7). This does not imply, however, that celibacy, in itself, must have been their first choice.

There are widows and widowers, abandoned spouses, men and women who, for various reasons have not found a fitting partner for a desired marriage or who, having accepted a heavy family burden or other life responsibility, have simply sacrificed the opportunity to marry. As Christians living under the law of grace, these celibates too can grasp somehow the meaning of their individual situations in view of the kingdom of God, and give deep meaning to their lives.

We cannot neglect another important reflection on how to help those who are celibates for the wrong reasons.

b) Celibacy and the capacity to grow in love

For Christians, the supreme concern is always and everywhere the person's capacity to love, to trust, to have faith. We speak of love incarnate, that love of God that implies joining him in his love for people, that loving trust in God that inspires trustful relationships, allowing us to discover in ourselves and in others ever greater potentialities to love and to serve generously and faithfully.

If, as celibates, we are able to love, to trust, and to promote loving communities, we shall never forget how much this capacity owes to the many generations of spouses and parents who have enriched each other and the whole world by their conjugal and parental love. Without that great resource and fundament, celibate love would be unthinkable.

In striving to love God with all our heart and mind and strength, we cannot allow the great powers of human affection, which are at least partially related to one's total sexual endowment, to disintegrate. The beauty of the mutual attraction between men and women in noble love and respect is a source of growth in the art of loving Jesus Christ, and with him, men and women.

Of course we distinguish sharply between loving and "falling in love". The celibate's vocation follows Jesus' example and therefore implies a special attention and affection for those with whom nobody falls in love. This special focus, however, does not imply renouncing those energies of ordered love that are increased by the complementarity of men and women.

Celibate persons should consciously accept their own manhood or womanhood, and honour their neighbour in his or her reality as a man or a woman. But this excludes paying attention first to the sex and only second to the person. A mature celibate meets everyone as a unique person to be honoured in the sight of God. But we do not meet abstract concepts of persons; we meet persons who are either men or women.

Occasionally one sees a self-defensive celibate who surrounds himself or herself with a kind of electric fence to ward off those of the other sex. These people try to disown their natural tendency to be attracted by persons of the opposite sex. To be watchful about one's inner freedom is necessary, of course. Care must be taken to be attracted in the right way. The eros that discovers the beauty, the inner wealth, the diversity and uniqueness of the other person has nothing to do with a possessive, erotic attraction. The mature celibate will communicate an atmosphere of liberty, freedom for the Lord, and freedom to love without fear or possessive desires.

Celibate men and women frequently join in the service of the Gospel, of the poor, the sick, and in many other noble activities. If their whole conduct breathes truthfulness and reverence, freedom from any desire to exploit or to manipulate, then these men and women will increase their own capacity to be truly an image and likeness of God for each other and for the others.

It is normal that, in certain moments of their lives, celibates feel that they could well fall in love with a person of the other sex, and the thought arises about how beautiful it would be to join hearts and hands for a married vocation. But faithfulness guarantees that this experience is thoroughly subordinate to the self-commitment to a celibate life, a commitment which is offered constantly to the Lord. The values of an attractive person of the other sex can be freely recognized, for a mature vocation to celibacy has nothing to do with a "sour grapes" renunciation of marriage. The celibate who is careful not to "fall in love" is also most careful not to diminish but to increase his capacity for love and friendship. This is the most powerful protection of one's celibate vocation.

It is always a matter of keeping one's heart open for the love of God and for that specific love of neighbour that is fitting for the celibate. This allows a liberating appreciation and gratitude for all the good qualities and generous love we receive from persons of either sex. It includes also the particular freedom to appreciate the complementarity that arises from friendship and cooperation with wonderful persons of the other sex.

c) True friendship

The celibate who wants to give to his or her life the full meaning and witness of celibacy for the kingdom of God will never seek a relationship with another person just for the sake of self-fulfilment. The other person deserves to be loved for his or her own sake. Even marriage reaches the fullness of sacramentality only when the spouses love each other and serve each other beyond the search for self-fulfilment. They come to genuine self-actualization in self-transcendence. Generous service offered with a warm heart, and grateful acceptance of goodness, kindness, gentleness, bring both persons nearer to genuine fulfilment of their dignity and vocation.

To live for Christ means to live for others. It is in this loving service, offered and received in the liberty of the children of God, that we grow, as persons, towards maturity.

Celibate love most radically excludes any possessive attitude. "Thou shalt not covet thy neighbour's wife". Healthy celibates will not be blind to the inner or outer beauty of persons whom they meet, but they know that admiring a flower does not include cutting it and making it wither. The mature celibate can admire and appreciate without coveting. If, in friendship, we love persons of the other sex as well as those of our own, we love them in full respect for the covenant relationships in which they live or for which they may be preparing themselves. This very freedom from coveting makes healthy human relationships possible.

An unmarried person uncommitted to celibacy may experience the desire for a person of the other sex whom he or she admires to become his or her spouse; but if the person desired is already committed to another covenant, whether of marriage or of freely-pledged celibacy, then the desire has to be renounced as covetous. The celibate for the kingdom of God may desire and accept friendship, but only a friendship that preserves his or her own freedom and promotes the other's freedom to live his or her covenant relationship in faithfulness.

d) Enthusiasm and asceticism

No one can live a healthy celibacy without enthusiastic dedication to a great cause. This cause must not be celibacy in itself, but a cause worthy of one's total dedication. Celibacy for the kingdom of God is expression of enthusiasm, joy in the Lord, grateful acceptance of the call to serve the Gospel and the needs of people for the Lord's sake.

A normal person surely does not become neurotic because of celibacy as such, but many celibates have become neurotic because their lives were not filled with an ideal equal to the task implied by celibacy. An initial or momentary enthusiasm does not suffice. To give full meaning to a celibate life, one has always to be on the road towards greater fullness of life in Christ Jesus, in an ever more dedicated service to humankind.

However, even people who have peak experiences of great joy in the service of the Lord and of neighbour should realize that they cannot keep this joy, so indispensable for authentic celibacy, unless they fit their style of life to this particular state of life. All Christians, but especially those embarking on celibacy, are warned by the Apostle: "Be most careful then how you conduct yourselves, like sensible people, not like simpletons" (Eph 5: 15).

Celibates as well as married people may not allow their fantasies to reach out for those things that contradict their commitment. Whoever wants to live celibacy in inner freedom will impose upon himself or herself clear criteria in the choice of friends, of the environment he or she creates, of entertainment, reading and so forth. A celibate who spends more hours watching senseless love stories on television than hours spent in meditating on the word of God and in joyous celebration should not be surprised by the increasing frustrations that befall him or her.

Celibacy requires a high degree of inner and outer freedom. They condition each other. We all shall become somehow manipulated manipulators if we fail to integrate the contemplative dimension into our lives in ever increasing freedom for the

Lord. For the celibate to live without dangerous frustrations, he or she needs a generous capacity to rejoice in the Lord, to contemplate the Word incarnate, and to bring all relationships and activities into the light of the Gospel.

e) Celibate chastity and sexual tensions

To identify perfect chastity simply with the state of celibacy is unrealistic. It is also unjust to the married state. Each Christian is called to tend towards perfect chastity in his or her own state of life. Faithful married people are on the road to perfect chastity according to their vocation, yet they will not easily think that their chastity is perfect when they understand it as condition and harvest of their mutual love in total self-bestowal. No mortal should ever think that he has perfectly acquired the virtues, but none should ever stop walking in the right direction.

Celibacy undertaken for the right motives and meaningfully fulfilled does not automatically and at once produce perfect chastity. This is, rather, a lifelong task. Temporary crises do not invalidate a faithful effort to give celibacy the right meaning and expression. There are men and women who live their celibate vocation in true dedication to a great cause, yet sometimes have trouble, for instance, with masturbation. Others who lack the same ideal and dedication may never have this difficulty or feel any attraction to people of the other sex; but their lack of ideals and their low capacity to love others generally signify an unfulfilled celibacy.

Temporary difficulties and even some faults may, through the grace of God, provoke greater zeal for the Lord and greater trust in him.

One's life as a celibate can greatly suffer if one has not been educated for discernment. Like anyone else, a celibate should learn to discern what his or her sexual tensions really mean. They can imply and express a basic selfishness, but not necessarily. Frequently they are caused by psychic conditioning or hormonal tensions. To be freed from overscrupulosity and from senseless guilt complexes can set free greater energies for the service to which one is committed, and also bring forth a greater capacity for self-control.

The more truthfully a person lives the celibate vocation, the easier he or she will overcome temptations and failures, and cope with those tensions that are not expressions of selfishness.

VI. SINS AGAINST CHASTITY

Moral theologians of the past centuries are frequently accused of having given disproportionate attention to sins against chastity, and a tendency to be more rigoristic in this field than in others. It seems to me that they should be censored not so much for giving special attention to this field as for having presented the prohibitive norms without giving enough attention to the meaning of sexuality and the virtue of chastity. Yet it cannot be denied that some moralists who were rather lenient in other domains were most severe in the matter of chastity. This has many historical reasons.

Sexuality was the most sensitive area for a moralist to explore in the post-tridentine Church. One example of its peculiar status is an order issued to all Jesuits in 1612 by Claudius Aquaviva, general of their order. Under the precept of obedience and under penalty of excommunication and removal from any teaching office, Aquaviva enjoined the Jesuits not to teach or counsel that there is generically any "smallness of matter" (*parvitas materiae*) in sexual sins.[144]

Sins against chastity should be treated with the same equilibrium and the same attention to behavioural sciences as other sins. The abiding truth in this matter seems to me to be this: in no area should the Christian think that he can transgress God's commandment up to a certain point, and that only beyond that point is God's commandment serious. But if a Christian recognizes that while every sin is serious, some are less or more serious than others, then this applies equally to matters of sex.[145] The borderline morality must yield to one of ongoing growth and conversion. An occasional lapse by a person, who generally and in the sexual domain is honestly striving towards healthy and honest conduct, has to be evaluated quite differently than that of another person whose overall picture is one of lack of growth or even of plain decay.

1. *Hygiene of fantasy and desire*

The basic evaluation of sexuality as a gift of the Creator and under the influence of the Redeemer, and the acknowledged need of a learning process, lead to the conclusion that sexual imagination is indispensable and, in itself, good. However, our knowledge of a disordered world with all kinds of degrading sex appeal, and the consciousness of concupiscence, make the hygiene of fantasy an important part of sexual ethics.[146]

Human thinking about bodily realities, including sexuality, is practically not possible without a minimum of fantasies. The ethical question is whether and how we shall cultivate our fantasy so that it serves healthy, respectful thinking and ordered desires in the matter of sexuality. To educate one's fantasy is not an easy task. Repression is surely the dangerous path, leading in most cases to obsession and guilt complexes that devour the best energies. A positive sexual education, including sobering words about the role of fantasy, offers helpful directives for cultivating imagination in view of creative liberty and fidelity.

The point of departure is that sexual fantasy is good if, according to gender, age and state of life, it helps in the growth process, reaching out towards a mature and healthy sexuality. Sexual fantasy becomes unhealthy if it becomes escapism, waste of time and energy in daydreaming, and/or when it leads to a way of thinking that degrades sexuality by disrespect or leads to an idolatrous cult of sex.

It is normal that healthy sexual fantasy gives rise to some pleasure, which is not the same as "turning on". It can be joyful admiration of the work of the Creator, the joy inherent in the eros. But as soon as sexual fantasy becomes the cause of unhealthy arousal or of disordered desires, the control of the will has to set in. Our thinking, including imagination about sexual reality or unreal dreaming about sexuality, has great impact upon our desires and intentions. Indulging voluntarily in unhealthy desires poisons the well-spring of our inner decisions and our conduct. The Lord warns us: "A man is not defiled by what goes into his mouth, but what comes out of it ... wicked thoughts, murder, adultery, fornication, theft, perjury, slander — these all proceed from the heart; and these are the things that defile a man" (Mt 15:11-20).

Jesus' solemn words in the Sermon on the Mount, "I tell you ... ", sharpen especially our responsibility for our inner acts, and that includes a responsible hygiene of sexual fantasy. Fantasy becomes evil not only when it actually becomes a part of planning sinful conduct but also if it weakens the inner resistance against evil. It can be a main cause of coveting or can cause the lack of freedom to resist coveting. "What I tell you is this: If a man looks on a woman with a lustful eye, he has already committed adultery with her in his heart" (Mt 5:28). This "lustful eye" means not only the internal act of planning adultery but also the so-called "ineffective desire", that evil desire which stops short of planning the action only because it is impossible or because of fear of the consequences. Of course, indulging in disordered fantasies that actually become part of planning the evil conduct is more sinful because there is generally a greater involvement of the free will.

The importance of a healthy hygiene of sexual fantasy reminds us again of the need to create a healthy environment for oneself by the judicious choice of friends, reading, leisure-time, activities, and so on. Habitual reading of magazines of the Playboy or Playgirl type surely does not make for a healthy fantasy and is no better than poisoning one's stomach or one's blood.

2. Amoral sexual conduct

The whole Judeo-Christian tradition, and especially the New Testament, condemns adultery as one of the gravest sins. If both partners in the sin are married, grave injustice is done to two marriages. It is also the sin of adultery for both partners if an unmarried person breaks into another's marriage. By adultery, the truth of the sexual act is thoroughly betrayed. It is falsity in view of the sacrament, in view of love, and in view of the meaning of sexual intercourse.

Similar to adultery is fornication with or by a person consecrated to celibacy for the kingdom of God by a free self-commitment. Tradition calls such fornication sacrilegious.

Rape is the total perversion of the meaning of sexual intercourse, a grave sin against the liberty and honour of the other person. The person raped must resist as far as possible without endangering her/his life (cf. Deut 22:23-27). Even more shameful is rape inflicted on mentally disturbed or retarded persons or on those subject to one's authority.

In all cultures we find the prohibition of incest, the sexual abuse of members of the same family. It is a sin not only against the meaning and purpose of sexuality but also against the spirit of family (*pietas*).

Traditional moral theology gives the name "fornication" to every sexual intercourse between two unmarried persons. The moral evaluation has always given additional attention to the sin of scandal or cooperation with the sin of another.

For education towards discernment, many theologians warn against using the one label "fornication" for such different actualities as prostitution, concubinage, promiscuity of unmarried persons, and the various degrees of premarital sex. In supporting the traditional rule that sexual intercourse has its truth and dignity only within marriage, we should not overlook that the digressions from truth can be of varying degrees with qualitative differences.

Prostitution, paid or unpaid, is total untruth and exploitation. Holy Scripture condemns particularly the temple prostitution, where sexual intercourse was used to celebrate fecundity in its sacredness. It is total falsification of the sacred. Promiscuity is surely downright untruth. It speaks mostly in a terminology of love, yet the persons contradict the very meaning of intercourse as mutual self-bestowal. In a concubinage (which, by definition, is a sexual communion without intention of irrevocable fidelity or stability), there can be various degrees, from a couple's lack of firm decision to commit themselves for a lifetime, to the direct intention to have this sexual community for only a limited time, always revocable.

We shall treat "pre-marital sex" here in the strict sense of sexual intercourse between two people who are betrothed and preparing for marriage, for we cannot use here the same argumentation as against the foregoing situations.

In view of today's actuality, we treat separately pre-marital sex, masturbation, homosexuality and other deviant forms of sexual conduct.

3. *Pre-marital sexual relationships*

Pre-marital chastity, in its manifestation and its difficulties, depends greatly on the cultural context. In past centuries, in Europe and in most parts of the other continents, marriage was arranged by the respective patriarchal or matriarchal family. The future spouses saw each other rarely and only under strict controls. There was great social interest that the future wife should have no intercourse before marriage while, at the same time, the double standard of morality gave the young man occasion to satisfy his sexual urge with prostitutes and quasi-prostitutes. In modern urban, industrialized cultures, the two sexes grow up together in school and in society. They themselves have to choose their future spouse, and they want to do so by knowing the person well. The main motive is love. All this poses the problem of pre-marital sex in a new way.[147]

It is evident that the two young people who meet each other with the prospect of a future marriage, do so consciously as sexual persons. The closer they come to marriage, especially through betrothal, the more they feel the need to express their affection by kisses, embraces and close physical contact. It is a learning process and a growth in togetherness that requires a high level of motivation and self-discipline.

The preparation for marriage must be, above all, truthful. No false expectations must be awakened and no untruthful promises made. This includes also the expression of affection, since it, too, can be understood as promise and can awaken false expectations.

Despite all the sensational talking and writing about the sexual revolution, there is still a high percentage of young people who want to abstain from sexual intercourse until the formal celebration of the marriage. However, a considerable number of them indulge (frequently with a good conscience) in pre-marital petting where orgasm is purposefully sought. Traditional moral theology considers this practice morally unacceptable. While tenderness, as such, is manifestation of affection in respect for the other person, this petting tends all too easily to use the other for one's own satisfaction. This statement, however, is contradicted by many young people who assert that even in heavy petting the main thing is the joy of being together, of enjoying each other. How true is this?

Empirical sociology has shown that a great number of Christians of all Churches refuse to accept the traditional doctrine that sexual intercourse must be reserved for marriage. We do not speak here of those who would justify any kind of intercourse if there is a bond of affection; we speak strictly of pre-marital intercourse: intercourse between two persons who have at least a prospect of a future marriage, intercourse with the hoped-for future spouse.

Surely the way to argue against this is not by quoting biblical texts that sharply condemn prostitution and particularly temple prostitution. The pre-marital intercourse is of a totally different nature. However, most of today's Catholic moral theologians and a good number of the moralists of other Churches, especially of the Orthodox Churches, strictly uphold the traditional rule that intercourse has its full truth only as expression of firmly committed married love.

The objection made by young people is, "But we know that when we are committed to each other, this does not depend on a ceremony". I respond: "Sexuality is, and for many reasons has to be, a social reality. Your escape into privatism and from social and ecclesial expression of commitment is against the truth of sexuality".

We may ask these young people, "How firmly committed are you?" A number of girls have told me in counselling that the fiance obtained sexual intercourse after insisting many times on his assurance, "We consider ourselves as huband and wife"; but as soon he got what he wanted and as often as he wanted, he said, "I like you very much, but I don't want to marry you … ". We have to be realistic about what would happen if moralists and even the official Church were to teach that it suffices for having intercourse if the two persons know each other well enough, are mature enough, and are firmly committed to each other. The temptation would frequently be enormous for young people, even in the first throes of attachment, to consider this to be their case.

While we must take into account the new situation, we can never simply yield to trends of the time that contradict the Christian normative ideal. We must have the courage to uphold traditional wisdom even if our word falls on the ears of a world that has made claims of "sexual freedom", rejecting social control and social norms regarding a reality that is so profoundly social. Rollo May expresses a balanced assessment of the disillusion of sensitive people: "The sexual freedom to which we were devoted fell short of being fully human".[148]

Frequently we hear the objection, "But we have to try out before marriage whether we are sexually suited to each other". I respond: Sexual intercourse as "trying out" another person is, in its deepest meaning and in its psychological experience something quite different from the conjugal act as expression of the total belonging to each other. To try out this total self-bestowal by using the other for "trying out" makes no more sense than trying out what death is by a long sleep. What gives truth to the intimate union is the firm commitment. The report presented to the British Council of Churches responds to this situation: "Where intercourse is undertaken to 'try out' so that the partner can decide whether he or she is suitable, this essential condition is lacking. Such intercourse could well be unsatisfactory and prove not a preparation for marriage but a reason — usually quite inadequate — for calling it off".[149]

What the same report says about casual intercourse is not said directly on this point but has also some bearing on it. "Casual sex is perilous unless you are prepared to be indifferent to the other person's feelings and hard-boiled enough to avoid being hurt yourself. Once acquired, these are not qualities which can be instantly discarded when you embark on marriage".[150] If one "tries out" the other person with promises of marriage and then dismisses her or him, feelings must be deeply hurt; the person can be wounded for his or her whole life.

Another argument that favours pre-marital sex is: "Traditional moral theology has argued against pre-marital intercourse by insisting that procreation outside marriage and before marriage is irresponsible. But now, through the calculated use of the infertile period or through other contraceptive practices, this danger can be avoided". I respond: Contraceptive practice between unmarried people separates thoroughly the unitive meaning of sex from the procreative purpose, so that the full truth and integrity of the sexual act is not preserved. Besides, even the unitive meaning itself is not given its full truth, since the two have not committed themselves to each other totally, or at least not yet in the socially valid language of public commitment.

To this, however, must be added an argument from experience: all contraceptive methods have their risks and uncertainties, particularly in the hands of young people. There is always the chance that they may fail, and in that case the temptation arises all too easily to think about abortion as "resolving" the failure. Moreover if the case is "pre-marital" only by an unpublicized mutual agreement and not by an announced betrothal, the man can rather easily deny and renounce his responsibility for the pregnancy, and leave the girl to face the situation alone.

The Vatican's declaration on certain questions concerning sexual ethics (December 29, 1975), reaffirms the traditional doctrine (n. 7): "Today there are many who vindicate the right to sexual union before marriage, at least in those cases where a firm intention to marry and an affection which is already in some way conjugal in the psychology of the subjects require this completion, which they judge to be co-natural. This is especially the case when the celebration of marriage is impeded by circumstances or when this intimate relationship seems necessary in order for love to be preserved. This opinion is contrary to Christian doctrine which states that every genital act must be within the framework of marriage".

The authors of "Human Sexuality, New Directions in American Catholic Thought", while rejecting pre-marital intercourse in the strict sense, argue in favour of the opinion that "pre-ceremonial intercourse" may be moral.[151] They accept fully the social dimension of sexuality and the need for a public manifestation of the spouses' mutual commitment. But they argue that society itself sometimes makes this public manifestation impossible. In consequence, they could approve intercourse by two mature people who are not only internally committed to each other but would make the public commitment (the celebration of marriage) if unjust situations would not hinder them. Having, then, intercourse in the marital spirit, they must consider themselves as irrevocably married. There must not be in their minds "Yes" and "No", but only a firm "Yes". In this case one could not speak of pre-marital intercourse but only of "pre-ceremonial intercourse". I am not sure whether this position can be harmonized with the declaration of the Doctrinal Congreation of the Vatican. But no one can deny that here clear limits are drawn, and that on principle, all pre-marital intercourse is excluded.

In my opinion, it is important to uphold the traditional doctrine and discipline of the Church in favour of the full truthfulness of the sexual act. At the same time, we must be pastorally concerned for and respectful of young people who, because of the influence of the environment and a deficient education in sexual morality, do not succeed in observing their own intention to abstain from intercourse until the marriage is celebrated. We must never dramatize the situation. And we should also consider the possibility that others are firmly convinced that, in their difficult situation, having reached a firm commitment to each other, they may have pre-marital intercourse. We will never approve it, but the confessor can give them absolution, not on the basis of new doctrines but simply on the basis of their sincere conviction. He should, however, clearly express this reasoning.

4. Self-stimulation

The phenomenon of which we speak here is treated under various names. "Masturbation" applied originally to the human male, probably from *mas* (male) and *turbare* (disturb), but possibly from *manus* (hand), meaning manipulation by hand. Some psychologists have suggested the word "ipsation" (centring on one's own self). The most rigoristic tradition since the eighteenth century frequently called it "onanism", the sin of Onan (cf. Gen 38: 9). Also, the word "autoeroticism" is used, meaning eroticism centred on oneself.

There are two quite different approaches to the problem. Manualists of the last century stated first the general principle that masturbation is always objectively a grave matter and does not allow "smallness of matter". Then they would agree that, at least sometimes, there might not be, subjectively, a grave sin. Today's moralists who follow this pattern would take into account the behavioural sciences after having stated the general principle.

The approach common today to ethicists and moralists out-side the Catholic Church, and to many moral theologians of today's generation, looks first to the diversity of the phenomena, and only then asks about the moral meaning, the moral danger, or possibly the sinfulness of the individual phenomenon. I con-sider this second approach the only appropriate one, for we cannot determine the norm and moral gravity until we have tried to understand the meaning of the phenomenon.[152]

The writings of the Old Testament have no direct word on self-stimulation. The same is probably true of the New Testa-ment. 1 Cor 6:10 was sometimes given this meaning, but the translation of The New English Bible expresses the mind of most of today's biblical scholars: "No fornicator or idolator, none who are guilty either of adultery or homosexual perversion ... will possess the kingdom of God". ("Homosexual perversion" includes the latin *"mollis"*.) The Jerusalem Bible has the same thought, translating "catamites, sodomites". Manualists not infrequently translated "masturbators" and called self-stimulation "mollities".

"As far as we can now ascertain, the Fathers of the Church are rather silent about this question".[153] We find the first clear position in some of the Irish-Scottish penitential books (*libri poenitentiales*). They foresee for youngsters a rather light penance, a more serious one for adult men, and a severe penance for members of the clergy. The most rigoristic evaluation is given by Pietro Damiani (1054) in his *Liber Gomorrianus,* with a letter of official approbation by Leo IX.[154] But there is no evidence that this position influenced the next centuries. The rigorism began to blossom under the influence of Calvinistic puritanism.

In 1711, the book "Onania, or the Heinous Sin of Self-pollution, and All Rightful Consequences in Both Sexes, Con-sidered with Spiritual and Physical Advice" was published. The author was most probably Dr Bekker. Referring to Genesis 38, he calls masturbation "a sin that cries to heaven" and "murder".[155] In 1760, the Calvinist Tissot published a disser-tation in Latin on ailments produced by masturbation. It was translated into the major languages and found an enormous readership. It was from these medical sources that the rigorism came into Protestant and Catholic moral theology. Until Sigmund Freud, it was an almost common conviction that masturbation,

and especially excessive masturbation, had to do with most sick-
nesses, although Galenus, the great medical authority of
antiquity, had justified masturbation on medical grounds when
necessary for the release of tension.[156]

At the beginning of this century, the research of behavioural
sciences radically changed the assessment of masturbation in
the secular world and almost equally within Protestant theology.
Only in the last decades, several Catholic theologians tried to
profit from the behavioural sciences. It is now commonly accepted
that self-stimulation among boys and men has not only a higher
frequency but also a quite different significance than among
girls and women. Earlier moralists had evaluated the self-
stimulation of women differently on the ground that there is no
loss of sperm. Today's ethicists refer chiefly to the psychological
difference.[157]

Psychologists and anthropologists have drawn our attention
to the fact that in most cultures self-stimulation is very frequent
in early childhood. It is a kind of play, of self-discovery, and
cannot enter into the same picture as adolescent masturbation
during puberty.

In the western countries, over 90% of boys and approximately 50% of girls have masturbatory phases during puberty.
It seems to be much more frequent among the school population
than among youths working in the fields and living in peaceful
villages. From the fact that such a high percentage of youth
masturbate, Kinsey and others draw the conclusion that this is
"normal". But we respond that if it is "normal" on the statistical
level, this does not at all prove it normal on the moral level.
We have to ask ourselves whether the environment that greatly
influences this phenomenon is "normal", healthy. Pomeroy, a
collaborator of Kinsey, expresses the extremist position: "It's
easy to do, requiring no special place or time. Anyone can do it,
and of all sex activity, it is the most easily learned. It releases
tensions and is therefore valuable in many ways".[158]

Some Catholic moral theologians assert the normality of
adolescent masturbation insofar as it is a phase through which
almost all adolescents go, although a phase to be overcome by a
general growth towards maturation.[159] The anthropologist and
experienced therapist, A. Jordi, warns: "It is, however, a somehow
lighthearted assumption of our time, overflooded with sexual

technical knowledge, to characterize masturbation as a banality of physiological processes of development".[160]

Gebsattel distinguishes four quite different types of self-stimulation. "First, the purely physical release under pressure, (Notonanie); second, desexualized self-stimulation, that is, self-stimulation for other than sexual goals; third, desexualized practice accompanied by or caused by fantasies, and fourth, the masturbatory syndrome, a symptom of attitude".[161] Most therapists see in the first two forms no moral problem, and many ethicists think in the same way.

It seems to me that we should focus on that kind of self-stimulation that manifests or is accompanied by self-centredness expressing itself not only in the sexual domain but in the whole of life, and which will be overcome by moral and psychological growth. The syndrome of masturbation is particularly serious if it manifests narcissism, an imprisonment in the selfish self. It can well be that others than the youngsters are accountable for this misery by refusing the child from the beginning, or at a certain age, genuine love and affirmation, and by failing to communicate to the young person liberating ideas and ideals.

Adolescents have to be helped by understanding, encouragement and discernment. But they must learn that "the need of the adolescent to control his own sexual urges, and his capacity to do so, is the measure of his advance towards adulthood".[162] Educators must be warned, however, that "immense mischief has been done by grossly overemphasizing the harm done by masturbation".[163] Guilt complexes or moral obsession with just this one problem not only lame the energies but also frequently perpetuate the problem. Only a moral teaching characterized by a dynamic vision and stressing the need for growth and maturation can help young people to overcome these difficulties and not to be discouraged by partial failures.

An approximate evaluation of the situation of youth who are not yet able to master the problem is only possible by giving attention to whether the overall picture is one of growth or of stagnation. Masturbation can be a serious symptom of stagnation or even of decay, or else a symptom of a disturbed environment and disturbed relationships.[164]

Habitual self-stimulation by adults can be a serious symptom denoting possibly a variety of difficulties or failures. But if it is a case of persons who are generous and sincerely striving, the presumption is that it is subjectively not a great sin but, rather, can be a mixture of suffering and not-yet-overcome egotism. Then the moral imperative is to accept patiently what cannot be healed, and at the same time to strive more generously towards maturity and generosity in all domains.

5. *Homosexuality and other forms of deviant sexuality*[165]

Both the Old and New Testaments present homosexuality as one of the most shaking perversions. The homosexual subculture was frequently linked to an idolatrous cult of a male god.

Paul, speaking not on individual homosexuals but on the phenomenon in pagan culture, has this sharp judgment: "For this reason God has given them up to the vileness of their own desires, and the consequent degradation of their bodies, because they have bartered away the true God for a false one ... In consequence I say, God has given them up to shameful passions. Their women have exchanged natural intercourse for unnatural, and their men in turn, giving up natural relations with women, burn with lust for one another; males behave indecently with males, and are paid in their own persons the fitting wage for such perversion" (Rom 1:24-27).

Homosexuality misses the given complementarity between man and woman. The homosexual or lesbian does not learn the different "language" of the other sex. There is fear of the other sex, the capacity to accept and to appreciate the sexual diversity, a lack of confidence that the other has something to tell.

Moral theology must carefully distinguish between persons with an exclusive homosexual orientation and others who, with good will, could fully develop the heterosexual mindset. To put oneself freely on the slippery road of homosexuality is a most serious sin against oneself and others. Our whole tradition holds the principle that persons with so strong a homosexual tendency that they are not fitted for marriage must abstain from all genital activity, just as other celibates are expected to do. But the counsellor has to be patient and discerning.

In the case of homosexuals who were running wild but are settling down to a friendship built on common ideals, and gradually reducing overt activity, the decisive criteria is that of growth in chastity and in the overall life and attitude. The sense of co-responsibility must be sharpened, so that no one should be accountable for perversion of others. Persons in the twenties can mostly be healed if they are strongly motivated and find a capable therapist. If one can overcome a deviant trend, he is duty-bound to do so.

Homosexuality, and even more, other sexual deviations like sadism and masochism, fetishism and bestiality, are grave pathologies and are to be treated in medical ethics.[166] The Christian attitude must be that of the Divine Physician, the merciful samaritan. But by the same love of the Redeemer, we must unmask those theories that justify these ways of conduct on the basis of grave errors about the meaning of sexuality.

Approaching the domain of human sexuality, Kinsey gives the following detestable advice: "The physician ... can reassure these individuals that such activities are biologically and psychologically part of the normal picture".[167]

Our own teaching must always convey the sublime message that God created male and female to his own image and likeness.

NOTES

[1] General works on sexuality and sexual ethics: J. Fuchs, *Die Sexualethik des hl. Thomas von Aquin*, Köln, 1949; M. Müller, *Die Ehelehre des hl. Augustinus von der Paradiesesehe und ihre Auswirkung in der Sexualethik des 12. u. 13. Jahrhunderts bis Thomas von Aquin*, Regensburg, 1954; H. Thielicke, *The Ethics of Sex*, New York, 1964; F.E. von Gagern, *Vom Wesen menschlicher Geschlechtlichkeit*, München, 1965; Id., *Eheliche Partnerschaft, Ehe als Lebens- und Geschlechtsgemeinschaft*, München, 1966[7]; L. Hodgson, *Sex and Christian Freedom*, New York, 1967; A. Auer, *Der Mensch und seine Geschlechtlichkeit*, Würzburg, 1967; M. Oraison, *The Human Mystery of Sexuality*, New York, 1967; "Hirtenbrief der deutschen Bischöfe zu Fragen der menschlichen Geschlechtlichkeit", in *Herderkorr.* 27 (1973), 280-296; T. Goffi, *Etica Sessuale cristiana*, Bologna, 1972; E. Borra, *Dizionario di sessuologia e dell'armonia coniugale*, Roma, 1974; L. Vereecke, "L'éthique sexuelle des moralistes post-tridentins", in *Studia moralia* 13 (1975), 175-196; B. Häring, "Sessualità", *Dizionario Enciclopedico di teologia morale*, Roma, 1976[4], 993-1006; 1420-1431; R. Volcha (ed.), *Dizionario di sessuologia*, Assisi, 1976; W. Rohrbach, *Humane*

*Sexualität. Analyse und Problemzusammenhänge in der theologischen Sexual-
ethik als Grundlage für sexualethische Entscheidungen*, Neunkirchen-Vluyn,
1976; G. Friedrich, *Sexualität und Ehe*. *Rückfragen an das Neue Testament*,
Stuttgart, 1977; St. Sapp, *Sexuality, the Bible and the Science*, Philadelphia,
1977; J. Dominian, *Proposals for a New Sexual Ethic*, London, 1977; A.
Chapelle, S.J., *Sexualité et saintété*, Bruxelles, 1977; G. Durand, *Sexualité
et foi. Synthèse de théologie morale*, Montréal, 1977; A. Kosnik, W. Carroll,
A. Cunningham, R. Modras, J. Schulte, *Human Sexuality. New Directions in
American Catholic Thought*, New York/Paramus/Toronto, 1977.
2 Sexuality: language-culture: A. Gardiner, *The Theory of Speech and Language*,
London, 1951; G. Siewerth, *Der Mensch und sein Leib*, Einsiedeln, 1963²;
Id., *Philosophie der Sprache*, Einsiedeln, 1957; A. Valeriani, *Il nostro corpo
come comunicazione. Linee fondamentali per una pedagogia del corpo umano*,
Brescia, 1964; L. Thoré, "Langage et sexualité", in *Sexualité humaine,
histoire, ethnologie, sociologie, psychanalyse, philosophie*, Paris, 1966, 65-95;
K. Rahner and A. Görres, *Der Leib und das Heil*, Mainz, 1967; O. Stevenson,
Ethics and Language, New Haven, 1969¹³; J. Fast, *Body Language*, New York,
1973; A. Guindon, *The Sexual Language. An Essay in Moral Theology*, Ottawa,
1976.
3 *Sex and Morality. A Report Presented to the British Council of Churches*,
London, 1966, 31.
4 l.c., 45.
5 Cf. E. Fuchs, *Glaube und Erfahrung*, Tübingen, 1965, 308 (referring to John
1: 1).
6 Cf. J. and I. Splett, *Meditation der Gemeinsamkeit*, München/Freiburg, 1970,
87-97.
7 Cf. Ph.S. Keane, *Sexual Morality. A Catholic Perspective*, New York, 1977,
4, 14.
8 Th. Bovet, *Die Liebe ist in unserer Mitte*, Tübingen, 1959, 123. Bovet was
one of the first writers who skilfully used the language paradigm for sexual
ethics.
9 Cf. J.B. Lotz, *Die drei Stufen der Liebe. Eros Philia Agape*, Frankfurt, 1971,
38.
10 Cf. F.E. von Gagern, *Eheliche Partnerschaft*, 38.
11 *Gaudium et Spes*, 49b.
12 Cf. J. Ratzinger, *LThK, The Second Vatican Council*, III, 323-325; T. de
Chardin, *Hymne de l'Universe*, Paris, 1961.
13 A. Guindon, *The Sexual Language*, 95.
14 D. Goergen, *The Sexual Celibate*, New York, 1974, 51.
15 R. May, *Man's Quest for Himself*, New York, 1953, 15ff.
16 U.T. Holmes, *The Sexual Person*, New York, 1970, 14.
17 Bibliography, Man-Woman relationship: M. Mead, *Male and Female. A Study
of the Sexes in a Changing World*, New York, 1949; D. Wendland, *Der
Mensch — Mann und Frau*, Aschaffenburg, 1962²; K. Barth, *Mann und Frau*,
München, 1964; J. Folliet, *Adam et Eve: Humanisme et sexualité*, Lyon, 1965;
D. von Hildebrand, *Man and Woman*, Chicago, 1966; G.N. Groeger, *Die
Geschlechter. Begegnung und Partnerschaft*, Wuppertal, 1966⁶; A. Zarri,
L'impazienza d'Adamo. Ontologia della sessualità, Torino, 1967; J.J. Envoy,
The Man and the Woman. Psychology of Human Love, New York, 1968;
A.B. Ulanov, *The Feminine in Jungian Psychology and in Christian Theology*,
Evanston/Ill., 1971; G.H. Tavard, *Woman in Christian Tradition*, Notre
Dame/Ind., 1973; R.R. Ruether, *Religion and Sexism: Image of Women in
the Jewish and Christian Tradition*, New York, 1974; P.K. Jewett, *Man as
Male and Female. A Study in Sexual Relationship from a Theological Point
of View*, Grand Rapids, 1975; J. Money and A.A. Ehrhardt, *Männlich-weiblich.
Die Entstehung der Geschlechtsunterschiede*, Reinbeck bei Hamburg, 1975;
E. Firkl, *Die selbstbewusste Frau. Zur Identitätskrise der Frau in der west-
lichen Welt*, Frankfurt, 1976; P. Washbourn, *Becoming Woman. The Quest
for Wholeness in Female Experience*, New York, 1977; F. Burri, *Mann und
Frau schuf Er sie. Differenzierung der Geschlechter aus moral — und*

praktisch — theologischer Sicht, Zürich-Köln, 1977; U. Erler, *Zerstörung und Selbstzerstörung der Frau. Emanzipationskampf der Geschlechter auf Kosten des Kindes*, Stuttgart, 1977; K. Forster, "Neue Ausgangsbedingungen der Frauenpastoral, Wandlung im vollen Verständnis und den religiösen Einstellungen der Frau", in *Herderkorr.* 31 (1977), 516-523.

[18] D.S. Baily, *The Man-Woman Relation in Christian Thought*, New York, 1959, 263; cf. Id., *Common Sense about Sexual Ethics*, New York, 1962.

[19] U.T. Holmes, *The Sexual Person*, 2.

[20] J.-M. Reuss, *Geschlechtlichkeit und Liebe*, Mainz, 1961, 12.

[21] K. Barth, *Church Dogmatics*, Edinburgh, 1958, III/1, 186.

[22] A. Guindon, l.c., 48.

[23] Cf. K. Wojtyla (John Paul II), *Amour et responsabilité*, Paris, 1965, 76-80.

[24] A. Guindon, l.c., 129.

[25] *Sex and Morality. Report...*, 37.

[26] M. Scheler, *Wissensformen und Gesellschaft*, Leipzig, 1926, 443; cf. F.K. Mayr, "Sprache", *Sacramentum Mundi*, IV, 704.

[27] S. *contra Gent.* IV, c. 11; cf. S.Th., II II, q 26, a 10.

[28] A.C. Kinsey, *The Sexual Behavior in the Human Male*, Philadelphia, 1948, 677.

[29] C. Villee, *Biology*, Philadelphia, 1972, 586.

[30] Cf. U.T. Holmes, l.c., 7.

[31] A. Guindon, l.c., 87; cf. Gagern, l.c., 164ff.

[32] Cf. A. Adler, *Superiority and Social Interest*, Evanston/Ill., 1964, 223.

[33] C. Hutt, *Males and Females*, Harmondsworth, 1972, 18; Guindon, 127.

[34] Cf. J. Müller, *Das sexuelle Leben der Völker*, Paderborn, 1935³; B. Häring, *Ehe in dieser Zeit*, Salzburg, 1964³; H. Schelsky, *Soziologie der Sexualität. Über die Beziehungen zwischen Geschlecht, Moral und Gesellschaft*, Hamburg, 1965; V. Packard, *Die sexuelle Verwirrung. Der Wandel in den Beziehungen der Geschlechter*, Wien-Düsselford, 1969; M. Mead, *Jugend und Sexualität in primitiven Gesellschaften*, 3 vols., München, 1970; J.L. Reiss, *Freizügigkeit, Doppelmoral, Enthaltsamkeit. Verhaltensmuster der Sexualität*, Reinbeck bei Hamburg, 1970; A. Valsecchi, *Nuove vie dell'etica sessuale. Discorso ai cristiani*, Brescia, 1972; J. Knoll, *Sexualität und Gesellschaftsreform*, München, 1972; E. Kennedy, *The New Sexuality: Myths, Fables and Hang-ups*, Garden City, 1973; H. Colton, *Sex after the Sex Revolution*, New York, 1973; W.B. Key, *Sublimal Seduction: Ad Media's Manipulation of a Not So Innocent America*, Englewood Cliffs, 1973; Id., *Media Sexploitation*, New York, 1977.

[35] S. de Beauvoir, *The Second Sex*, New York, 1953, 41.

[36] *Gaudium et Spes*, 52e.

[37] ibid, 52f.

[38] A. Guindon, l.c., 111.

[39] W. Cole, *Sex and Love in the Bible*, New York, 1959; P. Grelot, *Man and Wife in Scripture*, London, 1964; J.E. Kerns, S.J., *The Theology of Marriage. The Historical Development of Christian Attitudes Toward Sex and Marriage*, New York, 1964; T.B. de Kruijf, *The Bible and Sexuality*, De Pere/Wisc., 1966; L.M. Epstein, *Sex, Laws and Customs in Judaism*, New York, 1967.

[40] Cf. J. and I. Splett, l.c., 89ff.

[41] A. Guindon, l.c., 90.

[42] Cf. P. Fank, *Die Keuschheitsgebote in der Kindheit und Jugendzeit*, Linz, 1964; M. Oraison, *Learning to Love: Frank Advice for Young Catholics*, New York, 1965; J. Piaget, *The Moral Judgement in Childhood*, New York, 1965; Id., *Plays, Dreams and Imitation in Childhood*, London, 1967; W. Bockler/H. Fleckenstein, *Die sexualpädagogischen Richtlinien, Probleme der katholischen Theologie*, Mainz, 1967; B. Strätling, *Sexualethik und Sexualerziehung*, Donauwörth, 1970.

[43] A. Guindon, l.c., 87.

[44] J.-M. Reuss, l.c., 68.

[45] D. Goergen, *The Sexual Celibate*, 50-55.

[46] A. Guindon, l.c., 68.

[47] *Gravissimum Educationis*, 1.

[48] *Gaudium et Spes*, 49h.

49 Cf. F.M. Podimattam, A New Look at Chastity, Bengalore, 1974, 141ff.
50 F. Dantec, Voyez comme ils s'aiment, Quimper/Nantes, 1963; T. Goffi, Amore e sessualità, Brescia, 1964⁴; J.-M. Reuss, Modern Catholic Sex Instruction, Baltimore, 1964; H. Gilbert, Love in Marriage: The Meaning and Practice of Sexual Love in Christian Marriage, New York, 1964; F.X. Hornstein (ed.), Sex, Love, Marriage: A Handbook and Guide for Catholics, Freiburg, 1964; J. de Vinck, The Virtue of Sex, New York, 1966; Id., The Challenge of Love: Practical Advice for Married People and Those Planning Marriage, New York, 1969; S.C. Callahan, Beyond Birthcontrol. The Christian Experience of Sex, New York, 1968; B. Häring, Love is the Answer, Denville, 1969; Id., Married Love: A Modern Christian View of Marriage and Family Life, Chicago, 1970; M. Vidal, Moral del amor y de la sexualidad, Salamanca, 1972; P. De Neuter, "Amour, sexualité et religion: une bibliographie", in Compass 19 (1972), 473-480.
51 Cf. Th. Bovet, l.c., 103.
52 Cf. F. Dantec, l.c., 93ff.
53 Cf. above ch. IX on Eros-philia-agapé.
54 J.B. Lotz, Die drei Arten der Liebe, 17.
55 V. Frankl, Man's Search for Meaning, New York, 1965, 177.
56 F.E. von Gagern, l.c., 140.
57 Gaudium et Spes, 49b and c.
58 Cf. K. Wojtyla, Amour et responsabilité. Etude de morale sexuelle, Paris, 1965; S. Keil, Sexualität. Erkenntnisse und Massstäbe, Stuttgart, 1966; Bishop F.J. Mugavero, "Sexuality God's Gift: A Pastoral Letter", reprinted in Cath. Mind, May 1976, 53-58; Cardinal L.J. Suenens, "Amour et sexualité aujourd'hui", A Pastoral Letter, reprinted in Documentations Cath. 73 (1976), 679-690; P. Lippert, "Liebe als tragfähiges Kriterium sexualethischer Normenbildung", in Theol. d. Gegenw. 20 (1977), 94-102; F. Böckle (ed.), Menschliche Sexualität und kirchliche Sexualmoral. Ein Dauerkonflikt?, Düsseldorf, 1977.
59 Cf. Th. Bovet, l.c., 127.
60 Sex and Morality. A Report..., 48.
61 Gaudium et Spes, 48a.
62 H. Cox, The Secular City, London, 1965, 204.
63 Gaudium et Spes, 49a.
64 ibid, 52.
65 Cf. H. Schwenger, Antisexuelle Propaganda. Sexualpolitik in der Kirche, Reinbeck bei Hamburg, 1969; E. Kellner (ed.), Sexualität ohne Tabu und christliche Moral, München-Mainz, 1970; St. H. Pfürtner, Kirche und Sexualität, Reinbeck bei Hamburg, 1972; Ph. Schmitz, Der christliche Beitrag zu einer Sexualmoral, Mainz, 1972.
66 J. and I. Splett, l.c., 44ff.
67 E. Osborn, Ethical Patterns in Early Christian Thought, London/New York/Melbourne, 1976, 74.
68 Cf. B. Häring, "A Modern Approach to the Ascetical Life", in M. Marx, O.S.B. (ed.), Protestants and Catholics on the Spiritual Life, Collegeville, 1965, 72-85; Id., "Lebenswahre Askese", in Ordenskorr 5 (1964), 208-218; A. Grabner-Heider (ed.), Recht auf Lust?, Freiburg, 1971; L. Rossi, Il piacere proibito, Torino, 1977.
69 Gregory of Nyssa, De hominis opificio, 16, PG 44, 186A and 190; Id., De virginitate, 12, PG 46, 374D.
70 Sermo 51, c. 15, PL 38, 347ff.
71 ibid, 346.
72 Hugo of St Victor, De sacramentis I, PL 176, 156ff.
73 Gaudium et Spes, 49d.
74 S.Th. I, q 98, a 2.
75 K. Wojtyla, l.c., 17-25.
76 A. Maslow, Motivation and Personality, New York, 1970², 187ff.
77 V. Frankl, Der Wille zum Sinn, Berlin-Stuttgart, 1972, 21.
78 R. May, Love and Will, New York, 1969, 40.

[79] Cf. H. Doms, *Gatteneinheit und Nachkommenschaft*, Mainz, 1965.

[80] Cf. A. Guindon, l.c., 175ff.

[81] *Humanae Vitae*, n. 9.

[82] *Gaudium et Spes*, 50a and b.

[83] Cf. ibid, 50c.

[84] Cf. ibid, 50g.

[85] Cf. D. Ciotta (ed.), *Famiglia: spazio educativo*, Assisi, 1974.

[86] Cf. Th. Bovet, l.c., 125.

[87] *Gaudium et Spes*, 48.

[88] ibid.,

[89] "Sexualité humaine et fecondité africaine", in *Telema-Revue de réflexion et créativité chrétiennes en Afrique*, N. 4, 1976, 31-63.

[90] Cf. R. Fagley, *The Population Explosion and Christian Responsibility*, New York, 1960; P. Ehrlich, *Die Bevölkerungsbombe*, München, 1971; UN, *The Population Debates. Dimensions and Perspectives*, 2 vols., New York, 1974; L.H. Janssen (ed.), *Population Problems and Catholic Responsibility. Proceedings of the International Symposium on Population Problems in Developing Countries and Worldwide Catholic Responsibility*, Groningen/ Tilburg, 1975.

[91] *Gaudium et Spes*, 87.

[92] Alphonsus de Liguori, *Theol. mor.*, lib. VI, tr. VI, cap. II, n. 900.

[93] ibid, cap. I, n. 882; cf. Tr. VI, cap. II, n. 927: there Alphonsus seems to say that the same purposes which justify the marital contract make the petition of the conjugal act honest.

[94] Cf. B. Häring, "The Inseparability of the Unitive-Procreative Functions of the Marital Act", in Ch.E. Curran (ed.), *Contraception*, New York, 1969, 176-192.

[95] Pius XII, Discourse of Oct. 29, 1951, AAS 43 (1951), 835-854.

[96] *Gaudium et Spes*, 50; cf. R. Boudet, *Parents par amour*, Tournai, 1964; G. Martelet, *L'existence humaine et l'amour; pour mieux comprendre l'encyclique Humanae Vitae*, Paris, 1969; G. Campanini (ed.), *Sessualità e responsabilità*, Bologna, 1976;· N. Rigali, S.J., "The Historical Meaning of Humanae Vitae", in *Chicago Theol. St.* 15 (1976), 127-138; cf. R. McCormick in *Theol. Studies* 38 (1977), 59ff.

[97] Cf. Ph. Delhaye, J. Grootaers, G. Thils, *Pour relire Humanae Vitae. Declarations épiscopales du monde entier*, Gembloux, 1970; N.St. John-Stevas, *The Agonizing Choice. Birth Control, Religion, and the Law*, Bloomington/Ind., 1971; J. Horgan, *Humanae Vitae and the Bishops. The Encyclical and the Statements of the national Hierarchies*, London, 1972; D. Capone, *La coscienza morale nelle discussioni sulla "Humanae Vitae"*, Roma (Ac. Alph.), s.a.; J.-M. Reuss, *Familienplanung und Empfängnisverhütung. Uberlegungen im Anschluss an die Synodenvorlage 'christliche gelebte Ehe und Familie'*, sowie an die Enz. Humanae Vitae, Mainz, 1975; R. Olechwoski (ed.), *Familienplanung und Sexualmoral*, Wien, 1976; J.A. Komanchak, "Humanae Vitae and Its Reception", *Theol. Studies* 39 (1978), 221-257; J.C. Ford, S.J., and G. Grisez, "Contraception and the Infallibility of the Ordinary Magisterium", l.c., 258-312.

[98] K. Wojtyla, l.c., 227ff.

[99] Quoted by F.E. von Gagern, l.c., 364.

[100] *Gaudium et Spes*, 51a.

[101] ibid, 51c..

[102] ibid, 51d.

[103] *Humanae Vitae*, n. 14.

[104] ibid, n. 16; cf. G. Martelet, *Amour conjugal et renouveau conciliaire*, Lyon, 1967, 17. Card. K. Wojtyla argues exclusively in view of the exigencies of true conjugal love. See his stimulating lecture given a few months before his election: K. Wojtyla, "L'amore fecondo responsabile", *La famiglia in un mondo che cambia: Documenti* 2 (1978), 319-328; cf. l.c., 354-355; *Fruitful and Responsible Love*, Slough/New York/Sydney, 1978.

[105] ibid, 27.

[106] ibid, 34

107 ibid, 34ff.
108 ibid, 35ff.
109 Cf. chapter I of this volume, on truthfulness in conflict situations.
110 Cf. F. Dantec, l.c., 59ff.
111 A. Guindon, l.c., 174.
112 Cf. R. McCormick, "Conscience, Theologians and the Magisterium", in *New Catholic World* 220 (1977), 268-271.
113 *Die christliche gelebte Ehe*, Synodenbeschluss 11: 2.2.2.3.
114 Cf. Declaration of the Mexican Bishops of Dec. 1972, IV.
115 Cf. E. Schillebeeckx, *Marriage: Human Reality and Saving Mystery*, London, 1965; J. Höffner, *Ehe und Familie. Wesen und Wandel in der industriellen Gesellschaft*, Münster, 1965²; G. Krems/R. Mumm (eds.), *Theologie der Ehe.* Veröffentlichung des ökumenischen Arbeitskreises und katholischer Theologen, Regensburg/Göttingen, 1969; *La Famiglia*, N. 29 (1971), 401-512: "Famiglia per gli altri"; *Famiglia*, N. 35, 387-488: "*Matrimonio perché?*"; H. Rosenberg, *Familie als Gegenstruktur zur Gesellschaft. Kritik grundlegender Ansätze der westdeutschen Familiensoziologie*, Stuttgart, 1973; D. Ciotta (ed.), *Matrimonio oggi come?*, Assisi, 1974; Th. Rey-Mermet, *Ce que Dieu a uni. Le mariage chrétien hier et aujourd'hui*, Paris, 1974; J. Meyendorff, *Marriage. An Orthodox Perspective*, New York, 1975²; M. de Crispiero, *Il matrimonio cristiano*, Torino, 1976; J. Renker, *Christliche Ehe im Wandel der Zeit. Zur Ehelehre der Moraltheologen im deutschsprachigen Raum in der ersten Hälfte des 19. Jahrhunderts*, Regensburg, 1977.
116 *Gaudium et Spes*, 48b.
117 ibid, 47b.
118 ibid, 49g; cf. 52c and e.
119 ibid, 47c.
120 A. Guindon, l.c. 142.
121 *The Seduction of the Spirit*, New York, 1973, 235.
122 *Gaudium et Spes*, 47a and d.
123 ibid, 48d and e, f, g; cf. P. Anciaux, *Le sacrement du mariage aux sources de la morale conjugale*, Louvain/Paris, 1963; B. Häring, *The Sacraments in a Secular Age*, Slough, 1976, 185-212.
124 Council of Trent, Sessio XXIV, can. 2, Denz. Sch. 1802; cf. 1798.
125 Cf. E. Hillman, *Polygamy Reconsidered. African Plural Marriage and the Christian Churches* (Foreword by B. Häring), Maryknoll, 1975; B. Häring, *Evangelization Today*, Notre Dame, 1974, 145-159 (with more bibliography); cf. *Herderkorr.* 32 (1978), 435-438: Report on the fifth symposium of the African bishops in Nairobi, July 1978, where, after serious studies and preparation this thorny problem was approached frankly and realistically.
126 J. Jeremias, *Jerusalem at the Time of Jesus*, London, 1965, 93ff.
127 E. Schillebeeckx, l.c., I, 284.
128 J.L. McKenzie, in *The Critic*, Nov./Dec., 1970, 95.
129 H. Cox, *The Seduction of the Spirit*, 236.
130 Augustine, *De bono coniugali*, 18, PL 40, 395; cf. ibid, 25, PL 40, 387.
131 Cf. P.E. Harrel, *Divorce and Remarriage in the Early Church*, Austin, 1967; R. Pesch, *Freie Treue. Die Christen und die Ehescheidung*, Freiburg, 1971; D.J. Doherty, *Divorce and Remarriage. Resolving a Catholic Dilemma*, St. Meinrad/Ind., 1974; K. Niederwimmer, *Askese und Mysterium. Uber Ehe, Ehescheidung und Eheverzicht in den Anfängen des christlichen Glaubens*, Göttingen, 1975; cf. chapter I of this volume on fidelity in this time.
132 A. Denecke, *Wahrhaftigkeit. Eine evangelische Kasuistik*, Göttingen, 1975, 67; cf. Grundmann, *Das Evangelium nach Markus*, Berlin, 1959, 203.
133 Cf. P. Grelot, "The Institution of Marriage; Its Evolution in the Old Testament", in F. Böckle (ed.), *The Future of Marriage as Institution, Concilium* (London) N. 6, 1970, 39-50.
134 P. Hoffman, "Jesus' Saying About Divorce and its Interpretation in the New Testament Tradition", in *Concilium*, N. 6, 1970, 51-66.
135 ibid, 53.
136 ibid, 56.

[137] ibid, 53.
[138] J. Ratzinger, in J. Ratzinger, R. Schnackenburg, H.D. Wendland, *Theologie der Ehe*, Regensburg/Göttingen, 1969, 83.
[139] Cf. P. Hoffmann, l.c., 56-61.
[140] l.c., 63.
[141] Cf. B. Häring, "Pastoral Work among the Divorced and Invalidly Married", in *Concilium* (London) N. 6, 1970, 123-130; H. Heimer (ed.), *Verheiratet und doch nicht verheiratet?*, Wien-Freiburg-Basel, 1970; M. West and R. Francis, *Scandal in the Assembly. A Bill of Complaints and a Proposal for Reform on the Matrimonial Laws and Tribunals of the Roman Catholic Church*, London, 1970; J.T. Noonan, Jr., *Power to Dissolve. Lawyers and Marriages in the Courts of the Roman Curia*, Cambridge/Mass., 1972; L.G. Wrenn (ed.), *Divorce and Remarriage in the Catholic Church*, New York, 1973; L. Bressan, *Il divorzio nelle chiese orientali. Ricerca storica sull'atteggiamento cattolico*, Bologna, 1976; A. Zirkel, *Schliesst das Kirchenrecht alle wiederverheirateten Geschiedenen von den Sakramenten aus?*, Mainz, 1977; Ch.E. Curran, "Gospel and Culture: Divorce and Christian Culture", in *Issues in Sexual and Medical Ethics*, Notre Dame/Ind., 1978, 3-29.
[142] *In IV Sent.*, dist. 38, q 38, a 5.
[143] Cf. D. von Hildebrand, *In Defence of Purity. An Analysis of Catholic Ideals of Purity and Virginity*, London, 1945; Id., *Heiligkeit und Tüchtigkeit*, Regensburg, 1969; J. Pieper, *Zucht und Mass*, Münchcen, 1960; L. Weber, *On Marriage, Sex and Virginity*, New York, 1964; A. del Monte, *Il senso della verginità*, Torino, 1973; D. Goergen, *The Sexual Celibate*, New York, 1974.
[144] J.T. Noonan, Jr., *Contraception. A History of Its Treatment by Catholic Theologians and Canonists*, Cambridge/Mass., 1965, 357ff.
[145] Cf. *Free and Faithful*, vol. I, 407-410; *Declaration on Certain Questions Concerning Sexual Ethics*, Jan. 5, 1976, *Persona Humana*, Text in *Cath. Mind*, April, 1976, 52-65; *Herderkorr.* 30 (1976), 82-87; cf. R. McCormick, S.J., "Notes on Moral Theology", in *Theol. Studies* 38 (1977), 100-114 (on reactions to "Persona Humana"); M. Oraison, *Vie chrétienne et problèmes de la sexualité*, Paris, 1972; F. Leist, *Der sexuelle Notstand und die Kirchen*, Freiburg, 1972; J.E. Dedek, *Contemporary Sexual Morality*, New York, 1973; R. Ginder, *Binding with Briars. Sex and Sin in the Catholic Church*, Englewood Cliffs, N.J., 1975; J. White, *Eros Defiled. The Christian and Sexual Sin*, Downess Grove/Ill., 1977.
[146] A. Guindon, l.c., 223-244 treats "sexual fantasies" under the general heading "Issues of Sexual Growth". This could make sense as expression of a constructive, pedagogical approach; but the fact that he treats not only masturbation, but also premarital intercourse and even homosexuality under the same heading may make the reader critical.
[147] Cf. R.R. Bell, *Premarital Sex in a Changing Society*, Englewood Cliffs, N.J., 1966; F. Böckle/J. Kühne, *Geschlechtliche Beziehungen vor der Ehe. Die Lage der studentischen Jugend*, Mainz, 1967; B. Schlegelberger, *Vor- und ausserehelicher Geschlechtsverkehr. Die Stellung der katholischen Moraltheologie seit Alphons von Liguori*, Remscheid, 1970; J. McLaughlin, *Love before Marriage*, New York, 1970; W. Barclay, *Ethics in a Permissive Society*, New York, 1971; E. Daschbach, *Premarital Sex: Is Love Enough?*, Notre Dame, 1972; M. Vidal, *Moral y sexualidad prematrimonial*, Madrid, 1972; B. Häring, *Rapporti sessuali prematrimoniali e morale*, Francavilla al Mare, 1973; P. Scabini and G. Campanini (eds.), *Rapporti prematrimoniali e coscienza cristiana*, Roma, 1975.
[148] R. May, *Love and Will*, New York, 1969, 42.
[149] *Sex and Morality. A Report . . .*, 60.
[150] l.c., 56.
[151] A. Kosnicki, l.c., 149, cf. 165ff.
[152] Cf. E. Ell, *Junge und Mädchen in der leiblichen Pubertät*, Freiburg, 1962; A. Plé, "La masturbation; réflexions théologiques et pastorales", in *Vie spir.*, Supplément 19 (1966), 258-292; M. Petitmangin, *La masturbation;*

étude clinique, morale et pastorale, Paris-Liège, 1967; A. Alsteens, Tabu im Reifungsprozess: Masturbation — Symptom oder Vergehen, Münster, 1969; A. Jordi, Anthropologischer Beitrag zum Verständnis der Masturbation, Basel-New York, 1969; Ch. Curran, "Masturbation and Objectively Grave Matter", in Id., A New Look at Christian Morality, Notre Dame/Ind., 1970, 200-221; F.M. Podimattam, OFMCap., A Difficult Problem: Masturbation, Kotagiri, Nilgris/India, 1972; N. Brockmann, "Contemporary Attitudes on the Morality of Masturbation", in AER 166 (1972), 597-614; B. Häring, Masturbazione: fenomeno e guarigione, Catania, 1973.

153 A. Guindon, l.c., 255.
154 Pier Damiani, Liber gomorrianus, Migne PL 145, 159-180; Leo IX, Denz. Sch. 687/688.
155 Cf. K.F. Jacobs, Die Entstehung der Onanieliteratur im 17. und 18. Jahrhundert, med. Diss., München, 1963, 33 and 39; A. Jordi, l.c., 18ff.
156 S.A. Tissot, L'onanisme ou dissertation sur les maladies produites par la masturbation, Lausanne; cf. A. Jordi, l.c., 16.
157 Cf. A. Jordi, l.c., 15ff; E. Ell, Junge und Mädchen in der leiblichen Purbertät. Freiburg, 1962.
158 W.B. Pomeroy, Boys and Sex, New York, 1968, 50.
159 Cf. R. O'Neill and M. Donovan, Sexuality and Moral Responsibility, Washington, D.C., 1968, 107ff; cf. U. Holmes, l.c., 77. This is also the position of A. Guindon and others; A. Guindon, l.c., 251-297.
160 A. Jordi, l.c., 110ff.
161 V.F. von Gebsattel, Prologomena einer medizinischen Anthropologie, Berlin, 1954, 175-185.
162 Sex and Morality. A Report..., 39.
163 l.c., 61.
164 Cf. A. Alsteens, l.c.
165 Cf. E. Hooker, "The Homosexual community", in J.H. Ganon and W. Simon (eds.), Sexual Deviance, New York, 1967, 167-196 (Sexuelle Aussenseiter. Kollektive Formen sexueller Abweichungen, Reinbeck, 1970); H. Mais, Inzest, Hamburg, 1968; A. Schelkopf (ed.), Sexualität, Formen und Fehlformen, Göttingen, 1968; E. Chesser, Strange Loves. Human Aspects of Sexual Deviations, New York, 1971; M. Daniel/A. Baudry, Les homosexuels, Tournai, 1973; J. McNeill, The Church and the Homosexual, New York, 1976; B. Häring, "Omosessualità", in Diz. enc. di teol. mor., Roma, 1976⁴, 682-689; R. Woods, OP., Another Kind of Love. Homosexuality and Spirituality, Chicago, 1977; R.T. Barnhouse, Homosexuality: A Symbolic Confusion, New York, 1977.
166 To be treated in volume III.
167 A.C. Kinsey, The Sexual Behavior in the Human Male, Philadelphia, 1948, 677.

Index

Faith-education, 240-272
"Falsiloquium", 47
Family, nuclear, 519, 533
Family planning, 520, 522-523
Fathers of the Church, 46
Feast and celebration, 130-138, 410-411
Feuerbach, Ludwig, 337
Fidelity
— and commitment, 59-60, 62, 68-71
— and conscience, 66-67
— and discipline, 74-75
— and faith, 62-64
— and honour, 77
— and liberty, 68-69, 130, 137, 321-322, 416
— and memory, 66-67
— and tolerance, 75
— and trust, 64
— call to, 62
— counterfeits of, 60-61
— creative, 64-66, 68-70, 76, 287, 293
— dimensions of presence, 67
— sacramental quality, 71-74
— structures of, 70-76
— versus constancy, 69
Film industry, 173-176
Finiteness, 26
Flattery, 90
Forgiveness, 445-446
Formalism, 371-395
Fornication, 553-554
"Fossil Church", 387
Francis of Assisi, St, 109-110, 115, 219
Frankl, Viktor, 25, 37-38, 351, 400, 515
Fraternal correction, 456-458
Fraternal love, 427-428, 437
Freedom
— abuse and misuse, 389-390
— and communication, 165, 183
— and fidelity, 361-362, 373, 375, 398
— and hope, 384-385
— and suffering, 400
— and truth, 21-23, 29, 165, 192-193
— artistic, 125
Freud, Sigmund, 373, 495, 560-561
Friendship, 548-549
Friendship-love, 439-440, 441-443, 505
Fromm, Eric, 373
Fruitfulness, 27
Fundamental option
— against God, 363, 372, 472
— for brotherhood, 223
— for commitment to unity, 297
— for faith, 208-211, 213, 216, 223, 246
— for God, 222-223, 427, 443
— for integrity, 506

— for life-commitment, 59
— for love, 10-11
— for philia and agapé, 442-443
— for truth and goodness, 43
— for untruth, 43
Fundamentalism, 215

"Games People Play", 143
Garaudy, Roger, 144, 341
Gebsattel, V.F. Von, 562
Gide, André, 117
Gift-love, 441-444, 505
Gilkey, Langdon, 127, 408-409
Gnosticism, 512-513
Goal-commandments, 437-438, 478,
God   [540
— as Love, 21, 204, 232, 367, 374, 419-421, 423, 426-429, 432, 434, 439, 441-443, 467-468, 492-493
— of history, 399
— source of hope, 392
— the Faithful One, 22, 56-58, 384
— the Liberator, 204
— the Truth, 21, 36
Godlessness, 363-364
Goethe, Johann W. Von, 440
Good example, 453-456
Goodness, search for, 359
Gospel morality, 108
Grace
— and freedom, 321
— and hope, 391-393
Greeley, Andrew, 256-257
Gregory I (the Great), 514
Gregory XIII, Pope, 182
Gregory XVI, Pope, 182-183
Gregory of Nazianzus, 305
Gregory of Nyssa, St, 513, 520
Grotius, Hugh, 47
Guardini, Romano, 139, 260, 263
Guindon, André, 528
Gurvitch, George, 32, 33, 127
Gustafson, James M., 320

Haecker, Theodor, 145-146
Hartmann, Nicolai, 346
Haselden, Kyle, 166, 168, 179-180
Hatred and envy, 473
Healing and reconciliation, 375
Heidegger, Martin, 26, 211-212
Hemmerle, Klaus, 128, 140
Heresy, 233-237, 281-282
Heterodoxy, 233-237
Hinduism, 316
Hirscher, John Baptist, 81
Holiness, call to, 114, 416, 447-448, 451, 478
Holmes, Urban T., 497
Holy Spirit
— call to unity, 277-278, 305
— gifts of, 277, 288, 448, 450

Joy
— and beauty, 114-115
— and feasts, 131
— and freedom, 137
— and love, 137
— and suffering, 131-133, 136
Judaism, 315-316
Judith, 45

"Kairos", 228, 247, 249
Kant, Emmanuel, 118, 243, 442
Kern, A., 43
Kierkegaard, Soren, 478
King, Martin Luther, 219
Kinsey, Alfred C., 499, 561, 564
Knowledge
— forms of, 32, 33, 261
— of dominion, 35, 344
— of faith, 213-215
— of truth, 17-20
— partial, 16-17
"Knowledge of domination", 419
Kung, Hans, 141, 360

Laity, 465-466
Lambert, Bernard, 290
Laughter, 146, 148
"Law of Christ", 379
Law(s), 319-320
Laws, antitrust, 166
Leaders, Charismatic, 219
Leaders, Communist, 337-340
Leaders, Ecumenical, 310-311
Leaders, Military, 484-485
Leaders, Political, 484
Leadership, 455
Leeuw, Gerardus Van der, 139
Legalism, 75, 121, 133-134, 344,
    371, 415, 478, 502
Legaut, Marcel, 242
Legislators, 186
Leisure, 188-190
Leo XIII, Pope, 112, 183, 406
Lersch, Philip, 147
Lewis, Clive Staples, 442
"Liber Gomorrianus", 560
"Libertas", 183
Lies, children's, 44
Lies, jocose, 44, 46
Limbo, 229-230
Lindbeck, G., 295-296
Liturgical Worship, 111-113, 139,
    225, 257, 408-410
Locke, John, 28
Löhrer, Magnus, 270
Lotz, Johann Baptist, 442
Love
— and asceticism, 513
— and celibacy, 546, 548
— and humour, 147
— and justice, 466-471

— and mercy, 468-469
— and pleasure, 513-515, 520
— and sexuality, 505-506
— and truth, 419-486
— and unity, 424
— apostolic, 448
— as a sacrament, 434-435
— characteristics of, 431-438, 508
— commandments of, 425-429, 435,
    438, 444, 464, 471, 477
— conjugal, 500, 505, 507-508,
    513-514, 516-518, 521-522, 525,
— forms of, 439-446   [557
— Gospel message, 359-360, 363, 367
— Grateful, 433
— Healing, 444
— I-Thou-We relationship, 359-360,
    467-469
— Integrated, 506-507, 509
— Liberating, 433
— of enemies, 444-446
— Pathological, 442
— responsibilities of, 510-511
— sexual, 492-530
— sins against, 471-486, 509
— universal, 440-441
Lubac, Henri de, 423, 435-436
Luther, Martin, 46-47, 116, 292, 315,
    379, 532, 536
Lying, 41-48

McKenzie, John L., 537
McLuhan, Marshall, 169-171
"Magnificat", 218
Manicheism, 512-513
Manipulation, 180-181, 187, 256
Mannheim, Karl, 32
Marcel, Gabriel, 63, 71
Marconi, Guglielmo, 76
Marcuse, Herbert, 495
Maritain, Jacques, 117
Marriage
— and family, 450-451, 467, 492,
    507, 510, 512, 518, 530-532
— as a sacrament, 534-536, 538-539
— as a vocation, 534, 536
— as an institution, 531-534
— covenant of love, 506, 534-535
— indissolubility of, 59, 538-540
— law of, 325-327, 415, 539-543
— purposes of, 521
Marriage annulments, 543
Marriage courts, 257
Marriages, Mixed, 325-328
Martelet, Gustave, 526-528
Marx, Karl, 337, 373
Marxism, 335-337, 339-342, 348-349,
    360, 370, 374-375, 402
Mary, Blessed Virgin, 106, 218
    315-316, 407, 453
Mary Magdalen, St, 218-219

577